O Powerful Western Star!

PETER GOLDEN

O Powerful Western Star!

AMERICAN JEWS, RUSSIAN JEWS, AND THE FINAL BATTLE OF THE COLD WAR

gefen
publishing house
JERUSALEM • NEW YORK Est. 1981

Graphic Design: Damonza
Typesetting: Irit Nachum

ISBN: 978-965-229-543-9

1 3 5 7 9 8 6 4 2

Gefen Publishing House Ltd.
6 Hatzvi Street
Jerusalem 94386, Israel
972-2-538-0247
orders@gefenpublishing.com

Gefen Books
11 Edison Place
Springfield, NJ 07081
516-593-1234
orders@gefenpublishing.com

www.gefenpublishing.com

Printed in Israel

Send for our free catalogue

Library of Congress Cataloging-in-Publication Data

Golden, Peter.
  O powerful western star! : American Jews, Russian Jews, and the final battle of the
Cold War / Peter Golden.
     p. cm.
  Includes bibliographical references and index.
  ISBN 978-965-229-543-9
  1. Jews--United States--Politics and government. 2. Jews--Russia--Politics and
government. 3. United States--Foreign relations--Russia. 4. Russia--Foreign
relations--United States. 5. Jews--History--20th century. 6. Cold War--Social
aspects--United States. I. Title.
  E184.36.P64G65 2012
  973'.04924--dc23
                              2011048391

We are all trustees of our Jewish heritage…with an obligation to cherish it, improve it, and guard its future.

– Max M. Fisher (1908–2005)

Our father was, in the words of Howard Rieger, former United Jewish Community's president and CEO, "a giant in the world of Jewish volunteer leaders. He was known to all, whether heads of state in Israel or the United States, or the leadership of the Jewish and general communities in the United States, as a prime mover – someone who makes things happen."

The concept, genesis, and sponsorship of this book is attributable to our father (ז״ל), who passed away during its writing. Because he felt so deeply about the role of the United States in the world, the founding and flourishing of Israel, the rescue of Soviet Jewry and the American Jewish community, he wanted this story immortalized. He dedicated this book to his wife Marjorie, with eternal love and deep respect for her moral compass.

On behalf of my siblings Jane F. Sherman, Mary D. Fisher, Julie F. Cummings, and Marjorie M. Fisher, we were blessed to have had our father in our lives, shaping our principles and values for generations to come. We miss and love you, Dad!

Phillip Wm. Fisher

When an American says that he loves his country, he means not only that he loves the New England hills, the prairies glistening in the sun, the wide and rising plains, the great mountains, and the sea. He means that he loves an inner air, an inner light in which freedom lives and in which a man can draw the breath of self-respect.

– Adlai Stevenson

CONTENTS

PROLOGUE

CAPTURING THE PAST IMPERFECT

"Pity the poor historian," I said.

My son, Ben, a junior in high school, had come upstairs to my office and said that he had been assigned a group project about the origins of the Holocaust. Opening my browser and clicking on Amazon, I typed "holocaust" into the search box, hit Enter, and adjusted the monitor so Ben could see the results: 97,728 books were listed on the subject.

"The project's due in a month, Dad. I don't think I can read all those."

Smiling, I reached back, took a few books off a shelf, and handed them to Ben.

"The answers are in here?" he asked.

"I wouldn't bet my allowance on it," I said.

This exchange was part of a discussion Ben and I had been having over the last year, a result of both my son's schoolwork and the book I was writing on the American movement to free Soviet Jewry and its connection to the Cold War – a subject so multifaceted that the forces responsible for creating the connective threads resisted neat definition. One problem was the Gordian knot fastened around the neck of every historian: writing is a linear craft, but events don't march in line. Instead, they occur simultaneously and haphazardly, as though playing out on an infinite wall of separate movie screens.

One can occasionally peer into this deluge of sound and light and spot connections. For example, look to the screen on the left, where Tsar Alexander III lets loose with an antisemitic rant and orders his minister of the interior to drive the Jews from the empire. On the next screen over, a shtetl burns. Turn your gaze further to the right and there they are, a crowd of future Americans – Jews loaded down with bundles and lining up in the harbor of Odessa, waiting to board a ship bound for New York.

More frequently, though, events possess numerous fathers, and their paternity is obscured behind the distractions of drama or distributed across a timeline so long and crooked that it becomes difficult to connect the present to the past.

Consider the Cold War, and the American attempt to halt the spread of Communism in Southeast Asia. On the center screen a company of US Marines is pinned down on a jungle trail, ambushed by soldiers of the North Vietnamese Army. It's the fall of 1967, and the stalemate in the fighting during the last two years has created popular opposition among Americans. In October, one hundred thousand protestors march on the Pentagon. This antiwar movement, which emerged from the civil rights movement, will lead to more mass protests on behalf of other causes – including Soviet Jewry – but let's stay with the stalemated war and those ambushed Marines.

How could North Vietnam fight the United States to a standstill when the American military enjoyed such a technological advantage? You could cite the difficulties of fighting a distant jungle war; you could also shift your eyes from the ambush to another screen, where, during the summer of 1941, a young sergeant of the Red Army, wounded fighting the Nazi invaders, lies in his hospital bed. The sergeant, a tinkerer since childhood, promises himself that he will invent a weapon capable of driving the Germans from Russia. His name is Mikhail Timofeevich Kalashnikov,[1] and though the Nazis surrender two years before his work is complete, the assault rifle he designs, the AK-47, is later supplied to the Communist government in Hanoi and is among the chief reasons the North Vietnamese can counter the technologically superior US military.[2]

Unearthing the forces behind events has always required a strong back and sturdy shovel, but presently, in some postmodern quarters, the work seems to be considered a task for neurotic alchemists. Erstwhile Wall Street trader Nassim Nicholas Taleb, author of *The Black Swan*, an influential paean to the randomness of events, declares history "opaque"[3] and states that the impulse to identify its generators is the residue of human failing, since people are "generally incapable of accepting the idea of unpredictability."[4] Therefore, they traffic in illusion, unable to accept that the past is akin to a randomly performing hedge fund, its causes shrouded in perpetual mystery.

Taleb presents much of value to ponder in *The Black Swan*, and there may well be a reward in heaven for anyone injecting a measure of self-doubt into the hearts and minds of the doctrinaire. Yet Taleb soon falls prey to the intellectual hauteur that his book was intended to counter. By page ten, he has already gazed out across recorded time to inform us that "history does not crawl, it jumps."[5] And with this pronouncement Taleb is indistinguishable from the illusion-soaked, theory-laden scholars he condemns.

In our impressionistic age of blinding change and punditry unbound, history-on-a-pogo-stick is a seductive formulation: it allows us to dismiss facts altogether or, perhaps more appealing, not to fritter away our precious time uncovering them. But unfortunately for the pogo-stick theory, the crawl of history is often made apparent by an inspection of events and the testimony of participants and witnesses.

Frankly, had the history of the American Soviet Jewry movement jumped – materialized suddenly out of the postmodernist blue – this book would have been far easier to write. Initially, I had planned to limit my exploration to the movement itself, but as I examined documents, read through histories, newspapers, journals, and magazines, and conducted interviews – in short, searched for the causes and effects of events – I discovered that this history was made up of multiple stories as intricately entwined as Alençon lace.

The story begins in the Russian empire with the violent repression and social engineering of the tsars, and the exodus of Jews in the late nineteenth and early twentieth centuries – small bands of dreamers heading for Palestine to rebuild Zion, and hundreds of thousands sailing to America, with its promise of freedom and equality, to seek a better life. It is the story of what these refugees brought with them: an intimate acquaintance with the most persistent war against Jews ever conducted, a predilection for founding self-help organizations, and a habit of never forgetting the sorrows of the old country or the Jews who stayed behind. It is the story of the exalted culture built by the Jews of central and eastern Europe, and the destruction of that culture by the Nazis, along with two-thirds of European Jewry, which abruptly transformed American Jewry into the largest Jewish community in the world. Of course, American Jews had a story all their own – their struggle to assimilate into the melting pot, where their gentile neighbors frequently considered them less than a necessary ingredient.

Nonetheless, in a nation that prided itself (at some moments with more accuracy than others) as being the land of opportunity, Jews fought their way up the social ladder, often shedding pieces of their Jewish identity with each rung they climbed – sometimes happily, sometimes not. Still, following the Second World War, Jews in the United States were a haunted lot, convinced that they, the most politically powerful Jews in history, had failed to rescue the six million. Their response to this conviction was to raise staggering amounts of money to sustain the survivors of the Nazis as they lingered in the displaced persons camps across Europe, and the beleaguered Zionists in Palestine, who had, against all odds, finally declared a Jewish state.

Thus, it is also the story of the survivors and the new Israelis as they weathered economic hardship and constant armed conflict with their Arab neighbors. One of their options was to rely on the fund-raising and political activity of American Jewry; another was to attract immigrants with skills and education. Because it was difficult to persuade Jews to abandon the security of the United States, Israel reached out to the 2.3 million Soviet Jews living under the tyranny of Josef Stalin.[6]

So the story shifts to Stalin, whose enigmatic, controlling, suspicious, brutal personality was translated into a political system that was locked in a deadly competition with America for the fealty of the world. Gradually, Israel became a flash point of this competition, while Jews in the United States, with their own national stake in the Cold War, were also preoccupied with the survival of Israel, as though the survival of the Jewish state would ensure the survival of American Jewry, who, more than twenty years removed from the liberation of the camps, continued to grapple with their guilt and their ambivalence about vanishing into the beguiling embrace of gentile society.

As my research moved into the 1960s and the heart of the movement itself, I was startled to discover that in many respects the American effort to free Soviet Jewry had nothing at all to do with Soviet Jews. Rather, it was a collision between the past and present, a thunderclap of historical and cultural forces: the careening realities of family life in the wake of post-World War II prosperity and the coming of age of the baby boomers; the threat of nuclear war and the civil rights movement; the power of television; the music of Elvis, Dylan, and the Beatles; the Generation Gap, urban riots, Black Power, radical student politics, the raging argument over Vietnam, changing sexual mores, and doors swinging open for women.

Like the rest of the country, Jews in the United States were swept up by the high and low tides of the era, and yet, in one significant respect, they faced a unique circumstance: they were disappearing. American Jews were assimilating at an astounding rate: by May 1964, *Look* magazine was running a cover story entitled "The Vanishing American Jew." In part, this assimilation was an unintended consequence of becoming so successful and secure, but it also raised questions about their identity in the present and their survival in the future. By then, Soviet Jews were in trouble, and a movement to rescue them was born – a movement that, for the American Jewish community, would serve as a definitive statement about who they had been, who they had become, and who they would be: a movement rooted in yesterday and designed to secure tomorrow.

I have tried to capture this unfolding – the culmination of hundreds of years of history – and I have traveled numerous historical side roads to do so, in the belief that to narrow the story is to distort the record and ignore an intriguing chapter of the Jewish journey: how and why American Jewry came to play a crucial role in the Cold War and wound up on the frontlines of that war's final battle.

CHAPTER 1

THE WORLD OF ABRAHAM NADICH

Abraham Nadich stepped out into the rain.[1] It was a cold spring rain falling on the busy Russian port city of Rostov-on-Don, but as Nadich and his friend left the theater and went out into the street, Nadich seemed unaware of the evening cold and the falling rain. He was still dizzy from the news. He had just heard it. A minute ago, two minutes ago, Nadich wasn't sure. Time wouldn't move – stubborn time, lost time, time drowning in the rain.

Maybe, Nadich thought, the news wasn't true. After all, this was *Rossiyskaya Imperiya*, the sprawling violent land of Imperial Russia, the land of the tsar and the Cossacks, where truth was scarce and myths sprouted with ferocious abandon. And this news was startling. Even now, Nadich couldn't believe it. The evening had been going so well, too. Then the play had ended and his friend had been handed a dispatch in the lobby of the theater. Nadich stared at him as he opened it. He was still staring when his friend informed him that half a world away, in Washington, DC, President Abraham Lincoln had been assassinated.

Nadich, a Russian Jewish grain dealer, had no words, not then, for his anger or grief. Words about the death of the sixteenth US president wouldn't come to Nadich until early May 1865, when he sat down to write a letter in English to Timothy C. Smith, the United States consul in Odessa. For now, nothing. Silence, shock, just his blood "rush[ing] alternatively from heart to head," as he later wrote to Smith.

Nadich said good-bye to his friend outside the theater and "walked

1

about the streets…with a suffocating heart." Lincoln was the first US president to die by an assassin's hand. How could it have happened? Nadich believed that "the hideous doings of the slavedrivers [had] provoked the bloodshed and…threatened the Union," but what madness could have brought about this new tragedy now that the terrible American war was coming to an end? Lincoln's own secretary of state, William H. Seward, had once proclaimed that "assassination is not an American practice or habit."[2] And now Seward himself had been a target of the plot – stabbed as he lay in his very own bed. Such a fate seemed more appropriate for a tsar like Paul I, an arrogant man tone-deaf to the nuanced melodies of politics, who made enemies at every turn. On a freezing November night in 1801, a group of conspirators crept into his bedchamber in Mikhailovskii Castle and murdered Paul by bludgeoning him with a gold snuff box, beating him with fists, and strangling him with a scarf.[3]

Abraham Nadich, who would later admit that thinking about the Lincoln assassination left him feeling "lonely and quite indifferent to life," kept walking in the rain. The rain was cold and steady, and the streets went up toward the river bank, climbing steeply, and then down again, and Nadich would remember little from his solitary walk except the cold, steadily falling rain. He did not remember speaking to any friends or neighbors or hearing the squeak of the wagon wheels in the streets or the splashing sound of the horses' hooves in the puddles or seeing the misty light of the lamps in the windows or the dark surface of the Don dimpled with rain or the fog drifting over the warehouses and piers. All Abraham Nadich remembered was his loneliness and the rain.

He did not make note of how long he walked, but he must have been shivering and soaked to the skin when he arrived home and got into bed.

"Grief," he recalled, "was my sleep mate." And at last he "forced out heavy tears…[that] lightened my oppressedness."

In the morning, Abraham Nadich awoke exhausted, and for the next several hours we lose track of him. Did he sit by a window and brood? Was it still raining, or was Rostov-on-Don warmed by the spring sun? Did he wander the streets, or did he stroll by the river and stop to discuss the tragic news with other importers?

We have no idea, and so for now, let us leave Abraham Nadich. He will reappear by afternoon, and meanwhile there are other matters to consider, a dance through time, as it were. the matter of why a Russian Jewish grain dealer held such reverence for a president of the United States, and why, a century after that president was laid to rest in Springfield, Illinois, American Jews hurled themselves into the final battle of the Cold War.

◆ ◆ ◆

On clear, sunny days, if you look beyond the city of Rostov-on-Don, out past the silvery bend of the river, you can see the fields of wheat and maize rippling in the wind, a blaze of gold and green spreading out across the vast, grassy steppe, bright with wildflowers and noisy with the songs of birds floating on waves of brilliant blue air.

This flat, fertile land, blessed with waterways, rich with fruit and grain, and brimming with game, is part of the Eurasian Steppe. The ancient Scythians were among the first to ride their horses over these plains, and would become known for beheading their enemies. Other tribes of nomads – Huns, Khazars, Mongols, and Tatars – had also lived here for centuries, fighting and trading with each other, and blending their cultures through marriage.[4] Out of this mix came the Cossacks.

The Don Cossacks gradually settled in villages, but they retained their identity as a people, along with their fierce independence and love of battle. Two other aspects of their culture would color their relationship with Jews. First, the Cossacks were, like many Russians, wildly superstitious, and to alleviate their troubles and fears, and to escape the malicious power of the "evil eye," they sought advice from fortune-tellers, faith healers, witches, and wizards.[5] Second, the Cossacks were deeply devout Russian Orthodox Christians, a fact that would later tie them to the tsars.[6]

For Jews, living as a minority among superstitious, impoverished people prone to violence and devoted to Christian dogma was seldom a happy experience – and just how unhappy it could be was demonstrated in 1648 and 1649.

In those years, the Kingdom of Poland was seeking control of the Ukraine. The Cossacks were their allies, and as the Polish nobility built palaces and acquired property, they hired Jews to collect rental payments from the peasants for land and taxes, for the baptisms of peasant children, the marriages of peasant daughters, and, cruelest of all, for peasant funerals.[7] The peasants detested the Polish nobles and the Jews who worked for them, while the Cossacks, with their vigorous tribal loyalty, chafed at the control of any outsiders, especially the Poles with their Roman Catholicism. The conditions were ripe for revolt, and sure enough, a Cossack chief, or Hetman, was soon leading a rebellion against Polish rule.[8]

His name was Bogdan Chmielnicki. He had attended a university and was fluent in five languages, but his education, which was remarkable for a Cossack of that era, did not blunt his savagery.[9] His war against the Poles ignited the region, setting off a storm of indiscriminate butchery and plunder. The Cossacks and their peasant allies screamed for Jewish blood to avenge the crucifixion of Christ and swept through the Ukraine and the southern areas of Poland with their swords and axes.[10] Nathan Hanover, a witness to the Chmielnicki uprising, published an account of the carnage, *Abyss of Despair* (*Yeven Metzulah*). He recalled Jewish men, women, and children with their flesh flayed from their bodies being fed to dogs. Some were gutted like fish; others were buried alive or dismembered and left on the roads so carts and horses could run over them. Wives were raped in front of their husbands. Babies, still nursing at their mothers' breasts, were slaughtered like spring lambs. Towns and villages were looted and burned, and the air was thick with black corkscrews of smoke, the cries of the dying, and the stench of the dead.[11]

Over one hundred thousand Jews were murdered in these two years,[12] a wholesale slaughter that Russian Jews would not undergo again until the Ukrainian secessionist Simon Petlura led his troops in a civil war against Moscow that raged from 1918 until 1921. Spurring his soldiers on by allowing them to "slaughter the kikes," Petlura's men looted and burned their way through the Ukraine, southern Russia, and Belarus, murdering nearly two hundred thousand Jews.[13]

And all of this was a prelude to the Nazis.

Today, both Chmielnicki and Petlura are considered Ukrainian heroes. You can walk along Bogdan Chmielnicki Street in the city of Kiev and see a statue of Chmielnicki outside Saint Sophia Cathedral. As for Simon Petlura, celebratory days are declared to memorialize his courageous life, and on visits to Paris, where Petlura was shot to death in 1926 by a Jewish anarchist, the Ukrainian president has stopped by to lay flowers at Petlura's grave.[14]

◆ ◆ ◆

Between the barbarities of Chmielnicki, Petlura, and Hitler, Russian Jews endured periods of repression and less repression, because, as a rule, the government and popular sentiment regarded them, in the words of historian Irving Howe, "as pariahs, the stiff-necked enemies of Christ."[15]

As the nineteenth century approached, bringing with it the beginnings of industrial progress, the class structure of Russian society shifted. Previously divided into nobles, serfs, and clergymen, a middle class emerged, and Jews, who occupied their very own lower rung on the social ladder, rushed to fill its ranks. Catherine the Great believed that these new Jewish merchants and traders would benefit the economy, but before long, pressure to curtail Jewish economic advancement led Catherine to create, in 1791, an area where Jews were now ordered to live.[16]

This area would eventually be officially classified as the Pale of Permanent Jewish Settlement, and stretch across 366,000 square miles, running from the brackish waters of the Baltic Sea to the Black Sea.[17] The Pale occupied less than 5 percent of Imperial Russia, but 94 percent of Russian Jews resided there – often in poverty.[18] Still, the Jewish population grew: in 1820, there were 1.6 million Jews in the empire;[19] by 1897, when a "reasonably reliable"[20] census was taken, the number stood at 5.2 million. This was the largest Jewish population in the world, outnumbering all the Jews in Western Europe and the United States combined.[21]

Segregation protected the Jews from neither the government nor their countrymen. Jews were prohibited from leasing land and receiving advanced education, and they were taxed at twice the rate of Christians.[22] Spasms of violence, though initially less organized then the Chmielnicki uprising, were not uncommon and would add a new word to the vocabulary of Jewish agony: *pogrom*, from the Russian *pogromit*, meaning to wreak havoc. The term didn't become widely used in English until the late nineteenth century.

◆ ◆ ◆

In 1825, Nicholas I became tsar, and for the next thirty years of his rule more than six hundred decrees were issued against the Jews.[23] Nicholas I wasn't the most personally antisemitic tsar to sit on the throne: that distinction would belong to his grandson, Alexander III. In fact, Nicholas recognized that Jews could be productive subjects, but first they would have to "be cured of their religion,"[24] so he sought "to bring about," as one of his decrees stated, "[the Jews'] gradual merging with the Christian nationalities and to uproot those superstitious and harmful prejudices which are instilled by the teachings of the Talmud."[25]

Picking up where his grandmother, Catherine the Great, had left off, Nicholas decreed that the Pale would be the permanent Jewish residence inside the empire, and once again Jews were expelled from their homes. Nicholas also altered what was taught in Jewish schools, ordered that books in Yiddish and Hebrew be censored,[26] and, in 1827, established a yearly draft quota for Jewish males.[27] This was a grand attempt by Nicholas to separate Jews from their religion and erase any chance of a Jewish future. Once inducted, the conscripts were forbidden from fraternizing with Jews outside their units, speaking Yiddish, and practicing their faith. Their length of service to the tsar extended for twenty-five years, during which unrelenting efforts were made to baptize them into the Russian Orthodox Church.[28]

As if this was not painful enough, the governing body of the Jewish community, the *kahal*, was required to furnish the draftees.[29] This set Jew upon Jew. Desperate to protect their young sons, the parents who could afford it paid a fee or bribe or tapped their connections inside the *kahal* to keep their children out of the service.[30] Generally then, recruits were harvested from a bumper crop of beggars, vagabonds, servants, laborers lacking skills or talent, the chronically unemployed, and the terminally lonely, all those inhabiting the ragged edge of the social margins, where the only means of escape was through self-mutilation or to hide in the forests.

Intellectuals railed against the discrimination, but Nicholas I approved, for it removed the less productive segments of society, another goal of his ruthless foray into social engineering. The pressure to fill the ranks of the army never let up. If a Jewish community failed to meet its quota, then

Nicholas demanded that three additional recruits be added to their total, and one more would be required for every two-thousand-ruble shortfall in the community's tax bill. As communities throughout the Pale sunk deeper into debt and fell further behind in their quotas, Nicholas flew into a rage, believing the Jews were refusing to serve in his beloved military. First, he declared that the *kahal* leaders would be drafted if their failure persisted, and then he gave them permission to turn over any Jew they caught without a passport.[31]

Once the poverty-stricken margins had been stripped bare, the *kahal* turned elsewhere for conscripts. They sent children of eight or nine, because unlike many eighteen-year-olds they were not married and their absence would not rob a family of its chief breadwinner.[32] *Kahal* leaders also hired men, ofttimes members of the community, to round up boys for Mother Russia.[33] Jews referred to them as *khappers* (from the Yiddish *khapn*, to catch) and they roamed the Pale like famished wolves, snatching children from the arms of their mothers, breaking into homes and carrying out fresh conscripts, grabbing any stranger or unsuspecting boy off the streets – pursuing the commerce of cruelty and grief, trading souls for money, collecting salaries from the *kahal*, rewards from the government, and ransoms from families seeking to save their fathers and sons.[34]

Jews reserved a blind fury for these kidnappers, a fury that would repeat itself inside Hitler's ghettos, where the *Judenräte* sent Jewish policemen to select Jews for slave labor and for deportation to the concentration camps. As the draftees departed or disappeared, their parents lit the traditional mourning candles for them, believing they were lost forever,[35] which was often the case. A Russian officer at the time recalled that the "Jewish boys of eight or nine," without the love and care of their mothers and fathers, "tramping in the mud for ten hours a day" without much to eat, would "die off like flies."[36] An estimated seventy thousand Jewish conscripts entered the army between 1827 and 1855.[37] Most of them vanished into the unpitying darkness of Imperial Russia, dying from hunger or cold or disease or in battle, or converting to a strange religion and trying to restart their lives, never seeing home or their loved ones again.[38] A Christian Russian historian who lived under Nicholas described his reign as a "tyranny of madness, brutality, and misfortunes,"[39] and yet obliterating Jewish identity through military service, forced conversion, and harsh edicts proved harder than Nicholas I imagined. An official memorandum written in 1855, the year Nicholas died, noted that the "Jews do not abandon their religion during army service, in spite of the benefits offered to them for doing so."[40]

The death of Nicholas I was celebrated by Jews across the Pale,[41] and there was a burst of hope when Alexander II replaced his father as tsar and set about liberalizing the empire. Alexander II cut the army service of draftees, and permitted some Jews to attend universities, practice their professions, and travel outside the Pale to conduct business.[42] He also freed millions of serfs,[43] Westernized local government and the courts,[44] and oversaw the flourishing of the arts and sciences and the birth of the intelligentsia.[45]

No matter how hopeful Jews might have been about the reforms, there is evidence that in economic terms only a small minority escaped poverty,[46] and even fewer were able to blend into gentile society. Consider this excerpt from an 1872 report done at the request of US Secretary of State Hamilton Fish and written by his representative to St. Petersburg.[47]

> The spirit of modern Russian legislation is to fuse together the different races that inhabit the empire…. It is obvious that this object cannot be attained, so far as the Hebrews are concerned, while the laws exist which render them a separate and distinct body, and, by casting a slur on them, cause them only to shut themselves still more, and to resist all attempts to draw them into…the body politic."[48]

Seventeen years into the reforms of Alexander II, the Jews remained a people apart, just as they had been under Nicholas I. Nor was the overall situation of the empire improved. Alexander II may have freed society from his father's ironclad grip, but his reforms elevated expectations beyond his capacity to meet them, and the ensuing disappointment gave rise to a revolutionary movement that spawned a host of violent student radicals who declared war on the government – much like the American student radicals of the 1960s. In the spring of 1862, a little over a year after Alexander emancipated the serfs, arsonists set fire to St. Petersburg, spreading terror through every tier of society.[49] Wealth was no protection.

The rich as well as the poor were victims of the arsonists,[50] and thousands of people were left homeless, hurt, or dead.[51]

After a number of failed attempts on his life, Alexander II was assassinated in 1881. He was replaced by Alexander III, whose personal animosity toward Jews rivaled Hitler's.[52] To Alexander III, Jews were "Christ killers," and because this view was shared by a broad segment of his subjects, few objected when he supported the outbreak of pogroms two months into his reign. The pogroms, Alexander reasoned, were caused by the Jews themselves, and to punish them he issued the May Laws, which imposed further restrictions on Jewish life.[53] Nine hundred fifty thousand Jews, who had resided east or west of the Pale, were now herded like cattle into the Jewish region. Twenty thousand Jews were expelled from Moscow and two thousand from St. Petersburg, most of whom were taken out of the city in chains.[54]

Ironically, the cultural genocide launched against the Jews not only failed, it became an object lesson in the law of unintended consequences: what started in 1825 set Jews on a course that, in large measure, would help them to survive and prosper. Russian Jewry turned inward as never before, becoming a people separate from their religion, and a nation separate from a homeland. The yearning to return to Zion had played a central role in Judaism since the Romans destroyed the Second Temple in 70 CE, but so had a yearning for the coming of the Messiah; to Jews suffering under the tsars it must have appeared that God had scheduled both events for the very distant future.

In the end, all the Jews of *Rossiyskaya Imperiya* had was each other. A small minority managed to enter Russian society, and they would become visible in the wake of the 1917 Revolution and the rise of the Communists and the Soviet state.[55] Some Jews lived in towns and cities,[56] but for most, home was the shtetl, a hardscrabble island of safety in a sea of peril. The people imprisoned on that island survived by solidifying and enriching the very culture that Nicholas had tried to destroy.

They cultivated their intellectual and artistic gifts in their own schools and in their own languages – Yiddish and Hebrew. They conducted their lives by their own laws, prayed at their own synagogues, and formed their own economy, producing peddlers, shopkeepers, traders, and artisans.[57]

Because life was difficult for the average citizen of Imperial Russia, the shtetls developed their own network of charities. Dowries, medical care, and education were provided to the poor, and men unlucky enough to serve in the tsar's army were supplied with kosher food.[58]

Certainly, within the shtetl, Jews had their conflicts. As in any community, animosities surfaced among different economic and social classes – animosities that reached their apex over supplying conscripts to the tsar. Adding to that tension was the friction between traditional Jews and the Hasidim.[59] Furthermore, the German-born *Haskalah* movement had come to Russia,[60] and the *maskilim*, those under the spell of this Enlightenment, spurned the narrow confines of shtetl culture and the other-worldliness of religion and embraced the secular, which frequently annoyed everyone.[61]

Nevertheless, in the antisemitic eyes of the empire, a Jew was a Jew – he had the Lord's blood on his hands, whatever he believed – and as French philosopher Jean-Paul Sartre would observe in the immediate aftermath of the Holocaust, "What makes the Jew is his concrete situation; what unites him to other Jews is the identity of their situations."[62]

The flowering of shtetl life alone would have been more than enough irony for Nicholas I to bear, but as ironies go, it was tame in light of the unforeseen consequences that followed.

Across the Pale, Jews were whispering about a movement that would deliver them from the failed reforms of Alexander II and the prison that his father Nicholas had sanctioned.[63] The aim of this movement was to found a Jewish homeland, and the meetings were held in secret because in Tsarist Russia nationalism on the part of minorities was forbidden.[64] Eventually, these likeminded groups would be referred to as Hovevei Zion (Lovers of Zion).[65]

The roots of Zionism reach back to biblical days and the Jewish longing for the Messiah to deliver them from their enemies. By the nineteenth century, though, nationalism was blowing across Europe,[66] a gathering storm for princes and kings. In the Pale, Jews were aware that this notion had a sacred claim on the Cossack heart: the Cossacks wanted to have their own home and be free from the tsar. Yet the Jews had difficulty replicating this political vision; early attempts to update Zionism did not stray from the messianic vision until 1862, when the German Jewish journalist Moses Hess published *Rome and Jerusalem*, and the religious origins of Zionism were blended with the nationalist ideas of the Italian philosopher Giuseppe Mazzini.[67]

The book sold two hundred copies in its first five years and can hardly be considered influential.[68] In contrast, the pamphlet *Auto-Emancipation: A Warning to His Brethren by a Russian Jew*, published anonymously in 1882 by Leon Pinsker, would have a powerful influence. Among the first Jews to enroll at Odessa University, Pinsker studied law until it became clear that it was unlikely a Jew could become a lawyer. He transferred to the University of Moscow, where he earned a degree in medicine. After returning to Odessa to practice, Pinsker helped start a weekly newspaper that was written in Russian and preached the ideals of the *Haskalah*: assimilation and humanism would rescue the Jews from their tormentors.[69]

In 1871, a local pogrom caused Pinsker to reconsider his beliefs. This, along with the antisemitic outrages under Alexander III, led him to write the *Auto-Emancipation* pamphlet.[70] Pinsker now believed that "Judeophobia [was] a psychic aberration...a disease transmitted for two thousand years [that] is incurable."[71] Pinsker wrote that people dislike foreigners, and "since the Jew is nowhere regarded as a native, he remains an alien everywhere." The answer, then, was to "give up our endless life of wandering and rise to the dignity of a nation in our own eyes and in the eyes of the world."[72]

Auto-Emancipation struck a chord among Russian Jews, and shortly after its publication Pinsker found himself a leader of Hovevei Zion,[73] even though his imagined Jewish country did not necessarily have to be located in the Land of Israel. The evolution of Leon Pinsker's thinking reflects that of Russian Jewry as a whole. Upon reaching the cusp of middle age under the depredations of Nicholas I, Pinsker underwent a sea change when Alexander II instituted his reforms, but came to appreciate the utter hopelessness of the situation by the time Alexander III was crowned, since his approach was the same as the one favored by Nicholas I: Russifying the Jews by curing them of their religion. The goal of Alexander III was to quell the unrest set off by his father's reforms and to reestablish, through merciless repression, the absolute power of the tsar and the harmony that his grandfather had so brutally imposed on his subjects.[74]

Nicholas I would have been less than amused had he known that his efforts to extinguish Jewishness would ignite the desire to establish a Jewish state, and that once this state was founded in 1948, its citizens would help preserve the connection between Russian Jews and their religion by smuggling in prayer books and matzos.

Yet that state would not have been possible had the wheel of history not taken one of its most ironic turns – a turn that would, in a variety of ways, influence Jewish life into the twenty-first century.

As Alexander III picked up where his tyrannical grandfather had left off, Jews began to flee. Whatever their destination, getting there wouldn't be easy, but what did they have to lose? There was no end to the pogroms or the poverty: already, an estimated 40 percent of Russian Jewry relied on charity or financial assistance from outside the empire.[75] You could be poor anywhere, couldn't you? Maybe the children would do better.

The conflicts in the shtetl carried over to the subject of emigration. There were those who despaired of finding a hospitable place to live and those who were determined to stay and remake the empire – by revolution if necessary.[76] Another debate raged between those who believed it was their duty to build a Jewish home in *Eretz Yisrael* and those who had no desire to exchange the perilous whimsy of the tsars for the dangers of Middle Eastern swamps and deserts, and instead envisioned another Promised Land, also flowing with milk and honey – the *Goldeneh Medina*, they called it, the Golden Land: America.

It is tempting to dismiss this argument as erupting from the fear of the unknown, but there was an emotional and philosophical divide between the two camps, and it would resurface a century later, in a much more explosive form, when the Israeli government and the American Jewish community fought over the destination of Soviet Jews, and American Jewry itself was sorely divided on the issue.

As acrimonious as this battle would become, Jews were fortunate to be able to have it – since it meant that millions had survived not just the tsar, but later on, Hitler and Stalin. World Jewry owed much of their good fortune to the Jews who were brave enough to leave Imperial Russia. Some

Zionists, in a remarkable demonstration of idealism, hiked to Palestine. In this wave of immigration, which would become known as the First Aliyah,[77] ten thousand Jews from eastern Europe came to work the land. However, the majority of Russian Jewish emigrants opted to travel across the ocean to America.

The United States had already undergone two ripples of Jewish immigration. Between 1654 and 1820, the immigrants were predominantly Sephardic, originating in the Iberian Peninsula. The next ripple broke across American shores from 1820 to 1880, and these newcomers were primarily from central Europe. When they first disembarked, there were three thousand Jews and half a dozen synagogues in the country. Over the next sixty years, the Jewish population increased to three hundred thousand and Jewish religious and civic institutions proliferated. The leaders of this community were chiefly German Jews and belonged to the prominent families of New York: the Loebs, Guggenheims, Seligmans, Lehmans, Warburgs, Kahns, Rosenwalds, Morgenthaus, and Schiffs, to name just a few. The "Jewish Grand Dukes," some called them, but the members of this gilt-edged upper crust favored the understated style of the Protestant elite they emulated, and generally spoke of themselves as "our crowd."[78]

That all changed over the next generation as the Russians came, not in ripples but in waves. In 1914, their number reached 1.5 million, more than doubling the Jewish population of America. In addition, another nine hundred thousand eastern European Jews immigrated during the same period, speaking the lingua franca of the shtetl, Yiddish, and infused with attitudes and values similar to their Russian *landsleit*.[79]

By now, the first romance between American intellectuals and the Soviet Union was underway. Communism would succeed where religion had failed. The masses would not be saved by Scripture and the loving hand of God, but by the writings of Marx and the benevolent rule of Vladimir Lenin and the Bolsheviks. This combination of utopian longing and flawed thinking led America straight into a Red Scare. Godless Communism was a contagious disease spread by foreigners, and the cure was to pull in the welcome mat.[80]

In 1921, Congress curtailed immigration by enacting the Emergency

Quota Act, and in 1924 they passed the more stringent Johnson-Reed Immigration Reform Act. Louis Marshall, a lawyer and leader of the American Jewish Committee, tried to schedule an appointment with President Calvin Coolidge to ask him to veto Johnson-Reed, but Coolidge, who had written an article for *Good Housekeeping* which asserted that "Nordics deteriorate when mixed with other races," would not meet with him.[81]

By this point, 33 percent of eastern European Jews had emigrated, and their presence reenergized American Jewry. Charting the arc of their experience has produced more scholarship, journalism, literature, movies, music, art, and archives than can be absorbed in a lifetime. Some of that past has acquired a soft glow in the starlight of memory, as if the cobblestone streets of tenements on the Lower East Side or across the Hudson in Newark or down in Philadelphia and Baltimore were indeed paved with gold. The only sounds you heard were the faithful chanting in the synagogues and the joyous music of klezmer bands, and none of the Jews who walked across those rough stones ever worked too hard, died too young, or dreamt a dream that didn't come true.

Nostalgia is no friend of history; in this instance, it blinds us to the breadth of the immigrants' accomplishments. In spite of the hardships, at the close of the twentieth century these Jews and their descendants had become the prime movers in constructing the most economically and politically successful diaspora since the Babylonian Exile. And so here is one turn of the wheel: the culture that Nicholas had warred against had relocated and been reborn. It is likely that Nicholas would not have cared that his empire's Jews had fled; Alexander III surely did not. What neither tsar foresaw, however, was that down through the generations, these Jews never forgot their connection to Russia – even if that connection was limited to the stories their grandparents repeated at family gatherings.

The Holocaust provides another spin of the wheel. Two-thirds of European Jewry perished,[82] and even though American Jews had been unable to save them, at least their own community had been preserved and the horrific question never had to be answered: how many more would have died without the mass migration from eastern Europe?

One pressing question did arise as the Allies rolled through Europe and discovered the Nazi concentration camps: where would the Jewish survivors go?

◆ ◆ ◆

In February 1945, President Franklin D. Roosevelt, Prime Minister Winston Churchill, and Marshal Joseph Stalin gathered at the former palace of Tsar Nicholas II, in the Crimean resort city of Yalta, on the southern coast of the Black Sea, to discuss the shape of postwar Europe and coordinating the war against Japan. Twelve years before, FDR had ended "the sixteen years of estrangement"[83] between the United States and the Soviet Union by extending diplomatic recognition to Moscow, a decision that was not without controversy – namely that FDR was underestimating the harsh repressiveness of the Soviet regime and its philosophical hostility toward democracy.[84] Midway through the war, though, the Soviets were being touted, by and large, as friends: Hollywood churned out pro-Soviet films; the distinguished journalist, James Reston, called anti-Russian remarks "a shabby un-American game"; and *Collier's Magazine* reported that the Soviet Union was evolving "toward something resembling our own and Great Britain's democracy."[85]

At Yalta, however, Stalin made one of the opening moves in what would become the Cold War by signing – and then ignoring, as he tightened his grip on eastern Europe – an agreement pledging that in rebuilding their countries, "the liberated peoples" of Europe would be allowed "to create democratic institutions of their own choice."[86] FDR was criticized, at the time and by future historians, for being naïve with regard to Stalin and ceding too much to him at Yalta. This may or may not be true. FDR did tell his first ambassador to the Soviet Union, William C. Bullitt Jr., that he was gambling on Stalin not being the monster he was reputed to be. Yet in the name of historical fealty one must consider the options the president believed were available to him.[87] Prior to arriving at Yalta, FDR had admitted to the journalist Edgar Snow that his gamble was really no gamble at all, since "our alternative was to begin right then preparing for World War III."[88] By the winter of 1945, the facts supported FDR's assessment: the Russian Army had twelve million soldiers in the field and had already reached the Oder River; the United States had just four million soldiers and they were bogged down a good distance from Berlin.[89] The atom bomb was not yet a viable weapon – the invasion of Japan was coming, with high casualty estimates, and Stalin had pledged Soviet troops to fight the Japanese.[90] If, at Yalta, FDR made a deal with the devil, he did it to save a war-weary America from burying any more of its fathers and sons.

What role the survivors would play in the postwar world was unclear to FDR, but one evening, over dinner, he did raise their plight in his famously oblique way by saying that he was a Zionist and then asking Stalin if he was one as well.[91]

Yes, Stalin replied, he was a Zionist.[92] The Soviet leader already had detailed information about the death camps. In the summer of 1944, his army took the city of Lublin, Poland, and uncovered Majdanek. The Nazis had cleared the camp and burned it to obliterate their crimes, but the gas chambers had not been completely incinerated, and one photograph that appeared in the press, to the horror of the civilized world, showed a warehouse full of eight hundred thousand shoes that the Nazis had removed from their victims.[93] Over the next few weeks, Stalin's troops uncovered Belzec, Sobibor, and Treblinka.[94]

Before FDR could continue the conversation, Stalin qualified his position, claiming that he was only a Zionist in principle, because solving the Jewish problem was difficult.[95] He explained that the Soviet Union had set up the Jewish Autonomous Region, Birobidzhan, in the Far East, but the experiment had failed because Jews preferred to reside in cities.[96] What Stalin failed to mention was that in a 1936 speech he declared that for such a region to be classified as a Soviet republic it would require a population of over one million, a practical impossibility for Birobidzhan.[97]

Again, in a veiled reference to the resettlement of the survivors, FDR told Stalin that following the Yalta Conference he was scheduled to meet with the king of Saudi Arabia. Stalin inquired as to what gift he would give Ibn Saud. In his memoir, *Witness to History*, Charles E. Bohlen, who served as FDR's translator at Yalta, recalled that the president smiled and replied that he might offer "to give Ibn Saud the six million Jews in the United States."[98]

His humor was pungent with the genteel antisemitism not uncommon among American blue bloods of that era. Upon hearing it, perhaps Stalin felt that the president was relaxing his guard and sharing his genuine sentiments about Jews, because in response Stalin offered an opinion that would have cheered both Nicholas I and Alexander III. He called Jews "middlemen, profiteers, and parasites," [99] and then added a joke of his own. Referring to Yaroslav, a city renowned for its shrewd, aggressive businessmen, Stalin said that no Jew could live there.[100]

Out of politeness, one suspects, FDR smiled, but must have felt that he had uncorked more than he had bargained for, and he said nothing. A joke between men of refinement as they sipped martinis in front of the fireplace in Hyde Park was one thing, but hearing Stalin voice his bred-in-the-bone antisemitism – a visceral hatred of the all-powerful, magical Jew that was codified in the paranoid Russian fantasy *The Protocols of the Elders of Zion* – was quite another. It was a wise political choice, as Bohlen remarked in his memoir, that this exchange was excluded from the official transcript of their conversation.[101]

On Valentine's Day, an American warship, the USS *Quincy*, dropped anchor in Egypt's Great Bitter Lake,[102] and President Roosevelt and Ibn Saud spent six hours together.[103] In the photographs of their meeting the physical differences between the two leaders were startling. FDR was two years younger than Ibn Saud, but appeared older. The president had aged during the war, dropping weight, losing muscle tone, and developing heart disease.[104] At Yalta his blood pressure had jumped to dangerous heights – 260 over 150[105] – and as he sat on deck in his conservative suit with a coat draped over his left shoulder his face was pale and drawn. Ibn Saud was a true warrior-king with the leg wounds and cane to prove it, but seated in a chair between FDR and the kneeling American translator, Ibn Saud radiated the power of a monarch – a big, robust, dark-eyed man in black robes with a red-and-white-checked *ghutra* on his head.[106]

The translator, Col. William A. Eddy, was a Princeton-educated Marine hero from the First World War, who learned Arabic growing up in Lebanon as the son of Presbyterian missionaries.[107] He kept a record of the discussion aboard the *Quincy*, and in 1954 published it as the monograph *FDR Meets Ibn Saud*. The president and the king, wrote Col. Eddy, spoke about oil and logistical support when the Allies focused their full attention on defeating Japan, but at one point Roosevelt steered their talk to the fate of European Jewry.

FDR told Ibn Saud that "he had a serious problem," and asked for his advice and assistance. The Jews had "suffered terribly at the hands of the Nazis," FDR said, and he believed that he had "a personal responsibility" to assist the survivors. What were the king's thoughts on the matter?[108]

Ibn Saud had never ventured far from this desert kingdom, and at one point in his conversation with FDR referred to himself as an "uneducated Bedouin,"[109] but no one ever accused him of being slow witted. He understood exactly what FDR was asking, and he wanted nothing to do with it.

Ibn Saud replied, "Give them and their descendants the choicest lands and homes of the Germans who had oppressed them."[110]

"The Jewish survivors have a sentimental desire to settle in Palestine," FDR said, adding that they feared staying in Germany.[111]

The king refused to take the bait, replying that their fear was understandable, but how could the Allies leave the Nazis in a position from which they could harm anyone? The king would not allow a vanquished enemy to remain strong enough to strike again.[112]

The president pressed on, saying that he was counting on Arab hospitality and the king's personal assistance to solve "the problem of Zionism."[113]

Ibn Saud was unmovable. Yet there is a poignancy in his response, because it was so heartfelt in light of his inexperience with the complexities of Western geopolitics.

"Make the enemy and the oppressor pay," the king said. "That is how we Arabs wage war. Amends should be made by the criminal, not by the innocent bystander. What injury have Arabs done to the Jews of Europe? It is the 'Christian' Germans who stole their homes and lives. Let the Germans pay."[114]

Convinced that war would come between the Arabs and Jews unless a compromise could be reached,[115] FDR complained to Ibn Saud that he had been most unhelpful. Although the king found much to like and admire about Roosevelt, and always treasured the wheelchair that FDR presented to him as a gift, Ibn Saud had no intention of negotiating on the topic of Zionism.[116]

One portion of their conversation that Eddy left out of his monograph was revealed by Charles Bohlen. In *Witness to History*, Bohlen recounted that Ibn Saud gave FDR "a long dissertation on the basic attitude of Arabs toward the Jews."[117] The king's observations would prove to be tragically prescient.

Ibn Saud said that the conflict was not based on the fact that the immigrants to Palestine were Jews: it was that they came from eastern Europe, and they were "technically and culturally on a higher level than the Arabs," and thus the Arabs could not compete with them and would end up struggling to feed their families.[118]

"Arabs," Ibn Saud concluded, "would choose to die rather than yield their land to the Jews."[119]

Roosevelt did promise Ibn Saud that the United States would undertake no actions contrary to Arab interests nor alter its policy in Palestine without speaking to both Arabs and Jews, a promise the president reiterated in writing once he returned to Washington.[120] But FDR had been dispirited by his conversation with the king. Eleanor Roosevelt recalled that her husband told her that not reaching an agreement on Palestine with Ibn Saud was "his one complete failure."[121]

Not only did his failure add to his concern about the survivors, but by the early winter of 1945 the size and scope of Nazi atrocities were being confirmed – acts that were, as one correspondent wrote, "so wantonly cruel that, without such confirmation, they might have been discounted as propagandist inventions."[122]

It was as though Bogdan Chmielnicki had reemerged from the seventeenth century armed with modern technology that enabled an uncontrollable hatred to sweep across the landscape like the foul breath of a cockatrice. In Budapest, seventeen high Hungarian army officers were hanged for torturing and killing camp inmates.[123] In Lithuania, over one hundred Germans faced charges for their role in murdering 465,000 people.[124] In Algiers, a military tribunal was hearing evidence against the overseers of the Vichy concentration camps in North Africa.[125] In Germany, a captured Nazi corporal bragged to a journalist that he couldn't remember how many civilians he had killed – there were too many. Without a trace of guilt, he spoke about his fellow soldiers routinely robbing Jews in their homes, then raping the young girls and killing the families. He remembered witnessing German troops machine-gunning hundreds of Jews on the outskirts of Odessa, on the exact hill where the Nazis had previously mowed down fifteen thousand others.[126] He recalled Russian prisoners, still alive, being pushed into furnaces, and thousands of Jewish children being starved to death or dispatched with poison injections. He even added a tale of romance about a German solider who had fallen in love with a Jewish girl and begged a commanding officer to spare her. The officer had the lovers shot.[127]

In March, hoping to get a handle on the mounting crisis of the survivors, President Roosevelt appointed Earl G. Harrison as US representative to the Intergovernmental Committee on Refugees.[128] A former commissioner of immigration and naturalization, and later dean of the University of Pennsylvania Law School, Harrison was tall and square-jawed with an ample supply of energy, rectitude, and compassion.[129] He would need all three qualities to address the survivors' long-term problem – they had nowhere to go. Remaining in Germany, as Roosevelt had told Ibn Saud, was not appealing, and for most returning to their prewar homes was out of the question.

Towns, villages, and cities across the Continent lay in ruins. Sometimes the survivors did return, only to discover that their houses and possessions had been appropriated by their gentile neighbors or that their countrymen had not yet had their fill of Jewish slaughter. In Kielce, Poland, where the Nazis had killed or deported to Treblinka, Buchenwald, and Auschwitz almost all of the twenty-seven thousand Jews in the ghetto, 150 Jews who had survived or waited out the war by hiding in the woods sought refuge in the town's erstwhile Jewish community center. Soon, rumors were circulating: the Jews murdered a Polish boy to use his blood for matzo. No, not for matzo, according to the woman who went screaming through the streets – the Jews were murdering Polish children to drink their blood. Mobs formed outside the center. The Jews contacted the police and church leaders. No one would help and, in the ensuing pogrom, forty-two Jews were killed and dozens were injured.[130] The violence spread around the region with the speed of a plague. Thirty more Jews died, and the quarter of a million Polish Jews who had survived the Holocaust took flight.

◆ ◆ ◆

On April 12, 1945, Vice President Harry S. Truman was about to have a drink in Speaker of the House Samuel T. Rayburn's downstairs refuge in the Capitol when he was summoned by phone to the White House. There, in an upstairs sitting room, Eleanor Roosevelt informed him that her husband was dead.[131]

As the nation mourned, the new president went to work. Since 1943, when Truman was a senator, he had spoken about assisting the Jews who survived the Nazis and promised to support the creation of a Jewish homeland.[132] He had grown up next door to an observant Jewish family and become close with them, doing the chores that were forbidden to them on the Sabbath,[133] and one of his oldest friends, his former business partner Eddie Jacobson, was Jewish. Nevertheless, that did not prevent Truman from describing New York City as a "Kike town," and a poker player he considered "greedy" as a fellow who "screamed like a Jewish merchant."[134] His wife, Bess, like her mother before her, would not permit a Jew to enter their house in Independence, Missouri.[135]

David K. Niles, a Jew, was the White House liaison to ethnic minorities under FDR and Truman,[136] and he believed that Truman was genuinely sympathetic toward the survivors – a sympathy that Niles did not believe Roosevelt shared.[137] Truman had voiced his concern for their situation at the Potsdam Conference in July, where the leaders of the United States, Britain, and the Soviet Union gathered to follow through on the agreements made at Yalta. The president requested that the British permit the survivors to enter Palestine, but Britain was concerned about the Arab reaction, and Truman would not commit the military to protecting the new immigrants from the violence that would undoubtedly greet them.[138]

Truman turned to David Niles, who had been an enigma throughout his career. A wispy, balding, bespectacled man, he refrained from stepping into the spotlight, but offstage allegedly wielded substantial power. One story claimed that Niles was among FDR's most influential advisers during the New Deal. Another story posited that Niles had persuaded John L. Lewis, president of the United Mine Workers of America, to contribute half a million dollars to Roosevelt's 1936 campaign – a story that Niles refused to confirm or deny.[139] A reporter observed that "facts always have been in short supply for those seeking to talk or write about [Niles],"[140] but one did not have to look far to identify the wellspring of his sympathy for the survivors and his support for a Jewish homeland. In 1891, a year after Niles was born in Russian Poland, his parents, Sophie and Ascher Neyhus, had come to the United States, anglicized their last name, and settled in the slums of Boston's North End, where Niles grew up the poor, Yiddish-speaking son of a tailor.[141]

Following his death in September 1952, the *New York Times* ran an obituary in which the writer remarked that Niles was considered "instrumental in winning independence for Israel, yet again the part he played remains only in vague outline."[142]

That outline would have been less vague had more attention been paid to the statement President Truman issued to the press memorializing Niles: "In the work he did for displaced persons, untold numbers of people, many of whom may never know his name, have found a chance to live again in dignity.[143]

In part, Truman was referring to the fact that it was Niles who prevailed upon him, after Germany signed an unconditional surrender on May 7, 1945, to send Earl Harrison to Europe and produce a report on what could be done about the hundreds of thousands of survivors languishing in displaced persons camps.[144]

It was a decision that, in the end, would not simply address the predicament of the hurt and homeless, but would reverberate along the length of the Cold War, playing a pivotal role in the fate of nations. Steven L. Spiegel observes in *The Other Arab-Israeli Conflict*, his inquiry into the making of America's Middle East policy, that by dispatching Harrison "almost by accident and without any clear direction…Truman began to enmesh the United States in the Palestine question."[145]

History is a busy, crowded place, where the dead find eternal life by continuing to compete with each other for top billing, and historians, in a bid to leave their own mark, are constantly realigning the names on the marquee. As the heat of the present cools, accomplishments blend into the daily blur of events until even the most illustrious achievements are taken for granted, and players' names are removed from the lights, awaiting resurrection or disappearing permanently into the past.

David Niles was such a player – even more so, Earl Harrison. As much as any single individual, Harrison forced an America intent on celebrating the closing months of the war to see the wretched circumstances of the refugees, and made clear the moral imperative to help.

In Europe, Harrison discovered that survivors were still watching the days pass by through barbed wire, wearing the striped pajamas of the concentration camp inmate, or, when those clothes rotted off their bodies, donning old German SS uniforms.[146]

"It is questionable," he later wrote to Truman, "which clothing they hate the more."[147]

To Harrison, it appeared that the United States was "treating the Jews as the Nazis treated them except that we do not exterminate them. They are in concentration camps…under our military guard instead of SS troops. One is led to wonder whether the German people, seeing this, are not supposing that we are following or at least condoning Nazi policy."[148]

While Harrison toured the internment camps searching for a solution to the refugee problem, one man, a former subject of the tsar, was certain that he had the answer. Born in a shtetl in the Pale of Settlement, David Green had been just eleven years old when the journalist and playwright Theodor Herzl convened the first Zionist Congress in Switzerland in 1897. Herzl died in 1904, but his dream persisted, and two years later David Green boarded a cargo ship and sailed to Palestine. There he changed his last name to Ben-Gurion, and worked tirelessly to build a Jewish homeland – so tirelessly that the Ottomans, who ruled Palestine, deported him to the United States.[149] In 1917, while Ben-Gurion was traveling America beating the drum for Zionism, Dr. Chaim Weizmann, another Zionist born in a Russian shtetl and now a successful chemist in England, finally saw his efforts pay off when Britain's foreign secretary, Lord Arthur James Balfour, issued his declaration proclaiming that his government favored "the establishment in Palestine of a national home for the Jewish people."[150] Ben-Gurion volunteered for the Jewish Legion of the British Army – one of the twenty-six thousand Jews from Palestine who served His Majesty in the First World War. The Ottomans were defeated and their empire partitioned, and Britain was awarded a League of Nations Mandate over Palestine. Ben-

Gurion returned to *Eretz Yisrael* and became head of the Jewish Agency, a stand-in government for the Jews living under the mandate.

David Ben-Gurion rarely visited a synagogue and enjoyed eating ham for breakfast,[151] but there was something otherworldly about this thick-bodied, elfin dynamo with smoldering eyes and a crown of frizzy hair circling his bald, leonine head, this dreamer who spoke eight languages, immersed himself in the wisdom of Plato and Buddha, and amassed a library in his modest Tel Aviv home of twenty thousand books and periodicals.[152] In some respects, Ben-Gurion embodied the qualities of the *luftmensch* (literally, in Yiddish, "air man," meaning one who rejects the mundane in favor of the high altitude of the intellect – a scattered, absent-minded fellow who opts for the ideal over the pragmatic).

Yet when it came to the mathematics of survival, Ben-Gurion was as practical and plodding as a counting-house clerk, and tallied every soul. In 1922, there were 84,000 Jews and 590,000 Arabs in Palestine. In 1931, the Jewish population rose to 174,000, and the Arabs reached 760,000. Two years later, Hitler seized the reins of power in Germany, and by 1939, as the Second World War began, the flight from Europe swelled the Jewish population to 450,000, with the Arab population double that number.[153]

Forever a child of *Rossiyskaya Imperiya*, Ben-Gurion agreed with what the Russian Jew Leon Pinsker had concluded in *Auto-Emancipation* over sixty years before the death camps were uncovered – that Jews would remain hated and vulnerable until they had built a home of their own. For Ben-Gurion, the slaughter of the six million was possible "only because we were a nation without a homeland,"[154] and avoiding another catastrophe would require a state stocked with enough people to support and defend itself.

To call this a bedrock belief would underestimate the intensity with which Ben-Gurion felt immigration into a Jewish homeland would guarantee the survival of his people. The revelations of the Holocaust ripened his belief into an obsession that occupied Ben-Gurion well beyond the founding of Israel. For instance, in 1966, at a formal gathering at the Sheraton Hotel in Tel Aviv, when the American Jewish leader Max M. Fisher presented the former prime minister with an ancient glass vessel in honor of his eightieth birthday, Ben-Gurion said to him, "You should come live here." Fisher, who had grown up in a small Ohio town and spent his entire adulthood in Detroit, was a rather unlikely candidate for *aliyah*, but Ben-Gurion's comment was a measure of the depth of his conviction that a vibrant Jewish state was the most effective safeguard against another Hitler. His conviction would become a feature of the national psyche of Israel, so much so that on Holocaust Remembrance Day (Yom ha-Shoah) in April 1992, Ehud Barak, then chief of staff of the Israel Defense Forces, journeyed to Auschwitz and, in his speech, observed that although the IDF had at last arrived "under the gray skies of Poland," they were "fifty years too late."[155]

It was this profound faith in Israel as the protector of world Jewry that would, decades hence, inflame the debate between Israeli and American Jews over where the Soviet Jewish emigrants belonged.

If the Holocaust underscored for Ben-Gurion that perpetual wandering led Jews to the charnel house, it also provided him with a chance "to convert the great disaster of our people in exile into a powerful lever of redemption."[156] And so, as early as December 1944, after the Russian army liberated Bulgaria, Ben-Gurion traveled to the city of Sofia and addressed the Jewish survivors who had jammed into a movie theater to hear him speak. Cheers erupted when Ben-Gurion said that he was looking forward to them joining him in *Eretz Yisrael*.[157]

Over the next year, Ben-Gurion would visit the DP camps in Germany, seeing in the ravaged souls of his displaced people the rejuvenated future citizens of his unborn state. On one visit, he spoke to General Dwight D. Eisenhower and raised the art of chutzpah to new heights by requesting that the Supreme Allied Commander assign the Jewish DPs to their own mini-homeland in the south of Germany, where they could be readied to emigrate to Palestine by receiving training that would prepare them for sorely needed trades, with an emphasis on farming, and to serve in the armed forces. Eisenhower, though sympathetic to the hardships faced by the survivors, had no power to comply with Ben-Gurion's request.[158]

By then, Earl Harrison had delivered his secret report to Truman – but it did not stay secret for long. Less than a month later, his findings were splashed across the front page of the *New York Times*, elevating the sorrows of the refugees to a matter of national concern. The president had already ordered General Eisenhower to clean up the situation. The concentration camps were shut down, makeshift camps for Jews were created, and the responsibility for the care of the survivors was handed over to the United Nations.[159] In his report, Harrison made it clear to Truman that the survivors preferred "to be evacuated to Palestine now, just as other national groups are being repatriated to their homes."[160] He recommended that one hundred thousand of the refugees be permitted to enter Palestine.[161] Truman approved the recommendation and passed it along to the British government.[162]

Blocking the survivors' path to Palestine was the White Paper, which had been issued by the British government in the spring of 1939.[163] That year, disturbed about Nazi belligerence and wanting to keep the Arab countries on their side in the event of war, Britain reversed the Balfour Declaration's support for a Jewish national home by limiting Jewish immigration to just seventy-five thousand over a period of five years, and halting transfers of land to Jews.[164]

The White Paper was among the more inhumane pieces of realpolitik that the British Empire had concocted, as it left the Jews living under Hitler's baneful shadow desperate for a haven and unable to reach Palestine. Winston Churchill said as much to Prime Minister Neville Chamberlain and his government when the White Paper was published, reiterating that the promise of a home "was not made to the Jews of Palestine, but to the Jews outside Palestine, to that vast, unhappy mass of scattered, persecuted, wandering Jews."[165]

Six years later, despite the humanitarian crisis that emerged as the concentration camps were liberated, the British government, headed by Churchill, was reluctant to relax the constraints of the White Paper. This new reluctance was a result of the economic and geopolitical fallout from the war: The British had exhausted 25 percent of their wealth fighting the Axis, the nation was perched on the perilous ledge of bankruptcy, and its most valuable resource was the oil it controlled in the Middle East. Why should they alienate the Arabs? Moreover, between 1943 and 1947, as historian Howard M. Sachar points out, Britain "fulfilled their long-cherished ambition of maneuvering the French out of Syria and Lebanon," the realization of a longtime imperialistic goal.[166] Finally, by holding on to the mandated land in Palestine, Britain would discourage Soviet expansionism in the region.[167]

In Britain, the Conservatives were thrashed by the Labor Party in the 1945 election. Voters favored a "coherent plan of social welfare," and they were tired of what they perceived as "Tory apathy toward social change."[168] Churchill was replaced as prime minister by Clement Attlee, who named Ernest Bevin as his foreign secretary. Bevin had previously been an enthusiastic supporter of Zionism, but suddenly his support soured into an outspoken hostility toward Jews. In public, he stated that the Americans were trying to fill Palestine with Jews to prevent them from coming to America. Bevin followed up that charge by diving into the deeper end of the antisemitic cesspool, claiming that Jews were running a worldwide conspiracy from the United States against both Britain and Bevin, and he was convinced that the atrocities the Germans had perpetrated against the Jews had been taught to them by the Jews themselves.[169]

The British response to Truman's suggestion that they allow one hundred thousand survivors to enter Palestine was to delay by asking that a study group explore the question. Thus, the Anglo-American Committee of Inquiry was formed, and when they seconded Truman's suggestion, another group was born, the Morrison-Grady Committee. These delays met the immediate political needs of both the United States and Britain. Truman wanted to avoid all responsibility for whatever violence and economic needs would arise in Palestine, and the British were hesitant to relinquish a piece of their empire and, in the process, further irritate the Arab Middle East.[170]

In Palestine, the Hebrew Resistance Movement freed illegal immigrants from a detention camp and sabotaged railroads and British ships, infuriating the Labor government.[171] A more effective response to Britain's refusal to permit the survivors to emigrate, however, was an organized underground effort known as Brichah (escape).[172]

In the 1930s, hoping to save Jews from the Nazis, the Jewish Agency had supported illegal immigration (Aliyah Bet) and now the Agency assisted the Brichah, dispatching members of the underground to Europe, where they blended into the DP camps and organized Jews who had been living hand to mouth, walking from town to town, searching in vain for their vanished world.[173]

Slowly, this tattered ribbon of humanity started to wind through the Polish-Slovak mountains, through Upper Silesia and Bohemia, through Szczecin and into Berlin, winding steadily through crumbled cities and burned countryside. They continued through Prague and Bavaria, through Bratislava to Vienna, then on to Salzburg and Graz and into Germany, France, or preferably Italy, since the Italian coastline, jagged with inlets, seemed tailor-made for smuggling out human cargo.[174] Each voyage either brought Jewish immigrants to Palestine or, if the ship was caught in the net of the British blockade and the passengers were interned in the detention camps in Cyprus, generated sympathy for the Zionists by highlighting the heartlessness of Britain's policy toward the survivors.[175]

It is estimated that a quarter of a million Jews took advantage of the routes carved out by Brichah, making it "the largest organized illegal mass movement in modern times."[176] One little-noted feature of this illegal transit program was that it was partially funded by the American Jewish Joint Distribution Committee (JDC), a remarkable transformation for an organization whose charter members were generally opposed to Zionism.[177] This point becomes particularly interesting in the context of exploring the background of the Soviet Jewry advocacy that would arise in the United States.

The JDC had its origins in 1914, when US Ambassador to Turkey Henry Morgenthau Sr. cabled Louis Marshall and the financier Jacob H. Schiff, a giant in New York's banking world and one of the city's foremost philanthropists.[178] Morgenthau asked the two men to raise $50,000 to feed Jews in Palestine who were living under the Ottomans and on the verge of starvation. The money was raised and the JDC was founded, but Ambassador Morgenthau remained a doctrinaire anti-Zionist, a not uncommon position among the German Jewish upper class at the JDC and over at the older, more prestigious American Jewish Committee, which had been founded in 1906 as pogroms spread through Russia.[179]

A major part of the German Jewish establishment's argument against Zionism was that funds should not be earmarked for an unnecessary dream, when Europe already had sizeable Jewish centers that could be supported in place. And the JDC did help everywhere it could, including working with the Soviet government in the 1920s on the Agro-Joint, a program that resettled some seventy thousand Jews in the Ukraine and the Crimea and trained them for agricultural labor.[180]

As rational as their argument might seem on the surface, their hostility – or, at best, their indifference – toward Zionism was more psychological than practical.

On a superficial level was the fact that Zionism, in the main, was most ardently embraced by eastern European Jewry, while the German Jews, though feeling bound to assist their poorer, less educated brethren, tended to look down on them. Beneath this social conceit was a web of feelings that the historian Barbara W. Tuchman explored in her essay "The Assimilationist Dilemma." Tuchman recalled how her illustrious grandfather, Henry Morgenthau Sr., had been among the largest contributors to President Woodrow Wilson's campaign, but his reward was not, as he had hoped, a position in the cabinet. Instead, Morgenthau was handed "a minor ambassadorship" to Turkey. Tuchman recalled that her grandfather was pained by the appointment because "it was a post set aside for Jews," and he harbored such a "passionate desire to prove that a Jew could...be accepted in America on equal grounds." It was this desire and "the fear of being thought to have another loyalty" that made [Morgenthau] and others like him resist Zionism," which they felt "would supply an added cause for discrimination."[181]

So here is the nagging predicament of "dual allegiance," as though one confronted an existential choice between being an American and being a Jew. Behind this identity crisis was the unregenerate demon of antisemitism. Jews who had struggled to assimilate into wider Christian society were afraid to expose themselves to the antisemitic allegation that, because of their allegiance to Palestine (and later, Israel), they were incapable of being patriotic Americans.[182]

This is why the fact that the Joint Distribution Committee funded the Brichah operation deserves attention. It should be noted that at Earl Harrison's request, the JDC's European director, Dr. Joseph J. Schwartz, accompanied him on his tour of the camps; surely the traumatic revelation of German atrocities coupled with the dire straits of the survivors contributed to the JDC's uncharacteristic support for a blatantly Zionist undertaking.[183]

Not all assimilated segments of American Jewry were opposed to

Zionism: Louis D. Brandeis, for one, who was raised in Louisville, Kentucky, and was the first Jew to be appointed to the Supreme Court, was a friend to the cause. Brandeis was no stranger to antisemitism, not even in the rarefied atmosphere of the Court, where the openly antisemitic Justice James Clark McReynolds frequently insulted him.[184] Brandeis stated that "Jews [are] by reason of their traditions and their character peculiarly fitted for the attainment of American ideals," and these qualities would only be enhanced by establishing "a center from which the Jewish spirit may radiate and give to the Jews scattered throughout the world that inspiration which springs from the memories of a great past and the hope of a great future."[185]

Brandeis was revered by American Jews, though his public statements did not halt the argument about Zionism. In the 1930s, the Nazi assault on German Jewry muted the dueling voices long enough for the United Jewish Appeal to be created from other philanthropic agencies as an umbrella group. Yet from the outset, the UJA was plagued by internecine squabbling over whether to relocate the refugees to Palestine.[186] In 1941, the UJA raised $14 million; by 1945, the amount climbed to $35 million; and by 1946, as the horrific facts of the genocide and the resettlement needs of the survivors became widely known, contributions surpassed $100 million, a staggering figure by the standards of the day.[187]

Despite this success, Irving Bernstein, who spent forty years at the United Jewish Appeal and became its executive vice chairman, remembered the early UJA leadership as "hesitant."[188] From 1944 until 1952, 137,450 Jews immigrated to the United States from Europe, the overwhelming majority of them Holocaust survivors;[189] approximately three times that number would make their way to Israel.[190] Yet even after the founding of the Jewish state in 1948,[191] the argument over Zionism continued, at a less feverish pitch. It was rejuvenated following the 1967 Six-Day War by the New Left and persists until today, repudiating Leon Pinsker's assertion (shared by Theodor Herzl[192]) that a Jewish state would alleviate antisemitism; in reality, it has provided another target.

In the mid-1940s, the realization that the Nazis did not distinguish between Zionists and anti-Zionists when they selected their victims for the gas chambers temporarily quieted the debate, but another development had a more lasting impact, one that can been be seen by looking at the evolution of the United Jewish Appeal.

From its inception in 1939, the organization had been predominantly overseen by the German Jewish elite. However, by 1961, when *Time* magazine ran a story on the UJA with the headline "The No. 1 Charity," the baton of leadership had passed to the descendants of eastern European Jews. That year, the Baltimore real-estate developer Joseph Meyerhoff became the general chairman of the UJA. Meyerhoff was eight years old in 1907 when his parents fled from Tsarist Russia to the United States,[193] and his feelings about Zionism were unequivocal. As Meyerhoff told *Time*, "In my family, we took for granted that being a Jew and being interested in what was first Palestine and is now Israel were one and the same thing."[194]

Four years later, Max Fisher succeeded Meyerhoff as UJA chairman. Born in 1908 in Pittsburgh, Fisher's parents were Russian immigrants. Fisher was an unapologetic Zionist in the mold of Brandeis, and by 1969 he would unite the often competitive Jewish philanthropic organizations by heading not only the UJA but the Council of Jewish Federations and the United Israel Appeal.

The result of this change was the marriage between Jewish philanthropy and Israel. In 1961, this was hardly an earthshaking development. In a matter of years, though, as Israel became an increasingly important piece in an elaborate, ever-shifting geopolitical jigsaw puzzle, organized American Jewry, with its network of advocacy and charitable groups and its fund-raising machinery, haunted by its inability to save the six million, was suddenly caught up in the whirlwind of US-Soviet relations.

◆ ◆ ◆

It can become a guilty pleasure identifying the unintended consequences of the tsars driving the Jews from Russia. Consider the story of Blume and Moshe Mabovitch fleeing the "poverty, cold, hunger and fear"[195] of the empire with their children to settle in Milwaukee, Wisconsin, where not only did their daughter, Golda, grow so enthralled with Zionism that she moved to Palestine, but at the age of seventy-one she was elected prime minister of Israel.

For many American Jews the tale of Golda Meir endures as a satisfying irony, though as ironies go it is small in comparison to the more meaningful outcomes created by the influx of Russian Jews into the United States – an influx that would help define the issues of the Cold War and provide its final battleground. And so casting a discerning glance backward at Imperial Russia and the Jews who spurned her bitter embrace, it is not difficult to see that the seeds of the American movement to free Soviet Jewry, which began in earnest in the 1960s, were sown under the reign of Nicholas I, during those grim years between 1825 and 1855.

What is harder to spot, yet indispensable to understand, is the quintessentially American character of this movement. That part of the story belongs to a history that played out far from the palaces of the tsars and the shtetls of the Pale.

After all, the end result of a quarter-century of advocacy – opening the doors of the Soviet Union wide enough for 1.2 million Jews to leave – involved the efforts of Americans of diverse religious and ethnic backgrounds: for example, Father George Ford, [196] Sisters Ann Gillen[197] and Rose Thering,[198] Senator Henry M. Jackson, Congressman Charles A. Vanik, President Ronald W. Reagan, and Secretary of State George P. Shultz, along with millions of unnamed Americans who supported the ethical underpinnings of the cause.

One challenge to parsing any movement's origins and accomplishments is that as historians zoom in to examine the subject in detail, the events swirling around it are excluded from their field of vision. While this is a perpetual challenge to writers of history, it presents a minefield of complexities when exploring a movement born amid the accelerated social upheaval of the 1960s.

Another challenge is the frequently unacknowledged desire of the historian to apportion credit, to place events on a potter's wheel and shape them to fit a predetermined conclusion. With respect to the Soviet Jewry movement this desire has prolonged arguments, in recast forms, that occurred while the history was being created.

Take the conflict among the grassroots groups – notably the Union of Councils of Soviet Jews (UCSJ) and the Student Struggle for Soviet Jewry (SSSJ) – and the established organs of the American Jewish community, a fight that broke out as the movement gathered momentum in the United States. In *From Exodus to Freedom*, the author, Stuart Altshuler, credits the UCSJ and the SSSJ as "playing a decisive role in the overall making of policy for the Soviet Jewry movement."[199] At best, this claim is highly debatable. As we will see, it was the pressure to *form and sustain* a policy – no small accomplishment – that came from the grassroots, their unwavering dedication, and ceaseless public protests. Yet even if one rejected both of these assertions, I doubt that it would be possible to identify the exact calibration of decisiveness in a decades-long chronicle of a human rights struggle, with a lengthy list of dramatis personae. On the other hand, I am quite certain that the attempt only serves to distort the past by dismissing a number of the enlaced forces at play.

Fred A. Lazin, in his fascinating study *The Struggle for Soviet Jewry: Israel versus the American Jewish Establishment*, takes up an even older debate: Zionism. Lazin tailors the argument to the rescue of Soviet Jewry by focusing on the conflict that arose over whether the emigrants should go to Israel or the United States. Beneath this discussion you will find the larger question of whether the original Zionist dream succeeded or failed. While this is an interesting question, it hardly clarifies the forces behind the effort to free Soviet Jews. Nor does Lazin shy away from awarding blue ribbons. Early on, he repeats the claim of political scientist Daniel Elazar that "the American Jewish community had moved beyond Israel and evolved into the prime force in the Soviet Jewry movement."[200] He then proceeds to attack the claim by highlighting the continued involvement of the Israeli Liaison Bureau (*Lishkat Hakesher*).

The unadorned truth of the matter is that while both Israelis and Americans were intent on the rescue of Soviet Jews, their motivations and approaches were not identical – no surprise since, then and now, Israel and the United States face different challenges as nations and feature different cultures, and any homegrown movement must reflect these differences.

Granted, there were arguments over the destination of the emigrants, and yet, practically speaking, the arguments were beside the point, since the United States was never going to absorb hundreds of thousands of Soviet Jews in so short a time, and the sole realistic option for the great majority of emigrants was Israel. In addition, glancing in the rearview mirror to determine whose force was more or less prime is a pursuit of diminishing returns when compared to charting, as much as possible, the currents that gave rise to the movement and demonstrating how the combined efforts of all involved paid off.

To reengage in these narrow battles strips the Soviet Jewry movement of its context. For better or for worse, from its inception the movement was a chapter in the saga of the Cold War, as much a feature of that symbol-laden conflict as the Berlin Wall and the Fischer-Spassky chess match. Unquestionably, it was important to remove the bars from what Andrei Sakharov, the renowned Soviet physicist who coinvented the hydrogen bomb and later became one of the world's most famous dissidents, referred to as "the Soviet cage,"[201] but there were always bigger issues at stake.

Recalling the wars fought by Israel during those perilous years, Shimon Peres, who has held numerous positions at the highest level of the Israeli government, observes, "Israel against the Arabs – yes. Israel against the Arabs and Russians – no."[202]

This reality alone – that the United States was the ultimate guarantor of Israel's safety – highlights the distortion of examining Soviet Jewry as though unconnected to a larger narrative. The boundaries of the Cold War were drawn by President Dwight Eisenhower when he rejected the idea of limited nuclear strikes and ordered preparations for an all-out nuclear engagement. He believed that the potential of total destruction – not the delusion of a warhead here, a warhead there, and life goes on its merry way – would prevent the superpowers from either inching toward, or having their respective allies drag them to, a thermonuclear abyss.[203] His strategy worked. Save for the Cuban Missile Crisis and the aftermath of the Yom Kippur War, the superpowers never got close to Armageddon – even during the bloodiest fighting in Korea, Vietnam, and Afghanistan.

With the passing of time, with boys and girls no longer huddling in the hallways of their grammar schools in preparation for the inevitable hour of the Soviet attack, with suburbanites no longer investing small fortunes by installing bomb shelters under their homes, and with towns no longer sounding air raid sirens on Saturday afternoons, it is easy to forget the pervasive fear of pushed buttons and mushroom clouds, and how that fear informed every transaction between Washington and Moscow, coloring the lens through which events were interpreted, shaping the information by which decisions were made.

Whittled to its essence, the history of the Cold War is nothing more than the record of this fear.

Apart from the superpowers, the Israelis were wrestling with their own existential nightmares, and Soviet Jews, especially the brave refuseniks, had plenty to worry about. Yet one would still expect Israel to cast her eyes on Soviet Jewry, for the ingathering of persecuted Jews was her raison d'être, and the Jewish state was in dire need of citizens as a buttress against the numerical superiority of the Arabs. Nor is it hard to comprehend why the refuseniks desperately wanted out. But what of this American interest in the fate of Russian Jews? Where did that come from? And why did Russian Jews believe, decades before they conjured up those mythical twenty-four-karat paving stones and began to emigrate en masse to the United States, that America might help them?

Here is a mystery to be solved, a rich vein of history to be mined, and so, let us return to Rostov-on-Don, where we find Abraham Nadich on a May afternoon in 1865.

♦ ♦ ♦

Let's imagine the sun was shining, polishing the cloudless sky to a glimmering blue, and from our vantage point, on a hill overlooking the city, we can see great wooden ships entering and leaving the port, their hulls churning the water of the Don to foam, their white sails billowing in the wind. Past the gold onion domes of the cathedrals, glistening in the sunlight, and past the old Jewish prayer house, we see the bazaars, where women sell fish from woven baskets while peddlers, bent under their wares, troll for customers, avoiding the sharp-eyed men running card games, and the nimble-fingered pickpockets gliding through the crowds. The haggling and chatter fills the fragrant air like the lively music of lutes and zithers.

And there is Abraham Nadich, hurrying to the telegraph office with a jaunty spring in his step. He has recovered from his gloominess of the night before, because after he awoke from a fitful sleep, as he wrote, his "tired mind caught eagerly the idea that the report [of Lincoln's assassination] may be false."

Whether this was the temporary relief of self-deception or the healthy suspicion that news in Imperial Russia – and later in the Soviet Union – often bore scant resemblance to the facts, we cannot know for sure, but Abraham Nadich entered the office, sent a wire to the United States consul in Odessa and, with hope warming him like sunrise, waited for an answer.

It would appear that he did not have long to wait for the consul, Timothy Smith, to reply: "Lincoln killed in theatre."

Abraham Nadich did not leave us an account of his reaction when he read the response, but shortly thereafter he revealed his feelings in his letter to Smith.

> Who should live if he is dead, killed by human hands? It seems as if mankind were guilty for not having arrested the blow. But still, if the death of my only darling son could have redeemed him from his fate I would have accepted it as a boon.

This was no small thought for a nineteenth-century Russian Jew to transcribe onto paper, as his culture was neither noted for its shortage of superstition nor its ability to distinguish between an expressed thought and a cause.

Then, as if offering the life of his son in exchange for the slain president did not capture the extent of his pain, Nadich added:

> It is awful! How could the very dumb and motionless walls of the building allow that crime?... Poor America! Abraham Lincoln! Thou shouldest have been invulnerable to iron and fire, thy blood should not have flown when iron cut thee, for thou belongest not to thyself and America only but to the whole world!

Nadich's cri de coeur, if not his literary touch, brings to mind the reaction of the American poet Walt Whitman, who, in his elegy to Lincoln, wrote:

> When lilacs last in the dooryard bloom'd, And the great star early droop'd in the western sky in the night, I mourn'd, and yet shall mourn with ever-returning spring.... O powerful western fallen star![204]

Whitman was grieving along with millions of his countrymen. American Jewry, though, was not of one mind about the Civil War; their loyalty, like that of their countrymen, was generally determined by whether they resided north or south of the Mason-Dixon Line.[205] For instance, Jewish immigrants from eastern and central Europe, who wound up Free Staters in the Kansas Territory, fought alongside the radical abolitionist John Brown, while Senator Judah P. Benjamin of Louisiana, a Jew born in the West Indies, served the Confederacy as attorney general, secretary of war, and secretary of state. Still, even in Northern cities like Newark, New Jersey, where blacks were free, voters roundly rejected Lincoln and sympathized with the rebels, for by 1860 two-thirds of the goods produced in Newark, from saddles to jewelry, were sold to the South.[206] Jews were among the business people who profited from this trade, and yet as a group, Newark's Jews identified with Lincoln, referring fondly to him in Yiddish as "*Unser Avrohom*" (Our Abraham).[207] They, like tens of thousands of other Jews around the nation, turned out to watch his funeral train roll on to Illinois.[208]

Jewish identification with Lincoln reached unprecedented heights when Rabbi Isaac M. Wise, the most prominent American Jew of his era, stated that the president had informed him that he was "a descendant of Hebrew parentage."[209] Wise made this claim more than once – including during his eulogy for the president, which was published. There is no evidence to support his claim, and apparently Lincoln forgot to tell anyone else that he was Jewish.[210]

Over a century later, this feeling of kinship with Lincoln persisted. Phillip Roth explored it in his novel *Portnoy's Complaint* when Alexander Portnoy, on an eighth-grade field trip to downtown Newark, considers the statues of Washington and Lincoln, and concludes that the Father of our country was "obviously a *goy*," but Lincoln radiated the suffering of the chosen people. The sixteenth president was "so *oysgemitchet* [exhausted]," his emotional fatigue caused by laboring on behalf of the downtrodden – a career path the young Portnoy hoped to pursue.[211]

Lincoln died during Passover, and in American synagogues the sorrowful hymns and melodies of Yom Kippur replaced those that celebrated the exodus from Egypt. Many Jews who had not planned on worshipping changed their minds and went to services, seeking comfort among their friends and neighbors. In their sermons, rabbis compared Lincoln to Moses and the tradition of the biblical prophets, and a common theme resounding through their remarks was that everyone who had sinned bore some blame for the assassination, since "Lincoln's death was a visitation from God, punishment of America for all the evil of the war."[212]

Abraham Nadich was not so theologically minded or self-accusatory. In his letter to Smith, he fumed:

> Death is but a slight punishment to the murdering wretches. I only wish they might feel the awful atrocity of their crime twenty-four hours before they die, and [the] agony of death suffered a hundred times over, in its sharpest shapes would be a trifle compared with it.

At first glance, his rage is striking, because it flies in the face of the widespread perception that the Jews of the Russian empire were wistful, passive acceptors of those who harmed them. This perception – more myth than reality – would be immortalized by the Ukrainian-born Jewish poet Hayyim Nahman Bialik in his epic work "In the City of Slaughter," his account of the 1903 pogrom in Kishinev, which castigated Jews for standing helplessly by while their families were raped and murdered.

Nadich's rage is also striking since the most grievous violence directed at the Jews of Rostov-on-Don lay coiled in the future – the anti-Jewish riots in 1883, a pogrom in 1905 that included the burning of the synagogue, and finally the Nazis, who were welcomed by many Russians as a potential relief from the cruelty of Stalin, and thus had little trouble rounding up and slaughtering twenty-seven thousand Jews in 1943.[213]

To some degree, the depth of Nadich's feelings is understandable. By 1865, the Russian empire already had a barbarous relationship with its Jews dating back over two centuries. On a more personal level, Nadich grew up under Nicholas I, during his relentless campaign to wipe out Jewish culture, and in all likelihood Nadich passed some of his childhood afraid that he would be ripped from his parents and dragooned into the army.

Yet by that May afternoon Abraham Nadich was an adult, a businessman who evinced more than a casual knowledge of international affairs and who, for the past decade, had been living under the liberal tsar Alexander II. However, in his letter to Smith, Nadich made no mention of Alexander II. His sole focus was on Lincoln – not simply his death but his symbolic value to mankind.

Why, one wonders, was Lincoln a greater symbol to Nadich than Alexander II? After all, the tsar had not only relaxed the restrictions on his Jewish subjects, he had emancipated the serfs two years before Lincoln freed a limited number of slaves.[214]

So two questions arise: What might Abraham Nadich have known about Lincoln beyond the obvious? And more important, what might Nadich have known about America?

◆ ◆ ◆

In December of 1862, a month prior to signing the Emancipation Proclamation, President Lincoln sent a message to Congress in which he described the United States as "the last best hope of earth."[215]

By that winter, James M. McPherson writes that Lincoln was afraid that the United States was about to suffer "the fate of most republics," a plunge into disorder and oblivion. That fear was primary in his commitment to making certain that North held steady against the Confederacy, thus ensuring a future in which his country would be "governed by popular suffrage, majority rule, and the Constitution."[216]

Europe was less sanguine about the United States as the Promised Land. The London *Times*, which viewed America as "a nightmare," wished "success to the Confederate cause."[217] The French paper *La Patrie* crowed that "the work of George Washington has come to an end."[218] A Spanish journal, *Pensamiento Español*, expressed little surprise that brother was slaughtering brother since the United States "was populated by the dregs" of every country in the world and the fratricide was the logical result of a nation "constituting itself according to the flaming theories of democracy."[219]

McPherson observes that "anti-Americanism was the hobby of the European 'Right,'"[220] but it was a hobby cultivated in blood and sorrow. Europe had suffered through 1848, their Year of Revolution, which the French political thinker Alexis de Tocqueville described as a period when "society was cut in two: those who had nothing united in common envy, and those who had anything united in common terror."[221] How can you blame European aristocrats for preferring the established order to violent chaos? Also, Lincoln's "last, best hope" remark was an optimistic assertion, since his countrymen were embroiled in a savage war, and slavery persisted even though Britain had outlawed the practice and Russia had freed her serfs. Lincoln was claiming a moral high ground that, at that moment, the United States did not occupy. Since he – like the presidents who followed him – was never shy about preaching America's devotion to freedom, it was inevitable that when the United States fell short of its own standards, Europeans, weary of being preached at, would fire back.

George Washington had predicted that the War of Independence would reverberate through history, "for with our fate will the destiny of unborn millions be involved,"[222] and he lived to see his prediction come true. The aftershock of the American Revolution stirred intellectuals across Russia and shook the foundation of the House of Romanov. Copies of the United States Constitution were imported and recopied and passed from hand to hand,[223] a forerunner of the underground *samizdat* (self-published literature) that would be used two centuries later to spread the words of freedom under Soviet rule.[224] Long before Abraham Nadich wrote that Lincoln should have been "invulnerable to iron and fire," Russians elevated George Washington and Benjamin Franklin to the status of heroes, believing that the ideas nurtured by these men and their compatriots offered a possible respite from the tyranny of the tsars. Franklin was wildly popular. He was the first American invited to join Russia's national academy of sciences,[225] and the first American author to have his work translated into Russian. By today's standards, the translations of his *Autobiography* and *Poor Richard's Almanack* would have been best sellers.[226]

Invigorated by the upstart colonials' defeat of the British, the Russian social critic Aleksandr Radishchev wrote an ode to liberty, and in 1790 when he published part of it in his *Journey from St. Petersburg to Moscow*, Catherine the Great exiled him to Siberia, and his book was burned.[227] Burning books is a notoriously short-term solution to freedom's call, and by December 1825, on the ice-crusted streets of St. Petersburg, a group of army officers who favored a constitutional government gathered in the Senate Square with three thousand soldiers who refused to swear allegiance to the new tsar, Nicholas I. The rebels, many of whom were the sons of nobility, gathered around the statue of Peter the Great[228] while thousands of spectators braved the cold to watch them.[229] By nightfall, Nicholas ordered his cavalry to attack, but their sabers were too dull to disperse the rebels. At last, Nicholas ordered that cannons be fired into the square, and the grapeshot ended the insurrection.[230] The ringleaders of the "Decemberists" were arrested. Some were executed; others were shipped to Siberia – and Nicholas ordered that all information about America be strictly censored.[231]

Still, relations between Russia and the United States were friendly. The Russian-American Commercial Treaty of 1832 formalized trading rights between the countries and bestowed the economic blessings of most-favored-nation (MFN) status. During the Crimean War, political opinion in the United States was squarely on the side of the Russians, not the British and French. American physicians traveled to the war zone to help treat the wounded, an American submarine maker and salvage specialist cleared the sunken ships from Sevastopol harbor, and American shipbuilders furnished new warships to the Russian navy.[232]

After 1855, when Alexander II became tsar and a Western-style faith in progress and openness were in vogue, Abraham Nadich would have been exposed to copious amounts of information about America because the press was permitted to operate without much interference from government censors.[233] For the most part, Russians were favorably disposed toward Americans, admiring their pragmatism, creativity and can-do attitude.[234] With so many members of Russian society having served under arms, accounts of Civil War battles were avidly followed and discussed.[235] Alexander II demonstrated his support for the Union in 1863 by permitting his navy to sail to the United States, where his ships docked at New York, Philadelphia, Baltimore, Washington, Annapolis, and Alexandria. Russian officers, in their finest regalia, brought members of Lincoln's cabinet and the Congress aboard to celebrate the bond between the two nations. The overall Russian perception of the Civil War was that it had been necessary to rid the United States of the evils of slavery, and that reuniting the country under a single centralized government was morally right and advantageous for Russia, for an empowered America would prove a better ally for Russia against Britain.[236]

From the letter that Abraham Nadich sent to the consulate in Odessa it is clear that his opinion of the war was in synch with his countrymen and at the very least he was familiar with American political culture and the friendship between Russia and the United States. What is less clear is whether Nadich knew the reason that Lincoln held a special place in the hearts of American Jewry – the reasons they considered him "Our Abraham."

Did Nadich know of Lincoln's dear friend and political ally Abraham Jonas,[237] or his chiropodist, Dr. Isachar Zacharie, whom the president received at the White House and sent on clandestine diplomatic missions to the Confederacy, or the dozens of Jewish politicos, lawyers, merchants, and rabbis that Lincoln met and shared a cordial relationship with during the course of conducting official and personal business?[238] Was it possible that Nadich had read of Henry Wentworth Monk, a Christian mystic, who had proposed to Lincoln that he help return European Jewry to Palestine, and that after Lincoln replied that the Civil War had to take precedence over foreign affairs, he added, "I myself have a high regard for the Jews. My chiropodist is a Jew, and he has so many times 'put me upon my feet' that I would have no objection to giving his countrymen 'a leg up.'"[239] It is quite possible that Nadich had read of the controversy surrounding General Order No. 11, "the most sweeping anti-Jewish regulation in all American history."[240] It was issued on December 17, 1862, by General Ulysses S. Grant, expelling Jews from parts of Tennessee, Mississippi, and Kentucky, because "Jews, as a class," Grant claimed, "[were] violating every regulation of trade established by the Treasury Department."[241] It was not the first time Grant had issued orders excluding Jews, but on this occasion a merchant from Kentucky traveled to Washington and spoke to Lincoln in his second-floor office, showing him Order 11 and explaining that Jews "as a class" were guilty of no such thing. The president had a telegraph sent to Grant, telling him to rescind the order.[242]

One event that would surely have drawn the attention of Abraham Nadich was the arrest of Bernard Bernstein. He had been born in Isbica, a town in Russian Poland, and in 1845, under the threat of being forced into the army of Nicholas I, Bernstein fled to America, where he became a naturalized citizen. In October 1864 Bernstein returned to Isbica to visit his parents, and it was there that he was arrested. Under military guard, Bernstein was transported to Wloclawek and locked in prison. Someone must have pointed out to authorities that the government of Alexander I and the Lincoln administration enjoyed mutually beneficial relations, and an American citizen, even if he were a Jew, should be treated with care.[243]

Bernstein was permitted to contact the US legation in St. Petersburg, and the State Department in Washington was notified of his arrest. Bernstein was the first Jew to be mentioned in diplomatic correspondence between the United States and Russia.[244] He would not, as we know, be the last. In short order, Bernstein was released, but not before a prison official or guard stole most of his money. Bernstein had a number of notable lawyers who raised his case with Secretary of State Seward, but the secretary did not pressure the Russian government because Bernstein, under Russian law, was guilty of evading military service.[245]

It is easy to understand how Nadich might have seen the US government assisting one of its Jewish citizens as a consequence of Lincoln's principles, except there is no indication that Lincoln knew of Bernstein's arrest. Even had he known, it would have been a minor incident compared to the fighting raging at home in the autumn of 1864. Nor was it unusual for America to assist and protect her Jews – whether it was Ben Franklin donating money to build a synagogue in Philadelphia;[246] George Washington assuring Jews that his government "gives to bigotry no sanction, to persecution no assistance;"[247] or the claim made in the national publication the *Niles' Weekly Register* that the United States was "the most preferable country for the Jews.... Here they can lay their heads on their pillow at night without fear of mobs, of bigotry, of persecution."[248]

Abraham Nadich closed his letter to Timothy Smith by informing him that "some enlightened members of the Jewish community who are much grieved at the fatal occurrence expressed [to me] their sentiments of deep sorrow...[and we] collected between us...a sum of money to be united with any sum of money collected in America, for a monument or any benevolent institution in his name. Please sir, to ask...if such a proceeding could be allowed, and if it be granted, to ask the authorities to allow it."

History does not record if this contribution was ever sent, but we know that the qualities Nadich admired in Lincoln did not belong only to the president whom Nadich called the "holy martyr of humanity." Gazing back across those 145 years since Lincoln met his tragic end, we also know that the poet Walt Whitman was wrong. Yes, the great man was dead, but that western star Whitman wrote of had neither fallen nor disappeared, for it was not personified by any single individual. It was no less than the promise of American democracy.

This promise – the freedom of expression and opportunity for all, the ability to vote for leaders and to vote with your feet if you disliked your popularly elected government – was never wholly untainted by bouts of moral blindness and the unpleasant odor of hypocrisy, but it stands as the true beginning of the American movement to free Soviet Jewry. It is the reason that Jews in the Soviet Union had hope, and the reason that American Jewry dared hope to free them. It is the reason that the much-persecuted refusenik Anatoly Shcharansky (later Natan Sharansky) sent a congratulatory telegram to President Gerald R. Ford on the occasion of the Bicentennial, expressing his "gratitude to the American people for their devotion to the principles of liberty."[249] And it is the reason that the long, terrifying darkness of the Cold War did not end in the searing light that humanity had feared, but a gentler light, freedom's light: the light of a powerful western star.

CHAPTER 2

A CITY UPON A HILL

The Puritans were the first inhabitants of North America to connect democracy with a higher moral calling. In 1620, with their ship in sight of the Massachusetts coastline, they wrote and signed the Mayflower Compact. With its "civil Body Politick" and "just and equal Laws," and the promise of open meetings "for the general Good of the Colony," the compact was regarded as a marked improvement over the English monarchy and the religious conflicts from which the Pilgrims had fled.[1] Here in the New World they would be, in the words of John Winthrop, the first governor of Massachusetts, "as a city upon a hill."[2]

Enthralled by the Old Testament, which they read in the original Hebrew, and the ancient civilization of the Jews, the Puritans drew their concept of a righteous city from the promise that God made to the Israelites in the wilderness of Sinai, that they would be a "holy nation."[3] This concept was translated by the Founders into the hallowed covenant of democracy: that the government would draw its legitimacy through the consent of the governed. Even though slavery, the legal disenfranchisement of women, and other grim social realities of the fledgling republic tarnished the shining ideal, the bedrock of the Founders' creation was the unshakeable belief in the moral supremacy of American democracy.

Despite the significantly curtailed freedom and the rampant inequality in eighteenth-century society, Americans were proud of their new scripture, the Constitution, which, in the words of George Washington, would be

45

"sacredly maintained,"[4] and of the enumerated rights that would protect them from the domineering whims of monarchs, nobles, and clerics. In 1789, when Frenchmen stormed the Bastille and rose up against their king, Americans applauded their goals, seeing the uprising as a reaffirmation of their own beliefs. The French, in turn, tipped their plumed tricorns to their revolutionary brethren across the Atlantic by naming George Washington, James Madison, and Alexander Hamilton honorary citizens of their country. In September 1792, after France declared itself a republic, some Americans celebrated the development with the same gusto that had accompanied their liberation from the British crown.[5]

President George Washington watched these events unfold with alarm. He was disturbed by the possibility that the French Revolution could spread war to Europe and drag America into the conflict. This was no idle concern, for France was undergoing spasms of ghoulish violence. When Louis XVI was guillotined on January 21, 1793, children cheered and ran to taste his blood, and "one executioner did a thriving business selling snippets of royal hair and clothing."[6]

Washington was at home in Mount Vernon, his magnificent gardens beginning to brighten in the April sun, when he learned that, eleven days after Louis XVI was beheaded, France had declared war on England, Holland, and Spain. As Washington had feared, the French Revolution had metastasized into another round of battles that would beset the continent for two decades.[7]

Like most Americans, Washington was sympathetic to France. He was grateful to Louis XVI for his aid during the War of Independence and felt great "personal regard" for the Marquis de Lafayette, who fought so bravely for the Americans against the British.[8] But his goal that spring was to keep his country out of the hostilities in Europe, and he hurried to Philadelphia to consult with his advisers. Following a sharp debate, Washington announced his Proclamation of Neutrality, which emphasized that citizens of the United States should remain "friendly and impartial" toward the belligerents.[9]

The Neutrality Act did nothing to quell Americans' sympathy for France, and the drumbeat of war with Britain quickened in the States. Worried that his country, which lacked even a navy, was in no tactical or financial position to take up arms against England, Washington sent John Jay, chief justice of the Supreme Court, to London to conclude a final treaty with the Crown. The Jay Treaty contained provisions beneficial to the United States, including Britain's bestowal of the profitable most-favored-nation status on America, but it was met in some quarters with outrage. Thomas Jefferson thought the settlement was a sellout;[10] protests erupted in Philadelphia, Baltimore, and Charleston; and a mob outside City Hall in New York, hearing Alexander Hamilton defend the treaty, pelted him with stones.[11]

Washington was so pleased by the agreement that he dispatched Thomas Pinckney to Madrid to work out a comparable treaty with Spain. Yet the president had been enraged by the protests and, coupled with his physical ailments, his weariness with politics, and the personal attacks on him in the press, Washington decided not to seek a third term. A draft of a farewell address had been composed with the help of James Madison as Washington's first term was ending, but now the president thoroughly reworked the earlier version with the assistance of his closest adviser, Alexander Hamilton.[12]

Never intended to be delivered publicly, the address was a political testament, both an inspiration and a guide to future generations. It first appeared on September 19, 1796, in *Claypoole's American Daily Advertiser*, and was reprinted in newspapers around the country and as a pamphlet.[13]

Hamilton had been as adamant as Washington about the United States staying out of the war ignited by the French Revolution, and their feelings on the subject were apparent in the address, which implored Americans to avoid any "permanent, inveterate antipathies against particular Nations, and passionate attachments for others."[14] The address counseled the United States to steer its own course, in light of its own interests, and not to "quit our own to stand upon foreign ground" or "entangle our peace and prosperity" with the beating of distant drums.[15]

British historian Paul Johnson argues that heeding this advice only became impossible "when modernity finally overthrew the tyranny of distance" and the United States was forced into the international arena.[16] However, Johnson misses a facet of the American experience that forever altered the making of US foreign policy: the rising tide of immigrants whom the American Jewish poet, Emma Lazarus, would immortalize in a sonnet as "the huddled masses yearning to breathe free."[17]

Neither Washington nor Hamilton foresaw the changes the immigrants would bring. This was an understandable oversight by Washington, but Hamilton was the most forward-thinking of the Founders and seemed to possess the gifts of a fortune-teller when envisioning the future. And Hamilton was an immigrant. He was born a subject of King George II,[18] on the island of Nevis in the British West Indies,[19] and even though none of his political contemporaries would have accused him of being overly empathic, he showed enormous compassion for those he called the "children of adversity," the indigent French refugees who fled the furies bedeviling their country and poured into Philadelphia.[20]

It is curious that such an intelligent, multitalented visionary would miss how immigrants would affect foreign affairs. Hamilton understood that as a rule people were too "attached to their native countries to leave... and dissolve all their connexions," but his foresight probably failed him because his knowledge of the immigrants' lot was circumscribed by his own experience.[21] When the eighteen-year-old Hamilton boarded a boat to Boston, he was fleeing a tragic, poverty-stricken childhood and the shame of being the son of a common-law couple, and so, as Hamilton biographer Ron Chernow writes, the teenager "chose a psychological strategy adopted by many orphans and immigrants: he decided to cut himself off from his past and forge a new identity."[22]

Yet what of those immigrants who left loved ones behind and would never consider cutting themselves off from them? Culturally speaking, Hamilton was an Englishman, not much different from most Americans, but what about those immigrants whose new American identities were infused with the languages, customs, and religious practices of the homes they left behind? Washington's Farewell Address warned against "passionate attachments" to other nations, but for tens of millions of immigrants, renouncing their connections to all the people and the entire culture of the old country was a psychological impossibility.

Secretary of State George P. Shultz, who served in the Reagan administration from 1982 until 1989, would see this condition as a "unique aspect of American foreign policy."

"Everybody here is, in a sense, from somewhere else," explains Shultz. "So, if you're Secretary of State, you realize that there are all of these constituencies out there. For example, the biggest Polish city outside of Warsaw is Chicago. And so if you're going to do something about Poland, you'd better see what the people in Chicago think. And if you're not thinking about Poland, then they are going to remind you to think about Poland. It's characteristic of our foreign policy that we care more about what's happening in various countries than most other countries do about what's going on someplace else. And the reason is that we have this variety of constituencies. We shouldn't apologize for listening to…any [ethnic or religious] community."[23]

Long before the technology of communications, travel, and warfare brought the "foreign shores" mentioned in the Farewell Address to America's doorstep, citizens of the United States were influencing government policy by pressing leaders to help their erstwhile compatriots.

Irish Americans, for example, had railed against the John Jay Treaty in 1794; Dutch Americans had beseeched President Theodore Roosevelt to intervene in the Boer War; and German Americans had protested the United States joining the Allies in World War I.[24] For Jews, this was an especially complicated issue because their identity was not bounded by physical borders: it was tied to their coreligionists and an empathic response to the same hatred and violence that had driven them to emigrate.

As early as 1840, the fifteen thousand Jews in the United States were already showing a heightened interest in foreign affairs.[25] The incident that caught their collective attention occurred in Damascus, Syria, where Jews were charged with murdering a Moslem child and using the blood to bake matzo. With Franciscan monks supporting this blood libel, Syrian authorities arrested and tortured thirteen Jewish leaders and sixty children. President Martin Van Buren's secretary of state, John Forsythe, learned about the situation through a July protest held by British Jews in London.[26] Eventually it was pressure from European governments that forced Syria to renounce the charges and release the Jewish prisoners,[27] but the State Department sent cables in support, one of them saying that the president "cannot refrain from expressing surprise and pain, that in this advanced age, such unnatural practices should be ascribed to any portion of the religious world."[28]

American Jewry contributed next to nothing to the solution: they were too busy arguing over their protest arrangements[29] – the kind of quibbling that would plague them, on and off, all the way through the movement to free Soviet Jewry. At last, though, Jews attending a rally in New York City did draft a statement to send to the Van Buren administration, and shortly thereafter rallies were being held in Philadelphia, Charleston, Savannah, and Richmond. This was the first time the American Jewish community demonstrated enough confidence and cohesion to stage a national protest on behalf of persecuted Jews outside the United States.

Three years later, the B'nai B'rith was founded, but the community had been unable to capitalize on their momentary cohesiveness to create an effective group to mobilize a coordinated response to international injustice, a fact that became apparent in 1858.

On a June evening that year in Bologna, Italy, police entered the house of a Jewish merchant, Momolo Mortara, and his wife, Marianna, to remove one of their eight children, seven-year-old Edgardo. The police claimed that as an infant the boy had been secretly baptized by his nurse and could not legally be reared by Jews. Edgardo was sleeping, and his mother pleaded with police to leave him with his family. The police relented, but only until the next morning, when Edgardo was taken to Rome.[30] Despite the pleas to return Edgardo to his parents, Pope Pius IX refused, claiming that "God has given the Church the power and right to take possession of the baptized children of infidels, and that parental rights were subordinate to those of the Church."[31]

Rallies in support of the Mortaras went on in numerous cities. Newspaper editorials appeared, Protestant ministers spoke out, and the Republican Party and the anti-Catholic Know Nothing Party also condemned the act. The Jewish leader Rabbi Isaac Leeser did secure a meeting at the White House, but the Democratic president, James Buchanan, would not help. There were just fifty thousand Jewish Democrats, while Catholic Democrats numbered nearly one million, and Catholic sympathies were with their pope; one Catholic newspaper, the *New York Tablet*, stated that Edgar Mortara "deserved" to be raised in the church.[32] In addition, President Buchanan supported slavery, and he told Rabbi Leeser, in effect, that if he avoided taking a moral position on an Italian internal matter, it would encourage nations to refrain from exhorting America to free the slaves.[33]

Edgardo Mortara never returned to his parents. At the age of twenty-one, he was ordained a priest.

◆ ◆ ◆

For the next two decades, American Jews cobbled together what one historian calls "a tenuous unity."[34] In the main this unity was reflected by the creation of the Board of Delegates of American Israelites, which was modeled on a similar organization in Britain.

The board organized the first nationwide fund-raising campaign for needy Jews abroad. They approached the Lincoln administration and prevailed upon Secretary of State Seward to help the beleaguered Jews of Morocco by instructing his consul "to exert all proper influence to prevent repetition of the barbarous cruelties to which Israelites...have been subject."[35] And when the Romanian government instituted a rash of antisemitic laws and supported an eruption of pogroms, the board convinced President Ulysses S. Grant to send a Jewish consul to Romania, where he met Prince Charles in Bucharest and presented a letter from the president. In language drawn from the best traditions of that righteous city upon a hill, the letter said: "The United States, knowing no distinction of her citizens on count of religion or nativity, naturally believes in a civilization world over which will secure the same universal views."[36]

The letter led Prince Charles to have a change of heart. He spoke of his country's fondness for the United States and for "our Romanian Jews."[37] For the next five years, while the consul was in residence in Bucharest, the government-supported mob violence disappeared.

At the urging of Rabbi Isaac Mayer Wise, the Board of Delegates was integrated into the Union of American Hebrew Congregations in 1878. As the board was departing the scene, the treatment of Russian Jews was becoming the focal point of American Jewry's concern. This was primarily because of the tsar's brutality, and because the pogroms increasingly convinced Jews in the Russian empire to crowd into steerage class and sail across the ocean to the United States.

The immigrants were pouring into a nation that was rapidly expanding its public education system. Between 1878 and 1917, the number of high schools jumped from eight hundred to over eleven thousand, and there were plenty of night schools and libraries where adults could learn English and harvest the intellectual bounty of their new country. Freed from antisemitic constraints, eastern European Jews were quick to take advantage of the opportunity. Stripped of full rights by the House of Romanov, Russian Jews were ripe for an introduction to democracy, and once in possession of its power, they were eager to use it to confront the procession of tsarist regimes.[38]

Their chance arose after they had attained enough prosperity in the United States to travel back to the Russian empire for business or to visit family, and ran headlong into the antisemitism that had driven them to leave.

What followed was a preview of the struggle between the White House and the Kremlin over Soviet Jewry, and the argument over the propriety of one country interfering with the internal decisions of another. Like a chess game played again and again because neither master will accept a string of stalemates, this nineteenth-century pattern would repeat itself throughout the Cold War in a series of predictable moves and countermoves.

First would come a confrontation over Russia's repressive policies. Next, American Jewry would look toward Washington for relief. The US government would respond by lodging an official protest. Russia would find a cosmetic solution to the immediate concern and continue the repression. Yet in 1879, when an American Jew, Herman Rosenstraus, bought real estate in the Ukrainian city of Kharkov and the authorities would not release the title to him since Russian law prohibited Jews from owning this category of property, a new weapon in the fight for freedom was uncovered: the law.

Rosenstraus believed that as a US citizen he should be permitted to take title to his property; he was wrong. The Russo-American Commercial Treaty of 1832 stated that while Americans were inside the empire they were subject "to the laws and ordinances there prevailing."[39]

It was only logical that Jewish leaders would appeal to the Garfield administration to raise the renewal of the treaty with St. Petersburg. Their goal was clarified in an exchange between the investment banker Jacob

Schiff and Adolph S. Ochs, publisher of the *New York Times*. Schiff pointed out that once "Russia is compelled to live up to her treaties and admit the foreign Jew…on a basis of equality…the Russian government will not be able to maintain the Pale of Settlement."[40]

Secretary of State James G. Blaine did threaten the Russians that the agreement would be in jeopardy unless they changed their ways. Predictably, the discrimination did not end. The Garfield administration was no more successful in May 1881 when pogroms broke out and Secretary of State Blaine tried to enlist the British in a joint effort to alter Russian behavior. In a dispatch to the British Foreign Office, Blaine expressed his take on antisemitism, writing that the "patient industry [of the Jews] bred capital, and capital bred envy and envy persecution and persecution disaffection and special separation…. The Jews are made a people apart from other peoples, not of their volition, but because they have been repressed and ostracized in the communities in which they mixed."[41]

Unmoved by the dispatch and seeing no national interest at stake, Britain would not help.

The pogroms persisted, and the official position of the Russian empire remained the same. Their foreign minister, Nicholas de Giers, made it clear that the tsar had no interest in ethnic melting pots, and besides, Jews were "altogether unfitted for more liberty than they now possess."[42]

Russia was neither sorry to see the Jews leave nor anxious to have them return, and eight months after Herman Rosenstraus was refused title to his property, an American Jew working in a traveling circus was expelled from St. Petersburg. The US exerted diplomatic pressure and Russian authorities pulled off a tactical retreat, allowing the fellow to stay in the city. Then, to preserve their policy of antisemitism and to demonstrate their distaste of outsiders meddling in their business, authorities began arresting visiting Jews on highly suspect charges of draft evasion, the same charge that had been leveled at Bernard Bernstein in 1864. Once Bernstein had been let out of prison, Secretary of State Seward had not pursued his case with the Russians because of the charge, but in the spring of 1892, Congress entered the fray.[43]

Representative James Irvine Dungan, a Democrat from Ohio who had fought for the Union in the Civil War, introduced a joint resolution that directed "the President to sever diplomatic relations with the Russian Government until such time as that Government shall cease discrimination against the Hebrews because of their religions faith and remove the arbitrary and brutal restrictions now imposed upon them against the protest of the civilized world."[44]

The resolution was bounced to the Committee on Foreign Affairs.[45] At the suggestion of the Russian government, the State Department had temporarily avoided the problem by refusing to issue passports to erstwhile Jewish subjects of the tsar,[46] but the practice ended in 1892, when the Supreme Court ruled in *Geofroy v. Riggs* that "no treaty may authorize what the Constitution forbids."[47] The ruling also made it difficult for the State Department to turn away when citizens traveling outside the United States had their rights revoked, and it forced them to confront the Russian consulate in New York over their practice of denying visas to Jews on the basis of religion.

The assertiveness of American Jewry was intensified by the trial of Alfred Dreyfus, a Jewish artillery captain in the French army, who was falsely accused and convicted of treason, and sentenced to the penal colony of Devil's Island. For assimilated Jews who believed the democratic spirit protected them from maltreatment, the trial was alarming, since in 1791 France had been the first European nation to emancipate its Jews.[48] The novelist Émile Zola responded to the Dreyfus conviction by publishing an open letter to the president of France in a Paris newspaper. Entitled *J'accuse*, Zola's letter detailed the true events and claimed that Dreyfus was an innocent victim of the "'dirty Jew' obsession that is the scourge of our time."[49] To round out the full effect of the Dreyfus Affair it should be noted that it helped crystallize the thinking of the Paris correspondent for the *Neue Frei Presse*, the most influential newspaper in Austria. The journalist's name was Theodor Herzl. A Jew, originally from Hungary, Herzl had grown up in Vienna believing that secular enlightenment would deliver Jews from the contempt of Christian culture. Even before he covered the trial, with nationalist antisemitism rising in Europe, Herzl began to doubt that assimilation was the answer, and seeing the French crowds shouting, "Death to the Jews!" he determined that the solution was "the restoration of the Jewish state."[50]

During this period, the discrimination in Russia did not stop, nor did the appeals of American Jewry to the White House and Congress. On the surface it was a question of what would later be referred to as "human rights." Below the surface, the US government was worried about an entirely different issue.

The hundreds of thousands of Jews stampeding into America revealed a homegrown problem. The *New York Tribune* lamented that the "filthy condition" of the Jewish immigrants was ruining the parks;[51] progressive reformers asserted that Jews controlled the white slave trade; and the New York City police commissioner would claim that "alien" Jews, just one-quarter of the population, committed half the crimes.[52]

Secretary of State Blaine blamed the "oppressive measures" of the tsarist regime for the deluge of Jewish immigrants, adding that the "hospitality of a nation should not be turned into a burden." President Benjamin Harrison observed that banishing so many people from a country amounts to "an order to enter another." And by 1902, with Theodore Roosevelt in the White House, Secretary of State John Hay complained that the harsh treatment of Romanian Jews was driving them from their "native land" and forcing them to rely on "the charity of the United States."[53]

In time, Jewish leaders would use the fear of immigration to urge the administration to intercede with eastern European authorities on behalf of Jews. Philosophically, this strategy was a recognition by Jewish leadership that assistance for Jews abroad must serve the national interest and avoid the appearance of promoting the welfare of Jews to the detriment of Americans – an appearance that would engender the charge of dual loyalty.

Opinions on which actions are aligned with US interests are as fickle as a reluctant spring. Even so, Americans nurture a core value that elevates liberty above mundane interests, a basic belief that liberty threatened anywhere is a threat to the holy foundation of democracy. This value does not always trump selfish, shortsighted, or pragmatic concerns. Yet the notion that all people are entitled to their own city upon a hill persists, and this value was on display in 1903 when Jews in the tsarist province of Bessarabia endured what one journalist calls "the last pogrom of the Middle Ages and the first atrocity of the twentieth century."[54]

◆ ◆ ◆

The story began in February. A boy's body was discovered – a Christian boy, an heir to a substantial inheritance. His name was Michael Ribalenko. He had been dead for six days when they found him in the village of Dubossary,[55] twenty-five miles north of Kishinev, a bustling trading center and home to fifty thousand Jews.[56] A relative who stood to inherit a slice of the fortune had murdered the boy,[57] but the truth of Michael's death did not matter. Life under Tsar Nicholas II was hard, and for some it was only bearable with an enemy to loathe and to blame – a treacherous enemy who nailed our Lord to the cross and used the blood of Christian children to bake Passover matzos. Here was a tale worth being told in the *Bessarabetz*, a government-subsidized newspaper edited by Pavolachi Krushevan, a man who, like Emperor Nicholas II himself,[58] was sick with a malignant enmity toward Jews. For weeks, Krushevan published his invective, and on Easter Sunday mobs began rampaging through Kishinev.

Two days later, forty-nine Jews were dead and five hundred injured. Thirteen hundred houses and businesses were plundered and destroyed,[59] leaving ten thousand Jews homeless and at least as many in need of relief to survive.[60] As the details of the pogrom circled the globe – in newspaper reports transmitted via cable and in letters sent by the survivors to relatives in America,[61] it appeared as if civilized people everywhere were suddenly revolted by the hatred of Jews. The truth proved less dramatic: antisemitism had momentarily receded due to the culmination of events over a long arc of time. Almost two generations had gone by since the end of American slavery, the Industrial Revolution was on the march, President Theodore Roosevelt was flexing his nation's muscles across the seas, and progressivism and muckraking journalism were on the rise.

In Russia, the great novelist Leo Tolstoy and the crusading reporter Vladimir Korolenko decried the assault.[62] Jewish lawyers banded together to file suit for damages and publicly blamed tsarist officials for stirring up the attack. Protests attracted huge crowds in London and Paris, but in the United States the reaction was stunning. In churches and synagogues, in town squares and meeting halls, Christians and Jews spoke out in a single voice against the carnage with a feeling, as ex-President Grover Cleveland told a gathering in New York City, "that should stir every American worthy of the name."[63] Not only did the words of support for Russia's Jews reverberate with a passion that would not reappear until the Soviet Jewry movement reached its crescendo, but the condemnation of the pogrom was not limited to communities with sizeable Jewish populations: it also came from Texarkana, Texas; Omaha, Nebraska; Wichita, Kansas; Fort Smith, Arkansas; Sioux City, Iowa; Altoona, Pennsylvania; La Crosse, Wisconsin; Wheeling, West Virginia; Boise, Idaho; Terre Haute, Indiana; Salt Lake City, Utah; Birmingham, Alabama; Norfolk, Virginia; Toledo, Ohio and Tacoma, Washington.[64]

At the meetings people wept as they listened to accounts of the horrific events, and even the poorest members of the audience stepped forward to contribute to the funds being raised for the victims. According to the scholar Dr. Cyrus Adler, who charted the American reaction to Kishinev and published his findings in 1904, 77 protests were staged in 50 towns across 27 states. Three hundred sixty-three speeches were given; 107 letters of sympathy were read aloud; 29 sermons were delivered; 24 clubs, churches, and associations adopted resolutions excoriating the mob for the attack; and 80 newspapers printed 151 articles and editorials in reaction to the events of Kishinev.[65]

Three months after the pogrom, the book *Out of Kishineff: The Duty of the American People to the Russian Jew* was published. Written by the Rev. Dr. William Curtis Stiles, onetime pastor of the East End Congregational Church in Brooklyn, the thrust of the work was in synch with the national mood: the Jews are a good but long-persecuted people and America as a "world champion of justice and fair play, should teach autocratic Russia a lesson."[66]

Teaching Tsar Nicholas II a lesson must have appealed to President Theodore Roosevelt. Five years before the pogrom, the Russian army had marched into the industrialized Chinese province of Manchuria, and now they were refusing to abide by their agreement to leave. Russia was also attempting to block foreign commercial ships from docking at ports in Manchuria, a flagrant violation of the Open Door policy, the brainchild of Secretary of State John Hay. Early on, Hay had recognized that China was the new "storm center of the world…[and] a key to world politics for the next five centuries."[67]

Roosevelt had no intention of permitting the tsar to carve up the Chinese empire or interfere with US interests in the Far East, including the security of the Philippines, and he publicly proclaimed that while "we infinitely desire peace…the surest way of obtaining it is to show that we are not afraid of war."[68]

Roosevelt had been appalled by Kishinev and felt that it was fitting for the United States to lead the protests – if for no other reason than to "acknowledge the debt due to the Jewish race."[69] The president wanted to contribute one hundred dollars to a relief fund, but Secretary of State Hay and Secretary of War Elihu Root dissuaded him. Hay could be sarcastic about Jews, referring to them as "the Hebrews – poor dears!"[70] but he argued that a supportive pronouncement and contribution would be a diplomatic faux pas.[71] Secretary Root agreed, though his deepest concern about the ardent American outcry was the suggestion that public opinion had any legitimate role in the formation of foreign policy.[72]

After considering his secretaries' advice, Roosevelt made an interesting comparison: "I suppose," he said, "it would be very much like the tsar spreading his horror of our lynching Negroes."[73]

Lynching had become as newsworthy as pogroms: between 1882 and 1903, the Tuskegee Institute estimated that over four thousand blacks had been lynched.[74] By the early twentieth century, the fates of Jews and blacks were dovetailing in the minds of some Americans. In fact, three years after the Civil War, the fates of a Russian Jewish owner of a dry goods store in Franklin, Tennessee, and his black employee were identical: they were both lynched.[75] This pairing of Jews and blacks, which would be so crucial to the civil rights movement of the 1950s and 1960s, was formalized in the aftermath of a 1908 race riot in Springfield, Illinois, when the journalist and suffragette Mary White Ovington contacted Dr. Henry Moskowitz, a physician, and William English Walling, a labor reformer who had lived in Russia and married a Russian Jew. They met in New York City and founded an organization that would develop into the National Association for the Advancement of Colored People.[76]

Roosevelt felt that the plight of the Negro was his most urgent conundrum but, unlike the Jewish situation, it did not threaten to interfere with foreign affairs. On June 15, with Kishinev still a topic of sermons, meetings, and editorials around the country, the six-member executive committee of B'nai B'rith went to the White House to speak to the president.

After sixty years, the B'nai B'rith had become the unofficial representative of American Jewry, and Roosevelt listened as the executive-committee spokesman read a petition meant for Tsar Nicholas II. It characterized Russia as a land rife with "ignorance, superstition and bigotry…officials derelict in their duty…indefensible lawlessness… [and] misery suffered by the hapless Jews."[77] Roosevelt spent an hour with the group. He expressed his sympathy for the victims of the pogrom and recounted his warm feelings toward Jews. He told stories and quoted from the Henry Wadsworth Longfellow poem "The Jewish Cemetery at Newport": "How came they here? What burst of Christian hate, / What persecution, merciless and blind, / Drove o'er the sea – that desert desolate – / These Ishmaels and Hagars of mankind?"[78] Finally, he assured his visitors that he would study their petition.[79]

By June 27, Roosevelt was summering at Sagamore Hill, his home in Oyster Bay, New York. He was skeptical that the petition would carry any weight with St. Petersburg, but he approved the idea because it did not formally involve his administration.

But four days later, while B'nai B'rith was gathering signatures, a strange thing happened. The Russian ambassador, Count de Cassini, released a statement in Washington denying reports that the tsar's government had "offered any official explanations to the American Government" about Kishinev.[80]

The statement struck Roosevelt as odd, since no one had asked Cassini to explain anything. But when Cassini announced that Russia would reject "any petitions, presentations, or communications relative to its internal affairs,"[81] Roosevelt heard both a note of embarrassment about the pogrom and an unmistakable knock of opportunity.[82]

What happened next could have been billed as coming attractions for the Cold War, because the strategy Roosevelt employed would often be used to pressure the Soviet Union.

Even though the Russian government had no intention of accepting the B'nai B'rith petition, news of the written protest would keep the Kishinev massacre center stage, precisely where Roosevelt wanted it, just as later administrations would call attention to the distress of Soviet Jewry to discredit the Kremlin. Further embarrassing St. Petersburg gave Roosevelt a chance to firm up his support among American Jews and to wring a concession from Nicholas II on Manchuria – a welcome development for businesses hungry to trade in the Far East.[83] Future presidents would seek different concessions from the Soviet Union, but their game plan was essentially the same, right down to using the protests of organized American Jewry as a lever against the recalcitrance of Soviet leaders.

With Hay relaxing at his lakeside summer house in New Hampshire, Roosevelt barged ahead on his own.[84] From Oyster Bay he wired Acting Secretary of State Francis Loomis in Washington, telling him to release a public statement, in the name of the Administration and all our citizens, that conveyed "deep sympathy…for the…victims of the recent appalling massacres and outrages." Then the president gave Loomis instructions on what he wanted told to the press.[85]

On July 2, the following appeared in the *New York Times*:

> In speaking of the manner in which Russia has served notice of her intentions not to receive the petition, an official of the State Department…pointed out that it seemed somewhat strange…that the Russian Government should choose this particular method of making a statement to the American people at the very time when by methods which are certainly the reverse of friendly to the United States, it has sought to make China join in breaking the plighted faith of all the powers as to the open door in Manchuria.[86]

Obviously, the official was Roosevelt, and he intended the Russians to know it. Never one to let up when he sensed the battle turning his way, Roosevelt decided to send the petition to the Russian Minister of Foreign Affairs.[87] To preserve diplomatic niceties the cable inquired whether His Majesty, Tsar Nicholas II, might accept the petition. Roosevelt knew the answer would be no, and it was, but the content of the petition was disseminated all over the world,[88] and the next year was reprinted in *The Voice of America on Kishneff*, a 508-page tome of sermons, lectures, speeches, articles, editorials, resolutions, and relief measures that testified to the nation's revulsion for Russian marauding and murder.

◆ ◆ ◆

The Roosevelt family was still enjoying the sunny seaside pleasures of Oyster Bay when Russia declared that "certain cities in Manchuria" would now adhere to the Open Door policy.[89]

This retreat indicates that Roosevelt's gambit succeeded: St. Petersburg, having alienated China, Japan, and Britain, was hesitant to alienate the United States. Less successful was the condemnation over Kishinev, which did not prod Nicholas II to make any effort to rein in the mobs. Between 1903 and 1906, over three hundred pogroms occurred in *Rossiyskaya Imperiya*, blending into the social despair that was engulfing the empire: an escalating dissatisfaction with the feckless, corrupt autocracy among the proletariat, peasants, Socialist Revolutionaries, Social Democrats, and even the middle and upper classes – a strident, unremitting dissatisfaction that was not improved by the ninety thousand casualties Russia absorbed in her defeat by Japan in the Russo-Japanese War, a humiliation that so enraged the Russian people that not even another cycle of government-instigated pogroms could assuage them.

It was as though the accumulated weight of the empire's steel-hearted history was about to crush the House of the Romanovs. One could almost hear the despotic foundation quake on that cloudless Sunday morning in January 1905, when Father Georgii Gapon, a young, gifted orator and son of prosperous Ukrainian peasants, led thirty thousand workers on a peaceful march through the silvery cold of St. Petersburg. Dressed in their finest clothes and armed only with religious icons, the marchers passed under the sparkling onion domes of the cathedrals toward the Winter Palace with a petition for Nicholas II, a plea to lighten the burden of their poverty and grant them "justice and protection."[90] Before they arrived, the tsar's cavalry attempted to turn them back by walking their horses into the crowd and lashing out from their saddles with whips and sabers. When that failed, soldiers opened fire like sportsmen leisurely firing on herds of red deer in the foothills of the Caucasus, the crack of rifle shots sending men, women, and children running and screaming through the icy streets, slipping and falling and leaving shiny blood spoors on the snow until, in the gathering darkness of "Bloody Sunday," as many as one thousand marchers were dead or wounded, and the first Russian Revolution was underway.[91]

Although after Kishinev American Jewry had not blunted the spread of antisemitic fury in Russia, their success in mobilizing their country on behalf of the victims encouraged them to push ahead. Financier and philanthropist Jacob Schiff was so furious at the treatment of Russian Jews that he had his brokerage firm, Kuhn, Loeb and Company, underwrite $200 million of bonds to aid Japan during the Russo-Japanese War.[92] Schiff was knighted by the emperor of Japan, but his help was later viewed with some ambivalence by the Japanese. It contributed to their belief in the myth contained in *The Protocols of the Elders of Zion*, which today is still regarded as an accurate analysis in Japan – that Jews control the international economy. But Schiff was also remembered with gratitude during the Second World War when, despite the entreaties of their Nazi allies, the Japanese government would not single out Jews for persecution in the territory it controlled.[93]

Just how far Jews had come in the United States was highlighted when President Roosevelt selected Oscar Straus as his secretary of commerce and labor, the first Jew ever named to the cabinet.[94] A lawyer and former diplomat, Straus was a member of a New York merchant family active in philanthropy,[95] and Roosevelt explained his choice to Straus by telling him, "I want to show Russia and some other countries what we think of the Jews in this country."[96] That was a noble sentiment, and perhaps half true; the other half – the half that acknowledged the growing importance of American Jewry as a political bloc – was Roosevelt's desire to steer Jewish voters away from the hubristic booster of yellow journalism William Randolph Hearst, a Democrat, who was running against the Progressive Republican Charles Evan Hughes for governor of New York, an election that Hughes would win.[97]

From 1904 until 1908, as the situation rapidly deteriorated in Russia, 643,000 more Jews would emigrate to the United States.[98] Meanwhile, Nicholas II set out to stave off the revolution and end an empire-wide strike by signing the October Manifesto, permitting "civil freedoms,"[99] which never quite materialized, and a Duma (parliament), which had little power.

Jewish leaders in the United States understood that there was almost nothing they could do to halt the pogroms. (At one point, Jacob Schiff and other Jewish bankers attempted to stem the flow of investment capital into Russia, but French banks came to the tsar's rescue.[100]) Their most promising move was to focus on the passport issue by pressing Washington to abrogate the Commercial Treaty of 1832 and revoke Russia's most-favored-nation status. Roosevelt was not eager to take that step, and while he wrapped the passport question in spools of State Department red tape, Russia retreated an inch, promising visas to Jews sailing on Russian ships, though holding fast to their right to discriminate.[101]

William Howard Taft succeeded Roosevelt as president on March 4, 1909. During his campaign, Taft had spoken out against the discrimination, saying that he would try to end it, but once in the White House, Taft was reluctant to act. Regardless of his campaign rhetoric, deep down he thought that to advocate for these sorts of civil rights inside Tsarist Russia was unrealistic, and revoking the treaty would damage US commercial interests. On a pragmatic level, his position was hard to refute, but that did not stop American Jewry from refuting it.

On May 25, 1910, a delegation representing the American Jewish Committee, the Union of American Hebrew Congregations, and B'nai B'rith arrived at the White House to change the president's mind. Among the group was Jacob Schiff, a devout believer in his own judgment and in the moral imperative for the wealthy and powerful to assist the less fortunate.[102] Schiff was immune to intimidation by Jew or gentile, and would certainly not be cowed by the crowning symbol of American power: the White House. During the discussion Taft would not agree to keep his campaign promise on the treaty, and Schiff grew so frustrated that he abruptly stood up, his blue eyes flashing with anger, and said to the president, "We had hoped you would see that justice was done us but you have decided otherwise." Just before storming out, Schiff added, "We shall go to the American people."[103]

Schiff's fellow citizens were more understanding than the president, especially after reading articles on the subject in newspapers and magazines, or attending one of the sponsored meetings that were held around the country.

Congress introduced a resolution calling for an end to the treaty, and the House Foreign Affairs Committee conducted hearings on the proposal that were widely covered by the press.

A parade of prominent Americans testified: Judge Mayer Sulzberger, Jacob Schiff, Oscar Straus, Rev. Donald McLeod,[104] and the brilliant lawyer Louis Marshall, who, following a second pogrom in Kishinev in 1905, was the driving force behind the creation of the American Jewish Committee, a defense organization that drew its initial membership from the distinguished group of German Jews – men like Jacob Schiff, Oscar Straus, and Cyrus Adler. Marshall told the congressmen that the violation abroad of any citizens' rights, regardless of religion, was an insult to the sovereign power of the United States and "a betrayal of her most sacred principles."[105]

As the House of Representatives considered the treaty, Mendel Beilis, a Russian Jew employed as a superintendent of a brick factory, was arrested in Kiev. Beilis was charged with murdering a Christian boy. The child had been found dead in a cave in the hills above the city with forty-seven puncture wounds. At the child's funeral, the Black Hundreds, reactionary nationalists faithful to the tsar, distributed leaflets accusing "the kikes" of torture, stealing the boy's blood for their matzo, and imploring Christians to "Avenge the Unhappy Martyr!"[106]

Russian Jews braced for the inevitable pogroms, but the tsarist regime was momentarily averse to international criticism – influenced, perhaps, by the pending fate of the treaty and the unrest in their own streets, and violence was officially discouraged. Mendel Beilis was taken to prison, where he spent two years before being brought to trial.

On December 13, 1911, the House of Representatives voted 301 to 1 to abrogate the Commercial Treaty of 1832. Less than a week later, the Senate unanimously approved the measure, and the joint resolution was passed on December 21.[107] In August 1913, the Treasury Department removed the primary imports from Russia – wood, pulp, and paper products – from the most-favored-nation list.

The point had been made, though in Russia it was seen through a predictably antisemitic prism. One commentator dismissed it as a "scheme of the Russian Jews…to get hold of Russian trade and industry…using pressure through America," and another warned that "if the United States wishes to stretch a friendly hand to Russia it should not be across a Jewish bridge."[108]

That September, Mendel Beilis was tried in Kiev. Although the police were aware that the boy had been killed by a gang of thieves, the tsarist government, troubled by the liberalism unleashed by the 1905 Revolution, saw the trial as a means to reassert control. As with the Dreyfus Affair, there was an outpouring of support for Beilis – from inside and outside the empire. Leaders, clergymen, educators, literary lights, and the enlightened masses protested the "Jewish witch hunt."[109] Beilis was defended by a team of illustrious Jewish and Christian lawyers. Hundreds of foreign correspondents covered the trial, and had a man's life not been on the line, the proceedings would have qualified as farce: to prove Beilis's guilt, prosecutors had an expert testify that Jews were, by nature, evil.[110] Despite the overt prejudice of the jury – picture a black man charged with murdering a white child in 1950s Mississippi being judged by a jury of Klansmen – Beilis was acquitted and left Russia, emigrating to Palestine and then to the United States.

For American Jewry, one legacy of the 1903 Kishinev pogrom was discovering the domestic political rewards of organization and advocacy. Their ability to persuade Congress to abrogate the commercial treaty, while paying mixed dividends for the Jewish subjects of Nicholas II, would have loomed as an impossibility a few years before. The communal political activism would resonate with the Russian Jewish immigrants, enlisting new legions and, in not too long a time, new organizations that ushered in the modern era of the community's activism: the American Jewish Committee, the American Jewish Congress, the Joint Distribution Committee, the United Jewish Appeal, and the Jewish Federations.[111]

Perhaps the Russian immigrants' taste for activism was a cultural value instilled in them by the segregated Jewish environment of the shtetl, for Judaism is a faith that emphasizes deeds over theology. Or perhaps they brought their spirit for social activism with them from the Russian empire: a spirit that not even a brutally repressive succession of tsars could extinguish, a spirit that was on full display during the 1905 Revolution, led by Nikolai Lenin, a man dedicated to the concept of praxis – the unity of theory and action.

However, it was not simply public pressure that had mobilized Americans after Kishinev or moved Congress to call off the treaty: it was persuading a critical mass of the country of the moral rightness of the cause, demonstrating that the values at stake – fairness and freedom – were their own, and that preserving them beyond the borders of the nation was often in the interest of the nation itself.

This strategy was not always successful. In 1913, American Jewry faced a Dreyfus and Beilis affair of their own, with a much unhappier ending.

In April of that year, Leo Frank, a Jew who had relocated from Brooklyn to Atlanta to manage the National Pencil Factory, was arrested for strangling and apparently raping a pretty, blue-eyed, thirteen-year-old employee, Mary Phagan.[112] Her job was to operate a knurling machine, punching erasers into the metal ends of pencils. It paid just ten cents an hour, but Mary, like thousands of young women from red-clay Georgia, had quit school and gone off to the mills at the age of ten to chase the wolf away from her family's door.[113]

Little Mary Phagan, as she was memorialized in song, had died on Confederate Memorial Day, and her death inflamed the lingering bitterness over the Civil War. During the trial, which made national headlines, angry mobs besieged the courthouse. The Georgia Populist Tom Watson, publisher of the *Jeffersonian* and an accomplished demagogue with a pyrogenic hatred of Northerners, Jews, blacks, and Catholics, penned editorials about international Jewish conspiracies and called Frank "a rich depraved Sodomite…[and] satyr-faced New York Jew."[114] His opinions found a receptive audience in Georgia. In 1920, Watson was elected to the United States Senate, and after his death, a marble statue of him was erected outside the capitol in Atlanta.

Leo Frank was convicted of murder and sentenced to die. One of his attorneys described his client's trial as "the most horrible persecution of a Jew since the death of Christ."[115] In pleading for her husband's life, Lucille Frank suggested that the Russians, during the trial of Beilis, were "more disposed to principles of fair dealing."[116] The chief witness against Frank had been Jim Conley, a black janitor at the factory, no stranger to drunkenness and assault, whom historians would judge to be the true killer of Mary Phagan.[117]

On appeal, the case would go all the way to the United States Supreme Court, where it was argued by Louis Marshall. American Jewry raised money for Frank's defense. In response to the vitriol released by the trial, the Anti-Defamation League of B'nai B'rith was established. Editorials in support of Frank appeared across the country, and a petition on his behalf was signed by the "leading Gentile citizens of Texas."[118] Famed investigative journalist C. P. Connolly wrote a two-part series on the case for *Collier's Weekly*. Connolly lambasted "those who harbor the medieval picture of the fire-breathing, murderous Jew," and *Collier's* extended reprint rights of the series, free of charge, to ten thousand newspapers.[119] Upon reading the galley proofs, Leo Frank wrote to Connolly from his cell at the Fulton County Jail, opining that the muckraker "may prove to be my Zola," a reference to the *J'accuse* letter the French novelist had published during the Dreyfus Affair.[120]

In June 1915, with the appeals process exhausted, Governor John Slaton commuted Leo Frank's sentence to life imprisonment, saying that he uncovered troubling questions about his guilt and declaring that he would not sit by like "Pontius Pilate and turn Frank over to be executed."[121] Ten thousand protestors marched on his country home, hurling bricks at the security detail of National Guardsmen that had been summoned. A month later, after Leo Frank had been transferred from the Fulton County Tower to the State Prison Farm at Milledgeville, a hundred miles southeast of Atlanta, his throat was cut by a convict. The inmate explained the attack by saying it was "something that ought to be done."[122] Frank survived, but on the night of August 16, twenty-five armed men burst into the prison, allegedly overpowering the warden and guards, and kidnapped Frank, driving him over one hundred miles, past cotton fields and peach orchards, to a grove of oak trees two miles east of Marietta, and lynched him under the burnished morning sky.[123]

By foot or car or horse-drawn wagon people hurried to the grove – three thousand people as noisy and cheerful as the crowd at a carny sideshow. Some men wore overalls; some were in coats and ties. They stood around talking and backslapping their neighbors; one fellow fired his pistol in celebration. Children played, mothers held their babies, and all of them, at some point, stopped to gaze in wonder at the distended body dangling lifelessly from a rope, this thin, doe-eyed, barefoot, thirty-one-year-old Jew hanging from an oak, with blood dripping from his torn neck onto his white nightshirt – this sacrifice to the honor of Southern womanhood or maybe something darker, a human symbol of this community's own unquenchable bloodthirsty rebellion against the civilizing demands of a demanding God.[124] Some visitors to the grove wanted to hold onto this lustrous, late summer day forever; they took photographs and collected souvenirs – Leo Frank's shirtsleeves and the rope around his feet – and before the undertaker could remove the corpse, one man ground Frank's face under his boot heel, as if to make real the words St. Paul had written to the Galatians, telling them that they were free from Judaic law: "Christ redeemed us from the curse of the law, having become a curse for us: For it is written, Cursed is every one that hangeth on a tree."[125]

The identities of the men behind the execution were well known – and included some of the most prominent men in the state – but after interviewing eleven witnesses, a coroner's jury failed to name one of them, leading the *Boston Post* to ask: "Is Georgia in America?"[126]

By then, a picture of Frank hanging in the grove had been turned into a postcard. It would be sold around the South for decades to come.

In 1986, the Georgia State Board of Pardons and Paroles pardoned Leo Frank, conceding that the state failed to protect him and thereby denied Frank the "opportunity for continued legal appeal."[127] In 2000, Jonathan Turley, a law professor at George Washington University, renewed the call for the statue of Tom Watson to be removed from the front of the Georgia capitol.[128] In 2008, at the urging of the Anti-Defamation League, a state historical plaque was placed one hundred yards from the site where Leo Frank was hung. The tree had been cut down years before.[129]

◆ ◆ ◆

As the train brought Leo Frank's coffin to Pennsylvania Station in New York City, his lynching was roundly condemned. Former president Taft caught the prevailing mood by characterizing it as "a damnable outrage… that makes a decent man sick."[130] The post-Civil War South, where farmers constantly endured collapsing commodity prices and tightening credit, had seen a resurgence of the attitude that Jews were Christ-killers and

Shylocks, but Taft's assessment was seconded by major newspapers below the Mason-Dixon Line: the *Atlanta Journal*, *Macon Telegraph*, *Savannah Press*, *Columbus Enquirer*, *Louisville Courier-Journal*, *Richmond Times-Dispatch*, and the *Jackson Clarion-Ledger*. Elsewhere, if possible, the press was even less generous: the *San Francisco Bulletin* averred that Georgia was neither civilized nor Christian; the *Chicago Tribune* dismissed the South as "barely half educated."[131]

Jewish leaders – Rabbi Stephen Wise, Louis Marshall, and Macy's chairman, Nathan Straus – voiced their disgust, but down on the Lower East Side of Manhattan, among the tenements, sweatshops, synagogues, and pushcarts, men and women who had fled the pogroms of Imperial Russia gathered in the streets, weeping or standing in silence, stunned that this evil had trailed them across the ocean to the Golden Land.

Well in advance of the Friday morning on which Leo Frank was buried at Mount Carmel Cemetery in Queens, a conference on the tribulations of eastern European Jewry had been scheduled to take place in Manhattan. Chaired by Nathan Straus, the conference was slated for the Great Hall of Cooper Union, where, in 1860, presidential hopeful Abraham Lincoln had spoken out against the spread of slavery. The Great Hall had nine hundred seats, but on that Friday twenty thousand people showed up, many with tears streaming down their faces. Lines were long, tempers short, and once the doors were shut, the police, with assistance from the conference planners, narrowly avoided a riot.[132]

Inside, the mood was not much better, alternating between surges of sadness and anger. Talk of European Jewry was set aside to address the lynching. The Jewish establishment – that is, the American Jewish Committee and men like Nathan Straus; Louis Marshall; William J. Wollman, managing partner of the Wall Street firm J. S. Bache & Co.; and *New York Times* publisher Adolph Ochs – had been advocating for Georgia authorities to punish the guilty. This position required a large dose of self-deception, for had the authorities in the main been interested in justice, Leo Frank would not have been convicted or lynched. Beneath this position lurked a desire to banish the episode and, more important, the malevolence it revealed. It was as though some Jews, especially those who were highly visible and valued assimilation above all else, were embarrassed by the lynching. Even though Adolph Ochs, a Jew and son of the South, had long feared that his *New York Times* would be seen as "a Jewish newspaper,"[133] the publisher had made certain that the Frank story was prominently covered in the paper and the injustices were countered with editorials. Yet according to the author Garet Garrett, who penned editorials for Ochs, the publisher would come to suspect that "the outside interference of the Jews, led by the *Times*…had made it necessary to lynch Frank."[134] When the coroner's jury ruled that none of the guilty could be identified, the *Times* remained silent.

The majority of the audience at Cooper Union was unwilling to wait for Georgia authorities to act honorably. They believed American Jewry could create sufficient pressure that the state would have to arrest and punish the perpetrators. This position was articulated by Joseph Barondess, a popular union leader and Russian-born son of a rabbi, who asked why it was that Alfred Dreyfus had found justice, but Leo Frank had not. The audience was standing and applauding when Barondess answered his own question – because "the Jews of America are not organized. They are weaklings."[135]

One problem with blaming the tragedy on lack of organization was that it was demonstrably untrue. The American Jewish Committee and its president, Louis Marshall, had worked on behalf of Frank, and the Anti-Defamation League, founded in 1913 as a reaction to the case, had drawn 150 prominent Jews to its executive committee in just over a year.[136] After the conference at Cooper Union, there were more rallies; rewards were offered, notably $20,000 to any of the lynch party willing to testify; stores boycotted Atlanta's most famous export, Coca-Cola; congressional legislation was proposed to prevent Tom Watson from sending his *Jeffersonian* through the mail; and money was raised to hire private detectives to go to Marietta and apprehend the killers.[137]

And in the end none of these efforts made a difference, because organization was not the problem. Those well-meaning Jewish souls who believed otherwise were as deluded as the other well-meaning Jewish souls who believed that Georgia state officials would wake up one morning impatient to pursue justice.

Why so much self-deception? One answer is that in the aftermath of the Leo Frank lynching, American Jews were asking themselves if they had traveled as far as they had thought. When the unbearably painful answer was no, they needed a reason that was easily remedied – a reality that was in their power to change – and hence the applause for Joseph Barondess when he said that American Jews were "weaklings" because they neglected to organize.

What, then, was actually troubling American Jewry? Were they worried that the German princes of "our crowd" would be dragged from their resplendent homes and strung up from lampposts along Fifth Avenue? Did they fear that a lynch mob, letting loose with bloodcurdling rebel yells, would storm down Hester Street with knotted ropes in their hands?

Not likely.

Their fear was more complex, and hidden – an agonizing secret beating in Jewish hearts, a haunting awareness that despite their steady move into the wider gentile society, there was no escape from an inner reality that still featured an endless loop of nightmares. In their minds, Leo Frank, with his neck broken and bleeding, proved that even here, in America, they continued to be as powerless as the shtetl Jews they had left behind in the Russian Pale.

Inner lives of individuals or groups are legendary for their resistance to change and imperviousness to facts. And the facts are that in the South, blacks were lynched in far greater numbers than Jews, and for that matter, so were Italian immigrants, twenty-two of whom died at the end of an extralegal rope between 1891 and 1901.[138] The helplessness felt by Jewish "weaklings," however shameful to them, owed more to the past than to the present – an image, according to the cultural historian Sander L. Gilman, that was the result of the Jewish minority accepting "the mirage of themselves" held by the Christian majority.[139]

The mirage was created by Christians over centuries, the residue of their fearful imaginings, a magical hatred giving birth to twin Jewish phantoms: one as omnipotent as a king, the other as helpless as a newborn. Jewish kings were terrifying – stealing children's blood, poisoning wells to spread the plague, and ruling the world – and was it not more comforting for Christians to see Jews as the chosen lambs of God eager for slaughter and brimming with forgiveness for their butchers? Did Christ, nailed to the cross – did Leo Frank, hanging from an oak limb – satisfy their own homicidal lust and reassure Christians that the evil, inside and outside of them, was subdued? And most satisfying, weren't the Jews to blame for all this blood and sorrow – these Christ killers who invented the idea of Christ, these people of the book who set the law against the sinister chambers of humanity's heart, laying the moral foundation of Western society and producing the original charter for the city upon a hill?

To survive, a mirage must evolve, as Gilman writes, into myths "powerful enough to substitute for realities,"[140] and so one must ask: did Jews come to accept this mythological interpretation of their lives as real? Were the accused, after centuries spent as strangers in strange lands, finally willing to confess to the crimes of their accusers? Whether crying out from a Roman cross or flailing silently from a Georgia tree, did Jews take it on themselves to believe that powerlessness was their divinely commanded lot? And, having been convicted and repeatedly punished by the hostility surrounding them, did Jews embrace their earthly role as moral exemplars chosen by God, feeble scapegoats loaded up with the sins of mankind, hobbling off to die in the wilderness?

This is what Sander Gilman suggests, and nowhere was this "mirage of themselves" more evident than in the wake of the 1903 Kishinev pogrom.

At the time, an American newspaperman commented that "the scenes of horror attending this massacre are beyond description,"[141] and yet, owing to the genius of the Hebrew poet Hayyim Nahman Bialik, no prediction has ever been further off the mark.

The thirty-year-old Bialik was in Odessa, the hub of Jewish intellectual life in the Russian empire, when the pogrom took place. As part of a three-person committee, he was dispatched to Kishinev by a Jewish commission with the assignment of speaking with the survivors and reporting back on conditions in the city.[142]

His first report was the short poem "On the Slaughter," which railed against the killings and the Jewish victims who went to their deaths like animals under the knife of the ritual slaughterer:[143] "Hangman! Here's a neck – come kill! / Crop me like a dog, you have the axe-arm, / and all the earth to me is a block."[144]

His second report, a much longer poem, would become his most famous work, "In the City of Slaughter." In this poem, Bialik gave his rage over Jewish passivity full reign:

> And you will go down from there and come to the dark cellars
> where the pure daughters of your race were defiled among the pots and pans
> woman by woman under seven after seven uncircumcised,
> daughter in front of mother
> and mother in front of daughter,
> before slaughter, during slaughter, and after slaughter…!
> ·
> And see, oh see: in the shade of that same corner
> under this bench and behind that barrel
> lay husbands, fiancés, brothers, peeping out of holes
> at the flutter of holy bodies under the flesh of donkeys….[145]

One can feel Bialik's outrage as he detailed the ultimate disgrace – Jewish men cowering while their women were raped. As if this were not shameful enough, the poet writes that as the men hid they prayed that God would spare *them*, and when the violation ended, husbands hurried to the rabbi for a legal ruling as to whether their wives were sexually permitted to them.[146]

Yet this description of Jewish helplessness was thoroughly inaccurate. On April 24, a front-page story in the *Forward*, based on reports from eyewitnesses, detailed a different scene.

> Armed with knives and machetes, the murderers broke into Jewish homes, where they began stabbing and killing, chopping off heads and stomping frail women and small children…. Kishinev Jews are tough, healthy, strong as iron and fearless. When the murderous pogromists began their horrible slaughter, Jewish boys and men came running and fought like lions to protect their weaker and older brothers and sisters. Even young girls exhibited amazing heroism…. The Jews, however, fought with their bare hands and the murderers, [were] armed with machetes and knives.[147]

The vastly divergent accounts go beyond the dubious wisdom of sending a poet to do a reporter's job. By the spring of 1903, Bialik was incensed with what he saw as the willingness of Jews to wrap themselves in the sanctified shroud of victimhood, and there was no solace for him in the facts. Before departing for Kishinev Bialik had attended a meeting of the Conversation Club, a Jewish literary gathering, and heard Vladimir Jabotinsky, a twenty-two-year-old firebrand, lecture on *Auto-Emancipation*, the pamphlet by Leon Pinsker, which held that the only escape from "Judeophobia" was a homeland.[148] Bialik agreed, and though he did not live to see the founding of the Jewish state, Bialik is considered the national poet of Israel.[149]

Regardless of what we now know of the pogrom, the story of Kishinev still belongs to Bialik[150] – a story that would be reinforced in a small way by the lynching of Leo Frank, and on a grand scale by the Holocaust.

"Myths," it has been observed, "are beliefs which never were true and always will be,"[151] and the mythology of the Jew as hapless victim, as incapable of defending himself or his family, would not begin to erode until the Israeli victory in the 1967 Six-Day War. And it was this mythology, as much as any other hurdle, that American Jews would have to clear in order to organize themselves to rescue Soviet Jewry.

CHAPTER 3

THE LESSONS OF FIRE

My mother remembered the men in their threadbare overcoats with the collars turned up against the wind. They were standing in line shivering outside the basement soup kitchen on Mulberry Street, or huddled together on the corners of downtown Newark, stamping their feet to keep warm and glancing up and down Broad and Market as if a job – or maybe a day's work – might materialize out of the dull winter light. Beyond the jagged stone skyline of downtown there was another city, a sprawling city of shacks and tents running across the marshland with the smoke of cooking fires scudding across the sky like a pestilent cloud, and these images, as detailed as etchings, stayed with my mother forever.

She talked about them when I was a child and when I was grown and not long before she died, a narrative punctuated by an inconsolable memory of her father losing his business in the cataclysmic backwash of the crash and her family losing their home and a little girl leaving her house in the middle of the night, sitting until the last moment in the bay-window seat overlooking her beloved trestles of roses bordering the front porch. Fifty years on, the memories could be set off by a drive on the New Jersey Turnpike past those haunted marshlands or by a song on the radio: my mother found listening to "Brother, Can You Spare a Dime?" unbearable and made me turn it off no matter who was singing it – Bing Crosby or Peter, Paul and Mary.

These memories tormented my mother like recurring bouts of fever and chills, a chronic illness that was not alleviated by her husband's climb into the delights and security of the upper middle class that included a new suburban split-level with a circular driveway, central air conditioning, and rows of rose bushes she planted herself. The memories came packaged with one other unforgettable story that in my mother's telling seemed inseparable from her personal chronicle of the Great Depression, a story that shaped her vision of the humble plot of historical territory she occupied in the twentieth century, defining her irrevocable place in a world that, in her mind, never lost its dangerous edge.

She was eight years old and running through an empty schoolyard chased by two older boys. The boys had German names and they were calling her a kike. In the midst of her terror, my mother was stunned by the word. She had never advertised her religion, and with her blond-brown hair and cameo-perfect features she resembled Shirley Temple. Yet somehow the boys knew, probably because she did not attend school on Rosh Hashana and Yom Kippur – the Jew holidays, a girl in her class called them. Halfway across the schoolyard, on a dusty ball field, the boys caught her and pushed her to the ground. One of them had his knees on her chest – he was laughing – and the other boy had unwound a wire hanger and jabbed the point toward her eye. My mother recalled the scene as drained of color and sound, as if she were watching another girl, a stranger, writhing and screaming in the black-and-white flicker of a silent movie, and suddenly the principal appeared, a big, burly man in a three-piece suit, and pulled the boys off her, dragging them both back to the school, and my mother stood up and ran home.

This was 1936. In Hillside, New Jersey.

◆ ◆ ◆

Given the terrifying economic dislocation of the Depression – the failure of nearly ten thousand banks, the collapse of farm prices, shrinking world trade, and unemployment in the United States that hovered at 20 percent – and given that in Western culture explaining an assortment of plagues by blaming Jews was an age-old game, the attack on a little Jewish girl in the abstract judgment of a historian, as opposed to my outrage as that girl's son, is not shocking. After all, by Halloween of 1938 Americans were still so frightened by the dire economic climate, and the fighting in Europe and Asia, that during a radio broadcast, Orson Welles, directing an adaptation of the science-fiction novel *The War of the Worlds*, managed to convince many in his audience that Martians were invading the United States.

How different much of modern history would have been had the fear of the tumbling world economy been focused on lime-green creatures from outer space instead of Jews. In Germany, Hitler built his government by promising to address inflation, unemployment, and the humiliations Germans experienced after the First World War and the signing of the punitive Treaty of Versailles, and he connected these events with a mordant antisemitism. In the United States, President Franklin Roosevelt enacted his New Deal to counter his country's financial woes, and though antisemitism was not part of the program, Depression-era America was a halcyon period for Jew-hating rabble-rousers.

The writer and social critic H. L. Mencken, whose feelings about Jews were, at best, ambivalent, judged Gerald L. K. Smith "the greatest orator of them all…the Aristotle and Johann Sebastian Bach of all known ear-splitters, dead or alive."[1] Yet it was Father Charles E. Coughlin, thanks to the technology of radio, who reached more listeners. Dubbed the "Radio Priest," Coughlin broadcast his weekly show from his Shrine of the Little Flower in Royal Oak, Michigan. By the early 1930s he had thirty million listeners and received eighty thousand letters a week.

In spite of his antisemitism, Coughlin's archdiocese declared that his show did not contravene Catholic faith or morality. Not all Catholics agreed – for instance, Chicago Cardinal George Mundelein criticized both Coughlin and Hitler – but overall Church leadership did not publicly refute him until after the United States was at war with Germany, and Coughlin was ordered to leave the airwaves and politics.[2]

More threatening than these hate mongers was the pro-Nazi *Deutsch-Amerikanischer Volksbund*, because the group moved beyond rhetoric to action, eventually raising $123,000 in German bonds and nurturing three of the Nazi saboteurs who, in June 1942, landed on a beach at Amagansett, Long Island.[3] The fear of Nazi espionage would often be cited by Americans as a reason for restricting immigration from Hitler's Germany. Established in the mid-1930s, the German-American Bund was led by national "Fuehrer" Fritz Kuhn, a native of Germany who became a naturalized citizen of the United States. The Bund was vociferously opposed to Communism, whose "driving force" was supplied by Jews, as well as to the entry of the United States into any European war.[4] To press its agenda the organization published reams of propaganda, staged demonstrations, and set up bucolic retreats.

Popular reaction to the Bund across the United States was mixed. Reporter John C. Metcalfe, who joined the organization to write about it for the Chicago *Times*, later testified before Congressman Martin Dies and his Committee on Un-American Activities that the Bund had half a million American sympathizers.[5] Still, in 1936, when Fritz Kuhn traveled to Berlin, a photograph of him shaking hands with Hitler appeared in the stateside press, alienating many Americans. Hans Heinrich Dieckhoff, the German ambassador to the United States, quickly recognized the effect of the photo and suggested that his government publicly distance itself from Kuhn;[6] Hitler did not want to disturb the isolationism prevalent among average Americans and supported by a list of notables such as former president Herbert Hoover, who criticized the press for its anti-German bias, and the heroic aviator Charles Lindbergh, who characterized FDR's warnings about the Nazis as "hysterical chatter."[7]

Isolationism remained strong in the United States: the memory of the 320,000 doughboys who had been wounded or killed in fourteen months of fighting in 1917 and 1918 were less than two decades old, and so most Americans wanted to steer clear of quarrels across the sea.[8]

Consequently, as Hitler pressed on through the 1930s, it was tempting to believe that the Nazis were solely a European issue. If the price of keeping American boys from dying in another Belleau Wood was that the United States should stand idly by while Hitler rectified the unjust penalties of the Versailles Treaty and restricted the rights of German Jews, so be it. Why interfere? There was no shortage of antisemitism in America, and in practice the Nazis treated their Jews no worse than Negroes were treated right here at home.

Other voices objected. The revered, Pulitzer-Prize-winning newspaper editor William Allen White helped to form the Committee to Defend America by Aiding the Allies; playwright Robert Sherwood took out a newspaper ad headlined "Stop Hitler Now!";[9] and from 1933 onward Rabbi Stephen S. Wise spoke out against the Nazi threat.

As the summer of 1938 turned toward autumn it was apparent that Germany was not merely trying to right the wrongs of Versailles, but had goose-stepped all over the treaty, rebuilding its war machine, rushing in to reoccupy the Rhineland, annexing Austria, and taking control of the Sudetenland by entering into the Munich Agreement with Britain, France, and Italy. British Prime Minister Neville Chamberlain also signed a separate declaration with Hitler stating that both of them regarded "the agreement signed last night…as symbolic of the desire of our two peoples never to go to war with one another again."[10]

Upon returning to London, Chamberlain waved his piece of paper like a winning ticket in the Irish Sweepstakes, informing his wildly cheering supporters that he had secured "peace in our time," and thus would Chamberlain distinguish himself as one of history's greatest dupes for championing a deal that, over seventy years later, remains the very definition of appeasement.

Americans breathed a collective sigh of relief with the signing of the Munich Agreement. Maybe the Nazis would show some restraint. That line of thinking lasted right up until the night of November 9, when the Nazi government ordered an assault on Jews in Germany, Austria, and the Sudetenland.[11]

Witnesses would recall that you could hear the screaming and cries for help above the sledgehammers and shattering glass. Mobs of brown-shirted stormtroopers and apple-cheeked Hitler Youth and ordinary citizens were everywhere, all of them raging at the Jews. The noise was everywhere, too: the hiss of flames rising from synagogues, the joyous shouts of youngsters as they knocked over Jewish gravestones, the applause from smartly dressed young women who stood watching the show, wives sobbing over their husbands beaten to death in the street, mothers laughing and holding up their babies so the little ones wouldn't miss the fun.[12]

It was the glass that people remembered, the glass that gave this pogrom its name: *Kristallnacht*, the Night of Broken Glass. Over one thousand synagogues and prayer houses were ransacked and burned; over ninety people were murdered and many more, despairing of their future, committed suicide; over seven thousand Jewish businesses were looted and destroyed; and thirty thousand Jewish males were arrested, most of them dragged off to Dachau, Buchenwald, and Sachsenhausen.[13]

In a response that would recall the American response to the Kishinev pogrom in 1903, *Kristallnacht* sent shock waves down Main Street. For several weeks, accounts of the violence were front-page news. Nearly one thousand separate editorials condemning the action appeared, including one in the highly influential *New Yorker Staatzeitung und Herald*, a German-language publication that had been an apologist for Hitler's antisemitic policies. President Hoover changed his tune on a radio broadcast, and his views were echoed by a host of politicos.

In lieu of holding his usual free-for-all with the press, President Roosevelt read an unambiguous statement of condemnation, saying that he "could scarcely believe that such things could occur in a twentieth-century civilization."[14] FDR limited the government's official response by asking Hugh Wilson, the US ambassador to Germany, to come home to give him a personal report on the situation, a serious expression of the administration's disapproval of the violence.[15]

Despite the outrage over *Kristallnacht* and the fact that the Dies Committee was now investigating the German-American Bund, Fritz Kuhn continued his activities as national Fuehrer. By now, public opinion surveys showed that Americans viewed Kuhn as "the leading anti-Semite in the country,"[16] which did not inhibit his ability to raise money. Kuhn believed that support for Nazism – or at least a thriving antisemitism and a desperate desire to sit out another European war – had survived the outcry about German behavior, and he may well have proved his point on February 20, 1939, when twenty-two thousand of the faithful, paying between forty cents and $1.10 per ticket, jammed Madison Square Garden, where the stage was ablaze with light, the glow illuminating the thirty-foot-high portrait of Washington and the Stars and Stripes hanging behind the speaker's rostrum. The arena was festooned with swastikas and banners – one of them exclaiming, "Stop Jewish Domination of Christian America."[17] In his speech, Kuhn offered a rosy comparison between Hitler and Washington, exhorted the crowd to join a Fascist bulwark against Communism,[18] excoriated President Franklin D. "Rosenfeld," perpetrator of the "Jew Deal,"[19] and decried the "campaign of hate" directed at the Bund by newspapers, radio, and the movies – all of it, Kuhn claimed, originating with the Jews.[20]

Isadore Greenbaum, a young Jew from Brooklyn, was irritated by Kuhn's diatribe, and he scrambled up onto the platform toward the speaker. Bund guards in gray uniforms wrestled Greenbaum to the floor, which did little to soothe the young man. Several New York City policemen intervened and as they carried Greenbaum backstage, he tried to break free and managed to lose his suit pants in the struggle.[21]

Seventeen hundred policemen had been assigned to keep order. Some patrolled Fifty-Second Street and Eighth Avenue on horseback, the breath of their horses steaming in the wintry night, while others formed a blue serge wall to hold back the ten thousand anti-Nazi protestors who had gathered near the Garden. The rally ended just after eleven o'clock, and as Bundists poured into the streets, they ran headlong into angry bands of protestors, and fighting broke out. In all, thirteen people were arrested and eight suffered minor injuries, but by twelve o'clock, the *New York Times* later reported, "Eighth Avenue was as quiet as it usually is…on a midweek midnight."[22]

Fritz Kuhn suffered a not uncommon fate of American demagogues: he was convicted of embezzling funds from his organization.[23] His citizenship was revoked, and after serving his sentence in Sing Sing, he was interned until 1945, then deported to West Germany. The land of his birth put him on trial for his prewar efforts on behalf of the Nazis and incarcerated him. In 1951, shortly before Kuhn died, he gave voice to his disillusionment, musing to a guard, "Who would have known it would end like this?"[24]

◆ ◆ ◆

Two questions persist. Why, after *Kristallnacht*, didn't more Americans forcefully reject the Bund? And why didn't Roosevelt take any actions beyond scolding Germany and recalling Ambassador Wilson?

The answers to these questions are intertwined, but they are not the same. Frequently, antisemitism is cited as the unifying factor behind the inaction. It would be difficult to argue that antisemitism did not cast its shadow over both issues, but just as difficult is the argument that it was the cause of either one.

By the late fall of 1938, there was no shortage of antisemitism in the United States. A survey revealed that approximately fifty-six million Americans – 42.3 percent of the population – were convinced that the intense dislike of Jews was due to their own distasteful behavior and personality traits.[25] To some degree this explains why America as a whole didn't reject the Bund or any of the over one hundred antisemitic groups that were active during the Depression.[26] Yet if Jews were so roundly disliked by Americans, why all the excitement over *Kristallnacht*? That paradox becomes clearer when we examine the reaction of President Roosevelt.

Even the most generous portrait of FDR depicts a man who grew up infused with the cultural prejudices of his era, when antisemitism "was bred into the American ruling classes."[27] As a young woman, Roosevelt's wife, Eleanor, was equally indoctrinated, referring to a gathering as a "Jew party," and describing Jews as a "race [with] nerves of iron and tentacles of steel."[28] All the same, by the 1930s, it would appear that Eleanor and Franklin had outgrown the prejudices of their upbringing.

Certainly, the president and First Lady had Jewish associates and friends. Fifteen percent of FDR's top advisers were Jews, while only 3 percent of America was Jewish,[29] and Eleanor would eventually dedicate herself to the cause of saving Jewish refugees. Yet whether this represents an amelioration of their ingrained attitudes remains an open and irrelevant question given the nature of American antisemitism versus its more pathological European cousin.

Sociologist Peter I. Rose, in his study of small-town Jews and their neighbors, *Strangers in Their Midst*, offers a clue to this difference by suggesting that small-town "natives" managed to accept their Jewish neighbors by the psychological maneuver of "exemption," meaning that while they may have held fast to unpleasant Jewish stereotypes, they exempted "Jewish friends from these images and side-stepped their deep-seated prejudice."[30]

Thus, Americans could respond to the brutality of *Kristallnacht* and express their sympathy for the "underdog"[31] – always a potent American sentiment – while at the same time harboring a general antipathy toward Jews. They could also feel secure staying on the sidelines, convinced, as they were, that these Nazi thugs across the Atlantic had no connection to them and that this street violence, vile as it was, could not possibly lead to a world war.

Beginning in 1933, FDR was informed about the predicament of German Jewry. That year, after visiting Germany, the diplomat James McDonald reported to the president that the Nazis were planning to exterminate their nation's Jews. According to McDonald, Roosevelt "seemed deeply concerned and said he wanted to find a way to send a warning message to the German people over the head of Hitler."[32] Shortly after that meeting, Eleanor Roosevelt brought her friend Alice Hamilton to Hyde Park, where Hamilton, who had recently returned from a three-month sojourn in Germany, provided the president with "a detailed eyewitness account of German brutality against the Jews."[33]

Roosevelt conceded that the Nazis were "treating the Jews shamefully," and that Jews in the United States were "greatly excited."[34] Just how excited American Jewry was became evident on March 27, 1933, when an estimated one million Jews marched in a nationwide protest against Nazi antisemitism.[35] Still, FDR concluded that German antisemitism was not a matter for the White House; he could "do nothing except for American citizens who happen to be made victims."[36]

In approaching Berlin's internal policies toward Jews, FDR preferred "unofficial and personal influence" to official US government attempts to intercede,[37] the same position that would be adopted by President Richard Nixon when it came to dealing with the Kremlin on Soviet Jews. During the 1960s and 1970s, some of the most sustained efforts of the Soviet Jewry movement were directed at forcing official government recognition of the problem with the goal of pushing the administration and Congress to formulate a solution.

This approach would not prove successful in the United States during the Roosevelt administration, primarily because the country was so intent on preserving the illusion that Nazi belligerency did not concern them – an easily maintained illusion for those living in splendid geographic isolation. Whatever the inclinations of the president, FDR was an unerring reader of his nation's tea leaves, and he had no intention of getting too far out in front of the electorate. As pollster Elmo Roper observed, FDR was "tremendously interested in public opinion" and believed himself to be on far firmer ground "when he felt the public was behind him."[38]

And the public wanted to avoid a blood-drenched sequel to the Great War, a reality that was not lost on Congress, who passed the Neutrality Act of 1937, which withheld arms from belligerents.[39] A few years later, despite the widespread coverage of the Spanish Civil War and the newsreels showing the Axis powers on the march, a vast array of disparate groups – from committed isolationists to mothers who had lost sons to war – were vehemently opposed to a draft.[40] Once the war started in Europe, Congress hoped to help our allies – without direct US involvement – by allowing FDR to sell arms to England and France under a "cash-and-carry" arrangement.[41]

Nor did the public want to get involved in the business of rescue. Nazi propaganda minister Josef Goebbels had offered to send Germany's Jews to any country that wanted them, but Americans were opposed to any legislation that would expand immigration quotas. Polls found that two-thirds of the nation were against any refugees at all, a number that climbed to 83 percent after *Kristallnacht*.[42] These findings were not the result of idle opinion or barroom chatter, for during 1939 it became starkly clear just how profoundly opposed Americans were to accepting those in flight from Hitler.

That winter, Senator Robert F. Wagner, a Democrat from New York, and Congresswoman Edith Nourse Rogers, a Republican from Massachusetts, proposed rescuing twenty thousand German children over two years. A spate of national luminaries got behind the bill: New York City Mayor Fiorello La Guardia; the actress Helen Hayes; the Catholic leader His Eminence George Cardinal Mundelein; and former First Lady Grace Coolidge, who, along with her neighbors in Northampton, Massachusetts, pledged to take in twenty-five children.[43] One steadfast opponent of the Wagner-Rogers Bill was FDR's cousin Laura Delano Houghteling, wife of the commissioner of immigration. During a Washington dinner party, she observed that the problem with the measure was that "twenty thousand charming children would all too soon grow up into twenty thousand ugly adults."[44] It is doubtful that FDR agreed with his cousin, but despite the urging of Eleanor, the Wagner-Rogers Bill received no support from the president,[45] and the bill was never passed.[46]

In the spring, world attention was focused on the SS *St. Louis*, a liner owned by the Hamburg-America Line. The ship had sailed from Germany carrying 936 refugees,[47] all of whom held landing certificates for Cuba that had been purchased from the shipping company. However, the *St. Louis* was forbidden to dock in Havana because the Cuban government had revoked the permits, explaining that they were illegal.[48]

With the ship anchored in the port of Havana, American newspapers gave the incident front-page attention accompanied by sympathetic editorials that blamed Cuban officials and cited their moral obligation "to undo the blunder by letting these innocent victims land."[49] A smattering of papers, the *Christian Science Monitor* among them, criticized the passengers on the *St. Louis* for being too fussy about where they would agree to land and suggested they try "British Guiana, Dutch Guiana, North Rhodesia, Dominican Republic, and the Philippines."[50]

The US government and the Joint Distribution Committee were inundated with letters and telegrams from Jewish leaders and groups requesting that they intercede. Although the government and JDC pleaded with Cuban authorities to relent, and offered money to accept the passengers, no deal could be worked out. The ship left Havana, sailing along the coast of Florida. The refugees hoped that America would accept them and sent a telegram to FDR, asking for asylum. The president did not respond.[51] One newspaper opined that aiding these Jews would establish a "dangerous precedent" and the *St. Louis* would be "followed by other ship loads."[52] Indeed, more refugees were already sailing from Europe,[53] and even though from 1933 until 1940 approximately 105,000 refugees from the Nazis found a haven in the United States,[54] there would be no place for the men, women, and children crowding the decks of the *St. Louis*.

By the end of the war, 227 passengers from the ill-starred ship had been murdered by the Nazis.[55]

◆ ◆ ◆

As history has moved along and the actors have departed the stage, one question that defies a tidy explanation is why Roosevelt did not step in and help those seeking refuge from the Nazis.

Fifteen years before Hitler grabbed the reins of power in Germany, a wave of hostility toward refugees began to rise in the United States. Grappling with the end of the First World War had brought on a resurgence of nativism: Americans rejected foreign adventures, ideas, and people, although not without some ambivalence. For instance, First Lady Florence Harding opposed her husband's recommendation that humanitarian aid be provided to the twenty million people in danger of starving in Soviet Russia, claiming that before assistance was sent, Bolshevik leaders should be pressed to renounce Communism. But when a woman wrote to the First Lady about an elderly Russian Jew who was desperate to come to the United States, Florence Harding used her contacts to track down the man and arranged for him to emigrate.[56]

David S. Wyman, author of *The Abandonment of the Jews*, points out that through the 1930s and early 1940s the "anti-refugee sentiment was closely linked to anti-Semitism,"[57] and nowhere was this link more embodied than in the person of Assistant Secretary of State Breckinridge Long, who, beginning in January 1940, was in charge of the newly created Special War Problems Division, which oversaw the issuing of visas.[58]

Long was no man-of-his-times, run-of-the-mill American antisemite on the order of, say, Joseph P. Kennedy, the US ambassador to Britain, a staunch isolationist and supporter of Neville Chamberlain's appeasement of Germany. Kennedy referred to Jews as "sheeny" and "kike,"[59] though he demonstrated an equivalent enthusiasm for calling Italians "wops" and Irishmen "micks."[60] Kennedy defended himself against the charge of being a "Jew-hater" by citing his friendships with Jews in all walks of life.[61] Golf, in particular, seemed to kindle Kennedy's egalitarian spirit. In Florida, Kennedy refused to become a member of the Everglades Club, long suspected of excluding Jews,[62] and instead joined the Palm Beach Country Club, where, he liked to brag, he was "the only Christian member."[63] On Cape Cod, he proposed the Jewish secretary of the treasury, Henry Morgenthau Jr., for a guest membership at a golf club in Wianno, and when Morgenthau was rejected, Kennedy quit playing there.

Where Kennedy's feelings about Jews were a classic case of the psychological jugglery of exemption, Breckinridge Long was imbued with the antisemitism common to Europe, a hostility based on the belief that Jews were purveyors of a dark magic.[64] He felt that Hitler's autobiography and political tract *Mein Kampf* was "eloquent in opposition to Jewry and to Jews as exponents of Communism and chaos," and he made it clear in his diary that he believed the pressure to take in European runaways was emanating from "Communists, extreme radicals [and] Jewish professional agitators."[65] His answer to the pressure was to advise State Department officials that they could slow immigration by resorting "to various administrative devices which would postpone and postpone and postpone the granting of the visas."[66]

His reluctance to help infuriated Eleanor Roosevelt.[67] She referred to Long as a "fascist," and one afternoon, at lunch, when her husband reminded her that she should not say such a thing, Eleanor told the president: "Well, maybe I shouldn't say it, but he is."[68]

Long was not the worst of his ilk in the foreign service. There was Tyler Kent, scion of a venerable Virginia family and, like Long, a graduate of Princeton, who was convinced that the cause of "all wars" was the international banking community, a group "largely controlled by the Jews." Kent worked as a cipher clerk in the US embassy in London and, after reading the correspondence between Roosevelt and Churchill, passed the information along to a woman in touch with the Germans and Italians. When detectives from Scotland Yard arrived at his flat to arrest Kent, they discovered a filing cabinet labeled "This is a Jew's War."[69]

This charge was echoed in Congress by Rep. John R. Rankin, a Democrat from Mississippi and an unapologetic antisemite.[70] In June 1941, Rankin lashed out at "Wall Street and a little group of our international Jewish brethren" who wanted to drag the country into war. Rankin claimed that "international bankers" were so opposed to peace that the day before they had organized a rally in Wall Street to make certain that the fighting would not end.[71]

Rep. M. Michael Edelstein, a Jewish Democrat from New York City, was incensed by Rankin's words. Edelstein, who had been three years old when his parents fled the antisemitic violence of Imperial Russia and brought him to New York,[72] stood and asked Speaker of the House Sam Rayburn for the floor.

Rayburn recognized him, and Edelstein said that "Hitler started out by speaking about 'Jewish brethren.' It is becoming the play and the work of those people who want to demagogue to speak about 'Jewish brethren' and 'international bankers'.... The fact of the matter is that the number of Jewish bankers in the United States is infinitesimal. It is also a fact that the meeting which took place yesterday…was entirely controlled by persons other than Jewish bankers." [73]

The crosscurrent of discussion among the members was becoming so heated that Speaker Rayburn was forced to use his gavel repeatedly to call for order. Edelstein continued through the din, concluding: "As a member of this House I deplore such allegations, because we are living in a democracy. All men are created equal regardless of race, creed, or color; and whether a man be Jew or Gentile he may think what he deems fit."[74]

What happened next became a lugubrious nugget of congressional lore. Edelstein strode from the chamber and had a heart attack and died. He was fifty-three years old.[75]

One congressman unbowed by the isolationism of his colleagues was a Democratic wheeler-dealer from Texas, Lyndon Baines Johnson. According to Louis Gomolak, author of an unpublished 1989 doctoral thesis, "Prologue: LBJ's Foreign Affairs Background, 1908–1948," Johnson's aunt, Jessie Johnson Hatcher, belonged to the Zionist Organization of America, and she had a lasting influence on her nephew, encouraging him to befriend Jews. LBJ's grandfather, "Big Sam," and father, "Little Sam," both campaigned to save Leo Frank and earned the enmity of the Ku Klux Klan for doing so.[76] LBJ would later trace his antipathy toward antisemitism to Frank's lynching, and in 1940 he bent that antipathy to a just cause.[77] Along with a handful of likeminded individuals, including his constituent Jim Novy, a prosperous Jewish businessman who had emigrated from Russia as a teenager in 1913, Johnson set up Operation Texas, which helped European Jews obtain false passports and visas to Latin America and then relocated them to the National Youth Administration training camps in Texas. Novy shouldered the costs for the refugees to live in the NYA camps,[78] but it was illegal for foreigners to be there, so Operation Texas was kept quiet until December 1963 when Novy announced it during the dedication of a synagogue in Austin.[79] Estimates put the number of Jews rescued from forty-two to four hundred, but since the operation was illegal there was no written record.[80] Johnson's wife, Lady Bird, did recall that after the dedication, "Person after person plucked at my sleeve and said, 'I wouldn't be here today if it weren't for [your husband]. He helped me get out.'"[81]

◆ ◆ ◆

The antisemitism that precluded Jewish refugees from entering the United States was a challenge to the American covenant, but for Franklin Roosevelt the antisemitic mood of his nation went beyond the breaking of a promise. He saw it as potentially cataclysmic. FDR confided to Ambassador Kennedy that "if there was a demagogue around here of the type of Huey Long to take up anti-Semitism, there could be more blood running in the streets of New York than in Berlin."[82]

However, the resistance to providing sanctuary to European Jewry was a subset of a larger, more volatile isolationist movement that spanned the wings of domestic politics. The America First Committee (AFC), which claimed membership in excess of eight hundred thousand,[83] was supported by well-known antisemites: Charles Lindbergh, Henry Ford, and the publisher of the *Chicago Tribune*, Colonel Robert R. McCormack, who was more alienated by the alleged homosexuality of Nazi leaders than by their animosity toward Jews.[84] Yet the AFC also counted among its members the socialist leader and presidential candidate Norman Thomas; the liberal journalist John T. Flynn; and advertising executive Chester Bowles, who would later work for Presidents Roosevelt, Truman, and Kennedy.[85] In addition, Jews assumed important positions in the organization: Sidney Hertzberg was the first director of public relations, and James Lipsig played a significant role in writing AFC position papers.[86]

Roosevelt was concerned enough about the AFC to order a secret investigation of the group, using the FBI, a private investigator, and a grand jury.[87] In June 1940, speaking at the University of Virginia, FDR lashed out at isolationists, accusing them of clinging to the "obvious delusion that we of the United States can safely permit the United States to become a lone island…in a world dominated by the philosophy of force."[88]

By September 1940, with the Battle of Britain underway, Americans appeared to be inching closer to acknowledging the reality FDR had broached in his speech: Gallup pollsters discovered that opposition to a draft had changed; two-thirds of the country thought it wise to call up some young men; and Congress established the first peacetime draft in US history.[89]

In the midst of the German Luftwaffe's relentless air assault on Britain, Congress also passed the Hennings Bill, an amendment to the Neutrality Act, which allowed British children trapped by the bombing to enter the United States.[90] The bill was the first legislative victory for Americans pressuring the government to assist refugees, but it had not seen fit, a year earlier, to admit the refugee children of German Jews.[91]

Breckinridge Long vehemently opposed sanctuary for British children. Whatever his animosity toward Jews, his commitment to isolationism was unsullied by prejudice. "The very surest way," Long wrote, "to get America into this war would be to send an American ship to England and put 2,000 babies on it and then have it sunk by a German torpedo."[92] Long described the desire to reach out to these children as "an enormous psychosis"[93] and attributed it "to repressed emotion about the war, the chance finally to do something, however wrongheaded it may be."[94]

As coldhearted as this sounds, Long may have been onto something. The prevailing mood in the United States was akin to the family intent on a summer outing despite the rising wind and dark clouds in the near distance. After Dad spreads the blanket and Mom unpacks the potato salad, they stare out at their children on the sailboat in the middle of the white-capped lake and you can almost hear them reassure each other, in falsely cheerful tones, that they have nothing to worry about – no storm is coming – and even if it does there is an umbrella in the car.

FDR echoed Long's concerns about the rescue of the British children, but in September, when a German U-Boat sank the *City of Benares* in the North Atlantic, killing 260 people, including seventy-nine refugee children aboard, no call for war rose up from Americans.[95]

That fall, as FDR sought an unprecedented, and controversial, third term, his Republican opponent, Wendell L. Willkie, an internationalist at heart, saw an opportunity to defeat Roosevelt by accusing him of privately planning to ship Americans to fight in Europe, predicting that if the president were returned to the White House, the country would be mired in war in under six months.[96]

Even in the sparkling aura of one of FDR's free-flowing cocktail hours, it is unlikely that the president could have believed that the expansionist designs of Germany, Japan, and Italy would be thwarted without a significant commitment of his armed forces.[97] By September 1940, the best Roosevelt could do was help confront the German war machine by concluding the Destroyers for Bases Agreement with Britain, sending fifty destroyers to the Royal Navy in exchange for ninety-nine-year leases on British air and naval bases in Newfoundland, Bermuda, British Guiana, and across the Caribbean. FDR knew the deal would enrage isolationists, so he bypassed Congress and issued an executive decree that Attorney General Robert Jackson declared legal. Prime Minister Winston Churchill called the deal "a decidedly unneutral act."[98]

As the gap between FDR and Willkie narrowed, Roosevelt worried that the electorate would begin to believe Willkie's charge that he was dragging them into another cycle of European carnage. In an October campaign speech at Boston Garden, Roosevelt rebutted his opponent's allegation by telling the audience: "I have said this before, but I shall say it again and again and again: Your boys are not going to be sent into any foreign wars."[99]

FDR won the popular vote 54.7 percent to 44.8 percent, the narrowest margin since Woodrow Wilson defeated Charles Evans Hughes in 1916,[100] but his pledge would come to haunt him: one of his harshest critics, Claire Boothe Luce, the playwright and wife of *Time* founder Henry Luce, would comment that FDR had "lied us into a war he should have led us into."[101]

During the campaign Eleanor was able to intervene on behalf of eighty-three Jewish refugees. They had first arrived in New York Harbor on the SS *Quanza*. After the passengers with visas aboard the Portuguese freighter left the ship, the others begged to be allowed ashore, but official permission was not granted. The freighter headed south to Mexico, but Mexican authorities were no more hospitable than their northern counterparts. En route back to Europe, the freighter stopped in Norfolk, Virginia, to replenish her coal stores, and it was at this point that Eleanor Roosevelt was contacted by Jewish organizations desperate to assist the refugees. The president and First Lady were at Hyde Park, and Eleanor implored her husband to help. A Jewish lawyer, Jacob L. Morewitz, had already filed a suit in the US District Court to prevent the ship from leaving the port, a move that was guaranteed to prolong the controversy and attract the attention of humanitarians and editorialists.[102] Perhaps hoping to avoid another public skirmish over refugees so close to the election and to make certain that his Jewish supporters would come out to vote, FDR dispatched a representative to Norfolk, who soon approved any paperwork the passengers carried and certified everyone else as political refugees, thus allowing them to come ashore and leading a passenger to comment, "Mrs. Roosevelt saved my life."[103]

Breckinridge Long was not happy with the decision, but the assistance extended by FDR did not signal a change in his attitude toward refugees. In March 1941, though, the president signed the lend-lease bill, permitting the British Navy to receive American guns, ammunition, bomb charges, and PT boats, and the president promised $7 billion more in military aid. Yet FDR also took care not to shatter his country's conviction that direct involvement in the European war could be avoided. In October, after the USS *Reuben James* was sunk by Nazi U-boats off the coast of Iceland, an attack that took the lives of 115 men, the president commented that the incident would not alter the diplomatic relationship between the United States and Germany. Woody Guthrie was soon singing about the incident, but playwright Robert Sherwood, who also wrote speeches for FDR, "observed that the public seemed more interested in the Army-Notre Dame football game."[104]

As the fighting intensified overseas, Americans were reluctant to extend the same offer of sanctuary to Jewish children as they had to British youngsters. Thousands of Jewish children without parents were trapped in squalor in Vichy France and in danger of deportation to concentration camps. The Joint Distribution Committee set aside $1 million to rescue the children, but due to bureaucratic dithering, a reluctance to confront the restrictionist forces in the United States, and the fact that the Nazis had taken control of Vichy France, the children were not brought to America.[105]

Eleanor and Franklin's son James Roosevelt would later say that his mother's failure to convince his father to do more for refugees was "her deepest regret at the end of her life."[106]

FDR's refusal, writes historian Doris Kearns Goodwin, was his judgment that it would be futile to "pit his presidency against the xenophobic, anti-

Semitic mood of his country."[107] Yet it is impossible not to ask if FDR was too cautious. Could he have accepted more refugees *and* accomplished his ends? Perhaps, but how many would he have saved – hundreds, thousands, or hundreds of thousands? What number would have been worth the risk of strengthening the already strong hand of the isolationists? Rep. Samuel Dickstein, a Jew who chaired the House Committee on Immigration and Naturalization, felt that if Roosevelt had attempted to throw open the doors for European Jewry, then Congress would have reacted by voting to slam the doors shut, making the rescue of anyone nearly impossible.[108]

In hindsight, it is clear now that the early rounds of the Nazi persecution of Jews foretold a disaster the scope of which civilization had never seen – an eerie, bureaucratic, by-the-numbers genocide that rocked the foundations of Western civilization, destroying once and for all the faith born during the eighteenth century's Enlightenment, when, for a glorious instant, mankind believed, in the words of the scholar Lewis White Beck, that "reason [was] perfectly fitted for the wise conduct of life."[109]

Could Roosevelt possibly have envisioned the fiery dénouement in the opening scenes? Consider the recent past: the first bombing of the World Trade Center occurred in 1993; three years later, Khobar Towers in Saudi Arabia, home to US military personnel, was bombed; in 2000, al-Qaeda attacked the USS *Cole* in Yemen. So why was 9/11 so stunning for most Americans? Were we oblivious to the spread of theocratic fascism across the Middle East? Did we not hear or read about the earlier attacks? Were we unaware that Osama bin Laden had declared war on us? What explains our surprise? Because we wished our enemies would just go away? Because we are too occupied with our own work and families? Because we, as a people, prefer to be hopeful about the future? Because we cannot accept that others could hate our culture enough to trade their lives for the chance to murder innocent civilians as they sat on planes and in offices on a sunny September day?

In facing the developments in Germany, we know that at the outset, Roosevelt thought private diplomacy might temper the persecution of the Jews. German behavior shortly relieved him of his optimism. FDR was guilty of underestimating Hitler's commitment to the mass murder of Jews, but how could he have foreseen that the Nazis would so readily recruit willing accomplices in other European countries? In the main, Americans were no more prescient than FDR. Even as the slaughter began in earnest, Americans refused to believe it despite the evidence. In the summer of 1942, newspapers and radios in the United States and Britain reported that one million Jews had already been murdered – many in traveling gas chambers[110] – but a poll conducted six months later showed that fewer than half of Americans believed the reports.[111]

To educate the public, Hillel Kook, a Lithuanian-born Jew who had immigrated to Palestine, was sent to the United States. Kook adopted the pseudonym Peter Bergson and, along with other young Jews, formed the Bergson Group. Among their activities in 1943 and 1944 was organizing four hundred rabbis to march on the White House and running advertisements in hundreds of newspapers across the country that cried out for the rescue of European Jewry. One ad inquired: "How Well Are You Sleeping? Is There Something You Could Have Done to Save Millions of Innocent People from Torture and Death?" Another ad asked: "Time Races Death: What Are We Waiting For?"[112]

FDR complained to Eleanor that the Bergson ads were "hitting below the belt,"[113] and the *Washington Post*, which was owned by a Jew, splashed a series attacking the Bergson group across its front page.[114] Even though the advertisements did attract the attention of op-ed writers and Congress, Americans found it difficult to accept that a widespread genocide was underway. In December 1944, when reams of information had been published and William Randolph Hearst was beseeching the readers of his newspapers to "Remember... THIS IS NOT A JEWISH PROBLEM. It is a HUMAN PROBLEM,"[115] three-quarters of Americans had come to accept that the Germans were operating death factories, and yet, the overwhelming majority of those polled estimated the number of dead at no more than one hundred thousand.[116]

For some time Roosevelt had resisted Churchill's desire to widen the war to aid European Jewry. He thought that such a strategy would alienate Stalin, who had no special affection for Jews and no qualms against butchery.[117] But in October 1943, FDR relented to the British prime minister and affixed his signature, along with Churchill's and Stalin's, to the Declaration Concerning Atrocities. Secretly written by Churchill, the declaration warned that anyone whose hands were not already stained with innocent blood should not "join the ranks of the guilty, for most assuredly the three Allied powers will...deliver them to their accusers."[118]

Three months later, Roosevelt signed Executive Order 9417, establishing the War Refugee Board. The president had created the board at the urging of his longtime friend Henry Morgenthau Jr. Like his esteemed father, Secretary of the Treasury Morgenthau was a devoutly secular Jew with little sympathy for Zionism. But Morgenthau had been sickened by the growing evidence of the Nazi war against the Jews that Rabbi Stephen Wise, head of the American Jewish Congress, continually pressed on him, including the information that the remains of concentration-camp victims were processed into soap and that the Germans were "making lampshades out of the skins of the Jews."[119]

Working in concert with Jewish organizations, European resistance groups, and diplomats from neutral countries, the War Refugee Board did its best to rescue Jews living under Nazi occupation. The WRB was responsible for recruiting the Swedish businessman Raoul Wallenberg, who was credited with saving more than one hundred thousand Jews from extermination.[120] By the spring of 1945 it was estimated that in all the board saved twice that number.[121]

◆ ◆ ◆

Even before Germany surrendered, humanity had a new word for mass murder: *genocide*. It was coined by Raphael Lemkin, a Jewish lawyer born in 1900 in Imperial Russia. Prior to the war, Lemkin served as a prosecutor in the district court of Warsaw. In 1939, when the Nazis invaded Poland, Lemkin fled to the woods outside the city and joined the partisans fighting against the invaders. Forty members of Lemkin's family were killed by the Nazis, and Lemkin eventually made his way to the United States, where he taught at Duke University's School of Law.[122]

So began the literature of the Nazi destruction of European Jewry – a body of literature that has increased exponentially over the last sixty-six years. Because the writing was carried out over decades that saw a seismic shift in the circumstances of world Jewry, the motifs that emerge from the literature often reflect the shifting concerns of Jews.

To understand the impassioned underpinnings of the American movement to free Soviet Jewry (and why this chapter explores Depression-era antisemitism and America's reactions to Nazi Germany), it is essential to note a particular strand of Holocaust literature, one that has been described by J. J. Goldberg, author of *Jewish Power: Inside the American Jewish Establishment*, as "a long chain of blame"[123] that began in 1968 with the publication of Arthur D. Morse's *While Six Million Died*.[124]

A former television newsman who worked for the legendary Edward R. Murrow, Morse was no stranger to hard-hitting stories – he produced the first program for *CBS Reports* on the then-controversial connection between cigarettes and lung cancer[125] – and the subtitle of his book said it all: *A Chronicle of American Apathy*. Morse recorded what he deemed official apathy on page after page until it seemed the US government had reacted with no more alarm than if the Nazis had been exterminating ants.

The outrage Morse leveled at the "bystanders to cruelty [who] became bystanders to genocide"[126] was frequently repeated by historians as the years from 1933 to 1945 receded further into the past, a trend that reached its high watermark in 1984 when David S. Wyman, the grandson of Protestant ministers and a history professor at University of Massachusetts, Amherst, published *The Abandonment of the Jews: America and the Holocaust*.[127]

Wyman's study has endured as the monumental scholarly work of this genre, and he is no less harsh in his judgment than Morse, declaring that "the overall American response to the European Jewish catastrophe was a dismal failure."[128]

How could it have happened? American Jewry was keenly positioned to help Jews menaced by the Nazis. Beginning with the Damascus blood libel in 1840, the community had a proven track record assisting Jews persecuted abroad by utilizing its communal organizations and well-heeled and well-connected individuals to marshal public opinion and beseech the government to intercede. It should have been a simple matter. FDR had brought more Jews into his inner circle than any president before him, and the three congressional committees that should have been able to undertake the rescue of European refugees were headed by Jews: Rep. Dickstein oversaw Immigration and Naturalization, Rep. Sol Bloom was in charge of Foreign Affairs, and Rep. Emanuel Celler chaired the Judiciary Committee.[129]

Dickstein had shown some reluctance to open doors for refugees;[130] Bloom would be vilified by other Jews as "the State Department's Jew";[131] but Celler had been an outspoken critic of the Nazis. As early as September 1934, he had urged the United States not to participate in the 1936 Olympics that were to be held in Berlin, telling his colleagues in the House that "the Jew who is jeered in the streets simply because he is a Jew cannot be cheered in the arena because he is a champion."[132]

Wyman joins other critics in pointing out two main obstacles to a full-scale rescue effort: first, antisemitism, and second, the American Jewish community's lack of organization, its internal bickering, and shortage of leaders.[133] In *The Abandonment of the Jews*, and his earlier exploration of the refugee crisis, *Paper Walls*, Wyman does a masterful job of documenting these obstacles.

Curiously enough, neither Wyman nor Morse ever mentions World War I, a striking omission that ignores a critical influence on the American impulse to remain aloof from the turmoil in Europe. In 1937, a Gallup poll found that most Americans considered the country's involvement in the First World War "a mistake,"[134] and as the Depression ground on, the legacy of the War to End All Wars was still wafting in and out of the national consciousness.

Partially, this was because of the argument the United States was having with its former allies over their refusal to repay the more than $10 billion they had borrowed.[135] The four countries with the largest debts – Great Britain, France, Italy, and Belgium – suggested that the US cancel the repayments as another contribution to the cause.[136] Washington answered with a resounding no. France and Britain offered to relinquish their rights to reparations from Germany if the debts were canceled, but again, Washington said no. The London *Financial Times* summed up the prevailing Ameircan sentiment, opining that the country "may not take too kindly to an arrangement...she may regard as little short of a conspiracy to defraud."[137]

During the First World War, 4.7 million Americans served in uniform,[138] over 4 percent of the population,[139] and in 1932 the nation learned about the misfortune borne by some of these ex-servicemen. In the late spring, twenty thousand jobless veterans marched to Washington, DC, hoping that the government would advance them the few hundred dollars in bonuses that were scheduled to be paid in 1945.[140] The veterans, some joined by their wives and children, erected hovels on the mud flats of Anacostia. After touring "this strange city" a reporter from the Washington *Star* wrote that anyone "who can salvage an auto top from the dump has a mansion."[141]

The House agreed to a bill advancing the bonuses, and on June 17 – according to a local paper "the tensest day in the capital since the War" – thousands of veterans gathered at the Capitol, awaiting the Senate vote.[142] The bill was defeated 62 to 18, but thousands of the veterans hunkered down on the mud flats well into July, hoping to meet with President Hoover.[143] The president would not meet with them, and soldiers under the command of General Douglas McArthur removed the veterans and their families from the District. The hovels were burned, and as smoke smudged the summer-blue sky, mothers and fathers ran from the soldiers' bayonets with babies in their arms, while young children trailed after their parents, crying and coughing from the tear gas.[144]

When newsreels of the Bonus Riot were shown in movie theaters across the United States, audiences roundly booed the cavalry and infantry.[145]

At present, nearly a century removed from the horrors of World War I and with greater horrors to replace them, it is easy to discount the impact the Great War had on the Western psyche.

One can see that impact in the flourishing of antiwar literature in the 1920s and 1930s: the poems of Wilfred Owen and Siegfried Sassoon, *Three Soldiers* by John Dos Passos, *Goodbye to All That* by Robert Graves, *A Farewell to Arms* by Ernest Hemingway (and a number of his finest short stories), *Death of a Hero* by Richard Aldington, *All Quiet on the Western Front* by Erich Maria Remarque (a novel that so enraged the Nazis that they ordered the beheading of the author's sister, Elfriede, because her brother, an expatriate by then, was unavailable to them[146]), and *Johnny Got His Gun* by Dalton Trumbo. For the less literary, there were movies, where the cinematic depiction of the Great War drew large audiences: *The Four Horsemen of the Apocalypse*, *Wings*, *Hell's Angels*, *A Farewell to Arms* (which also appeared as a Broadway play), *All Quiet on the Western Front*, and *Grand Illusion*.

The American poet Archibald MacLeish, who saw action in the war and whose brother, a fighter pilot, was killed, accused his longtime (and former) friend, Hemingway, and other postwar writers of having "educated a generation to believe that all beliefs are fraudulent, that all statements of conviction are sales-talk, that nothing men can put into words is worth fighting for," and concluded that their work had "done more to disarm democracy in the face of fascism than any other single influence."[147]

During the war it was the doctors in field hospitals and wards far from the front who saw the mass psychological trauma that "the liquid fire, high explosives, tanks, poison gas, [and] bombing planes" produced. This new form of total war gave rise to a new psychological malady, "shell shock," the alliterative predecessor of post-traumatic stress disorder. Symptoms included "staring eyes, violent tremors, a look of terror, and blue, cold extremities,"[148] and some soldiers, untouched by bullets or shrapnel, were unable to see, hear, speak, or walk.

Notwithstanding the fact that some of the isolationism in the United States was infected with antisemitism, isn't it also reasonable to maintain that Americans were less than eager for their fathers, husbands, and sons to march into another overseas convulsion?

Clearly, the First World War influenced one of America's foremost isolationists, Ambassador Joseph Kennedy. Granted, the ambassador would never be a favorite of the Anti-Defamation League, but Jews were the last thing on his mind on an April evening in 1938, as he ate dinner in the beautifully lit Garter Throne Room at Windsor Castle with King George VI and the queen consort, Elizabeth.

"What the American people fear more than anything else is being involved in a war," Kennedy told his hosts. "When they remember 1917 and how they went in to make the world safe for democracy and then they look now at the crop of dictatorships, quarrels, and miseries arising out of that war they say to themselves, 'Never again!'"[149]

None of this is intended to suggest that antisemitism was not a notable feature of the American landscape during the years of the Third Reich. Morse is muted on the subject in *While Six Million Died*, but in *The Abandonment of the Jews* Wyman cites data that is startling: "[S]urveys from August 1940 on through the war found that from 15 to 24 percent of the respondents looked on Jews as 'a menace to America.' Jews were consistently seen as more of a threat than Negroes, Catholics, Germans, or Japanese (except during 1942, when Japanese and Germans were rated more dangerous).… An alarming set of polls taken between 1938 and 1945 revealed that…as much as 35 to 40 percent of the population was prepared to approve an anti-Jewish campaign [in the United States]."[150]

Even so, Wyman believes that FDR could have overcome the obstacles of isolationism and antisemitism "if he had wanted to…by speaking out on the issue."[151] On the other hand, Morse allows Eleanor Roosevelt to testify on behalf of her husband, citing her comments from *This I Remember*.[152] In her memoir, the First Lady wrote that "Franklin frequently refrained from supporting political causes in which he believed, because of political realities."[153] Among these causes were support for the democratic government in the Spanish Civil War, anti-lynching legislation, and the rescinding of the poll tax. FDR's reasoning, according to his wife, was that he wanted to avoid fighting with senators and congressmen whose votes he would need on more important matters, and once the Nazis were on the march, Eleanor recalled, "preparation for war had to take precedence over everything else."[154]

These roadblocks are not sufficient to alter the conviction of either Arthur Morse or David Wyman – and the other writers in the chain of blame – that American Jews, a widely loathed minority, should have been able to persuade their government to rescue Europe's Jews from the homicidal insanity the Nazis had unleashed.

In a 1967 pre-publication interview with the *New York Times*, Morse observed that had it not been for the widespread apathy "there is no doubt from the evidence at hand that additional thousands of refugees could have been saved."[155]

Wyman estimates the numbers to be far higher. In a 2008 interview with the author, he said: "Had President Roosevelt gone directly into action in November 1942 when the government received the first evidence Hitler planned to exterminate European Jewry; had the president not waited fourteen months to establish the War Refugee Board and had he seen to it that the board received sufficient funding from Congress, then the United States could have rescued up to one million Jews."[156]

Since even one life is precious, how wondrous that would have been:

the preservation of one million souls. Yet, if that miracle had occurred, wouldn't the great tides of history remain unaltered?

Would history not remember the five million as a catastrophe? Would Hitler and Nazism not be synonymous with unspeakable cruelty? Would the gas chambers and crematoria not stand as emblems of genocide?

Even had there been less sorrow, wouldn't the sorrow of Jews run just as deep?

Wouldn't the survivors have filled the displaced persons camps? Wouldn't Ben-Gurion have gone to Europe to bring them to Palestine? Wouldn't Jews, including those who had been hostile to Zionism, have finally decided that a Jewish homeland was necessary to protect them from another Hitler?

And had there been five million ghosts haunting American Jews, wouldn't they still have done everything in their power to rescue Soviet Jewry?

◆ ◆ ◆

The debate over the possibility of rescuing Jews from the Nazis goes on, a dirge without end.

In 2006, historian Robert Rosen published *Saving the Jews: Franklin D. Roosevelt and the Holocaust*. On his website, Rosen states that following five years of research he discovered that "the main charges against the Roosevelt Administration – FDR's alleged 'abandonment of the Jews' and 'complicity in the Holocaust' – were not true," and that the president was "not silent" nor "were American Jews who protested, held memorial services, and demanded action."[157]

Four years later, the journalist and author, Robert Shogan, answered with *Prelude to Catastrophe: FDR's Jews and the Menace of Nazism*. Shogan found the polar opposite of Rosen, writing that "by the time Franklin Roosevelt died in office in 1945, six million European Jews had been murdered by the Nazis with neither FDR nor American Jews lifting much more than a finger to help them."[158]

Wherever one stands in this debate, what is most important is the immediate effect the Holocaust had on Jews in the United States, Europe, and Palestine. In 1945, as Jews struggled to absorb the grisly specifics of the Nazi genocide, illusions were dying and realities were being born. The writer and publisher Alexander Donat, a Polish Jew who survived the camps and later immigrated to New York, succinctly described the disillusionment, observing that Jews had been victims of their "faith in mankind...[their] belief that humanity had set limits to the degradation and persecution of one's fellow man."[159] The result was that each new nightmarish radio report or newspaper account or newsreel or letter from a desperate European relative or story from a returning solider challenged the community's collective faith. It was as though in a sublime instant of clarity, Jews realized that, as a people, they were alone, fully apart from their gentile neighbors, and accepted the coarse wisdom in the old Yiddish adage "Scratch a *goy*, find an anti-Semite."[160]

This attitude was spotted by twenty-three-year-old Robert F. Kennedy, the third son of the ambassador. Robert graduated Harvard in March 1948, and as the ambassador had done with Robert's older brothers, Joe Junior (who had been killed flying a mission against Nazi V-1 rocket sites) and John, he sent Robert abroad for some seasoning. The ambassador also arranged for his son to receive correspondent credentials from the *Boston Post*, and in one of his dispatches from Palestine Robert wrote that the Jews there, pursuing the dream of a homeland, "believed the time had long since passed for the Jewish people to expect anything but treachery and broken promises from the outside world."[161]

American Jews, now the biggest Jewish community in the world, set about trying to preserve the remnants of their European *landsleit* by raising money – more money than they had ever raised before. Montreal-born Henry Montor, a hard-charging dropout from Hebrew Union College with a reputation for abundant self-regard, was appointed executive vice chairman of the United Jewish Appeal and directed to oversee the UJA's fundraising campaigns. Montor demonstrated a genius for the task, sending out field representatives to organize communities and setting up national "big gifts" campaigns in cities across the country with a minimum contribution of $10,000. The meeting in Washington, DC, drew 350 guests; after Edmund I. Kaufman, head of Kay jewelry stores, announced a pledge of $250,000, he read the names of the attendees and asked for their pledges. The financier Bernard Baruch, not known for his munificence toward Jewish charities, gave $100,000. Montor also devised ways to reach out to small business owners, professionals, and college students, and in 1946 the UJA raised $101 million,[162] an amount equal to four times the donations made by the entire country to the American Red Cross.[163]

This effort would become an invaluable template for Jewish philanthropy and organization in the future, but fund-raising did little to expiate what the psychoanalyst and scholar Dr. Mortimer Ostow diagnosed as "a kind of survivor guilt."[164] Ironically, as American Jews wrestled with their inability to prevent the catastrophe, a newspaper poll conducted in 1945 indicated that two-thirds of Americans believed that Jews had too much power in the United States.[165] Jewish magazines and journals punctuated American Jewry's guilt by ladling out heaping portions of blame: "Sleep On, American Jews" was the title of one poem; "Why Were You Silent?" was the title of another;[166] and both encapsulated the spirit of the outpouring of words castigating the community for not putting its alleged power to better use.

The community needed no assistance when it came to objurgating itself. Perhaps half of the Jews in postwar America could trace their origins to the European community that the Nazis had all but ground to dust, and turning around to confront the ashes of the camps, the piles and pits of bones, the blank stares of the emaciated survivors, and the accusations of six million ghosts, American Jews accepted the gentile perception of their undue influence, discounting the impassable roadblocks to rescue and assigning themselves an obligation that they had never possessed the power to fulfill – saving a substantial percentage of European Jewry from their murderers.

Their guilt left them with a hunger to redeem themselves, and Soviet Jews would provide the opportunity for their redemption, their chance to create a movement dedicated to both the future and the past. It would take time, though. The Cold War would have to begin, providing American Jews a common cause with their countrymen and concerns that could be aligned with the goals of their government. The State of Israel would have to be born, which offered hope to Jews trapped behind the Iron Curtain and provided the increasingly secular and assimilated American Jewish community with a civil religion that, as Jonathan Woocher writes, gave "meaning to their identities as Jews by connecting them to a great historic drama of destruction and rebirth."[167] They would need a new American approach to organized and theatrical protest, tactics they would learn from the civil rights and antiwar movements. Above all, they would need history and fate to join hands, and it would be then, and only then, that American Jewry would finally answer the accusatory voices of the dead.

CHAPTER 4

GENESIS – A DRAMA IN FIVE ACTS

ACT I: THE MOST POWERFUL MAN ON EARTH

The Cold War erupted in a blaze of words. In just two weeks during the winter of 1946, these words – a speech and a diplomatic cable – shaped the course of history for the next forty-five years.

On February 9, 1946, Soviet Premier Josef Stalin approached the rostrum at the Bolshoi Theater in Moscow to thunderous applause. The pre-election speech was being broadcast on the radio, and the audience of electors applauded him for five straight minutes before he even spoke.[1]

The sixty-six-year-old Stalin, born in the poverty-stricken region of Georgia in the looming shadows of the Caucuses, the son of a semiliterate washerwoman and drunken, wife-and-child-beating cobbler, accepted the applause and cheers as his due. Pictures and newsreels of the Soviet premier left the impression that he carried himself with a regal bearing, possessed a Spartan discipline, and ruled the Soviet empire by virtue of his pure faith in Communism and his shrewd pragmatism.

Yet up close that evening at the Bolshoi, it was as if you could see through that legerdemain right down to his vengeful, necrotic soul. Stalin was short and paunchy, and his stiff, imperious bearing owed much to his withered left arm. His hair had gone gray and thin, and his teeth, when visible under his bushy moustache, were crooked and brownish-black. It was his face, though, that told most of his story, a face pitted with smallpox scars[2] and marked with a "Kremlin complexion" – a ghostly pallor blotted with red from the long hours spent in his office,[3] the late nights of movie-watching in the cinema on the second floor of the Great Kremlin Palace, and the lavish dinners with his apparatchiks in his dacha at Kuntsevo. These political banquets featured food fights, stag dancing, the courtiers' omnipresent fear of Stalin's ever-changing moods, and, fueling it all, drinking until dawn so that guests frequently had to wobble away from the table to vomit or be carried out by their chauffeurs.[4]

Historian Alan Bullock would describe Stalin as someone whose "suspicion never slept"[5] – an amusing illustration of British understatement, for by 1946 Stalin's record of savagery would have shamed the worst of the tsars: the execution of his rivals in the Communist Party; the collectivization of farms, with a special emphasis on the land of wealthier peasants – the kulaks – that downgraded Soviet agriculture and killed 14.5 million people through starvation, execution, forced labor, and deportation;[6] the Great Purge of the 1930s, in which six hundred thousand party members died from torture, execution, or laboring in the Gulag; and the purging of his military's officer corps, which left his country unprepared for the start of the Second World War.

The applause faded, and Stalin launched into his speech, which lasted just under an hour. His first language was Georgian – he hadn't studied Russian until after his eighth birthday – and as an adult, he spoke slowly in public, his words as meticulously crafted as his image. At the Bolshoi, he was relaxed, speaking informally and without theatrics.

He began by blaming the Second World War on capitalism and suggested that catastrophes of this sort could be avoided if "periodic redistribution of raw materials and markets between…countries existed in accordance with their economic needs." He credited the Soviet system for his nation's victory in the war, and someone cried out, "Under Comrade Stalin's leadership!" and the audience was on its feet again, cheering and clapping.[7]

Stalin paused to let the ovation wash over him. When the theater grew quiet, Stalin spoke of the future, announcing that the Soviet Union would pursue a new Five-Year Plan to raise its industrial and agricultural capacity, adding that he was certain that if the government gave "the necessary assistance to our scientists they will be able not only to overtake but…surpass the achievements of science outside the boundaries of our country."[8]

This was a veiled reference to the production of atomic weapons, and it drew another round of deafening applause.

Stalin believed that the mushroom clouds over Japan were a message to him, and he concluded that advanced weaponry would be crucial to the Soviets if they wanted "to talk to the great shopkeeper Harry Truman and keep him pinned down where we want him."[9]

At the Bolshoi, Stalin hid his aggressive plans for expanding Soviet influence behind the charge that it was capitalism that led nations to compete "by means of armed force" and kept the world on the edge of catastrophe. Consequently, it was only by forging ahead in industry and science that the Soviet Union could "be insured against any eventuality."[10]

Less than two weeks after Stalin delivered his speech, George F. Kennan, a young diplomat at the US embassy in Moscow, composed an eight-thousand-word overview of Soviet strategy, which he cabled to the State Department. This "Long Telegram"[11] was the foundation of US strategy throughout the Cold War.[12]

The genesis of the "Kremlin's neurotic view of world affairs," Kennan explained, came from a "traditional…insecurity. Russian rulers have invariably sensed that their rule was…unable to stand comparison or contact with political systems of Western countries. For this reason they have always feared foreign penetration [by the West]."[13] In addition, Kennan said, the dogma of Marxism was necessary to justify the Soviet's "dictatorship without which they did not know how to rule."[14] For Kennan, Soviet leaders were, like the tsars, "impervious to the logic of reason" and "highly sensitive to the logic of force."[15]

Keenan felt that the Kremlin believed peaceful coexistence with the United States was impossible and "the internal harmony" of our society and the "international authority of our state" had to be destroyed "if Soviet power [were] to be secure."[16]

Former British prime minister Winston Churchill believed that the Soviets were already well along in the process of securing their power. On March 5, Churchill arrived at Westminster College in Fulton, Missouri, to accept an honorary degree. He was introduced to the crowd in the gymnasium by President Truman, and in his address Churchill delineated the geopolitical challenge of the hour, observing that "an iron curtain has descended across the Continent." The citizens behind this curtain were increasingly living under Soviet control, Churchill said, and it fell to the United States, now "at the pinnacle of world power," to roll back the Communist tide.[17]

Kennan would later suggest that to roll back this tide the United States had to adopt "a long-term, patient but firm and vigilant containment of Russian expansive tendencies."[18] However, more than a year would pass before President Truman decided on an approach: his hand had been forced when the British withdrew aid from Greece and Turkey, and the two countries were threatened with being hauled into the Soviet orbit.

On March 12, 1947, Truman told a joint session of Congress that he believed the United States must "support free peoples who are resisting attempted subjugation by armed minorities or by outside pressures" and suggested the support should "primarily" be financial, and he asked Congress for $400 million for Greece and Turkey.[19]

At this moment, the Truman Doctrine was born. It was not universally applauded in the United States. The influential journalist Walter Lippmann thought the speech sounded as if the president were trading the current peace and prosperity for a global crusade.[20] Congress, on both sides of the aisle, also objected, some decrying the cost, others seeing it as representing a permanent fracture in US-Soviet relations.[21]

The geopolitical roiling was easier to comprehend once it had a name. And five weeks after Truman addressed Congress, Bernard Baruch, the legendary investor and adviser to every president since Wilson, gave it one: "Let us not be deceived," Baruch warned, "we are today in the midst of a cold war."[22]

◆ ◆ ◆

The Soviet Union claimed that it had rescued more Jews from the Holocaust than Britain and America combined.[23] While there is some truth in the claim, the rescue was not a consequence of any desire to shield Jews from the Nazis, but rather the result of the Nonaggression Pact that Germany and the Soviets signed in August 1939. The pact contained a secret protocol that carved up eastern Europe like a Christmas goose, apportioning separate "spheres of interest" to the Nazis and the Communists.[24] Hitler had pushed for the pact so Britain and France could not secure Soviet support when Germany launched its planned invasion of Poland. Stalin hoped that the agreement would allow the Soviet Union to sit by and consolidate its new territory, while the Western democracies got bogged down in a war with Germany and Italy.

The Nonaggression Pact lasted until June 1941, when Hitler invaded the Soviet Union. The secret protocol, by partitioning Poland between Germany and the Soviet Union, provided a haven for the 1.8 million Polish Jews who escaped the Nazi advance by fleeing behind Soviet lines. Also, by 1940, Stalin controlled the Baltic States, increasing the total Jewish population living under Soviet rule to 5.2 million, which exceeded the Jewish population in the United States. This unforeseen consequence of the pact did save Jews, but it did not spare Jews in Soviet-controlled areas from the genocide – far from it. The Germans murdered between 2.5 and 3.3 million Jews in these regions.[25] And they did not do it alone – they drew support from eastern Europeans warped by centuries of antisemitism.

The most infamous joint effort between Germans and their eastern European helpmates occurred following the Nazi capture of Kiev on September 19, 1941. Once the Red Army was chased from the city, the Ukrainians treated the Nazis as deliverers from Stalin, who had attacked their long-cherished desire for independence by starving them to death by the millions and executing the more troublesome among them.

Members of the Soviet security police, a forerunner of the KGB, had stayed behind to harass the Nazis, and the next day Soviet saboteurs retaliated. The commanding general of the German artillery, along with his chief of staff, were killed in the opening round of blasts, and over the next week or so, buildings where the Germans were quartered were rocked with explosions. The sabotage was blamed on the Jews – the standard bureaucratic excuse the Nazis used to justify annihilating civilians.

Jews were ordered to report to a spot near the rail yards on September 29. Rumors were rife that they were only being relocated to ghettos and no harm would come to them, a credible assumption because during World War I the Germans had not abused civilians. On Monday morning, Jews began arriving in the cold, blustery dark, thousands and thousands of them, walking miles from the center of the city, carrying their belongings in flimsy suitcases or strapping them on their backs or wheeling heavier loads in carts or baby carriages."[26]

Crowds gathered to watch the ragged shoulder-to-shoulder procession advancing in fits and starts toward the cemetery and the ravine beyond it, Babi Yar (grandmother ravine). Most Jewish men healthy enough to fight were serving in the Red Army, and so the Jews inching up Melnikov Street, moving past the brick wall of the cemetery under the cruel stares of German soldiers and Ukrainian policemen in their ominous black uniforms, were mostly mothers and children, the aged and infirm, and they went ahead in a great slow river of humanity, none of them appearing to hear the faint echo of machine-gun fire in the distance.

The Ukrainian police and German soldiers instructed the Jews to drop their belongings in the pile and hand over their papers to soldiers seated at the desks. These were men from the *Einsatzgruppen*, the Nazi mobile killing units. Tossing the documents aside, the Nazis behind the desks directed the Jews to keep moving up past where soldiers, armed with batons, waited with their barking dogs. The soldiers formed a corridor, and as Jews walked between them they were beaten. The blood seemed to amuse the soldiers, who, according to an eyewitness, were "laughing happily, as if they were watching a circus act."[27]

Terrified, the Jews filed into a field, where Ukrainian militia forced them to remove their clothing and then herded them into the ravine, where they were machine-gunned by German soldiers and Ukrainian police.[28] As the hours passed, corpses were stacked upon corpses, a vision of hell that would have taxed the frenetic imaginings of Bosch and Dante. A woman who miraculously survived remembered holding onto her son and falling under "a heap of warm, bloody bodies. The bodies of old men rested on the bodies of children, who lay on the bodies of their dead mothers."[29]

Over two days, 33,771 Jews were executed. The Nazis built the Syrets concentration camp above the ravine, and during the next year, executions were scheduled for Tuesdays and Fridays.[30] By 1943, when the Red Army expelled the Germans from Kiev, 100,000 to 200,000 Jews, Gypsies, Turkmen, and Soviet POWs had been murdered at Babi Yar.[31]

Violent antisemitism in the Ukraine is an old story, but what would make this history so remarkable is that it took the Kremlin so long to officially acknowledge that it had occurred and a full half century to admit that Jews had been the primary victims.

As the Great Patriotic War ground on and the losses mounted into the tens of millions, the Soviet government, desperate for loyal troops, dampened its animosity toward religion. This strange interlude of tolerance survived briefly after the war, but it never extended to Soviet citizens still imbued with a hatred of Jews so integral to Russian culture it seemed inseparable from the snow and sun. Nonetheless, the antisemitic myth that Jews had not helped to defend the Soviet Union persisted despite that fact that 500,000 Jews fought in the Red Army; 200,000 of them died; and 160,000 of them were decorated for bravery, with over 150 receiving the highest award, the Gold Star and the honorary title "Hero of the Soviet Union."[32]

The inability of Soviet Jews to improve their status despite their sacrifices hardened their sense of identity and gradually soured into despair. Jews had ample opportunity to share their feelings with each other as they made pilgrimages to attend the memorial services held for the Soviet war dead. The net effect of these circumstances is illustrated by the response of one much-decorated Jewish veteran to the legacy of Masha Bruskina.

Masha's story goes back to the autumn of 1941 and the city of Minsk, where the Nazis had sentenced three Belarusian partisans – a man, a sixteen-year-old boy, and a seventeen-year-old girl – to death. On October 26, the condemned were escorted from prison and led through the streets; the girl wore a dove-gray sweater, a dark skirt, white socks, and a large placard around her neck that said: "We are partisans and have shot at German soldiers."[33] As a crowd gathered to watch, the man and the two teenagers were hung from a gate of the Yeast Generator Plant, and their lifeless bodies were left there for three days as a warning to any budding resistance fighters. It was the first public execution of Russian partisans in the Soviet Union, and a member of the Lithuanian auxiliary working with the Germans had photographed it. After the war the pictures became some of the best-known images among the Soviet people, images celebrated for documenting their heroism. In the photographs the man was identified as

Kiril Trus and the teenage boy as Volodia Shcherbatsevich, but the teenage girl was designated "unknown,"[34] although by then she had been identified as Masha Bruskina. It turned out that Masha was a Jew, and thus she was not entitled to her name or her status as a heroine.[35]

Commenting on Masha's imposed anonymity, the Jewish veteran said that this insult explained why Soviet Jews were convinced that "the only correct decision is to leave."[36]

This comment illuminates the hopelessness of postwar Soviet Jewry – the polar opposite of the optimism exhibited at the same time by American Jewry – and to some degree it was this bottomless despair that drove Russian Jews to apply for exit visas and to withstand the abuse that the Soviet government heaped onto the refuseniks (one of whom, Benjamin Bogomolny, the acknowledged champion of stubborn resolve, waited for two decades[37]).

If they were to leave Mother Russia, where would they go? The answer, by 1948, was Israel, which, in what surely must stand as one of the most astounding twists of fate on record, may well not have survived her birth without the help of Stalin.

◆ ◆ ◆

Almost to a man, President Harry Truman's most trusted foreign policy advisers opposed him recognizing Israel when the British Mandate ended on May 15, 1948. This was especially true of those six advisers who had a guiding hand in formulating the strategy of the Cold War and would later be christened "the Wise Men": Dean Acheson, Charles Bohlen, Averell Harriman, George Kennan, Robert A. Lovett, and John McCloy.[38] Equally forceful opposition came from Secretary of Defense James V. Forrestal and Secretary of State General George C. Marshall.[39] The reasons for the opposition were reduced to the essentials by Forrestal in a conversation with Truman's White House counsel, Clark M. Clifford. Forrestal said: "Forty million Arabs are going to push four hundred thousand Jews into the sea. And that's all there is to it. Oil – that is the side we ought to be on."[40]

Clifford disagreed with Forrestal. It was true: fighting between Jews and Arabs had escalated since that Saturday afternoon, on November 29,

1947, when the United Nations General Assembly had voted to partition Palestine into an Arab and a Jewish state. The Arabs had rejected the plan, but Clifford believed that the Jews could hold on if the United States would put its prestige on the line and recognize the Jewish homeland. Clifford pointed out to Truman that traditionally America had been morally committed to stopping persecution and that recognizing the Jewish state would be a modest start in addressing the suffering of European Jewry. Truman was sympathetic to that line of reasoning, but Clifford also argued that a democracy in the "unstable Middle East" would help dilute the influence of the Soviet Union.[41]

This was the stronger argument, for containing the Soviets was the central strategic goal of US foreign policy and the motivation for the billions of dollars being spent on the Marshall Plan. The secretary of state had outlined his plan on June 5, 1947, in a commencement address at Harvard.[42] Standing on the steps of Memorial Church, Marshall spoke in a hushed voice, telling the audience that the United States must "assist in the return of normal economic health to the world" so as to restore political stability and to assure peace."[43] Written by Charles Bohlen, the speech was based on a report by George Kennan.[44]

Marshall claimed that the plan was not "directed against any country or doctrine, but against hunger, poverty, desperation and chaos."[45] It was a disingenuous claim. Two months prior to his speech, Marshall had met with Stalin in Moscow and determined that the Soviet leader favored chaos in Europe, since it enabled him to extend the Kremlin's power. Already Stalin was tightening his grip on the Balkans;[46] the royalist government in Greece was engaged in a civil war with Communist guerillas, a conflict in which one hundred thousand people would die;[47] food shortages in France and Italy ignited a round of rioting, leading local Communist leaders to push for a general strike; and Britain, burdened by war expenditures, was withdrawing from the far-flung corners of its empire, leaving behind fertile ground for the spread of Communism.[48]

The Marshall Plan was a policy aimed right between Stalin's eyes. At Harvard, Marshall stated that the assistance to Europe would "permit the emergence of political and social conditions in which free institutions can exist,"[49] a development that the creators of the plan knew Stalin would never countenance in Eastern Europe. Furthermore, the plan was used to fund the anti-Communist operations of the Central Intelligence Agency. Congress approved $13.7 billion for the plan, and any government receiving assistance was mandated to hold aside equal funds in its own currency, 5 percent of which – some $685 million – would be funneled to CIA stations around the world.[50]

This arrangement, according to Tim Weiner, author of *Legacy of Ashes*, a history of the CIA, "stayed secret until well after the cold war ended,"[51] but even had Stalin known about it, he had no intention of accepting US aid even though his people were suffering. To stave off the postwar famine, Stalin had accepted assistance from the United Nations Relief Administration, but the Soviet leader was worried about the returning veterans. As he confided to the author Konstantin Simonov, the war had shown the Russian soldier his strengths as an individual, "his mother-wit, his intelligence, his courage,"[52] and this individualism could embolden them (as it had emboldened the Jewish veterans) and lead them to challenge Stalin's power. Then, too, the soldiers had seen living standards across Europe that exceeded their own, and Stalin had no intention of allowing money from the West to make Soviet lives easier, or democratic ideals to seduce his people with the possibilities of dreams.[53]

Since Truman had gone to great lengths to set the Marshall Plan in motion as a bulwark against Stalin in Europe, it would only be logical to hold off the Soviets in the Middle East by being at the head of the line to welcome the Jewish state into the family of nations. This was the course recommended by Eleanor Roosevelt, who, since her husband's death, had exercised an influential voice in Democratic Party politics.[54] Domestic opinion favored recognition, which was made plain to the president during the first three months of 1948 when hundreds of thousands of postcards, letters, and telegrams arrived at the White House, not all of them from Jews.[55] The American Jewish community was especially adamant. Not only were political leaders besieged with a blizzard of mail, but small groups of American Jews, a number of them veterans, ventured into the shadowy byways of European and Central American arms dealing.[56]

They had taken that step because although the United Nations Partition Resolution called for the Arab and Jewish states to have "an armed militia...to maintain internal order and to prevent frontier clashes," the State Department announced an arms embargo to Palestine and its Arab neighbors less than a week after the UN vote.[57] Ostensibly, it was a prudent reaction, but as the United States discovered in the run-up to World War II, neutrality tends to favor one side over the other. In this instance, neutrality favored the Arabs, since it was obvious that once the Jews declared a state in Palestine it would be invaded, and Great Britain was still supplying Arab countries with arms, claiming that it was satisfying "longstanding orders."[58] Beset by severe financial woes, the British were protecting their oil and pipeline agreements with Arab leaders, and to that end they also turned over their abandoned fortresses and military facilities in Palestine to the Arabs and cracked down on Jewish attempts to sustain an army or import weapons.

And so approximately one thousand Americans, primarily Jewish war veterans (with at least one notable exception, Charles Winters, an Irish Protestant from Boston), banded together to assist the Israelis, who called their group *Machal* – a Hebrew acronym for "volunteers from outside Israel."[59] Led by Connecticut native Adolph "Al" Schwimmer, the *Machalnik*s purchased and restored old military planes, loaded them with munitions, and saw to it that the equipment was delivered to the Israelis. Winters even went so far as to hop into the pilot's seat of a B-17 and fly the heavy bomber from a Miami airfield across the Atlantic to Czechoslovakia.[60]

Regardless of the sympathies Truman might have felt for the Jewish state, he was adamant about keeping US military hardware out of the Middle East. Accordingly, his administration was not inclined to look the other way when the weapons embargo was ignored, and Schwimmer, Winters, and another volunteer, Hank Greenspun, were arrested, tried, and convicted of violating the Neutrality Act. The three men were fined, and Winters was sentenced to eighteen months in prison. In 1961, President Kennedy pardoned Greenspun; in 2000, President Clinton pardoned Schwimmer; in 2008, Winters, who had died and was buried in Israel, was pardoned by President Bush.[61]

The work of the *Machalnik*s would have been impossible without the money provided by American Jewry. In 1948, $214 million was raised from a total Jewish population of 5.5 million. More important, as a sign of community support, the money rolled in from across the economic spectrum – from industrialists to students – money pledged at grand dinners and money handed out to volunteers walking door-to-door.[62] It was as though American Jewry had, all at once, anticipated the words that Rabbi Abraham Joshua Heschel would one day write: "Israel enables us to bear the agony of Auschwitz without radical despair."[63]

Truman grew annoyed with the pressure from Jewish leaders, but remained sympathetic to the Zionist cause; he always denied that politics influenced his decision to recognize Israel, though just then he was terribly unpopular. A Gallup poll pegged his approval rating at 36 percent, and a cover story in the *New Republic* advised the president to quit.[64] Meanwhile, the Democratic Party was busy fragmenting into incompatible left and right wings: ex-Vice President Henry A. Wallace, who opposed the Cold War and became, according to Arthur Schlesinger Jr., "a Soviet apologist,"[65] ultimately led the left, and Governor Strom Thurmond of South Carolina, who considered Truman overly serious about ending segregation, led the right.[66]

Years later, when the storm of the debate was over, Eddie Jacobson, Truman's old friend and ex-partner in a Kansas City haberdashery, was credited with influencing the president; the paradigm of the heroic individual who intercedes on behalf of his people and alters the path of Jewish history has long appealed to Jews. Jacobson did urge Truman to meet with Chaim Weizmann, who would become Israel's first president, and continued to communicate with his old friend about why he should back a Jewish state, but several factors led Truman to his decision, not the least of which was his disgust with those despicable "striped pants conspirators"[67] in the State Department, who appeared confused about who made foreign policy.

Secondly, Truman agreed with Eleanor Roosevelt that it was not in the interest of the United States to permit the Soviets to take the lead on recognition. There was also – and perhaps decisively – the beckoning of history; Truman was not unaware of what it meant for Jews to return home after nineteen centuries of wandering.[68] Just how important the call of history was to Truman was clarified in 1961, when the former president stopped by a New York City hotel suite to talk with David Ben-Gurion.[69] Toward the end of their talk, the Israeli prime minister told Truman that he occupied "an immortal place in Jewish history," and, Ben-Gurion recalled, "tears suddenly sprang to [Truman's] eyes."[70]

All of these factors informed Truman's decision on May 14, 1948, when, at 6:11 PM, eleven minutes after David Ben-Gurion had stood up at the Tel Aviv Museum and proclaimed "the establishment of the Jewish state in Palestine,"[71] the White House announced the *de facto* recognition of Israel. The next morning, Israel was attacked by Egypt, Syria, Lebanon, Jordan, Iraq, and Saudi Arabia. Truman was steadfast in his refusal to involve the United States, and would not permit arms shipments to Israel.[72]

The embargo was an opening that Stalin was quick to exploit.

◆ ◆ ◆

For a quarter-century, Zionism had been derided in the USSR as another incarnation of "bourgeois imperialism."[73] As late as May 10, 1948, the US chargé d'affaires in Moscow was cabling his superiors that the Kremlin would oppose a Jewish state as a "Zionist tool of [the] west, inevitably hostile to [the] Soviet Union."[74]

It would not be the last time the United States would misread Soviet intentions.

On May 14, the Soviet representative, Andrei Gromyko, announced to the UN General Assembly that his government favored a two-state solution. Gromyko said that it was the failure of the West to "safeguard" the Jewish people "against the violence of the fascist executioners" that accounted for the Jewish desire to establish their own country.[75]

Gromyko made no mention of Zionism developing in the nineteenth century as a means to escape Russian brutality, but his statement stands as one of the most lucid connections ever articulated by a diplomat between the Holocaust and the creation of Israel.

The calculation behind the Soviet endorsement was unmistakable: driving the British out of the Middle East appealed to Stalin, and the friction that Zionism engendered between Britain and the United States was an added fillip.

Yet no less a critic of the USSR than Golda Meir – a champion grudge holder who never forgave the Russians their pogroms or their later encouragement of the Arabs, with advisers and arms, to attack Israel – saw something else at work, an empathic response "because of the terrible toll that the Russians themselves had paid in the world war and their resultantly deep feeling that the Jews, who had also suffered so bitterly at the hands of the Nazis, deserved to have their state."[76] Equally critical to Israel, Meir remembered, was the military assistance from the Soviet bloc for without "the arms and ammunition that we were able to buy in Czechoslovakia and transport through Yugoslavia and other Balkan countries in those dark days at the start of the war, I do not know whether we actually could have held out until the tide changed."[77]

In 1949, Israel signed cease-fire agreements with the invading Arab countries, and the armistice lines became the borders of Israel. By then, the US government was focused on Berlin, which was still split between East and West. To jump-start West Berlin's flattened economy, the United States introduced a new currency.[78] Stalin, who quite reasonably feared a resuscitated Germany allied with America, Britain, and France, introduced a new currency in the Soviet-controlled Eastern sector and prevented supplies from reaching West Berlin by instituting a blockade.[79] The United States answered with an airlift that supplied the city until the blockade was officially lifted in May 1949.[80] By this point, the North Atlantic Treaty Organization had been assembled, giving Stalin a mutual defense pact of Western allies to face. By September, however, the West was confronting a terrifying wrinkle in its own relationship with the USSR.

That month, a US B-29 weather plane detected increased radiation over the northern Pacific. Other planes soon confirmed the findings, and scientists concluded that the Soviet Union had tested an atom bomb. In a prediction that would shortly seem more like an understatement, Senator Arthur Vandenberg, chairman of the Foreign Relations Committee, observed that it was now "a different world."[81]

Israelis toiled far away from the Cold War, preoccupied with protecting their borders and struggling to house and feed the rush of immigrants – over 340,000 in the first two years of the state's existence. The Red Army was not seen as a threat; it was revered for its valiant defeat of the Nazis and for liberating the concentration camps. In the communal dining areas of the leftist collective farms – the kibbutzim – it was not uncommon to see a red flag and a picture of Stalin adorning a wall, and throughout the Jewish state one often heard deeply committed socialists refer to the Soviet Union as *ha-moledet ha-shniya* (the second homeland).[82]

On a rainy September afternoon in 1948, Golda Meyerson (later Hebraized to Meir) landed in Moscow to take up her post as the first Israeli minister to the Soviet Union.[83] Curious about what had become of Jews living under the Kremlin's official disapproval of religion and nationalism, Golda and her legation set off one Sabbath morning to attend services at the Great Synagogue. They found, at most, 150 "weary-looking, shabby old men and women," who stared at Golda after the rabbi mentioned her name but did not approach her.[84] Golda was walking back alone to the Hotel Metropole when an elderly man bumped into her and whispered, in Yiddish, that she should follow him without speaking. Not far from the hotel, the old man stopped, turned to Golda and recited a Hebrew prayer of thanksgiving.[85] Then he vanished down the windy Moscow street, leaving Golda to wonder if she had dreamt the whole "strange pathetic encounter."[86]

By 1948, antisemitism was on the rise in the Soviet Union. Stalin had encouraged the resurgence, but since the Nazis had temporarily given antisemitism a bad name, it was not the Jews who came under attack but "rootless cosmopolitans," intellectuals with their unpatriotic worship of Western ideas. Stalin was particularly unhappy with the Jewish Anti-Fascist Committee, which had been organized in the spring of 1942 to solicit funds and political support from Jews in the West to aid the Soviet fight against the Nazis. After the war, the JAC had an impressive list of contacts in the United States and Great Britain and was still seen as playing a leadership role by Soviet Jewry. Stalin mistrusted the former and could not abide the latter, and he ordered the murder of the JAC leader, Solomon Mikhoels, the famed Jewish actor and director of the Moscow Yiddish Theater, who was renowned for his King Lear and who had performed privately for Stalin on several occasions. Mikhoels was dispatched to Minsk, ostensibly to evaluate a play for the Stalin Prize, but Lavrenti Tsanava, chief of the Belorussian security services, brought Mikhoels to his country house, where the actor was shot. His body was dumped in the snow on a back street, and it was announced to Mikhoel's adoring fans that the actor had died in a car accident. He was honored with a state funeral. Two weeks later his killer was awarded the Order of Lenin at a secret ceremony. Stalin dissolved the JAC and had its director, Solomon Losovsky, a former assistant foreign minister, arrested and executed.[87]

Stalin had shown flashes of antisemitism throughout his life: his son, Yakov, and his daughter, Svetlana, both married Jews, and Stalin proved to be a less-than-desirable father-in-law, sending Yakov's wife to prison and exiling Svetlana's husband for a decade. Nikita Khrushchev, who succeeded Stalin as general secretary, thought the animosity Stalin exhibited toward Jews in the final five years of his life was a symptom of the Soviet leader's emotional breakdown, but this observation reveals as much about Khrushchev and the Soviet interpretation of reality as it does about Stalin, for it suggests that in decades past Stalin enjoyed the utmost mental health while he ordered millions executed or sent to the Gulag.[88]

More helpful for charting the course of the Cold War and the ontogeny of the American movement to free Soviet Jewry is to explore how Stalin saw the external and internal situation of the Soviet Union in 1948. He recognized that the world was being cleaved in two, one allied with him, the other with the West. The United States was on firmer financial ground than the USSR, and America possessed the atom bomb. Stalin believed that the bomb his scientists were building would stave off his enemies outside the USSR, and economic recovery would defeat his enemies within. Wages for the workers were on the rise, and the shortages plaguing his people would be dealt with by a reinvigorated Marxism.

What of his other goal, the goal that had occupied his thoughts for a quarter-century, the goal that had eluded the tsars: crafting a Russia of one common language and culture? Stalin had renounced his roots as a Georgian and transformed himself into a Russian. Shouldn't his people follow in his footsteps? Like the father of the revolution, Nikolai Lenin, Stalin had anticipated that ethnic and religious identities would dissolve as the Kremlin "offered the carrot of modernization with the stick of forced assimilation."[89] Stalin had long been disgusted with the "bourgeois nationalism" of the Ukrainians and Caucasians for refusing to become Russified, and continuing to clamor for their own national and cultural identity.[90]

And now the Jews! Ingrates whom Stalin had rescued from the Nazis! Treasonous Jews with their own country because of Stalin! On their New Year, Golda Meyerson arrives at the Great Synagogue, and fifty thousand Jews materialize from every nook and cranny in Moscow to see her. Fifty thousand![91] "The entire older generation is contaminated with Zionism," Stalin told his daughter, "and now they're teaching the young people too."[92] And on that October morning, this multitude – the parents with babies in their arms, the grizzled army officers and boyish soldiers – ignore the price for incurring Stalin's wrath and flock to the Israeli minister, crying out, "Our Golda, our Golda, *shalom*," and touching her, kissing her dress. And what does this woman say to them in Yiddish? "Thank you for having remained Jews."[93] Not Russians – Jews! Then someone takes a photograph of this Jewish ocean and everywhere copies are passed, like a sacred document, from Jew to Jew, humiliating Stalin, making his goal of Russification seem like nothing more than the woolgathering of a doddering fool.[94]

Stalin, the truest of true believers, never doubted that Marxism would defeat capitalism, but he kept an even grander dream locked in his heart – that the Soviet Union, teeming with hundreds of ethnic identities and languages and with people who nurtured smoldering nationalistic aspirations and religious loyalties, could be molded through education, dictates, suppression, and terror into one state with one prevailing ideology.

Stalin, though, was the opposite of reflective; self-criticism escaped him. Had it been otherwise he might have understood that trying to obliterate the identity of Soviet Jews only led them to identify more strongly with Israel. So there sits Stalin, a lonely monster at dusk. The interminable nights of drinking in his dacha at Kuntsevo are catching up with him, the endless chain of cigarettes, the countless hours of smoking his pipe. His blood pressure rages; the pain of angina is like a thunderbolt in his chest. And as he sits there, fuming at the news that fifty thousand Jews had the gall to show up for a pathetic glimpse of Golda Meyerson, one wonders if, for an excruciating moment, reality did not lift its veil and allow Stalin to see that his quest was an exercise in self-delusion and hovered even beyond the reach of the man who was arguably the most powerful individual on earth.

Stalin's fury, fed by the noxious gases of his decomposing dream, was volcanic, and he set out to eradicate Jewish culture with a single-mindedness that recalled the efforts of Nicholas I. Jewish publications were shut down; Jewish books were removed from libraries; Yiddish printing presses were demolished; Jewish theaters were closed; Jewish schools, which had been shuttered during the war, were forbidden to reopen; Jewish writers were arrested and murdered; and the wife of Foreign Minister Vyacheslav M. Molotov, a Jewish woman who had exchanged pleasantries with Golda Meyerson at a reception honoring the anniversary of the Russian Revolution, was sent to a prison camp.[95]

This is only a sampling of the cruelties of the "black years" of Soviet Jewry, and Stalin himself appeared to perceive that his paranoia was consuming him. On vacation in the Caucasus, he walked out onto the porch of his dacha and, according to Nikita Khrushchev, who was watching him, said aloud, "I'm finished. I trust no one, not even myself."[96]

The repression went on. During the show trials – another round of Communist Party purges – in Hungary, Czechoslovakia, Poland, and Romania – Stalin was able to both remove Jews from power and lambaste Israel. In Czechoslovakia, eleven of the fourteen party and government officials who were tried in Prague were Jews, including the party secretary general, Rudolf Slansky. All were accused of being "Zionist, bourgeois-nationalist traitors."[97]

Stalin preyed upon people who had been faithful to him for decades: his bodyguard, personal secretary, and physician. The latter was arrested along with other doctors who worked at the Kremlin hospital and clinic used by government luminaries. Allegedly, the doctors were plotting to murder Stalin and other leaders through improper medical care. Stalin ordered his physician locked in chains while the others were beaten, and he warned that if the minister of state security was unable to make the doctors confess, Stalin would "shorten [the minister] by a head."[98]

On January 13, 1953, *Pravda* announced that the doctors had been arrested.[99] Six out of the nine were Jewish.[100] The Israeli Foreign Ministry responded by stating that it would bring the plight of Jews behind the Iron Curtain before the UN General Assembly; the World Zionist Organization asked the Kremlin to "Let My People Go"; and Rabbi Israel Miller, president of the Zionist Organization of America, put a resolution before the ZOA that passed unanimously and stated that "if the so-called Jewish 'bourgeois elements' and 'cosmopolitans' are undesirable...they should be permitted to emigrate to Israel."[101]

These pleas were not enough to satisfy members of the Kingdom of Israel, a small underground organization of ultranationalist Israelis who were enraged that with Hitler's death camps less than a decade in the past, Israel, which had been founded to protect the survival of Jews everywhere, was doing nothing beyond threatening to complain to the United Nations. The reaction of the underground to the Slansky trial and the Doctors' Plot proved to be a harbinger of things to come – not in Israel but in the United States – as the Soviet Jewry movement gathered momentum in the late 1960s. The group lobbed a hand grenade at the Czech mission in Tel Aviv, and followed up on the night of February 10 by setting off a bomb in the city's Soviet embassy, which wounded four people inside, the ambassador's wife among them.[102]

The Soviet Union severed diplomatic relations with Israel. The doctors, and much of Soviet Jewry, were nervously awaiting their fate when Stalin died on March 5.

◆ ◆ ◆

Prime Minister David Ben-Gurion was steeped in Zionist theory, but theories were of little use to him when confronting the central challenges to his tiny nation's existence: Israel was geographically surrounded and vastly outnumbered by its enemies. The solution would be a massive influx of immigrants, and in 1950 the Israeli government enacted the Law of Return, granting every Jew the right to immigrate and become a citizen. Conditions in Israel, however, were not favorable for attracting immigrants. The Jewish state teetered on the perilous edge of financial ruin; integrating new citizens into a tattered economy, teaching them a language, and caring for the sick, elderly, and destitute are lengthy and expensive processes; already hundreds of thousands of immigrants were housed in the squalor of the *ma'abarot*, the refugee camps of tents and tin shacks, where drinking water had to be boiled and sanitation facilities and schools were wholly inadequate.[103] The immigrants Ben-Gurion longed for were European Jews with skills and professions who could contribute immediately to building the economy.[104]

The Soviet Jews were perfect; they frequently had experience in the trades or the benefit of a rigorous Soviet education, and the threat presented by Stalin appeared to outweigh the dangers of an untamed desert. Yet Ben-Gurion had to be careful; his two biggest benefactors – the Soviet Union and the United States – were butting heads, and the prime minister had to try to avoid alienating either one. Israel reassured the Kremlin that it would never assist any nation that was an enemy of the Soviet Union.[105]

In May 1950, Ben-Gurion requested that the Kremlin permit Jews to emigrate from the Soviet Union to Israel. The prime minister was not interested in embarrassing the Soviets – a tactic that would later be used effectively by American grassroots organizations. Ben-Gurion had his foreign minister, Moshe Sharett, meet with his Soviet counterpart, Andrei Vishinsky, a Stalin loyalist and the former lead prosecutor at the Great Purge trials of the 1930s. Sharett suggested that it would be compassionate for the Soviets to allow families separated by the war and devastated by the Holocaust to reunify in Israel.[106] In other words, Israel was not requesting that every Jew should leave the USSR. Not surprisingly, the Kremlin did not undergo a paroxysm of mercy.

In spite of Ben-Gurion's caution, his government was forced to take a public position on the Cold War. In June, North Korean dictator Kim Il-sung, with the assent of Communist China's Mao Zedong and the direct military assistance of Stalin, ordered his forces to cross the 38th Parallel and attack South Korea. Not only were the North Koreans invading a US ally, they had violated an internationally recognized border – the first time this had happened since the conclusion of the Second World War.[107] Hitler had taught the world that appeasing aggression invites more aggression, and Truman believed that if the attack went unanswered "no small nation would have the courage to resist...[its] stronger Communist neighbors."[108]

Intent on rousing world opinion against the invasion, the United States pressured Israel to condemn North Korea. Being in no position to alienate the American government or American Jewry, whose philanthropy kept the struggling state afloat, the Israeli government relented, and the relationship between Jerusalem and Moscow went steadily downhill, with the Soviets withholding support from the Jewish state when the Security Council took up the issue of Arab-Israeli armistice agreements.[109] Consequently, with few exceptions, Israel developed a muted approach to the predicament of Soviet Jewry, following a course designed to avoid a head-on collision with the Kremlin. Nonetheless, Israeli leaders, foremost among them the Ukrainian-born Moshe Sharett, were confident that in time any Soviet Jew who wanted to emigrate would be granted an exit visa,[110] a belief that during Stalin's reign appeared as realistic as Theodor Herzl's assertion, at the First Zionist Congress in Basel in 1897, that a Jewish state would be established within fifty years.

In 1952, Isser Harel, who had emigrated from the Soviet Union in 1931 and was now head of the Mossad, and Shaul Avigur, whom Golda Meir referred to as the "underground minister of defense"[111] for his dazzling success smuggling immigrants into Palestine, called a meeting at a house outside Tel Aviv. The purpose of the meeting was to discuss whether Israel, through operatives in its Moscow embassy, should establish a program to help Soviet Jews. Neither Harel nor Avigur thought that such an operation would work given Stalin's repression and the KGB's monitoring of Israeli diplomatic personnel, but the consensus was that Israel was morally obligated to try.[112]

With the approval of the prime minister, a department was formed. Overseen by Harel and Avigur, and code-named "Nativ," the department would evolve into the innocuous-sounding *Lishkat Hakesher* (Liaison Bureau), but its mission remained the same: do everything possible to reinforce Jewish identity behind the Iron Curtain in the event that one day these Jews might be brought to Israel.

Assigned to lead the mission to Moscow was a kibbutz farm manager, Nehemiah Levanon, who had lived in Estonia under Soviet rule. Cautiously, the Liaison Bureau began to approach Soviet Jews; in time, cultural and sporting events with Israelis were arranged; packages of clothing, financed by the American Joint Distribution Committee, were sent; books and pamphlets were smuggled past the censors and distributed;[113] and at one concert, which reverberated for Levanon more than forty years after the final notes had faded, a Latvian folksinger performed a Yiddish rendition of the African American spiritual "Go Down Moses (Let My People Go)," a song that the predominantly Jewish audience responded to with "thunderous applause."[114]

In 1970, Levanon summed up his activities during those early years for Richard N. Perle, then a young assistant to Senator Henry "Scoop" Jackson and the future author of the controversial legislation that occupied center stage of the American movement to free Soviet Jewry, the Jackson-Vanik Amendment – a bill that linked US trade concessions to the relaxation of USSR emigration restrictions. "The Soviets thought I was interested in raising potatoes," Levanon told Perle. "I was interested in raising Jews."[115]

Obviously, the Kremlin realized that Levanon had more than farming on his mind, because in the fall of 1955 he was expelled. Avigur and Harel assured him that the outreach would continue inside the USSR, but they wanted Levanon to pursue a course of action he had been recommending: stimulating support for Soviet Jewry in the West.[116] This section of the bureau was code-named "Bar."[117]

Six months later, a cultural sea change was underway in the USSR. Officially it began on February 25, 1956, at the final session of the Twentieth Party Congress held in the Great Kremlin Palace, when Stalin's successor, Nikita Khrushchev, approached the microphone, shoulders thrust forward as he moved across the stage with that almost delicate grace which is so striking in short, stocky men. Dressed in a baggy suit with the light gleaming on his bald head, Khrushchev spoke for almost four hours with just a single intermission.[118] He denounced Stalin's "cult of personality," criticizing the dead leader as "capricious, irritable and brutal,"[119] and condemning his "mass arrests and deportation of thousands and thousands of people, and executions without trial or normal investigation."[120] Khrushchev also stated, contrary to Stalin's position, that a third world war was not inevitable and that countries could travel different paths to socialism and arrive there without violent revolution.

The speech had been closed to foreign delegates and journalists, but by summer *Pravda* was publishing an admission from the Central Committee that the Congress had addressed the "harmful consequences" of Stalin's rule.[121] This era of de-Stalinization would become known as "the thaw" (a name drawn from the title of a novel by the Jewish writer and Soviet apologist Ilya Ehrenburg[122]). Initially, there was cause for hope among Soviet Jews, and among all Soviets who valued freedom and hoped for an improved standard of living.

One young lawyer, a Communist Party loyalist whose paternal grandfather had been sentenced to the Gulag under Stalin for resisting the collectivization of his farm, recalled that the thaw "proclaimed the possibility of preventing a third world war…and of peaceful revolution.… I remember the appearance of truthful and moving films…and hundreds of grateful listeners flocking to the Polytechnic Museum to listen to readings of the young poets."[123]

The lawyer's name was Mikhail Gorbachev, and it was this era that he would try to rejuvenate when he became the leader of the Soviet Union in 1985.

With an assist from the Israeli government, the West was informed of the new Kremlin policy. Copies of Khrushchev's speech had been circulated among leaders in the Eastern bloc, and Polish journalist Viktor Grayevsky secured a copy from his girlfriend, a secretary in a Communist Party office. Grayevsky was Jewish, and he took his copy to the Israeli embassy. The speech was photographed and sent to Israel, where it wound up in the hands of Amos Manor, head of the Shin Bet security service. More than a half century later, Manor told Yossi Melman of *Haaretz* that at the time he thought that if the document was authentic, it was "an atom bomb," and after Manor showed it to the prime minister and the Mossad, he had the document delivered to James Jesus Angleton, who was in charge of the Israeli desk at the Central Intelligence Agency. After informing President Eisenhower and determining that the speech was authentic, the CIA leaked the speech to the *New York Times*.[124]

Khrushchev's speech indicated that he could imagine a better future and possessed the bravery to express it, and during his decade of power, from 1954 until 1964, there were encouraging signs for Soviet Jews: while the Kremlin had allowed only seven Jews to emigrate between 1948 and 1953,[125] thousands would be permitted to go back to Poland and then on to Israel in 1958 – released in the name of family reunification, which provided an excuse for the Kremlin to permit emigration without opening up the gates wide enough to create a stampede.[126]

In addition, the existence of antisemitism was publicly aired. One of the young poets that Gorbachev had gone to hear at the Polytechnic Museum was a gangly, fourth-generation descendant of Ukrainians. His name was Yevgeny Yevtushenko, and he would achieve international renown by his literary response to some myopic civic planning by the Kiev town council. The council wanted to build a park and stadium on the site of the Babi Yar massacre. The Soviet novelist Viktor Nekrasov suggested a memorial to the Jews who had died there would be more appropriate.[127] The council pledged that "an obelisk with a memorial plaque to Soviet citizens exterminated by the Nazis will be erected at its center." From that description one might have thought not one Jew died there, and so Yevtushenko corrected the record with his poem "Babi Yar," an outcry against the Nazi and Russian slaughter of Jews.[128]

Overall, though, life did not meaningfully improve for Soviet Jewry under Khrushchev. In 1963 the Ukrainian Academy of Sciences published *Judaism without Embellishment* by T. K. Kichko, a tract that purported to be a history of Judaism and featured, among other viciously antisemitic observations and images, a cartoon of a man with a nose hooked like a scimitar who was identified as a Zionist leader doing the bidding of the "Hitlerite" invaders of the Ukraine.[129] In one respect, Khrushchev proved to be harsher toward his Jews than Stalin, who had not launched total war against religious observance. In 1917, an estimated three thousand synagogues flourished, but between 1956 and 1963, Khrushchev's police whittled that number down to fewer than one hundred.[130] The Kremlin also outlawed the production of matzo, a significant hardship for observant Jews, because bread was the ballast of the impoverished Soviet diet, and therefore during Passover religious Jews had to choose between going hungry or violating the Torah's injunction against eating leavened bread.[131]

Most frightening, the Russian practice of scapegoating Jews reappeared as shortages beset the USSR. Intent on catching up economically with the United States, Khrushchev promised his people in 1957 that within four years their per capita consumption of meat would be on a par with Americans. His prediction fell woefully short. In 1962, the Kremlin had to increase the price of meat by 30 percent, while the production of other crucial commodities – grain, milk, and wool – either nosedived or stayed flat. Embezzling became so rampant that the Kremlin warned economic crimes would be punishable by death. It was no idle threat. Over half of the 250 people executed were Jews, and even if an alleged crime did not involve Jews, the government-controlled press managed to accuse them. When a pair of Russian Orthodox priests were identified as "drunkards and fornicators" and charged with "exploiting the faithful," an elderly Jewish couple was accused of giving them "sin-supplies."[132]

Despite the persecution, the Israeli government persisted in its just-below-the-surface outreach to Jews inside the USSR. Israel wanted to avoid antagonizing the Soviet Union, which had restored diplomatic relations with Israel after Stalin's death. Distributing literature to Soviet Jews was risky: the police routinely searched homes, incarcerating anyone in possession of Jewish printed materials – on one night alone, ninety Jews were arrested, principally in Moscow and Leningrad, charged with being aware of Zionist groups and receiving Israeli newspapers. And finally, Israel recognized the limits of what it could accomplish; evidently, under Khrushchev, the harshness of the regime toward Jews could only be modified by economic assistance from the West, the proof being that when shortages led the USSR to arrange a billion-dollar purchase of Western wheat, the Kremlin suddenly permitted the publication of a Yiddish periodical and the baking of matzo.

This was a lesson for the future Soviet Jewry movement – the ability of the Western powers to bend the will of the Kremlin when the USSR required assistance. For the time being, though, the Liaison Bureau contented itself with discreetly reinforcing cultural identity. One prime example of how this was accomplished, and the way in which it rippled across generations of Soviet Jews, was the use of the novel *Exodus*.

Published in 1958 and written by Leon Uris, a thirty-four-year-old American Jew, *Exodus* recounted the birth of Israel, celebrating the exploits of the Jewish underground smuggling Jews into Palestine and emphasizing the connection between the creation of Israel and the violent antisemitism of the Russian empire and Nazi Germany. The novel proved to be a publishing phenomenon: the hardcover was on the best-seller list for over a year, nineteen weeks at the top spot (and would go on to be translated into dozens of languages and sell upwards of twenty million copies). Uris was by no means a literary master, but in *Exodus* he constructed an emotion-packed, nation-building, page-turning, heroic Zionist tale that David Ben-Gurion would describe as the greatest "piece of propaganda…ever written about Israel."[133] Increasing the novel's popularity was the movie, which opened in 1960 and starred Paul Newman and Eva Marie Saint, and the 1961 hit song, performed by pop idol Pat Boone.

Soviet Jewry would come to accept *Exodus* as if it were an extension of the Bible, referring to it, in reverential tones, as "The Book." This did not occur by accident. Since the Kremlin would not allow a pro-Zionist work to be published or distributed in the USSR, Israeli diplomatic personnel had English-language editions of *Exodus* delivered via diplomatic pouch to their embassy in Moscow and furtively distributed the books to Soviet Jews who could read English. Soon, dissident networks were busy translating the 599-page-paperback into Russian. The groups did the translating independently of each other, sometimes with interesting results: one translator, irked by the romance between the Jewish soldier, Ari Ben Canaan, and the American Christian nurse, Kitty Freemont, proceeded to cut out the storyline.[134]

Since Soviet law forbade individuals from owning photocopiers or mimeograph machines, once the translations were completed they were typed, with carbon paper backing the originals in order to produce more copies, and then handed out across the Soviet Union. *Exodus* became a mainstay of the body of *samizdat* (self-published) underground literature. The impact of the novel, according to Eliahu Essas, a mathematician who emigrated from the Soviet Union to Israel after a thirteen-year wait, "was enormous. It was our first encounter with Jewish history. It gave us inspiration, and turned almost everybody who read it into more or less convinced Zionists."[135]

A half century after the publication of *Exodus*, in an age of advanced technology when information is available and easily copied and communicated even in countries where governments try to suppress it, one struggles to fathom that once upon a time the Soviet Union, with its huge military and vast array of weaponry, could have been threatened by a melodramatic American best seller. But it was, and the penalty for being caught with the banned book could be severe. Even in the mid-1980s, a decade after tens of thousands of Soviet Jews had emigrated to Israel and had communicated their own impressions of the country to relatives and friends in the USSR, the Kremlin kept jailing individuals for their connection to the novel. Yakov Levin, a Hebrew teacher, and Leonid Volvovsky, a computer expert, both spent over two years in prison for anti-Soviet activities that included handing out *Exodus*.[136]

Without question, the Israeli government's program to reinforce Jewish identity inside the Soviet Union was effective – a program that featured piping in Hebrew, Yiddish, and English radio broadcasts, meeting with Jews whose friends and family had come to Palestine in the 1920s and 1930s, and attracting the attention of Jews across the Soviet Union by driving into the hinterlands in cars flying the Israeli flag. But it was another development in 1956, undervalued at the time, that would rearrange the conditions of the Cold War and play a far larger role in prying open the gates of the Soviet Union.

ACT II: SUEZ AND THE NEW MIDDLE EAST

For Jews in the United States and Israel the 1956 Suez Crisis tumbles through history with the momentary glimmer of a falling star before vanishing into the brighter, more emotionally charged record of Israel's other wars: the relief that followed the War of Independence in 1948; the rejoicing at the end of the Six-Day War in 1967; the sobering aftermath of the Yom Kippur War in 1973; and the wrenching political and ethical gyrations that accompanied the subsequent fighting in Lebanon, the West Bank, and Gaza.

When it comes to the Cold War, however – and by extension, the fate of Soviet Jewry – no Middle East conflict had a greater geopolitical impact than what happened at Suez.

The crisis evolved from an attempt by the United States to diffuse Middle East tensions and prevent Egypt from entering the Soviet camp. The immediate source of tension was that Egypt had blockaded the Gulf of Aqaba, closed the Suez Canal to ships destined for Israel, and sent fedayeen to conduct raids into the Jewish state from the Gaza Strip. Israeli civilians were killed by the guerrillas, and in a show of force meant to discourage further raiding parties, Israel undertook a brigade-sized assault on Egyptian army headquarters in Gaza, where buildings were leveled and thirty-six Egyptian regulars died in the fighting.[137] President Gamel Abdel Nasser of Egypt, a magnetic, secular nationalist who four years earlier had participated in the military overthrow of the feckless, corrupt regime of King Farouk,[138] announced a deal intended to alter the balance of power in the region; Nasser would use the next dozen years of Egypt's cotton crop to buy $320 million worth of state-of-the-art Soviet weaponry from Czechoslovakia.[139]

Trying to halt the bloody tit for tat between Egypt and Israel, President Eisenhower sent former secretary of the navy Robert B. Anderson on a secret mission to negotiate a settlement between Nasser and Ben-Gurion. Anderson flew between Cairo and Tel Aviv, inaugurating a practice that would become known as shuttle diplomacy. The settlement died in its cradle; the leaders could not even agree on how to proceed. Behind the mundane objections, Ben-Gurion was concerned about the influx of modern weapons into Egypt, and Nasser was opposed to the Baghdad Pact, a mutual security agreement among Turkey, Iraq, Iran, Pakistan, and Britain that was designed to contain Soviet expansionism,[140] and that Nasser viewed as colonialism decked out in new clothes.[141]

Eisenhower was not pleased by the Egyptian leader's blossoming friendship with the Soviets. Early on, the Central Intelligence Agency had courted Nasser, funneling $3 million to him directly and setting up a state radio station for his use[142] – a safer approach than the one the CIA had employed in Iran in 1953, when they engineered the overthrow of Prime Minister Mohammad Mossadegh, who had nationalized British oil interests. Seeing no possibility of overthrowing Nasser at this point, Eisenhower was considering offering him a carrot: the administration would ask Congress for funds to assist Egypt with the construction of the Aswan High Dam, a project that Nasser felt would win him acclaim beyond the immortal veneration reserved for the pharaohs who built the pyramids. And why not? The dam would lift Egypt out of poverty, furnishing water to irrigate over one million acres of soil and producing enough electricity to meet more than half the nation's needs.[143]

But on July 19, 1956, Secretary of State John Foster Dulles informed the Egyptian ambassador to the United States that no congressional request would be made. Nasser had accepted Soviet arms, militated against the

Baghdad Pact, and recognized the Communist government of the People's Republic of China.[144] In short, he was no friend of America.[145]

Nasser was enraged. On July 24, he lashed out, telling the West to "go choke on your fury."[146] His remarks were broadcast on the radio, earning him sympathy among the Arab masses that mushroomed into idolization two days later when Nasser took to the airwaves again and announced that he was nationalizing the Suez Canal and its future revenues would be applied to the construction of the dam. Celebrations erupted from North Africa to the Arabian Gulf. Here, at last, was an audacious Arab leader staring down the imperialists. And before long, writes Nasser biographer Said K. Aburish, the Egyptian leader's picture was on display "in the tents of the Yemen, the souks of Marrakesh, and the posh villas of Syria."[147]

The British owned 44 percent of the Suez Canal Company, with private French investors owning most of the other stock, so neither Britain nor France shared the Arabs' celebratory mood; they were ready to go to war. Beyond the lost revenues, two-thirds of Western Europe's oil was shipped through the canal, and they had no intention of being at the mercy of a fickle, rabidly nationalistic Egyptian populist who had supported the revolution in the French colony of Algeria and cozied up to the Soviet Union and Communist China.[148]

Through a round of meetings and diplomacy, Eisenhower attempted to muffle the talk of war. The president believed that something would have to be done about Nasser, but in the near term any outbreak of hostilities – whether by coup or invasion – would cut off oil to Western Europe with dire economic consequences. Worse, Eisenhower told British prime minister Anthony Eden, war would turn the Arabs against the West and toward the Soviet Union.[149]

In the fall of 1956, as the talk went on and ships bound for Western Europe sailed through the Canal without interference, Eisenhower thought that the dilemma was momentarily behind him.[150] He was wrong. The British, French, and Israelis had devised a secret plan to attack Egypt. Israel would land paratroopers near the Suez Canal. The British and French would demand that both sides withdraw. Nasser, his stature among the Arabs on the line, would refuse, and Britain and France would have a pretext to strike.[151]

On Monday, October 29, Israel attacked. Eisenhower was livid; he had been tricked by his allies. The British and French issued their ultimatum for withdrawal. When Nasser refused, the British and French bombed Egyptian airfields. Eisenhower phoned Prime Minister Eden and vented his outrage in a spate of language more familiar to an enlisted men's barracks than to the stately rooms of 10 Downing Street.[152] On Wednesday, Eisenhower shifted his attention to the more vulnerable Jewish state, warning Prime Minister Ben-Gurion that "despite the present temporary interests that Israel has in common with France and Britain, you ought not to forget that the strength of Israel and her future are bound up with the United States."[153]

The Israelis did not withdraw, and by November 5, they controlled the Sinai and the Gaza Strip. Before Eisenhower could ratchet up the pressure, he was distracted by developments in Hungary, where hundreds of thousands of workers, students, and intellectuals were clashing violently with Soviet soldiers in the streets of Budapest.[154] Protestors had persuaded a smattering of Red Army troops to support them, and Soviet tanks could be seen flying the Hungarian flag. At the city park, welders used an acetylene torch to cut off the tall bronze statue of Stalin at the knees,[155] and a mob hauled the statue through the streets like a condemned man,[156] leaving the severed head on the paving stones as though fresh from the guillotine.[157]

Khrushchev had to act, though he was wary of employing too heavy a hand. In pursuit of de-Stalinization, Khrushchev had installed Imre Nagy as prime minister of Hungary in 1953; Nagy had been toppled by a rival two years later, but now, with the country spiraling into armed insurrection, Khrushchev had Nagy reappointed as premier with the proviso that he ask the Red Army to restore order in Budapest.[158] Due to an unquenchable thirst for freedom and perhaps a diminished capacity for self-preservation, Nagy disregarded his instructions. Over the radio, he told Hungarians that the hated secret police would be disbanded; that a democratically elected multiparty coalition would replace the dictates of Moscow with self-rule;[159] and that Hungary would resign from the Warsaw Pact,[160] the military coalition that the Soviet Union had foisted on Eastern Europe to counterbalance the West's North American Treaty Organization.

Nagy's announcements were greeted with less than good cheer in the Kremlin, as well as in the Sea Palaces compound in Beijing, where Chairman Mao Zedong, a devotee of Stalinism,[161] quickly concluded that the uprising had to be suppressed, a conclusion that Mao shared with Khrushchev.[162] Nagy may have spoken so boldly because he was banking on the Eisenhower administration for support. Possibly, he had heard that Eastern European defectors, trained by the CIA, were infiltrating across the Austrian border into Hungary.[163] Surely, Nagy had heard Radio Free Europe bombarding the Soviet satellites for many years with the message that the West was standing by ready to help them cast off the Soviet yoke. And as the rebellion spread from Budapest to the outlying provinces, Radio Free Europe urged the people of Hungary to resist the Red Army, providing the recipe for Molotov cocktails and exhorting Hungarians to choose "Freedom or Death!"[164]

On November 4, Khrushchev ordered two hundred thousand troops and four thousand tanks into Hungary,[165] and as the Red Army conducted its ferocious business, a Hungarian announcer on Radio Free Europe maintained that "the pressure upon the government of the US to send military help to the freedom fighters will become irresistible."[166]

Apparently, the announcer was unfamiliar with realpolitik as practiced by Eisenhower, or maybe he had seen too many Hollywood westerns. No American soldiers would ride to the rescue of Hungary. Eisenhower did not believe the insurgency could succeed, and direct US military intervention in the Soviet's back yard was unthinkable, since it could trigger World War III, complete with the use of nuclear arms.[167] This concern trumped all others for Eisenhower, even though his decision led both friends and foes to doubt American resolve and criticize the rhetoric about freedom as hollow. And so the United States stayed on the sidelines as the revolution was crushed. In three days, an estimated twenty thousand Hungarians and two thousand Soviets died.[168] Two years later, Khrushchev had Imre Nagy tried and hanged, and his body dumped in a prison grave.[169]

Eisenhower was also concerned about the conflict widening at Suez – and with reason. Moscow notified Washington, London, and Paris that the Soviet Union was contemplating the use of force to halt the attack on Egypt. Because keeping the Soviets out of the Middle East had been one of his primary goals, Eisenhower responded to the threat by informing Moscow that the United States would not sit by while the Soviets intervened. To emphasize his response, the president began a mobilization of the armed forces.[170]

Simultaneously, though, Eisenhower's warnings to Jerusalem became more menacing. He said that there could be severe repercussions if Israel did not evacuate the Sinai and Gaza: UN condemnations, counterattacks by Soviet "volunteers," and the termination of all US governmental aid and philanthropic assistance – a move that contained the threat of a Justice Department investigation into the tax-exempt status of charities that furnished funds vital to Israel.[171]

Eisenhower's arm-twisting was effective. The following morning, Ben-Gurion announced that his soldiers would withdraw.

Richard M. Nixon, who, as vice president under Eisenhower, was close to the Suez Crisis, recalled his boss's thinking in 1956.

"Eisenhower," said Nixon, "never had any illusions about Nasser. First, there were Nasser's impolitic statements at that time – to put it mildly. And there were so many interests to consider: we had French interests, British interests, Israeli interests. But what really happened in 1956 was that it came at a very bad time politically. It came right after the Hungarian Revolution, after we had bashed Khrushchev as the Butcher of Budapest. So it was difficult to say, 'Well, we're going to support our own people when they are doing the same thing.' Although ours was justified – and the two were not the same – nevertheless, it was difficult. The second thing is that it came shortly before [a presidential] election, which we were going to win anyway as it later turned out. But on the other hand it was an election in which we were running on the platform of peace and prosperity. And so all of these factors led to Eisenhower's decision to force the Israelis out."[172]

Eisenhower easily won reelection, but beyond the issue of domestic politics is whether he made the correct decision at Suez. In his two-volume memoir he gave no indication of second-guessing himself. Nor did he question his actions during the time he spent talking to Stephen E. Ambrose, who wrote a two-volume Eisenhower biography.[173] Regarding Suez, Ambrose would later record that Eisenhower "never wavered on or regretted his decision to force the invading parties out of Egypt, no matter what."[174]

That was the Eisenhower position for public consumption – but he had long hidden much of his thinking behind platitudes and his omnipresent grin. Although Eisenhower appeared to be the opposite of vain, his biographers Chester J. Pach Jr. and Elmo Richardson wrote that he actively tried "to shape the judgments historians would make."[175]

By the mid-1960s Eisenhower could see that the US position had slipped badly in the Middle East while the USSR had gained a solid foothold by encouraging the growth of a Red Fertile Crescent. Egypt was squarely in the Soviet camp; Iraq had withdrawn from the Baghdad Pact;[176] the Soviets had set their sights on Iraq's oil reserves,[177] and they had become, in conjunction with some of the Eastern bloc, the chief weapons suppliers to Syria.[178] Presumably, these developments led Eisenhower to reconsider his choices, and on an October afternoon in 1965, on the glass-enclosed sun porch of his Gettysburg farm, Eisenhower raised the 1956 crisis with Max Fisher, general chairman of the United Jewish Appeal and a rising star in Republican Party politics, who had come to invite Eisenhower to accept an award marking the twentieth anniversary of the liberation of the concentration camps.[179]

The two men had been discussing the state of the Republican Party following Barry Goldwater's resounding defeat by Lyndon Johnson in the 1964 presidential election when Eisenhower abruptly, and somewhat wistfully, said, "You know, Max, looking back at Suez, I regret what I did. I never should have pressured Israel to evacuate the Sinai." Then the former president added that if he'd had "a Jewish adviser" working for him he doubted that he "would have handled the situation the same way."[180]

This was news to Fisher, and while it helped define his later career as a presidential adviser, forcing Israel out was just a small facet of the geopolitical problem created by the handling of the crisis. Around the same time Eisenhower spoke with Fisher, he also told Richard Nixon that "he thought that the action that was taken [at Suez]…was a mistake."[181] Eisenhower, said Nixon, saw the end of the crisis as "the beginning of Britain withdrawing as a world power east of Suez…. After Suez, the writing was on the wall."[182]

That writing had profound implications for the United States. What became clear to Eisenhower, said Nixon, was that "as a result of our turning on the British and the French when they were trying to protect their interests in the Canal, it meant that they were finished in other parts of the world as well. That was a very unfortunate thing because it meant that the United States then virtually had to act alone."[183]

As the Cold War shifted into a mano-a-mano competition between the United States and the Soviet Union, it was inevitable that the enmity between the superpowers would filter into the Middle East and expand a regional dispute into a geopolitical one – precisely the expansion that Eisenhower had hoped to avoid with his more evenhanded approach to the Arabs and Israelis. The dangers created by the widened conflict would become obvious in the prelude to the 1967 Six-Day War and its more dangerous aftermath when the Soviet Union broke off diplomatic relations with Israel, provided money, arms, training, and logistical support to Arab terrorist organizations, and supplied sophisticated anti-tank and surface-to-air missiles to Egypt and Syria along with technicians to operate them. In a region where the pot forever threatened to boil over, a head-to-head exchange between the United States and Soviet Union, and the wholesale destruction that would entail, seemed to be waiting right around the bend.

The geopolitics that brought the Cold War to the Middle East also dragged Soviet Jewry onto the global battlefield. Prior to the Suez crisis, the treatment of Soviet Jews was a topic the United States government would raise in the same way it raised any rough treatment the Kremlin meted out to its citizens or satellites: as a means for scoring points in the ideological debate between democracy and authoritarianism. This was no small matter. In the opening decade of the twentieth century Ambrose Bierce defined politics as "a strife of interests masquerading as a contest of principles,"[184] and while Bierce's cynical definition applied in greater and lesser degrees at various junctures of the Cold War, to understand the origin of the American movement to free Soviet Jewry it is critical to remember the barrages of charges and countercharges exchanged by the United States and Soviet Union – imperialism, racism, religious repression, censorship, the exploitation of the poor – all of them fired off with the goal of maintaining and winning allies by controlling the moral high ground.

Once the hostility between Washington and Moscow infected the clash between Arabs and Israelis, Soviet Jewry moved past its status as a premise in a philosophical argument and became a tactical asset, a tangible addition to the arsenal of the Cold War.

Israel, the bedrock American ally in the region, remained in dire need of immigrants – a need that grew desperate after the Six-Day War when the Israelis found themselves in control of twenty-six thousand square miles of new land and 1.1 million Arabs.[185] Not only did Israel have to formulate an approach to dealing with this territory, but it also faced the possibility that its Jewish population would be surpassed by the Arabs with their higher birth rate, a demographic contest that the Israelis, with their commitment to living in a Jewish, *democratic* state, could not afford to lose. Despite the spike in idealistic American immigrants after 1967, it was evident that the Zionist endgame of ingathering world Jewry into its historic homeland was more dream than reality. Still, there were between two and three million Jews in the USSR, a great number of them educated and skilled and anxious to leave, and for the Israeli government these potential immigrants were the only realistic solution to their nation's most pressing existential problem.

The Kremlin was not unaware of this problem. Moreover, Soviet leaders understood that the United States, seeking to ensure Israel's safety and stabilize the Middle East, had a stake in the immigration of Soviet Jews into the Jewish state. But the Kremlin had its own concerns beyond the Middle East, concerns grounded in its central ideological flashpoint with the West. In his memoir, Khrushchev wrote that for the USSR to trumpet that it was constructing a "paradise," while keeping its borders "bolted with seven locks" was to "discredit the Marxist-Leninist ideals on which our Soviet way of life is based."[186] It was a salient point, and Khrushchev was eminently qualified to raise it, since this was the challenge confronting him in East Berlin during the summer of 1961, when citizens of the Communist sector of the city were fleeing to West Berlin at an astounding rate, most of whom, according to Khrushchev, were "the best and most qualified people". Frightened that the economy would collapse if the flight wasn't stopped – hence proving communism inferior to capitalism – Khrushchev felt that his sole option was to build a wall, even though he later admitted that it was a "hateful thing".[187]

The Berlin Wall, nearly one hundred miles of concrete block twelve feet high, with guard towers from which soldiers could shoot anyone trying to flee, became the predominant symbol of the Cold War. It also provided President Kennedy with a tremendous public relations victory at Khrushchev's expense. On a June 1963 visit to West Germany, where an estimated three million West Berliners poured into the streets to cheer him, JFK pummeled the Soviet system by saying, "Democracy is not perfect, but we have never had to put a wall up to keep our people in."[188]

For the Kremlin, Soviet Jewry would represent the same harsh reality as the Berlin Wall. The initial line of defense adopted by Khrushchev was to proclaim that no Jews had filed applications for emigration to Israel. However, Golda Meir, the Israeli foreign minister, repudiated Khrushchev in the *New York Times*, saying that 9,236 Jews had requested applications to leave.[189] Internally, Soviet propaganda continued to deny that Jews wanted to go; for example, one internal memorandum to the Central Committee of the Communist Party of the Soviet Union (CPSU) blamed the "imperial powers and Israel" for spreading these rumors.[190]

In spite of the denials, Soviet officials were not above using exit visas as a bargaining chip when dealing with the United States. Better still, for the Kremlin, if at some moment the decision was made to curtail Jewish emigration, there was a ready excuse – namely, the need to accommodate the Soviet Union's Arab friends – because unlike the majority of American Jews in the 1950s and 1960s, Arab governments did not fail to connect Soviet Jewry with Israeli survival. In 1953, in a protest that would have been comical had it not been so tragic a situation, a high-ranking Egyptian official decried the antisemitism that had reasserted itself in Eastern Europe because, like the Nazi persecution, antisemitism would increase Jewish immigration to Israel "with a concomitant resurgence of Zionist pressure against the Arabs."[191]

When President Harry Truman reluctantly recognized the Jewish state, he did not anticipate Israel becoming the lynchpin of US security in the Middle East. His lack of foresight was understandable given the odds Israelis faced in 1948: a ragtag collection of idealists, Holocaust survivors, and refugees encircled by enemies and shoehorned into a sliver of deserts and swamps with the Mediterranean at their backs. Almost equally unimaginable, and certainly not envisioned by Truman (or Eisenhower or Kennedy), was how the Cold War would alter the region, and how the region would in turn alter the Cold War. The process began in 1956, gathering force imperceptibly at first, like the trickiest of sandstorms – just a slight breeze picked up and the air grew faintly gritty until, all at once, the wind howled and the sky went black with whirling sand. The changes did not take long. In a little over three years – between the Six-Day War and December 1970, when Soviet dissidents were sentenced for attempting to hijack an Aeroflot airliner in Leningrad with the hope of flying to Israel[192] – the United States and the Soviet Union, the Arabs and Israelis, had come to comprehend that they were entwined in a new, potentially disastrous reality, and all of the participants, each for their own reasons, fixed their eyes on Soviet Jewry.

◆ ◆ ◆

Acting on the recommendation of Nehemiah Levanon, the Liaison Bureau began reaching out to the West. Levanon saw that Israel was not in a position to pressure the Kremlin. Only the White House and Congress had that ability, and the best approach to the US government, Levanon reasoned, was not through the assortment of nascent grassroots groups dedicated to the Jews behind the Iron Curtain, but by enlisting the help of the established communal organizations of American Jewry.[193]

At first glance, it seemed a reasonable plan. But neither Levanon nor anyone else at the Liaison Bureau noticed that it mirrored the strategy used by American Jewish organizations in response to Hitler. In all likelihood, no one noticed the inauspicious reflection due to a combination of how desperately Israel wanted the immigrants, and the erroneous conviction that these same organizations had stood silently by while Germany redefined the limits of depravity. There is no question that the United States, Great Britain, and other nations could have saved some of Hitler's victims by providing sanctuary, but had the outrage expressed by organized American Jewry in meetings, protests, editorials, letters, petitions, rallies, and conferences been effective in thwarting the Nazis, no Holocaust would have occurred.

In 1951, the American Jewish Committee, hoping to spread the word to the wider community, supported the publication of two excellent books: *Jews in the Soviet Union* by Solomon Schwartz, and *Jews in the Soviet*

Satellites by Peter Meyer.[194] Neither one was a best seller. A year later, during Stalin's Doctor's Plot, the United Jewish Appeal, the Zionist Organization of America, and Hadassah sprang into action by condemning the Soviet Union, planning a nationwide rally, and firing off memos. President Eisenhower and Secretary of State Dulles added their voices to the chorus of disapproval, and the Senate and House of Representatives passed three resolutions regarding "the persecution of the Jewish people."[195] After the doctors were freed, the criticism did not let up. In 1954, with Stalin dead and Khrushchev tightening his grip on power, Senator Herbert H. Lehman, a Democrat from New York, was telling an audience at a UJA dinner that Russian Jews "need our constant and unremitting efforts."[196]

Not long afterwards the American Jewish Committee made an interfaith appeal to Khrushchev and produced a petition signed by scholars and clergymen requesting that he call a halt to the abuse of his Jewish citizens.[197] For years, newspapers and magazines in the United States and Western Europe published well-documented stories and irate editorials on the oppression of Soviet Jewry.[198] Confronted with the information at press conferences, Soviet spokesmen denied the charges, citing as evidence the numerous Soviet officials married to Jewish women, a claim that was mocked in the press with the headline "Some of Our Best Wives Are Jewish."[199] In 1959, the activist and writer Moshe Decter, with the assistance of the Liaison Bureau, filled one whole issue of the *New Leader* with an examination of Jewish suffering in the USSR.[200] Nobody seemed to care, even though the journal spoke with an authoritative cultural voice, having printed, among other groundbreaking work, Dr. Martin Luther King Jr.'s "Letter from Birmingham City Jail"[201] and "Prose Poems" by Aleksandr Solzhenitsyn.[202]

That same year, in September, conservative writer William F. Buckley Jr., angered by the invitation Eisenhower had extended to Khrushchev to hold a summit in the United States, told the 2,500 people assembled in Carnegie Hall to protest the visit that Khrushchev "not only discriminates against Jews, he kills them."[203] Eisenhower knew the summit would attract critics, but he was determined to reduce the chances of a nuclear showdown by attempting "to soften up" Khrushchev. The strength of the president's feelings about the meeting was unmistakable when a journalist asked him if he was concerned about damaging his prestige. Eisenhower, who waged a lifelong war against his quick temper, snapped, "We are talking about the human race and what's going to happen to it."[204] Although Eisenhower was trying to cultivate warmer relations with Khrushchev, when the president met with him at Camp David he mentioned that American Jews were deeply disturbed by Soviet antisemitism. The president did not advance an official position on the topic; he left that job to Secretary of State Christian Herter, who informed Soviet foreign minister Andrei Gromyko that the United States was troubled by "the status of Jews in the USSR."[205]

After Kennedy replaced Eisenhower, the bipartisan drumbeat on behalf of Soviet Jews grew louder. Two powerful senators, Jacob Javits and Abraham Ribicoff, the former a Republican and the latter a Democrat, shepherded a resolution through the Senate condemning religious persecution in the USSR.[206] The House Foreign Affairs Committee then contacted Soviet Ambassador Anatoly Dobrynin with a request for the Kremlin to "alleviate the reported conditions affecting Soviet Jewry."[207] Along with Supreme Court Justice Arthur Goldberg, one of the most esteemed Jews in America, Javits and Ribicoff met with Secretary of State Dean Rusk to enlist his assistance. Rusk suggested assembling an international committee of prominent representatives of world Jewry in lieu of State Department officials to meet with the Soviets. Rusk was not unsympathetic; however, he objected to promoting the plight of Soviet Jewry to the status of a tactical feature of the Cold War.

Dissatisfied with Rusk's proposal, Justice Goldberg and Senators Javits and Ribicoff went to see the president. Owing to presidential counsel Myer Feldman, Kennedy was well versed on the travails of Soviet Jewry, and willing to explore it in private with Khrushchev and Gromyko.[208] JFK also took the opportunity, in an address before the UN General Assembly, to chastise the USSR with the observation that members of the United Nations were bound by its charter to respect human rights, and "those rights are not respected when…a synagogue is shut down."[209] All the same, Kennedy agreed with Rusk. He thought it counterproductive to fold Soviet Jewry into the Cold War portfolio, particularly by linking economic assistance sought by the Kremlin to permission for Soviet Jews to emigrate.[210]

This recap of the energy expended on behalf of Soviet Jews during the Eisenhower and Kennedy administrations is woefully incomplete. To appreciate the full scope all one has to do is page through the magnificent study by Yaacov Ro'i, *The Struggle for Soviet-Jewish Emigration, 1948–1967*. In his book, Ro'i aptly establishes that "it was the Israelis who provided virtually everyone engaged in the struggle with detailed and updated information on the day-to-day situation of Jews in the USSR."[211] Yet Ro'i then concludes that it was "Israel's guiding hand and persistent efforts in cultivating prominent figures and institutions…[in] the United States, that made the struggle an organized and meaningful one."[212]

This Israel-centric view of the movement to free Soviet Jewry is not uncommon among Israeli scholars. Nevertheless, it is unsupported by the record, a fair amount of which is contained in Ro'i's own book. After all, how successful was this movement if Presidents Eisenhower and Kennedy, Secretaries of State Herter and Rusk, a majority of the Congress and such venerable organizations as the American Jewish Committee and the United Jewish Appeal accomplished so little in terms of ameliorating Kremlin-sanctioned antisemitism or persuading Khrushchev to let the Jews leave?

My intention here is not to buy a ticket to the hackneyed sideshow of who deserves more credit for the later success of the movement. Rather, it is to explain the reason for what happened or, more precisely, from the 1950s well into the 1960s, what did not happen.

Ultimately, the decisive difference between the Soviet Jewry movement and the frantic exertions of the American Jewish community to save Europe's Jews from Hitler was that saving European Jewry was not deemed in synch with US interests. Not so the Soviet Jews, at least not once Richard Nixon occupied the Oval Office. As Nixon enacted his policy of détente – seeking a relaxation in the geopolitical tensions between the superpowers – the American grassroots Soviet Jewry advocates attempted to do exactly the opposite through demonstrations, vigils, harassment of Soviet diplomatic personnel, and the occasional bombing. In this manner, the advocates managed to infuriate both Soviet officials and the president, who accused the groups – and rightly so – of intentionally interfering in the Cold War.[213] Their antics also attracted the attention of the established Jewish organizations, which, after much dithering over territory and funding, began to focus on the problem.[214]

By brute-forcing Soviet Jewry onto the Cold War agenda, the grassroots groups created an essential condition for garnering the popular support of Americans and their government – the indispensable keys for unlocking the Soviet cage. This is not to denigrate the contributions of the Liaison Bureau, but as a rule the Israelis did not forge bonds with grassroots advocates, for as is often the case with freelancers, they were resistant to control by outsiders.[215] Moreover, when the Liaison Bureau first looked to the American Jewish community for help, the community at large was otherwise engaged, journeying through the Great American Funhouse at mid-century, where identities were eradicated and reborn. And it was only when American Jews came out the other side, changed by events at home and abroad, that they would embrace the cause of Soviet Jewry.

Act III: Boom!

During the Second World War, some fifteen million Americans were mobilized, and in the fall of 1945, the lucky ones began coming home.[216] For veterans, the joy of surviving was nearly matched by the discovery that the Great Depression was over, vanquished by the herculean labors of wartime.[217]

Veterans, in a mad dash to make up for their years in olive drab and khaki, hopped onto the 1940s version of the fast track. They enrolled in college, paying their way with the GI Bill. They married, found jobs, and started their climb into the upper reaches of the middle class. With the economies of Europe and Japan in tatters, with China trying to feed its people and the Soviet Union forgoing the production of consumer goods to pursue military parity with the United States,[218] and with the rest of the world grappling with the complexities of industrialization or living under colonial rule, America stood alone, ablaze with opportunities.

In the first five years after the war, the White House and Congress jump-started a building boom with an infusion of $20 billion. The Veterans Administration offered low-cost mortgages that required no down payment, and overnight, it seemed, in lonely cornfields and overgrown woods, boxy two-bedrooms, split levels in pastel pink, blue, and gray, and low-slung ranches in redwood or white brick sprang up, attracting young marrieds eager to flee dreary cityscapes for suburbia.[219]

During World War Two, 11 percent of Jews in the United States had been in uniform – fully half of the men ages eighteen to forty-four – and they came home anxious to cut themselves a hard-won slice of the American dream.[220] Prejudice against Jews was receding; in 1947, two popular movies attacking antisemitism appeared, *Gentlemen's Agreement* and *Crossfire*, both of which were nominated for the Best Picture Oscar. Jews were also swapping blue collars for white with astonishing speed. In 1940, just one in ten American Jews wore a coat and tie to work; by 1957 that percentage had increased to well over half.[221]

Young Jewish couples were in the forefront of the exodus to the suburbs, relocating at four times the rate of non-Jews, and in the 1950s alone more than doubled their suburban presence.[222] Exchanging candy stores for malt shops, recapturing the camaraderie of a crowded front stoop in the airy spaces of a backyard barbecue, and transplanting the nucleus of family life from a rusty, metal-legged kitchen table to a teak Danish modern dinette set all had their rewards, but Jewish newcomers to these wonderlands also harvested their share of loss, a nagging feeling that they were cut off from who they were. To be a Jew in the city, all you had to do to behold a reassuring touchstone of your identity was to stop at the corner deli for a pastrami on rye and an earful of gossip spiced with Yiddish.

To buttress their wobbly identities and counteract their social isolation in suburbia, Jews built over one thousand synagogues, primarily Conservative and Reform, between 1945 and 1965,[223] at an estimated cost of $1 billion,[224] and congregation membership jumped by 60 percent from the Depression years.[225] However, as the theologian Will Herberg wrote, these houses of worship with their soaring roof lines and fiery walls of stained glass had more to do with "belonging" than "orienting a life to God."[226] Not only were Jews shoring up their cultural identity, they were joining their gentile neighbors in the passion for religious affiliation that dominated 1950s America, where to conservatives and liberals alike religion was another manifestation of patriotism, a rebuke to the godless Communists of the Soviet Union.

As the Cold War devolved into a terrifying nuclear standoff between the United States and the USSR, Americans obsessed about Communism at home. The House Un-American Activities Committee was revived, and HUAC made a splash by summoning Hollywood moguls, actors, directors, and writers to ask them if they were, or had been, Communists. When ten of those appearing before the committee refused to answer, stating that their opinions were protected by the First Amendment, HUAC and the courts judged the Hollywood Ten guilty of contempt of Congress; they were punished with prison sentences of up to one year.[227] A blacklist was drawn up, drumming alleged Communists and those who were uncooperative with the hunt out of the entertainment business. HUAC was then shoved out of the limelight by the most aggressive witch hunter, Senator Joseph R. McCarthy.[228] In speeches and hearings McCarthy employed the ugly art of innuendo and slander, and he saw Communist influence everywhere – at the Voice of America, on library shelves, in the State Department, and in the Army. His ungainly pirouette through the limelight lasted until December 2, 1954, when he was censured by his Senate colleagues.[229] Two and a half years later, he was dead from alcoholism.[230]

Communism was a sensitive subject for American Jewry because there was "a disproportionate presence of Jews as members"[231] of the Communist Party – from 50 to 60 percent, according to an FBI estimate.[232] Since the 1920s Jews had been attracted to Communism, with its theoretical assurance of economic and social justice, and its atheism, which offered a reprieve from religious-based animosity toward Jews. Even though the justice of Communism proved illusive, true believers did not easily renounce their misplaced faith.

As folksinger and activist Pete Seeger recalled, "I thought Stalin was the brave Secretary Stalin and had no idea how cruel a leader he was. I got out in '49, though.... I should have left much earlier. It was stupid of me not to.... I didn't realize the danger the world was in."[233]

After the Soviet Union turned from a US ally to a prime antagonist, many Americans, like Seeger, were embarrassed by their earlier Communist connections, but the American Jewish community was especially appalled due to the courtroom revelations of the large number of Jews involved in espionage. There was the Judith Coplon case, the *Amerasia* affair, the Canadian spy ring,[234] and, worst of all, the arrest of Ethel and Julius

Rosenberg for passing atomic secrets to the Soviet Union. Testifying in his own defense, Julius denied that he was a spy, but admitted that he was "emotional" about the Soviets "destroying the Hitler beast who killed six million of my coreligionists."[235] The Rosenbergs, parents of two small boys, were convicted and sentenced to die in the electric chair at Sing Sing.[236]

As appeals were filed, the verdict was assailed by the Left. William L. Patterson of the Civil Rights Congress, which had been officially listed as a Communist front by the US government,[237] predicted that if the innocent Rosenbergs were executed, "a wave of Hitler-like genocidal attacks" would be launched against American Jews.[238] The literary critic Louis Harap declared that "the fight to reverse the death sentence against the Rosenbergs is the fight against the anti-Semitic implications of the whole affair."[239] In general, when it came to witch hunting, Harap was not entirely incorrect – Red baiting was frequently rank with antisemitism. Indeed, the floridly antisemitic newspaper columnist Westbrook Pegler was a zealous supporter of McCarthy. Harap's charge was echoed by Communists across Western and Eastern Europe, though somehow they did not see antisemitism at work in the Slansky trial in Czechoslovakia or in the resulting execution of eight Jews.

In spite of the pronouncements of intellectuals and the cacophony of protests, ascribing the Rosenbergs' conviction to prejudice found scant traction among the majority of American Jews. A significant number of Jewish communal groups criticized the Rosenbergs' defenders as "Communist-inspired," and the American Jewish Committee advocated for the death penalty to be carried out.[240] Support for the verdict did not soothe the collective sense of shame that lingered among Jews long after June 19, 1953, the day the Rosenbergs were executed. In 2009, when the Jewish real estate and media baron Mort Zuckerman was asked to comment on the impact of Bernard L. Madoff and his $50-billion Ponzi scheme, Zuckerman replied that no one since Julius Rosenberg had "so damaged the image and self-respect of Jews."[241]

Even so, unlike the nativism of the 1920s and the financial collapse of the 1930s, the Red hunting of the 1950s did not spawn any mass antisemitic movements. The immigrants the nativists had feared were now well down the path of assimilation, and the economy was revved up as Americans embarked on the longest, giddiest shopping spree in history.[242]

Cars were rolling off Detroit assembly lines, and the new government-financed highways were chockablock with Country Squire station wagons, the rustic, faux-wood trim on the doors a fitting detail for suburban pioneers. Gas was cheap; Americans were on the move – and they appeared to agree with Ronald Reagan, a corporate spokesman for General Electric, who was fond of reminding audiences that "progress is our most important product."[243] Freshly minted suburbanites painted their living rooms in colors bold enough to blind Jackson Pollock and, enchanted by the *au courant* absurdity that promised a future of infinite leisure, stocked up on the latest gadgetry: televisions (free entertainment, who could believe it?), built-in wall ovens, push-button electric ranges, and vacuum cleaners that resembled affable, hard-working creatures from outer space. A 1958 article in *Cosmopolitan* foretold of a miraculous time to come when ultrasonic closets used vibrations to clean clothes, while another machine created disposable dishes for every meal, and technology relieved women "of virtually every household chore except the diaper switch."[244]

Diapers were a much-discussed topic with the baby boom in full swing. The girls and boys born between 1946 and 1964 would change the world – not into the global love fest they would naïvely imagine while under the spell of flower power, but by their overwhelming numbers, which guaranteed that whatever choices they made would influence the culture around them. One impact was economic. In 1951 *Fortune* magazine was already rhapsodizing about "a civilian market growing by the size of Iowa every year"; and the financial optimism was still alive and well seven years later when *Life* ran a cover story with the headline "Kids, Built-in Recession Cure – How 4,000,000 A Year Make Millions in Business."[245]

Another impact was on education. By 1970, there would be 48.7 million students enrolled in kindergarten through high school, a record that would not be broken until 2003.[246] Jewish parents were happy to send their sons and daughters to good public schools, but they were concerned about preserving their children's Jewish identity. It was a complicated task because parents were encouraging their children to assimilate and not to assimilate – to move into gentile society and partake fully of the educational, cultural, social, and career opportunities available, all the while remembering that when they grew up they should marry other Jews. The rate of intermarriage was low in the 1950s – in the neighborhood of 5 percent.[247] And generally speaking, Jewish parents of baby boomers wanted to keep it that way.

Parents turned to their synagogues for help, and as the 1950s drew to a close, 80 percent of Jewish elementary-school students were also attending some kind of Sunday or afternoon Hebrew school program,[248] many of which required youngsters to participate in junior congregation, the student-run Sabbath services. In addition, there were local, state, and national Jewish youth groups that sponsored dances and conventions, and community centers for basketball and swimming; Jewish sleepaway camps and day camps; bat- and bar-mitzvah extravaganzas in catering halls so opulent King Solomon would have blushed; and piles of Chanukah gifts so the children would not feel left out at Christmastime.

Strangely enough, despite this focus on Jewish learning and identity, the hardships of Soviet Jews did not attract any notable attention from the American Jewish community at large. Stranger still were the findings of sociologist Nathan Glazer, who conducted the sole scholarly survey of the community during the 1950s and judged that the six million victims of Hitler "had had remarkably slight effects on the inner life of American Jewry."[249]

What happened? How is it possible that American Jews were so hesitant to discuss, or so indifferent to, the mass industrialized murder of their European *landsleit*? And how did that event become so significant to American Jews? What was the trajectory of their interest in the Holocaust?

The answer to that question leads to their determination to free Soviet Jewry.

◆ ◆ ◆

In 2009, historian Hasia R. Diner published *We Remember with Reverence and Love*, her rebuttal to the "often repeated 'truth'" that from 1945 until 1962 American Jewry was "silent" on the subject of the Holocaust.[250] Diner unearths a treasure trove of public interest in the six million – discussions, lectures, sermons, temple bulletins, museum exhibits, movies, radio and TV shows, plays, novels, and scholarly tomes – all of which prove her thesis with respect to silence. However, less obvious is whether, during that time frame, the Holocaust escaped what historian Jonathan Sarna refers to as "the periphery of American Jewish life."[251]

Diner cites Leo Shpall, "a constant observer of the Jewish book scene," who in 1958 wrote that the "Jewish persecution and extermination by the Nazis has, in the course of years, created a vast literature."[252]

Exactly how vast seems to be in the eye of the beholder: A book search on Amazon using the keywords "Nazis and Jews" returns 13,461 results, but just 101 of the books are listed as being available by 1962.

In the 1950s, commercial publishers in the United States did not appear to be in any rush to bring books about the Holocaust to the mass market, perhaps believing that the broad audience of book buyers was unwilling to read about the atrocities so soon after they occurred. In 1950, John Hersey published *The Wall*, a novel about the Warsaw ghetto; Anne Frank's diary appeared in the Netherlands in 1947, but five years passed before its American publication; Primo Levi's *If This Is a Man* was completed in 1947, but was not translated into English until 1958; Elie Wiesel's *Night* did not arrive until 1960, two years after it came out in France;[253] and Raul Hilberg, author of *The Destruction of the European Jews*, had trouble locating a home for a book that would later be hailed as a classic. It was printed in 1961 only after a wealthy benefactor promised the publisher he would buy thirteen hundred copies and donate them to libraries.[254]

One can attribute the reluctance to publish Hilberg's book as a commercial decision made by professionals who, after all, are in the guesswork business, but that does not account for the choice made by the Jewish Publication Society. A nonprofit organization founded in 1888, the JPS augmented its earnings from sales with dues from subscribers who had a demonstrable interest in reading about things Jewish.[255] However, from 1950 until 1965, the JPS offered just a single title dealing with the Final Solution.[256]

Given the response of moviegoers, publishers had accurately gauged the marketplace. *Judgment at Nuremberg*, with its previous incarnation as a television play and a movie cast of Hollywood royalty, and *The Diary of Anne Frank*, which had sold well in bookstores and won a Pulitzer Prize as a Broadway play, were both disappointments at the box office.[257]

The public reticence extended to situations as diverse as a memorial in New York City's Riverside Park that was dedicated but never built[258] and a survivor who was warned by his aunt that "if you want to have friends here in America, don't keep talking about your experiences.... [T]hey'll be afraid to come see you."[259]

There are a variety of explanations for the genocide's move from the quiet margins of American Jewish life to the noisy center. The simplest explanation is that the 1950s was simply a more socially constricted period, when the norm was to refrain from public displays of emotion and to avoid unpleasantness in polite conversation; once that reserve gave way, the six million became a more frequent topic of discussion. Another view holds that the shift was consistent with the psychoanalytic dance of trauma and repression: a terrible event occurs, its memory is repressed, and then it returns in an exaggerated form.[260] The Holocaust scholar Deborah E. Lipstadt ascribes the blossoming interest to the curiosity of "baby boomers who felt entirely comfortable as Americans and Jews [and] wanted to know more about this cataclysmic event."[261]

The most controversial explanation for the change came in 1999, when University of Chicago historian Peter Novick published *The Holocaust in American Life*, which – along with Norman Finklestein's *The Holocaust Industry*, published a year later – was cited by Diner as falsely perpetuating the myth that American Jews were silent about the Holocaust in the immediate postwar period.[262] Novick rejects the position that the American Jewish community was traumatized by the destruction of European Jewry, and accepts at face value Glazer's findings that the community was basically indifferent.[263] Novick believes that after the 1967 Six-Day War, the genocide was used by Jewish community leadership to strengthen political and financial backing for Israel, to combat assimilation and intermarriage, and to take "permanent possession of the gold medal in the Victimization Olympics."[264] And all of this was accomplished with the assistance of the Jewish handmaidens who play "an influential role in Hollywood, the television industry, and the newspaper, magazine, and book publishing worlds."[265]

Undeniably, the six million were cited as a rationale for supporting Israel and nurturing Jewish identity, and singled out as a unique calamity worth exploring in films and books. Logically speaking, though, one cannot illuminate the cause of an action by a simple reference to the action. In the 1960s, when American Jews raised the Nazis in the context of their fear for Israel and the threats of Egyptian President Nasser to drive the Jews into the sea, what does that tell us? If we read a book – say, Novick's own – are we to assume that there were no Jews employed by his publisher? Or did his publisher only hire Jews sufficiently enlightened to exhibit an indifference to genocide?

More interesting is that after Novick rejects the theory of trauma and repression he points out that "contemporary American Jewish religious thinkers had nothing to say about the Holocaust."[266]

Save for the ultra-orthodox Lubavitch Hasidim, who saw the tragedy as the "last labors prior to the arrival of our Messiah,"[267] and for Louis Finkelstein, chancellor of the Conservative movement's rabbinical seminary, who during an interview with *Time* magazine speculated that God had sent Hitler to force the Jews to repent,[268] the religious significance of the Holocaust was initially left unexplored. The theological quiet was permanently disturbed in 1966 when Richard L. Rubenstein took on the religious implications of the death camps in *After Auschwitz*.

Even allowing for Novick's support of Nathan Glazer's questionable findings, or acknowledging Diner's observations that in 1952 the American Jewish Congress produced the Ritual of Remembrance to be recited during the Seder and that suburban rabbis spoke about the six million to their congregations,[269] how could scholarly Jewish theologians brush aside the implications of their deaths? Addressing the existence of an omnipotent and good God while evil thrives is an essential chore of the theologian. Their avoidance, whether conscious or unconscious, was telling, and it spoke louder than the Lubavitchers' mysticism and Finklestein's vision of a ravenously vindictive God.

In *After Auschwitz* Rubenstein suggested that it was the almost unfathomable scope of the tragedy that had kept his confrères quiet. "It would have been better had six million Jews not died," he wrote, "but they have. We cannot restore the religious world which preceded their demise nor can we ignore the fact that the catastrophe has had and will continue to have an extraordinary influence on Jewish life."[270]

One can empathize with the shock that accompanied learning of the gruesome Nazi behavior in newspapers, magazines, and newsreels, and at the war crimes trials in Nuremberg; it must have seemed as though the laws of gravity had been repealed. Today, sixty-five years on, after reading shelves of books, inspecting stacks of grainy photographs and watching untold hours of film, after listening to the stories of survivors and standing in the Hall of Names at Yad Vashem, after reflecting on the exhibits at the US Holocaust Museum and touring the gas chamber at the Dachau concentration camp, we rebel at the evidence, stubbornly resisting what we know to be true – that between 1933 and 1945 Germany rejected its centuries-old position as a lodestar of scientific and artistic achievement, and degenerated into a cesspit of barbarians.

Here is one cause of the reluctance to talk about the six million during the 1950s: the scale of the transgression was virtually inconceivable. This mindset contributed to the Israeli government's decision to dispatch spymaster Isser Harrel and a team of Mossad and Shin Bet agents to capture the fugitive SS colonel Adolph Eichmann, who had overseen the logistics of the Final Solution, and was living in Buenos Aires under an assumed name.[271]

As Israeli attorney general Gideon Hausner, the lead prosecutor at the Eichmann trial, told the *Saturday Evening Post*, "While the purpose of the trial was to probe into charges preferred [*sic*] against one man, we also wanted to…bring the enormity of…the Nazis' crimes down to a point where average people could comprehend it."[272]

More than any other event, it was the 1961 trial of Adolph Eichmann that brought the American Jewish community's reticence about the genocide into focus and marked the beginning of its end. The four-month trial was held in Jerusalem, in the spacious new Beit Ha-Am Theater,[273] where Eichmann sat in his bulletproof glass cage and listened to the survivors relate their tales of horror with "his head tilted, lips tight and twisted, mouth moving as though he were tasting something unpleasant, eyes darting…like a silent-movie actor playing a villain."[274] As the survivors recounted scenes of rapes, sterilization, starvation, gassings, and watching their children being murdered before their eyes, spectators fainted. "Not one of us," a journalist commented, "will leave here as he was before." But the audience was not limited to the Beit Ha-Am;[275] the proceedings were broadcast on the radio with simultaneous translations from Hebrew into English, German, and French. Thirty-eight countries received daily, airmailed videotapes to be shown on television, the first time an international trial had appeared on TV. Print reporters from around the world were also out in force. There were 756 seats in the theater and 474 were set aside for the press. Journalists could also adjourn to the pressroom to watch a closed-circuit broadcast.[276]

As the world listened, the Nazi destruction of European Jewry was converted into a separately defined event from the Second World War. This was markedly different from the treatment of Nazi atrocities at the 1945 Nuremberg trials or in the 1960 best seller by William L. Shirer, *The Rise and Fall of the Third Reich*, which "put Nazism and World War II on the American cultural map," but only dedicated some thirty pages out of twelve hundred to the annihilation of the Jews.[277] At the Eichmann trial, the annihilation was the story, and the American and European audience was given a new name for it: Holocaust, a translation of the Hebrew word *shoah* (catastrophe), which Israelis used in reference to the six million.[278] Originally, Holocaust was spelled with a small *h*. In effect, the capitalization was an editorial comment emphasizing the singularity of the events, and it initially appeared in the trial dispatches of Paul Jacobs.[279]

Jacobs was an assimilated American Jew, but reporting on the trial he felt as though his identity had been upended and admitted that he "started to wonder if the American gentile world has always regarded me as a Jew who is also incidentally an American.... I shall certainly be troubled until I find out."[280]

His dilemma was shared by much of American Jewry and explains the discomfort they had in acknowledging the Holocaust, both in casual conversation and in formal contexts such as sociological surveys. Adding to the general discomfort of American Jews was that their communal organizations were worried that the Eichmann trial, by spotlighting Jewish identity, would engender an antisemitic backlash. Judge Joseph M. Proskauer, president of the American Jewish Committee, was so concerned that he wrote Prime Minister Ben-Gurion, asking him to allow West Germany or an international tribunal to prosecute Eichmann.[281] The

Anti-Defamation League went to great pains to separate itself from Israel's claim that it had the right to try Eichmann, and an ADL memorandum expressed the fear that the trial would sully the perception Christians had of Jews as "fair-minded and merciful."[282]

The ADL memo may have been overly optimistic about Christian impressions of Jews. The *National Review*, whose editor-in-chief, William Buckley, had resigned from the *American Mercury* allegedly because he thought the magazine antisemitic,[283] accused Israel of bending the law "to give assassination a juridical rationale." As if that wasn't enough, the *National Review* treated its readership to a fictional conversation between a crude husband and wife living on Central Park West in which "Sylvia" talks to "Myron" about Eichmann – along with gold and hairdressers – as she does her nails.[284] The *Wall Street Journal* declared that the trial aided the Soviet Union by stirring up anti-German sentiment and was rife with "an atmosphere of Old Testament retribution."[285] In the *Unitarian Register*, a minister declared that ethically he could not distinguish "the Jew-pursuing Nazi" from "the Nazi-pursuing Jew,"[286] an opinion expressed in more scathing tones by the Catholic newspaper *The Tablet*, which excoriated "some influential people around who – like Shylock of old – demand their pound of flesh."[287]

Other than releasing Eichmann, none of these publications suggested what Christians might do with a man who was a prime mover in the murder of millions of innocents. And while the opinions appear to assume a moral stance, one wonders if they were also a reaction to the charge of Christian complicity in the Holocaust – a charge that was made in two novels that were climbing the best-seller lists: *The Last of the Just* by André Schwarz-Bart, a Jewish Frenchman whose parents had died in the camps, which traces the murder of Jews from the Crusades to the Holocaust;[288] and *Mila 18* by Leon Uris, an account of the Warsaw ghetto uprising.

No wonder then that Irving Howe characterized the postwar years of American Jewish life as "inherently 'schizoid,'" years of being buffeted by irreconcilable forces – increasing prosperity and social comfort at home while across the Atlantic the remains of Hitler's ovens and gas chambers marked the Continent like a livid scar.[289] Furthermore, public displays of antisemitism were in the news. In December 1959, West

German synagogues were defaced with swastikas, and soon synagogues across Europe and in the United States were also smeared with the icon. An American Nazi Party had sprung up under the leadership of George Lincoln Rockwell, and rallies were held in New York City and Washington, DC, where Rockwell promulgated his view that 80 percent of Jews were Communist traitors who should be gassed.[290]

Nonetheless, there was no widespread eruption of antisemitism during the trial, nor after Eichmann, who maintained that he was no more than a "small fry" duty bound to follow orders,[291] was found guilty by the three-judge panel[292] and executed by hanging in the Ramla prison on May 31, 1962.[293] The ambivalence of American Jews about their identity – whether huddled together in decrepit city walkups or in new gilded suburban shtetls – was partially diminished by the prosecution of Eichmann, because it transmitted the Holocaust to the public realm and uncoupled antisemitism from unpleasant characterizations of Jews, instead linking it to unadulterated evil. Then, too, by demonstrating the unprecedented heights to which the Nazis had raised the bar of Jew hatred, the testimony about the camps and the mass shootings in villages and outside cities made the social antisemitism in America – the antisemitism of restricted clubs, housing covenants, and quotas at prestigious universities – inconsequential by comparison. Lastly, Israel had shown itself to be a competent defender of the Jewish people, even those – in the words of Attorney General Hausner – "whose graves are scattered the length and breadth of Europe."[294]

Still, the suffering of Soviet Jewry did not filter down to the grassroots of the American Jewish community. As the Communist witch hunts abated, Jews in the United States no longer felt imperiled – a respite that would end in the spring of 1967 – but for now they were in hot pursuit of their postwar dreams and enmeshed in another cause for social justice, a cause with which they had long identified, that felt closer to home, and that did not throw their Jewishness into bold relief: the civil rights movement.

ACT IV: ROCK 'N' ROLL IS HERE TO STAY

The connection between blacks and Jews and their mutual stake in civil rights was formalized in 1909, when social activist Mary White Ovington cofounded an organization that would evolve into the National Association for the Advancement of Colored People.[295] Her cofounders were the journalist William English Walling, who had caught Ovington's attention with his account of race riots in Springfield, Illinois; and Dr. Henry Moskowitz, a reformer and vocal critic of social and political antisemitism.[296] Walling had traveled extensively in Russia, and his understanding of persecution had been so marked by the experience that at the group's first meeting in New York City, Walling remarked "that the Negro was treated with greater inhumanity in the United States than the Jew was treated in Russia."[297]

This pairing of the lugubrious circumstances of blacks and Jews was partially responsible for attracting Jewish leaders to the organization. In 1914, when Joel Spingarn, a former literature professor at Columbia University who helped to found the publishing house Harcourt Brace,[298] was elected chairman of the NAACP, he brought Jacob Schiff, Jacob Billikoppf, and Rabbi Stephen Wise to the board.[299] By the 1930s, the African American press was repeatedly stressing the shared suffering of the two minority groups, citing the state-supported harassment in Germany and the Jim Crow laws and lynching in the South.[300]

This is not to say that either group was free from prejudice about the other, but during the Depression they managed to unite their causes, whether it was the Union of American Hebrew Congregations protesting "the lynching evil" and commending "the Rabbis and lay leaders who… have taken a courageous position on the question,"[301] or the historically black colleges providing teaching positions to Jewish refugee scholars from Germany and Austria.[302]

During the Second World War, over 2.5 million African Americans registered for selective service; approximately one half were inducted into the military, with 75 percent of those assigned to the Army. Black units were segregated and primarily relegated to support roles, with only 15 percent permitted to join combat units.[303] The perverseness of African Americans fighting for freedoms in Europe and the Pacific that they themselves did not enjoy at home was never clearer than in Southern towns, where German POWs in transit were served inside restaurants, while the black

GIs guarding them, many of whom had seen combat against the Nazis, were forced to wait outside, victims of Jim Crow.[304]

Like Soviet Jews who had fought in the Red Army and returned to find that their country still regarded them as a people apart, black veterans learned that their sacrifices for the nation did not alter their status as second-class citizens. In Mississippi, four black soldiers recently home from overseas were thrown out of army trucks and beaten. In Georgia, two black men and their wives were pulled from a car and murdered by a mob; one of the men was a veteran. And in South Carolina, a young black sergeant was dragged off a bus, then beaten and blinded by policemen.[305]

Fortunately, unlike Soviet Jews trapped under the iron hand of the Kremlin with scant opportunity to improve their situation, African Americans were soon organizing politically and turning toward the White House, Congress, and the courts for relief. On June 3, 1946, the Supreme Court ruled that "seating arrangements for the different races in interstate motor travel require a single, uniform rule to promote and protect national travel,"[306] and the following April a group of sixteen men, eight white and eight black, set off on the Journey of Reconciliation – a bus trip through Virginia, North Carolina, Tennessee, and Kentucky, to determine whether the South was behaving in accordance with the ruling. Only six days after the journey began, Jack Roosevelt Robinson, a black son of Cairo, Georgia, trotted out onto Ebbets Field in a Dodger uniform, forever changing the national pastime – and the nation itself.

By the early 1950s Jim Crow would be under full-scale assault.

◆ ◆ ◆

Nine months after Jackie Robinson broke baseball's color barrier, President Truman decided to bypass the obstructionist segregationists in Congress and to integrate the armed forces through executive order. That task, like so much of the initial headway against Jim Crow, was finally accomplished during the Eisenhower administration.[307] In 1953, blacks won a favorable settlement in a bus boycott in Baton Rouge, Louisiana,[308] and by 1956 a year-long bus boycott in Montgomery, Alabama, set off by the resistance of Rosa Parks and sustained by the eloquence of Martin Luther King Jr., concluded with the desegregation of the city's buses. In between came the unanimous 1954 Supreme Court decision *Brown v. Board of Education*, which held that state laws establishing separate public schools for black and white children were unconstitutional. In October of that year, as the Supreme Court prepared to consider briefs on the implementation of *Brown*, President Eisenhower, over the objection of southern senators, appointed John Marshall Harlan II to the court. Like his grandfather, Justice John Marshall Harlan, the sole dissenter in the 1896 *Plessy v. Ferguson* Supreme Court decision that upheld segregation, Harlan II was pro civil rights.[309] In 1955, Eisenhower appointed E. Frederic Morrow to his staff, the first African American to fill an executive post in the White House,[310] and a year later the president put William J. Brennan, a liberal Catholic, on the court.[311] Just how determined Eisenhower was to see civil rights rulings implemented was evident in 1957, when, to enforce the *Brown* decision, the president dispatched a thousand paratroopers from the 101st Airborne to Little Rock, Arkansas, to hold back the white mobs and to escort the black children to school. Sending the 101st had both practical and public relations benefits. With their protection, the children were not harmed,[312] and by using the Screaming Eagles, the most storied unit in the Allied victory, Eisenhower, the beloved general who had engineered the defeat of Hitler, was making a subtle statement about his opinion of segregationists: they were no better than Nazis.

Wherever one looked, Jews were in the thick of the struggle. At the NAACP Legal Defense Fund, Jack Greenberg was a top assistant to Thurgood Marshall, the lead attorney in *Brown*. In that case, African American sociologist Kenneth Clark submitted a study to the Supreme Court demonstrating that segregation scarred black children. Financed by the American Jewish Committee, the study was incorporated into the amicus curiae brief the AJC presented to the court. Amicus curiae briefs were also presented by the Anti-Defamation League and the American Jewish Congress, and on the heels of the *Brown* decision, Jewish organizations inundated the courts with a cascade of briefs attacking segregation.[313]

The Union of American Hebrew Congregations and the Synagogue Council of America were swept into the fray, bringing with them congregants from all those new synagogues,[314] as was the B'nai B'rith, which had long urged its sizeable membership to "protest whenever the

Negro's rights are abridged."[315] Soon, the majority of organized American Jewry was threaded through the movement, and the activism began filtering down to the grassroots.

At the Temple, the oldest and wealthiest Jewish congregation in Atlanta, Georgia,[316] Rabbi Jacob M. Rothschild was a proponent of civil rights. In his sermons, Rothschild pressed his congregants to take up the noble cause. His campaign did not stop even though from the autumn of 1957 through the autumn of 1958 bombers targeted Jews across the South – in Birmingham, Charlotte, Gastonia, Jacksonville, Miami, and Nashville.[317] As a chaplain Rothschild had been in combat on Guadalcanal, so perhaps this experience enabled him to press on.[318] His efforts were effective enough that by the early hours of October 12, 1958, a group calling itself the Confederate Underground, who declared blacks and Jews to be "aliens," blew up part of the Temple with dynamite,[319] the blast rocking the houses along Peachtree Street[320] and leaving a twisted pile of pipes and rubble topped by a shattered rainbow of stained glass.[321]

Officials in Atlanta and local clergy of all faiths and hues publicly objurgated the bombing, and President Eisenhower added his voice to the chorus, labeling the Confederate Underground "a bunch of Al Capone gangsters."[322] One consequence of the bombing harkened back to the 1915 lynching of Leo Frank, who had been a member of the Temple.[323] Witnessing the flood of concern from her Christian neighbors, Rabbi Rothschild's wife, Janice, referred to the attack as "The Bomb That Healed,"[324] a phrase still in use fifty years later.[325] Another consequence was that Rabbi Rothschild redoubled his efforts on behalf of racial equality. He developed a close relationship with Dr. King, and some of the Temple's congregants, who earlier had hesitated to get involved, became active participants and would play an influential role in the integration of Atlanta's public schools.[326]

As civil right protests accelerated after 1960, Jews, especially from up North, flocked to the movement. Two-thirds of the white Freedom Riders were Jewish.[327] So were at least one-third of the whites[328] who helped register black voters and picket segregated stores, restaurants, and amusement parks.[329] Reform rabbis were arrested in St. Augustine, Florida, for trying to integrate a swimming pool,[330] and Rabbi Arthur J. Lelyveld was beaten in Hattiesburg, Mississippi, where he was participating in a voter registration drive. Lelyveld delivered the eulogy for family friend and CORE worker Andrew Goodman, who was shot to death near Philadelphia, Mississippi, along with another young Jewish New Yorker, Michael Schwerner, and their black colleague, Mississippi-born James Chaney.

One frequently cited explanation for Jews gravitating toward the civil rights movement is the religious concept of *tikkun olam* (repairing the world), the requirement to take on the task that God intended for the Jewish people as an ethical light among the nations. This was the motivation Rabbi Lelyveld was expressing when he said, "I do not serve the cause of Negro emancipation because I expect the Negro to love me in return. The command to remember the stranger and the oppressed is unconditional."[331]

Jews had stocked left-wing movements in the United States from the outset of the twentieth century; it was a tradition born in response to the antisemitism of Europe and imported by immigrants. Betty Friedan, who kicked off the women's movement in 1963 by publishing *The Feminine Mystique*, had a Russian Jewish immigrant for a father,[332] and she later said that her "passion against injustice…originated from my feelings of the injustice of anti-Semitism."[333] No matter how profoundly one believes in the altruistic impulse of *tikkun olam*, it would be inaccurate to dismiss self-interest in the leftward tilt of the Jewish community, since any political enterprise that increased religious and social tolerance benefited Jews, as did any undertaking that sought to safeguard or expand the rights of minorities – at least until affirmative action became widespread and some Jews were excluded from schools and jobs because of their accomplishments, a change that would exacerbate tensions between the African American and Jewish communities.

Another contributing factor revolved around blacks and Jews identifying with each other. This phenomenon was explored in a February 1948 essay by James Baldwin that appeared in *Commentary*, at that time a publication of the American Jewish Committee. Reflecting on his native Harlem, Baldwin wrote that "the Negro identifies himself almost wholly with the Jew. The more devout Negro considers that he is a Jew, in bondage to a hard taskmaster and waiting for a Moses to lead him out of Egypt."[334] Another African American writer, Julius Lester, who in 1968 was seen as "a personal emissary of Black Power,"[335] and who in 1982 converted to

Judaism,[336] has observed that what blacks have failed to understand about most Jews is that they "don't see themselves as white."[337]

Thus, whatever hard-won comforts Jews enjoyed, the political connection between put-upon minorities persevered. But something else was at work on young men and women by the early 1950s and '60s – an identification between blacks and whites forged by the cultural bond of popular music. In 1936, *Billboard* magazine's new hit parade categorized the music of black artists as "race" records. In 1949, the magazine bestowed a hipper name on the category, designating it "rhythm and blues," but the intent was the same: to keep the races separate. Pop records were white; R&B was black.[338]

Regardless of commercial distinctions, a trend that was clear to Leo Mintz, owner of the Record Rendezvous store in Cleveland, Ohio, was that his customers were rejecting jazz and standard pop fare for R&B. Mintz brought this information to Cleveland disc jockey Alan Freed, host of a late-night pop show that was scrambling to attract advertisers. Mintz urged Freed to play R&B records and backed it up with sponsorship money.[339] On July 11, 1951, Alan Freed signed on as the "Moondog,"[340] and suddenly he was deejaying the most popular show in Cleveland.[341] The next month, a little-noticed event occurred that would be as meaningful to the music industry as Jackie Robinson's debut was to baseball. In August, the blatantly sexual blues song "Sixty Minute Man," recorded by the black group the Dominoes, and already an R&B hit, crossed the color line to the pop charts.[342] It was a lyric from this song that inspired Allen Freed to christen this new sound "rock 'n' roll."[343]

The hold this music was gaining on black and white teenagers was demonstrated on March 21, 1952. Freed had promoted a concert, the "Moondog Coronation Ball," to be held at Cleveland Arena, which had a seating capacity of ten thousand. More than twice that number showed up, and the police had to shut down the concert after one song.[344]

In 1953, another black rock 'n' roll group crossed over to the pop charts: the Orioles, with "Crying in the Chapel." The next year, the Crows' "Gee" and the Chords' "Sh-Boom" made the trip.[345] This sound would become known as "doo-wop," and city street corners in the Midwest and Northeast were awash in these hand-clapping, finger-snapping a cappella harmonies that originated in the black church. And whites were not just listening to doo-wop; they were performing it.

Carl Foushee, a member of the Monotones, a New Jersey group that would go on to record the doo-wop classic "Book of Love," remembered that "kids were singing doo-wop all over Newark. And it wasn't only black kids. White kids were down with it too."[346]

Teenagers in the South had even more choices of R&B stations than their peers in other sections of the country. Because of segregation, southern cities often had their own black radio stations, and white youngsters were becoming a notable portion of their listening audience.[347]

In 1954, a *Billboard* headline announced: "The Latest Trend: R & B Disks Are Going Pop."[348] Classifying it as a trend was an understatement. That year, the white musician Bill Haley covered "Shake, Rattle and Roll," originally recorded by the older black singer Big Joe Turner, and by the beginning of 1955 Haley's version had crossed over from the pop to the R&B charts and sold one million copies. Then black rock 'n' roller Chuck Berry released "Maybellene," and Berry was followed by Little Richard with "Tutti Frutti," another pop hit.[349]

And then Elvis Presley arrived, his dancing and singing steeped in the black and white musical traditions of the South. Mothers and fathers, with the backing of journalists, disc jockeys, clergymen, and civic leaders, disapproved of the nimble-hipped Elvis with his big glossy pompadour and sexy leer. *Time* magazine compared Elvis to an oversized sausage, and a *New York Times* critic deplored his facial expressions as "singularly distasteful." Across the country, radio stations refused to play his music, and the performer was hung in effigy and burned. But it was Reverend William Shannon, condemning Elvis in the *Catholic Sun*, who pinpointed his appeal: "Presley and his voodoo of frustrations and defiance have become symbols in our country."[350]

Exactly. Chafing against the narrow social mores of the 1950s, teenagers were adopting a lingua franca all their own. Their common language of rebellion filled the malt shops, high-school gyms, basement rec rooms, and cars parked under the moonlit leaves of lover's lanes. These teenagers – thirteen million of them by 1956 – were the wealthiest in the history of the republic. They had $7 billion a year in pocket money,[351] and they bought records by the ton – in April 1956, Elvis was selling over $500,000 worth of records a week.[352]

For white middle-class youth to identify with black culture was not new. The Roaring Twenties, for instance, had produced Mezz Mezzrow. Born in 1899 to Russian Jews who immigrated to Chicago, Mezzrow exchanged the opportunity to take over the family drugstore for a career as a jazz saxophonist, convicted marijuana dealer, and self-anointed "voluntary Negro."[353] But the 1950s were different; it was the age of the American rebel and anti-hero. In the movies, actors Marlon Brando and James Dean inhabited these roles; astutely, the entertainer Jackie Gleason judged Elvis to be "a guitar-playing Marlon Brando."[354] By 1959, Norman Mailer was writing about a "new breed" of hipster who "had absorbed the existentialist synapses of the Negro, and for practical purposes could be considered a white Negro."[355] James Baldwin viewed the romanticizing of the mean circumstances of African Americans as a delusion,[356] and Tom Wolfe would later satirize it in *Radical Chic*, his portrait of the Black Panthers attending a party at Leonard and Felicia Bernstein's penthouse on Park Avenue, where the new-moneyed upper crust was chasing "the gauche thrill of taking on certain styles of the lower order."[357]

However true the critiques of Baldwin and Wolfe, the connection between the cultural earthquakes of rock 'n' roll and integration was undeniable, and both were being spread by television. The civil rights movement was gathering steam as ownership of TV sets was increasing from approximately half the homes in the United States to over 90 percent. Portable cameras made it easier to film on the fly, and nightly news programs were widening their time slots from fifteen minutes to half an hour, and extending their coverage of the national scene.[358] Reading about southern policemen beating nonviolent protestors with billy clubs was disturbing enough for most Americans; watching it on TV was almost unbearable.

The black-and-white images of racial discord saturating living rooms were balanced by the joyful noise and motion of rock 'n' roll. Teenagers could tune in to local shows like *Milt Grant*, *Buddy Deane*, and *Clay Cole*, and by 1957, youngsters across the country could come home from school every day and watch *American Bandstand*.[359] Elvis finally won a seal of approval from the arbiter of respectable family entertainment, Ed Sullivan. On Sunday evenings at eight o'clock, the poker-faced, buttoned-up Sullivan hosted the most popular variety show on television.[360] Careful not to offend his viewing audience, Sullivan resisted booking Elvis until he started drawing huge ratings on other programs. Between September 1956 and January 1957, Elvis made three appearances on Sullivan, and more than 87 percent of American households with TV sets tuned in.[361] At the conclusion of the final show Sullivan assured the country that Elvis was "a real decent, fine boy," who was "thoroughly all right".

The Pulitzer Prize-winning journalist David Halberstam, who in the 1950s was a reporter in the Deep South, would deem Sullivan's approval of Presley as "a critical moment for the whole society: the old order had been challenged and had not held. New forces were at work, driven by technology. The young did not have to listen to their parents anymore."[362]

And the shockwaves were just beginning. Film clips of Presley's performances migrated over the Atlantic to Britain, and one day, in a suburb of Liverpool, a middle-aged widow, Mimi Smith, cast a disapproving eye on the teenage nephew she was raising. All the boy talked about was Elvis. Finally driven to distraction by her nephew's rhapsodizing, Smith said, "Elvis Presley's all very well, John. But I don't want him for breakfast, dinner and tea."[363]

By that summer, John was in a band with a fifteen-year-old who had taught himself to play and sing a wild, throaty version of Presley's "All Shook Up." His name was Paul McCartney.[364]

◆ ◆ ◆

Some twenty-three centuries before rock 'n' roll, Plato asserted that musical innovation threatened the order of the state.[365] In a visceral way among listeners, as an evolving, highly profitable industry, as a soundtrack of adolescent rebellion, and as the embodiment of African American efforts to assume their rightful place in society, rock 'n' roll did indeed upend the status quo.

But it was a different strain of music that took aim at the state: music that emerged from the coffee houses of Greenwich Village and Boston – a pastiche of traditional English, Irish, Scottish, and Welsh ballads;

American blues, spirituals, and country and western; the songs of Woody Guthrie and Pete Seeger, and the hyperkinetic lyricism of beat writers like Jack Kerouac and Allen Ginsberg. Unlike rock 'n' roll, much of this new folk oeuvre was sharply political and arose from two overriding concerns that Suze Rotolo – Bob Dylan's lover and sometime muse – recalled in her memoir: "A dislike of injustice and fear of the bomb."[366] By 1963, folksingers had become so closely linked with the civil rights movement that the organizers of the March on Washington for Jobs and Freedom invited some of the hottest young acts to play.

On August 28, as two or three hundred thousand people crowded around the reflecting pool and the Lincoln Memorial,[367] Joan Baez sang "Oh, Freedom"; Peter, Paul and Mary led a group singing one of their latest hits, Bob Dylan's "Blowin' in the Wind"; [368] and Dylan performed "Only a Pawn in Their Game," which had been inspired by the assassination of Medgar Evers.[369] On the evening of June 12, the NAACP leader had been gunned down outside his home in Jackson, Mississippi, just one day after President Kennedy had delivered a televised address stating that civil rights legislation was needed to confront "a moral issue...as old as the Scriptures and...as clear as the American Constitution."[370]

This was the essential message of the March on Washington, and television was there to cover it – the first mass demonstration ever broadcast to the nation.[371] Before Dr. King walked out to deliver the finest speech of the twentieth century, Rabbi Joachim Prinz, the spiritual leader of Temple B'nai Abraham in Newark, New Jersey, and president of the American Jewish Congress, stepped up to the microphone. In his slightly accented English, the urbane, fifty-nine-year-old refugee from Nazi Germany spoke of the "complete identification" Jews had "for the black people of America," which was "born of our own painful historic experience."[372] The history Prinz expanded on was his own. "When I was the rabbi of the Jewish community in Berlin under the Hitler regime I learned many things," he told the crowd, the most important of which was that "the most urgent...the most shameful and the most tragic problem is silence."[373]

The reference to Hitler underlines a not insignificant feature of Jews filling the ranks of the civil rights movement – that their activism coincided with their increasing knowledge about the Holocaust. When Prinz spoke there were four other rabbis on the platform, while out among the multitude there were thousands of Jews, some of them carrying signs with words from the Torah that appeared on the Liberty Bell:[374] "Proclaim Liberty throughout the land, and unto all the inhabitants thereof."[375] Nevertheless, why Jews, especially those with the social conscience to join the March, were not moved to end their silence on Soviet Jewry is a good question.

The suffering of Soviet Jews was reported in the press, though not with the immediacy of the horrors in the South. There was the pragmatic challenge of time: if you were committed to one movement, where would you find the opportunity to be committed to another? Then there was the lack of leadership from the organized community. And finally, one wonders if Jews were still growing accustomed to their newfound feeling of belonging – a feeling that was affirmed by their civil rights activism – and were unwilling to risk returning to being seen by gentiles solely as Jews and thereby confined to the outskirts of the American scene.

The destructiveness of silence was not unfamiliar to Rabbi Abraham Joshua Heschel. In 1938, the Gestapo deported him to Poland, and he made his way, via England, to the United States, where he eventually became a professor at the Jewish Theological Seminary in New York City. Heschel had escaped the Holocaust, but his mother had died in the Warsaw ghetto and his sister at Treblinka.[376] Heschel was an illustrious theologian who, like Dr. King, had a deep interest in the prophets. The two men met in January 1963 at the first "National Conference on Religion and Race."[377] They became fast friends, and two years later marched together from Selma to Montgomery, whereupon Heschel announced that he felt as if his legs were praying. Because of his untamed shock of white hair and white beard he was affectionately known to civil rights workers as "Father Abraham." To King, he was "my rabbi."[378]

Heschel would become the Jewish leader most closely associated with King, and his involvement with civil rights led him to wonder why the worsening situation of Soviet Jews was not on the top of the agenda of organized American Jewry.[379] In Moscow, Kiev, and Minsk, Jewish cemeteries had been shut down; there were few rabbis, fewer prayer books, and no matzo; and Soviet publications pumped out a steady stream of antisemitic propaganda.[380]

One week after the March on Washington, Heschel spoke to the Conservative movement's Synagogue Council of America,[381] accusing American Jews of the same apathy that they had demonstrated between 1940 and 1943, and warning the audience that it was up to American Jewry to prevent the twentieth century from entering "the annals of Jewish history as the century of physical and spiritual destruction!"[382]

More effective than scolding was the bureaucratic threat that Heschel leveled at leaders of the National Jewish Community Relations Advisory Council.[383] NJCRAC was the umbrella group for the Community Relations Councils that flourished in cities with large Jewish populations, and the local CRCs were perfectly positioned to dispense information on Soviet Jews and to raise money and oversee political activities.[384] Heschel told NJCRAC leaders that either they must found a separate entity to deal with Soviet Jewry, or Heschel would launch his own drive for such an agency.[385] Established Jewish organizations rebel at the mention of new organizations, since they divert resources from the fund-raising pipeline, but Heschel was serious about his threat and possessed enough prestige to carry it out.

Heschel also had a high-profile ally. At the convention of the United Synagogue of America, the representative body of Conservative synagogues, Martin Luther King publicly praised Heschel for upholding the tradition of the prophets by criticizing the failings of their own community. The following day, King traveled to Chicago to speak to the annual convention of the Reform movement, and during his speech King raised the hardships of Soviet Jewry.[386]

Heschel kept moving up the organizational food chain. He met with the Conference of Presidents of Major American Jewish Organizations, which, at the time, represented twenty-four groups, both secular and religious, and was as close to a collective voice as the community had.[387] After making his case to the Presidents Conference, bureaucratic dart throwing ensued, and no one could agree on what to do for Soviet Jews or who should do it.[388]

When in doubt, hold a bigger and longer meeting. On April 5 and 6, 1964, hundreds of representatives from two dozen Jewish organizations descended on the Willard Hotel in Washington, DC, and created the

American Jewish Conference on Soviet Jewry.[389] The AJCSJ was charged with coordinating efforts to assist Soviet Jews.[390] Supreme Court Justice Arthur Goldberg came to speak at the Willard, as did Senator Ribicoff.[391] George Meany, president of the AFL-CIO, and Dr. King sent along spirited messages of support; and the Kremlin was guaranteed to hear about it because reporters from *Pravda* and *Izvestia* were on hand.[392]

Decisions reached during the meeting would plague the Soviet Jewry movement for the next six years, although this was not yet evident as preparations got underway for a rally at Madison Square Garden, sponsored by the New York Conference on Soviet Jewry, an affiliate of the AJCSJ.[393]

Just before the rally, a letter appeared in the *New York Times*, signed by two Soviet Jews, the physicist Lev Landau, and the economist Evsei Liberman, both of whom had been awarded the Nobel Prize. In no uncertain terms the letter stated that antisemitism was "a non-existent problem" and beseeched Americans "not to participate in the provocative meeting, which will do nothing but harm mutual understanding between our countries."[394]

The answer to the letter came on the evening of June 3, 1965, when approximately twenty thousand people streamed into Madison Square Garden. Among the speakers were Senator Robert Kennedy and longtime civil rights leader A. Phillip Randolph; President Johnson also sent a message, a promising sign since a goal of the rally was to begin collecting one million signatures on a petition requesting LBJ to intervene with the Soviets on behalf of Jews in the USSR.[395] Especially adept at stirring up the assemblage was Morris B. Abram, a Georgia-born lawyer and Rhodes Scholar who had a minor role on the American legal team at the Nuremberg trials and came away convinced "that the veneer of civilization is thin, and that when it cracks…the Jew is the first victim."[396] Abram had been involved in civil rights since the late 1940s, when he spearheaded the legal campaign to roll back Georgia's "county unit rule," a favorite of segregationists since it gave undue weight to voters in rural counties. Abram won that fight in a 1963 Supreme Court decision that struck down the Georgia rule.[397] By that evening at the rally, Abram was practicing law in New York City, involved with the UN Humans Rights Commission, and president of the American Jewish Committee. In his speech he delighted twenty thousand hopeful souls by saying that until the Kremlin stopped discriminating against Jews or permitted them to leave, "we shall protest – we shall march – and we shall overcome."[398]

Three months after Madison Square Garden, the American Jewish Conference on Soviet Jewry staged an Eternal Light Vigil in Lafayette Park across the street from the White House,[399] the first major Soviet Jewry protest in Washington.[400] Ten thousand demonstrators from over one hundred cities participated.[401] The final act of the demonstration was a march to the Soviet Embassy, where a delegation – civil rights activist Bayard Rustin; folksinger, actor, and civil rights supporter Theodore Bikel; Rabbi Seymour Cohen of the AJCSJ; and Reverend John Cronin from the National Catholic Welfare Council – planned to drop off boxes of signed petitions.[402] When no one answered the door, Bikel bent down and slid a petition inside the embassy. CBS and ABC captured the scene for television, and the Voice of America broadcast news of the demonstration to Eastern Europe.[403]

In December, the AJCSJ released an official evaluation of its progress, stating that in less than two years it had conducted "a vigorous" effort to expose the maltreatment of Soviet Jews, and the resulting worldwide "condemnations" were so harsh that they could not be dismissed by the Kremlin.[404] Then, at its conference in April 1966, the AJCSJ declared that as long as Soviet Jewry suffered, the AJCSJ would not stop proclaiming its "indignation."[405]

Rabbi Abraham Joshua Heschel had heard enough. Nothing had changed on the ground for Soviet Jews, and he was losing patience with the inability of Jewish organizations to make any meaningful headway. Perhaps it was that Heschel had seen what was possible to achieve against bigotry when the Civil Rights Act of 1964 became law, and the next year when President Lyndon Johnson signed the Voting Rights Act. In addition, Soviet repression at its worst had recently been in the news. In February 1966, two Soviet writers, Andrei Sinyavsky and Yuli Daniel, had gone on trial in Moscow, charged with slandering the state for work they had published abroad.[406] But their real crime, according to London-based writer and Soviet émigré Jeanne Vronskaya, was that "being a Russian, Sinyavsky took a Jewish pseudonym while Daniel, who was Jewish, took a Russian pseudonym, and this pair – 'agents of international Zionism,' as they were called – challenged the whole Soviet system."[407] Shilling for the Kremlin, writers in the weekly *Literaturnaya Gazeta* said that the two men deserved to be executed.[408] After a four-day show trial that would have pleased Stalin, the writers were sentenced to hard labor – Sinyavsky for seven years, Daniel for five.[409]

And so on May 15, when Heschel arrived in Toronto, Canada, to address five hundred Conservative rabbis, a number of whom had studied under him at the Jewish Theological Seminary, he gave full vent to his frustration. "Over and above the noise of our banquets and testimonial dinners," he said, "I hear the cry of Russian Jews: 'The Jewish people forsakes us, the Jewish people has forgotten us.' Their dismay is mixed with disdain for those whose voice is loud but whose hearts are made of stone."[410]

With a barely controlled fury worthy of the prophet Amos, Heschel rebuked organized American Jewry for "spending [its] energy on dealing with marginal non-vital issues, rather than on the most important emergency of our day."[411]

Here was an unambiguous statement that Heschel had reordered his priorities; at that moment, he believed the civil rights movement should take a back seat to addressing the hardships borne by Soviet Jewry.

Heschel had witnessed blacks chip away at state-sanctioned racism not with a couple of circus-like events where notables made speeches and basked in the limelight, but through incessant demonstrations comprised of grassroots folks, an approach that fulfilled a dual purpose: it kept the discrimination in the news and recruited even more people to the cause. Heschel blamed the Conference of Presidents, saying that it had "consistently frustrated efforts of many of us to cry out our anguish over the plight of Russian Jewry."[412] As if it weren't embarrassing enough to be accused of neglecting your moral responsibilities by a former professor and an esteemed clergyman, Heschel summoned six million ghosts, his own family among them, and said, "I do not want future generations to spit on our graves saying: 'Here lies a community which, living in comfort and prosperity, kept silent while millions of their brothers were exposed to spiritual extermination.'"[413]

The five hundred rabbis were not done hearing about the Holocaust. It was brought up at another session by the writer Elie Wiesel, whose family had perished in the death camps and whose introduction to the American reading public was *Night*, his memoir of a childhood spent surviving Auschwitz and Buchenwald. Wiesel had recently traveled through the Soviet Union, writing a series of features for the Israeli newspaper *Yediot Aharonot*.[414] The Liaison Bureau, hoping to jumpstart compassion in the West for Soviet Jews with an eye toward bringing them to Israel, had been behind Wiesel's visit, going so far as to set up his interviews. By May, when Wiesel was speaking to the rabbis in Canada, he had almost completed transforming his articles into the book *The Jews of Silence*. A member of the Liaison Bureau recalled that someone at the American Jewish Committee had helped drum up interest in *The Jews of Silence*,[415] which was serialized in the *Saturday Evening Post*, beginning on November 19, 1966 and then published in the United States by Holt, Rinehart and Winston. Decades later, when historian Fred Lazin asked Wiesel about the role of the Liaison Bureau, he did not deny their influence but said that as a newspaper reporter he would have gone to the USSR anyway.[416]

At the session in Toronto, Wiesel reiterated a theme that was in his book: Soviet Jewry "had a sense of being thrown out of Jewish history" and felt as though they were "the stepchildren of the Jewish people."[417] Dipping into the haunted past, Wiesel suggested that American Jews were abandoning their Soviet brothers and sisters just as they had abandoned European Jewry to Hitler, and he blamed the community's organizations, saying that the only interests "some Jewish leaders" had in the issue was as a means of "self-aggrandizement and fund-raising" instead of waking up "the conscience of the world."[418]

The remarks of Heschel and Wiesel appeared in the *New York Times* and set off a firestorm. Rabbi Prinz, by then chairman of the Presidents Conference, denied the criticism, and Rabbi Israel Miller, head of the AJCSJ, lashed out at Heschel for his "vocal demagoguery," a charge that was repeated in Jewish newspapers from Maine to California. However, an editorial published in Washington, DC's *Jewish Week* opined that portraying Heschel's words so censoriously "sounded very much like the indignation of a disturbed conscience," a view not infrequently heard from American Jews who were members in good standing among the establishment groups.[419]

The issues identified in Toronto – and the two major stumbling blocks to setting up an effective movement – were an outgrowth of the 1964 meeting that created the American Jewish Conference on Soviet Jewry.

The first obstacle is discernible in an engaging book chapter on the history of the AJCSJ written by Albert D. Chernin, who worked as a coordinator for the organization.[420] Chernin writes that "for the AJCSJ, a top priority of the Soviet Jewry issue was to put it on the agenda of US-Soviet relations," and for that purpose AJCSJ representatives met with Presidents Johnson and Nixon, Vice President Hubert H. Humphrey, Secretaries of State Dean Rusk and William P. Rogers, National Security Adviser McGeorge Bundy, and a solid-gold array of special assistants, undersecretaries, and ambassadors.[421]

Despite these meetings with important people, no progress was made, and Chernin writes that though the officials were sympathetic, "there seemed to be some reticence in vigorously pressing the case officially through diplomatic channels. They seemed to acquiesce in the Soviet contention that the issue was an internal matter, not the business of the US government."[422]

Chernin does not mention how the AJCSJ could have possibly expected different results. After all, Eisenhower had raised Soviet antisemitism with Khrushchev, and Secretary of State Herter had done likewise with Soviet Foreign Minister Gromyko, and nothing had come of it.[423] President Kennedy had dispatched Justice Goldberg and Senators Javits and Ribicoff to talk about the subject with Ambassador Dobrynin, and before his trio of heavyweights went to the meeting JFK had his adviser on Soviet affairs and a former ambassador to Moscow, Llewellyn Thompson, explain to Dobrynin that the three men were speaking for the president. Still, during the discussion with the trio, Dobrynin denied the charge of Soviet antisemitism and issued a diplomat's version of a threat, saying that to raise the conditions of Soviet Jews would interfere in the harmonious relationship that the Kremlin sought to establish with America.[424]

The reason that the Kremlin was able to cut off the entreaties from the American Jewish Conference on Soviet Jewry was that at the founding meeting the two dozen participating organizations of the AJCSJ had to pledge "not to exacerbate cold war tensions."[425] Strategically, this was a grievous error, and the polar opposite of the strategy adopted by the civil rights movement, which, given its success, should have provided an easy template for the AJCSJ to follow. Far from avoiding the Cold War, civil rights advocates rarely passed up a chance to insert, generally to the discomfort of the White House, the cause of racial equality into the moral debate between the United States and the USSR.

In 1946, after Secretary of State James Byrne criticized the Kremlin for suppressing voting in the Balkans,[426] W. E. B. Du Bois, the first African American to earn a doctorate from Harvard and director of special research for the NAACP, went to Byrne's home state of South Carolina and told the Southern Negro Youth Conference that Byrnes ought to "establish in his own South Carolina something of that democracy which he has been so loudly preaching to Russia."[427]

This approach was often used, and administrations had to be concerned about it because they were competing with the Soviets for the hearts and minds of the international community, and the Kremlin was appealing to the Third World based on its hatred of European colonialism and its attendant racism.[428] The American rejoinder was that the Soviet Union was repressive, a response that would have been easier to swallow had Jim Crow not been in full flower.

This was the gist of the argument that the Justice Department made when it submitted its amicus curiae briefs in the school desegregation cases that were folded into *Brown v. Board of Education*. If the Supreme Court were to rule that segregation was in synch with democratic ideals, argued the Justice Department, then the United States would have no moral authority among the people of the world, most of whom were not white.[429]

Even the jazz trumpeter Louis "Satchmo" Armstrong spoke up, an opportunity that arose because popular culture was employed as a marketing tool for democracy, and the Voice of America jazz program hosted by Willis Conover had an enormous fan base in the USSR.[430] The radio broadcasts were augmented with government-sponsored tours by entertainers,[431] and among the most popular was Armstrong. With his big smile and gravelly voice it is easy to understand why the State Department considered him one of its best goodwill ambassadors. Also, unlike the popular African American actor and singer Paul Robeson, who was active in the fight against segregation beginning in the 1930s and later won the Stalin Peace Prize, Armstrong had no ties to the Communist Party and was seen as apolitical. Nevertheless, given what happened after the State Department scheduled a tour for Satchmo to the Soviet Union, some wide-awake official would have been wise to note that Armstrong had recorded the tune "(What Did I Do to Be So) Black and Blue," a song that laments the treatment of African Americans.[432]

In September 1957, as Armstrong's tour date approached, Orval Faubus, the governor of Arkansas, directed his National Guard to prevent the integration of Central High School in Little Rock. A federal judge ordered Faubus to stop interfering, and Faubus responded with a statement assailing the judge's authority. Before Eisenhower could intercede, Armstrong called off his trip to the Soviet Union, explaining, "The way they are treating my people in the South, the Government can go to hell,"[433] and then he summed up the racial situation by saying, "It's getting almost so bad a colored man hasn't got any country."[434]

In Moscow, radio commentators spoke of the "racist outrages" in Little Rock and "new acts of anti-Negro terror."[435] To counter the Soviet commentators and to frame racism as unpatriotic, Eisenhower delivered a televised speech from the Oval Office, informing the country that its enemies were "gloating over this incident," and warning that "it would be difficult to exaggerate the harm that is being done to the prestige and influence, and indeed to the safety, of our nation and the world."[436]

Beginning on the cold January day that he was sworn in as president, John Kennedy was exquisitely sensitive to the symbolism of race on the foreign stage. Television coverage was live from early morning until evening, and not only would the inauguration be witnessed by sixty million Americans, it was the first time the ceremony and festivities would be seen by a substantial audience overseas.[437] Shortly after taking the oath of office and delivering his address, JFK went to review the inaugural parade. As a detachment of Coast Guard Academy cadets marched by, Kennedy noticed that there were no blacks among them. Summoning one of his speechwriters, Richard Goodwin, Kennedy said, "Call the commandant and tell him I don't ever want to see that happen again."[438]

Kennedy would soon be complaining that the politics of race were "just in everything,"[439] a justifiable complaint from a president who had to wage the Cold War while the world watched civil rights advocates being attacked and even saw a journalist from the *London Daily Sketch* die during a riot in the fall of 1962, when James Meredith integrated the University of Mississippi.[440]

Meredith was not surprised by the lethal drama: "I considered myself engaged in a war from Day One," Meredith recalled on the fortieth anniversary of his walk across the campus to register. "And my objective was to force the federal government…into a position where they would have to use the United States military force to enforce my rights as a citizen."[441]

Forcing the hand of the government had been the hallmark of modern civil rights advocacy ever since A. Phillip Randolph told FDR that he would bring one hundred thousand protestors to the capital unless the president did away with discrimination in defense plants. In June 1963, when JFK tried to dissuade Randolph from planning the March on Washington, Randolph again said no.[442] And when Kennedy encouraged Dr. King to move gradually, King answered him in his speech to over two hundred thousand marchers and the millions watching on television, emphasizing the "fierce urgency of now," and rejecting JFK's suggested pace by saying that this was not the time "to take the tranquilizing drug of gradualism."[443]

By this juncture organized American Jewry should have seen that launching a relentless public relations campaign against Soviet antisemitism had the potential to ameliorate the Kremlin's behavior. Even though the Soviet government had greater control of the information that breached its borders, that control was not total, and Soviet leaders were vulnerable to being embarrassed – maybe even more so than their American counterparts – because the Kremlin was still failing to provide the majority of its citizens anything close to the standard of living that middle-class Americans enjoyed. It should also have been clear to the organized American Jewish community that if the US government was reluctant to take a tougher position on Soviet Jewry with the Kremlin, then the community would have to become as publicly critical as civil rights advocates were with the White House and Congress. If American leaders were embarrassed, so be it. The civil rights movement had shown that elected officials could be spurred into action by embarrassment.

In one sense, the disinclination of the American Jewish Conference on Soviet Jewry to employ the tactics of the civil rights movement – and the impetus for extracting the promise that its twenty-four member organizations would not interfere in the Cold War and make trouble for political leaders – was consistent with a centuries-old precedent, when diaspora Jews lived as a minority under kings whose munificence they depended on to survive: the Talmudic principle of *dina de-malkhuta dina* – the law of the land is the law – dates to the third century in Babylonia and promoted avoiding conflicts with the state.[444]

Principally, however, the reluctance of the AJCSJ was a consequence of the contentious relations among its membership. The paranoid antisemitic fiction that Jews control the world was most assuredly not invented by someone acquainted with the alphabet soup of Jewish communal organizations. These groups are frequently at odds with each other over philosophy, turf, and strategy, and suffer ego clashes among the honorary leaders and the professionals who handle the operations.[445] In 1959, when Khrushchev accepted Eisenhower's invitation to a summit, *Newsweek* reported that the organized American Jewish community was so divided that it would be difficult for the community to select representatives to meet with the general secretary.[446] Merely creating an umbrella organization in 1963 did not alchemize discord into harmony.

Fueling the differences among the established communal groups was that they were in a competition for funds, because their budgets were furnished from the same philanthropic pockets – the American Jewish community. Traditionally, the bulk of the money budgeted for overseas needs had gone to Eastern European Jews. That stopped in 1948 when the fiscal woes besetting the Israelis started consuming a growing percentage of charitable dollars. Yet when Heschel threatened to see to it that an agency dedicated to Soviet Jews would be created, the establishment knew that it had to act and formed the AJCSJ. They dealt with their own budgetary demands by not allocating any money to the AJCSJ for hiring staff or renting office space and by circumscribing its latitude in the coordination of activities.[447]

Their lack of financial commitment did not equal lack of concern; it was an outgrowth of their institutional past. Organized American Jewry produced assistance through established procedures of harvesting donations and doling out funds. Soviet Jewry was uncharted territory, demanding not simply money but an ongoing political program, and this was a new challenge to the establishment. Now, the classical approach just would not do. What was needed was rock 'n' roll. And that music was composed through individual initiative and the efflorescence of the grassroots.

Act V: O Pioneers

In the beginning, it was lonely work, with days stretching into nights. There was William Korey, sitting at his desk in a pool of light, methodically reading through stacks of books.

Korey had been with one of the first army units to enter Berlin in 1945, and he was soon raising funds to help displaced Jews get to Palestine. Returning from the war, Korey became a Russian history professor at the City College of New York, but when McCarthyism infected the campuses of universities, Korey left to head the Illinois-Missouri chapter of the Anti-Defamation League. One day, late in 1959, Korey received a phone call from Philip Klutznick, a Chicago real estate developer and president of B'nai B'rith, who had been named a delegate to the United Nations by President Eisenhower. Klutznick was familiar with Korey's interest in Soviet Jewry and the issue of freedom of movement. He was calling to offer Korey the chance to pursue his interests as the director of the United Nations Office of B'nai B'rith.[448]

Korey accepted, moved to Washington, DC, and started producing detailed reports that connected emigration to human rights.[449] The right to leave a country had roots in ancient Greece, where Socrates judged it to be an "attribute of personal liberty." The first legal charter to enumerate the right was the Magna Carta in 1215, which saw it as inherent in "natural law." The French Constitution of 1791 seconded that position, and an 1868 act by Congress guaranteed Americans that expatriation was "indispensable to the enjoyment of the rights of life, liberty, and the pursuit of happiness." Moreover, the United Nations' own Universal Declaration of Human Rights, passed by the General Assembly in 1948, stated: "Everyone has the right to leave any country, including his own, and to return to his country."[450] This enumerated freedom does much to explain why the Soviet Union refused to ratify the Universal Declaration.[451]

Korey's work was used in a UN study of discrimination against people seeking to leave their homelands. Overseen by Judge José D. Inglés, a highly respected legal expert from the Philippines, the 115-page report was delivered in 1963.[452] It was, according to Korey, "a landmark in the evolution of human freedom," because it so ably demonstrated that "next to the right of life, the right to leave one's country is probably the most important of human rights."[453]

By 1963, the Berlin Wall stood as a stark assertion of the Kremlin's attitude toward the right of citizens to vote with their feet. Nonetheless, as with much that occurred during the days that kindled the American movement to free Soviet Jewry, it was impossible at that point to see the chinks in the monolithic armor of the Soviet Union, impossible to gauge its vulnerability to global embarrassment, impossible to predict that the Kremlin would sign the Helsinki Final Act on August 1, 1975, and that the agreement, which contained a section mentioning freedom of movement, would spark a long-repressed desire for democracy throughout Eastern Europe and bring about the end of the Cold War.

◆ ◆ ◆

As Korey pressed on with his research and writing, Rabbi Pinchas Mordechai Teitz, a Latvian-born Orthodox leader in Elizabeth, New Jersey, packed his bags for the first of his twenty-two trips to the Soviet Union. In 1953, Rabbi Teitz became a celebrity of sorts when he began hosting "The Talmudic Seminar of the Air," a weekly radio program in New York that drew two hundred thousand listeners and stayed on the air until 1989.[454] Rabbi Teitz had received the approval of the Kremlin to travel through the Soviet Union to teach Judaism, but with the proviso that he not publicize his mission. Rabbi Teitz agreed and remained opposed to demonstrations attacking the Kremlin, but he was not averse to bringing along kosher salamis to distribute to his students.[455]

His salami supplier was his close friend Rabbi David H. Hill, who owned a delicatessen business on Rivington Street on the Lower East Side. In 1961, Hill had been elected president of the National Council of Young Israel, a modern Orthodox movement founded in the United States right before World War I.[456] One of the first people Hill spoke with about Soviet Jewry was Israeli foreign minister Golda Meir, who told him that whatever actions were taken to help the Jews in Russia, the Israeli government could not jeopardize its relations with the Kremlin by being publicly involved. That did not stop the Liaison Bureau from dispatching Meir Rosenne, a diplomat with a doctorate from the Sorbonne, to America to help garner public support for Soviet Jewry.[457] Hill let Rosenne operate out of his office on Rivington Street, but by then Hill was trying to find ways to assist Soviet Jews without adding to their burden.

From an Israeli who had traveled extensively in the USSR, Hill had a list of names and addresses of Jews, and he began shipping goods to them – fine clothes, leather gloves, chocolates, anything that could bring a high rate of exchange on the black market, the proceeds of which were used to finance underground Jewish schools. Hill discovered that so many American Jews were willing to pay for the goods that he ran out of names. Seeking a new list, Hill went to Crown Heights, Brooklyn, to speak with the Lubavitcher Rebbe, Rabbi Menachem Mendel Schneerson, leader of the worldwide network of Lubavitch Hasidim. Though it was not widely known, the Lubavitchers had been running an underground operation inside the USSR since the 1920s. They smuggled in money and smuggled out information and people, and preserved Jewish life by covertly supporting education, prayer houses, and even mikvahs.[458]

Seated in the rebbe's book-lined study, Hill spoke to him in Yiddish. Originally from the Ukraine, Schneerson had been a brilliant student as a young man, studying mathematics and science at the University of Berlin and the Sorbonne. In 1941 he had to hide from the Nazis for several days before escaping Germany and emigrating to the United States.[459]

Taking note of Hill's accent, Schneerson asked him where he had been born. When Hill answered, "Latvia," the rebbe spoke of a family member who had been rescued by Mordechai Dubin, a prominent member of the Latvian parliament. [460]

Hill said, "I'm related to Dubin."

The rebbe eyed Hill. Then he said, "I can trust you. What do you really want of me?"

Hill replied that he wanted more contacts inside the Soviet Union and that he was hoping to send in people to teach Jewish history and Torah.

Secrecy was all that protected the rebbe's network, all that stood between the Lubavitchers in the Soviet Union and the hostility of the Kremlin. Therefore, while the rebbe promised Hill that he would open the door of his community, he added, "I have one condition – no publicity."[461]

The rebbe kept his word, and for the next thirty years Hill never told anyone how he reached the far-flung Jewish communities with his teachers. This tactic would contribute to the return to Judaism inside the Soviet Union, and this *ba'alei teshuva* movement, as it would become known, would be a palliative to the Kremlin's crusade to stamp out Jewishness and an inspiration to refuseniks who now had a religious context for their desire to leave.[462]

◆ ◆ ◆

Hill was so pleased with the results of his meeting with Rabbi Schneerson that he decided to speak with the Satmar Rebbe, Rabbi Yoel Teitelbaum. The rabbi had been saved from the Nazis when he was ransomed from the Bergen-Belsen concentration camp and, after a brief stay in Jerusalem, relocated to Williamsburg, Brooklyn.[463] Hill thought Rabbi Teitelbaum might join in his project of shipping goods to the Soviet Union because there were still Satmar Hasidim living in the Carpathian Mountain region of the USSR.

Rabbi Teitelbaum said that he would help with the goods, and Hill asked him if he had any other suggestions.

The Satmar Hasidim are well known for their opposition to secular culture, and their resulting social isolation, and so Hill was stunned when the Satmar Rebbe replied, "This cannot be a Jewish movement. No. It cannot. We tried that with the Nazis. You must find Catholics and Republicans and Democrats and Protestants and what have you. This must be an American movement."

Hill brought that advice to the Presidents Conference. "I told them, 'I have a message from the Satmar Rebbe,' and everyone in the room looked at me like I had horns on my head. But I repeated the rebbe's advice, and that was one reason why when we planned the Eternal Light Vigil in Washington we invited Christian clergymen."[464]

◆ ◆ ◆

In Cleveland, Ohio, as Alan Freed was spreading the gospel of rock 'n' roll, Dr. Louis Rosenblum was helping to found Beth Israel, a small Reform congregation. An infantryman who was awarded the Bronze Star for his actions at the Battle of Okinawa, Rosenblum returned from the Pacific to complete a doctorate in organic chemistry at Ohio State University, and by 1961 he was married and employed as a research manager at NASA.[465]

Beth Israel expanded through a merger with the West Side Jewish Center, and Rosenblum, along with a handful of members, began gathering to discuss the Holocaust. The group, Rosenblum recalled, was distressed by the "angry anguished essay, 'Bankrupt,'" which was written by Chaim Greenberg and appeared in *Yiddishe Kemfer* in February 1943. In "Bankrupt," Greenberg attacks American Jewish organizations for not renouncing their "normal behavior of in-fighting and advantage-seeking" to help the Jews of Europe.[466]

Rabbi Daniel Litt of Beth Israel had encouraged his congregants to extend themselves to Jews beyond Cleveland, and the logical focus for Rosenblum and the other group members, steeped as they now were in the history of the Holocaust, was Soviet Jews, since they were the second largest Jewish community in the world and their predicament eerily resembled the situation of European Jewry as the Nazis began to solidify their hold on the Continent. In October 1963, after ascertaining that almost nothing was being done for Jews in the USSR, the Beth Israel group founded the Cleveland Committee on Soviet Anti-Semitism.[467]

Rabbi Litt and committee member Herb Caron, a psychologist, intuitively grasped the advice the Satmar Rebbe had given David Hill: any movement to assist Soviet Jews had to be an American undertaking, and Litt and Caron reached across boundaries of religion and race to assemble a board. The honorary chairman was Cleveland mayor Ralph Locher, and he was joined by Msgr. Lawrence Cahill, president of St. Johns College;

Bruce Whittemore, director of the Cleveland Area Church Federation; Leo Jackson, an African American who sat on the Cleveland City Council; and Reform rabbi Philip Horowitz.[468]

A month later, the committee released its first publication, *Soviet Terror against Jews: How Cleveland Initiated an Interfaith Protest*, and from that moment the committee was off and running, doing everything that volunteers with little time and less money could do to publicize the grim circumstances of Soviet Jews. They advertised in newspapers, produced another publication appealing directly to Soviet leaders with a signed petition, published a newsletter, and developed a substantial mailing list with names from people across the United States and in Europe who contacted the committee requesting information and seeking advice.[469]

In the spring of 1964, Rosenblum was encouraged when he heard that an American Conference on Soviet Jewry was being organized in Washington.[470] Rosenblum, along with Litt and Caron, secured delegate credentials, and off they went to the Willard Hotel, where they promptly convinced other delegates to support their proposed resolution to create and adequately fund a national group dedicated to Soviet Jewry.[471]

"The delegates we spoke with were ready to help," Rosenblum says. "They probably thought here are these Jews from Cleveland – not a city one associates with a big, active Jewish community – and they're helping. We should help, too."[472]

On the last day of the conference, the resolution was offered from the floor, but Isaiah Minkoff, the executive vice president of the National Jewish Community Relations Advisory Council, who was chairing the meeting, did not like it. An immigrant from Poland and a former yeshiva student, Minkoff was the ultimate organization man of American Jewry, and he had no tolerance for grassroots movements that challenged the establishment.[473]

Minkoff admonished "these unspeakable Bundists from Cleveland, who circulated among the delegates this destructive resolution."[474]

Delegates became angry. Someone shouted up from the floor, "Is this a democratic meeting or not?" When Minkoff saw that he might have a mutiny on his hands, he allowed the resolution to be offered, and it was passed by an overwhelming vote.[475]

Minkoff and the establishment outmaneuvered the grassroots by creating a Soviet Jewry organization without a budget. For Rosenblum, it was a rerun of the failure Greenberg had written of in his 1943 essay, "Bankrupt." He, Caron, and Litt returned home intent on redoubling their efforts and transforming their organization into a more potent force.[476] They changed the name to the Cleveland Council on Soviet Anti-Semitism, incorporated as a nonprofit in Ohio, and recruited a dynamic chairman of the board, Abe Silverstein, a prominent aerospace engineer and director of the NASA research center where Rosenblum worked.[477]

The membership of the council, and its visibility, was greatly enhanced by a rally to protest Soviet antisemitism held on March 5, 1965, at Cleveland Heights High School. The local Jewish federation contributed money, and over twenty-two hundred people wedged into the auditorium, with others lining the hallways and listening to the speeches over the portable speakers that had been set up. Well-known Protestant and Catholic clergy, and local, county, and state officials all joined in with expressions of support and concern.[478]

Suddenly, Rosenblum was receiving phone calls from representatives of the Israelis' Liaison Bureau. Both Meir Rosenne and Nehemiah Levanon furnished Rosenblum with documentation of Soviet Jewish suffering, and the information was incorporated into the council's literature and presentations.[479] By May, the Cleveland Council was passing out a petition of concern for Soviet Jews to the Moiseyev Folk Dancers, a Soviet dance company touring the United States. Since Soviet performers in America traveled with KGB agents, the council knew word of its petition would be transmitted to the Kremlin. The entire process was staged to generate maximum press attention. Thirty or forty volunteers from the council stationed themselves outside the theater and the incoming audience was presented with printed material about Soviet Jews and a copy of the petition. After the performance, a half dozen council representatives went backstage and gave a petition to the dance company.[480]

The Cleveland Council on Soviet Anti-Semitism employed this tactic repeatedly. These were local protests, however, and Lou Rosenblum was convinced that if Soviet Jews were ever to be saved, the protests had to be nationwide. That necessitated an aggressive organizing campaign, and though the American Jewish establishment was positioned to lead the charge, it was not inclined in that direction. The Israelis had assisted the Cleveland Council with information, but Rosenblum could see that the Liaison Bureau was backing the American Conference on Soviet Jewry, most likely, he suspected, because the Israeli government wanted to oversee the rescue of Jews in the USSR, and did not want Americans too involved.[481]

Rosenblum wondered if the Cleveland Council could build a national network of like-minded activists. It was a long shot, but there was really no other alternative. Rosenblum was often on the road for NASA, and so whenever possible he stopped to see if there was any action on Soviet Jewry down among the grassroots.[482]

◆ ◆ ◆

Up in Washington Heights, a tall, thirty-seven-year-old Englishman with a neatly clipped Van Dyke beard was striding through the chill of an early spring day in 1964 with the sort of fur wedge cap on his head that was commonly seen on the streets of Moscow. The man's name was Jacob Birnbaum; he had arrived in the United States the year before and taken up residence in a room rented from the chief librarian at Yeshiva University. If Birnbaum did not have the manic gleam of the proselytizer in his eyes, then he should have, because he was hurrying to the dorms at Yeshiva to inform the students that they must stand up and save Soviet Jewry.[483]

Birnbaum was no stranger to Jewish intellectual and political ferment. His father, Solomon, was a leading Yiddish scholar, and his grandfather, Nathan, was a famed speaker, thinker, and writer, who coined the term "Zionism" in 1885[484] and who was elected secretary general of the first Zionist congress in Basel, Switzerland, in 1897.[485] As a child, Jacob had lived in Hamburg, Germany, until Nazis beat his father in the street and Jacob was set upon by German boys who assaulted him and crammed his mouth full of dirt.[486] The family fled to London, where during the war Jacob's father worked in the Uncommon Languages Department of the government censor's office, which gave him access to the "desperate letters" written by European Jews. Years later, Jacob remembered that as he watched his father sink into despair because he was unable to do anything about the unfolding tragedies in those letters, his father's "helplessness seared itself into my soul."[487] In the 1950s, after Jacob earned a degree in history from London University, he worked with teenage survivors in England and Ireland grappling with the psychological aftermath of the Holocaust. For a while he tried to assist Algerian Jewish immigrants, and then he was the director of the Manchester Jewish community council, but when he landed in America he was preoccupied with a single goal: the rescue of Soviet Jews.[488]

Birnbaum had been appalled by the dog-and-pony show at the Willard Hotel that produced the American Jewish Conference on Soviet Jewry – a "toothless, fumbling group" was how he saw it.[489] And as he spoke to the students at Yeshiva, and moved on to Columbia University, the Jewish Theological Seminary, and Queens College, he told the students that their grandparents and parents had kept silent while the Nazis prepared to destroy European Jewry and now they must not repeat that mistake – they must not remain silent.[490]

Aware of what had been transpiring among the youth in the United States, Birnbaum did not base his appeal solely on the memory of the six million. The movement he envisioned was set squarely in the American idiom of the moral immediacy and nonviolent protest of the civil rights movement, and this was made plain on the leaflet that announced the first meeting of the College Students' Struggle for Soviet Jewry: "Just as we, as human beings and as Jews, are conscious of the wrongs suffered by the Negro and we fight for his betterment, so must we come to feel in ourselves the silent, strangulated pain of so many of our Russian brethren."[491]

Birnbaum was plugging into the percolating culture of protest. A future study of his organization would reveal that 28 percent of the membership had been involved in the civil rights movement, 26 percent had joined in some variety of activism on college campuses, and over half would participate in antiwar activities.[492]

One of the students Birnbaum brought onboard was Glenn Richter, a lanky teenager with thick-rimmed glasses whose sartorial style was marked by an olive-green trench coat and peddler's cap and who could spout humorous patter with the ease of a Borscht Belt comic.[493] Richter had been raised in a Conservative Jewish family in Queens, and his uncle,

Rabbi Paul Teicher, had gone down to Birmingham to work with black ministers. In 1963, as Richter completed his freshman year at Queens College, he had wanted to sign on with the Freedom Riders (a choice made by another student at his school, Andrew Goodman, who would be murdered in Mississippi), but Richter decided that he was too young to go into the Deep South, so he settled for volunteering at the New York City office of the Student Nonviolent Coordinating Committee. SNCC – pronounced "Snick" – was an outgrowth of the 1960 student sit-ins for integration in Greensboro, North Carolina, and it was a mainstream civil rights group until 1965, when it slid over to the radical Left.[494]

When Birnbaum invited Richter to his organizational meeting on the campus of Columbia University, Richter was eager to go. Not only was Richter a political science major attracted to social justice movements, he had recently read Moshe Decter's article "The Status of the Jews in the Soviet Union" in *Foreign Affairs*, a piece that Decter had written with research from the Liaison Bureau.[495]

At Columbia, two hundred young men and women gathered in the graduate students' lounge of Philosophy Hall. The feeling, Birnbaum recalled, was "electric," with students promising that they would not be silent in the face of Jewish suffering and declaring that they wanted to act now.[496] Impatience is among the virtues of grassroots protest movements, and Birnbaum harnessed it by proposing a demonstration outside the Soviet mission to the United Nations on May 1 – May Day, International Workers' Day, a holiday in the USSR.[497]

"We ran around New York City handing out flyers at colleges," said Richter. "We worked in Jacob's room writing press releases and signs, calling Hillel Houses and Jewish youth groups. A lot of us were interested in civil rights, but now we felt that if we could act on behalf of others, then we could act on behalf of our own people."[498]

Birnbaum had a rubber stamp made that said, "Students Struggle for Soviet Jewry," but Richter told him that "Student Struggle for Soviet Jewry" sounded better, and when Birnbaum agreed, Richter completed the renaming by surgically removing the final "s" with a razor.[499]

Nearly one thousand marchers spent four hours walking outside the Soviet UN mission on East 67th Street between Lexington and Park

Avenues, carrying signs in English, Russian, and Hebrew: "Open Up Jewish Houses of Worship"; "Why No Matzos?"; "We Cannot Keep Silent Any Longer."[500] The plan had been to march in silence to underscore the silence encasing Soviet Jewry,[501] but there was singing, notably the Hebrew song *"Ani Ma'amin"* (I believe), which was often heard from the columns of Jews en route to the gas chambers.[502]

A *New York Times* reporter captured the Soviet response to the rally, and it anticipated the Kremlin's underestimation of the outrage its repression of Soviet Jewry would engender in the United States: "For the most part, Soviet officials and employees ignored the demonstration. A young boy walking past with his father asked in Russian, "What is it all about?" The father replied, also in Russian, "It's a First of May celebration.""[503]

In retrospect one of the most important results of the May Day rally was that local congressman Leonard Farbstein, who marched outside the Soviet mission with the sign "Let My People Pray," bought an ad in the *Daily News* for his reelection campaign in which he asked voters to "Support Congressman Farbstein's Fight Against Soviet Anti-Semitism."[504]

Here was a congressional candidate promoting Soviet Jewry as an issue worthy of a campaign for national office. Although there was nothing earth-shaking about a Jewish congressman using a Jewish cause to appeal to Jewish constituents, it was a start at inserting Soviet Jews into electoral politics.

The members of Student Struggle for Soviet Jewry (SSSJ) – referred to in conversation as "Triple-S J" – were pleased with the coverage of the rally and began planning a follow-up.[505] However, not everyone was so enamored of the demonstration, and the mixed reviews mirrored the divisions in the American Jewish community. Birnbaum heard from some irate parents who accused him of exposing their sons and daughters to danger; the complaints were tempered by other parents who expressed their gratitude to Birnbaum for removing their children from the violence that increasingly surrounded the civil rights movement and turning them toward the needs of other Jews.[506] A more official disapproval was levied at SSSJ member Jimmy Torczyner, a student at Yeshiva University who was suspended by the school for efforts on behalf of Soviet Jewry. In contrast, the activism of another member, Arthur Green, a rabbinical student at the Jewish Theological Seminary, was supported by JTS professor Rabbi Heschel.[507]

Believing that the attention in the press might make the Student Struggle more appealing to the leaders of the Jewish establishment, Birnbaum went to speak with the chairman of the steering committee of the American Conference on Soviet Jewry. Birnbaum proposed mailing information packets to Jewish summer camps, but since SSSJ relied on three-dollar membership dues and passing the hat to survive, Birnbaum asked the chairman if the conference would share the costs. The chairman responded by accusing Birnbaum of contacting him simply to dig up financing. It would not be the last time SSSJ was rejected by the establishment.[508]

In June, SSSJ was back outside the Soviet mission to the United Nations, leading a service with Jewish, Catholic, and Protestant clergy that included a week of prayer and fasting.[509] Two months later, Birnbaum led his volunteers to the Democratic National Convention in Atlantic City, New Jersey. SSSJ hoped to convince Democrats to insert a Soviet Jewry plank in their platform.[510] On the balmy Tuesday evening of August 25, the group gathered on the Boardwalk and prayed for the deliverance of Soviet Jews, concluding their prayers with the sounding of the shofar.[511] A position on Soviet Jews was not adopted, but Attorney General Robert Kennedy did stand on top of a car and speak out on the issue, and Birnbaum got a preview of the divisive black militancy that would afflict the civil rights establishment.

The 1964 Democratic Convention is remembered for two parallel dramas: Bobby Kennedy memorializing his slain brother in an emotional speech to the delegates, and Fannie Lou Hamer, a black forty-six-year-old former sharecropper and one of the top organizers at SNCC, asking the Convention Credentials Committee to seat the interracial Mississippi Freedom Democratic Party in place of the official Mississippi state delegation, which was all white and pro-segregation. President Johnson had no intention of dividing Democrats in the South before the election, and he cut a deal that offered the Mississippi Freedom delegates guest status and two nonvoting seats in the official state delegation. Furious, they refused.[512]

Stokely Carmichael, a devoted activist from SNCC, was a member of the Mississippi Freedom Democrats. Carmichael was disgusted by what he saw in Atlantic City. Like the young activists in the Student Struggle for Soviet Jewry, he was losing his faith in the establishment to bring about change; the slow, steady course of nonviolent integration had failed to win blacks their fair share of the American dream. During the next two years Carmichael would become more militant, coining the phrase "Black Power," supplanting the less radical John Lewis as the chairman of SNCC, and drumming out the white members of the organization.[513]

That process, according to Jacob Birnbaum, was underway as Carmichael stood on the Boardwalk that August and spoke into a portable microphone, advocating for seating the Mississippi Freedom delegation. Birnbaum was in the crowd listening, and when Carmichael finished, Birnbaum walked over, introduced himself, and told Carmichael that he agreed with what he had said. Nodding, Carmichael turned to walk away, and Birnbaum asked him if he might use the microphone to speak about Soviet Jewry.[514]

"No," Carmichael said. "This is a black microphone. Not a white one."[515]

Not infrequently, coincidence is the handmaiden of history, and no cultural happenstance would have a greater effect on the American movement to free Soviet Jews than the rising black militancy. This shift would validate the practice of identity politics, especially among the youth culture of protest, and, in the smoldering aftermath of urban riots and the antisemitic rhetoric during the New York City teacher's strike, it would separate much of the American Jewish community from the civil rights movement, leaving the community free to seek social justice for their own, and turning them toward the Soviet Union.

Over the next few years, the Student Struggle was relentless. Two months after the Democratic Convention, SSSJ arranged a rally on the Lower East Side of Manhattan that drew over two thousand protestors; both US senators from New York; a statement from New York Senate hopeful Bobby Kennedy; and Myer Feldman, special counsel to President Johnson, who brought along a message from LBJ that encouraged the assembled to continue their protests against the Kremlin's policies.[516] SSSJ disseminated a constant flow of information about the travails of Soviet Jews.

Jacob Birnbaum even prevailed upon the folk-singing rabbi Shlomo Carlebach to compose an anthem for the movement, an idea borrowed from the civil rights protestors singing "We Shall Overcome." Birnbaum asked Carlebach to use the phrase "*Am Yisrael chai*" (the Jewish people live). In 1948, when Golda had landed in Moscow, Russian Jews had greeted her with those words, and Carlebach set them to music.[517] The song, which would be sung by American Soviet Jewry activists and Jewish refuseniks in the USSR, was unveiled during the Jericho March in New York City on April 4, 1965,[518] when three thousand protestors marched around the Soviet mission and seven shofars were sounded seven times to recall how the walls were toppled at the Battle of Jericho.[519] In May, SSSJ brought its shofar sounding to the street outside the Soviet embassy in Washington, DC. Later, on the White House lawn, Birnbaum presented LBJ with an SSSJ lapel pin.[520] By the following spring, SSSJ returned to the Soviet mission in Manhattan, this time with fifteen thousand marchers.[521]

Beyond the demonstrations was the ongoing recruitment of new volunteers. Glenn Richter, who in 1966 would leave NYU Law School to work as SSSJ's national coordinator for the next quarter-century, recalled that one day a young member, Larry Fetterman, volunteered to travel to college campuses around the country to spread the word about Soviet Jewry. Richter told Fetterman that SSSJ did not have much money to give him.[522] "We may be Jews," Richter liked to say, "but we're not Rothschilds."[523] Fetterman, whom Richter remembered as "a gentle soul with a pony tail," was not worried about funding, and left on his trip, camping out, sleeping in barns, or crashing on borrowed beds or couches in dorms or student apartments.[524]

One youngster that Richter enlisted was Yossi Klein Halevi. They met one afternoon in 1965 in an area of Borough Park that was "populated mostly by Orthodox Holocaust survivors."[525] Richter was on a corner passing out leaflets and imploring the passersby to help save Soviet Jews. Halevi's father was a survivor, and the twelve-year-old eagerly accepted the leaflets Richter gave him, along with a tongue-in-cheek appointment as "Borough Park elementary school chairman of SSSJ."[526]

By his own account, Halevi would become an obsessive activist, first at SSSJ and then at the more radical Jewish Defense League. After his youthful tour in street politics, Halevi would go on to a distinguished career as a journalist and author, and in 2004 he wrote a retrospective of SSSJ that succinctly identified the strategic principles driving Jacob Birnbaum, a man whom Halevi would come to admire for his selflessness and conviction.

Birnbaum planned to use the grassroots to rouse American Jews and pressure "the establishment to transform the Conference on Soviet Jewry into an effective organization."[527] This was crucial because Birnbaum understood that only the establishment possessed the membership and finances to carry on an extended national campaign. In a tactic employed by the civil rights activists against the US government, Birnbaum was intent on humiliating "the Soviet Union by exposing its false pretensions as a model society," all the while promoting the White House and Congress as protectors of Soviet Jews. In this way, Birnbaum hoped to insert their plight into the US-USSR competition for hearts and minds, which would elevate the issue to a battle in the Cold War. And finally, since Birnbaum felt that the battle would drag on for years, the movement had to offer encouragement and succor to Soviet Jews.[528]

This vision would come to pass, but not solely through the efforts of SSSJ. The visions of William Korey, David Hill, Lou Rosenblum, and many others would energize and shape the American movement to free Soviet Jewry. Nevertheless, despite all the public hoopla, by the end of 1966 American Jews had not risen up en masse for Soviet Jewry. In November, the *Saturday Evening Post* ran an excerpt from Wiesel's *The Jews of Silence*, and hailed the excerpt on its cover as "a major report from Russia."[529] Over the next year, however, the magazine did not publish a single letter to the editor about the excerpt, presumably because the editor received none. In December, Wiesel's book was published; it was respectfully reviewed and "highly recommended" by the *Library Journal*,[530] but the book was not a best seller. All the same, something – a free-floating sense that the hardships of Soviet Jews were not irrelevant to their prosperous coreligionists across the ocean – was alive below the contented surface of the American Jewish community. *The Fixer*, a novel by Bernard Malamud, popped onto the *New York Times* best-seller list on October 2, 1966,[531] where it stayed for the next six months, and in 1967 won the author a National Book Award and Pulitzer Prize.[532] *The Fixer* was based on the case of Mendel Beilis, the Jewish superintendent of a Kiev brick factory who was falsely accused and imprisoned in 1911 for the murder of a Christian boy.[533] American indignation over the treatment of Beilis would contribute to the House of Representatives abrogating the Commercial Treaty of 1832 with the Russians.

Still, some unifying component was absent that would persuade American Jews that their fate was inseparable from Jews in the USSR. Then in mid-May 1967, Egyptian President Gamel Abdel Nasser ordered the UN observers out of Gaza and Sharm el-Sheikh and closed the Straits of Tiran in apparent preparation for an attack on Israel. Thus began what the Israelis referred to as *ha-hamtana* (the waiting), and as the American Jewish leader Morris Abram observed, it was this period that revived the "fearful collective unconscious" of Jews in the United States and focused them not only on the survival of Israel but, in not too long a time, on the rescue of Soviet Jewry.[534]

CHAPTER 5

GOODBYE, KISHINEV

Beginning in the autumn of 2007, the Jewish world celebrated the fortieth anniversary of the Soviet Jewry movement. In the United States forums and receptions were held in cities across the country, and Friday, December 7, during Chanukah, was observed in synagogues as Soviet Jewry Shabbat. In Israel far more was made of the anniversary: it was marked by the Knesset; a commemorative postage stamp; educational programs for children, new immigrants, and soldiers; academic conferences; radio and TV broadcasts;[1] and kicking it all off, on October 30, a magnificent exhibit, "Jews of Struggle: The Jewish National Movement in the USSR, 1967–1989," at the Museum of the Jewish Diaspora in Tel Aviv.

Selecting 1967 as a starting point was a curious choice since the movement clearly started much earlier. Dr. Jonathan Dekel-Chen, an American by birth who made aliyah as a teenager and is currently a professor of modern history at Hebrew University, was on the exhibition committee that set 1967 as the start date. "We had to begin somewhere," says Dekel-Chen. "And it seemed to be a reasonable choice, if not wholly accurate."[2]

The choice of 1967 also marked the fortieth anniversary of the Six-Day War and, according to the exhibition website, this was just as it should be because it was that "epic week" that "catalyzed" the demand of Soviet Jews for the right to immigrate."[3]

This is a predominantly Israeli perception of the movement – designed, in part, to collect kudos for the eventual exodus of Soviet Jews – but it does not fully conform to the facts.

Vitold Kapshitser, a writer, was the first publicly recognized Soviet Jew to renounce his citizenship, and he announced his decision in May, prior to the war.[4] The most famous of the early Soviet Jews to reject his status as a citizen and to request permission to emigrate to Israel was Yasha Kazakov, a nineteen-year-old engineering student at Moscow State University. However, it was in January 1967, five months before the fighting broke out, that Kazakov slipped past the Soviet militiamen stationed outside the Israeli embassy in Moscow and asked a clerk inside for instructions on emigrating to Israel.[5] His visits to the embassy ended during the second week of June when Moscow severed diplomatic relations with Jerusalem in response to the war with its Arab allies. So Kazakov decided to try his luck at the US embassy. He was arrested by an officer of the Soviet militia, questioned for hours, and expelled from school.[6]

Kazakov would become famous for a letter he sent to the Supreme Soviet, the nation's highest legislative body, stating: "I am a Jew, and, as a Jew, I consider the State of Israel my fatherland…and I, like any other Jew, have the indubitable right to live in that state."[7]

The letter soon became a wildly popular part of the *samizdat* literature traveling the underground, and it was handed off to Western tourists, who smuggled it out of the country. The letter made its way to Washington, and to Nehemiah Levanon, who was overseeing the Soviet Jewry desk at the Israeli embassy. Never missing a chance to press the case for the emigration of Russian Jews to the Jewish state, Levanon passed the letter along to the *Washington Post*. On December 19, 1968, Kazakov's cry for freedom appeared in the paper, and from there it was picked up by journalists throughout the West. The Kremlin, deeming Kazakov a walking, talking public relations disaster, issued him an exit visa, and by February Kazakov was en route to Israel, where he would go on to a distinguished career in the Foreign Service and, fittingly, a seven-year stint as director of the Liaison Bureau.[8]

The narrative of Yasha Kazakov has the dramatic and emotional appeal of a Zionist fable, and without question Israel inspired and assisted him. Nonetheless, to see his story as solely a chapter in the Soviet Jewry movement is a distortion, for it suggests that Kazakov existed in a supernatural realm exempt from the shaping hands of history.

Kazakov composed his letter in May 1968, when, as Paul Berman writes in his exploration of the generation that came of age during that year, a "utopian exhilaration"[9] ignited the "pure flame of political rebellion" around the globe.[10] More young people than ever before were pursuing higher education. (In the United States, the numbers tripled from 1955 to 1970; Mexico exhibited the same growth rate between 1964 and 1970.[11] In France, the numbers increased by a factor of four; in the USSR, by a factor of 2.5; and in China, they doubled.[12]) In the United States alone, between January and June 1968, there were 221 major demonstrations on 101 college campuses; 39,000 students were involved,[13] and a *New York Times* survey found that 20 percent of the activists were Jewish. The 550,000 US troops fighting in Vietnam, unregenerate racism, and the desire to expand students rights were cited as the causes of the uprisings, but the reasons behind the unrest, according to a Gallup poll, were more universal – a conviction that a blind allegiance to the conventions of the Establishment was destroying the hope for a future free of arbitrary authority, hatred, war, and poverty.

That year, the best-known campus revolt occurred in April, after the assassination of Dr. King, at Columbia University on the Upper West Side of Manhattan. The local chapter of Students for a Democratic Society, a militant organization belonging to the New Left, demanded that Columbia stop its research for the Defense Department – research, SDS said, that was designed to oppress the Vietnamese and to enact "mass genocide" against African Americans.[14] Further raising the revolutionary hackles on the Ivy League campus was that Columbia was building a gym and proposed separate entrances for students and the mainly black residents of Harlem, which smacked of Jim Crow. Students marched on the site of the gym, then on an administration building and the library, and ransacked the office of President Grayson Kirk. Before long, students were occupying buildings around the campus. One thousand police were summoned; over seven hundred people were arrested and some 150 were injured.[15]

In 1962, Marshall McLuhan had predicted that the "electric media" would create a "global village,"[16] and six years later his prediction had come to pass. The modern town criers of radio and television rapidly disseminated news and popular culture, and for young protestors in this new borderless hamlet the common denominator was rock 'n' roll. Not even the Iron Curtain was "soundproof,"[17] observed Géza Ekecs, a Hungarian-born disc jockey who hosted a show on Radio Free Europe, an operation funded by Congress through the CIA.[18] The Czech playwright Václav Havel, a political prisoner later elected president of his country and enamored with rock 'n' roll, was described by historian Gale Stokes as "a Lennonist rather than a Leninist,"[19] and since the message of rock was to assail the older generation's most cherished shibboleths and cultural norms, the Beatles, Rolling Stones, Jimi Hendrix, Jefferson Airplane, and the Doors provided the perfect soundtrack for dissent.

"We have learned a great deal from the student revolt [in the United States]," a young West German activist told the Associated Press; so had his contemporaries in Latin America, England, Spain, Japan, and China, all of whom were testing the limits of the old order.[20]

In France, student anger at the university system escalated into violence and crippling labor strikes that led President Charles de Gaulle to declare that he was "not in charge of anything anymore."[21] In Italy and Belgium student revolts led to the collapse of the governments, and in the Soviet satellites the authority of the Kremlin was under siege. In Yugoslavia, after police dispersed a raucous crowd at a concert with nightsticks and water cannons, students marched through the streets of Belgrade, fought with police, and took over the university. In Poland, state censors stopped the performance of a play considered "anti-Soviet," and within weeks tens of thousands of students and workers were brawling with police and the militia in Warsaw. As students called for "freedom of expression, of assembly, mass meetings and demonstrations," the violence spread to other cities. Leaders of the Polish Communist Party blamed "reactionary elements, Zionists and demagogues," and proceeded to purge Jews from the party ranks and to announce that they were stepping up government control of colleges.[22]

The Polish demand for freedom had partially been a reaction to the Prague Spring, those hopeful months when Alexander Dubcek, head of the Communist Party in Czechoslovakia, pledged to introduce "socialism with a human face."[23] Students and intellectuals had long been clamoring for the restoration of personal liberties, an end to the corrupt, inefficient, centralized economy, and for improved relations with the West. As the government moved ahead with these reforms, a broadside appeared, signed by a host of the country's luminaries, stating that since 1948 Czechoslovakia had been in "the hands of the wrong people...[pro-Moscow] egoists avid for rule, calculating cowards and unprincipled people."[24]

Soviet General Secretary Leonid Brezhnev was livid. That August, in a move similar to Khrushchev's retort to the 1956 Hungarian Revolution, Brezhnev sent two hundred thousand Warsaw Pact troops with five thousand tanks into Czechoslovakia.[25] (Khrushchev, living in retirement in a villa on the Istra River, belittled Brezhnev's subjugation of the Czechs by saying, "What kind of socialism is this? What kind of shit is it when you have to keep people in chains?"[26]) Over one hundred protesters were killed by the soldiers, and Dubcek was arrested and carted off to Moscow. In the last week of August, he returned to Prague to tell his people that the reforms were finished. Gustav Husak, amenable to doing Moscow's bidding, replaced him,[27] and in the fall the Brezhnev Doctrine was announced, formalizing the USSR's commitment to invade any country that sought to exchange Marxism-Leninism for capitalism.[28]

Out of this upheaval came Yasha Kazakov. Undoubtedly, he was a child of the Russian past; equally certain was his delight in the Israeli triumph in 1967. His May 1968 letter to the Supreme Soviet, however, reverberated with accusations that could have been copied from the leaflet of a student radical on any campus in America: Kazakov charged Soviet leaders with suppressing the freedoms of their citizens, conducting an imperialistic foreign policy, and facilitating genocide.[29]

The legions of young Soviet Jewish dissidents who followed Yasha Kazakov were influenced by the same global convulsions. This is not to say that the outcome of the Six-Day War was unimportant. The Soviet Jews who hoped to leave knew they needed another home and, up until the late 1970s when they set their eyes on the United States, Israel was the one country they could rely on to accept them.[30] The results of the war proved that the Jewish state now had a highly skilled and technologically superior military that could stave off destruction.

Practically speaking, the 1967 war had no impact on the American

Jewish community, except that on trips to Israel it was now possible to visit the Western Wall and the Golan Heights. But psychologically, the community would never be the same again. The collective fear of annihilation, much of which was buried beneath the concerns of economic advancement and rearing children, would bubble to the surface, and that fear and the courage to confront it would rearrange the priorities of the community, change its politics, and spur the growth of the movement to free Soviet Jewry.

◆ ◆ ◆

Ha-Hamtana – the waiting, but waiting for what? The unthinkable? The inevitable? The final chapter of the Final Solution?

By the third week of May, aerial photographs taken by Israeli planes revealed that the Egyptians had deployed eighty thousand troops supported by 550 tanks and one thousand artillery pieces.[31] Other Arab armies were mobilized, and Yossi Peled, a company commander of an Israeli armored division who had survived the Holocaust through adoption by a Christian family,[32] remembered that his fellow citizens "had already started thinking in terms of annihilation."[33] Five years before, Nasser had intervened in the civil war in Yemen, and the photographs of dead Yemenis, killed by Egyptian poison gas, reignited the nightmares of Nazi vans filling with carbon monoxide and death-chamber walls stained blue by Zyklon-B.

The intelligence reports read by President Johnson indicated that in a confrontation with the Arabs, Israel would win a fast and decisive victory.[34] LBJ had heard similar predictions about Vietnam, but between May 25 and June 1, US forces suffered 2,929 killed and wounded, a new high for a single week of fighting.[35] The last thing the president needed was another foreign war against Soviet proxies, and he had warned Israeli prime minister Levi Eshkol that the "United States cannot accept any responsibility for situations that are liable to occur as a result of actions on which we were not consulted."[36] Thus, if the Israelis were to launch a preemptive strike and the fighting spun out of control, then no American troops could be counted on to assist the Israel Defense Forces.

Yitzhak Rabin, the IDF chief of staff, concluded that it was "about time we realized that nobody is going to come to our rescue."[37]

Unlike the situation during the rise of Hitler in the 1930s, when information was slow to travel across the Atlantic, American Jews were able to track the crisis in the newspapers, on the radio, and on television, and they reached the same conclusion as Rabin. Coloring their perceptions of the danger to Israel was the rhetoric from Cairo, which was as vitriolic as the worst of the Nazi propaganda. When one congregant asked his rabbi what would happen if Israel was destroyed, the rabbi's reply seemed to course through the bloodstream of the American Jewish community: "You will find a sign outside our synagogue that we are closed."[38]

Now, as Elie Wiesel commented, all Jews were children of the Holocaust.[39]

With the ghosts of the six million hovering just above their heads, American Jews were not inclined to sit this one out. On May 28, in New York, 150,000 people rallied in support of Israel, the largest Jewish event of its kind in US history.[40] By then, the State Department had advised the hundreds of American students in Israel to return home. The official warning was followed by frantic cables from parents, but only a handful returned; many of those who remained volunteered to work at schools, kibbutzim, and hospitals. Another ten thousand Americans – most of them young men and women – offered their services, even though the Israeli government asked them not to come and the State Department prohibited travel to the war zone. Few were able to get to Israel before the fighting ended, but during the summer, 7,500 of them finally made it.[41] This was a stunning development, since between 1948 and 1968 there had been just ten thousand applications from the United States for resettlement in Israel; from 1968 until 1970, twelve thousand new applications were filed.[42]

Polls discovered that 99 percent of Jews identified with and supported Israel,[43] and these findings were borne out by the emergency fund-raising campaign that was set up. Although the majority of local communities had recently completed their annual United Jewish Appeal drives, donations poured in. Synagogues froze their expansion funds; businessmen applied for personal loans and donated the proceeds. In fifteen minutes, a sum of $15 million was raised at a New York luncheon. In Boston, fifty families contributed $2.5 million. Overnight, the Jews of St. Louis raised $1.2 million; those in Cleveland, in excess of $3 million.[44] In Baltimore,

Shoshana Cardin (who would later assume a leadership role in the Soviet Jewry movement), was working at a table in a bank lobby, collecting donations from Jews who emptied their accounts for Israel. When they ran out of money, they handed her their jewelry.[45] On street corners children were collecting money in bottles and cans, and the donations did not come from Jews alone. The president of Fordham, a Catholic university, contributed $5,000; former army secretary Robert T. Stevens, who had gone into the textile business, gave $250,000; and in Minnesota, a young girl phoned a rabbi to ask how she could convert to Judaism because she wanted to donate to the cause.[46]

It was the most successful campaign ever conducted by the American Jewish community. During 1967, a total of $240 million was raised and $190 million in Israeli bonds were sold.

◆ ◆ ◆

As the smoke cleared, the majority of American Jews experienced a new feeling of pride in their Jewishness. Even Jews who had opposed the founding of Israel because they worried it would make them vulnerable to accusations of not being patriotic Americans put aside their fears. Shortly after the war, a Reform Southern Jew, who had fretted over the charge of dual loyalty, received a phone call from his neighbor, a retired admiral, who said, "I'm glad you Jews kicked the shit out of 'em."[47] The admiral appeared to be speaking for most Americans, who were, momentarily, able to identify the geopolitical connection between the United States and Israel. A Harris poll that appeared during the fighting concluded that nearly 70 percent of Americans thought the Kremlin had engineered the war to weaken the United States in Vietnam.[48] That the Israelis had defeated Soviet proxies was reason for high praise. As one newspaper announced, "The glorious fighters of Israel have made an automatic hero of every Jew in America."[49]

Pride, however, can be more nuanced than it appears. In *We Are One!*, an inquiry into the relationship between American Jewry and Israel, Melvin I. Urofsky writes that after the Six-Day War, "one no longer had to be ashamed of being a Jew." The etiology of the shame was illuminated by a secular Jewish woman with no Zionist leanings who told a reporter that the Israeli victory was a relief "from seeing the Jews as the long-suffering victims."[50]

Pride, then, was partially the absence of shame, a respite from a chronicle stretching across centuries in which Jews were a despised minority subjected to cultural and physical assault who, so goes this story, responded by becoming passive victims.

In this narrative, there was no Maccabean revolt against the Seleucid Empire or Bar-Kochba revolt against Rome. The Jews did not ally themselves with Berber tribes to fight the invading Arab armies. The Jewish Queen Judith of Ethiopia did not overthrow the repressive rule of the Axum dynasty. Fast-forwarding a millennium, the Jews of Kishinev did not try to defend their wives and children. Why not? Because Hayyim Bialik bent his genius to composing "In the City of Slaughter," a poem based on his fantasies instead of the realities of the fierce Jewish defense. As for the Holocaust, there were no Jewish partisans, there was no resistance at the death camps – none at Treblinka, Sobibor, Auschwitz, Kruszyna, Krychow, or Kopernik.[51] There was no uprising in the Warsaw ghetto or active undergrounds in some one hundred other ghettos across eastern Europe.[52]

Alas, history is no match for myth, and while the jubilation experienced by American Jews after the war was there for all to see, it also sharpened their existential concerns for Israel and reawakened a sense of responsibility for the six million.

While American Jewry underwent this sea change, Israel was elevated to the status of full-fledged participant in the Cold War. The process that had begun in 1956 with the withdrawal of Britain and France from the Middle East was now complete: the United States and the USSR had divided the region into friends and foes.

As political scientist Robert O. Freedman points out, "Soviet leaders never quite made up their minds as to how to handle Jewish emigration, whether permissively or through harsh crackdowns," though they understood that if they wanted to improve their relationship with the West, emigration would be a topic of conversation.[53] In December 1966, Premier Alexei N. Kosygin had attempted to soften the Soviet stance when he stated that he favored emigration for the purpose of reunifying families, and his statement was published in *Izvestia*, but the outcome of the Six-Day War atomized Soviet goodwill.[54]

The Communist bloc, save for Romania and Cuba, broke off diplomatic relations with Israel; the Soviets began funding, arming, training, and encouraging Palestinian guerillas to attack Israel, and churned out anti-Zionist propaganda laced with an antisemitic poison that harkened back to the tsars. In an update of *The Protocols of the Elders of Zion* that substituted Zionism for Judaism,[55] Jews were charged with being members of a worldwide "Zionist Corporation [whose] well-camouflaged aim [was the] enrichment by any means of the international Zionist network."[56]

The Third World lined up behind the Kremlin, and debates at the UN General Assembly began to resemble rallies in the Third Reich. Ambassador Jamil Baroody of Saudi Arabia (who four years hence would be described by then UN ambassador George H. W. Bush as "an unguided missile"[57]) injected some religious enmity into the grotesque carnival at the General Assembly by emphasizing that Jews were the ones who had murdered Christ.[58]

Because of the American Jewish community's identification with Israel, once the Jewish state was inducted into the Cold War the community threw itself into the politics of the conflict. Moreover, American Jews, newly obsessed by the memory of Hitler, became increasingly worried about their brethren behind the Iron Curtain, who, owing to the Kremlin's internal and external antisemitic campaign, were further alienated from Mother Russia and even more eager to emigrate.[59] The timing was propitious. The Six-Day War was a riposte to the mythic Jewish impuissance, and although the change had required the slow turning of time's wheel, it seemed that suddenly Jews in the United States realized that they were captains of their own fate, a realization that enabled them to bid farewell to Bialik's Kishinev and soon energized them on behalf of the Jews in the USSR.

The Soviet Jewry movement was also on the verge of receiving an influx of American Jews who were being driven from their longtime homestead on the political left, when it became apparent that not everyone was pleased by the tarnishing of a cherished myth.

Among the first to express their displeasure were the young radicals of the New Left, a substantial portion of whom were Jews.[60] In the summer of

1967, at the national convention of the Students for a Democratic Society, Israel was condemned to the same imperialistic hell as the United States with its adventurism in Vietnam.[61] SDS was the most influential group of the New Left, and by September its condemnation was seconded at the luxuriously appointed Palmer House in Chicago, where over two thousand people from two hundred organizations were attending the National Convention for a New Politics.[62]

This anti-Israel stance was not limited to young radicals. The esteemed theologian, Henry P. Van Dusen, the former president of the Union Theological Seminary,[63] likened the Israeli strike to the Nazi blitzkrieg of Europe in 1940 and opined that Israel was "aiming not at victory but at annihilation,"[64] an opinion that was shared by the Jesuit antiwar activist Rev. Daniel J. Berrigan, who claimed that Israel's "militarism" and "domestic repressions" of the Palestinians were reminiscent of the Nazis.[65] An answer to this charge was provided by another prominent Christian theologian, Franklin H. Littell, who declared that what "the Christian humanitarian cannot grasp is the Jew who is a winner…who does not have to beg protection of a patron or toleration of a so-called Christian nation."[66]

The problem Littell identified was exacerbated by the zeitgeist of the 1960s, which favored bestowing sainthood, deserved or not, on the underdog – from the Viet Cong to the New York Mets. This development alone would have been sufficient to alienate American Jewish champions of Israel from the Left, but their exit was hastened by the antisemitism that erupted from a quarter considered a haven from such hatred: the civil rights movement.

◆ ◆ ◆

In September 1963, in the heady wake of the March on Washington, Abraham Joshua Heschel assured a gathering of rabbis that "the Negroes will be ready to join us on behalf of equal rights for Jews in Russia."[67] Dr. King was ready to join; so was Bayard Rustin. But for several years the movement had been torn between the opposing visions of King and Malcolm X, the older generation siding with the former, and the younger attracted to the militancy of the latter. As far back as the Washington march, there were clashes between the two age groups: when the twenty-three-year-old chairman of SNCC, John R. Lewis, was slated to address the hundreds of thousands of people gathered on the Mall, and proposed admonishing the Kennedy administration for the weakness of its civil right legislation, his elders stepped in to red pencil his criticism.[68] By 1967, a national Black Power conference was calling for the separation of the United States into two nations, one black, the other white,[69] and with the dream of integration dead, young African Americans dismissed King as an Uncle Tom and attacked white society in general and Jews in particular.[70]

Malcolm X was assassinated in 1965, but not before setting the gold standard for the antisemitism of black militants by commenting that the six million had brought their destruction on themselves,[71] a position that appealed to CORE official Clifford Brown, who, during a discussion of school desegregation in Mount Vernon, New York, proffered that Hitler had not done away with enough Jews.[72] To be clear, black antisemitism was not invented in the 1960s. James Baldwin, born in 1924, remembered that during his Harlem childhood he met no Negroes "in my family or out of it, who would really ever trust a Jew, and few who did not, indeed, exhibit for them the blackest contempt."[73] Their hatred, Baldwin said, was because Jews, as the local businesspeople, exploited their Negro customers. This was a not uncommon complaint in the North, while in the South antisemitism had more classic origins. When the black writer Alice Walker brought her future white Jewish husband and civil rights lawyer Mel Leventhal home, her mother "smiled a little" before saying, "You're one of the ones who killed Christ."[74]

What happened, however, over the course of 1967 and 1968 would open up such a terrible schism between the Jewish and African American communities that more than forty years on, it has not fully healed.

Young politicized blacks saw themselves as part of the Third World, and after the Six-Day War their sympathies lay with the Arabs.[75] SNCC's newsletter printed cartoons that could have been plucked from the pages of the Nazi newspaper *Der Stürmer*. One cartoon was of the most famous Israeli soldier and current defense minister, Moshe Dayan, with his trademark eye patch and dollar signs decorating the epaulets of his uniform. Another cartoon, this one of Muhammad Ali, repeated this theme, showing the boxer with a noose around his neck; the hand holding the rope was marked by the Star of David and a dollar sign.[76] The black playwright and poet Leroi Jones chimed in with a rebarbative cliché, referring to Judaism as "a dangerous, germ culture,"[77] and the Black Panther Party, a radical organization that had been formed in Oakland, California, in 1966, proposed a Final Solution redux.[78] In its publication, *Black Power*, the editors promised: "We're gonna burn their towns and that ain't all. We're gonna piss upon the Wailing Wall. And we'll get Kosygin and de Gaulle. That will be ecstasy, killing every Jew we see."[79]

Dr. King would state publicly that "When people criticize Zionists they mean Jews, you are talking anti-Semitism,"[80] but young radicals were no longer listening to him, and Jews started flooding out of liberal organizations.[81] Major national Jewish groups – among them the American Jewish Committee, American Jewish Congress, and the Central Conference of American Rabbis – attempted to close the widening rift by adopting an understanding attitude toward the desire of blacks to distance themselves from whites, but for Jews events did nothing to cast the slogan "Black Power" in a charitable light.[82] The summer of 1967 proved to be a long hot summer of looting, arson, and gunfire, when rubble-strewn streets of mostly black neighborhoods were shrouded by the smoke of firebombs and patrolled by National Guardsmen and federal troops carrying rifles with fixed bayonets. The riots in Newark, New Jersey, and Detroit, Michigan, attracted the most attention from the press, but violence broke out in 114 communities across thirty-two states. Eighty-eight people died; four thousand were injured; and over twelve thousand were arrested. Financial losses were in the hundreds of millions of dollars.[83]

Between 1945 and 1965 most Jews had moved away from the riot-torn areas, but some still operated businesses there. A number of these businesses were now lost, and many of those who had stubbornly hunkered down in their homes as their neighbors lit out for the suburbs finally decided to leave, refugees from charred cityscapes rampant with poverty and crime. It was then that an unrelated issue – a struggle over local control of schools – escalated into a conflict so rife with antisemitism that it shattered what remained of the alliance between blacks and Jews like a brick thrown through a storefront window.

◆ ◆ ◆

With the assistance of a Ford Foundation grant,[84] the Board of Education of New York City undertook an experiment in decentralization by establishing three local school districts with boards of parents and community leaders overseeing budgets, curricula, and the selection of teachers.[85] The United Federation of Teachers and its president, Albert Shanker, were unhappy with the experiment, especially when on May 9, 1968, just five weeks after the assassination of Dr. King and the new round of civil uprisings that followed, Rhody A. McCoy, an articulate, pipe-smoking, experienced black educator and the chief administrator of the school board in the poor, predominantly black Ocean Hill-Brownsville neighborhood of Brooklyn,[86] attempted to replace some of its white teachers and principals with African Americans.[87]

The teachers' union fought the move, and given the fractious state of race relations and that the union was 90 percent white and 60 percent Jewish,[88] it was not long before the controversy intensified. Black militants from outside Ocean Hill-Brownsville showed up to organize and preach, and meetings of the board degenerated into opportunities for each side to revile the other with such choice phrases as "Jew pigs" and "black Nazis."[89]

When McCoy refused to reinstate the teachers, Shanker and the union called for strikes, and from September 9 to November 18, 1968, the 1.1 million students in New York City missed thirty-six days of classes.[90] A leaflet appeared in mailboxes at two schools[91] that referred to Jewish teachers as "Middle East Murderers of Colored People" and "Bloodsucking Exploiters."[92] To win sympathy for the strike Shanker had half a million copies of the leaflet made and distributed.[93] Some of his aides had attempted to dissuade him, saying that this was not a fight between blacks and Jews, and that the leaflet obviously contained the declamations of a madman and had not originated with the board in Ocean Hill-Brownsville.[94] But the union president was a no-holds-barred tactician and so famously combative that in Woody Allen's futuristic movie *Sleeper*, the Allen character awakes from a deep freeze after two hundred years to discover that the world he had known was destroyed when "a man by the name of Albert Shanker got hold of a nuclear warhead."[95]

The leaflet, along with Shanker's public statements, engendered the backlash that the union leader had been counting on. Opinion turned against the local board, and the city shut down its experiment with community control of the schools.[96] Still, the controversy was not finished. Julius Lester, the host of a show on WBAI-FM on which he interviewed black and white radicals, invited Leslie Campbell to appear on the radio one evening. Campbell was black and taught history in Ocean Hill-Brownsville, and the union had identified him as the most "militant" teacher in the district. Lester wanted to inform his listeners about the feelings being engendered by the dispute, and he urged Campbell to read a poem, dedicated to Shanker, that had been written by a student, a fifteen-year-old girl. The poem began, "Hey, Jew boy, with that yarmulke on your head/You pale-faced Jew boy – I wish you were dead."[97]

Time magazine would headline the whole affair as "a falling out of allies,"[98] but to a Jew hoping to leave the Soviet Union, the antisemitism that came bundled with the racial strife in America must have seemed like the flicker of a remote star. And yet it was this discord that led a Brooklyn-born rabbi, Meir Kahane, to found the Jewish Defense League, which, for all of its grievous faults, finally convinced the established American Jewish community to reach out to Soviet Jewry and helped boost their plight onto the agenda of the Cold War.

◆ ◆ ◆

Call Rabbi Meir Kahane a lunatic; racist; womanizer; tool of the FBI, Mossad, and right-wing Israeli politicians; or a "gangster with a Messiah complex," the phrase favored by journalist and author Christopher Hitchens,[99] and there will be no shortage of erudite men and women, Jew and gentile alike, willing to agree with you. Yet no matter how richly Kahane deserves the pejoratives, the indignation he engendered obscures not only his substantial contribution to the American movement to free Soviet Jewry, but also precisely how he was able to make it.

The Six-Day War may have demonstrated that Jews could defend themselves, but the sentiment experienced by Israeli soldiers, according to their reminiscences in the 1970 book *The Seventh Day*, suggested that they were reluctant victors without much animosity toward their enemy.[100]

American Jews, in significant numbers, were in a less charitable mood, and Kahane knew it. Their participation in the civil rights movement had been betrayed by the black militants; the riots had destroyed the urban Edens of their youth. The sweet shop with the marble-topped soda fountain was gone, and the parks and school yards where they used to play were now treacherous kingdoms ruled by ambulatory skeletons craving dope, mini-skirted purveyors of the cheap trick, and muggers convinced that knocking an elderly woman to the sidewalk and stealing her purse was an exalted act of revolution.

The feelings of loss for some Jews, Kahane understood, were overpowering and fueled their smoldering ire, as did the dissension in Ocean Hill-Brownsville, and it was during that controversy, on May 24, 1968, that Kahane, three months shy of this thirty-seventh birthday, placed an ad in the *Jewish Press*, an Orthodox weekly hostile to gentiles at home and Arabs abroad, to which Kahane was a regular contributor. The ad sought people devoted to "Jewish Pride," and thirty-five of the faithful, most of them professional men, showed up on Tuesday evening, June 18, for the inaugural meeting at the West Side Jewish Center in Manhattan, a synagogue whose rabbi was Kahane's first cousin. Using Ocean Hill-Brownsville as an object lesson, Kahane said that "Black Jew-hatred" was growing by perilous leaps and bounds, warning that Jewish survival was at stake and declaring that turning "the other cheek is not a Jewish concept. Do not listen to the soothing anesthesia of the establishment. They walk in the paths of those whose timidity helped to bury our brothers and sisters less than thirty years ago."[101]

This last comment explains the dual motto of the Jewish Defense League: "Never Again" and "Every Jew a .22." Pairing the fear of street crime with the Holocaust was a master stroke and demonstrates that Kahane perceived that there was more feeding Jewish ire than a controversy in Brooklyn.

Egypt had recently started the bloody War of Attrition against Israel that would drag on for two years, and there were signs of worse battles to come. Humiliated by its Egyptian client's crushing defeat, the Kremlin had provided Nasser with advisers and $3.5 billion in aid, including surface-to-air missile batteries that were manned by Soviet crews,[102] a move that

Henry A. Kissinger would remember as a "terrifying escalation," since the SAMs were capable of neutralizing Israel's air superiority.[103]

Further eroding American Jewry's sense of security were reminders that even assimilated Jews – the suburbanites Kahane mocked in his columns for the *Jewish Press* as building temples akin to ostentatious burial chambers and hiring rabbis best suited to catering bar mitzvahs[104] – were not fully accepted by society. This point had been driven home by an earlier school board dustup, this one in the small, overwhelmingly white community of Wayne, New Jersey. In the winter of 1967, five candidates were seeking three seats on the board. Two of the candidates – Jack Mandell, a lawyer, and Richard Kraus, a corporate executive – were Jews. Just prior to the vote, the board vice president, Newton Miller, told the town paper, "Most Jewish people are liberals, especially when it comes to spending for education. If Kraus and Mandell are elected…[and join with the other Jewish board member] that's a three-to-six vote. It would only take two more votes for a majority, and Wayne would be in real financial trouble. Two more votes and we lose what is left of Christ in our Christmas celebrations in our schools."[105]

The school board and township council censured Miller, but the story was spread by the national media. Elected officials and clergymen condemned the remarks, and in the closing days of the campaign Miller apologized, but held fast to his opinions. Right-minded individuals anticipated that the rejoinder to Miller would be the outcome of the election. One community leader posited that "open political anti-Semitism simply is no longer tolerated in American life," a position that was contradicted by the vote: Mandell and Kraus lost in a landslide, and so did the school budget they backed.[106]

As the media continued to report on Wayne and Ocean Hill-Brownsville, and Kahane opened the Jewish Defense League office in Manhattan and began recruiting members, television viewers were treated to some crude, old-time antisemitism courtesy of the legendary political boss of Chicago, Mayor Richard J. Daley. At the Democratic Convention, while Senator Abraham Ribicoff was at the podium, he stared down at Daley and denounced him for using Gestapo-like tactics to suppress the antiwar demonstrations outside.[107] The cameras cut to Daley, and though the audio was off, the mayor's lips were easily read as he screamed up at Ribicoff, "Fuck you, you Jew bastard."[108]

All of these occurrences were accentuated by the appearance of Arthur Morse's best-selling *While Six Million Died: A Chronicle of American Apathy.*[109] The lede of the front-page review in the *Washington Post Book World* indicates why Kahane was able to find an army of sympathetic listeners: "This is an angry book by an angry author, and impossible to read without sharing the anger."[110]

After the Six-Day War, Israel gave the world the image of the humanistic soldier. Kahane produced a much different, and perhaps more accurate image – an image perfectly suited to the political moment: the Angry Jew. And Kahane found them in all walks of life: doctors, lawyers, dentists, college professors, businesspeople, Vietnam veterans, survivors of the Nazi camps, youngsters from the yeshivas in traditional black garb, and college kids decked out like East Village freaks.[111]

In August, the Jewish Defense League held its first demonstration. Kahane and fourteen other picketers marched outside New York University, protesting against NYU naming John E. Hatchett as director of the Martin Luther King Jr. Afro-American Student Center.[112] Hatchett, who had been a substitute teacher in the New York City schools until he was fired for bringing his grammar-school class to a memorial rally for Malcolm X, had published an article in the journal of the African American Teachers Association accusing "antiblack Jews" of inflicting "misery, degradation, racism and cultural genocide daily against my people."[113]

From there Kahane and his followers would go on to drive through black neighborhoods in a sound truck, announcing that the residents had better leave Jews alone. His minions also picked fights at school board meetings; phoned in death threats to black leaders and well-known Jewish liberals; raided WBAI after Leslie Campbell had read the student's poem on the radio;[114] and when blacks harassed the crowds at a synagogue-sponsored carnival, the Rockaways Jewish Community Council of Brooklyn brought in the JDL for protection.[115]

Jewish self-defense groups were nothing new in the United States. During World War I, Abner "Longy" Zwillman, who would become one of the founding fathers of organized crime, protected Jewish peddlers in

Newark from marauding Irish teenagers with a gang of Jewish youngsters calling themselves the "Happy Ramblers,"[116] and by the 1930s Zwillman was dispatching his toughs to disrupt meetings of the pro-Nazi Friends of the New Germany and the German-American Bund.[117]

Kahane both politicized this paradigm and updated it. The portfolio of the JDL would expand to include antisemitism everywhere, and it was modeled, ironically, on the Black Panthers, with whom the JDL would brawl in May 1970 outside the Panthers' New York headquarters in Harlem.[118] Kahane was a diligent student of black radicals;[119] he even adopted the Black Power salute of a raised fist for the JDL logo – a fist punching through the center of the Star of David. His reasoning was obvious. Kahane saw the appeal these romanticized rebels with a cause had among the young, the same demographic he was recruiting and, just as important, with reporters.[120] Grim-faced, hard-eyed JDL members made for compelling images in print and on television with their berets and combat fatigues, and armed with lead pipes, baseball bats, or chains. For Kahane, though, violence was more than a matter of public perception: before long, the JDL was offering paramilitary training at a camp in the Catskills, and an elite group known as *Chayas* (a Hebrew and Yiddish word meaning animals) studied the art of bomb making.[121]

The government of Israel had shaped the organized American Jewish community's quiet response to Soviet Jewry, but in December 1969, a right-wing member of the Knesset, Geula Cohen, arrived in the United States for a speaking tour. Her trip was paid for by a Jewish businessman and Orthodox rabbis working to persuade Congress to help Jews in the USSR. Cohen was unhappy with Israel's official stance on the situation, and during a visit with Kahane in New York City she suggested that he make the issue his own. Other Israeli politicians – the future prime minister Yitzhak Shamir among them – would support the move.[122]

Kahane did not need much encouragement. The quiet response favored by the Israeli government had created a vacuum, and if the JDL could fill it the organization might transform itself into a major political player. By the closing days of December the Jewish Defense League was assaulting what Kahane dramatically identified as "the institutions of Soviet tyranny."[123] The JDL occupied the offices of Tass, Intourist, and Aeroflot, and painted the Hebrew words *Am Yisrael Chai* on a Soviet airliner that had just flown from Moscow to Kennedy International Airport.[124] The next day, over one hundred JDL members showed up outside the Soviet mission in New York City and a riot ensued.[125]

Israeli prime minister Golda Meir condemned the actions,[126] and the American Jewish Committee railed against the JDL's "wanton violence and repeated harassments."[127] Kahane answered the objections with a full-page ad in the *New York Times* in which he jabbed the secret shame beating in millions of American Jewish hearts: "Our leaders went to President Roosevelt and asked him to bomb the rail lines carrying the cars packed with Jews to the gas chambers. He refused. We did nothing.... In 1970, when we know of the national and spiritual destruction of Soviet Jewry... where are all the demonstrators who bleed for every people, every cause, every group – except the Jew? We, by our silence, doom the Soviet Jew."[128]

The grassroots activists – the Student Struggle for Soviet Jewry and the new confederation that was about to enter the fray, the Union of Councils for Soviet Jews – agreed with Kahane. After six years of traveling across the United States to talk to like-minded individuals, Lou Rosenblum managed to unite the Cleveland Council on Soviet Anti-Semitism with five similar groups in California, South Florida, and Washington, DC. Rosenblum saw the Union of Councils "as a visible manifestation of the Jewish establishment's failure to produce any kind of a viable organization to help Soviet Jews."[129]

Even Jewish students, unaffiliated with any group, were pressing the establishment. Hillel Levine had gone to Soviet Jewry protests when he was enrolled at Yeshiva University high school, and he was suspended for ten days and told that his record would now contain the charge that he was an "anarchist." In the fall of 1967, Elie Wiesel, whom Levine had met, asked him to visit the Soviet Union. Levine went to Israel and was prepped by Nehemiah Levanon. Arriving in Moscow via Vienna, Levine traveled to Odessa, where he spoke to refuseniks. One of them was Avraham Shifrin, who would lose a leg during his decade spent in Soviet labor camps for trumpeting Zionism, and who would go on to write *The First Guidebook to Prisons and Concentration Camps of the Soviet Union.*[130]

"Avraham gave me a letter," says Levine. "It was written in broken

English and basically said that we are Jews and want to live in Israel. I memorized it and hid it in my shoe. I was picked up for questioning by the KGB, but they never got the letter. All they did was leave me on the Romanian border."[131]

Levine flew to London and went directly to the Israeli embassy. An official took the letter and refused to give it back to him. After flying back to the United States, Levine spoke with a reporter at the *New York Times*, told him what had happened, and recited the letter, but the newspaper, unable to verify his account or the contents of Shifrin's letter, would not print the story. Something had to be done, Levine thought, and by 1969, when he was enrolled in a PhD program at Harvard, he brought hundreds of young people to stage a sit-in at the annual meeting of the general assembly of the Council of Jewish Federations and Welfare Funds in Boston. The CJF controlled the budget allocations of the federations, and the students wanted the CJF to appropriate funds for Soviet Jewry. Levine was told they would consider it.[132]

As noble as the grassroots efforts were, none of the organizations or activists commanded national attention. Of all the lessons that Kahane learned from black radicals, the most crucial was that violence drew reporters, cameras, and microphones, and seduced them with the promise of a narrative as exciting as a Hollywood shoot 'em up. Kahane saw that for some reason, Americans were more disposed to take movements seriously if they were violent. Maybe it was the headlines and the stories on the evening news that were needed – the stamp of approval that sliced through the ever-increasing distractions and the information glut in the global village and made you worthy of everyone's rapidly dwindling attention. Or maybe it was that violence appealed to some facet buried in the recesses of the American character – back to the movies again, the Western, the war film – and, in part, this might have been what the black radical H. Rap Brown was referring to when he explained blacks rampaging through the cities by quipping, "Violence is as American as cherry pie."[133]

◆ ◆ ◆

As Kahane planned his next step, Brezhnev waffled on emigration. In 1969, the Kremlin permitted 2,979 Jews to go – as opposed to 223 the year before[134] – and the huge jump was apparently intended to mollify the United States government and to prevent it from taking sides in case the fighting between China and the USSR along the Ussuri River metastasized into a war.[135] Once the situation on the Sino-Soviet border stabilized, the Kremlin decided that too many of its citizens – particularly the scientists and engineers needed for military and industrial purposes – were applying for exit visas.[136]

The Soviets had already made an object lesson of Boris Kochubievsky, a secular Ukrainian Jew who had grown up in an orphanage after his father, an officer in the Red Army, died at the Babi Yar massacre and his mother fled from the Nazis. After the Six-Day War Kochubievsky refused to join his fellow trade unionists when they were ordered to condemn Israel as aggressors. Berated, then shunned, Kochubievsky quit and produced an essay that was circulated underground in the Soviet Union, then smuggled out and published in the *New York Times*. Entitled "Why I Am a Zionist," the essay explained that Soviet Jewish youth, ignorant of their cultural background and with no belief in God, were attached to Israel because of antisemitism, "the new brand which was implanted from above and, as a means of camouflage, is called anti-Zionism."[137]

In June 1968 Kochubievsky married Larisa Aleksandrovna, a Ukrainian woman and a fourth-year student at the Kiev Pedagogical Institute, whose father was a KGB agent. The couple applied to OVIR (the Russian acronym for Department of Visas and Registration) for permission to emigrate to Israel.[138] Their applications were denied, and Larissa was jettisoned from the institute.[139] That fall, Boris and Larisa reapplied to OVIR and were assured that the exit permits would be forthcoming.[140]

At the end of September the couple was in the audience at a state-sanctioned memorial for the "Soviet citizens, Russians, Ukrainians and others who were slaughtered by the Nazi barbarians" at Babi Yar. Boris was enraged by the fraudulent revisionism which denied that Jews had been the primary victims of the slaughter, and he made his feelings known to authorities.[141] Five weeks later the couple received word that their visas had been granted and were told to pick up the paperwork at the offices of OVIR. While Boris and Larisa were out, their apartment was searched and documents were removed, and in December Boris was arrested for "disseminating fabrications alleging that the Soviet state oppresses and keeps down Jews."[142]

The repetitiveness of history can be illuminating, and so it was with the three-day trial of Boris Kochubievsky, which began on May 13, 1969 – fifty-six years after Mendel Beilis had been tried in the same court for allegedly murdering a Christian child.[143] The proceedings featured a judge who was harsher in his questioning of Kochubievsky than the prosecutor and who did not silence the antisemitic catcalls filling the courtroom.[144]

Beilis had been acquitted of the false charges; Kochubievsky was not as fortunate. He was found guilty and sentenced to three years of hard labor, becoming the first activist imprisoned for applying to emigrate to Israel. In protest, fifty-two Soviet intellectuals sent a petition to the United Nations, and Rita Hauser, appointed by Nixon as his delegate to the UN Human Rights Commission, raised the problem with the General Assembly.[145]

After leaving prison in December 1971, Boris departed for Israel. Larisa did not want to accompany him. She remained in the Soviet Union with their daughter.[146]

◆ ◆ ◆

Evidently, Soviet leadership determined that the treatment of Kochubievsky was an insufficient deterrent, because the Kremlin was soon undertaking a widespread, coordinated crackdown against Jewish activists. It began on the morning of June 15, 1970, when police arrested twelve Soviet citizens at Smolny Airport in Leningrad as they boarded a single-engine Aeroflot plane that was scheduled to fly to Priozersk, a city forty miles from the Finnish border.[147] Nine of those arrested were Jews, and they were accused of intending to hijack the plane – "without causing a single scratch," one defendant later said – so they could go to Israel.[148]

During the next two hours, and for weeks afterwards, in Leningrad, Moscow, Riga, Kishinev, Odessa, and Kharkov, scores of Jews were arrested for their alleged (and highly unlikely) involvement with the hijacking. Homes were searched, and materials confiscated: the works of Hayyim Bialik, Leon Uris, and Howard Fast; Israeli picture postcards and petitions ready to be mailed to the UN; textbooks on Jewish history and Hebrew; albums of Jewish songs and even a Communist newspaper,

Folksstimme, published in Poland and written in Yiddish.[149]

The KGB had responded so promptly that in all probability they had known about the plot in advance or may have used one or more of its agents to contrive the affair to provide the Kremlin with the justification for suppressing the Jewish emigration movement,[150] which had spread like a flash fire after the Six-Day War and, as Ambassador Anatoly Dobrynin recalled, was seen by Soviet leadership as "a reproof to our socialist paradise" and "a rank insult."[151] The Kremlin's failure, Dobrynin believed, was that it did not distinguish between those who simply wanted to emigrate and pestiferous dissidents like the author Aleksandr Solzhenitsyn, who pilloried his government by chronicling the horrors of the Gulag, and the physicist Andrei Sakharov, with his outspoken advocacy for disarmament and human rights.[152]

Dobrynin ascribed the mistake of lumping the Jews and dissidents together as enemies of the state to the "heavy heritage of Stalin,"[153] but the Soviet Jews clamoring to emigrate presented Brezhnev with two challenges that Stalin had not faced.

Because the Cold War had evolved into a feverish competition for the hearts and minds of the world, the expressed desire of Jews to leave created the same public relations quandary as the runaway East Berliners had presented to Brezhnev's predecessor, Nikita Khrushchev. In 1961, Khrushchev concluded that he had no choice but to order the building of the Berlin Wall. Brezhnev did not have that option. Even more challenging for the general secretary, as Sakharov pointed out in an open letter to Congress, Jews were not the only ones who wanted to leave. Soviet labor camps and mental hospitals were stocked with Germans, Russians, Ukrainians, Lithuanians, Armenians, Estonians, Latvians, Turks, and members of other ethnic groups who had "at the cost of endless difficulty and humiliation" sought to emigrate, a right that had been enumerated in 1948 by the United Nations Universal Declaration of Human Rights.[154]

Secondly, Stalin had enjoyed better relations with Israel than the current Soviet leadership; since Stalin had backed the founding of the Jewish state there was, as Dobrynin notes, a "huge reservoir of goodwill" between the two countries.[155] That reservoir had been drained dry by the Six-Day War and the ensuing Soviet-encouraged attacks on Israel by Palestinian guerillas and Egypt. Moreover, with Israel squarely in the American camp, the Kremlin had to keep its Arab allies in the fold, and so the Leningrad arrests – engineered in lieu of a wall to stop emigration by discrediting and frightening people who tried to leave – can be seen as both a rebuke to Israel, which desperately needed immigrants, and as an attempt to reassure the Arabs. The longtime Arab dread of a massive influx of Soviet Jews into Israel had intensified after the 1967 war. In the four years from 1966 through 1970, only 5,675 Jews were able to leave the Soviet Union.[156] Then a report published in the USSR and leaked to the international press mentioned that up to three hundred thousand Soviet Jews were hoping to emigrate. The report embarrassed the Kremlin, and so a commentator in *Pravda* dismissed the estimate as "fantastic" and "absurd," and denigrated the report by saying it was crafted by the "American-Zionist lie machine" and designed to scare the Arabs and undermine the relationship between the Arab world and the Soviet Union.[157]

The Arabs were not noticeably comforted by the Kremlin's house organ. When a Soviet delegation arrived in Lebanon, Lebanese Premier Saeb Salam reminded his visitors that "every new Jew who arrives in Israel is more dangerous than a tank, cannon or fighter plane."[158]

The *New York Times* reported that to calm the diplomatic waters, the delegation leader replied that those who were being permitted to go to Israel were too young to serve in the army and that "the number of Soviet Jews who had expressed their wish to go to Israel was not large."[159]

The *Times* reporter did not record whether Salam accepted the Soviet answer, but the Arab press rejected it and accused Soviet authorities of facilitating Israeli colonialism by stocking the Jewish state with new immigrants.[160]

◆ ◆ ◆

Six months after the arrests at Smolny Airport the trial began. No outside observers or members of the foreign press corps were permitted inside the Leningrad courtroom. The sole source of information was the Soviet news agency, Tass, whose heavily edited dispatches were tilted to vindicate the Kremlin.[161] The state wanted to avoid stirring up its citizens by releasing details from the courtroom. The reports from Tass were directed at the foreign market; internally, the media swamped the Soviet Union with accounts of American antiwar protestors being dragged off to jail and the legal troubles of black militant and Communist Angela Davis, who in October had been arrested by the FBI for her alleged role in a kidnapping and escape from a Marin County, California, courthouse, in which Judge Harold Haley, Jonathan Jackson (the teenager who planned the abduction), and two convicts were shot to death.[162]

The Kremlin was wise to keep the proceedings in Leningrad hidden from public view, for it would have appeared that Stalin had risen from the grave to demand one of his showcase trials,[163] an outcome that was anticipated by American Jews. Even before the proceedings were underway, a vigil on behalf of Soviet Jewry began across from the Soviet embassy – a residence formerly owned by the family of sleeping car manufacturer George Pullman – on Sixteenth Street in Washington.[164] A few days later the Greater New York Conference on Soviet Jewry and SSSJ staged a rally at Madison Square Garden that drew an audience of twenty thousand. Theodore Bikel performed a selection of songs he called "Silent No More," which were based on music and lyrics that had been recorded on tapes by Soviet Jews and smuggled out of the USSR. Rep. Gerald R. Ford, a Republican from Michigan and the House minority leader, urged President Nixon to press the case of Soviet Jews when he met with Brezhnev, and Senator Henry Jackson, a Democrat from Washington, demanded that the Kremlin grant Soviet Jews the rights they deserved.[165]

The Leningrad court judged the hijackers guilty of violating Article 64-A, which made it treasonous to flee abroad and equated a planned crime with one that had been committed. The sentences were handed down on Christmas Eve. Eleven of those arrested were tried,[166] and nine of the defendants were ordered to serve prison-camp terms ranging from four to fifteen years. Two other defendants – both of whom had applied for exit visas to Israel – were sentenced to die before a firing squad.[167]

Suddenly, Brezhnev was dealing with a public relations disaster of epic proportions. If he had been betting on the designation of "hijacker" to demonize the defendants he had bet his rubles on the wrong horse. In the West, political hijackings, often accompanied by murder, as pursued by the Palestine Liberation Organization, were judged to be despicable, but hijacking a plane to fly to freedom, with no intention of harming anyone, was as inspirational as the accounts of slaves escaping the inhumanity of their masters via the Underground Railroad. Thus not only did the trial and sentences fail to suppress the yearning of the refuseniks to leave, they elevated the hijackers to heroes,[168] and turned world opinion against the Kremlin, which was seen as so repressive it could not allow these poor innocent people to emigrate.

Demonstrations erupted in Europe, Israel, the United States, and the Soviet Union, with the anger exceeding the reaction to the invasion of Czechoslovakia.[169] Andrei Sakharov telegrammed Brezhnev pleading with him to commute the death sentences,[170] and the Kremlin was inundated with the same message from abroad – from U Thant, secretary general of the United Nations; from Christian religious organizations and leaders, with Pope Paul VI pledging to intercede; and from the US Congress, which passed a resolution, introduced by Rep. Edward Koch of New York, deprecating the sentences.[171]

One development in Washington, DC, nicely encapsulated how a specific Soviet injustice not only temporarily raised the level of indignation, but led to an ongoing expression of outrage. The Washington Committee for Soviet Jewry had started in 1968 by mailing Rosh Hashana greeting cards to synagogues across the USSR. The committee then graduated to protesting outside the Soviet embassy, but now, spurred on by the outcome of the Leningrad trial, the committee moved to institutionalize the protest. In the District of Columbia demonstrations were outlawed within five hundred feet of an embassy. However, the headquarters of the International Union of Electrical Workers was across the street from the Soviet embassy, and the committee arranged with the union to permit a daily, silent noontime vigil outside their building.[172] The vigil would go on for the next twenty years.[173]

Brezhnev could not even discount the reaction as the skullduggery of capitalists and Zionists. The Communist parties in France and Italy declared that they were also bewildered by the verdicts, and as if that were not embarrassing enough a cartoon in a European newspaper likened Brezhnev to the Spanish dictator Francisco Franco by portraying the two leaders dancing around a Christmas tree festooned with hanged men, a reference to the Basque separatists who had recently been sentenced to die. The Kremlin, through the Soviet press, had assailed Franco, the former Fascist enemy of the USSR, for the sentences, and Franco had commuted them on the day after the sentencing in Leningrad. Now Brezhnev had to decide if he would follow suit.[174]

Soviet law stated that the convicted had seven days to file their appeals with the Russian Federation's Supreme Court, and by December 30, only twenty-four hours remained for the condemned. A Jewish leadership conference had been convened in Washington to approach the Nixon administration for help with the Leningrad case. Max Fisher, president of the Council of Jewish Federations and Welfare Funds and, more important, a longtime supporter and trusted adviser to President Nixon, met with congressional leaders through the morning and then, along with Dr. William Wexler and Rabbi Herschel Schacter, paid a call on Secretary of State Rogers at Foggy Bottom. They implored Rogers to intercede, but, in keeping with the State Department practice of remaining aloof from the internal affairs of other nations, Rogers said that his hands were tied.

"What about the president?" Schacter asked. "This is an apolitical cause – purely humanitarian."

Rogers left the room to phone Nixon and returned five minutes later. "Let's go," he said. The four men took the back elevator to the garage and rode over to the White House in the secretary's limousine. At 4:20 PM, they walked into the Oval Office. Nixon sat behind his desk. Chief of Staff H. R. Haldeman and George P. Shultz, director of the Office of Management and Budget, were talking to the president. Before entering the Oval Office, Rogers had cautioned the three Jewish leaders that Nixon's schedule was tight and not to engage him in an extended dialogue. So they hastily repeated their request – could he intercede with Brezhnev?

The president did not rush them, nor did he immediately answer their question. He reminisced about his 1959 kitchen debate in Moscow with Khrushchev. Nixon recalled telling Khrushchev that "a real test of a society is the manner in which a government treats its Jewish citizens." The president then remarked on his admiration for Israel and said that had the Leningrad hijackers been Israeli pilots, they would have escaped with the plane.

Nixon said that he would be glad to help, "but you know I'm Public Enemy Number One in the Kremlin. The minute I try, they'll probably shove these guys up against a wall and shoot them." He paused. "There's a way, though. Listen, last time [Prime Minister] Golda [Meir] was here I said to her, 'Trust me.' Which is what I'll say to you: 'Trust me.'"[175]

On New Year's Eve the Russian Supreme Court commuted the two death sentences to fifteen-year prison terms and reduced the length of time the others would have to serve.[176] In reversing itself, the Kremlin was probably influenced by a combination of the widespread condemnation and the intercession of the White House. None of the Jewish leaders ever learned how Nixon had managed it, but Max Fisher speculated that the president spoke to Kissinger, who contacted Ambassador Dobrynin, who in turn contacted Moscow and suggested that since Brezhnev planned to enter negotiations with Nixon, granting the president's request would be an investment in the future.[177]

The machinations of Soviet leaders in Leningrad exhibited how out of touch they were with sensibilities in the West. All the same, it would have been inconceivable for the Kremlin to anticipate that offering clemency to the hijackers would prove as counterproductive to muffling the outcry for emigration as trying to extinguish a campfire by emptying a bottle of vodka on the orange-hot coals. In March 1971, Soviet Jews fought back against the Kremlin with tactics straight from the civil rights playbook, conducting a sit-in inside the Soviet Parliament on the eve of the Twenty-Fourth Party Congress and voicing their complaints to the foreign journalists who had descended on Moscow to cover the congress. With the counterproductive ambivalence that the Soviet government would repeatedly demonstrate toward its Jews, Brezhnev approved moving forward with more trials, but he also opened the gates wider for Jews wanting to leave the country:[178] in March, a thousand Jews were allowed to emigrate, and another thirteen hundred left in April.[179]

In the United States, the grassroots Soviet Jewry activists – along with many American Jews who sympathized with them but, without a national organization leading a high-pressure membership drive, stood on the sidelines – saw the Kremlin's relenting as proof that quiet diplomacy would not rescue the Jews in the USSR and that the only effective means available was to vilify the Soviet government, in as loud and unified a voice as could be summoned, for denying people's basic human rights.

Even had Nixon's intercession, and not the negative publicity, been decisive, it would not have mattered to the activists, chiefly because they were unaware of it. And there is some question whether Nixon would have crawled out on a limb with the Soviets had he not been keeping a wary eye on the mushrooming activist movement in America.

At the heart of Nixon's foreign policy was détente – the relaxation of tensions between the United States, the Soviet Union, and China[180] – and to pursue it he needed flexibility and a country that was not in turmoil. Already, antiwar demonstrators had limited his options in Vietnam. On April 30, 1970, when Nixon announced that the US had invaded Cambodia to attack the bases of the Viet Cong and the North Vietnamese Army, it was, as the Associated Press said, like "putting a match to a giant fuse."[181] Demonstrations broke out at 1,350 colleges and universities, five hundred of which had to close.[182] Four students were shot dead at Kent State University in Ohio, and a student and teenage grocery store clerk walking across campus after work suffered the same fate at Jackson State College in Mississippi. In response, more than two hundred employees of the State Department publicly denounced the Cambodian incursion with a petition,[183] and one hundred thousand protestors descended on Washington.[184] All of this led the Senate to rebuke the White House by voting fifty-eight to thirty-seven in favor of the bipartisan Cooper-Church Amendment to the Military Sales Act, which denied funds for fighting in Cambodia.[185] It was the first time in American history that the Senate had curtailed the ability of the president to wage war.[186]

The House defeated the amendment, but Nixon was keenly aware that activists could hinder his foreign policy goals. He did not want a Soviet Jewry movement bludgeoning Congress until the White House had no room to maneuver with the Kremlin, and beyond the humanitarian considerations for the hijackers, this may have been the deciding factor in Nixon's decision to urge the Soviets to be more lenient. Fifteen years after leaving the White House, Nixon admitted that the Jewish Defense League, which even before the Leningrad trial and sentences had taken to stalking Soviet diplomats and spitting and cursing at them, was complicating his relations with Brezhnev and "interfering in the Cold War,"[187] and a secret memorandum from the KGB to the Central Committee backs up Nixon's claim. The memo blamed the "Zionists" – KGB-speak for anyone favoring Soviet Jewish emigration – for striving "to counteract any rapprochement in relations between the US and USSR." KGB agents were particularly disturbed by Kahane; they reported that the JDL leader had "developed an entire program of action against the Soviet Union for fascist elements in the US."[188]

With all due respect to KGB paranoia, Kahane was never disciplined enough to concoct a realistic program that could be sustained over the long haul. Fringe groups rarely play this role. By nature, they are reactive – outlandishly so; it is precisely this outlandishness that furnishes the catalyst for more sober political undertakings. However, while the Soviets worried about Kahane, they again discounted their provocative actions in Leningrad, the round-up of Jews across the USSR, the ignominious parade of Stalinesque trials, and, by the summer of 1971, the forty-two Jewish activists wasting away in prison cells[189] – all of which provoked a lurid stint of JDL violence that would enlist the Jewish community and Congress in the campaign to save Soviet Jewry and, just as Nixon had feared, confront his administration with an act of Congress that threatened to scuttle détente and alter the terms of the Cold War.

◆ ◆ ◆

In New York City, the Jewish Defense League set off bombs outside the offices of Intourist and Aeroflot, and inside Amtorg, the Soviet trade center. In Washington, DC, a bomb blew out the windows and destroyed the gate of the Soviet cultural building, and the bombing was followed up by calls to news outlets saying, "This is a sample of things to come. Let our people go. Never Again!" The cars of Soviet diplomats were firebombed, their counterparts in Europe received letter bombs,[190] and an eighteen-year-old JDL member was arrested by the New York police carrying a rifle that had just been used to fire four shots through an apartment window of the Soviet mission.[191] Two gift shops stocked with Soviet goods, one in New York and the other in Minnesota, were bombed. Plots to attack a Soviet-owned estate on Long Island, to assassinate Ambassador Dobrynin, and to fly a large model airplane loaded with explosives and steered by remote control into the Soviet mission were derailed by authorities.[192]

The White House, Justice Department, and the NYPD were not the only ones concerned about the uptick in violence. In a secret memo to the Central Committee, the KGB also wanted to put a stop to it and recommended taking "measures to compromise the leadership of the Jewish Defense League in foreign public opinion." To accomplish this aim, one tactic the KGB proposed was emphasizing that even "the leaders of the New York Jewish community have distanced themselves from the actions of the league."[193]

It was a logical strategy, a way for the Kremlin to make it permissible for non-Jews to reject Kahane without fearing the charge of antisemitism – but it was out of date. Initially resistant to Kahane, the Jewish movers and shakers in New York, some of the most influential players among American Jewry, were growing more sympathetic to the JDL, a measure of their disgust with the Soviet hostility toward Israel and the mistreatment of the refuseniks.

Emanuel Rackman, rabbi of the Fifth Avenue Synagogue on the Upper East Side of Manhattan, a respected scholar and the provost at Yeshiva University, set up private talks for Kahane that raked in as much as $50,000 in contributions from donors like the financier and philanthropist Joseph S. Gruss,[194] who had fled Poland to escape the Nazis.[195] According to Kahane's uncle, Isaac Trainin, the director of the Federation of Jewish Charities, wealthy donors publicly rejected Kahane while lining up to "give him money under the table." During a federation dinner the billionaire Max Stern, founder of Hartz Mountain, told Trainin that easily "twelve of the twenty or thirty people sitting on the dais…had given [his nephew] $10,000 or more."[196] One well-known Jew who was not ashamed to approve of Kahane was counterculture hero Bob Dylan, who told a reporter that he greatly admired the JDL and called Kahane "a really sincere guy" who has "put it all together."[197]

More than money and endorsements, though, Kahane was collecting headlines. From the JDL's first demonstration outside NYU in August 1968 until New Year's Eve 1971, the Jewish Defense League was mentioned in the *New York Times* on 388 occasions. During that same period, the

American Jewish Conference on Soviet Jewry was mentioned thirty-four times and the Student Struggle for Soviet Jewry fifteen. Also, by then, the JDL boasted a membership in excess of ten thousand in the United States, Britain, France, and South Africa.[198] Most important, Kahane had focused attention on the anguish of Soviet Jews and forced the Jewish establishment to address that anguish.

Shoshana Cardin, who at this juncture was rising through the leadership ranks of Jewish philanthropic organizations in her hometown of Baltimore, recalled that over the years the rescue of Soviet Jewry had been a frequent topic of conversation among the establishment groups, but just as frequently the discussions circled back to the bedrock issue of money. Regardless of whether the hundreds of thousands of potential Soviet Jewish emigrants wound up in Israel or the United States, the question remained: who would pay the staggering costs to resettle them?

"American Jews, of course," says Cardin. "But we already had plenty of organizations to fund, and we were emptying our pockets for Israel.[199]

Still, by the fall of 1970, the organized American Jewish community made a start. At the annual meeting of the general assembly of the Council of Jewish Federation and Welfare Funds in Kansas City, CJF leaders kept their word to the student protestors who had come to Boston the year before, and appropriated $100,000 for a campaign on behalf of Soviet Jews. In February 1971, a World Conference on Soviet Jewry was held in Brussels. Eight hundred delegates from thirty-eight countries and a plethora of nongovernmental organizations were invited.[200] Morey Shapira, who got involved in Soviet Jewry activism in Boston during the early 1970s and was later elected president of the Union of Councils, said, "Brussels was a joke. More infighting. More bickering over turf."[201] His judgment was seconded by an editorial in the student Jewish newspaper *Genesis 2*, which held that the conference featured "opportunism, organizational self-aggrandizement, bureaucratic buck-passing, cowardice and cynicism," and the "same penchant for disunity that paralyzed world Jewry while six million died."[202]

At last, in the summer of 1971, there was a step in the right direction. The ineffectual AJCSJ was replaced by another, better-funded umbrella agency, the National Conference on Soviet Jewry (NCSJ).[203] During the transition Rabbi Herschel Schacter served as the chairman; he was succeeded by Richard Maass, an investment manager long involved in civil rights and a prominent member of the American Jewish Committee.[204] Maass made sure that organizations like B'nai B'rith and the Council of Jewish Federations would pay the dues necessary to finance NCSJ.[205] To run the National Conference, Maass tapped Jerry Goodman from the American Jewish Committee. Born in Brownsville, Brooklyn, Goodman was in his early twenties and had been active in both the civil rights and antiwar movements. Goodman was offered space in the Presidents Conference offices, but he believed that "we needed to be seen as an independent, free-standing operation."[206] An office was opened in Washington, but Goodman doubted that he would be there for long. Maass had assured him that he would only be taking a two-year leave of absence from his job overseeing European affairs for the AJC. It was an overly optimistic prediction; Goodman would serve as executive director of the NCSJ for the next seventeen years.[207]

Goodman says that NCSJ was created as a direct result of Kahane. "There had been some talk by the establishment about starting an organization dedicated to Soviet Jews, but nothing had come of it until it became obvious that the JDL had the field to itself, and then there was great concern that the fate of Soviet Jews had been left to crazy people."[208]

◆ ◆ ◆

In January 1972, bombs exploded in two Manhattan talent agencies, Columbia Artists and the offices of impresario Sol Hurok. Both agencies booked Soviet entertainers, but Hurok, who had immigrated to America from the Ukraine, was the most famous for it, bringing the Bolshoi Ballet, the Moiseyev dancers, and many other Russian luminaries to perform in the United States. The sound of the blasts had barely faded when the Associated Press and NBC received anonymous calls claiming that the bombings were a protest against "the deaths and imprisonment of Soviet Jews."[209] For some time, Hurok had been an object of Kahane's wrath, the JDL leader commenting that the impressario's "appetite for profits leads him to abandon his obligations as a human and his loyalties as a Jew."[210] Two years before the bombings Kahane had sent some of his less savory representatives to Hurok's office, where one burned a hole in his carpet with a cigarette to threaten him.[211] No one was hurt at Columbia Artists, but a twenty-seven-year-old Jewish secretary, Iris Kones, who worked for Hurok, died from smoke inhalation, and a number of others, including Hurok, were injured. Kahane was in Israel, and he characterized the bombings as "insane."[212] Nonetheless, the damage was done: in one fell swoop the JDL lost much of its support. Kahane's first cousin, David Kahane, rabbi at the Sutton Place Synagogue in Manhattan, conducted the funeral of Iris Kones and in his eulogy observed that her death was the "bitter fruit of the climate of violence."[213]

Less than a week later, the celebrated Russian poet Yevgeny Yevtushenko, author of "Babi Yar," appeared in front of a sold-out crowd at Madison Square Garden's Felt Forum, though not before police, responding to a bomb threat, had searched the theater. "Flailing his arms and howling with indignation," Yevtushenko read "Bombs for Balalaikas," which he had written after the tragedy at Hurok's office.[214] Yevtushenko reflected on "poor Iris, victim of the age…fragile, dark-eyed Jewish girl suffocated by smoke, as though in a Nazi gas chamber," and then the poet threw a haymaker at the JDL: "Damn you, servants of Hell, who seek coexistence between peoples, by building bridges of cadavers."[215]

The Jewish Defense League did not disappear; in fact, Malcolm Hoenlein, head of the Greater New York Conference on Soviet Jewry, an organization affiliated with NCSJ, would apprise the JDL of rallies and encourage an occasional, restrained show of civil disobedience, still an effective method for attracting the press.[216] But after the Hurok bombing the Jewish Defense League was relegated to the sidelines, and Kahane, upon winning a seat in the Knesset, sank into a morass of hatred until his assassination on November 5, 1990, after a speech at the Marriott Hotel in midtown Manhattan. The assassin was an Islamic radical, El Sayyid Nosair; his accomplices were eventually linked to the first World Trade Center bombing,[217] and Nosair's defense, it was later revealed, was partly funded by Osama Bin Laden.[218]

Regardless of how repugnant one might find Kahane, he bequeathed a legacy to Soviet Jews, pressuring the US government and the organized American Jewish community to take up their cause, and posing enough of a challenge to détente that the Kremlin started to open the doors of the USSR. The number of Jewish emigrants jumped from approximately three thousand in 1969, when the JDL began to ratchet up its campaign against the Soviet Union, to nearly forty-five thousand in 1971 and 1972.[219]

The methods Kahane used to accomplish these ends were scorned by the vast majority of American Jews, but equally certain is that his exclamation "Never Again!" reverberated in the souls of all Holocaust-haunted Jews and endured as the rallying cry of the American movement to free Soviet Jewry.

CHAPTER 6

TIME-OUT – THE COLD WAR AND OTHER CONFLICTS

By and large, after the Six-Day War, the American Jewish community seemed to be entwined in a rapturous embrace with Israel. The rapture was conveyed in the exclamation "We are one!" and it was on full display in late September 1969 when Prime Minister Golda Meir arrived at the airport in Philadelphia before traveling to the White House for her first visit with President Nixon. Mobs of people greeted Meir when she landed, with lines of schoolchildren holding up banners and singing *"Hevenu Shalom Aleichem."* More hosannas awaited the prime minister when she was driven to Independence Square, where a crowd of thirty thousand had been standing for hours behind police barricades to hear her speak.[1]

Yet, at the policy level, the rapture and oneness were greatly exaggerated, and the sharp differences over policy altered the relationship among Israel, the Nixon administration, and American Jews and left its claw marks on the Cold War, US domestic politics, and the approach to helping Soviet Jewry.

◆ ◆ ◆

Golda Meir would recall that she felt comfortable with Richard Nixon because they spoke "the same language,"[2] meaning that both leaders saw the Kremlin as an untrustworthy, aggressive, implacable enemy

231

of democracy.[3] All the same, Meir entered the Oval Office with some trepidation. In 1965, during the India-Pakistan War, the United States had embargoed arms to both countries even though Pakistan belonged to SEATO and CENTO, which should have assured the Pakistanis of US aid, a move that led Yitzhak Rabin, then chief of staff of the IDF, to say that America "didn't come through on its commitments."[4] It was not an uncommon sentiment among Israeli leaders, especially because right before President Johnson left the White House he had finally promised to sell fifty Phantom jet fighters to Israel and the jets were slow to arrive.[5]

Meir spent a couple of hours with Nixon and asked him for twenty-five more Phantoms and eighty Skyhawk jets and a low-interest loan to pay for the hardware.[6] With the euphoria of the 1967 victory erased by the War of Attrition, American Jews were so overwrought about the safety of the Jewish state they may well have approved of Nixon lending Israel half the aircraft in the US Air Force. Nixon was worried about the Soviets arming the Egyptians and tried to convince Moscow to institute a joint arms embargo.[7] Nixon had reason to worry about the fighting in the Middle East spinning out of control. In July, National Security Adviser Henry Kissinger had forwarded the president a memo saying that since the Israelis "are one of the few peoples whose survival is genuinely threatened," they would be "more likely than almost any other country to actually use their nuclear weapons."[8]

In his memoir, *RN*, which appeared in 1978, Nixon recounts little of his conversation with Meir other than that he "reassured her that our commitments would be met."[9] Meir is not much more forthcoming in *My Life*: she confirms Nixon's assurance, says that the Palestinians belong in Jordan, and that Nixon concurred with her that no land captured in the Six-Day War should be returned until an "acceptable agreement with the Arabs was reached." Then, intriguingly, Meir adds that in 1969 she had promised not to quote Nixon on "the more substantive matters" they discussed, and she would not break that promise six years later in her memoir.[10]

As time passed, Nixon was less constrained. In a 1989 letter to the author, the former president wrote that he spoke "very bluntly" to the prime minister, telling her that "Israel should make peace with its neighbors when they are weak rather than waiting until later when their strength forces

Israel to do so." Nixon reasoned that for Israel "to remain on a war footing with whatever arms are necessary to defeat its neighbors…is good short-term politics…[but] bad long-term statesmanship. Within Israel itself and also eventually even within the United States, support for such a policy will inevitably erode."[11]

No wonder Meir would not repeat this advice: she was seeking arms to hold off the Arabs, and Israel still needed those arms in 1975 when *My Life* was published. Nixon would have been mauled politically in 1969 if he had repeated it. Besides, his goal, back then, was to pursue détente with the Soviets, and the chief tactic he used was linkage. During the transition after the 1968 election, Nixon and Kissinger had agreed that it was "unrealistic to separate or compartmentalize areas of concern" between the competing superpowers and so decided "to link progress in such areas of Soviet concern as strategic arms limitations and increased trade with progress in areas that were important to us – Vietnam, the Mideast, and Berlin."[12]

Nixon could not very well provide jets to Israel and expect to lessen tensions with the Kremlin or decelerate the arms race in the Middle East. Furthermore, from the outset of his administration, Nixon believed that there was slim hope for diplomatic success in the area, and he distanced the White House from the political siroccos that, with depressing regularity, whipped across the region. The president also restricted Kissinger from becoming involved; the national security adviser would be busy enough with Vietnam, the Soviet Union, Europe, and the secret prize, China. Then, too, Kissinger's Jewishness would be a liability with Arab leaders,[13] and Nixon himself felt that Kissinger would lack objectivity about Israel. Kissinger deplored Nixon's cultural antisemitism and the crude comments that emanated from it, but he doubted his own ability to be objective about the Jewish state, saying, "How can I, as a Jew who lost thirteen relatives in the Holocaust, do anything that would betray Israel?"[14] Nonetheless, in 1973, in the aftermath of the Yom Kippur War, Israelis and American Jews would accuse him of just such a betrayal.

When Nixon named William Rogers, his old friend and former attorney general under Eisenhower, to the post of secretary of state, the president saw his main function as handling "the recalcitrant bureaucracy of the State Department."[15] Rogers had other ideas. He introduced a plan to push Israel back to her pre-June 5, 1967, borders, a slightly altered form of UN Security Council Resolution 242, which drew noisy objections from American Jewry and brought one thousand Jewish, Protestant, Catholic, and black organizational leaders and members to the Statler-Hilton Hotel in Washington to express their disapproval. Nixon had a reassuring letter delivered to the hotel stating that "the United States stands by its friends [and] Israel is one of its friends."[16]

The Israelis rejected the Rogers Plan. After the Six-Day War, then prime minister Levi Eshkol had offered to trade land for peace treaties, and the Arabs, conferring in Khartoum, had answered that there would be no recognition of Israel, no negotiations with Israel, and no peace with Israel.[17] Nor would the Soviets play ball with Nixon: the Kremlin poured weapons into Egypt. So Kissinger brought Yitzhak Rabin, the Israeli ambassador to Washington, to the Oval Office, where the president said that the weapons would be forthcoming, but he would not expose his pledge to public debate. Nixon told Rabin, "The moment Israel needs arms, approach me, by way of Kissinger, and I'll find a way of overcoming bureaucracy."[18]

Kissinger led Rabin to Attorney General John N. Mitchell, a chief political adviser to Nixon, who had been his law partner.

"We had a situation," says Mitchell, "where Henry Kissinger was Jewish…and Bill Rogers was a little mixed up in his perception of the Middle East. And so we handled things like the Phantoms outside of the state department and the national security council. I saw to it that the Phantom deal received proper consideration. I worked on it with [General Alexander M. Haig Jr.], who was on Kissinger's staff…. And that's how Israel got her Phantoms."[19]

As Israel secured its weapons pipeline, the War of Attrition took a dangerous turn. The Egyptians and Soviets kept moving the SAM batteries closer to the Suez Canal and Soviet pilots began flying MiG-21s overhead to protect the missile sites from Israeli air strikes. On June 30, 1970, the missiles destroyed two Israeli planes, and a month later Israel retaliated against the Soviet pilots by setting an aerial ambush, and a dozen Israeli Phantoms and Mirages shot down five MiGs in a few minutes, while the other eleven Soviet fighter jets flew away.[20]

A spike in Israeli-Soviet dogfights was guaranteed to raise the temperature of the Cold War, and a cease-fire was declared in August, but Israel would not enter into peace talks until Nasser removed the SAMs from the cease-fire zone on the Egyptian side of the Suez Canal.[21] In September, while Golda Meir was back in Washington meeting with Nixon, King Hussein of Jordan was undergoing an assault on his leadership by Soviet-backed Palestinian guerillas, the fedayeen. It was also an assault on an American ally. When Nixon took office, Jordan was the only Arab country that had an official relationship with the United States; the others had rejected their governmental connection to Washington after the Six-Day War.[22]

And the Jordanian situation was about to worsen. Just when Hussein's army had quashed the Palestinian insurrection, Syrian tanks invaded Jordan. Kissinger saw this as a Soviet test of American steadfastness,[23] and Nixon believed that the region was on the edge of total war, since Israel would "take pre-emptive measures against a Syrian-dominated radical government in Jordan; the Egyptians were tied to Syria by military alliances; and Soviet prestige was on the line" with its Arab clients. If Israel were pushed to the brink of destruction, the United States would have to enter the fight, which elevated the possibility of a confrontation with the Soviets. Nixon felt as though he were watching "a ghastly game of dominoes, with a nuclear war waiting at the end."[24]

With uncharacteristic understatement, Kissinger remembered this moment as "a challenge [that] had to be met."[25] The question, though, was how to meet it. Given that nearly half of Americans wanted an immediate withdrawal from Vietnam, it would have been politically disastrous for Nixon to dispatch soldiers to the Middle East.[26] Still, talking to reporters the president would not take intervention off the table if the Soviets inserted their forces, and the headlines carried his message: "Nixon Warns Reds: Keep Out."[27]

The crisis came to a happy conclusion for the United States and its allies. At the request of Washington, Israel readied its army and air force. At the same time, Nixon put twenty thousand troops on alert and increased US naval presence in the Mediterranean as a signal to the Soviets. The Jordanian military was effective and successfully threw back the Syrians and cleared the fedayeen from Amman.[28] When Palestinian leader Yasser Arafat at last agreed to a halt of the hostilities with Jordan, two thousand people had died.[29] That month of carnage would be added to the list of Palestinian grievances under the name "Black September."

Calm returned to the region – or rather a Middle Eastern version of calm. Four days after Arafat accepted the truce, Nasser died; he was succeeded by Anwar el-Sadat and a sedate interval of Egyptian confusion while Sadat contemplated the paths to war and peace. American Jews were relieved to see the Nixon White House assuming a sympathetic posture toward Israel, furnishing weapons and backing away from the Rogers Plan.[30] The relief was partially attributable to their perception that Nixon had never been considered a friend of the Jews and had won only 17 percent of the Jewish vote in the 1968 election.[31]

But all was not as it seemed. For Nixon, assisting the Israelis was based on the same geopolitical strategy as assisting the South Vietnamese. In a memorandum he dictated to Kissinger, the president explained that he backed Israel because it was "the only state in the Mideast which is *pro-freedom* and an effective opponent to Soviet expansion. We will oppose a cut-and-run policy either in Vietnam or Cuba or the Mideast or NATO or anyplace else in the world.... It is a question of all or none."[32]

This pitted the White House against most of the American Jewish community just as the Soviet Jewry movement coalesced and readied itself to approach Congress on legislation designed to punish the Kremlin for its intransigence on emigration. Lyndon Johnson had had to cope with the same disagreement. Jews had been in the forefront of Vietnam protests, and not solely among student radicals and card-carrying intellectuals like Noam Chomsky, Paul Goodman, and Norman Mailer, who had been among the thirty-five thousand antiwar protesters marching on the Pentagon in October 1967[33] (a march that Mailer recounted the next year in his Pulitzer-Prize-winning nonfiction novel, *The Armies of the Night*). As early as January 15, 1966, the Synagogue Council of America, which represented 3.5 million Jews affiliated with Orthodox, Conservative, and Reform synagogues, implored LBJ to refrain from escalating the war. According to the Jewish Telegraphic Agency, the primary news source for the Anglo-Jewish press, "The appeal to President Johnson marked the first time that the entire Jewish religious community took a position on an international issue going beyond immediate Jewish concern."[34]

How Johnson felt about Jewish antiwar activity was revealed when Abe Feinberg, a Jewish adviser and one of his significant fund-raisers, mentioned to the president that his standing by the Republic of Vietnam demonstrated that he would stand by Israel. LBJ replied, "Then why the hell don't the Jews of America believe that?"[35]

It was a fair question with an answer that, during the Johnson administration, was in the process of being born. Jews were intent on clinging to their historical roost on the left wing, while simultaneously advocating for the maximum protection of Israel, a relatively recent addition to their political to-do list and a position associated with the political right. Examined more closely, though, the advocacy for Israel was also a reaction to exclusion at home, a defense against Jew haters from the Midwest to the Middle East and a fundamental component of the evolving civil religion of American Jewry – a faith with its own duality, the proud, majestic light of Israel's existence and the guilt-laden darkness of the Holocaust.

By the 1972 presidential election, and the subsequent exertions to pass the Jackson-Vanik amendment, it would become clear that the politically ambivalent posture of American Jewry was drifting rightward. The ambivalence, quite understandably, annoyed Johnson, and it would frustrate and then enrage Nixon. "I used to see Jewish leaders on the news at antiwar demonstrations," recalled Nixon. "Three days later I'd see these same leaders again in the Roosevelt Room asking us to ship more planes to Israel. I used to say to them, 'But [Vietnam and Israel are] the same war, don't you understand? It's the same war.'"[36]

Complicating this dispute for American Jews was that the Israeli government and military establishment sided with Nixon on Vietnam. More ominous, from Israel's perspective, was the belief that the United States was going to lose. In 1966, the Israeli newspaper *Ma'ariv* engaged Moshe Dayan, the erstwhile chief of staff of the IDF, as a war correspondent. After traveling through South Vietnam, patrolling with US troops, and getting caught in a firefight, Dayan predicted that if the North Vietnamese stuck to guerilla tactics they would prevail.[37] Two years later, when Yitzhak Rabin arrived in Washington, he angered the syndicated columnist Joseph Alsop by telling him essentially the same thing.[38]

By March 1971, halfway through Rabin's tenure as ambassador, a poll revealed that public confidence in the president had plummeted to 50 percent, Nixon's lowest rating since his inauguration. According to another survey, support for US actions in Vietnam was down to 34 percent, with over half of Americans believing that the war was "morally wrong."[39] And all of this came *after* Nixon had appointed William Scranton, a Republican and former governor of Pennsylvania, to head the Commission on Campus Unrest, which reported that the divide between Americans over Southeast Asia was "as deep as any since the Civil War" and suggested that "nothing was more important" than concluding the fighting in Vietnam.[40]

The Israeli government was uneasy with the growing isolationism in the United States. With varying shades of accuracy, isolationism had been blamed for the murder of the six million, and it would be catastrophic for Israel if America withdrew from the region, thereby removing the counterweight to the Soviet Union. Nixon remembered Rabin telling him, on a variety of occasions, that his country "had a stake in the United States not failing in Vietnam and thought that [Israel's friends] in the American Jewish community were in error,"[41] a point that Golda Meir tried to make in 1971 at the Waldorf Astoria when she met with several hundred students of *Habonim* (Builders, in Hebrew), a culturally Jewish socialist Zionist youth movement.[42]

"Three of my closest friends stood up to ask Golda questions," says J. J. Goldberg, who attended the gathering and later became the editor in chief of the *Forward*. "And it was very weird because we felt burned by Golda's embracing Nixon's Vietnam policy. In the 1930s she had been the first emissary from Israel to the first *Habonim* summer camp in the Catskills. And everyone in the room at the Waldorf knew that."

Marty Salowitz broke the ice, saying, "We, as your fellow socialists, had a dream of a democratic Jewish country that stood for enlightened values."

Golda, never fêted for her patience, retorted, "Dreams are for children."

Then David Twersky got up and said, "We're only trying to say that we have a different view, and we're trying to reconcile the socialism we learned in your movement with Israel and your position on Vietnam."[43]

Making a brief stab at an explanation, Golda replied, "The best socialist I know is Lee Kuan Yew [the prime minister of Singapore]. And he has said to me that Nixon is holding the line for democracy and small countries depended on him to do that."

That was not the answer the young men and women had come to hear, and another student, David Mandel, stood and, trying to relieve the obvious tension, said to the prime minister, "Your anger is understandable. But we are living in an atmosphere where these views are widespread and, as much as we try to influence our fellow students, sometimes we are influenced by them as well."

Like a mother disapproving of her wayward teenager, Golda said, "In my generation Zionists, activists, and radicals worked for a living. And got haircuts."

The discussion was over, but as J. J. Goldberg recalled, the fight went on: "I was told that our current emissary from Israel spent the better part of the night in Golda's room trying to talk her out of cutting off our funding."

◆ ◆ ◆

Golda Meir was not alone among Israelis of her generation in her distaste for the youth culture. When the Beatles emerged as a cultural phenomenon they were known in Israel as *Hipushiot Haketzev* (the beat beetles). As if referring to the band as bugs did not express enough disdain, adults added to it with a touch of wordplay, calling the Fab Four *Hipushiot Hazevel* (the dung beetles). This snide disapproval by those on the older side of the generation gap was not unknown in other democracies, but in Israel it reached a higher level. In 1965, after the Beatles arranged to appear there, a government committee refused to permit foreign funds to be used to pay for the concert and explained its decision to cancel the performance by stating that the band "cannot add to the spiritual and cultural life of the youth in Israel."[44]

To a government that believed its nation's survival relied on preserving the tough, ascetic, egalitarian spirit of its pioneers and depended on its youth to fill a military faced with perpetual danger, one can understand the aversion to a blithesome quartet of British mop-tops whose songs, even at their most poignant, reaffirmed the delights of being young, carefree, and alive.

One Israeli, a bar mitzvah boy in 1965, remembered the cancellation with bitterness. "We still had no television and only official radio stations. We were living in a cultural ghetto; the country was Bolshevik. Teenagers and their parents debated it for weeks. Every teenager was furious."[45]

Nevertheless, whatever hostility existed in Israel toward the politics or music of the young, it paled beside the enmity the Israeli government bore the grassroots Soviet Jewry activists in the West, an enmity that would persist right up until the Jews were free.

◆ ◆ ◆

In 1968, Zev Yaroslavsky was a nice, twenty-year-old Jewish boy who often demonstrated against the war in Vietnam and loved the Beatles, both of which, one might say, were part of his heritage, since Zev grew up in the Los Angeles of the placid fifties and rambunctious sixties and was enrolled at UCLA. Zev also loved Israel and detested the repression in the Soviet Union. This, too, was part of his heritage. His parents had emigrated from the Ukraine, Zev attended a Labor Zionist summer camp, and he never forgot a greeting he received on his bar mitzvah from his aunt in the Soviet Union that said, "Happy Thirteenth Birthday."[46]

"My aunt was afraid to write 'bar mitzvah,'" explains Yaroslavsky.[47]

She was also afraid to speak about her Jewish compatriots in public, which Zev learned when he visited his aunt and cousins in Moscow. They were strolling through Red Square when Zev asked, "How is it for the Jews in Russia?" and his aunt replied, "Shhh, the walls have ears."[48]

Upon returning home, Zev was determined to do something to help Soviet Jews.

"I had always wondered how the calamity of the six million could have occurred," says Yaroslavsky. "I believe a lot of Jews my age held our parents' generation accountable for the silence of that period, so Soviet Jewry gave my generation the opportunity to retroactively fight the Holocaust. That's what was going through our minds. Whether true or not, that's what we believed."[49]

Zev had no idea where to begin but, he says, "this was the 1960s, so if you had a problem you took it to the streets." He formed the California Students for Soviet Jews and got in touch with his friends, a number of whom he knew from antiwar rallies and the Jewish student newspaper he founded at UCLA. They made picket signs and ran off announcements on a mimeograph machine, distributing them to students and the press. The plan was to picket the Los Angeles Coliseum, where Soviet and American track teams were engaged in a meet.[50]

"I was warned by the local Jewish Federation Council not to do it, because Jews would suffer for it in the Soviet Union," says Yaroslavsky. "In my youthful arrogance, I said, 'I'll take the chance.' We picketed at four in the afternoon. About the worst time for publicity. What did I know? Maybe thirty people showed up. But the media came and it was the lead story on the evening news on radio and TV. It captured the public imagination and, all of sudden, people around LA were asking, 'Why haven't we done this before?'"[51]

Si Frumkin had been asking himself the same question. A Lithuanian by birth, Si had been liberated from Dachau in 1945 not long before his fifteenth birthday. His father had died two weeks before, and his grandfather had been shot by the Nazis in front of his house before the family was taken away. Once Si was reunited with his mother and immigrated to the United States, he completed college at New York University and moved to Los Angeles to work in the textile business.[52]

"Up until the late 1960s, I never thought of Jews in Russia," says Frumkin. "I was pro-Israel, but that was as far as it went. In 1968, I heard William Korey lecture about official Soviet antisemitism at the Jewish Federation Council. It really upset me. Someone asked if I wanted to volunteer to help, and I filled out a form and wrote that I spoke and read Russian fluently. I was never contacted. I stopped by the federation, and I was told a meeting was being held of the LA Commission on Soviet Jewry. I went to the meeting, but the commission's idea of action was to place an extra chair at the Seder. That was ridiculous, and I looked over at this young guy and could see that he thought it was ridiculous, too. That young guy was Zev."[53]

The two men thought a candlelight walk might draw some publicity, and they were sure Zev could mobilize a few dozen students to march around Westwood. Then Si had a brainstorm. He picked up the phone and called George Putnam, the undisputed heavyweight champion of TV news in Los Angeles, a tall, distinguished anchorman with wavy hair, a slow, distinctive style of speaking, and an unforgettable baritone voice. On the phone Frumkin said that he was a professor who had a student that returned from the Soviet Union and wanted to address the treatment of Jews there. An archconservative who loathed the Russians and was devoted to Israel, Putnam invited Si and Zev to eat dinner with him at Nicodell's. As they ate, Putnam assured the two men that during his broadcasts over the next couple of weeks he would push the idea of a downtown walk on the first night of Chanukah.[54]

"The Commission on Soviet Jewry got angry with us," says Frumkin. "Putnam was advertising like crazy. The commission said he was too conservative, but I think they didn't want us being too upfront about Soviet Jews. My answer was to call [the entertainer] Steve Allen and invite him to walk. Allen said, 'Sure, I'll come.'"[55]

Neither Si nor Zev were optimistic about the numbers the walk would draw – perhaps a few hundred – but as the native-Californian Richard Nixon observed about George Putnam, "Some people didn't like what he said; some people liked what he said. But everybody listened to [him]."[56]

In 1969, the Candlelight Walk for Soviet Jews brought five thousand people to downtown Los Angeles, including Mayor Sam Yorty and an assortment of politicos and celebrities; the next year, the walk drew ten thousand. By then, Hal Light had been in touch with Si and Zev. Light and his wife, Stella, had experience with grassroots organizing; they had put together Parents Mississippi while their son was a civil rights worker in the South. After a visit to the Soviet Union, they formed a tax-exempt advocacy group, the Bay Area Council on Soviet Jewry,[57] and Light encouraged Si to do the same. The result was the Southern California Council for Soviet Jews,[58] and Si, along with Zev's California Students for Soviet Jews, banded together with Lou Rosenblum and the Union of Councils.[59]

It was not long before Si and Zev saw that to garner West Coast media coverage it helped to set aside the more staid forms of protest from the civil rights movements – marches, sit-ins, picketing, and leafleting – and employ the zanier guerilla theater as practiced by Abbie Hoffman and the Youth International Party, the Yippies. Before the Soviet water polo team was going to play in Santa Barbara, they poured red dye in the swimming pool; when oilman Armand Hammer, the son of Russian Jewish immigrants who maintained business and personal relationships across the USSR, refused a request to visit the longtime refusenik Ida Nudel on his next trip to the Soviet Union, they burned a Star of David on the lawn of Hammer's home;[60] they rented a helicopter to fly over the Super Bowl with a banner proclaiming, "Save Soviet Jewry!";[61] and they rented a motorboat to reach a Soviet freighter in the Port of Los Angeles and hurriedly spray-painted "Let Jews Go" on the side of the ship, steadying their motorboat against the waves by slapping toilet plungers on the side of the freighter.[62]

"The *LA Times* printed a picture of it," says Yaroslavsky, "and the Soviets obviously heard about it because another year the captain of the freighter turned out to be a Jew and the spitting image of the comedian Myron Cohen. The captain's last name was Goldberg, and he invited us and the press up on the ship, and we had something to eat and drink and when I came down a reporter asked me what I thought of the Jewish captain. I said, 'He's great. Like the grandfather I never had. I just wish the other three million Soviet Jews could come to us on a ship.'"[63]

Imagine. Three million Soviet Jews steaming into the ports of America. For Zev and other American activists, it was dream. For the Israeli government, it was a nightmare.

◆ ◆ ◆

Beginning in 1948, Jerusalem was nonconfrontational with Moscow in its outreach to Jews in the USSR, avoiding any appearance of an anti-Soviet posture. This strategy was dictated by Israeli military, financial, and diplomatic reliance on the Soviet Union and the United States, and Prime Minister David Ben-Gurion's decision that it was in his country's interest to stay out of the wrestling match between the superpowers.

After the Six-Day War and the War of Attrition, though, this strategy appeared futile. The Cold War had landed on Israel's doorstep. Diplomatic relations between Moscow and Jerusalem were gone, with denunciations crackling like rifle fire between the two countries. The Soviets had thrown themselves behind the Arabs, and Israeli security was now tied to the geopolitical premise that the United States would not tolerate the Soviet Union, directly or indirectly, destroying one of its allies.

Despite the drastically altered circumstances, Israel did not ratchet up its rhetoric about Soviet Jewry, and discouraged others from doing so. Michael Sherbourne, a London schoolteacher who had fought for Israel in 1948 and later taught himself Russian, literally made thousands of phone calls from England to the Soviet Union to speak with refuseniks, a word coined by Sherbourne.[64] The calls were taped and transcribed by Sherbourne, who then forwarded the transcripts to the British Board of Deputies to be reprinted in a bulletin, "Jews in the USSR." Often, the information would not be released, and Sherbourne would learn that it was the Liaison Bureau who had prevented the refuseniks' stories from being told.[65]

Yasha Kazakov was perplexed by the Israeli attitude. After all, Moscow had only permitted him to emigrate to Israel when his letter to the Supreme Soviet, declaring his "indubitable right" to live in the Jewish state, made him a cause célèbre.[66] Kazakov felt that Israel should be leading an offensive to win open emigration for Soviet Jews, and he set out to encourage just such an endeavor by paying a visit to Shaul Avigur,[67] the secretive master of clandestine immigration who had been summoned out of retirement from his kibbutz near the Sea of Galilee to direct the Liaison Bureau.[68]

Kazakov came right to the point. "Why is it that Russian Jews are not afraid to risk their lives by sending letters and petitions to the West, yet the Israelis, living in safety and freedom, are fearful of publishing them?"[69]

Avigur hewed to the party line: an outright demand for the Kremlin to let the Jews go would end any emigration at all; behind-the-scenes negotiations were the safest and wisest choice.[70]

Given his experience, this reply could not have made sense to Kazakov, and so, in March 1970, in a plea placed by the Student Struggle for Soviet Jewry in the *New York Times*, Kazakov asked the world to "Protest against the Soviet Government's Spiritual Annihilation and Forced Detention of Soviet Jews." Then he said he was going on a hunger strike to protest the treatment of his family by the Kremlin and invited everyone to join him at the Isaiah Wall of the United Nations.[71]

One man who would not join Kazakov was Yoram Dinstein, the Liaison Bureau representative working out of the Israeli consulate in New

York. Dinstein's opposition to Kazakov's appearance in the United States disgusted the American activists[72] and, more than forty years on, some have not forgiven him.[73] The Liaison Bureau grew concerned enough about the grassroots organizations that it placed an informant inside the Student Struggle for Soviet Jewry[74] and pressured the Union of Councils to halt their activities.

Dinstein contacted Lou Rosenblum and threatened "to destroy him."[75] He phoned Zev Yaroslavsky and said he was troubled that his California Students for Soviet Jews was listed on the stationery of the Union of Councils; in fact, Dinstein said, it was "a declaration of war." If Yaroslavsky did not remove his organization's name from the stationery, Dinstein promised that he would see to it that Yaroslavsky lost his job at the Jewish Federation.[76] Yaroslavsky refused, and he was fired.[77]

The reaction by the Israeli government to the activists was harsh, but the harshness was a reflection of its deep-seated anxiety that it would lose the chance to bring the Soviet Jews to Israel. One can appreciate the Israeli fear. The Cold War was an unpredictable contest, and the Kremlin ran hot and cold on emigration: in 1970, just over one thousand Jews were permitted to leave; in 1971 Jewish emigration surpassed thirteen thousand.[78] The fluctuation was tied to the grassroots activists' unrelenting dedication to spotlighting Soviet antisemitism and calling for the Kremlin to let the Jews go, and because the Soviets needed the cooperation of the White House and Congress to conclude trade and arms-limitation deals.

Until 1974 almost every Soviet Jewish emigrant went to Israel.[79] But suppose, for a moment, that the Kremlin, desirous of US cooperation or determining that its restricted emigration was extracting too high a price in worldwide reprobation, abruptly chose to unlock the cage and stand aside. In all likelihood hundreds of thousands of Jews would flee. And where would they go? Israel possessed neither the infrastructure nor the financial wherewithal to absorb a stampede. The United States and American Jewry possessed both in abundance. If the great majority of Soviet Jews were to wind up in America it would be a repudiation of Zionist ideology (which maintained a powerful hold on the older generation of Israeli leaders), a challenge to Israel's self-appointed role as the representative of world Jewry, and a threat to its future survival since it desperately needed an influx of Jewish immigrants to build its economy and stock its military.[80]

Still, the emotional charge in the disagreement between Israeli leadership and the American grassroots activists was not a byproduct of the practical or abstract aspects of rescuing Jews in the USSR; it was a consequence of the divergent ways in which Israelis and American Jews (with some exceptions) coped with the Holocaust.

Israel had no lingering guilt about the destruction of European Jewry; it had not even been theoretically feasible for the state-in-the-making to save a substantial percentage of the victims or to stop Hitler's march to war. Consequently, Israel's answer to the six million was the willingness to fight and die to preserve a Jewish state – the national realization of "Never Again!" On the other hand, the American Jewish community, living in comfort and safety, resolved to atone for its inability to save the Jews from the Nazis by saving the Jews from the Soviets. The debt was settled by their rescue, not by their final destination. Thus it was that much of the community favored "freedom of choice" for the emigrants in lieu of imposing the "Israel option" on them, an imposition that struck some as hypocritical since Soviet Jews were in flight from a cruelly authoritarian state that denied them freedom of movement.[81]

In light of this profoundly different relationship to the Holocaust and attitude toward the meaning of freedom, and because Israel could only absorb a slow-moving line of immigrants, the Israeli government worked long and hard to muffle the grassroots clamor, to shape the American Jewish establishment's quiet response, and to ensure that the Soviet Jews immigrated to Israel by pressuring communal leadership to advocate for that option. One strategy for blocking US resettlement was to cut off the money. For example, at a meeting of Jewish establishment leaders, Prime Minister Golda Meir requested that the Hebrew Immigrant Aid Society stop assisting the Soviet Jews in Vienna hoping to enter America. Max Fisher reportedly told colleagues to "give Golda what she wants."[82]

Pragmatism, not philosophy, was behind Fisher's recommendation; he believed that Israel was in need of immigrants and America was not. But while Fisher was endorsing Golda's request with establishment leaders, he was also privately working the other side of the street with Attorney General John Mitchell, who served as Nixon's campaign manager in 1968 and would resign from the Justice Department to reprise that role in 1972. The big, gruff, pipe-smoking attorney general had shown himself to be sympathetic to Israel and the problems of Jews in the USSR, a sympathy that Mitchell biographer James Rosen attributes to a combination of "innate decency" and the "calculations of realpolitik."[83]

Fisher urged Mitchell to use his parole authority to bring Soviet Jews to the United States as political refugees, a designation that allowed them to enter outside the fixed quota limits,[84] and Fisher accompanied Mitchell to the airport in Philadelphia when the first group arrived. As the Russians deplaned and headed for the terminal, Mitchell began to cry, and he stood there, silent and motionless, without even bothering to wipe the tears from his face.[85]

The political reward, Fisher predicted to Mitchell, would come in the 1972 presidential election, where the administration's outreach to Soviet Jewry would increase the Jewish vote for Republicans.[86]

And indeed it would – but more than just a means to appeal to Jewish voters in 1972, Soviet Jewry would be formally ensconced in the Cold War when Senator Henry Jackson and Representative Charles Vanik introduced an amendment that would drag the Jews of the Soviet Union to the center of the geopolitical stage, where they would stay, a moral focal point, until the Cold War ended.

CHAPTER 7

IN SEARCH OF THE WESTERN STAR

On February 17, 1972, all three major television networks ran a live broadcast of President Richard Nixon boarding Air Force One to begin his historic journey to the People's Republic of China,[1] a trip that would be watched by 98 percent of the families in America.[2] National Security Adviser Henry Kissinger had negotiated the arrangements for the visit in secret to skirt the inevitable uproar at home and abroad that would have likely sabotaged the plans had they been bandied about in public.

Nixon was hoping that the Chinese, who provided North Vietnam with small arms and enough rice to feed its people,[3] would help Washington conclude a peace agreement with Hanoi.[4] The inducement for China to lend a hand was Beijing's fear of the hostility directed at it by the Soviets, who had more troops stationed along the Chinese border than they had in Eastern Europe.[5] Chairman Mao had already forbidden the Soviets to use Chinese airfields or airspace to resupply the North Vietnamese, explaining his decision by telling the Kremlin, "We do not trust you."[6] Nixon had pledged that he would not permit the Chinese to be "smashed" by the Soviet Union, a surprising declaration from the formerly rabid anti-Communist,[7] and yet one that was consistent with the Nixon administration's commitment to maintaining an international order that none of the major powers would feel compelled to overturn.[8]

The overarching purpose of the trip, though, was to unnerve the Soviets by forming a Sino-American alliance based on a shared distrust of the

Kremlin, and to alter the geometry of the Cold War, creating a triangular diplomacy that enabled the president to play two US adversaries against each other.[9] In May, Nixon planned to work the other side of the triangle when he flew to Moscow for his scheduled summit with Brezhnev.

Understandably lost in the fanfare, overshadowed by pictures of the president deplaning in Beijing, smiling and standing at the Great Wall with his wife, Pat, and receiving a lesson in the use of chopsticks from Premier Chou En-lai,[10] bills had been quietly introduced in the Senate and House to spend $85 million to assist the Israelis with the absorption of Soviet Jews.[11] At the same time, Samuel Rothberg, the general chairman of the Israel Bond Organization, was preparing to make some history of his own at the Fontainebleau Hotel in Miami Beach, where he would announce his goal of selling a record $450 million in bonds, the proceeds earmarked to help the Jewish state resettle the seventy thousand new immigrants predicted to arrive during the year, mostly from the Soviet Union. The sale would not be limited to the Jewish community. Banks, labor unions, and other financial institutions were ready to buy up to 20 percent of the bonds.[12]

Although foreign aid for Israel and a bond drive would appear far removed from the opening to China, it became clear, after Nixon received an impromptu invitation to Mao's quarters in the old Forbidden City and spent an hour talking to him in his book-filled study,[13] that the issues raised by the events were connected and weighed heavily on both leaders' minds.

The seventy-eight-year-old Mao had been thoroughly prepped for the meeting, and he was unusually alert, as though the import of the occasion provided him with the energy to transcend the ravages of his heart condition, Parkinson's disease, and several strokes.[14] During the conversation he joked that he had voted for Nixon "when your country was in havoc, during your last electoral campaign."[15] Underneath the humor the chairman was expressing his own anxiety about the havoc in China, which had undergone a massive surge of unrest led by its educated young after Mao set off the Great Proletarian Cultural Revolution in 1966. In the name of preserving the passion of the revolution, Mao turned his Red Guards against the national establishment and his political opponents, whereupon China spiraled into anarchy. An estimated four hundred thousand to one million people died, and Mao did not regain control until the end of 1969 when he forced millions of the student revolutionaries into the rural hinterlands, where, according to the *People's Daily*, the official newspaper of the Chinese Communist Party, they were "re-educated by workers, peasants, and soldiers."[16]

Still, Mao faced internal resistance, and it was apparent to Nixon that the chairman harbored a deep concern for preserving order in his country. And while Mao was distressed by the actions of the Soviet Union toward China, he was aware of the strife inside the USSR. By the winter of 1971 Soviet Jewry was an international news story, as was the American movement demanding that the Kremlin let the refuseniks go, a story that prominently featured mass demonstrations and bombings carried out by the JDL. So toward the conclusion of their conversation, with Mao visibly tired, Nixon sought to reassure him by saying, "What brings us together is a recognition on our part that what is important is not a nation's internal political philosophy. What is important is its policy toward the rest of the world and toward us."[17]

One can construe this statement as Nixon assuring Mao that the debate between capitalism and Communism would not color their relationship, but that seems too trite a difference to raise in the context of establishing their new geopolitical alliance. Certainly, it was a reference to the dispute over Beijing's claim that Taiwan was part of China and therefore an internal matter, but since the disagreement about Taiwan would shortly be addressed in the Shanghai Communiqué, the statement can also be interpreted as Nixon promising that China's record of abuse toward its own people would not be used to foment internal dissent and external condemnation – as the record of Soviet abuse was being used against the Kremlin. Given Mao's concern about internal mayhem, this is a likely interpretation. Moreover, later that evening, at the banquet in the Great Hall, which was broadcast live for four hours by the three networks in the United States, Premier Chou En-lai toasted the president and specifically cited the "non-interference in each other's internal affairs" as one of the principles underpinning the Sino-American friendship.[18]

A final point that Nixon made to Mao and Chou was that he kept his word: "I never say something I cannot do," the president assured, "and

I will always do more than I can say."[19] It was a point that Nixon and Kissinger would also make repeatedly to Brezhnev and Gromyko – that the administration would do whatever was necessary to surmount the obstacles of Congress and public opinion to deliver on its promises.

Such a pledge is comforting to authoritarian leaders disquieted by the unpredictable outcomes produced by democracy. Americans, on the other hand, were becoming impatient with Nixon end-running Congress and defying the popular demand for a full withdrawal of US troops from the fighting in Southeast Asia. That impatience would be given voice by historian Arthur M. Schlesinger Jr. in *The Imperial Presidency*, which began appearing in the *Atlantic Monthly* in 1973 and was published as a book that same year. Schlesinger conceded that "vigorous presidential leadership…enabled the American republic to meet the great crises of its history," but argued that Nixon's conception of the office was too "preemptory"[20] and while the president should not be a "puppet," neither should he be a "czar."[21]

Long after the storm of his presidency had passed, Nixon looked back without regret to his formulation of foreign policy outside official channels – an approach that both circumvented the bureaucracy of the State Department and prevented the American people and Congress from peering disapprovingly over his shoulder.

Said Nixon: "You'll see all these experts burbling about the need to do things through official channels. Let me tell you: if we had done things through channels, we wouldn't have had the opening to China; we wouldn't have had [the Strategic Arms Limitation Talks]; we wouldn't have had negotiations to end the war in Vietnam. Generally, you should try to get it through channels so that you have an orderly procedure. So that you have a record and so forth. But when you have highly controversial issues, very complex issues, it is necessary in a negotiation to have private talks."[22]

Granted, these tactics may have been necessary and, more often than not, effective, but they could not protect a president from issues that attracted public support strong enough to mobilize Congress to assert its constitutional authority – a lesson that Nixon would learn with respect to freedom for Soviet Jewry. Even more challenging for the president was that the charge would be led by a senator and congressman, and in the end not only would the White House lose the two-and-a-half-year battle, but the policy of détente would become collateral damage.

◆ ◆ ◆

On March 30, 1972, Hanoi launched a spring offensive. One hundred twenty thousand North Vietnamese regulars and thousands of Viet Cong guerrillas rushed into the northern provinces of South Vietnam, across the central highlands and the Cambodian border region above Saigon.[23] Nixon had been steadily withdrawing US forces from the theater since the summer of 1969 when he announced his intention to turn over responsibility for fighting to the South Vietnamese – a plan known as "Vietnamization" – so there were just seventy thousand American troops in-country to meet the Communist offensive and only 10 percent of these were combat troops. Nixon was under no illusion about the eventual outcome of the war, writing in his diary that "the real problem is that the enemy is willing to sacrifice in order to win, while the South Vietnamese aren't willing to pay that much of a price in order to avoid losing."[24]

Nixon wanted a negotiated settlement in Vietnam, and to show the Saigon and Hanoi governments that he felt free to exercise American power to get and maintain such a settlement, he unleashed a ferocious bombing on North Vietnam to counteract the Communist invasion, and ordered the mining of North Vietnamese ports to choke off the supply of oil[25] and shipments of Soviet weapons.[26] A Soviet cargo ship was sunk and two Russian sailors died,[27] but the Kremlin did not threaten to cancel the upcoming Nixon-Brezhnev summit, a measure of how unnerved it was by the US rapprochement with China and its own economic desperation.

The Politburo, according to Yuri Andropov, had determined by the mid-1960s that it could no longer "settle" for food shortages, because if trends persisted, Soviet citizens "would have to go on starvation rations soon."[28] Stocking cities with adequate food supplies had bedeviled Russian leaders and imperiled the stability of the society since the days of the tsars and had led to the Russian Revolution in 1917 and the civil war that followed.[29] And in 1962, when the price of meat and butter rose sharply, thousands of people had rioted in Novocherkassk and the army had to be summoned, an uprising that went unreported by the Soviet press.[30] By 1972, because of a cold spell and drought, the Soviets were suffering through their worst grain harvest since 1963,[31] their economy was stalled, and dissidents were sprouting like spring flowers – and not just inside the Soviet Union. In Poland, protests broke out over soaring food prices, which the army quelled by firing on and killing protestors in Gdansk and Gdynia.[32] (In the Gdansk shipyard one of the observers to the violence was a mustachioed fireplug of a man, Lech Wałęsa, who six years later would be fired from his job for attempting to organize a labor union.[33]) Revealing the extent of its concern about the connection between social turmoil and abysmal living standards, the Kremlin did not respond to the unrest by invoking the Brezhnev Doctrine and ordering troops into Poland, but stepped up the production of consumer goods and sought to buy food and technology from Western Europe and the United States.[34] Soviet leaders were still unwilling to institute any liberal reforms, but they recognized that they had to reach out to the West as a means of addressing the rising discontent across the USSR.[35]

Whether Nixon realized the fragility of the Soviet circumstances and how vulnerable the Kremlin must have been if its solution was to seek assistance from its sworn ideological enemies is unclear, but the president had three overriding goals for the summit: showing demonstrable achievements from his policy of détente, seeking Soviet help to reach a negotiated end to the war in Southeast Asia, and generating a favorable reaction among the American people that would assure his reelection in November. Because Nixon would be the first president to visit Moscow and he was slated to approve an Anti-Ballistic Missile Treaty and the Strategic Arms Limitation Treaty Interim Agreement (both of which had been forged by negotiators in Helsinki and Vienna), much was made of the upcoming summit in the media, and American Jewish activists used the press attention to add their concern about the treatment of Russian Jews to the president's agenda.

Malcolm Hoenlein, executive director of the Greater New York Conference on Soviet Jewry, was unique for his ability to work easily with both establishment groups and grassroots activists, and three weeks before Nixon left for Moscow, the GNYCSJ, in conjunction with the National Conference on Soviet Jewry, organized the first Solidarity

Sunday demonstrations.[36] In Chicago, a rally was staged outside the Civic Opera House; in Dallas, thousands of Jews and Christians gathered at a mass meeting; in Philadelphia, a round-the-clock protest began with a Saturday-night prayer vigil; in Los Angeles, telephone conversations between American Jews and their relatives who had been imprisoned by Soviet authorities were played in public; and in New York City, forty-five thousand people marched down Fifth Avenue to Dag Hammarskjold Plaza.[37]

Demonstrations were held in ninety communities across the country, an indication that Soviet Jewry was becoming a cause for concern among Americans. The large crowds were also indicative of two cultural shifts in the Jewish community. The first was spotted by a reporter covering the rally in New York, who wrote that "the plaza was filled with young people in blue jeans, older couples in their best clothes and children scurrying for vantage points."[38] Here, at last, was a common purpose capable of bridging the generation gap that often painfully divided parents from their children, a respite from the standard arguments over hair, clothes, music, and politics. Looking back at his years as an activist, Yossi Klein Halevi said that he got along fine with his father at Soviet Jewry rallies, but "when we stopped being Jews together and switched to being Americans, we fought as bitterly as any father and son in the 1960s."[39]

How Jews actually expressed their Jewishness accounted for the second cultural shift. As social barriers for American Jews began to fall after the Second World War, assimilation accelerated, a trend that was noticeable in the rate of intermarriage – from 5 percent in the 1950s to 28 percent in the 1970s.[40] Leaving religion behind, however, frequently made Jews more active in secular Jewish life. Israel had been one cause tying them to their Jewish past; now, Soviet Jewry was another.

"I met Jews during this time who hadn't been in a synagogue in years," says Carmi Schwartz, who would serve as the executive vice president of the Council of Jewish Federations. "Some of them were proud that they didn't belong to a synagogue. But they gave money to their federation and the United Jewish Appeal, and they were willing to do anything they could for Soviet Jews."[41]

Before departing for the summit Nixon met with American Jewish leaders in the White House and promised to discuss Soviet Jewry with Brezhnev. The president was not unaware of the advantages that their immigration would have for Israel or that the American Jewish community's concern for Russian Jews would be a matter for debate in the run-up to the election. Max Fisher had told Nixon's campaign manager, John Mitchell, that he felt a strong stand on behalf of Soviet Jews would win Republicans a meaningful percentage of the Jewish vote, never a bountiful harvest for Nixon.[42]

At the summit, the president was good to his word and privately raised the subject with Brezhnev, asking him straight out, "When will you let the Jews go?" Brezhnev countered, "When will you release Angela Davis?"[43] The black militant and Communist was currently on trial in California for her alleged role in a shooting and escape at a Marin County courthouse.[44]

"It wasn't a helpful exchange," Nixon recalled.[45]

Kissinger had more success working his back channel with Dobrynin,[46] handing him lists of refuseniks "who were barred from emigration by some technicality of security regulations or for other difficulties," and he received assurances that some thirty-five thousand Jews would be permitted to emigrate each year.[47] Nixon and Kissinger also discussed improved trade relations with the Soviets. The Kremlin was seeking most-favored-nation status, which sounds more advantageous than it is: a country granted MFN from Congress is given access to the US market and pays the same tariffs as other countries pay. More precisely, MFN status represented the normalization of trade relations, and Kissinger saw it as "more important to the Soviets for symbolic rather than for commercial reasons," bestowing on the USSR "the appearance of equality in the economic field."[48]

Nixon was reluctant to finalize a trade agreement. He had asked Brezhnev for help with a settlement in Vietnam and felt it prudent to wait and see if the assistance would be forthcoming before rewarding the Kremlin with a trade deal. So Nixon and Brezhnev agreed to form a commission that would negotiate a plan in which the Soviets would receive MFN status and Export-Import Bank credits if they paid their lend-lease debt from the Second World War.[49]

The summit was hailed as a victory for détente, and yet, despite all the talk about the policy, détente was little else than a tactic disguised as a strategy – a grandiloquent term that evoked the royal European courts of a vanished past replete with fairy-tale castles and amatory intrigue. Stripped of its romantic veneer, the word was a substitute for the more prosaic expression "playing for time." The Soviets would not stop their struggle against capitalism and, Kissinger admitted, the United States was hoping to avoid a US-USSR nuclear conflagration long enough for the "historical process of erosion" to break up the Soviet empire.[50]

The summit did produce a signed Strategic Arms Limitation Talks (SALT) agreement – though as Nixon commented to Brezhnev, both sides retained arsenals deadly enough to "destroy each other many times over,"[51] – and an Agreement on Basic Principles of Relations, which promised that the superpowers would cooperate to prevent nuclear war, to stifle regional conflicts, and to maintain the balance of power around the globe. Nonetheless, neither Washington nor Moscow intended to stop spreading their influence and protecting their allies or employing détente as a shield behind which each would attempt to outflank the other.[52]

One weapon that Nixon had no intention of publicly deploying against the Kremlin was the situation of Soviet Jews. The first principle of the agreement stated that the development of normal relations would be based, in part, on the "noninterference in internal affairs," and the third principle reaffirmed that pledge by saying that the US and USSR would not "be subject to outside interference in their internal affairs."[53] As if that was not adequate to placate the Kremlin, Nixon gave a speech that was carried on Soviet radio and television, saying that peace could only be attained through "mutual respect," and hence the United States supported "the right of each nation to chart its own course…without interference from other nations."[54]

Nixon readily consented to these conditions because he thought it fruitless to stress the human rights abuses perpetrated by the Kremlin.

"If someone wanted to do the Soviets in," Nixon said, "I was all for it. But no great nation can allow itself to be forced into doing something internally by another nation."[55]

On this subject, Kissinger was in perfect alignment with his boss. He believed that "other imperatives imposed limits on our ability to produce internal changes in foreign countries," and since the Soviet Union was a nuclear superpower there was "no rational alternative to the pursuit of a relaxation of tensions."[56]

Consequently, Kissinger did not bash the Kremlin in public on the question of Soviet Jewry because he thought it served no useful purpose. As the Cold War was ending, he would change his mind.[57]

Another outgrowth of the summit, not much commented upon at the time, was that Nixon agreed to allow preliminary discussions to proceed on a Conference on Security and Cooperation in Europe (CSCE). Brezhnev had been asking Nixon about it since January, writing to him that he considered it important "to undertake further concrete steps that would consolidate the détente and safeguard security in Europe…. A confidential exchange of views, suggested by you…would, I believe, be useful indeed."[58]

Soviet leadership had been angling to convene such a meeting since 1954, when Foreign Minister Molotov proposed it. The emergent conflicts of the Cold War interfered with any further discussion until Brezhnev revisited it in 1966 at a gathering of the Warsaw Pact in Bucharest.[59] In his authorized biography, published while he was in power and authored by the Academy of Sciences of the USSR, Brezhnev claimed that the significance of such a conference would be clear to Europeans "who belong to the generation that experienced the Second World War," and to those "who grew up and are living in conditions of peace and who rightly consider that this is as it should be."[60]

Although the people of Hungary, Czechoslovakia, and Poland – to say nothing of the Soviet dissidents and refuseniks – may well have objected to Brezhnev's assertion that they were living in peace, Kissinger told Nixon that his impression of Brezhnev was of a man whose horrific memories of the Second World War retained their hold on him and who truly hated war.[61] Perhaps, but Nixon thought that behind Brezhnev's noble rhetoric was the less lofty desire of the Kremlin to get the West to sign a document legitimizing Soviet control of Eastern Europe.[62] Nixon was hesitant, but once leaders in Western Europe endorsed the idea of a Conference on Security and Cooperation, Nixon decided it was pointless to stand in their way.[63]

It is no small irony that ultimately the accords born at the CSCE and heralded by the Kremlin as a triumph did more than any other document to hasten the collapse of the Soviet empire.

◆ ◆ ◆

Détente had its muscle-bound detractors in the USSR and the United States, and the first to lash out at it after the summit was the number two man in the Communist Party and its most forceful ideologue, Mikhail A. Suslov,[64] a humorless man who had risen to prominence under Stalin. Suslov had assisted with the purges during the 1930s, the deportation of ethnic minorities from the Caucasus and the crackdown on Eastern Europe in the 1940s, and had urged the Kremlin to take an iron fist to the 1956 Hungarian revolt and the 1968 Prague Spring. Intoxicated by the mists of a glorious past more imagined than real, Suslov advocated for stepping up Marxist indoctrination in schools and factories. He was hostile to any strain of dissidence, whether from Jews clamoring to emigrate or teenagers emulating their "bourgeois" Western counterparts with their taste for long hair, Levi's, and rock 'n' roll.[65]

Suslov pushed for a head tax on emigrants, with a graduated scale from $5,000 to $25,000, to reimburse the state for their higher education,[66] and cleverly applied it to all emigrants to avoid the charge of antisemitism. But the decree, according to historian Henry Feingold, fooled no one, since Jews "disproportionately possessed higher education degrees and were overwhelmingly the candidates for emigration."[67]

The "diploma tax" had been discussed as far back as July 1971, and it was enacted during August of the following year while Foreign Minister Gromyko and General Secretary Brezhnev were on vacation at the Black Sea,[68] leaving Suslov in charge of the Kremlin.[69] Gromyko did not accept that freedom of movement was a "chief human right," a designation he reserved for the right to life; it was only the West, he thought, that interpreted human rights so narrowly.[70] Nonetheless, he thought the tax was a gross political misstep,[71] and when the Politburo took up the tax at a meeting, Premier Alexei Kosygin and Brezhnev were appalled by it. After KGB chief Yuri Andropov said that he had received the directive from Suslov,[72] Kosygin commented that "we are creating the Jewish problem for ourselves," and Brezhnev added, "Zionism is making us stupid."[73]

The Soviets would later argue that too much was being made of the tax. Israel had paid for Romanian Jews to be released by Communist dictator Nicolae Ceausescu, and West Germany had a similar deal with the Kremlin, though instead of a paying a tax West Germany provided loans to the Soviet Union.[74] From the outset, though, the Soviets realized that the new diploma tax would be assailed, the evidence being that initially the directive was kept under lock and key. It was a Jewish emigrant in Kiev who copied and sent it to the Liaison Bureau's Nechemia Levanon, who forwarded it to Israeli and American officials.[75]

Prime Minster Meir denounced the tax in the Knesset as "a shameful decree,"[76] but it is hard to imagine that the prime minister was shocked about a country asking Israel to pay for immigrants. The Mossad had put together a secret deal with Morocco that, between 1962 and 1964, brought one hundred thousand Moroccan Jews to Israel at a cost estimated between $5 million and $20 million.[77] Meir was more likely concerned about the Kremlin training, arming, and inciting the Arabs, and took the opportunity to turn opinion – especially in the United States – against the Soviets. She was not disappointed. Twenty-one Nobel Prize winners and six thousand professors called for an end to the tax, and Max Fisher, president of the Jewish Agency's board of governors; Jacob Stein, chairman of the Presidents Conference; and Richard Maass, president of the National Conference on Soviet Jewry, met with Secretary of State Rogers to express the anger of the Jewish community.[78]

"We called the exit tax a 'ransom,'" says Jerry Goodman, then the executive director of the NCSJ. "It was a ridiculous move by the Soviets. What was it, slavery? Like putting Africans on an auction block and saying, 'Look, he's worth $25,000.' Only now it was Jews up on the block."[79]

The comparison that was soon being made was not to the nineteenth-century American South but to Nazi Germany, where in the wake of *Kristallnacht* Hermann Goering levied a "flight tax" on Jews, and the banker and economist Hjalmar Schacht concocted a ransom plan that could be used to rescue Germany's Jewish population.[80] The comparison between the situation of Jews under Hitler and Jews in the Soviet Union was imprecise, and is further evidence of the past casting a distortive shadow across the present. While Soviet society was rife with antisemitism, the outcry against the tax obscured the geopolitical objections that Suslov and other Soviet leaders had to détente – objections that highlight how Soviet

Jewry was becoming entwined in the intricacies of the Cold War.

◆ ◆ ◆

Kissinger would recall that Dobrynin explained the tax to him by saying that "some middle-level functionary had made a routine decision mechanically ratified by the relevant minister who himself was a technician."[81] It was a lame excuse. Kissinger knew that the Soviet system would not permit decisions impacting foreign policy to be finalized at that level, and Kissinger guessed that the tax was an attempt by the Soviets "to refurbish their credentials" in the Arab world.[82]

It was a good guess. Indeed, in the midst of one Politburo conversation about restricting Jewish emigration, Brezhnev commented that he was hoping to avoid a quarrel with the Arabs.[83]

One Arab leader who was angry with Brezhnev was Egyptian president Anwar el-Sadat. He had been blindsided by the summit, because the Agreement on Basic Principles of Relations appeared to preclude Soviet help in recovering the Sinai Peninsula and the Gaza Strip, which Egypt had lost during the Six-Day War. So in July, in a bid to see if the United States might assist him in approaching Israel for a return of the territory, Sadat ordered fifteen thousand Soviet advisers to leave Egypt.[84]

Nor was Sadat alone in his fear of Soviet Jewish emigration into Israel. Palestinian radicals were also worried. The rumors of thirty-five thousand Jews per year being allowed to go might have been seemed low to Soviet Jewry activists, but to Arabs at war with Israel every immigrant translated into another soldier protecting the Jewish state. The response was a wave of terror. In May 1972, four Palestinian Black September terrorists hijacked a flight from Vienna and forced it to land at Lod Airport in Tel Aviv, and three weeks later a trio from the Japanese Red Army massacred twenty-four people in the passenger area of the Tel Aviv airport. Then in June of the following year, a Palestinian terrorist placed a bomb on the autobahn near the Schoenau Castle in Vienna, a way station for Soviet emigrants en route to Israel, but the bomb went off prematurely, killing the terrorist.[85] In August, two Arab terrorists murdered five travelers at the airport in Athens, Greece, when they mistook a TWA plane loading for New York for another TWA flight boarding passengers for Israel.[86] That fall, an Arab terrorist organization, calling itself the Eagles of the Palestinian Revolution, directly aimed their violence at the emigrants when a pair of armed terrorists commandeered a train with thirty-seven Soviet Jews onboard.[87] The train was passing through Czechoslovakia to Austria, from where the Jews would travel to Israel. When the train reached Austria, the terrorists took four hostages – three of them Jewish and the other an employee of Austrian customs – and drove to an airport in a van, where they asked for a plane to take them to an Arab country. They released the customs employee and then flew to Libya. In Tripoli, the terrorists held a press conference to announce that they were dedicated to halting Soviet Jewish emigration "by any means."[88]

As a result of their hijacking and kidnapping, Austrian chancellor Bruno Kreisky – a Jewish socialist hostile to Israel who was later convicted of defaming Nazi hunter Simon Wiesenthal, acquiesced to shutting down the Schoenau transit center.[89]

Spurred on by this small victory, the Eagles of the Palestinian Revolution claimed that they would not limit themselves to operations against countries aiding the Soviet emigrants. Even the USSR, despite its role as the chief ally of Arab terror, was threatened. In the Beirut newspaper *An Nahar*, the Eagles stated that if the Kremlin did not desist from issuing exit visas to Israel, then they would begin targeting their embassies and interests in the Middle East.[90]

This sentiment was echoed by no less a beneficiary of Soviet largesse than the Popular Front for the Liberation of Palestine. In an interview with a Viennese journalist, a PLFP spokesman said that guerillas would attack any country "actively and passively supporting [Soviet Jewish] emigration."[91]

Egypt, the Soviet Union's largest Arab client state, was also enthralled with the work of the terrorists. The Egyptian press wrote of them in heroic terms and heaped praise on the Austrian chancellor for closing the transit station. President Sadat went so far as to dispatch a representative to Vienna to deliver his personal thanks to Chancellor Kreisky.[92]

Two years later, as Egypt was contemplating peace with Israel in the rocky period that followed the Yom Kippur War, their foreign minister, Ismail Fahmi, commented that no agreement would be reached unless immigration was halted or drastically curtailed, since Israel would be "expanding at our expense and jeopardizing our security."[93] His comment was a remarkable request for one sovereign nation to make of another, and yet it was a retreat from his position of a year before, when Fahmi contended that a final peace settlement with the Israelis would only come to fruition if they stopped immigration for a half century.[94]

Arab nations and terror groups continued to complain bitterly to their Soviet enablers about the ongoing issuing of exit visas to Jews, and there is some indication that Soviet diplomats got tired of hearing it. In response to one overly strident Arab critic, a Kremlin point man brought up the Jews who had been systematically thrown out of Arab lands and said, "You Arabs have permitted one million Jews to emigrate to Israel; do not criticize us for allowing one hundred thousand to go."[95]

◆ ◆ ◆

Senator Scoop Jackson, a Democrat from Washington State, was a staunch opponent of détente. He had entered the presidential primaries in 1972 and been rebuffed, but his rejection and the chatter about him as a potential candidate in 1976 had no impact on his stance as an anti-Soviet hardliner. Jackson thought that the American objective in the Cold War should be the dismantling of the Soviet empire or the destruction of its totalitarian system, and that US policy should prudently seek that outcome, sooner rather than later, with every means at its disposal.[96] Jackson was unhappy with the summit because he thought the SALT agreement conceded too much to the Kremlin and that MFN status and Export-Import Bank credits would benefit the Russians without wringing any concessions from them.[97]

Trade with the Soviet Union was becoming a touchy subject in the United States because of a deal that critics would deride as the "Great Grain Robbery."[98] In the spring of 1972, following the disastrous harvest in the USSR, Secretary of Agriculture Earl L. Butz negotiated an arrangement whereby the Soviets would buy American wheat with $750 million from the Commodity Credit Corporation (CCC), a government entity created during the Depression to stabilize and protect agricultural prices.[99] Unbeknownst to Butz, the Kremlin was also covertly buying grain from private American export companies in the United States. By the summer of 1972, the Soviets had bought up one-quarter of American wheat just as farmers were barely meeting their domestic and foreign orders.[100] Prices doubled, inflation jumped, and, adding insult to injury, since the Soviets had acquired the grain with funds from the CCC, it meant that American taxpayers had subsidized the Soviet purchase.[101]

Furious about the grain robbery, Jackson grew more suspicious of agreements between the administration and the Kremlin that were made in the name of détente,[102] and less than a month after the Nixon-Brezhnev tête-à-tête, Jackson had his staff exploring how to scuttle the deal that Secretary of Commerce Peter G. Petersen was working out with the Soviets on repaying their lend-lease debt to the United States.[103]

The senator was renowned for the quality of his staff, and two of his finest were Dorothy "Dickie" Fosdick and Richard Perle. Fosdick, a petite, tough-minded woman with a doctorate in public law from Columbia University, was in charge of Jackson's cramped office on Capitol Hill, which was known alternatively as "the bunker"[104] and "a détente-wrecking operation,"[105] and she adopted such an uncompromising position toward the Soviet Union "that her colleagues sometimes had to remind themselves that she was…the daughter of the Rev. Dr. Harry Emerson Fosdick, the pacifist pastor of Riverside Church."[106] Perle, young enough to be the son of Jackson and Fosdick, was a small, intense, chain-smoking intellectual whose soft voice and formal manner belied his hardline views toward the Kremlin,[107] his disdain for détente, and his reputation as a no-holds-barred bureaucratic in-fighter, a skill that led his opponents to refer to him as the Prince of Darkness – a nickname that did not suffice for Henry Kissinger, whose preferred sobriquets for Perle were "ruthless," "a little bastard," and "a son of Mensheviks who thinks all Bolsheviks are evil."[108]

Perle had grown up a secular Jew in Hollywood, California, and as Jackson began to discuss tying trade to freedom for Soviet Jews, much would be made of the fact that Perle was Jewish. However, Jackson, a Norwegian Lutheran by birth, was far more passionate than his young aide on the subject of the Holocaust and defending Israel. Friends and colleagues traced the source of these strong feeling to April 1945, when Jackson was a month shy of his twenty-ninth birthday, and he and six other congressmen were invited by General Eisenhower to tour the Buchenwald concentration camp. Jackson came away with the impression that "the atrocities are the most sordid I have ever imagined."[109] By 1970, Jackson was offering an amendment to the Defense Procurement Act that basically removed the limits on the amount of military hardware that could be provided to Israel. From then on he had been such an unwavering friend to the Israelis that Jamil Baroody, the Saudi UN ambassador, wondered aloud, "Who is this Senator Jackson, who hails from a distance of six thousand miles from the Middle East, to be the arbiter of the people of Palestine, when he gives the impression that he is more Zionist than the Zionists, more Jewish than the Jews?"[110]

By July, Perle had jettisoned the notion of attacking the lend-lease deal and focused on linking trade to improving the lot of Soviet Jews. The approach had a historical precedent – the battle that began in the nineteenth century when the tsar would not stop discriminating against American Jews conducting business in the Russian empire or curtail the cycle of pogroms and persecutory trials. American Jewry began to call for the abrogation of the Russo-American Commercial Treaty of 1832 in order to revoke Russia's most-favored-nation status. The call was finally answered in December 1911, when Congress voted to abrogate the treaty.[111]

An updated version of this tactic – connecting trade to emigration – had been circulating in government and intellectual circles ever since Lou Rosenblum of the Union of Councils for Soviet Jewry had started talking about it in the late 1960s.[112] By 1971, some 250,000 Soviet Jews had applied for exit visas, and that fall, Lou Rosenblum and the Union of Councils discussed the backlog of applications at their convention and decided to press for legislation in Congress that levied economic sanctions against countries restricting freedom of movement. On New Year's Day, 1972, Rosenblum met with Professor Harvey Lieber of American University's School of Public Affairs and the illustrious trial and appellate attorney Nathan Lewin, both of whom were associated with the Washington Committee for Soviet Jews. Shortly afterwards, Lewin drafted an amendment for the Export Administration Act that was slated to be renewed. Lieber lined up graduate students to help prepare position papers and devise legislative tactics.[113]

Si Frumkin enlisted California congressman Thomas M. Rees, a member of the House Banking and Currency Committee, to introduce Lewin's legislation, and on May 4, with several cosponsors, Rees introduced HR 14806, *A Bill to amend the Export Administration Act of 1969 in order to promote freedom of emigration*. Lieber tried to round up support from the National Conference on Soviet Jewry, but found NCSJ to be "very timid" about wading into a legislative slugfest.[114] In July, the bill died in committee, losing by two votes, but Rosenblum thought the effort was a marked improvement over the customary congressional resolutions scolding the Soviets.[115]

So did a trio of Jewish congressional staffers often referred to as the "Washington group," which included Perle; Morris Amitay, an aide to Senator Ribicoff; and Mark Talisman, an aide to Representative Charles Vanik of Ohio.[116] Talisman, a native Clevelander, also had close ties to Union of Councils founder Lou Rosenblum.[117] In August, after word of the exit tax leaked, Perle and Amitay, with the assistance of I. L. "Sy" Kenen, the lobbyist from the American Israel Public Affairs Committee, convened a meeting in the Red Cross Bandage room of the Old Senate Office Building with congressional staff, Jerry Goodman from the NCSJ, and Yehuda Hellman, director of the Presidents Conference. Perle and Amitay raised the idea of tying MFN status to emigration, but Goodman, Hellman, and Kenen did not favor linking them.[118] Their hesitancy was understandable, since Perle was effectively proposing that they join the fight against détente, a move that would alienate the White House – and alienating the president was not usually in the best interest of the American Jewish community or Israel.

But the link between Soviet behavior and trade gained some currency when Senator Javits spoke at a rally in New York City's garment district and then on the floor of the Senate, warning that if the diploma fee was not rescinded, agreements desired by the Kremlin would be hard-pressed to earn congressional approval.[119] The other senator from New York, the conservative James Buckley, issued a similar warning, as did Senator Ribicoff.[120]

Seeing trouble brewing, Nixon had the State Department inform the Soviet embassy that the exit tax would be a roadblock to Congress passing bills "we both feel are beneficial and important to our relations."[121] By then,

Perle and Amitay had met again with Senate staffers, but a satisfactory conclusion had not been reached,[122] and Perle, with Jackson urging him on, barged ahead on his own.

"For Scoop, it all came down to freedom of movement," says Perle. "He thought it was the seminal human right – different from all of the others. You could talk about freedom of speech and the press and all the rest, but if people were free to vote with their feet, then the pressure would be on their government to make a decent life for them so they would not leave."[123]

Perle was the consummate night owl, much to the chagrin of Dorothy Fosdick, who often went looking for him in the morning at the office only to find that he was still home sleeping. Perle lived on Capitol Hill, so he and Fosdick developed a system where he wrote at night and left the completed drafts in his mailbox, which Fosdick emptied in the morning and brought to work.[124]

"That's how I wrote the first draft of the amendment," says Perle. "During the night, at home, in one sitting, and Dickie picked it up. I had pretty clear directions from Scoop. Originally, we started out thinking of tying most-favored-nation status to freedom of movement for all people – not only Jews – but then somebody in a meeting said, 'Well, the credits are even more important,' and so we said, 'Great idea, let's do credits, too.' Hence, the ultimate language."[125]

The amendment stated that its raison d'être was "to assure the continued dedication of the United States to fundamental human rights," and therefore "no nonmarket economy country shall be eligible to receive most-favored-nation treatment or to participate in any program…which extends credits or credit guarantees, directly or indirectly…[if that country] denies its citizens the right or opportunity to emigrate to the country of their choice [or] imposes more than a nominal tax on emigration or on the visas or other documents required for emigration for any purpose or cause whatsoever."[126]

While the draft was checked for legal precision by the Senate Office of the Legislative Counsel, Jackson campaigned to win Jewish backing for his amendment on September 26 by addressing the National Conference on Soviet Jewry, which was holding an emergency session in Washington to discuss the exit tax. Boiled down to its essence, Jackson's message to the one hundred twenty people in the audience was that they should lend their unwavering commitment to his amendment.[127]

As Jackson was speaking to the NCSJ, Nixon was in New York at a hospitality suite in the Waldorf-Astoria speaking to thirty-one Jewish leaders from around the country.[128] Three weeks earlier, Nixon had disappointed many Americans by not recalling the US Olympic team after Palestinian terrorists murdered eleven Israeli athletes and coaches in Munich[129] – a feeling summed up by *Los Angeles Times* sports columnist Jimmy Murray: "Incredibly, they're going on with it," wrote Murray. "It's almost like having a dance at Dachau."[130] The Jewish leaders did ask the president about the Middle East and terrorism and hiring quotas, which much of the Jewish community opposed because, as former Nixon speechwriter William Safire observed, for Jews "a quota is a sign on a closed door that says, 'Stay in your place.'"[131] However, the most pointed questions focused on Soviet Jewry, and Nixon was repeatedly asked what he intended to do about the Kremlin's "ransom" demands.

"I'm concerned about Soviet Jewry," Nixon replied. "I've had much experience dealing with the Soviets. This sort of thing must be dealt with quietly. And that's what I am doing – Kissinger constantly mentions it to them. We're getting results. Between 1968 and 1971, only fifteen thousand Soviet Jews were allowed to emigrate. This year over thirty-five thousand will leave. I ask you to trust me."[132]

Quiet diplomacy was attacked the next day in the press by two leaders who were not at the Waldorf-Astoria and who were not supporting Nixon's reelection: Rabbi Arthur J. Hertzberg, president of the American Jewish Congress, and Harold Ostroff, president of the Workmen's Circle.

Rabbi Hertzberg said, "The abhorrence our government feels over the persecution of Soviet Jewry is consoling but ineffective as long as it finds no expression in practical action. We do not see it as confrontation for the president to make clear both to the American people and to the Soviet leadership that the United States will not grant major economic benefits to the Soviet Union while that country continues to blackmail Russian Jews seeking to emigrate."[133]

Ostroff stated that he was "shocked" at the view that pressuring the Soviet Union to eliminate exit fees for Jewish citizens constituted unwarranted harsh confrontation and that the issue was not worthy of public debate. Voicing additional "shock" at the administration's opposition to withholding most-favored-nation treatment until the ransom demands were withdrawn, Ostroff claimed that "gains for Soviet Jews have surely been abetted by vigorous public activities on their behalf."[134]

This same argument – quiet diplomacy and behind-the-scenes persuasion versus noisy indignation and the legislative headlock of exchanging trade benefits for human rights – would rage until the final days of 1974, whereupon it would move, with equal acrimony, into the history books, where, until the present day, the argument goes on.

◆ ◆ ◆

On October 2, after spending the morning with Soviet foreign minister Gromyko in preparation for the next day's signing of the ABM Treaty and the interim agreement, Nixon invited Gromyko to stay overnight at Camp David so they could continue talking.[135] Kissinger and Gromyko joined them, and there, in the stillness of the Catoctin Mountains, Nixon reiterated that the diploma tax might make it impossible for the Soviets to win a trade deal.[136] Gromyko replied that the tax would "fade away."[137] This was the message that Secretary of State Rogers delivered to Max Fisher, Jacob Stein, and Richard Maass, who publicly let his members at the National Conference on Soviet Jewry know, via the press, that he was in contact with presidential assistant Leonard Garment and that the State Department and White House were doing everything possible to roll back the tax, adding that he thought the president understood how important the issue was to the American Jewish community.[138]

The next day, at the White House, Nixon and Gromyko signed the two pacts limiting the use of nuclear arms. With all the media attention focused on what Nixon characterized as a "first step in reducing the danger of war," it is understandable why journalists were not overly curious as to why, after the signing, the president and Senator Jackson took a forty-five-minute stroll through the Rose Garden. Jackson had objected to the pacts with the Soviets, calling the interim agreement a "bum deal" because it permitted the Soviets heavier throw weights in missiles. But Jackson had not come to talk missiles; he wanted to talk trade.[139]

Jackson said that he would be introducing an amendment that denied most-favored-nation status and credit to any Communist country restricting emigration in any way – including the use of an exit tax. Yet, Jackson explained, with the election looming, he was willing to do some horse-trading with Nixon. The senator said that he would neither turn his amendment into a campaign issue, nor press the Ninety-Second Congress to vote on it, if the president would release the Republican senators who refused to cosponsor the amendment without Nixon's blessing. Nixon cut the deal.[140]

On October 4, Jackson brought his amendment before the Senate. It had an astounding seventy-two cosponsors. (Six days later, Vanik sponsored the amendment in the House.[141]) Two weeks later, a comprehensive US-USSR trade agreement was signed. The administration agreed to seek congressional approval to bestow MFN status on the Soviet Union, while the Soviets agreed to repay the United States $722 million of its lend-lease debt. The president also approved Export-Import Bank credit for the Kremlin, which was in the process of purchasing $1.4 billion worth of grain. Nixon stated that extending the credit served American national interests. Whether true or not, it was demonstrably helpful to Soviet Jews. Nineteen Soviet Jewish families emigrating to Israel were abruptly informed by authorities that they were exempt from the diploma tax, an exemption that countermanded what they had been told two days before. More exemptions from the tax were forthcoming from the Soviet Council of Ministers,[142] and during October, 4,500 Jews – the most yet in a single month – were allowed to emigrate.[143]

Congress voted to approve the SALT agreement and treaty but adjourned on the evening of October 18 without having voted on the trade bill or Jackson's amendment, postponing that drama to the New Year when the Ninety-Third Congress would be seated.[144]

◆ ◆ ◆

It is almost inevitable in piecing together a history of the American movement to free Soviet Jewry that the writer will lose the thread of other events and thereby discount the political and, every bit as decisive, emotional impact they exerted on the unfurling of the past. Vietnam, or "that goddamn war," as Nixon frequently called it,[145] was just such an event, and its impact on the administration's reaction to Jackson's link between trade and emigration – a reaction that was tied to the pressure that Nixon and Kissinger were under to nail down a settlement and extract the United States from – cannot be discounted. Nixon bore the brunt of the domestic criticism, but it was Kissinger who, since February 21, 1970, when he walked into a small rundown house in a gritty Paris suburb, had been dueling with Le Duc Tho, the North Vietnamese negotiator.[146]

In his late fifties, with a preternatural calm that precluded both warmth and humor, Le Duc Tho was a founder of the Indochinese Communist party, and had fought the French and helped organize the insurgents inside South Vietnam – a man whom Stanley Karnow, a journalist who had covered Southeast Asia since 1959, would describe as "a professional revolutionary for whom negotiations were a form of protracted guerilla warfare."[147] That warfare of negotiations with Kissinger persisted into 1973. As the years went on and the US troops rotated home, and Hanoi demonstrated that it was willing to suffer horrendous casualties in bombing campaigns to sustain its presence in the South, Kissinger watched his options dwindle away. One option he did retain was Moscow's ability to squeeze Hanoi: the Soviets supplied the North Vietnamese with a variety of sophisticated military equipment – notably, given Nixon's tactic of employing air strikes to counter Hanoi's intransigence, surface-to-air missiles and radar.[148] When the Kremlin approached the White House on trade, Kissinger, quite reasonably, was more interested in negotiating an end to the Vietnam War than in open emigration for Soviet citizens.[149]

By October, Kissinger had hammered out an understanding with Le Duc Tho that let North Vietnam hold onto the areas it controlled in the South, and established a transition coalition governing body that, as a practical matter, would surely feature some Communists.[150] At a White House press conference Kissinger announced that "peace is at hand," even though President Nguyen Van Thieu of South Vietnam rejected the terms and resented that the United States had made an agreement behind his back and intended to impose it on him, an imposition that would simply require the United States to cut off aid to Saigon and to stop using the Air Force to restrain the North Vietnamese.[151]

Nixon dispatched General Alexander M. Haig Jr. to Saigon to talk with Thieu, "soldier to soldier, without regard to diplomatic niceties."[152] Thieu would not retract his demand that the North Vietnamese leave his country: "If Russia invaded the US," he asked Haig, "would you accept an agreement where they got to stay and then say that it was a peace?"[153]

Thieu's logic was much more unassailable than his position on the ground, but trying not to appear as though America was selling out an ally – American reliability being another cornerstone of détente – Kissinger returned to Paris in November and handed over a list of the sixty-nine modifications that Thieu wanted to the accords. Le Duc Tho responded with a lecture about the centuries-long predilection of colonial powers to deceive Vietnam. No substantive changes were made, and Kissinger flew home empty-handed.[154]

Nixon then ordered the "Christmas bombing," three thousand sorties dropping an estimated forty thousand tons of bombs on the sixty-mile stretch between Hanoi and Haiphong. His purpose was to demonstrate American power in the absence of troops, thus pressuring the North and reassuring the South. For the moment, it worked. Hanoi said it was willing to talk once the bombing stopped. Nixon halted it on December 30.[155] Nixon was so frustrated by Thieu's recalcitrance that he would tell Kissinger he was willing to "do any damn thing" to get the accords signed, including cutting off the South Vietnamese leader's head.[156] In lieu of a guillotine, Nixon sent a message to Thieu that was as effective as an execution: "You must decide now whether you desire to continue our alliance or whether you want me to seek a settlement with the enemy which serves US interests alone."[157]

The meaning was unmistakable: sign or lose American aid. Thieu had no choice, and on January 27, 1973, the agreement was signed in Paris. Nixon declared it a "peace with honor," a poetic rendering of an arrangement that proved to be, as Nixon and Kissinger had feared all along, a temporary cease-fire.[158]

◆ ◆ ◆

In December 1972 Senator Hubert Humphrey traveled to the Soviet Union with a congressional delegation and spoke with Premier Kosygin, telling him that Jackson's amendment was not a chess move related to the election. Congress felt strongly about the right of Soviet Jews to emigrate and would not drop it in the new session. Kosygin disregarded the warning, and Soviet authorities stiffened on the diploma tax, announcing that while they might approve exit visas, the Kremlin did "not intend to act as a philanthropist" toward citizens with advanced education.[159]

This intransigence had multiple causes. To some degree it was the consequence of a political problem for the Soviets with their Arab allies and a psychological one for themselves. Obviously, the Arabs wanted the Kremlin to refrain from fortifying Israel with Russian Jews. Less obvious among the Soviet leadership was what Henry Kissinger observed and the journalist C. L. Sulzberger noted: the Soviets were "not entirely rational on Israel. There is a hysterical edge. They are basically anti-Semitic and hate being licked by Jews."[160] Moreover, Anatoly Dobrynin would concede that the assessment of Soviet leaders was that they would have no trouble with trade legislation since they "always underestimated the influence of American public opinion on US foreign policy because they were free from such pressure at home."[161]

The most fractious aspect of foreign affairs in the United States – Vietnam – was now erased from the headlines and no longer the lead story on the evening news; headway had been made reducing nuclear weapons; in November, the Pepsi Cola Corporation concluded a deal to produce and sell Pepsi in the Soviet Union while marketing Soviet vodka and wine in the United States; and Chase Manhattan Bank had received the Kremlin's go-ahead to open a branch in Moscow.[162] Given all these factors, Soviet optimism about trade does not, in hindsight, seem farfetched nor did its judgment that the American people – and hence, Congress – would be more favorably disposed toward improved relations with the USSR.

Unlike the Kremlin, Henry Kissinger did not underestimate the impact of public opinion on foreign affairs. Yet Kissinger, along with the administration's point man on the trade bill, Peter M. Flanigan, executive director of the Council on International Economic Policy, believed, according to one staff member at the National Security Council, that the objections to the trade bill were "controllable."[163] To be fair, Kissinger was distracted by buttoning up the Paris Peace Accords, but that does not fully account for his initial disregard of the storm brewing over Soviet Jewish emigration – a disregard that Paula Stern, author of *Water's Edge*, a thorough examination of the creation of the Jackson-Vanik amendment, diagnoses as "malign neglect."[164]

Stern's verdict, though harsh enough to satisfy fans of Jackson-Vanik, is insufficient to explain Kissinger's myopia. Like the Soviet leadership, Kissinger may have calculated that recent accomplishments would put the wind at the administration's back when the hour arrived to pass the trade bill. If that did not pan out, Kissinger may have thought that since Nixon was in his last term, the administration was freer to operate without factoring in the electoral costs of bucking popular sentiment.

In his memoirs Kissinger lays the blame for the trade bill coming under fire at the feet of Jackson's ambition to occupy the Oval Office, opining that the senator "wanted an issue, not a solution,"[165] and another development that Kissinger deems as rare as "an eclipse of the sun."[166]

He was referring to the coalition of traditional conservatives like the governor of California, Ronald Reagan, who, as an aspirant to the presidency, would soon be comparing détente to the relationship that "a farmer has with his turkey – until Thanksgiving Day,"[167] and the acolytes of an emerging political philosophy, christened "neoconservatism" by writer Michael Harrington, that was anti-Soviet and dedicated to old-time, color-blind liberalism.[168]

As a rule the so-called neocons – for example, Norman Podhoretz, the editor of *Commentary* magazine, his wife, Midge Decter, and Irving Kristol, editor of the *Public Interest*[169] and the godfather of neoconservatism, whose definition of his newfound faith was that of "a liberal who has been mugged by reality"[170] – had opposed American involvement in Vietnam. Nixon would later say it was to their "great credit"[171] that they had changed their minds and come to see that free nations were imperiled if the United States, as Kissinger wrote, "abdicated its concern for regional balances of power against countries armed by the Soviets."[172]

Kissinger dates the epiphany of neocons – a significant percentage of whom were Jewish – to the aftermath of the October 1973 Middle East war, but the political sea change had predated the 1972 election and was unmistakable in the returns.

The issue of Soviet Jewry had been raised frequently during the campaign. Democratic presidential candidate Senator George S. McGovern had accused Nixon of ignoring the question at the summit, and at the Republican National Convention in Miami Beach, Richard Maass, chairman of the NCSJ, stopped during his presentation to the platform committee to deplore the Soviet education tax. Senator John Tower, chairman of the Republican Resolutions Committee, made certain that a forceful Soviet Jewry plank was written into the party platform,[173] and Rita Hauser, an international lawyer who was a cochair of the Committee to Reelect the President, continued urging the White House to reach out to a Jewish community incensed by the diploma tax.[174]

Max Fisher had been active trying to bridge the racial divide in his hometown of Detroit, especially in the wake of the devastating 1967 riot, and he had firsthand experience with the civil rights movement rejecting the ways of Dr. King and embracing the New Left with its antisemitic rhetoric. McGovern drew support from the New Left, and at the same time scared many Jewish communal leaders – who often furnished Democratic presidential hopefuls with generous campaign contributions and spoke with some influence to their constituencies – with his dovish pronouncements on the defense budget and foreign affairs; his criticism of Israel's dependence on military action, as opposed to negotiations, to provide security;[175] and his call for the "internationalization" of Jerusalem.[176]

Fisher saw an opportunity and conducted a nonstop campaign to bring Jews to the GOP. He arranged for Rabbi Herschel Schacter, a former chairman of the National Conference on Soviet Jewry and the presiding head of the Religious Zionists of America, to deliver the opening prayer at the Republican National Convention; Schacter would serve as vice chairman of Democrats for Nixon. Enlisting Jewish support was easier than Fisher had imagined, and the list was long and the individuals prominent: George Klein from Bartons Candy; Dr. William Wexler, former head of B'nai B'rith and the Presidents Conference; Joseph Meyerhoff, one of the biggest builders in America and a former chairman of the United Jewish Appeal and Israel Bonds, along with his daughter-in-law, Lynn Meyerhoff; Edward Ginsburg, a former chairman of the UJA and current chairman of the Joint Distribution Committee; and Louis Boyar, a Los Angeles real estate investor who for years had contributed heavily to Democratic candidates but endorsed Nixon in 1972 and invited dozens of his wealthy Democratic friends to his Beverly Hills home, where Fisher converted most of them to the cause.[177]

Fisher recalled that the one statistic he repeatedly cited was that "the Nixon administration has given $1.1 billion of military and economic aid to Israel – as much as the United States expended in the previous nineteen years."[178]

Nixon defeated McGovern in a landslide, winning 60.7 percent of the popular vote and carrying every state except Massachusetts and the District of Columbia.[179] Among Jews, Nixon won 39 percent of the vote, more than double his percentage in 1968.[180] The Jewish vote should have alerted the administration that a new game was afoot – mainly a rising animosity toward the Kremlin that came packaged with American Jewry's concern for Israel – but for the moment the newly reelected president anticipated that in his last term he would extend the gains won by détente and sign a SALT II agreement with Brezhnev that would create a safer world.

Like Kissinger, Nixon ascribed the fight over his trade bill to his administration getting wedged between "the liberals and the American Zionists [who] had decided that now was the time to challenge the Soviet Union's highly restrictive emigration policies...[and] the conservatives, who had traditionally opposed détente because it challenged their ideological opposition to contacts with Communist countries."[181]

To be sure, liberals, even those who eschewed neoconservatism, saw the Soviet Union as a blot on the moral landscape. For example, the Rev. Robert Drinan, a Democratic representative from Massachusetts, had run on an antiwar platform, becoming the first Roman Catholic priest elected to Congress, and while in Washington he cofounded the National Interreligious Task Force on Soviet Jewry.[182] Yet historians would give less weight to Kissinger and Nixon's analysis of the unusual coalition, dismissing the anti-détente hardliners – save for Perle and Jackson – and citing the amendment as a triumph for the Jewish lobby.[183] This is not wholly accurate: AIPAC helped, but the National Conference on Soviet Jewry and the Union of Councils were tax-exempt organizations and not permitted to lobby. Then, too, many Jewish leaders opposed the amendment.

Not only the two most prominent Jewish Republicans, Fisher and Stein, but Rabbi Hertzberg, Charlotte Jacobson, president of the World Zionist Organization's American section, and even Jerry Goodman from NCSJ had reservations, sounding a cautionary note to Jewish student activists at the University of Maryland, remarking that it was dangerous to sever all trade ties with the Soviets.[184] The fact is that in the early stages of the amendment, the Jewish lobby consisted of three congressional staffers: Perle, Amitay, and Talisman.[185]

They were aided by forces more decisive than any lobby – the tides of history and culture, which Nixon and Kissinger constantly underrated.

Before his inauguration in 1969, Nixon decided on linking "such areas of Soviet concern as strategic arms limitation and increased trade with progress in areas that were important to us,"[186] and once he was in the Oval Office he appeared to think that progress – most notably in Southeast Asia – would validate the soundness of linkage and détente, and keep his critics at bay. Yet progress was slow. The deal reached on Vietnam in 1973 had been available four years earlier;[187] in the meantime, over twenty thousand more US troops had died,[188] and the country fractured along fault lines that have never quite healed. Nixon was adept at reaching out to foreign leaders, but he was unable to persuade the American people and, more important, Congress, that the game of détente was worth the candle.[189]

Kissinger knew that Americans were uncomfortable with an international agenda "based on the calculation of the national interests and relationships of power," preferring an idealistic approach that trumpeted the great cause of "human rights."[190] But it just was this approach, Kissinger thought – born of sentiment and not of reason – that had brought the nation to grief, leading it to "lurch toward either isolationism or global intervention," since claiming the moral high ground leads "as easily to crusades as abstinence."[191]

From his days as a graduate student at Harvard, where his doctoral dissertation explored the means by which two statesmen, the Austrian Prince Klemens von Metternich and the British Viscount Castlereagh, brought peace to Europe in the early nineteenth century by restoring equilibrium and preserving balances of power, Kissinger eschewed the conception of a foreign policy forged by morality or influenced by a preoccupation with the behavior of countries within their own borders.[192] It was a conviction he carried with him into the Nixon administration – one that he shared with his president – and as Jackson began to seek backing for his amendment Kissinger concluded that "the most important task" before the administration was "psychological" and consisted of educating Americans about the compromises and lack of clear-cut moral delineations inherent in pursuing the balance of power.[193] This education would help the public comprehend "the complexity of the world we would have to manage"[194] – a world, he was confident, that would be safer if free from disorder even if the price was accepting injustice.[195]

Kissinger was aware that one challenge to détente was that "containment and coexistence has no automatic consensus behind it" to stoke up the broad-based public approval needed to thrive.[196] The lack of approval, though, was not the result of conflicting philosophies – say, a spitball fight between supply-siders and the tax-and-spend crowd – nor a consequence of an America drunk on its own rectitude. There was scant popular support for détente due to the inescapable reality that Nixon and Kissinger were not practicing their brand of realism in nineteenth-century Europe, but in the midst of the Cold War, which, in its theoretical form, was a moral contest between divergent visions.

On one side stood those who believed earthly salvation lay in selecting their own government and freely choosing their own path, while the other side subscribed to a totalitarian imagining of Eden, where the state dominated nearly every facet of public and private life. As it played out, the Cold War was a slow-motion fencing match between the superpowers: the not infrequently blemished democracy of America, with its messy, energetic individualism and with dissent both a sign of political health and a source of civic entertainment, versus a cruel, repressive, paranoid political system where – except for those who found favor with the ruling clique – hope was as hard to find as consumer goods, and where the gray, faceless masses occupied an Orwellian nightmare, forbidden to challenge those behind the towering stone walls of the Kremlin and trudging off to factories and Gulags with the same stony expression on their faces.

In their respective memoirs, Nixon and Kissinger avoided the topic of the *specific* moral basis for the American people's opposition to the Soviet

Union. Kissinger does mention that he sympathized with the objections but rejected them as a basis for policy.[197] However, in 1994, twelve years after the second volume of his memoirs appeared and with the Soviet Union now grazing land for historians, Kissinger published *Diplomacy* and discoursed at length on the moral underpinnings of the Cold War, acknowledging that the United States could not "have sustained four decades of grueling exertion on behalf of a policy which did not reflect it deepest values and idcals." Kissinger then cites a National Security Document (NSC-68) from April 1950, which asserts that "a defeat of free institutions anywhere is a defeat everywhere…and it is only by practical affirmation, abroad as well as at home, of our essential values, that we can preserve our own integrity, in which lies the real frustration of the Kremlin design."[198]

There should be no surprise in reading NSC-68. Postwar America was shaped by its unabashed pride in defeating the murderous totalitarianism of Nazi Germany and Imperial Japan – a totalitarianism for which Americans felt an intense revulsion – and so it does not seem remarkable, glancing backward, that in the United States of the early 1970s, where only recently African Americans had won full legal citizenship, a cry arose to insert moral principles into the nation's foreign policy. What is perplexing is that such a widespread outcry had not occurred much sooner.

The veterans of the Second World War and their peers, the members of Tom Brokaw's Greatest Generation, were in middle age, and their children, who had gone off to college in record numbers, had long been railing against injustice, filling the civil rights movement, enlisting to fight in Vietnam – to answer, as Philip Caputo writes in *A Rumor of War*, President Kennedy's call to "ask what you can do for your country"[199] – and joining the Peace Corps, the antiwar movement, the women's liberation movement, the environmental movement, the gay liberation movement, and the Soviet Jewry movement. Here was a return to a history that reached back to the seventeenth century, when the Puritans proclaimed that democracy was inseparable from the word of God.

Despite Nixon's experience and his willingness to navigate uncharted and contentious waters, despite Kissinger's intellect, his dexterity as a juggler of situations, and his skills as a negotiator, the two men did not factor in that by 1972 these feelings were at high tide and unlikely to be held back by rational education. Furthermore, while Kissinger was willing to accept that détente was in perpetual search of a constituency, he seemed to brush aside another of its salient flaws: playing for time carries with it the inherent risk of running out of time. Americans would have waited indefinitely to sidestep a nuclear showdown, but as schoolchildren were no longer scrambling from behind their desks to duck and cover, the Cuban Missile Crisis vanished into the ethers of the past, and US involvement in Southeast Asia was coming to a close without anyone in Moscow or Washington having pushed the doomsday button, it was inevitable that the American preference for a morally driven foreign agenda would reassert itself. Cultural norms live in the bloodstream of a society, and to think you can escape them for long is wishful thinking – and so it was that the realism of Nixon and Kissinger deserted them.

"No other single question," Anatoly Dobrynin would recall, "did more to sour the atmosphere of détente than the question of Jewish emigration from the Soviet Union,"[200] and this, too, was a complication for Nixon and Kissinger.

Nixon never comprehended the American Jewish community's tortured emotional relationship with the Holocaust beyond its fear for Israel, most likely because of his own ambivalence toward Jews. His internal world was populated by conniving, traitorous Jewish enemies who as a people, he said, harbored a death wish,[201] while simultaneously he admired Benjamin Disraeli, Louis Brandeis, Felix Frankfurter, and Herman Wouk,[202] and nurtured friendships with Jews, making more space for them in his government than any other previous president, and treated the Israelis, as William Safire remembered, "with special affection" and spared nothing in their defense.[203]

Kissinger, raised an Orthodox Jew in a family that fled Nazi Germany when he was fifteen, appeared as removed from the community's complex relationship to the Holocaust as Nixon, albeit with better reason. The concentration camps claimed more than a dozen of his relatives,[204] and so the Holocaust was no mythological catastrophe to Kissinger, engendering in him the kind of guilt experienced by American Jews who had not been touched directly by the annihilation, but who had largely come to accept the conclusions in Arthur Morse's *While Six Million Died* – that the antisemitism of their government and countrymen, combined with their own powerlessness as a community, had contributed mightily to the cataclysm.

This guilt, and the pledge that such a disaster would never again befall the Jewish people, was the animating emotion of the Soviet Jewry movement, and that the cavalry charge to rescue Soviet Jews was now being led by a gentile senator from Washington State and a gentile congressman from Ohio made it unthinkable for the American Jewish community to sit on its hands while the administration expounded on the necessity of moral compromise.

Nixon and Kissinger were sailing into a perfect storm, but neither one seemed aware of the wind picking up or the white-capped water or any of the signs that were all around for them to see.

CHAPTER 8

STAR LIGHT, STAR BRIGHT

The first sign of trouble appeared as the trade agreement was taken up by the House of Representatives. Because most-favored-nation status impacted tariffs, Nixon was constitutionally bound to win a House vote in order for the agreement to go into effect.

Before coming to the floor, the trade bill would have to clear the Ways and Means Committee, which oversaw the drafting of revenue legislation and was chaired by Democrat Wilbur Mills from Arkansas, a portly country lawyer and banker with a razor-sharp mind.[1] He was the undisputed master of the cabalistic involutions of the Tax Code, much of which he wrote, and the minutia of trade legislation. Mills took great pleasure in his undisputed power as the manipulator of the federal purse strings,[2] and fortifying this power was the fact that Democratic members of Ways and Means were in charge of assigning Democratic representatives to all House committees, which enabled Mills "to nearly make or break a House career."[3]

But Nixon had a possible chance to coax Mills into his corner, because the Ways and Means chairman was not averse to the publicity that accrues to a legislator who facilitates a meeting of the minds between the administration and Congress. Yet another member of Ways and Means was Charles Vanik, and he would be a much higher hurdle for the White House – and the Kremlin – to clear.[4]

Vanik's grandparents had come to the United States from Czechoslovakia. He was elected to Congress in 1955, representing a slice of Cleveland and the suburbs along the city's eastern edge,[5] where 11 percent of his constituents were Jews and a larger percentage were of Slavic descent – men and women well versed in the assorted inhumanities of the Soviet Union.[6] Vanik was a lawyer and former judge with a strong moral streak who was just as comfortable chatting with voters at the grocery store as he was decked out in his usual bow tie and suit, hurrying through the Capitol to buttonhole colleagues.[7] Vanik had interceded on behalf of hundreds of his constituents who were trying to bring family members from behind the Iron Curtain, and he had met refuseniks in the Soviet Union. At first, Vanik was worried that any legislation would lead to more persecution for them. He told the refuseniks of his fear, asking, "Are you sure you want this white hot light on you?" And they replied, "Turn off that light and we're dead."[8]

That was all Vanik needed to hear. For over two years, he remained focused on linking the trade bill to increased emigration. Ably assisting him was his top staffer, Mark Talisman. This was not happy news for Nixon and Brezhnev. A Harvard graduate with thirteen years of legislative mud wrestling behind him, Talisman had roots that reached back to the brutality of Tsarist Russia, and his feelings ran deep about his own Jewishness. He would later serve as a lobbyist for the Council of Jewish Federations and Welfare Funds, and as founding vice president of the US Holocaust Memorial Museum.

Talisman recruited backers for the Jackson-Vanik amendment by phoning every representative and talking about the Nazi death camps. He then pointed out that PepsiCo was doing business with the Soviets, but the United States had received nothing in return. The coup de grâce was intended to rile every member of the House: the administration, Talisman said, was orchestrating another of its end runs around Congress, not even bothering to consult with legislators when the trade bill was conceived.[9]

"Kissinger," said Talisman, "wouldn't even waste a gallon of gas to come up to the Hill to testify."[10]

AIPAC mailed a letter backing the amendment to one thousand Jewish leaders, but as an AIPAC employee told Paula Stern, "Vanik's office did 80 to 90 percent of the work,"[11] and much of that work was being done by Talisman, who kept dialing his phone and piling up backers. Careful not to arouse the opposition, Talisman did not advertise his success, answering inquiries from the press and State Department with a noncommittal "I'm working on it."

When Talisman began collecting signatures they walked the amendment around the floor.

"We didn't want to let it out of our hands," says Talisman. "When Dobrynin heard what we were doing, he kept stopping by and asking how many signatures we had. We always gave him the same answer – fifty."[12]

◆ ◆ ◆

Another ominous development for Nixon and Kissinger was that the Watergate scandal was beginning to sap the moral sway of the White House, a key presidential weapon in any standoff with Congress. In August 1972, two months after the burglary at the Democratic National Committee headquarters, Nixon called a press conference and assured the American people that no one presently employed in his administration had been "involved in this very bizarre incident."[13] The following month the *Washington Post* reported that John Mitchell, during his tenure as attorney general, had been in charge of a Republican slush fund that paid for intelligence-gathering against the Democrats,[14] and by the end of January 1973, five Watergate burglars had pleaded guilty before Chief US District Court Judge John J. Sirica, while two other men involved in the break-in – former Nixon aides G. Gordon Liddy and James W. McCord Jr. – had been found guilty of conspiracy, burglary, and wiretapping.[15]

As the abuses – suborning perjury, payoffs, and spying on US citizens, to name a few – were revealed, demands for Congress to respond grew more insistent, and in early February 1973, the Senate voted 77-0 to establish the Select Committee on Presidential Campaign Activities – soon to be known as the Watergate Committee – chaired by Senator Sam Ervin, a jowly, bushy-eyebrowed, deceptively folksy Democrat from North Carolina,[16] who, as a reporter observed, "came across as a stern father figure who wasn't confused about what was right and wrong."[17]

Not long after the Senate voted, Talisman reached 279 cosponsors for the amendment.[18]

Recalls Talisman: "To get two-thirds of the representatives is rocket fuel for legislation. Not only will it pass the House, but the Senate – by design the more sober deliberative body – has to take that level of support seriously when it votes."[19]

The one man who could scuttle the amendment was Wilbur Mills, but the Ways and Mean chairman, for multiple reasons, agreed to cosponsor it. First, AIPAC's Sy Kenen contacted a Jewish supporter of Mills from Little Rock, Philip Back, and requested that he appeal personally to the congressman.[20] Next, Mills heard from the Irving Stone family of Cleveland, owners of American Greeting Card Company who were active in Jewish philanthropy and who had a factory in Arkansas.[21] And lastly, Mills was shrewd enough to insinuate himself into the lead on developing legislation with broad appeal, since it enabled him to share credit or to make his mark on the final draft.[22]

Anxious to prevent a House vote on the amendment, the president prevailed upon the Israelis to recommend that organized American Jewry accept a compromise on Soviet trade. Ambassador Rabin talked to Richard Perle, but got nowhere. Prime Minister Meir promised Nixon that Israel would "cool it" on the amendment,[23] though Nehemiah Levanon was in constant discussion with the National Conference on Soviet Jewry and the Presidents Conference. Their eventual endorsement of Jackson-Vanik can be seen, in some measure, as a result of the Liaison Bureau's advocacy, with its implied permission that Israel, always in dire need of presidential empathy, did not object to the Jewish organizations lining up against the White House.[24]

In addition to playing the Israel card, Nixon had his lead man on international economic policy, Peter Flanigan, arrange for Georgy Arbatov[25] to address eight hundred leading American businesspeople who had come to Washington for a conference on Soviet trade. Arbatov was the head of the Soviet Institute of American Affairs and reputedly a trusted adviser to the Politburo,[26] but he was tone deaf when it came to US domestic politics. At bottom, his strategy was to threaten Soviet Jewry, claiming that passing the amendment would lead to a spike in antisemitism because it granted preferential treatment to Jews.[27] Taking umbrage at the threat, Senator Abraham Ribicoff told Arbatov "to mind his own damned business"[28] and requested that he be directed to return to Moscow.[29]

Apparently more fruitful for the administration and the Kremlin was the tête-à-tête Mills conducted with V. S. Alkhimov, the Soviet deputy minister of foreign trade, who was a more astute observer of the American scene than Arbatov. After speaking with a group of congressmen, Alkhimov told Mills, "I can see we are not going to get MFN out of this Congress and my job is to tell Moscow that."[30]

Unlike Jackson, Mills was not an implacable foe of détente and, truth be told, he was a halfhearted backer of the amendment.[31]

"I was worried that Mills might sink the bill," says Talisman. "He was the paramount legislator of the century."[32]

His fear was well founded. Mills was contemplating a compromise that would ease Soviet Jewish emigration as well as getting the Kremlin its trade package. He told Alkhimov that if the Soviets rescinded the education tax, then Mills would personally pull every lever possible so that the agreement would be approved without the amendment.[33]

Nixon had sent Secretary of the Treasury George Shultz to Moscow, where the secretary explained to Brezhnev that the White House could not, by itself, grant MFN status to the USSR; Congress would have to vote for it – an unlikely occurrence if the exit tax was not repealed. Shultz flew home convinced that Brezhnev intended "to tackle the problem in very real terms."[34]

On March 15, Scoop Jackson introduced his amendment to the East-West Trade Relations Bill in the Senate with seventy-three of his colleagues lined up behind him as cosponsors. Jackson had no intention of limiting his assault to the diploma tax. His amendment called for biannual accountings of the Kremlin's emigration practices and left Congress the prerogative to revoke trade arrangements with the USSR if the Kremlin hindered free emigration.[35]

Five days later, as news of the Kremlin's intention to refrain from collecting the diploma tax spread, the Export-Import Bank officially pledged $101.2 million in direct loans to the USSR and guaranteed the same amount from US lending institutions for the Soviets to buy American industrial equipment.[36] But Jackson wasn't fully satisfied. He told an audience at the National Press Club that he opposed the Kremlin's restrictive emigration policies in general, not the exit tax in particular, saying that he had heard "the Soviets are going to keep the ransom tax on the statute books but they won't apply it in practice. I say that we are going to put the Jackson amendment on the statute books but in the hope that it won't apply to the Soviet Union because they will be in compliance with the free emigration provision."[37]

On April 10, 1973, Nixon presented his Trade Reform Act to Congress complete with a proviso for the president to raise or lower tariffs for countries as he saw fit and a specific mention of granting the Soviet Union most-favored-nation status.[38] Jackson turned around, on the very same day, and attached his amendment to the Trade Reform Act.[39] In doing so, Jackson declared that he did back East-West trade, but Nixon's bill was providing "economic assistance" to the Soviets. In choosing that phrase Jackson was tipping his hat to another powerful supporter of his amendment, George Meany, leader of the AFL-CIO and the most influential labor boss in America.[40]

Meany had predicted that McGovern would lose badly in the election, and he had seen to it that the AFL-CIO did not endorse him or waste any money on his campaign, a stunning turnaround for a labor union that traditionally threw its weight behind the Democratic nominee. Over drinks and cigars on the porch of the Burning Tree Club in Chevy Chase, Maryland, Meany had told Nixon, long a bête noire of unions, that he wouldn't vote for him, but he wasn't voting for McGovern, a victory of sorts for the president.[41] But Meany was a diehard anti-Communist, and organized labor was dead set against providing credits to foreign nations, for it eventually moved jobs overseas,[42] and the AFL-CIO not only lined up behind Jackson-Vanik, the union opposed any trade bill at all with the Soviets.[43]

This represented another threat to the administration, and by spring, the six months of thrusts and parries over the amendment was about to intensify into an all-out war. Watergate, with its egregious ethical violations, made it politically more difficult for Nixon and Kissinger to argue for their brand of realpolitik to the exclusion of moral considerations, since the lack of a moral compass was cited as the cause of what the president of the American Bar Association termed "a domestic crisis of unparalleled proportions."[44]

◆ ◆ ◆

As hope for a compromise between the White House and Congress on Jackson-Vanik dimmed, Nixon focused his attention on an essential pillar of the amendment's support: the organized American Jewish community. The president approached the community via two Jewish Republicans: Max Fisher, who was en route to earning his reputation as the "dean of American Jewry," and Jacob Stein, chairman of the Presidents Conference, which came closer than any other body to being the official political voice of American Jewry.

Fisher was a secular Jew from small-town Ohio who had made his mark as an oilman and philanthropist, while Stein was a religious Jew from Brooklyn who had developed shopping centers on Long Island.[45] Fisher had recruited Stein to the GOP in 1960 with the argument that it was a mistake for Jews "to be locked in by the Democrats because they were taken for granted. Every election the Democrats knew they could count on 75 or 80 percent of the Jewish vote. They didn't have to work for it."[46] As Jewish Republicans the two men were rare birds; both belonged to the liberal wing of the party and neither was excessively ideological. A bedrock pragmatism was the quality that they most had in common, and it was their pragmatism that led them to object to Jackson-Vanik.

Fisher had met privately with Jackson and, after going back and forth with the senator, asked, "How many Jews a year do the Soviets have to let go before you'd vote for granting them MFN status?" When Jackson replied, "about a hundred thousand," a number both men knew the Kremlin would reject out of hand, Fisher concluded that Jackson was more interested in sustaining the emigration issue – whether as a means to undermine détente or to pave his path to the White House – than he was in saving Soviet Jews.[47]

Kissinger had met with Fisher and Stein and assured them that the Soviets would stop levying the exit tax and were already talking about an annual rate of Jewish emigration in excess of thirty thousand. Kissinger also said that the administration's ability to influence the Soviets on emigration would be strengthened if freedom of movement was not coupled with trade, but linked to a range of enticements that touched on every aspect of the US-USSR relationship. Fisher thought that made sense, and so did Stein, with some reservations – but Stein was the one who would have to sell the idea to the Presidents Conference, where Jackson-Vanik had gained significant traction among the member organizations.[48]

Fisher and Stein led a parade of Jewish leaders through the White House to meet on Jackson-Vanik. "It was," Nixon later said, "a bloody scene at times."[49]

One of these scenes occurred on April 19, when Fisher and Stein and thirteen other Jewish leaders gathered for over an hour in the Cabinet Room at the White House with the president and Kissinger. Nixon reiterated his sympathy for Soviet Jewry, but he emphasized the difficulties that would arise in his quest to reduce East-West tensions if the Jackson-Vanik proposal passed – difficulties that he believed would negatively impact Soviet Jewish emigration. Kissinger shared his private assurances from the Kremlin regarding the exit tax and Jewish emigration.[50] However, several leaders were not satisfied, and when they belittled Nixon's quiet diplomacy, the president became visibly angry and said, "You gentlemen have more faith in your senators than you do in me. And that is a mistake. You'll save more Jews my way. Protest all you want. The Kremlin won't listen."[51]

After leaving the Cabinet Room, Fisher, Stein, and Charlotte Jacobson issued a statement to the press reaffirming their determination to aid Russian Jews and expressing their appreciation to Nixon for his help. At Fisher's insistence, the statement was vague regarding whether American Jewry would advocate on behalf of Jackson-Vanik. Fisher thought that the vagueness would cool the public debate and permit the rising emigration statistics to demonstrate that Nixon's methods were effective.[52]

It was a reasonable response, but American Jews were in no mood for reason on the subject of Soviet Jewry. Energized by a combustible fusion of sorrow and guilt created by the Holocaust, American Jewry's intense emotional commitment to deterring any semblance of a repeat performance was heightened several days after the meeting, when one hundred Soviet Jewish dissidents forwarded an open letter to American Jewish leaders pleading for their assistance by raising the memory of the six million. "Remember," their letter warned, "the history of our people has known many terrible mistakes. Remember – your smallest hesitation may cause irreparable tragic results. Our fate depends on you. Can you retreat at such a moment?"[53]

The answer to that question, from much of the American Jewish community, was a resounding no. In April, when the Presidents Conference met in New York to vote on endorsing Jackson-Vanik, Stein attempted to dissuade the assembled leaders from supporting it. He was answered with accusations of treason, and the group voted by a huge margin to back the amendment.[54] That same month, Yossi Klein Halevi and six other American students, who had entered the USSR as tourists, were detained by Soviet authorities for demonstrating outside the Moscow visa office, where they sang Hebrew songs and chanted "Let our people go!" The students were held for several hours and then released, but their timing was impeccable. Their demonstration had occurred as a member of the Politburo, addressing a Lenin birthday rally, decried the Americans opposing the trade agreement. The students' escapade made the *New York Times*,[55] and it was merely a warm-up for the outpouring of support for Jackson-Vanik that appeared the first week of May when the Greater New York Conference on Soviet Jewry sponsored a parade and rally that brought one hundred thousand protestors marching down Fifth Avenue and then toward the United Nations, singing "*Am Yisrael Chai*" and carrying signs that read "Free the Prisoners Now," while youngsters in striped prison garb held up signs printed with the names of imprisoned refuseniks.[56]

Stretched across Dag Hammarskjold Plaza was a canvas reproduction of the entranceway to the Potna Labor Camp, where Soviet Jewish activists were incarcerated, and a platform with loudspeakers had been set up. The demonstrators cheered when Mikhail Shepsholovich, a twenty-nine-year-old Russian Jew who had just emigrated to Israel, said that the "hope for Russian Jewry lies with the United States."[57] Senator James Buckley was rewarded with an approbatory roar when he said, "Before we grant the Russians privileged access to our markets, let us first insist that they grant their own citizens not the privilege of emigration, but the fundamental right of emigration,"[58] and Senator Jacob Javits won a loud ovation when he told the crowd that the "Soviets read the newspapers...I am sure that through demonstrations such as this they sense this deep-rooted feeling for the plight of Soviet Jewry."[59]

One man who was cognizant of the deep-rooted feelings was Henry Kissinger. Before traveling to Moscow to prepare for the Nixon-Brezhnev summit scheduled for June in the United States, Kissinger asked Fisher and Stein to meet with him again. The administration had tried to exclude Richard Maass, chairman of the National Conference on Soviet Jewry, from the discussion, because NCSJ was now openly urging the adoption of the Jackson-Vanik amendment. Fisher and Stein refused to exclude Maass; they understood that if the administration could not bring Maass and his organization to rethink their stance, then the administration had no hope of changing the collective mind of American Jewry.[60]

Nothing came of the discussion, and Kissinger left for Moscow.

◆ ◆ ◆

By the time Leonid Brezhnev landed at Andrews Air Force Base on Saturday afternoon, June 16, Richard Nixon had bigger problems than a congressional revolt against his trade bill.[61] Watergate had taken an ugly turn. H. R. Haldeman, the White House chief of staff; John Ehrlichman, assistant to the president for domestic affairs; and Attorney General Richard Kleindienst had resigned because of the scandal. The Senate Watergate Committee had begun televising its hearings, and after White House counsel John Dean was fired by Nixon, he told Watergate investigators that he had discussed the cover-up with the president on some thirty-five occasions.[62]

Nixon was hemorrhaging political capital, which put him at a disadvantage with Brezhnev, who relied on the president to deliver on his promises. One promise that Nixon had made to the Soviet leader, when they had first met in Moscow, was that if Brezhnev visited the United States, he would enjoy "a good reception" and would not have to "worry about demonstrations…we know how to handle them."[63] That was an easier guarantee for Nixon to offer in May 1972 than in June 1973, but the National Conference on Soviet Jewry, perhaps at Kissinger's request, only organized small protests to greet Brezhnev, a decision that exasperated the grassroots activists, who were already planning a demonstration of their own.[64]

On Monday evening, a state dinner in honor of Brezhnev was held at the White House. Along with the usual government officials, the guest list included numerous celebrities and business leaders: June Allyson, Van Cliburn, Cornelius and Marylou Whitney, Teamster head Frank E. Fitzsimmons, Marjorie and Max Fisher, and Jean and Jack Stein.[65]

Many leaders in the American Jewish community were irate at Fisher and Stein for attending the dinner, and activists were irritated enough to picket in front of Stein's home on Long Island.[66] Six years later, when the generally fair-minded William W. Orbach published his history of the American Soviet Jewry movement, that anger seeped into his narrative. He wrote that Stein sided with the administration because he was afraid to lose "his White House links" and that Stein and Fisher had gone to the dinner because they were "flattered" to be asked.[67]

Fisher and Stein thought that explanation was patently absurd.

"Max and I went that evening," Stein explained more than thirty years after the dinner, "because yelling into a microphone at somebody who is five thousand miles away on an issue that we felt strongly about didn't make sense to us – not if we had a chance to sit across the table and talk to him."[68]

Nixon knew that by inviting Fisher and Stein he was signaling Brezhnev that Soviet Jewry could not be swept aside if he hoped to win most-favored-nation status.[69] And Nixon took no chances that Brezhnev would miss the signal. As the guests walked down the receiving line in the Blue Room, Nixon introduced the Fishers and Steins, emphasizing that the two men were Jewish leaders. Brezhnev got the message. Stein remembers that when the interpreter translated Nixon's introduction, he used the Russian word for Hebrew, *Yevrey*. Brezhnev nodded.[70]

During the cocktail hour, Fisher and Stein cornered Soviet foreign affairs minister Andrei Gromyko. They began to talk, warily at first, and then Stein started peppering Gromyko with questions: "Why are you doing this to the Jews? Why can't we sit and talk this thing out? Why do you need people in your country that you don't want? Why are you jeopardizing your MFN status?"[71]

Gromyko listened. Finally, he said, "Everything will be all right. The road will be wider."[72]

The foreign minister spotted Soviet ambassador Anatoly Dobrynin nearby, and requested that he join the conversation. Then he recapped what had been said and asked Dobrynin, "Why don't you talk this out with Mr. Fisher and Mr. Stein?"[73]

Dobrynin answered that he would do so in the near future. Dinner was announced and the four men went to their tables.[74]

On Friday, June 22, after Nixon and Brezhnev signed the Agreement for the Prevention of Nuclear War, the two leaders flew to the president's house in San Clemente, California, to continue their talks. That afternoon, Fisher phoned Stein at his office. There was a Soviet Jewry demonstration planned in California, Fisher said. Was it really in everyone's best interest to heap more public embarrassment on the Russians? We know that Nixon is behind us and has been talking to Brezhnev about getting the Jews out to Israel, he said. Was it possible to do something to avert the protest?[75]

The protest had been planned by the merry pranksters of the Soviet Jewry movement, Si Frumkin and Zev Yaroslavsky, and their brainstorms had a propensity to attract attention. Stein called Frumkin and said, "Si, don't do this. You burn flags at demonstrations; you pour red ink into swimming pools. This is two heads of state we're talking about. It's not appropriate."[76]

Frumkin replied that he and Zev had only taken a small ad in the *Los Angeles Times*, asking people to come to San Clemente and carry candles so Brezhnev would see them. It would not be as over-the-top as their other demonstrations. Of course, says Frumkin, the call came before someone dreamt up standing outside the Western White House and releasing balloons printed with "Let My People Go!" on them in English and Russian; before one of the most popular disc jockeys in Southern California, Dick Whittinghill, heard about the scheme; and before Whittinghill, on the air, phoned the police in San Clemente to ask what would happen when protestors arrived with balloons.[77]

"I'll arrest them," said the police officer.

"Arrest them for what?" said Whittinghill.

"For littering," the officer replied.

"Littering?" Whittinghill said.

"Littering," the officer said. "If they release those balloons then the balloons have to come down and the minute they touch the ground that's littering."[78]

Eight thousand people demonstrated. No one was arrested for littering. The summit concluded without Nixon and Brezhnev making much progress on SALT II, though they did agree to sign an arms limitations agreement by the end of the following year.[79]

◆ ◆ ◆

Brezhnev had met with congressional leaders while he was in Washington to defend Soviet emigration practices, which gave Senator J. William Fulbright, a Democrat from Arkansas and member of the Foreign Affairs Committee, an opening to decry the influence of the "Jewish lobby."[80] On *Face the Nation*, Fulbright would declare that 80 percent of the Senate was controlled by Israel, adding that its power "in the House of Representatives is even greater."[81] Jackson answered Fulbright's charges by saying that his amendment was nothing but an attempt to create "a tiny bit of freedom for Jew and Gentile in the USSR," an attempt that Fulbright dismissed as "idealistic meddling."[82]

In July, Ambassador Dobrynin invited Fisher and Stein, with their wives, to lunch at the Russian embassy in Washington. Neither Marjorie Fisher nor Jean Stein wanted to go, but Jean relented because in a roundabout way Dobrynin insisted that at least one of the wives come along so it did not appear that he was courting American Jews on substantive concerns.[83]

Before riding over to the Russian embassy, Fisher and Stein met with Kissinger at his NSC office in the White House. When Kissinger was asked if certain issues should be avoided during their lunch, he replied, "You can say things the administration can't say. You can raise issues we can't raise. Go ahead and raise them."[84]

From Kissinger's instructions to Fisher and Stein, it would seem that he was using the pressure generated by the American Jewish community to help force concessions from the Soviets.[85]

In the embassy dining room the ambassador sat at one end of the long table, his wife at the other. As soon as everyone was seated, Jacob Stein took out his reference notes and unloaded on Dobrynin; Fisher, for the moment, hung back. Stein recalled that he gave the ambassador an earful of "the whole Soviet Jewry line – straight out – names, dates, facts and figures."[86]

When Stein finished, Dobrynin said, "I do not know why right now the Jewish community is pushing for Jackson-Vanik. I do not understand it. The levels of immigration are going up. I, myself, have a lot of Jewish friends in the Soviet Union; I play chess with them when I go home."[87]

Dobrynin's wife, obviously angry with the way Stein had gone after her husband, said to the ambassador, "Why don't we put all of our Jews on a TWA plane and send them to the United States?"[88]

"Could you do that?" Fisher asked. "We would be happy to pay their way."[89]

No one answered that question, and as they ate, the conversation proceeded on a softer note. Ambassador Dobrynin said that the matter of the Russian Jews had to be seen in the context of the Soviet Union's overall relations with the United States and that it could be worked out if it were done "without confrontation." Fisher said that the drop in exit visas to Israel during May and June had many Americans skeptical of the Kremlin's willingness to let the Jews go. The ambassador replied that this was deliberate because the Soviets did not want Brezhnev's visit keyed to a rise in immigration.[90]

But, Dobrynin said, the annual immigration figures would be forty thousand. Fisher and Stein said that it would be helpful if that level could be maintained for the rest of the year. It also would be helpful, Fisher said, if Kissinger could get confirmation on Soviet emigration statistics. For example, Fisher said, of the eight hundred names submitted to Kissinger, only fifty or sixty could be confirmed. If the ambassador could provide the names of the other 750, then perhaps Americans might have more confidence in the Kremlin's sincerity.[91]

"That is a fair request," Dobrynin said. "I will see what I can do."[92]

Fisher broached the subject of harassment of the Jews who applied for visas, but as Fisher later told Leonard Garment at the White House, he was "not confident that much will happen in this regard." Dobrynin said that the activists who were in jail would eventually be released, but "not now, because doing so would create an internal problem." Dobrynin said that no activists were allowed to roam the streets of the Soviet Union – Jewish or otherwise.[93]

The final issue Fisher raised was that Brezhnev had stated that 90 percent of the Jews who applied for exit visas would receive them. Yet, Fisher said, reports from the National Conference on Soviet Jewry and other groups indicated that roughly one hundred thousand people hoped to secure visas. Was there any way to reconcile these reports with – and confirm – Brezhnev's statement?[94]

"No," Dobrynin replied, and shortly thereafter, the luncheon was over.[95]

◆ ◆ ◆

In August, Fisher asked Attorney General Elliot Richardson to use his parole authority to bring eight hundred Soviet Jews into the United States.[96] Richardson agreed, but the grassroots activists were unmoved by these efforts.[97]

A month later, the Soviet Union ratified two international covenants on human rights that had been adopted by the UN General Assembly in 1966. Most of the provisions were roughly equivalent to those in the Soviet Constitution that Stalin had approved in 1936. But the UN Covenant on Civil and Political Rights enumerated one right that Stalin never would have countenanced: it stated that "everyone shall be free to leave any country, including his own." The ratification was announced in a single sentence in *Pravda*, which was followed by a self-congratulatory editorial in another Communist Party newspaper, *Sovetskaya Rossiya*. The covenants were not published and the list of protected rights that appeared excluded any mention of the right to emigrate. Hedrick Smith, Moscow bureau chief for the *New York Times*, judged the ratification to be an attempt "to influence voting in the United States Congress on Soviet-American trade."[98]

◆ ◆ ◆

Watergate was now threatening to overwhelm the president. Alexander P. Butterfield, the administrator of the Federal Aviation Administration and an erstwhile White House aide, disclosed to the committee that listening devices and taps had been installed in all the president's offices and phones for the purpose of preserving Nixon's conversations for posterity. Now, the committee wanted to hear the tapes and Nixon refused; the committee slapped him with a subpoena. Judge Sirica stepped in and ordered Nixon to hand over nine tapes for the judge to listen to in private – the first of several legal rulings that would go against the president.

Meanwhile, Nixon had fired Secretary of State Rogers, and he hoped that Kissinger, his nominee to fill the post, would have a chance to discuss the necessity of quiet diplomacy before the Senate Foreign Relations Committee during his confirmation hearings – providing a counterargument to the fans of Jackson-Vanik and distracting the public from the Watergate proceedings – but Kissinger was confirmed without a hearing.[99]

By September, the Jackson-Vanik amendment had 77 cosponsors in the Senate and 285 in the House. Jackson published an op-ed in the *New York Times* in which, paraphrasing Thomas Mann and Aleksandr Solzhenitsyn, he wrote that "a regime that denies the rights of man can never be reconciled to membership in the community of civilized nations."[100] Later that month, the most famous dissident in the USSR, Andrei Sakharov, wrote a letter urging the adoption of Jackson-Vanik, suggesting that the amendment was not interfering in internal matters but was "a defense of international law, without which there can be no trust," and that "the abandonment of a policy of principle" would be "tantamount to total capitulation of democratic principles in the face of blackmail, deceit, and violence."[101]

The Kremlin responded to Sakharov with a spate of denunciations,[102] and shortly the KGB would be interrogating his wife, Yelena, calling her mentally ill – with the implication that she would be locked away in a psychiatric hospital – and threatening their children.[103]

Senator George McGovern attacked the crux of Nixon and Kissinger's argument against the amendment by asking a simple question: "If we don't interfere in internal affairs, what the hell were we doing in Vietnam?"[104]

The trade bill emerged from the Ways and Means Committee on September 26, but less than two weeks later Washington and Moscow were dragged into another Arab-Israeli war.

◆ ◆ ◆

Egyptian President Anwar el-Sadat was not impressed with détente. To avoid an increase in tensions the superpowers had maintained the status quo in the Middle East, which meant that neither Moscow nor Washington would help Egypt recover the territory it had lost in the Six-Day War.

Even after Sadat expelled Soviet advisers in the hope of bringing the United States to his aid nothing changed. So Sadat altered the prevailing geopolitical arrangements by sending his forces across the Suez Canal on Yom Kippur, while Syria stormed the Golan Heights.[105]

That evening, October 6, the leadership from the heavyweights of organized American Jewry – the Presidents Conference, the United Jewish Appeal, and Council of Jewish Federations and Welfare Funds – had gathered in New York City. Given the decisive Israeli victory in 1967, the leaders were confident that Israel would repel the attack. Fund-raising programs were mapped out, and a national leadership convocation was scheduled at the Shoreham Hotel in Washington, DC, for Tuesday, October 9.[106]

By Tuesday, however, the Egyptians had barreled into the Sinai, planting their flags on Israeli bunkers, and the Syrians had captured the high ground on Mount Hermon in the Golan. Israeli losses were unprecedented. Egypt's Soviet-supplied surface-to-air missiles had neutralized Israeli air superiority, and the Soviet Union was determined to strengthen its ties to the Arab world by beginning an airlift to resupply Syria and Egypt.[107]

The top priority for Israel and American Jewish leaders was to persuade the administration to resupply Israel. Prime Minister Golda Meir was phoning Simcha Dinitz, the indefatigable Israeli ambassador to Washington, "at all hours of the day and the night."[108] Dinitz, in turn, kept calling American Jewish leaders and Kissinger. At first, when the fighting broke out, Kissinger had told Dobrynin that if the Kremlin showed restraint, then he would keep pushing for MFN, and he told Dinitz that he would resupply Israel if American leaders stopped their crusade to pass Jackson-Vanik. Kissinger's efforts at linkage fell apart by October 9, when it became clear that Israel was in dire straits and was readying its nuclear missiles.[109] That afternoon, Max Fisher went to the Oval Office to speak with the president. Nixon was still battling against the release of the tapes and waiting to accept the resignation of Vice President Spiro Agnew, who was being investigated on suspicion of accepting kickbacks while governor of Maryland. Fisher handed Nixon a letter from the Presidents Conference asking him to resupply the Israelis, and then added his own voice to the request. Nixon assured him that Israel would get everything it needed.[110]

But by the sixth day of the war, the American airlift had still not begun. Columnists blamed Kissinger,[111] as did Senator Jackson and Senator Javits, who charged that the administration was more interested in preserving détente than protecting Israel.[112] The cause of the delay has persisted as a historical debate, and now, as well as then, the blame is often dropped on Kissinger's doorstep.

Former NSC staffer William B. Quandt recalled that "when Dinitz complained about the slow American response, Kissinger blamed it on the Defense Department, a ploy he repeatedly used with the Israeli ambassador over the next several days."[113] Buttressing this claim was Kissinger's own admission that when he had bad news for Dinitz he "was not above ascribing it to bureaucratic stalemates."[114] And lastly there was Kissinger's statement to Secretary of Defense James R. Schlesinger, at the outbreak of hostilities, that stability would be best achieved "if Israel came out a little ahead but got bloodied in the process, and if the US stayed clean."[115]

To the charge that he deliberately stalled to accomplish American objectives Kissinger says, "Who are the people who could claim this? There has to be a limit to ingratitude. The war started Saturday morning [October 6], and we were delivering weapons to them – over violent bureaucratic opposition in our government – by Saturday night [October 13]. The Israelis had told us that they were going to win the war by Thursday. They grossly overestimated their own capabilities. So initially our priority was not to resupply them during the war, but after a cease-fire. The first time we knew the extent of their needs was on Tuesday morning [October 9]. By Friday night [October 12], they had the all-American military airlift operating. Sure, we explored the possibility of civilian airlifts. That took all of thirty-six hours. Before you put your whole military-airlift capability at the disposal of a foreign country, you do look at alternatives."[116]

Former president Richard Nixon also cites a bureaucratic wrestling match for the holdup. "There was great opposition in the Defense Department and among some in the foreign-service bureaucracy to coming down on the side of Israel in this conflict," says Nixon. "Their opposition was due, in part, to the threat of an [oil] embargo. Consequently, when we got the request from Golda Meir, there was a Soviet airlift to Syria operating. I said to Kissinger: 'Let's see what we can do about this.'

So [the National Security Council] came up with all these cockamamie schemes – we'll paint over the Star of David on the Israeli airplanes; we'll charter planes from private companies. It was all nonsense. Finally, we agreed upon a position. Kissinger said we should send three C-5A military transport planes. I said: 'How many do we have?' Kissinger said: 'Twenty-six.' I said: 'Send them all.' Kissinger repeated the bureaucratic objections. 'Just send them all,' I said. My point was that if you send three, then we were going to get blamed by the Arabs just as much as if we had sent twenty-six."[117]

General Alexander Haig, who had replaced Haldeman as White House chief of staff, believes that it was a bureaucratic dust-up between State and Defense delaying the airlift.[118] But Haig, after speaking with Kissinger, had already intervened. On October 6, Haig contacted the Israelis, saying that the United States had a recently developed weapon – a tube-launched, optically tracked wire-guided missile, a devastatingly effective tank killer – and he offered these TOWs to the Israelis. It was an extraordinary offer: the TOWs had only been "shared" with Britain and West Germany, and it was an indication of how precarious Haig thought the Israeli situation to be. By nightfall, a CIA plane was bringing forty Israeli officers to Fort Benning, Georgia, where they were trained to use the missiles. By Sunday, October 14, when the first official US resupply planes touched down at Lod Airport, the Israelis had already decisively deployed the TOWs.[119]

The story of the TOW missiles is generally absent from historical discussions of the airlift controversy. In 2003, Kissinger confirmed that whether to ship Israel the missiles was "one of the considerations"[120] that had to be decided. Arming the Israelis with a new weapon – which had first been tested against Soviet tanks in 1972 to blunt North Vietnam's spring offensive[121] – attests to how far out on the geopolitical limb the United States was willing to go to preserve the balance of power, but it also spotlights the weakness of détente.

Notwithstanding all the talk of lessening tensions since 1969, Washington and Moscow found themselves up to their eyeballs in a Middle East war: Israel was prepared to launch a nuclear strike. Washington was shipping state-of-the-art weaponry to the Israelis, along with a massive airlift and forty new F-4 Phantoms.[122] Moscow was landing planes in Arab states at the rate of eighteen every hour, and, after the IDF surrounded the Egyptian Third Army in the Sinai, readied fifty thousand troops to go to Egypt's rescue – a move that Washington answered by putting US conventional and nuclear forces on alert.[123]

So much for détente. This point was not lost on the American Jewish community, and made it nearly unimaginable to argue that the administration's policy was worth preserving by granting the Soviet Union – clearly no friend of Israel – most-favored-nation status. Once the illusion of Israeli military invincibility was gone, the omnipresent survival fears of the Jewish community were inflamed. Leaving aside what Nixon euphemistically referred to as the "limitations" of détente,[124] this made it harder to oppose an amendment that might save Jews in distress and bring them to Israel, where it was now evident they were sorely needed. Last but not least, the Yom Kippur War had proven that the United States, by virtue of the Cold War, could not permit Soviet clients to defeat Israel, a position that would not be reversed by amending the Trade Reform Act, regardless of how strongly the administration felt that the amendment should not be attached to the legislation.

◆ ◆ ◆

None of this prevented Kissinger from trying to persuade Jewish leadership to help defeat Jackson-Vanik. On October 25, after the secretary of state returned from Moscow, where he had gone to work on a Middle East cease-fire agreement, he spoke with Fisher, Stein, and Maass and told them that Soviet cooperation would be required for peace – cooperation that could be secured by eliminating the amendment.[125] Kissinger might as well have been preaching to himself. No one's mind was changed by his appeal: Maass and the National Conference on Soviet Jewry would stick with Jackson-Vanik; Fisher and Stein expected that if the amendment passed, the Kremlin would not modify its emigration practices, except to cut back on the number of Jews that were let go. Nonetheless, the three men told Kissinger that they would speak with Jackson.[126]

There were, says Stein, "some harsh words between Scoop and us."[127] The senator said that Nixon's methods would not get the Soviet Jews out, and he would personally make that known to the Jewish community –

going over the heads of the Presidents Conference, Fisher, or anyone else who got in his way.[128]

According to Stein, by the late fall of 1973, American Jews from the established bodies he represented as chairman of the Presidents Conference, along with the network of grassroots activists, were ardently pro-Jackson-Vanik. Stein and Fisher were willing to talk privately of their anxieties about the doors slamming shut for Soviet Jews if the amendment was hardened into law, but Stein says that because he and Fisher knew "you can't be a leader if you don't have followers," they wound up signing statements of support that "neither one of us believed in."[129]

While Kissinger was off on a round of shuttle diplomacy in the Middle East, Nixon made an appeal to the House. Unfortunately for the president, there would be no backroom workaround with Wilbur Mills. The Ways and Means chairman had been absent from Congress because of back surgery, and upon his return he became embroiled in a scandal that would shortly cost him his chairmanship. On October 7, Mills had been stopped at 2 AM by the US Park Police while he was driving near the Tidal Basin. He was drunk; his face was cut; and he was accompanied by Annabell Battistella, a stripper twenty-seven years his junior, who performed under the name "Fanne Foxe," and was billed as the "Argentine Firecracker."[130]

Nixon wrote to Speaker of the House Carl B. Albert and requested that the House either defeat Jackson-Vanik or remove most-favored-nation from the trade bill. Normally, such a direct appeal from the president would receive the utmost consideration from Congress, but Nixon, drowning in Watergate, had all but exhausted the moral authority of the Oval Office, and on December 11, the House passed Jackson-Vanik by a margin of 319 to 80, while an amendment to scratch MFN from the trade bill was rejected by a vote of 298 to 106.[131]

The trade bill moved into the Senate and, on March 6, two days after Kissinger returned from jump-starting negotiations between Israel and Syria, he began to negotiate with Jackson, Ribicoff, and Javits, trying to forge a compromise on the amendment. The plan was for the Senate to grant MFN status to the Soviets, but to retain oversight on their emigration policy. Backed by Ribicoff and Javits, Jackson responded that he wanted a written guarantee from the Kremlin that one hundred thousand Soviet citizens would be allowed to emigrate every year and that the emigrants would not be heavily weighted toward Jews in the provinces, where they were less educated, but would also come from the cities – the Jews the Israelis most desired. The requests, Kissinger thought, were pure pie-in-the-sky, intended to humiliate the Soviets – a humiliation, Kissinger was convinced, that would lead to a reduction in the thirty-five thousand a year the Kremlin was currently permitting to emigrate.[132]

In his memoirs, Kissinger railed against the absurdity of the demands: "I was being asked to triple Jewish emigration from the Soviet Union…on top of the hundredfold increase we had already achieved…and to specify from what region emigrants should be drawn – all in return for giving the Soviets the same trade treatment already enjoyed by over one hundred other nations."[133] No wonder Kissinger later said that his conversations with Jackson made him "long for the relative tranquility of the Middle East."[134]

In the last week of March, as Kissinger arrived in Moscow to discuss the upcoming Nixon-Brezhnev summit in June, *Pravda* warned the United States not to interfere with Soviet emigration and accused "international Zionism" of conducting a concerted effort to destroy détente and any cooperation between the US and USSR.[135] Undaunted, Kissinger brought the senators' requests to Gromyko. The Soviet foreign minister said that forty-five thousand emigrants a year could be mentioned to the senators as indicative of a "trend," but not as a firm commitment, since no one knew how many applications for exit visas would be submitted. Then, demonstrating that he was not without a sense of humor, Gromyko explained that the Kremlin "did not want to put itself in a position where it had to recruit citizens to emigrate to fulfill a moral obligation to the United States."[136]

With such wittiness in the air, Kissinger went for broke and inquired about the geographic distribution of emigrants. In a voice as cold as the Siberian winter, Gromyko replied that he would "check with Moscow."[137]

Nixon made one last public gesture to defend the administration's position on Jackson-Vanik. In a June 5 speech at Annapolis, the besieged president discounted an American foreign policy burdened by "eloquent speeches"[138] and "appeals"[139] to pursue a human rights agenda inside other nations, saying that "we would not welcome the intervention of other countries in our domestic affairs and we cannot expect them to be cooperative when we seek to intervene directly in theirs."[140]

The speech had been written by Kissinger's staff, and the following day when Jewish leaders stopped by to see the secretary of state before going to the White House, Kissinger advised that they avoid mention of the speech, since the president had gone "a bit too far," and he promised to talk to him about it. The leaders were not fooled by the gambit, which only reinforced Kissinger's reputation for duplicity – a reputation that would be front and center in the closing scene of the Jackson-Vanik drama.[141]

♦ ♦ ♦

On August 9, 1974, Richard Nixon resigned, and Gerald Ford, a straight-shooting, former longtime congressman from Michigan who had replaced Agnew, was sworn in as president. Five days later Ambassador Dobrynin came to the Oval Office with Kissinger. Dobrynin said that Brezhnev would promise to allow fifty-five thousand Soviet Jews to emigrate each year, but that the promise would not be formalized in writing so Jackson could "use it for his own political purposes."[142]

The next morning Ford ate breakfast in the White House with Jackson, Ribicoff, and Javits, and the president recounted the pledge Dobrynin had made. Ribicoff and Javits were satisfied with the offer; Jackson was not. He said that the administration was "being too soft on the Russians." [143] When the breakfast ended Ford was hoping for a compromise, though he doubted Jackson would agree to one because he "had a strong constituency among American Jews. He was about to launch his presidential campaign, and he was playing politics to the hilt."[144]

However, by September, the inexhaustible Kissinger had cobbled together a semblance of a deal between Dobrynin and Jackson. On its surface, the deal was so childish that to give it proper historical attention, one has to remember that the alleviation of the suffering of the refuseniks was at stake. Richard Perle and Kissinger aide Helmut Sonnenfeldt would draft three letters:[145] Kissinger would deliver one letter to Jackson affirming that the Kremlin would increase emigration. Jackson would send a letter back to Kissinger claiming that a minimum of sixty thousand visas would be issued annually. In the third letter, Kissinger would answer Jackson by stating that he saw no reason to contradict his visa projections.[146]

The one caveat to this ridiculous formulation was that Jackson could not officially release the letters, only leak them, which is exactly what he did, making it sound as though the Kremlin had signed on the dotted line to release sixty thousand Jews. Brezhnev, under assault from Kremlin hardliners, signaled his displeasure with the news. As pleased as organized American Jewry was with the notion of an official commitment from the Soviets, the more pragmatically minded perceived that an ongoing dispute over the letters threatened the arrangement, and the warnings of Fisher and Stein about drastically reduced emigration, once so angrily dismissed, could come true.[147]

Kissinger retreated. He had National Security Adviser Brent Scowcroft inform Jackson that there would be just two letters, not three, meaning that the secretary of state would not tacitly confirm Jackson's estimate on yearly visas. Jackson and Perle were enraged by the maneuver, but they devised countermoves of their own.[148] The two letters were exchanged at the White House on October 18, 1974. Kissinger's letter did not define the amount of emigration allowed, and Jackson's letter specified that he "would consider a benchmark – a minimum standard of initial compliance – to be the issuance of visas at a rate of 60,000 per annum."[149] Jackson was invited to the White House pressroom to brief reporters. At times, the senator tended to be somewhat out of touch with his audience, perhaps a result of the faith he placed in his own moral uprightness,[150] and his briefing sounded as though he were testing out a presidential stump speech, all the while disregarding the extreme sensitivity of the Kremlin to being upstaged before the world: "I think it is a monumental accomplishment considering the fact that so many said it could never be accomplished." As Jackson congratulated himself, Richard Perle and Morris Amitay distributed the letters to the press – the official release that Kissinger had excluded from the deal.[151]

Kissinger said that Jackson's performance demonstrated a disconcerting lack of judgment, a charge that Perle thought showed Kissinger at his duplicitous worst.

"Kissinger saw the text of Scoop's remarks in advance," Perle said.

"I had taken a draft of them the night before to the Jockey Club, where Sonnenfeldt was having a drink." Perle also asseverated that President Ford, responding to a request from Jacob Javits, had sanctioned the dissemination of the letters. In Perle's opinion, "you would have to be living on another planet to think they wouldn't be released."[152]

President Ford was not living on another planet, and he was appalled at the pressroom imbroglio. He said that Jackson had "behaved like a swine" and then told reporters that the Soviets had not furnished specifics on exit visas.[153]

And Brezhnev was evidently living on the same planet as Ford, because a week later, when Kissinger went to Moscow to prepare for the summit in Vladivostok, Brezhnev was "livid," and Gromyko handed the secretary of state a letter that, in the bland-speak of diplomacy, charged Kissinger with being an outright liar for distorting Soviet commitments on emigration. The "elucidations" the Kremlin had made regarding emigrants had been translated into "assurances" and "some figures were being quoted with regard to an anticipated increase in emigration," when, in reality, the Soviets had cited "a tendency toward a decrease in the number of persons wishing to leave the USSR."[154] Gromyko's letter closed with the admonition that diplomatic games of telephone would not be tolerated: "No ambiguities should remain as regards the position of the Soviet Union."[155]

◆ ◆ ◆

As harsh a rebuke as the letter contained, it did not negate the prospect of a compromise, particularly if Kissinger forgot to mention it to anyone and assumed that in all likelihood the letter was nothing but a means for the Soviet leaders favoring emigration – Brezhnev, Gromyko, and Dobrynin – to cover their hindquarters were the Kremlin hardliners to make a fuss.[156]

Momentarily, tactical forgetfulness appeared to be a masterstroke. Less than a week before Thanksgiving, when Ford spoke with Brezhnev at the Vladivostok summit, the secretary general told the president that the Kissinger-Jackson letter exchange had been troubling, but emigration would proceed as planned.[157] On December 3, Kissinger testified before the Senate Finance Committee. The committee was about to approve the Trade Reform Act, complete with MFN for the Soviet Union, the Jackson-Vanik amendment, and a provision granting the president the ability to suspend the amendment if Soviet emigration policy was acceptable. Kissinger said nothing about the Gromyko letter, since if the senators heard that Soviet "assurances" were really the less promising "elucidations," then the compromise would have gone up in smoke.[158]

George Meany and the labor movement stayed steadfast in their opposition to the Trade Act of 1974, but President Ford was now pushing for its adoption, and Senate offices were flooded with phone calls from Jewish groups urging a yes vote on the bill, though the Jewish Defense League labeled the waiver provision a "sell-out."[159] And it was then that another, less publicized amendment attached to the Trade Act – this one the brainchild of Democratic senator Adlai Stevenson III of Illinois – became an issue that would sound the death knell for détente.

◆ ◆ ◆

Back on June 30, 1974, the presidential authority to utilize the Export-Import Bank was scheduled for renewal by Congress, which Kissinger judged "a routine decision" that had been made "biannually for decades without controversy."[160] But the zeitgeist was anything but routine, and Senator Stevenson (chairman of the International Finance Subcommittee) and several other senators were tired of giving Nixon free reign to pursue détente. Reportedly at the suggestion of organized labor,[161] Stevenson went to work on an amendment that would lay down a limit of $300 million on total loans from the Export-Import Bank to the USSR during a four-year period. If the president wanted to increase the loan amount, then Congress would have to approve it.[162]

According to Stanley J. Marcus, the subcommittee counsel, "Stevenson saw Jackson-Vanik as too narrow because it was limited to emigration, and he thought his amendment could substitute for it. Circumscribing credit from the Export-Import Bank was a more subtle lever than interfering with the internal policies of a superpower, and it gave Congress the choice to reward or punish the Soviets across a whole range of their behavior. But it was hard to explain this to the public. Besides, the times were overheated, and the Soviet Jewry movement was not the most rational movement in American history."[163]

Jerry Goodman, the executive director of NCSJ, recalls that the Jewish leaders who understood the Stevenson amendment were distressed because it would dilute the emphasis on emigration in Jackson-Vanik. But, says Goodman, "We felt we couldn't oppose [Stevenson] openly. We would have been seen as apologists."[164]

On the other hand, Henry Kissinger, in the 1982 volume of his memoirs, *Years of Upheaval*, says that he was "caught flat-footed" by the Stevenson amendment owing to a preoccupation with other events.[165]

Richard Perle and Stanley Marcus are perplexed by that explanation.

"Scoop and I spoke with Stevenson and Marcus in Scoop's office," says Perle. "I'll never forget the meeting. Stevenson told us about his amendment. Before Scoop could say a word, I said, 'Why do we want this? It replaces what we're doing. No, we don't like it all.' Then Stevenson said, 'I've discussed it with Kissinger, and he has no problem with it.' That kind of pulled the rug out from under my argument, and Scoop wound up co-sponsoring Stevenson's amendment, and Stevenson co-sponsored Jackson-Vanik."[166]

Marcus points to Kissinger's December 3 testimony before the Finance Committee. After Senator Robert C. Byrd asked the secretary of state if he opposed the $300 million ceiling on loans to the Soviet Union, Kissinger replied that "from the point of view of flexibility in the conduct of foreign policy, I would prefer no ceiling be placed on these loans." Byrd asked if Kissinger was seeking a blank check, and Kissinger responded, "No... [but] I do believe we would be better off without a ceiling."[167]

In a 1975 monograph on East-West trade, Marcus wrote, "Those looking for evidence of strenuous administration opposition to a ceiling on Eximbank credits will be hard put to find it in those words of the secretary of state. A preference for no ceiling...yes; but adamant opposition no."[168]

Perle concurs with this assessment, mainly because Stevenson had no reason to lie about sharing a draft of his amendment with Kissinger.[169] Which leads to a fascinating historical question: In light of Kissinger's intelligence, his ability to handle multiple complexities, and yes, his tactical duplicity – is it possible that the Stevenson amendment, which in its own way was as heavy-handed and humiliating to the Kremlin as Jackson-Vanik, escaped Kissinger's attention? Or is it possible that

Kissinger believed he could secure MFN for the Soviets and thereby not only wring concession from them in other areas, but still have the stick of the Stevenson amendment to wield against the Kremlin?

If one operates on the principle that the simplest explanation should suffice, then Kissinger's distraction is sufficient to account for the oversight. An alternative explanation may be more intriguing, but in a 2003 interview with the author, all Kissinger would say about the Stevenson amendment was, "It got by me. I was too focused elsewhere."[170]

◆ ◆ ◆

On December 13 – by now a full year after passage in the House – the Senate passed the Trade Reform Act with both the Jackson and Stevenson amendments by a vote of seventy-seven to four. On December 18, just two days prior to the Christmas recess and the adjournment of the Ninety-Third Congress, before a conference committee had even had a chance to iron out the minor variations of the bill passed by the House and Senate,[171] Tass, the official Soviet news agency, released a statement saying that the Kremlin rejected any efforts "to interfere in the internal affairs that are entirely the concern of the Soviet State and no one else." [172] The statement was accompanied by a copy of the letter that Gromyko had given to Kissinger and which the secretary of state had neglected to mention.[173]

Kissinger was having breakfast with Dobrynin when he learned of the revelations from Tass. The Soviet ambassador remembered Kissinger's reaction as "indignant."[174] More likely, he was embarrassed, but he was later said to suggest that the deal fell apart because Perle and Amitay had humiliated the Kremlin by distributing the letters in the White House press room, which made plain how desperately the Kremlin wanted a deal and how anxious Soviet leaders were to hide their desperation.[175] Jackson dismissed the Tass statement as fodder for internal Soviet consumption and advised his supporters to stay calm. Again, Jackson had misread Soviet leadership, who were genuinely angered by the internal meddling demanded by the Jackson amendment and perhaps, even worse, the stingy, demeaning credit restrictions of the Stevenson amendment.[176]

In January, after the entire trade package was passed and signed by a reluctant President Ford, who knew his veto would be overridden by

Congress,[177] the Soviet Union officially withdrew its request for MFN status and announced that it would neither honor its pledge to ease emigration restrictions nor repay its Lend Lease debts.[178]

It was at this moment that the efficacy of Jackson-Vanik entered the realm of eternal historical argument.

◆ ◆ ◆

For opponents of the legislation like Max Fisher and Jacob Stein, whose opposition was based in their belief that the Kremlin could not be humbled into adopting the West's human rights agenda, the passage of the trade bill was, as Nixon and Kissinger had predicted, a nightmare come true. In 1973, 34,733 Soviet Jews were allowed to emigrate; in 1974, that number shrank to 20,944, and to 13,221 in 1975. Save for 1979, when the Kremlin wanted Congress to approve the SALT II agreement and permitted a substantial uptick in emigration, the 1973 numbers would not be reached again for sixteen years.[179]

Disillusionment among supporters of trade restrictions was apparent by 1976, when three original and influential backers – Bertram Gold from the American Jewish Committee, Phil Baum from American Jewish Congress, and Marshall I. Goldman, an internationally recognized expert on the Russian economy[180] – publicly expressed their disenchantment with the attempt to arm-twist the Soviets into revising their emigration practices and were chastised by the Student Struggle for Soviet Jewry and the Union of Councils for their alleged betrayal.[181]

In measuring the tangible impact of the Jackson-Vanik and Stevenson amendments, the disheartening conclusion is unassailable: the Soviet reaction to the legislation was to drastically scale back emigration. Détente was a casualty as well. In 1976, after the Kremlin sent five thousand Cuban combat troops, armed with $100 million of weapons courtesy of the Soviets, to fight in the Angolan civil war,[182] President Ford no longer believed that détente was a realistic strategy. The SALT talks stalled, leading Brezhnev to delay a trip to the United States; the administration cancelled three US-USSR cabinet-level discussions; and Kissinger said that he would stop asking Congress to repeal trade restrictions or to approve multibillion-dollar investments in developing Soviet oil fields and natural gas deposits.[183] As tensions mounted between Washington and Moscow – especially in the five years from 1982 to 1986 while the Soviets were waging war in Afghanistan – the Kremlin only let seven thousand Jews leave, a disheartening total that had not been seen since the bad old days of the 1960s.[184]

Then there is the intangible impact of the amendments – a trickier measurement, since American Jewish supporters of trade restrictions were left to wonder if, by rejecting Nixon and Kissinger's quiet diplomacy, they were responsible for leaving the refuseniks trapped in the Soviet cage, the exact sort of Holocaust-inspired guilt from which the American Jewish community had been trying to extricate itself by railing against détente.

Yet, Anatoly Shcharansky, a refusenik who spent nine years in Soviet prisons in part because of his championing of Jackson-Vanik, feels that the Kremlin never had any "intention of allowing masses of Jews to leave," and the amendment, by placing the plight of Soviet Jews on the international stage, convinced the refuseniks that "the regime could not act toward us with impunity and that this forced restraint would embolden more and more Soviet Jews to join our struggle."[185] For Shcharansky (who would adopt the first name of Natan once he reached Israel) and his Jewish compatriots, the amendment meant that "the sands in the hourglass of the Soviet's fear society were running out."[186] Every Jew who was permitted to go decreased "the level of fear,"[187] and though Soviet leaders "could continue to violate the rights of their own people...it now would come with an expensive price tag."[188]

The ramifications of the legislation for American Jews were just as profound. While they had not entirely rid themselves of their guilt over the six million, they had made a start and were now full-fledged players in the Cold War.[189] The problems that had plagued the American Jewish community during the 1930s – the warring political and religious factions, the confused messages sent to policy makers, and the internecine squabbling among leaders – had been handled adroitly, even if they weren't completely gone, and did not destroy the effort. When it counted, the center had held.[190]

Some overestimated the Jewish contribution to the victory: after all, Jackson's primary target was détente, and he was torpedoing a president aboard a leaky ship. Mark Talisman sees the amendment as a great legislative "illusion."[191] Nothing changed, and yet everything changed, because Soviet Jews were now full-fledged participants in the Cold War, and American Jews had proven that they could labor in the political vineyard and come away with more than empathic pronouncements from the White House or bromides masquerading as congressional resolutions. Even if some American Jews had second thoughts once the legislation became law, they had been energized by the results – particularly the grassroots – and this energy was crucial, because in 1975 the Soviet Union still loomed as an obdurate monolith, and the majority of foreign policy experts believed that the Cold War would continue with no end in sight.[192]

The argument over Jackson-Vanik persists because both sides are right and wrong, depending on which perspective – tangible or intangible – is assumed. But one fact, as unassailable as the decrease in emigration, is that the American Jewish community had joined the fight, and the fight would go on.

CHAPTER 9

COLD WAR REDUX

I learned to touch history before I learned to read it, in the form of an olive-drab US Army knapsack that belonged to my Uncle Leonard, my father's older brother. My uncle was a stocky, barrel-chested man with a booming voice, and as a lieutenant with the 119th Infantry Regiment, 30th Infantry Division, he had landed in Normandy less than a week after D-Day. In the sun-dappled pastures between the walls of hedgerows the war moved one bloodstained inch at a time; at last, after the Germans were driven from Saint-Lô, my uncle fought in Belgium and Holland and assaulted the Siegfried Line, where on October 3, 1944, he was severely wounded by artillery fire.

As a child in the 1960s, I frequently asked my uncle about the war, and he showed me his three bronze stars and told me about the captured SS officers he took a grim satisfaction in interrogating with his fractured Yiddish. He was fiercely proud of his service, and at the end of every Seder he made the entire family stand and sing "The Star Spangled Banner," his response to anyone who might question whether his love for Israel encroached on his fealty to America.

Touching those artifacts from my uncle's war and listening to him talk, I was bitten by the history bug, and augmented my small pool of knowledge with comic books – *Sgt. Rock* and *Sgt. Fury and His Howling Commandos*, both of which confirmed the idea that the United States had single-handedly saved the human race from the Third Reich. I remember reading a history of the Marine Corps written for children and seeing the movie *The Longest Day*, and then on a family outing to the Lower East Side discovering my first used bookstore and investing my allowance in a history of the 101ˢᵗ Airborne published in 1948, collections of Ernie Pyle dispatches, and Bill Mauldin cartoons.

I do not ever recall, in my reading or in grammar school, junior high, or high school, ever learning about the Red Army – the men whom Stalin described as fighting "from Stalingrad to Belgrade – over thousands of kilometres of [their] own devastated land, across the dead bodies of [their] comrades and dearest ones."[1] Also missing were the mind-numbing statistics of the gruesome Nazi handiwork inside the USSR, the seventy thousand cities, towns, and villages that were destroyed along with six million houses, ninety-eight thousand farms, eighty-two thousand schools, forty-three thousand libraries, six thousand hospitals, and endless miles of roadways and rail lines.[2] An estimated twenty-seven million Soviets died in their Great Patriotic War against Hitler, two-thirds of whom were civilians.[3]

In due course, I came to understand that during the Cold War the US government – and therefore the public schools that were charged with educating the duck-and-cover kids – thought it best to downplay the decisive Soviet contribution to victory in the Second World War. (Even the Soviet Union's most famous war photographer, the Ukrainian-born Yevgeny Khaldei, who captured the image of a Red Army soldier hoisting a Soviet flag over the Reichstag, was relegated to anonymity until 2008, when his photographs were honored with a retrospective at the Martin-Gropius-Bau museum in Berlin.[4]) Still, the fact that my perceptions about World War II had been so incomplete bothered me.

More important, as regards the American movement to free Soviet Jewry, it bothered many Russians, including the men – with long, unappeasable memories – who ruled the USSR.

For a moment, let's skip to the year 1999, when Mark Talisman – yes, that Mark Talisman, by then no longer an aide to Charles Vanik or a lobbyist for the Council of Jewish Federations – was retained to assemble a museum exhibit, *World War II through Russian Eyes*. (Among the gems Talisman located was a film of Dwight D. Eisenhower stating that D-Day would have been impossible without the millions of Russian troops holding down the Nazis on the Eastern Front.) The exhibit was a resounding success across the United States, and Talisman then took it to the former Soviet Union. One night, in Moscow, he entered a crowded restaurant with a government official and, as they went to their table, people began to applaud.

"You must be very popular," Talisman said to the official.

"They're not clapping for me," the official replied. "They've seen you and your exhibition on television. They're clapping for you."

An older woman walked over to Talisman, took his hand, and kissed it. "Thank you," she said. "Thank you for telling the world what we did."[5]

I mention all of this as a way of broaching one of the most intriguing events of the Cold War: the signing of the Helsinki Final Act, which proved to be, as Henry Kissinger wrote, one of those "turning points [that] often pass unrecognized by contemporaries."[6]

◆ ◆ ◆

By the end of July 1975, the Conference on Security and Cooperation in Europe had given birth to the Helsinki Final Act, and thirty-five leaders from Europe, the United States, and Canada gathered in the Finnish capital to sign the agreement. The Final Act would deal with three sets of issues, known as baskets: Basket I dealt with security; Basket II with trade; and Basket III with human rights, notably, "the freer movement of people and ideas,"[7] and a requirement that any nation signing the accords would "expedite" the issuing of exit visas to facilitate the "reunion of families."[8] These provisions were inserted by the West through a clever diplomatic ploy engineered by George Vest, a career State Department official. To prevent the preparation of the accords from degenerating into a mano-a-mano between the superpowers, Vest had quietly prodded the West Europeans to insert a human rights agenda.[9]

It had taken months of highly charged negotiations to produce the agreement, and because the Soviet foreign ministry had been unable to clear every word with the Politburo, when the Soviet leaders met to consider the sixty-page, forty-thousand-word document[10] they were, according to Anatoly Dobrynin, "stunned."[11] Particularly taken aback were President Nikolai Podgorny, a stubborn, unsentimental man;[12] Mikhail Suslov, an inflexible ideologue even by the standards of the Kremlin; Yuri Andropov, head of the KGB[13] and notoriously intolerant of dissidents;[14] and the prime minister, Alexei Kosygin, an economic reformer with enough vision to see that the liberalizing principles in the accords were a diplomatic invitation for the West to meddle in the internal affairs of the Soviet Union.

A contentious debate broke out. Foreign Minister Gromyko, whose ministry had negotiated the agreement, was its primary defender. Gromyko said that the Kremlin had long wanted the West to accept the Soviet borders in Eastern Europe, and the Final Act accomplished this goal, which would be "a major political and propaganda victory for Moscow."[15] Basket II of the accords would pave the way for trade with the West, another Soviet goal. And while Basket III obliged the Soviets to make some progress in opening up their society, the United States, with their Jackson-Vanik and Stevenson amendments, had tried, unsuccessfully, to coerce the Kremlin into accepting such adjustments. "We are masters in our own house," Gromyko said. Brezhnev accepted Gromyko's formulation, as did the Politburo, since no one among the Soviet leadership had any intention of complying with the demands in Basket III.[16]

◆ ◆ ◆

President Gerald Ford was locked in a contentious debate of his own about his scheduled trip to Helsinki. Ford agreed with Kissinger's analysis that the Final Act should be signed by the United States because "the philosophy which permeates most of the…declarations is that of the West's open societies."[17]

However, opponents in the United States were fixated on the same issue as the Kremlin: the acceptance of the borders in Eastern Europe, which, in the minds of critics, permanently ceded those countries to Soviet control and rekindled the memories of FDR's alleged sellout at the Yalta Conference when the president secretly consented to hand over Eastern Europe to Stalin. Whether FDR had any choice short of going to war with the USSR, whose troops vastly outnumbered US forces in Europe, is still subject to debate, but in the context of Helsinki it was the sellout – the abandonment of millions of people by the West – that was raised. Lithuanian, Latvian, and Estonian organizations protested outside the White House,[18] and no less an authority on Soviet subjugation than Nobel laureate Aleksandr Solzhenitsyn, now living in the United States, publicly predicted that this "amicable agreement of diplomatic shovels will bury and pack down corpses still breathing in a common grave."[19]

In addition to the Yalta argument, opponents of the accords did not trust that the Soviets would abide by the human rights provisions, nor did they want Ford, while he was in Finland, to conclude a SALT II treaty with Brezhnev. In a rare instance of political alignment, the editorial page of the *Wall Street Journal* implored the president not to go to Helsinki,[20] and the *New York Times* denigrated the trip as "misguided and empty."[21] Two of Ford's most outspoken opponents were also being touted as potential candidates for the presidency – Senator Jackson, who with much public fanfare said that Ford was "taking us backward, not forward, in the search for a genuine peace,"[22] and Governor Ronald Reagan, who announced that he was against the Final Act and thought "all Americans should be against it."[23]

Ford was optimistic about the future use of the human rights provisions, and he wanted a SALT II agreement. En route to Helsinki, Ford stopped in Poland to speak with First Secretary Edward Gierek and, after discussing trade, détente, and the odds of reaching an arms treaty with the Kremlin,[24] Ford became the first American president to visit Auschwitz, a gesture that let the world know that even though he planned to sign the Helsinki Final Act, he would not forget the lessons of the Second World War.

Ford and Brezhnev could not resolve their differences on arms in Helsinki, but the president had a message for the general secretary when he stood up to speak to the heads of state in Finlandia House. Brezhnev had already promised the gathering that he would "implement the understandings" contained in the Final Act, but Ford was no naïf when it came to Soviet commitments, and during his speech he paused dramatically, then stared at Brezhnev and said, "To my country these principles are not clichés or empty phrases.... It is important that you realize the deep devotion of the American people and their government to human rights and fundamental freedoms and thus to the pledges that this conference has made regarding the freer movement of people, ideas, and information. History will judge this conference...not by the promises we make but the by the promises we keep."[25]

The press reaction to the speech was favorable, but critics still spoke of a sellout and decried the apparent propaganda victory the Kremlin had won.[26] Brezhnev must have been delighted. It was working out as Gromyko had foreseen. Now all that Brezhnev had left to do was to return to Moscow and, in light of Soviet designs, commit one of the biggest strategic blunders of the Cold War.

◆ ◆ ◆

In September 1975, just a little over a month after the Final Act was signed, the Kremlin had the full text of the accords printed in *Pravda*[27] and *Izvestia*.[28]

Here was the "turning point" that Kissinger had written about in the third volume of his memoirs, because contrary to the outcome the Kremlin had intended, it was the human rights provisions – not the settlement of borders – that received the most attention in the Soviet Union and across Eastern Europe, and as Anatoly Dobrynin would recall, became a "manifesto" for dissidents and "caused the fundamental changes…that helped end the Cold War."[29]

The British Soviet Jewry activist Doreen Gainsford preferred a simpler description of the Final Act. She called it "a gift from God."[30]

But that gift would have been useless if Brezhnev and the Politburo had not permitted the accords to appear unedited in *Pravda* and *Izvestia*. And so the question is, why did the Soviet leadership make that decision?

Dobrynin thought that the Kremlin was under the impression that since the Soviet people had "sacrificed so much" in World War II they would be gratified that, after thirty years, there was a tangible accomplishment to show for their suffering.[31]

On the other hand, David Satter, the Moscow correspondent for the *Financial Times* of London, believed that "words in the Soviet Union, like any totalitarian state, had no real meaning, so the Politburo was not concerned that someone would take the human rights aspects of the accords seriously."[32]

There are elements of truth in both statements, but Soviet behavior tends to give more weight to the perception that the decision demonstrated how haunted the Soviet leaders were by the Great Patriotic War and how insulted – hurt, actually, if one dare ascribe such tenderness to members of the Politburo – they were that the free world had refused to recognize the exorbitant price the USSR had paid, and the majestic valor it had shown, in defeating the Nazis.

In 1973, when the Soviets ratified the United Nations Covenant on Civil and Political Rights, the Kremlin had been judicious enough to prohibit any newspapers in the USSR from mentioning that Soviet leaders had agreed to extend the right of emigration to citizens of the Soviet bloc.[33]

However, two years later they reversed their policy about publicizing the possibility of freedom of movement, and the major difference between the two events was that a reward of the Helsinki Final Act was connected to the Second World War, while the United Nations covenant did not offer a similar benefit. And though it is true, as David Satter says, that the Kremlin reserved the right to interpret words in any manner it wished, the blunder was not limited to publishing the text, but doing so when Eastern Europe had been clearly listing toward the openness of the West, with its rollicking culture and promise of unending opportunity.

Perhaps this was unavoidable. Even in the United States leaders inside the Beltway enter a bubble that can lead them to lose touch with the people they represent. One could argue that the greatest mistake Nixon made in handling Watergate was that he underestimated the anger over the half truths and outright lies told by American leaders regarding Vietnam, and all of that rage came crashing down on him once the cover-up was revealed. Hence, it should be no surprise that the stagnant, self-perpetuating ruling class of the USSR would also misread its subjects, and that no one in the Politburo would see that even inside the great gray dungeon of the Soviet Union, the times they were a-changin'.

◆ ◆ ◆

One individual the Kremlin would not permit to leave the country was Andrei Sakharov, and so, two months after Helsinki, it was his wife, Yelena Bonner, who traveled to Oslo to accept her husband's Nobel Peace Prize, while Sakharov stayed behind in Vilnius, the capital of Soviet Lithuania, where he hoped to gain access to a courtroom to witness the trial of a dissident. At the ceremony, Bonner read a statement from her husband in which the physicist said that he shared the honor of the prize with "all prisoners of conscience in the Soviet Union and in other Eastern European countries as well as with those who fight for their liberation."[34]

In this heady atmosphere Soviet Jews reacted to the Helsinki Final Act as though it were a lifeline. During the last few months of 1975 and through the following year nearly 40 percent of the Jews applying to emigrate cited the accords provision to reunify families.[35] But there was an even greater potential contained in the Final Act, and it was Yuri Orlov, a dissident Soviet physicist, who was the first to spot it. Since the signatories of Helsinki had consented to international accountability on human rights, it was only logical that there should be a method for transmitting "to the participating states information on violations of the humanitarian provisions," and that to interfere with the transmittal of this information would be "a fundamental violation of the spirit and letter of the Final Act."[36]

After all, Orlov later commented, "if the Soviet government said [Helsinki] was important, it was, in fact, important."[37] Consequently, in keeping with the accords, Orlov founded the Moscow Helsinki Watch Group with Anatoly Shcharansky, Vitaly Rubin, Vladimir Slepak, and other refuseniks and dissidents. They announced the formation of their group in April 1976.[38]

The spread of the dissident movement was a boon to Western journalists, because, as Kevin Klose, Moscow bureau chief of the *Washington Post*, recalled, "Reporters suddenly had live bodies who could tell them what was truly going on."[39] Before long other watch groups were flourishing in the USSR and across Eastern Europe, and dissidents were citing the accords in reaction to government heavy-handedness. When members of the underground Czechoslovak rock band the Plastic People were arrested after eight years of secret performances, several hundred intellectuals responded by signing Charter 77, a document that exhorted the Czech government to respect Helsinki's guarantee of freedom of expression. A number of those who signed Charter 77 were then arrested, including the writer and rock-music aficionado Václav Havel, who spent four years in prison churning out essays and plays that lay bare his generation's disgust with Communism, surely not the future that Brezhnev had envisioned when he had the Czech government sign the Final Act.[40]

And the United States government was also getting into the monitoring business. The sparkplug behind it was a flinty, sixty-five-year-old, pipe-smoking Republican congresswoman from New Jersey, Millicent Fenwick. A passionate supporter of the civil rights movement[41] and a former writer and editor at *Vogue*, Fenwick was described by a former aide as the "Katherine Hepburn of politics." She was reputed to be the inspiration for Representative Lacey Davenport in Gary Trudeau's *Doonesbury* comic strip.[42]

In August 1975, Fenwick was part of a congressional delegation that went to the Soviet Union. During a reception at the embassy, she encountered Christopher Wren, the Moscow bureau chief of the *New York Times*. Wren took her to meet dissidents, an experience Fenwick compared to being in a "spy movie." In his white Volga sedan clouded with Fenwick's pipe smoke,[43] Wren drove her to meet Valentin Turchin, director of the Moscow office of Amnesty International; Yuri Orlov; and Anatoly Shcharansky, who, with his excellent English, sharp wit, and infectious passion persuaded Fenwick that the United States should push the Kremlin to comply with Helsinki.[44]

NCSJ had arranged a meeting for Fenwick with refusenik Lilia Roitburd. The woman told Fenwick that her husband had lost his job as an engineer and was excoriated in public as "an imperialist puppet" for no other reason than that he had applied for exit visas for himself and his family, and Lilia pleaded with Fenwick to help. Later, Fenwick would say that she had been terribly moved by Lilia's "ravaged face."[45] Soon, other refuseniks, despite KGB surveillance and the omnipresent threat of arrest, were stopping by to speak with Fenwick at her hotel rooms in Moscow and Leningrad and recounting their troubles. Struck by the courage of the refuseniks, Fenwick asked them why they risked the visit, and she was told, "Don't you understand? That's our only hope. We've seen you. Now they know you've seen us."[46] By the final day of her trip Fenwick had heard enough heartbreaking tales. Meeting Brezhnev, she recapped some of them for the general secretary and requested that he look into what might be done for these people. Brezhnev would claim that Fenwick was "obsessed."[47]

It was an accurate assessment. By September, Fenwick was bringing a bill to the floor of the House that called for the creation of the Commission on Security and Cooperation in Europe, a bipartisan panel comprised of members from both houses of Congress and representatives from the State, Defense, and Commerce departments.[48] Known as the Helsinki Commission, its function would be to evaluate whether the signatories of the Final Act were complying with their responsibilities regarding individual rights and the reunification of families.[49] Because the commission would report its findings to the House and Senate, its creation would also establish a public forum for embarrassing the Kremlin if it ignored the human rights demands of the Final Act.

In November, hearings began on the Fenwick bill before a subcommittee of the House International Affairs Committee. The chairman was Dante B. Fascell, a veteran Democratic congressman from Florida who was as passionate about human rights as Fenwick, and as feisty, but far surpassed her and the majority of his colleagues when it came to the art of getting things done, whether digging up a budget for a commission or securing office space for a staff of thirteen, ten of whom were researcher-analysts – both of which Fascell did once he was selected as a chairman of the Helsinki Commission.[50] Jerry Goodman from the National Conference on Soviet Jewry testified before the subcommittee, reeling off examples of the Kremlin's shameful treatment of refuseniks and a host of other violations of the accords. Fascell was deeply affected by Goodman's testimony and thanked the NCSJ for "the excellent work you have done" raising the "awareness" of the Soviet Jewish problem. This was the beginning of a beautiful friendship between Fascell and NCSJ, which would run its own monitoring operation and pass its findings along to the Helsinki Commission.[51]

The bill passed the House, and Republican senator Clifford Case from New Jersey shepherded it through its passage in the Senate. Secretary of State Kissinger and National Security Adviser Scowcroft objected to the commission, seeing it as a blatant encroachment on the territory of the executive branch.[52] Their objections were valid, but the television images of the last helicopters lifting off from the roof of the US embassy in Saigon during the frantic American exit still smarted like a cinder in the mind's eye of the nation, and coupled with the wounds of Watergate, it was not the most propitious moment to argue against reducing the power of the White House.

Moreover, if the Kremlin had missed the trap of the human rights provisions in the Final Act, there was some sign that all the talk leading up to the Helsinki Commission had attracted the attention of Soviet leaders. Even before the bill was brought to the floor for a vote, Fenwick announced that the dissident Victor Abdalov, who was married to an American student, had been released by Soviet authorities. Lastly, President Ford would have to stand for election in November, and the commission was backed by a wide, dynamic swath of voters – Jews; Polish, Hungarian, and Czechoslovak émigré groups; and the Baltic-American Committee.[53] On June 3, 1976, the president signed the bill into law.

Fascell turned the Helsinki Commission loose, holding public hearings and making news. Research was funded around the world. In Israel, émigrés from the USSR were interviewed. Anyone with a justifiable complaint against the Kremlin would find a sympathetic ear at the commission, and if someone had stories to share or wanted to contact monitoring organizations behind the Iron Curtain the commission could provide assistance. By 1978, the information gleaned was published in nine volumes and given to Congress and nongovernmental organizations that dealt with human rights.[54]

The Helsinki Commission did not lead to a profound reversal in the Soviet treatment of dissidents, but the United States government had traveled a great distance in the six years since Scoop Jackson had introduced his amendment in the Senate. Human rights no longer had to enter US international relations through a back door fashioned from an add-on to a trade bill. Human rights were now generally accepted as a framework for foreign policy, and the government had sanctioned a body to evaluate which nations were meeting its standards. For Soviet Jews this evolution would ultimately stand as the most effective weapon in the American arsenal.

◆ ◆ ◆

Even before Jimmy Carter was inaugurated in January 1977, Secretary General Brezhnev signaled the president-elect that he was hoping his administration would work with the Kremlin to renew the SALT agreement, liberalize trade relations, and resume the Geneva Middle East Peace Conference. To underscore this desire, the Soviets turned to their tried-and-true signal flares, Soviet Jews, who during the final two months of 1976 were allowed to emigrate at an increased rate. Undoubtedly, Soviet leaders were pleased that Carter had publicly supported a new SALT agreement and proposed up to a $7 billion decrease in defense spending and a staged withdrawal of US troops from Korea. Less pleasing was that during the campaign Carter had expressed his approval of the Jackson-Vanik amendment, saying that he was deeply concerned about "the protection of human rights and freedom of emigration in the USSR," and shortly after election day Carter sent a supportive telegram to refusenik Vladimir Slepak.[55]

Then in January 1977, one day after the inauguration, Martin Garbus, the famed civil rights attorney, returned from Moscow and headed to the White House. Garbus had already represented a Georgian refusenik at trial, at the request of NCSJ, and now he was delivering a letter from Andrei Sakharov to the new president.[56] Sakharov had written to ask Carter to "defend those who suffer because of their non-violent struggle for an open society, for justice, and for other people whose rights are violated."[57] Sakharov was invited to the US embassy in Moscow and presented with the president's reply: "Human rights is a central concern of my administration," Carter wrote, and he promised that he would "seek the release of prisoners of conscience."[58] The State Department opined that the Kremlin's harassment of Sakharov represented a violation of the Final Act, an opinion that did not sit well with the Politburo.[59] Sakharov forwarded another letter to the White House, this one telling Carter that members of the Helsinki Watch Group had been arrested. Incensed, Brezhnev proclaimed that he deplored the "outright attempts…to interfere in the internal affairs of the Soviet Union."[60]

Predictably, Soviet leaders moved to show Carter that he could not push them around. The dissident, Aleksandr Ginsburg, was arrested, and George Krimsky, a reporter for the Associated Press, was expelled.[61] In February, Yuri Orlov was arrested; he was tried on a charge of anti-Soviet activity and sentenced to seven years in prison and five in internal exile.[62]

The next month, the KGB grabbed Anatoly Shcharansky; he was accused of being a CIA spy.[63] The Kremlin had also reverted to fomenting the hatred of Jews, producing two antisemitic films, one of which was shown twice on nationwide television while the other played in movie theaters, and, as a warning to Jewish activists, the films featured their names and addresses.[64] Meanwhile, editorials in the Soviet press fired bursts of invective at the moralizing president, but that did not dissuade Carter from meeting with Vladimir Bukovsky, a Soviet dissident who had left his homeland for the United States in a swap for the Chilean Communist leader Louis Corvalan. This meeting was also denounced in *Pravda*.[65]

In May, two hundred thousand people marched from New York's City Hall to Battery Park in the annual solidarity demonstration sponsored by the Greater New York Conference on Soviet Jewry. Carter sent a personal representative, White House aide Margaret Costanza, to speak, the first president to have done so in six years. Costanza reaffirmed to the marchers that in the context of the US relationship with other countries, "human rights will occupy a place of prominence."[66]

Soviet leaders would not be the last people that Jimmy Carter, while in or out of the Oval Office, would offend with his high moral tone. In fairness to Carter, though, his commitment to his vision of morality was inseparable from who he was and not easily amenable to strategic flexibility. On occasion, Carter did try to rein himself in. Commenting on the arrest of Anatoly Shcharansky, the president said that he would not meet with his wife, Avital, but he did add that, contrary to the claims of the Kremlin, Shcharansky was not an American spy. The president also interjected his human rights commentary with concessions that he thought would mollify the Kremlin. On June 30, 1977, Carter said that the United States would not build the B-1 bomber, but he then put the Kremlin on the defensive by adding that he would proceed with the neutron bomb and MX missile.[67]

The president seemed genuinely perplexed by the angry reaction to him in Moscow, and in July, during an address to the two thousand attendees of the Southern Legislative Conference in Charleston, South Carolina, he attempted to explain himself. After declaring that he was committed to curtailing strategic weapons like the development of the cruise missile if the Soviets would limit their heavy intercontinental missiles, Carter said that he believed Secretary General Brezhnev was sincere in his desire for peace and explained that his raising the subject of human rights was an expression of American values and intended for the entire world. It was not meant as an attack on the Soviet Union nor was it designed, as Soviet editorials had suggested, "to heat up the arms race or bring back the Cold War."[68]

The Kremlin was not impressed. Some Soviet leaders saw the ambivalence of American foreign policy as a reflection of Carter being pulled in divergent directions – to the left by his practical, conciliatory secretary of state, Cyrus R. Vance, and to the right by the aggressiveness of his Polish-born national security adviser, Zbigniew K. Brzezinski, a less pragmatic Henry Kissinger.[69]

Undoubtedly, there was tension between Vance and Brzezinski, but it was Carter himself who lacked dexterity when wielding carrots and sticks. For example, in a move guaranteed to endear himself to the Kremlin, Carter asked Congress to reconsider the Jackson-Vanik amendment, removing the requirement for the Soviets to promise a certain level of emigration and replacing it with the discretion of the president, who would grant trade benefits if it were determined that annual emigration was "adequate."[70] Then, in a move that was sure to garner worldwide attention and enrage Soviet leaders, when the president's mother, the ever-so-popular and quotable "Miz Lillian," visited the Vatican, her son had her deliver a letter from him to Pope Paul VI, which beseeched the Catholic Church to become more actively involved on behalf of human rights inside the Soviet Union and other socialist countries.[71]

At first, Foreign Minister Andrei Gromyko, the Soviet official most experienced in dealing with Washington, thought that Carter, who "was not overburdened with foreign policy expertise,"[72] was being unrealistic – a charge that was repeated by *Pravda*.[73] Gromyko was a famously cagey, reserved man who never uttered two words when one would do. Legend has it that an American reporter once asked him if he had enjoyed his breakfast, to which Gromyko replied, "Possibly."[74] Gromyko was so put-out by the censoriousness of the Carter administration, with the president "sounding like a zealous TV commercial,"[75] that in a response highly unusual for him, the foreign minister summoned the press and said that all the talk of human rights was poisoning the relationship between Moscow and Washington and interfering with working on the concerns between the two countries.[76] Much to the displeasure of Gromyko, the censoriousness went on, and after one White House meeting with Carter, when the president had delivered a lengthy sermon on the evils of Soviet repression, Gromyko returned to his embassy and indulged in an uncharacteristic tirade, letting loose with a spate of curses at the president for insisting on poking his nose into "the internal affairs of the Soviet Union."[77]

What Carter failed to grasp, and Nixon understood, was that the problem Washington encountered in engaging Moscow was – when stripped of stock phrases, tactics, and strategy – a collision of cultures. By and large, the aging men who controlled the Kremlin were a conflicted lot, their cynicism and love of untrammeled power at war with their idealistic devotion to Communism and their exquisite sensitivity to public perception – especially when compared unfavorably to the West. This sensitivity was more Russian than Soviet – it dated back centuries to the tsars – but during the Nixon and Carter administrations it was intensified by the fact that the Soviets were seeking arms reduction, technology transfers, grain shipments, and credit from their avowed foes, the capitalist Americans, whose system was supposed to collapse and prove that the Kremlin's faith in Marx and Lenin had not been misplaced.

Unlike their Soviet counterparts, American leaders were accustomed to having their power checked by the people, the press, and political rivals. If they were to thrive in the arena, then it was incumbent upon them to make an uneasy peace with the slings and arrows of differing and often harshly expressed opinions. With his constant harping on the abominable human rights record of the Kremlin, President Carter may have seen himself as a fluent practitioner of this American idiom – the rock-'em-sock-'em campaign, verbally squaring off with an opponent to achieve an objective.

Lamentably, for Carter, that is not how his rhetoric played inside the Kremlin, where it was heard as the discordant music of a president intent on humiliating the USSR and destroying détente. Even a decade later, when Gromyko published his memoirs, he accused Carter of dragging out "the myth of the 'Soviet threat'" and proceeding "steadily towards confrontation."[78] Brezhnev was particularly angry about it, and his emotional resources for coping with it were diminishing. Afflicted with atherosclerosis and medicating himself with opiate-based sedatives to which he became addicted, he was growing progressively more suspicious and irritable, and less tolerant of the give-and-take inherent in geopolitical maneuvering.[79]

As tempting as it may be, for it coincides with the pop-culture Russian stereotype of the era, one cannot dismiss Soviet suspicions as florid paranoia. The general secretary and his foreign policy entourage were keenly aware that Carter had command of a nuclear arsenal that was more than a match for their own; they had a rough idea that their defense burden was approximately three times that of America, while their gross domestic product was just one-sixth the size of their enemy's GDP;[80] and they were worried about the revived friendship between Washington and Beijing, which had rejected Soviet overtures to come to terms on their border dispute. The Carter administration was not shy about turning the Sino-Soviet animosity to its own advantage. After traveling to China to discuss US strategy in the region, National Security Adviser Brzezinski derisively referred to the USSR in public as "the polar bear." Brezhnev was not amused. He called the "cynical" use of the China card against the USSR "a dangerous policy."[81]

Because of these realities, because Soviet leadership was unaccustomed to gales of criticism, and because Carter was relentless in his critiques, it was almost a foregone conclusion that Moscow would come to see the president as an unforgiving enemy, his words like troops massing on Soviet borders, a prelude to invasion, the coming of another terrible war.

Yet it is no small irony that the Soviet leaders themselves, and none more than Brezhnev, were responsible for the recurrent tongue lashings – not simply due to their disregard for human rights or that they had been the ones who had campaigned for a Conference on Security and Cooperation in Europe and had signed the Helsinki Final Act, but because the accords called for the signatories to participate in a follow-up conference in Belgrade, Yugoslavia, which presented another opportunity to drag the miserable human rights record of the Soviet Union into the glare of the international limelight.

The conference began in October 1977 and lasted until March 1978.

Arthur Goldberg, erstwhile secretary of labor and Supreme Court justice, was appointed to lead the American delegation to Belgrade.[82] The Moscow Helsinki Watch Group submitted twenty-six documents to the conference, laying out the broken Soviet promises on Jewish emigration and detailing the official cultural and religious hostility directed toward Jews, all of which was prohibited by the Final Act.[83] The NATO delegations were not eager to poke the Soviet bear, and they objected, to no avail, when Arthur Goldberg himself raised Shcharansky's arrest and other similar cases, his tone ripe with moral indignation, as though Émile Zola had materialized out of the gloaming of history to point a finger at the Kremlin and shout, "*J'accuse!*"[84]

On the face of it, though, the conference was not a success: the final report that was produced did not even discuss human rights.[85] But the fuse that was lit in Belgrade set off an explosion in the fall of 1980 at the next conference in Madrid, which *Le Monde* would accurately label the "city of dissidence," because Eastern European dissidents, refuseniks, and champions of democracy descended on the Spanish capital in droves to meet with Americans and Western Europeans. Madrid was awash with leaflets, posters, books, and films, and the rallies, protests, and press conferences seemed to run around the clock.[86] The Moscow Helsinki Watch Group forwarded 138 documents delineating violations of the Final Act.[87] The new head of the US delegation, Max M. Kampelman, persuaded the American allies in Europe to muffle their complaints about raising human rights abuses, and then Kampelman and his team, adhering to a strategy Kampelman referred to as "shaming," cited sixty-five specific instances, "including almost all of the major refusenik cases."[88]

"These forums that allowed governments and activists to take the Soviet Union to task were invaluable," says William Korey, author of *The Promises We Keep*, the definitive study of the Helsinki process, "and without a doubt they contributed to the conclusion of the Cold War."[89]

That conclusion, at the moment, defied the imagination of all but the most Pollyannaish among foreign affairs prognosticators as relations between Washington and Moscow worsened, the ever-fragile détente shattered like a crystal goblet hurled against a stone wall, and the future looming on the horizon appeared even more ominous than the past.

◆ ◆ ◆

The Soviet Union had been pushing the Carter administration to restart Middle East peace talks, because the disengagements produced by Kissinger's shuttle diplomacy after the 1973 war had decreased Soviet influence in the region. However, in November 1977, Egyptian president Anwar Sadat delivered another blow to the Kremlin by traveling to Jerusalem and declaring before the Knesset that he welcomed Israel "to live among us in peace and security,"[90] a statement that was the first step on the road to the Camp David Accords and that effectively severed Moscow's relationship with Cairo.

A week later, the Soviets stepped up their commitment in the Horn of Africa by flying twenty thousand Cuban troops to Ethiopia and lending three generals to the Ethiopian military, which was locked in a war with Somalia.[91] Coming just two years after the Soviets had interceded in Angola, the move was disconcerting to the Carter administration for it appeared that Moscow had declared war on Washington in the Third World.[92] NSA adviser Brzezinski advised the president to link the SALT talks to the situation in Africa, while Secretary of State Vance counseled against it.[93]

Carter sided with Vance. In public, the president remained optimistic about US-USSR relations, but when Shcharansky went on trial for treason, Carter scrubbed a sale of sophisticated oil-drilling equipment to the Soviet Union, refused to let his science adviser make a scheduled trip to Moscow, and withdrew the US participants from the joint Soviet-American Commission on Scientific and Technological Cooperation.[94] Still, the president seemed open to a SALT treaty, and Carter, much to the dismay of the Student Struggle for Soviet Jewry and the Union of Councils,[95] was talking about asking Congress to waive the Jackson-Vanik amendment and grant most-favored-nation status to the Soviet Union. Romania had been granted MFN status by Ford, and Carter would do the same for China and Hungary.[96] Sixty-eight refuseniks from across the Soviet Union implored Congress not to waive the amendment. Senator Jackson would not back the president, and the Israeli government, though keeping its feelings out of the press,[97] did not want the amendment waived, perhaps because upwards of 60 percent of the Jews leaving the Soviet Union were entering the United States and not Israel.[98]

With all the talk of waiving Jackson-Vanik and revisiting the Stevenson amendment to raise the $300 million limit on Soviet credit, the Kremlin responded with grand humanitarian gestures designed for a maximum public relations payoff in the United States. Brezhnev pardoned five of the alleged hijackers who had been convicted in the Leningrad trial in 1970, all of whom received exit visas for Israel. Two others convicted in Leningrad were packaged with the Jewish dissident Aleksandr Ginsburg and two Ukrainian dissidents and swapped for a pair of Soviet spies captured in the United States.[99] The Kremlin also permitted a jump in emigration: 28,865 Soviet Jews were allowed to leave in 1978, and the following year 51,333 were allowed to go.[100]

Nevertheless, by then it was apparent that Soviet leaders were playing a double game with respect to human rights. Andrei Sakharov, who would soon be exiled to the industrial Russian city of Gorky, was putting together a report for the US Helsinki Commission that was published in the *Boston Globe*. Sakharov said that more than forty members of the Moscow Helsinki Watch Group were now in prison. The KGB had also incarcerated most of the watch group in the Ukraine, and Victoras Piatkus, a Catholic stalwart from the Lithuanian watch group, had been convicted at a show trial and sentenced to ten years in prison and five years in exile. Then there were all the others who had been arrested – not formal members of any watch group, but people who worked on behalf of human rights.[101]

Carter pushed on to Vienna, where on June 19, 1979, he and Brezhnev signed the SALT II treaty. Although the two leaders had scrawled their names across a treaty, they were no closer to reaching any understandings on their differences in Africa, Asia, and the Middle East, differences that were an ongoing threat to world peace. During their talks in Vienna, Brezhnev had gone on the offensive, reiterating that the Soviet Union would continue to express solidarity and furnish aid to "liberation struggles," and he challenged Carter by asking, "Where would the United States be, perhaps still a colony, if it had not received aid from abroad in its own 1770s liberation struggle?"[102]

There was no meaningful discussion of reducing troop levels in Europe or on nuclear testing or chemical weapons, and no future meetings were scheduled. Carter did seem to warm up to Brezhnev. He prevented the obviously ailing general secretary from falling down, and after a dinner at the Soviet embassy, the president clasped Brezhnev's left hand as they moved slowly down a walkway while a Soviet aide held onto Brezhnev's other hand. It was, as *Washington Post* reporter Don Oberdorfer wrote, "a curious and touching scene."[103] But such sentimental images did nothing to alter the fact that by summer, with the SALT II treaty awaiting ratification by Congress, the Soviet Union appeared to have gained the upper hand in the Cold War.

This perception did not wholly emerge from a reading of the geopolitical scoreboard, but was also attributable to the cultural ambience in the United States that President Carter identified on July 15, during a televised primetime address from the Oval Office, which would be remembered as his "malaise speech."[104] With one hundred million people tuned in, Carter spoke of a "crisis of confidence," the "doubt" afflicting Americans "about the meaning of our own lives…the loss of a unity of purpose for our nation…[and] the growing disrespect for government and for churches and for schools, the news media, and other institutions."[105]

This pessimism should not have been unexpected in the dispiriting aftermath of Vietnam and Watergate, together with the befuddling societal realignment that resulted as the traditional roles of women were revised and the divorce rate neared its historic peak.[106] In his speech Carter downplayed a recession that would send unemployment up to nearly 8 percent,[107] nor did he wish to dwell on the fact that in January, after the shah of Iran was overthrown by Islamic fundamentalists, another oil crisis ensued complete with another round of gas lines. By the fall of 1979, Nicaraguan dictator and American ally Anastasio Somoza had been driven from the country, replaced by the Marxist Sandinistas,[108] and Islamic radicals had stormed the US embassy in Teheran and taken dozens of diplomatic and military personnel hostage, delivering a blow to American prestige as inflation climbed to 12 percent.[109]

With Americans distracted by these events, and the tendency for détente to conceal the political and economic vulnerability of the USSR, it was easy to miss that the Soviets faced tremendous problems of their own. The East

Germans publicly applauded West German Chancellor Willy Brandt when he visited the city of Erfurt, violent protests erupted over food shortages in Poland, and the Soviets were in the grips of a bottomless addiction to oil revenues to buttress up a chronically ill economy.[110] One bright spot was that SALT II had been sent to the US Congress, and assistance in the form of most-favored-nation status and expanded credit might be forthcoming – but then the Kremlin was suddenly confronted with a potential revolution in Afghanistan.[111]

In 1978, a coup had left a Marxist government in charge in Kabul. The Soviets reacted with massive amounts of aid as the Marxist government attempted to modernize the country, instituting land reform, expanding rights for women, and supporting secular education. However, with Ayatollah Khomeini ruling Iran, there was a resurgence of militant Islam in Afghanistan,[112] and in March 1979 an uprising in Herat claimed the lives of five thousand people, fifty Soviet advisers and their families among them. Afghan prime minister Nur Mohammed Taraki admitted to Soviet premier Alexei Kosygin that he had no popular support; the Kremlin contemplated an invasion, but instead opted to preserve the tattered remnants of détente.[113]

That all changed nine months later. Taraki was assassinated by a rival, Hafzullah Amin, who was allegedly on the payroll of the CIA.[114] The KGB believed that Amin was about to pull "a Sadat."[115] Soviet leaders were reluctant to accept a diminution of their influence, and they were alarmed by the establishment of a "pro-imperialist bridgehead of military aggression on the southern borders of the USSR."[116] An invasion was planned, and in an eerie reminder of the attitude of Johnson administration officials toward escalating the US commitment to South Vietnam, Brezhnev predicted that "it will be over in three to four weeks."[117] Soviet forces entered Afghanistan on Christmas Eve, and the full-scale invasion was in motion by morning. Amin was executed by the Soviets, a puppet Marxist government was installed, and shortly thereafter some one hundred thousand Soviet troops were occupying Afghanistan.[118]

In what was deemed "the toughest diplomatic exchange of his presidency," Carter sent a message to Brezhnev on a hotline installed for emergencies, warning the general secretary that if he did not withdraw his troops it would have "serious consequences" for the US-USSR relationship.[119] Brezhnev did not comply, and Carter responded with a salvo of sanctions, embargoing grain and high technology, restricting Soviet fishing in American waters, delaying the opening of new Soviet consulates, forbidding American athletes from competing in the 1980 Olympics slated to be held in Moscow, and withdrawing the SALT II treaty from the Senate.[120]

Détente was finished and so, for the next nine years, was any significant emigration of Soviet Jews. When Ronald Reagan was elected in November, the bad old days of the Cold War were with us once again.

CHAPTER 10

THE COWBOY AND AN EMISSARY
FROM THE EVIL EMPIRE

From the beginning, Soviet leadership viewed President Ronald Reagan with "great indignation and suspicion"[1] that, according to General Oleg Kalugin, who oversaw foreign counterintelligence for the KGB, "bordered on hysteria."[2]

The central problem for the Soviets was that Reagan had no use for détente. At his first press conference after his inauguration Reagan characterized détente as "a one-way street that the Soviet Union has used to pursue its own aims." The Kremlin, he asserted, felt entitled "to commit any crime, to lie, to cheat."[3]

His hatred of Soviet oppression was visceral, and on May 28, 1981, Reagan heard firsthand testimony of Jewish suffering in the Soviet Union, when Avital Shcharansky, along with a young Jewish dissident who had languished for a decade in the Gulag, came to the White House. Avital said that her husband, Anatoly, who was still imprisoned by the Soviets, was quite sick and that his weight had dropped to one hundred pounds. The president promised that he would do "everything I could to obtain his release."[4]

Recording the meeting in his diary, Reagan wrote of the Soviets, "D-n those inhuman monsters."[5]

The president kept his word to Avital. He wrote to Brezhnev, asking if he could "find it in your heart" to release Anatoly Shcharansky, promising that if Brezhnev did so Reagan would not reveal his kindness or use it to embarrass him. [6]

Brezhnev would not hear of it, replying to Reagan that Shcharansky had been convicted of committing "grave anti-Soviet crimes."[7]

By 1981, as the scholars Ivan Caine and Jeffrey Tigay wrote in the *Philadelphia Inquirer*, the US-Soviet relationship was so fractured that in Moscow "authorities feel they have nothing to lose by harassing the Jews." For example, the refuseniks Yuli Kosharovsky and Pavel Abramovich were threatened with violence if they did not stop teaching Hebrew, and another Hebrew teacher, Yosef Begun, was convicted of parasitism and sentenced to Siberia. Some five hundred demonstrators from the University of Pennsylvania protested the treatment of Begun, and members of Student Struggle for Soviet Jewry conducted a hunger strike and placed hundreds of phone calls to the Soviet embassy in Washington, only to have embassy personnel hang up on them.[8]

The early days of embarrassing the Kremlin with local demonstrations were over. Paradoxically, it had been the success of the American Soviet Jewry movement that was responsible for the change. Soviet Jews were now intricately threaded into the Cold War and their fate was inextricably bound up with that conflict. With the polarization between Washington and Moscow, the Kremlin cut off Jewish emigration. In 1981, just under 9,500 left; in 1982, that number dropped to under three thousand; then, from 1983 until 1986, only an average of one thousand per year were allowed to go.[9]

American Jews had few cards to play on behalf of Soviet Jewry, so they contented themselves with assisting the emigrants who were already in the United States, and one other action that, strangely enough, the Kremlin did not prohibit: traveling to the USSR to visit Soviet Jews.

"It was to give moral support to the refuseniks," says Rabbi Norman R. Patz, who was then the spiritual leader of Temple Sholom of West Essex in Cedar Grove, New Jersey. "I don't know who started it, but we never stopped."[10]

The National Conference on Soviet Jewry supplied the names, and the visits had an extraordinary impact on both Americans and Russian Jews.[11]

"One year we sent a Protestant minister," says Patz. "When he came back he told me that the first thing he did was put up an American flag on his porch because we don't know how lucky we are to live in the United States."[12]

Arlene and Martin Kesselhaut from West Orange, New Jersey, will never forget a man they visited in Moscow.

"It took us a while to find him," recalls Martin Kesselhaut. "He lived in one of those rundown clusters of towers. We finally found his apartment and knocked on the door. We heard someone moving around inside, but no one answered, so we kept knocking."

At last, the door opened a crack.

The Kesselhauts said hello, using the man's name.

"How do you know who I am?" the man asked.

Martin said, "Because in the United States you are famous for your courage."

The man let them in. The first thing the Kesselhauts noticed was a noose dangling from a ceiling pipe with a chair below it.

"It was awful," says Martin Kesselhaut. "He had been getting ready to commit suicide. He was distraught because he wanted to go Israel, but wasn't allowed to leave and had been fired from his job after applying for an exit visa. We spoke to him for a long time and took down the noose."[13]

The refusenik survived and later moved to Israel.[14]

These visits were not isolated incidents, but came in waves. The visitors had to be careful carrying the names and addresses of refuseniks. It was not unusual for Soviet officials to confiscate notebooks and lists of names from visitors when they entered the country, and one creative soul used Juicy Fruit gum wrappers as an address book, printing the information in letters so tiny they were difficult to see.[15] More often than not, American visitors brought badly needed goods with them. Levi's and Marlboro cigarettes were popular items, because they could be traded by the jobless refuseniks for enough food to feed a family for a month. Morey Schapira, who would serve as the president of the Union of Councils of Soviet Jewry, recalls people being sent to smuggle in the components of fax machines that could then be reassembled and used to communicate with friends in the United States.

"People also brought in Flintstones vitamins," says Schapira. "You could get them past customs because the vitamins looked like candy. Then the vitamins could be passed to refuseniks in prison, since their diet was terrible and they needed vitamins."[16]

Israel was also involved in sending American Jews into the USSR. Richard Stone, a young law professor at Columbia University, received a phone call from his friend Joseph Telushkin, who asked him if he would like to visit refuseniks in the Soviet Union.

"The Israeli government paid for it," said Stone. "And the Israelis briefed us for twelve hours in New York before we left. I wasn't the only one Israel sent. There must have been hundreds of us."[17]

Joseph Smukler, who had come to the Soviet Jewry movement after a 1974 trip to the USSR with his wife, Connie, remembers people smuggling in parts of the Leon Uris novel *Exodus*.

"Everyone carried a different section," says Smukler, "and after they were handed over to the refuseniks, they were put together, copied, and passed on."[18]

The Smuklers belonged to the Soviet Jewry Council of Greater Philadelphia, which was an especially active organization, sending both Jews and Christians. SJC instituted a separately funded travel program, developed a handbook for travelers, and conducted lengthy briefings before the trip. The Smuklers even redesigned their home to make it easier to conduct briefings and hold SJC meetings. The same was done by Bernard and Lana Dishler, and the briefings were so successful that eventually Bernard Dishler became the chairman of NCSJ's briefing committee.[19]

A catalogue of these visits could fill volumes, and the efforts of American Jews stand as a testament of their commitment to help. But it would be the fissures in the Soviet system, and Reagan's willingness to exploit them while highlighting the Kremlin's cruelties, that would be required to free the Soviet Jews.

◆ ◆ ◆

The initial controversy between Reagan and the Kremlin centered on nuclear weapons. In a bid to upset the balance of nuclear power in Europe, the Soviets had deployed their SS-20, a medium-range missile that could hit Western European nations when fired from inside the USSR. Reagan offered to keep the US ground-launched Pershing II missiles out of Europe if Brezhnev would get rid of the SS-20s and other intermediate range missiles. Brezhnev refused, and Reagan went ahead with the deployment of Pershing II and land-based Tomahawk cruise missiles. None of these weapons were capable of a first strike at Moscow, but the meaning of Reagan's reply was obvious: if the Kremlin struck at Western Europe with nuclear weapons, then the United States would retaliate.[20]

Reagan's countermove gave rise to a disarmament movement. During the nineteenth century America-bashing had been the avocation of elitist European right-wingers,[21] but during the Cold War the European Left had taken over as the assailers-in-chief of US foreign policy. Their criticism began in earnest during the Vietnam War and now extended to the deployment of American missiles to the Continent. In October 1981, when 150,000 protesters marched to London's Hyde Park for a rally, Michael Foot, leader of the Labor Party, tucked that history into one statement by telling the crowd that the goal of the protest was to rekindle the passion of the antiwar movement of the 1960s.[22]

Looking back, one can barely fathom the images that must have popped up in the collective imagination of the millions of protesters who gathered in Madrid, Rome, Paris, Brussels, and Bonn to rail against positioning missiles in their back yards. Did they believe that if the missiles remained in North America and there was a nuclear exchange between the United States and the Soviet Union, Europe would be spared from Armageddon? Did they imagine themselves sitting outside at a café enjoying the soft blue evening and sipping an apéritif while Intercontinental Ballistic Missiles flew overhead like geese migrating back and forth between the superpowers?

The nuclear disarmament movement also attracted proponents in the United States. In the summer of 1982, pollsters discovered that over two-thirds of Americans favored freezing the nuclear arsenals of the superpowers, and nearly one million anti-nuke protestors jammed the streets of Manhattan in what the *New York Times* judged to be the "largest political demonstration in American history."[23] Understandably then, the Kremlin may have calculated that the peace movement would sap Western resolve as it had undermined US policy in Southeast Asia,[24] but the fine points of nuclear arms negotiations would ultimately prove to be beyond the average citizen. The geopolitical chess game couched in a linguistic hodgepodge of scientific measures and Defense Department acronyms had become too confusing a game to comprehend, and as Henry Kissinger saw in retrospect, "the debate shifted to an issue…which had a greater resonance with the public at large – the proposition that human rights should rank among the principal goals of American foreign policy."[25]

Mothers and fathers and children trapped by the failing anachronistic shell of Stalin's paranoia brought the argument back full circle to the philosophical roots of the Cold War, the great cause of individual liberty versus the oppressive hand of the state. In that competition, the United States enjoyed every advantage, and the new president was anxious to seize it.

◆ ◆ ◆

To the discomfort of Soviet leaders, Ronald Reagan did not embrace the unending stalemate of détente, but saw the Cold War as a zero-sum game. "We win," he said, "and they lose."[26]

A simple formulation, but not an easy one to accomplish. Yet Reagan thought it was inevitable. In 1975, when he was the host of his own syndicated radio show, Reagan said that "Communism is neither an economic [n]or a political system – it is a form of insanity – a temporary aberration which will one day disappear from the earth because it is contrary to human nature."[27] One can hear the echo of these words seven years later when President Reagan assured the British Parliament that the USSR was a country "that runs against the tides of history by denying human freedom and human dignity" while "unable to feed its own people,"[28] and therefore "the march of freedom and democracy…will leave Marxist-Leninism on the ash heap of history."[29] His certainty, says George Shultz, who would replace Alexander Haig as Reagan's secretary of state in 1982, was not based on "detailed knowledge," much to the dismay of numerous foreign policy professionals and pundits, but on "instinct."[30]

Reagan had two strong allies in Europe: British prime minister Margaret Thatcher and Pope John Paul II, both of whom agreed with the president that the Cold War need not be permanent.[31] In June 1982, Reagan went to Vatican City and spoke privately with John Paul II. Like the president, John Paul II had been wounded during an assassination attempt in 1981. Unlike Reagan, who had been shot by the deranged John W. Hinckley Jr. in a psychotic gambit to impress the actress Jodie Foster, the attempt to murder the Polish-born pope in St. Peter's Square was an outgrowth of his hostility toward Communism, specifically his backing of Lech Wałęsa and Solidarity, the pro-democratic Polish workers movement.[32] His would-be assassin was a young Turkish man, Mehmet Ali Ağca, who claimed – and then recanted his claim – that Bulgarian intelligence and the KGB were involved. Italian authorities believe that Moscow had a hand in the plot, which was carried out in the hope of stemming the rising tide of democracy in Poland.[33]

In their private discussion, Reagan found John Paul II to be committed to his fight against the Kremlin, but then, the Catholic clergy in the United States had been sympathetic to the cause of Soviet Jewry. There was Father Robert Drinan, a congressman, who had been involved with the Interreligous Task Force for Soviet Jews, and Sister Rose Thering, Sister Ann Gillen and Sister Margaret Traxler, who persuaded R. Sargent Shriver, the first director of the Peace Corps and a Democratic vice-presidential candidate in 1972, to lend his name to the task force as its honorary chairman.[34]

Not only did John Paul II promise Reagan that he would speak out on the religious repression in the USSR, he also promised tactical assistance. The pope said that he would do everything possible to encourage the Poles to chip away at their ties to the Soviet Union and that he would never support the nuclear freeze movement. Reagan came away from the meeting with an idea that he later wrote about in a letter to a friend, saying that he had a hunch "religion may turn out to be the Soviets' Achilles heel."[35]

Despite his hunch, Reagan was more earthbound in formulating US policy toward the Soviet Union. It was clear that economically the USSR was inching toward disaster. In 1980, the Soviets had sold their standard amount of gold: ninety tons. Then, in the first ten months of 1981, despite the fact that the demand for gold was declining, the amount sold jumped to 240 tons.[36] William J. Casey, director of the Central Intelligence Agency, was quick to spot the meaning of the gold sales. Casey had a background in utilizing economic frailties to defeat an enemy, a tactic with which he had become acquainted during the Second World War when the Allies used it against Germany. Reagan had already been briefed on the Soviet Union's overreliance on Western credit to stabilize its economy, and in November 1982, at Casey's urging, the president signed a national security directive that declared war on the Soviet economy.[37] In addition, Reagan signed two other NSA directives – one designed to "neutralize" the Kremlin's control over Eastern Europe through the use of covert action and the other declaring that the administration was dedicated to altering the nature of the Soviet system.[38]

♦ ♦ ♦

As Reagan was planning his offensive, an event – apparently unrelated to the central actors of the Cold War – led Moscow to conclude that its economic troubles were going to make it difficult, at best, for the Soviets to maintain its military parity with the United States.

In June 1982, Israel went into Lebanon to stop the PLO from firing artillery barrages into the Galilee, and Syria moved to protect Palestinian positions. Israeli pilots, manning US F-15 and F-16 fighters fitted with state-of-the-art microelectronics and computer systems, shot down eighty-one Syrian pilots flying Soviet-made MiG-21 and MiG-23 fighters over the Bekaa Valley without a single Israeli aircraft being destroyed.[39]

"At the time," says David Satter, "you heard the usual comments about the skill of Israeli pilots when matched against Arab pilots. But what the battle over the Bekka demonstrated was the immense superiority of American weapons systems compared to what the Soviets were producing. And Brezhnev, as well as the rest of the Soviet leaders in the Kremlin, knew it."[40]

Brezhnev died in November 1982, and was replaced by spymaster Yuri Andropov. By the winter of 1983, Reagan was halfway through his first term, and except for meeting Brezhnev during a reception at Nixon's home in San Clemente while Reagan was governor of California, he had never engaged in a meaningful dialogue with an important Communist official. During a dinner with Secretary of State Shultz, Reagan indicated that he would like to participate in such a discussion.[41]

Few of his advisers favored the idea, so instead of bringing Ambassador Dobrynin to the Oval Office, Shultz brought him to the Reagans' private residence on the second floor of the White House. Their talk lasted nearly two hours. Dobrynin said that Andropov was interested in "More deeds, less words."[42] The president was infuriated by the official repression practiced by the Kremlin toward religion – Jews or Christians, it didn't matter to Reagan, since "we all worship the same God."[43] After raising the treatment of Soviet Jews with the ambassador, he turned to the matter of a half dozen Siberian Pentecostals who wanted to emigrate and had been living in the basement of the US embassy in Moscow for the last five years. Reagan had spoken of their plight, years before, on his radio program,[44] and now, he was about to cut what his secretary of state, George Shultz, characterized as his "first deal" with the Kremlin.[45]

The president told Dobrynin it would be helpful to relations between Moscow and Washington if the Pentecostals were permitted to leave the country, promising that he wouldn't trumpet his success. It was the same variety of quiet diplomacy that President Richard Nixon had employed, and it was Nixon himself who had convinced Reagan that this was the sole way the Soviets would relax their harsh treatment of dissidents – if the Kremlin would not be publicly humiliated in the process.[46] Indemnified against international embarrassment, the Kremlin permitted the Pentecostals to go, and Reagan was good to his word.[47]

But his word did not exclude him from assaulting the Kremlin. On March 8, 1983, in a speech to the National Association of Evangelicals in Orlando, Florida, Reagan referred to the Soviet Union as an "evil empire." Henry Steele Commager, one of the most distinguished presidential scholars in the United States, said that "it was the worst presidential speech" in history because it "so flagrantly allied the government with religion."[48] A world away, in Siberia, Anatoly Shcharansky and his fellow prisoners gave the speech a more charitable review. After Shcharansky learned what Reagan had told the evangelicals, he shouted the phrase into the toilet pipes in his cell, and he and the other political prisoners were "ecstatic" that an American president had at last told the "truth."[49]

Fifteen days after Orlando, Reagan gave a televised speech to the nation and announced his answer to the nuclear stand-off theory of Mutual

Assured Destruction – the Strategic Defense Initiative (SDI), a futuristic missile defense system that "could intercept and destroy strategic ballistic missiles before they reached our own soil or that of our allies."[50] As *Time*'s Strobe Talbott observed, Reagan was "a nuclear abolitionist,"[51] who asserted that the goal of SDI was to make nuclear weapons "impotent and obsolete."[52] SDI would mockingly be referred to as "Star Wars" by critics who were unaware that the Buck Rogers imaginings of Ronald Reagan would obsess the Soviets and go a long way to convincing them that technologically and economically they would soon be incapable of maintaining parity with the United States.[53]

Andropov was so terrified by the announcement that he thought Reagan might be planning a preemptive strike. The Kremlin was infected with this fear, which was responsible for the order being given to shoot down a South Korean passenger jet that mistakenly flew into Soviet air space in September 1983. Two hundred sixty-nine people died on KAL flight 007, and sixty-three of them were Americans.[54] Reagan called it "an act of mass murder."[55]

That same month, Scoop Jackson, still a force to be reckoned with in the Senate, died from an aortic embolism at the age of seventy-one. His final curtain call on the political stage had come during a press conference earlier in the day at the Old Federal Office Building in Seattle, where he condemned the Soviets for their malevolence and called their attack on KAL 007 "a dastardly, barbaric act against humanity."[56]

Nearly a decade had passed since Jackson had first connected increased Jewish emigration from the Soviet Union to economic benefits from the United States. Although Reagan and George Shultz were not overly enamored of the Jackson-Vanik amendment, both embodied the belief that Jackson had embraced – that human rights should play an important role in the US-Soviet relationship. When Reagan awarded Jackson the Presidential Medal of Freedom posthumously in June 1984, he praised him by saying that he had understood "political decisions must spring from moral convictions."[57] Jackson's Democratic colleague, Senator Daniel Patrick Moynihan of New York, paid homage to his colleague's contribution by pointing to how unique Jackson's view had been when he proposed his amendment. Jackson, said Moynihan, was "proof of the old belief in the

Judaic tradition that at any moment in history goodness in the world is preserved by the deeds of thirty-six just men who do not know that this is the role the Lord has given them. Henry Jackson was one of those men."[58]

One can debate the value of the senator's amendment, but a better measure of Jackson's contribution is that the issue of Soviet Jewry had become inseparable from the Cold War itself, and thus, unlike the 1930s, the US government and the American Jewish community were aligned on policy. It was this alignment that would save Soviet Jewry.

◆ ◆ ◆

Andropov remained on edge about Reagan. A NATO exercise in the late fall of 1983 convinced the Soviet leader that a nuclear strike was imminent, a miscalculation that would have led straight to Armageddon. The fact was not lost on Reagan, who learned of the Kremlin's misjudgment through the work of Oleg Gordievsky, a KGB officer in London who was on the payroll of British intelligence.[59] The president tempered his rhetoric, reminding everyone, in one of the most sentimental speeches ever delivered by a president (and in words that Reagan had written himself), that the Jims and Sallies and Ivans and Anyas of this world did not start wars.[60]

Andropov died shortly after the speech and was replaced by the ailing Konstantin Chernenko, who Reagan saw as "a tough old-line Communist addicted to Lenin's secular religion of expansionism and world domination."[61]

Reagan handily won reelection, and on February 6, 1985, he delivered his State of the Union address to Congress, declaring that the United States "must stand by all our democratic allies. And we must not break faith with those who are risking their lives on every continent…to defy Soviet-supported aggression and secure rights which have been ours from birth."[62]

Here, finally, was a clear statement of his policy toward the Soviet Union. It was seen as a profound shift from both the policies of containment and détente and recalled the "Roll Back" strategy employed by Eisenhower's secretary of state, John Foster Dulles. Unlike Dulles, Reagan was brazenly public about his opposition to the Kremlin.[63] Two months later the columnist Charles Krauthammer, writing in *Time* magazine, christened the president's position as the "Reagan Doctrine," a policy of "democratic militance...[that] proclaims overt and unashamed American support for "anti-Communist revolution," whether for the contras in Nicaragua or the *mujahadeen* in Afghanistan or the members of Solidarity in Poland.[64]

The next month, Chernenko died, leading Reagan to ask his wife, "How am I supposed to get anyplace with the Russians if they keep dying on me?"[65]

The answer to that question was the new leader of the Soviet Union, fifty-four-year-old Mikhail Gorbachev.

◆ ◆ ◆

Vice President George H. W. Bush had presented a letter from Reagan to Gorbachev after Chernenko's funeral, inviting him to Washington for a summit,[66] but the vice president returned home with a warning for his boss. Gorbachev, Bush said, may be young, dynamic, and better educated than the Kremlin leaders of the past, but that would only enable him to present the old Soviet shibboleths "much more effectively than any (I repeat any) of his predecessors."[67]

Nonetheless, Reagan was ready to talk. A summit was arranged for November at a neutral site – Geneva, Switzerland – and then a controversy erupted which revealed that despite all the progress of the American Jewish community from the dark days of Hitler, the wounds inflicted on the community by the Holocaust had not healed.

President Reagan was slated to visit West Germany in May for the G6 conference in Bonn. Chancellor Helmut Kohl, facing a tough regional election cycle, asked the president to make a symbolic gesture of reconciliation between the two countries by visiting the German military cemetery in Bitburg. To thank Kohl for his strong backing of placing US missiles on the Continent, Reagan agreed. The White House advance team had failed to uncover that dozens of Hitler's SS troops were buried in Bitburg, men who had not only cold-bloodedly murdered Jews but American GIs as well. The visit was widely condemned in newspapers, and by Jewish and veterans' groups. Another stop was added to Reagan's itinerary: the Bergen-Belsen concentration camp – but the controversy did not abate.[68]

On April 19, the president awarded a Congressional Gold Medal to Elie Wiesel in the Roosevelt Room of the White House, and the world's most famous Holocaust survivor thanked the president for the help he had extended to Soviet Jewry. After stating that the medal was not his alone, but "belongs to all those who remember what the SS killers have done to their victims," Wiesel asked Reagan not to visit Bitburg: "That place, Mr. President, is not your place. Your place is with the victims of the SS."[69]

Reagan kept his promise to Kohl, but at Bergen-Belsen he echoed the cry of the Soviet Jewry movement: "Never again!" he exclaimed. "I promise you we will never forget."[70]

When the president met Gorbachev, he indeed did not forget.

◆ ◆ ◆

By November 1985, when Ronald Reagan landed in Geneva to meet Mikhail Gorbachev, the US assault on the Soviet economy, with the help of Saudi Arabia, was about to pay off. The Saudi royal family had long believed that Israel was created by the Bolsheviks to separate the Arabs from the United States, and that the Jews and Communists were working to undermine the world order.[71] Saudi paranoia was not improved by the Iranian revolution, the Soviet invasion of Afghanistan, or the Iran-Iraq War. The Reagan administration had sold the Saudis Airborne Warning and Control Systems, flying radar systems that are used to pinpoint incoming aircraft or missiles and to direct the launching of defensive or offensive missiles. According to Alexander Haig, then secretary of state, "the Israeli government was prepared to accept the sale, but much of the American Jewish community, and Congress was not."[72]

Reagan spent a fair amount of political capital to complete the sale, and the administration went further by assuring the Saudi government that the United States would protect the Kingdom from upheaval in the region.[73] The rise of Islamic Jihad in Saudi Arabia and a spate of bombings in Riyadh further eroded the royal family's sense of security, and William Casey flew to the Kingdom and offered King Fahd CIA assistance. He also subtly suggested that lower oil prices would be helpful, since it would deprive Iran and the Soviet Union of revenue.[74] Fahd did not give Casey an answer – not until the end of 1985 when the Saudis stepped up oil production and in a matter of months drove the price of a barrel of oil from $30 to $12. Overnight, the Soviet Union lost in excess of $10 billion in hard currency.[75]

On a personal level, the summit proved to be a success: Reagan and Gorbachev established a rapport. However, by then, an estimated four hundred thousand Soviet Jews had applied to emigrate,[76] and the president handed the general secretary a list of Soviet citizens who had been denied exit visas.[77] Nothing had changed for Soviet Jews: the emigration numbers for 1985 would top out at 1,140.[78] Gorbachev was more interested in discussing SDI and tried to talk Reagan into killing the program; Reagan refused.[79]

A year later, at their summit in Reykjavik, Iceland, Reagan gave Gorbachev a list of twelve hundred Soviet Jews who wanted to leave.[80] While the behind-the-scenes method may have avoided public enmity, there is some indication that even alone with the president and their translators, Gorbachev bristled at the pressure.

In an interview with the author, Gorbachev recalled: "The United States must lead by example, but [it] has no right to lecture other countries. To be their teacher or to impose their will. The United States has to show more patience and cannot just demand change. It took thirty-five years for the United States to put into practice their beloved Constitution. Yet it wants other countries to achieve in thirty-five hours what took the United States thirty-five years to accomplish.

"I remember a meeting I had with President Reagan. He was lecturing me, and I said: 'You are not my teacher, and I am not your student. You are not the prosecutor, and I am not the accused. If you continue to lecture me, we can stop right now, and I will walk away. If you treat me as an equal, we can work together.'"[81]

Ultimately, Reagan felt that Gorbachev came to see himself and the president "as partners making a better world,"[82] but this didn't prevent Reagan from exhorting the general secretary to open up Soviet society.

Even though Gorbachev was a proponent of *glasnost* and *demokratizatsiia* (openness and democratization), neither one had translated into widespread freedom for Soviet Jews. The emigration numbers for 1986 were even lower than they had been the year before, dropping to under a thousand.[83] When Edgar Bronfman, president of the World Jewish Congress, and Morris Abram, chairman of the National Conference on Soviet Jewry, traveled to Moscow in an attempt to secure exit visas for Jews and the Kremlin's permission to relax the laws against the practice of Jewish culture and religion, they were rebuffed.[84]

However, before the summit, Gorbachev made it plain that he was at least contemplating charting a new course for the Soviet Union. On February 11, 1986, Anatoly Shcharansky was freed. He was exchanged for captured Communist spies and walked across the Glieneke Bridge into West Germany. He was driven in a limousine to Tempelhof Airport, where he flew to Frankfurt and was reunited with his wife. Yitzhak Ben-Ari, the Israeli ambassador to West Germany, presented Sharansky with a passport bearing his new Hebrew first name, Natan (he also simplified the English spelling of his last name), and then he and Avital boarded a plane to Tel Aviv.[85]

At first, in Reykjavik, Reagan and Gorbachev appeared to take a giant leap toward the most radical arms reduction agreement ever reached between the United States and the Soviet Union, but it fell apart because Reagan would not confine SDI to the laboratory.[86]

In 1987, the details were worked out for an Intermediate-Range Nuclear Forces Treaty that called for the United States and Soviet Union to discard all of their nuclear and conventional ground-launched ballistic and cruise missiles with ranges of 500 to 5,500 kilometers. The INF Treaty was the first time the superpowers had agreed to downsize their nuclear arsenals, wipe out a whole class of nuclear weapons, and permit thorough on-site inspections to make certain that both countries were in compliance.[87]

A summit was planned to begin in Washington on December 7, 1987, with the treaty signing the next day. It was then that leaders of the organized American Jewish community decided the moment had come to show Gorbachev that a full rapprochement with the West would only be possible if he recognized the right of freedom of movement. There had to be a demonstration in Washington – a march that would compare in size to the 1963 march for civil rights.

"We thought the situation was starting to change for the better," says Shoshana Cardin, who was then the president of the Council of

Jewish Federations. "In 1987, the Jewish emigration numbers were over eight thousand. And Gorbachev knew he would have to reach out to the administration for economic assistance, and both Reagan and Shultz were not shy when it came to pressuring the Soviets for concessions at the bargaining table. In June, Reagan had stood before the Brandenburg Gate and asked Gorbachev to tear down the Berlin Wall."[88]

David A. Harris, who in 1987 was working in Washington as a lobbyist for the American Jewish Committee, remembers that there was a good deal of anxiety about planning such a large demonstration.

"The American Jewish community had never had much success with demonstrations in Washington," says Harris. "The best was only twelve or thirteen thousand, back when Brezhnev came in 1973. That turnout would have been a disaster with Gorbachev. What level of support would he believe Soviet Jewry had with those kind of numbers? We thought that maybe we should just invite five hundred Jewish leaders for a meeting and say they represented millions."[89]

Then along came Natan Sharansky, who since his release had become a tireless advocate for those still trapped in the Soviet cage. He heard the plans and commented, "That's rubbish. Go for broke."[90]

Sharansky suggested a goal of four hundred thousand people, one for each Soviet Jew who had applied to emigrate.

"I thought that was overly optimistic," says Cardin. "But I thought a quarter of a million was possible."[91]

Freedom Sunday for Soviet Jewry was scheduled for December 6. Harris was the national coordinator.

"It was like planning the biggest bar mitzvah in the world," says Harris. "We set up a war room at 2027 Massachusetts Avenue, where the American Jewish Committee and the National Conference on Soviet Jewry had their offices. We had less than six weeks to arrange everything. We had to get permits, organize transportation, rent a stage and sound system and publicize it. And this was before the days of the Internet and e-mail."[92]

Shoshana Cardin traveled around the country, speaking to audiences, making certain people knew the stakes if the march did not draw a significant crowd.

"Bob Loup, chairman of the United Jewish Appeal, also did a lot of traveling and speaking," says Cardin. "We were lucky we had David Harris and David Saperstein and Carmi Schwartz handling the logistics. They were three accomplished professionals, and they certainly knew what they were doing."[93]

Sunday, December 6, was a freezing cold day, but fortunately no snow had come to shut down the city. David Harris was outside by five o'clock in the morning.

"People were supposed to gather at the Ellipse, the grassy area behind the White House," says Harris, but as he stood there, peering into the darkness, he saw nothing. As streaks of light began to appear in the sky, Harris noticed a group of people walking toward him. Then he saw another group. And another.[94]

They're coming, Harris thought, they're coming. He began to cry. By dawn, people were coming from every direction. In all, the US Park Police estimated that some 250,000 people were at the rally. Later, as Harris stood on the stage and gazed out at the mass of humanity standing in the cold bright air of the Mall, he was reminded of the photographs he had seen of the 1963 March on Washington.[95]

Says Harris, "I was looking at the American Jewish community's belated expiation for its failure to rescue more Jews from Hitler."[96]

The demonstrators marched up Constitution Avenue from the Ellipse, past the IRS and the Department of Justice, to the foot of Capitol Hill, carrying placards and chanting, "Let our people go!" They sang "God Bless America" and "*Hatikva*," the Israeli national anthem.[97] *New York Times* reporter Andrew Rosenthal described the march as "an emotional collage of religion and politics," and a Soviet film crew was on hand to transmit the demonstration to Moscow.[98]

Mary Travers and Peter Yarrow performed; so did Pearl Bailey. And there was a long, distinguished lineup of speakers – human rights advocates, leaders of American Jewish and Christian groups, and a selection of presidential aspirants.[99] Natan Sharansky said, "We all heard that it would be impossible to make American Jews come to Washington in the winter. Here you come and it is winter," and then he helped translate the meaning of the march for the Kremlin: "The Soviets have to know that no missiles and tanks, no camps and prisons, can extinguish the light of the candle of freedom." Vice President Bush, an obvious candidate for president in 1988, said, "It would be easier, safer, more diplomatic to remain silent – to negotiate our treaties and never raise the question of human rights. But that would be untrue to ourselves, and it would break our promise to the past." Another potential Republican presidential candidate, Senator Robert J. Dole, made what stands out as the most trenchant observation about Gorbachev up to this point. "Whatever *glasnost* is," said Dole, "it is not freedom."[100] Elie Wiesel reminded the marchers that too many had been silent in the 1940s, but "we are not silent today." Morris Abram, the chairman of the National Conference on Soviet Jewry, read a letter from President Reagan, and then Shoshana Cardin approached the microphone.[101]

"Most of what I said that day escapes me," recalls Cardin. "But what I've never forgotten was my feeling that it wouldn't be long before the Soviet Jews were free."[102]

◆ ◆ ◆

At the opening White House meeting of the summit, Reagan and Gorbachev were alone except for their translators, and the first subject Reagan brought up was human rights, asking Gorbachev why the Kremlin would not get rid of the restrictions on Jewish emigration. Gorbachev was put off by the opening, muttering to his translator, "*Ohn boltayet yeschchyo*, he's blathering on again."[103] When Reagan finished, Gorbachev replied that the United States had a heavily guarded border with Mexico – a logically flawed response that Reagan countered with the obvious: keeping people out was far different from keeping people in.[104]

The discussion moved on but the point had been made: as long as the United States and the Soviet Union were involved in negotiating – on any issue – the question of human rights would not go away.

The point was not lost on Soviet leadership. By the time Reagan was preparing for his final summit with Gorbachev, scheduled for Moscow in the spring of 1988, the Kremlin had loosened its restraints, permitting Bibles to be shipped into the country and Hebrew to be taught. The first kosher restaurant had opened in Moscow, and doctors from the American Psychiatric Association and National Institute of Mental Health had been allowed inside Soviet psychiatric hospitals, which in the past had frequently served not as treatment centers but as jails for the politically untamed. Laws for freer emigration were being considered, as was a judiciary that dispensed rulings based on independent laws and not on the whims of the Kremlin.[105]

Yet Reagan would not let up. En route to Moscow, he gave a speech in Helsinki's Finlandia Hall, stating that "the greatest creative and moral force in this new world, the greatest hope for survival and success, for peace and happiness is human freedom," and the president wondered aloud "why Soviet citizens who wish to exercise their right to emigrate should be subject to artificial quotas and arbitrary rulings."[106]

It was Nancy Reagan who suggested to her husband that while in Moscow they visit the home of a family of Jewish refuseniks, Yuri and Tatayana Zieman, who had applied to emigrate in 1977. Appearing to approve the plan, the Kremlin had the family's living quarters painted and repaired their street, but a message was sent to Reagan saying that the family would be permitted to leave "if the issue was not forced."[107] The visit was called off, and two months later the Ziemans moved to the United States.[108]

In Moscow, the Reagans did spend close to an hour with ninety-six dissidents and refuseniks and their families at a tea held in the ballroom of Spaso House, the residence of the US ambassador. At the tea, the president gave a warm welcome to the seventy-seven-year-old refusenik Abe Stolar, shaking his hand and telling him, "I've just spoken to Mikhail Gorbachev about you. I told him we [both] came from [Illinois] and were born at the same time."[109]

Stolar, who had been waiting for thirteen years to emigrate, had one of the strangest and saddest stories to tell. He'd been born in Chicago to parents who were true believers in Communism, and in the name of ideological purity had moved to the Soviet Union in 1931. Six years later, during Stalin's purges, Stolar's father was arrested and sent to a labor camp, where he died. In the aftermath of the Second World War, his sister, Eva, and her husband were also sentenced to labor camps. Stolar's mother passed away in 1949, about the same time as Abe lost his job as an English translator and editor for Radio Moscow in a convulsion of antisemitic purges. His brother-in-law died in the labor camp, but after his sister served five years she was able to leave for Israel and finally settled in Los Angeles.[110]

Despite the series of setbacks and tragedies, Abe Stolar remained a devout Communist, and following the death of Stalin, he was given another job as a translator at Tass. Interestingly enough, Stolar continued to exercise his rights as an American citizen, going to the US embassy in Moscow and voting in presidential elections. In 1975, Stolar, his Russian-born wife, Gita, and son were granted exit visas from the Soviet Union. Yet, without warning, security pulled them off their flight and their visas were revoked. It was unclear why the Kremlin had such a sudden change of heart, but the official explanation was that Gita, a chemical engineer, had once worked in a laboratory where she had allegedly been exposed to scientific knowledge too important to share with another country. It was a standard Soviet excuse for canceling visas.[111]

In time and without further explanation, the Stolars were issued new visas. By then, Abe's sister in Los Angles had died, but Gita had brothers living in Israel. Now another wrinkle in their plans emerged. The mother-in-law of Abe and Gita's son would not sign a waiver of obligations, giving her permission for her daughter to emigrate, and so the Stolars remained stuck. Perhaps Gorbachev would have someone speak to the reluctant mother-in-law.[112]

Not all of the refuseniks and dissidents the Reagans met in the embassy ballroom were Jews. A Lithuanian nationalist, just freed from a prison camp, attended, as did a Russian Orthodox priest, and the gathering did have a lighter moment. One of the attendees, Lev Timofeyev, an editor of a journal not officially sanctioned by the state and a director of a group who kept watch on human rights violations, told President Reagan that when he was arrested, the KGB told his young daughter that he was "the president's right-hand man in unleashing a new world war." Reagan thought that was funny, the ridiculous height of Soviet paranoia.[113]

As the tea drew to a close, the president assured the gathering that he would pursue their freedom and ended his remarks with a quote from the nineteenth-century Russian poet and author Aleksandr Pushkin: "It is time, my friend, it is time."[114]

The most perplexing aspect of the last Reagan-Gorbachev summit was the ambivalence exhibited by the Kremlin toward human rights. While the Soviet government was not prepared at this point to fully repeal their restrictive policies, they were also hesitant to return to the past and the tighter controls on free expression. Perhaps because Gorbachev realized that he was going to need an ample infusion of economic assistance from the United States to save the Soviet Union, it made sense for him to provide Reagan with a forum from which to rhapsodize about democracy.

But it doesn't explain why the Soviets permitted Micah Naftalin and Pamela Cohen of the Union of Councils for Soviet Jews, and Glenn Richter, Rabbi Avi Weiss, and other members of the Student Struggle for Soviet Jewry to enter the country during the summit. The Soviets had been denying some of these outspoken activists visas since the 1970s.[115]

Glenn Richter recalls, "We had been demonstrating in Helsinki before we went to Leningrad and Moscow, so it wasn't as if the Soviets didn't know what we were doing. The Soviet Union had denied me entrance since my last trip in 1974. I was mildly surprised they let us in, but I suppose they were trying to be on their best behavior."[116]

The demonstrations in Helsinki had been splashed across the front pages of the European press, and according to Naftalin, it was only due "to the direct intervention of General Colin Powell, Reagan's national security adviser," with the Kremlin that enabled the activists to enter the country.[117]

In Leningrad, Richter, Weiss, and their group met with the refusenik Elena Keis, whose mother had been committed to a Soviet psychiatric institution because she had mailed her sister Anna's violin to her in Israel, where Anna performed with the Israel Philharmonic Orchestra. As Richter spoke to Elena, he noticed a quartet of KGB agents nearby trying to overhear their conversation. Still, the KGB allowed members of the Student Struggle for Soviet Jewry to talk with Keis and go on with their trip.[118]

The Americans staged a protest prayer service in Red Square and then demonstrated with refuseniks outside Spaso House and the Lenin Library.[119] The KGB attended as well, and one burly, tough-looking agent, pretending to be a reporter, walked up to Richter, stuck a mini tape recorder in his face, and angrily asked, "Who are you? Why are you here?"[120]

Behind the agent, several genuine journalists caught Richter's eye, silently mouthing the word "KGB," and Richter refused to answer.[121]

By the time the activists and refuseniks moved their protests outside the Lenin Library, the KGB had had enough *glasnost* for one summit. They waded into the crowd, pushing and hitting the demonstrators. A Canadian television van pulled up and a cameraman threw open the back doors, shouting at the Americans to climb in, and after they were safely inside, the van drove away.[122]

In all probability the ambivalent posture taken by the Soviet government was simply a reflection of the ambivalence that it felt about *glasnost*. The Kremlin may have thought its cause would be well served by displaying improvement, but the halfhearted show of openness proved to be a public relations disaster and scored few points with democratic countries, because it provided the opportunity for American officials and activists to highlight continuing Soviet repression.

In addition to the three public speeches President Reagan gave in Moscow extolling the virtues of freedom,[123] he handed another list to Gorbachev, this one boiled down to fourteen human rights cases. When Gorbachev was later asked if action would be taken on behalf of these cases, he snapped, "There are too many lists."[124]

During the summit, the Coalition to Free Soviet Jews staged a rally of support in New York City, where the mayor, Ed Koch, briefly renamed Times Square "Red Square." City and state politicians spoke to the thousands of demonstrators from a rostrum built to resemble Lenin's Tomb. Gorbachev was accused of using *glasnost* as a ploy, not a policy, and Koch told the cheering demonstrators that the president deserved credit for raising the issue of emigration with Gorbachev, for had Reagan not raised it, "we would not be here waiting for that signal to let our people go."[125]

Back at Spaso House in Moscow, at Reagan's final press conference of the summit, the president appeared concerned about the fallout from his public display of concern for the refuseniks and dissidents. Perhaps he had pushed Gorbachev too far, threatening his position with Soviet hardliners, and the president tried to let him off the hook by blaming "a bureaucratic bungle" for the stalled progress on emigration.[126]

Reporters weren't buying that explanation. They peppered him with questions about the restrictive Soviet policy, and Reagan responded with an amusing story from his experience in the Second World War: he had asked his superiors if he could get rid of some filing cabinets crammed with old files, and he was told that he could dump the cabinets "providing copies were made of each file destroyed."[127]

The comic relief didn't alter the questions, and Reagan replied with a vote of confidence for Gorbachev. He said, "I just have to believe that in any government some of us do find ourselves bound in by the bureaucracy, and then sometimes you have to stomp your foot and say, unmistakably, 'I want it done...' I have great confidence in [Gorbachev's] ability to do that."[128]

At his own closing session with journalists, Gorbachev acted unimpressed with Reagan focusing on dissidents and refuseniks during the summit, saying that he "did not have a lot of admiration for that part of the trip."[129]

In reaction to the press conferences, the National Conference of Soviet Jewry opined that Reagan had "raised the [human rights] issue in a forceful fashion and is now waiting for a Soviet response."[130]

But Abraham H. Foxman, national director of the Anti-Defamation League of B'nai B'rith, came closer to the truth when he said that President Reagan's comments had been "a diplomatic way of trying to save face for the Soviets after he had made the point as loudly, dramatically and vigorously as he could."[131]

◆ ◆ ◆

Secretary of State George Shultz was not as generous as the president about Soviet failings because, as a Cabinet secretary who was not negotiating face-to-face with Gorbachev, he didn't have to be. Throughout the Reagan administration, Shultz rarely missed an opportunity to chide the Kremlin in public regarding their record on emigration, and he would be beloved by the American Jewish community for doing so. In Helsinki, prior to the Moscow summit, Shultz attended a Seder,[132] and the secretary was still hammering home his point months later on election day, 1988, when Reagan vice president George H. W. Bush defeated the Democratic candidate, Governor Michael Dukakis of Massachusetts.

Even though Shultz's tenure at Foggy Bottom was coming to a close, he hosted a photo exhibition in the lobby of the State Department in which the thirty or so black-and-white photographs in the exhibit were the work of Sergei Petrov, a Soviet photographer with dreams of emigrating to the United States. The Kremlin would not even issue Petrov a travel visa to the West, claiming that his employment at a physics institute, a decade before, had provided him with state secrets.[133]

Purported knowledge of such secrets – whether gained through work in a technological field or by service in the military – had been a primary weapon in the Soviet bureaucratic arsenal for denying exit visas to their citizens. In discussions with representatives from the American Jewish community, journalists, and the US government, Soviet officials had promised to work on resolving this issue. Of course, Soviet officials had also said that the secrecy designation would be removed from an individual's status after a decade, but that hadn't been true for Petrov or refuseniks like Yuli Kosharovsky, Leonid Shabashov, Boris Strelchik, and Vladimir Kislik, who together had spent sixty years with that designation hanging over their heads.[134] Kislik had been employed at an atomic plant in the 1960s and had been waiting for a visa since 1973. Yet in spite of the hardships he suffered, Kislik managed to hold onto his sense of humor when he wrote directly to Gorbachev, saying, "Nowadays, these 'secrets' are known even to the more curious high school students. What do you need me for?"[135]

Shultz, after observing that Sergei Petrov had been forbidden to attend his own exhibit, said, "I want all of you to know that we will continue to press for Sergei's release as long as he is held against his will in the Soviet Union. Perhaps we should take some consolation at Sergei's attitude about this and other exhibitions. In a letter to a friend, he wrote, 'At least when my works get out, part of me gets out too.'"[136]

Evidently, the prospect of dealing with a new Republican president who was unlikely to deviate from Reagan's posture toward the Kremlin, and Shultz's ongoing drumbeat for freedom, were not lost on Moscow. On Saturday, four days after the election, Shultz received a phone call from Yuri Dubinin, the man who had replaced Anatoly Dobrynin as Soviet ambassador to the United States when, in 1986, Dobrynin had been summoned home to Moscow to head the International Department of the

Communist Party's Central Committee and become one of Gorbachev's chief advisers.[137]

Dubinin told Shultz that he was returning to Washington on Sunday, and he hoped Shultz could see him immediately.[138] Shultz had been playing golf in Augusta, Georgia, over the weekend, and on Sunday evening, he went straight from Andrews Air Force Base to his office at the State Department and met the ambassador. Dubinin told Shultz that Gorbachev had decided, after more than three years in power, to address the United Nations for the first time. Dubinin said that it would be a groundbreaking speech, and he wanted to know if the general secretary could meet with President Reagan and President-elect Bush when he was in New York City.[139]

It was an opportune moment for Gorbachev to pursue foreign policy. He planned to travel twenty thousand miles during December, visiting the United States, Cuba, and Britain. After the May summit with Reagan, Gorbachev had forged ahead with his policy of *perestroika*. His political and economic restructuring had produced mixed domestic results. The top leadership in the Kremlin had changed, and nationalism was sweeping though Armenia and the Baltic states, but the Soviet economy was still in a shambles with scant hope of immediate improvement, a fact that threatened the future viability of Gorbachev's reforms.

Despite all the discussion and debate about *perestroika* and the man who brought it into being, it seemed that Mikhail Gorbachev's most notable success since taking over the Soviet Union had been his ability to impress democracies with his promise of a new era to come, and perhaps this explained his sudden desire to address the United Nations.[140]

Eager to support a Soviet leader who had finally seen the light of liberal democracy and free markets, Shultz "recommended to President Reagan that he be gracious about the visit."[141] Reagan was happy to meet with Gorbachev, but even before arrangements could be finalized, Soviet officials expressed concern about the general secretary's safety. They did not reveal any specific information about a threat, but they were worried that once Gorbachev was in the United States, a coup would be launched in Moscow. At the same time, an assassin would be dispatched to murder Gorbachev in New York, and the assassination would be staged to make it appear as though an American were responsible.[142]

Reagan was unsure of how seriously to regard the threat, though he knew Gorbachev had made himself as many enemies as friends.[143]

Indeed, within the Soviet Union, hardliners were dismayed not just at the economic dislocation at home, but with the erosion of their nation's global power. In private discussions with Gorbachev they gave vent to their dissatisfaction with his repudiation of socialism and his cozying up to the West.[144]

Under Gorbachev, the Soviets had curtailed their longtime strategy of fomenting revolution as a method for confronting the West and had gone so far as to stop jamming the broadcasts of Radio Liberty and Radio Free Europe. Pressed by Gorbachev, and with the help of US mediators, Cuba had promised to recall its forces from Angola, and Vietnam would shortly quit Cambodia.[145] Soviet clients would no longer be supplied with weapons systems for free, a fact that Gorbachev passed along in Moscow to President Hafez al-Assad of Syria, his most important client in the Middle East. At a dinner in honor of the Syrian president, Gorbachev pointedly asked him why he was wasting so much money on weapons. Shouldn't he use the funds to buttress up his sagging economy? Assad had no answer for Gorbachev, but then the general secretary wasn't really looking for one. He was making a point: Moscow would see to it that Damascus had adequate equipment for defense but the Kremlin would not be underwriting any military adventurism.[146]

As Gorbachev reined in Assad, he reached out to repair the diplomatic relationship between the Soviet Union and Israel. Gorbachev sent a Soviet consular delegation to Israel and accepted an Israeli delegation in Moscow.[147] It was not the same as an official exchange of ambassadors; the consular delegations had nothing close to the status of embassies, though it was a hopeful step in that direction.

Gorbachev stated publicly that any arrangement between Israel and the Palestinians must take into account Israeli security needs, a position that endeared him to Israeli prime minister Yitzhak Shamir, who called the general secretary "a great man and a great leader."[148]

In a move that would reshape the region, Gorbachev ordered his government to back off its restrictive emigration policy, allowing more Soviet Jews to leave. In 1988, over twenty thousand left, almost tripling the number from 1987, but a rather modest amount compared to what was to come in the next two years.[149]

The increase in emigration alarmed the Arab world more than Gorbachev's apparent evenhandedness on the Middle East conflict. Initially, Arab spokesmen denied the reality, a reliable indication of anxiety among their leadership. An associate of Yasser Arafat claimed that the rumored emigration of Soviet Jewry was a plot hatched by the United States and Israeli media to interfere in the friendship between the Palestine Liberation Organization and the Kremlin. When it became clear that more Jews were departing, Egypt suggested that the Soviets cancel the visas until a Middle East peace plan was in place, and the Popular Front for the Liberation of Palestine requested that the Kremlin halt Jewish emigration because the policy was exerting "pressure on Palestinian Communist elements...to recognize the Zionist state."[150]

The rise in emigration coupled with the lack of Soviet support was also a factor in setting the Palestine Liberation Organization on a new tack. Three weeks before Gorbachev came to the United Nations, Yasser Arafat convened a session of the Palestinian National Council in Algiers. At the PNC meeting a "Palestinian state" was declared in the West Bank and Gaza with Arafat as president. Implicitly, the geography of the state recognized the existence of Israel, a first for the PLO. By the end of the year, at the urging of Shultz, Arafat publicly recognized Israel (although the PLO charter itself was never changed to reflect Arafat's statement), and the United States rewarded him by rescinding its ban on direct discussions with the organization.[151]

Five days before Gorbachev left to address the General Assembly of the United Nations, Soviet officials announced that over one hundred longtime refuseniks would no longer be refused exit visas based on their alleged possession of state secrets.[152]

Celebration at the news was muted by tragedy. Matus Poberezhny, a doctor of technical sciences, had been waiting nine years to emigrate to Israel. Despairing of ever securing a visa, he talked his wife and son into leaving without him. After being notified that his secrecy classification had at last been lifted, the fifty-four-year-old Dr. Poberezhny suffered a fatal coronary.[153]

The relaxation of the overall policies toward Jews by the Soviets was accompanied by a notable improvement in the cultural and political relationship between the USSR and Israel.

During the first week of December, the Hapoel volleyball team traveled from Israel to Moscow to play the Soviet champions in the opening round of the European Cup tournament. The televised contest was the first time since 1967 that Israeli and Russian sports teams had competed on one or the other's home turf. The crowd and the press, Jews and non-Jews alike, warmly greeted the Israeli team, with many of the Jewish spectators waving Israeli flags and calling, "Hapoel! Hapoel!" The Israelis lost, but a rematch was slated to be held in Israel. In addition, the Israeli championship basketball team had a series of games scheduled against the Red Army sports club team in Moscow and Tel Aviv.[154]

Less than seventy-two hours before Gorbachev departed for New York, another incident played out in the newspapers and on television that not only demonstrated the fundamental changes that had taken hold inside the Kremlin, but softened the relationship between Moscow and Jerusalem, establishing the context for further cooperation between the two countries – cooperation that was soon going to be crucial to resettling hundreds of thousands of Soviet Jews.

The incident began in southern Russia, in the town of Ordzhonikdze, when four gunmen kidnapped thirty children, a teacher, and a driver on a school bus. The leader of the gang was a convicted criminal and drug addict, and a deputy chairman of the KGB security police was sent to negotiate with him.

The gang demanded to be granted passage to the airport at Mineralnyye Vody, 110 miles to the northwest, where they wanted the government to furnish them with a cargo plane so they could drive the bus aboard and be flown to a capitalist country.[155]

Soviet authorities cooperated. In exchange for releasing the hostages, they provided the men with an Ilyushin-76 jet transport, an eight-man Aeroflot crew, drugs, $2 million in cash, and let one of the gang bring his wife aboard. The hijackers had planned to go to Pakistan or Iraq, but after the plane had lifted off, Israel was chosen as a destination because the hijackers had heard that the recently elected government was staunchly anticommunist and would not harm them.[156]

On Friday morning, the Israeli Civil Aviation Authority received three telexes from its Moscow counterpart, the first such direct communication in years. The initial telex was in broken English. Israeli officials thought it was a hoax, then worried that they were dealing with Jewish refuseniks who had tired of waiting for approval to emigrate, or maybe Arab terrorists launching an attack.[157]

When subsequent communications made it clear that they were dealing with hijackers without a political agenda, a hurried round of high-level discussions took place in Israel and with Moscow and Washington. The hijackers were cleared to land in Israel, and Defense Minister Yitzhak Rabin and Israel Defense Forces chief of staff General Dan Shomron established an operational headquarters at Ben-Gurion Airport.[158]

That evening, as the Aeroflot plane neared Israeli air space, an F-15 fighter jet was dispatched to serve as an escort. From above, the only runway lights visible in the darkness were along a military airstrip on the remote northern edge of the airport, which was ringed with ambulances, fire trucks, snipers, commandos, and police.[159]

Once the Ilyushin-76 had taxied to stop, a hijacker asked the Aeroflot flight engineer if they were in Israel or Syria, adding, "If this is Israel, we'll stay."[160] The door was opened, and three crew members deplaned with a request for a Russian interpreter.[161] The hijackers demanded evidence that they were really in the Jewish state. Unable to decipher the lettering on an Israeli soldier's ID card, they asked for an item with a Star of David on it or to hear someone speak Yiddish.[162] When that was done, an interpreter quickly negotiated the release of the entire crew, and then the hijackers walked out, several of them still wearing their fur hats, and surrendered a shotgun, four pistols, and a suitcase stuffed with money to the Israeli authorities.[163]

They were incarcerated for the night in the Tel Kabir jail in Tel Aviv. Israel had no formal diplomatic relationship with the USSR, so no extradition treaty existed between the two countries.[164] However, both nations had signed an international agreement outlawing air piracy,[165] and under the Israeli Law of Entry anyone who enters the country illegally can be deported without the thirty-day wait that accompanies a court-ordered expulsion.[166]

Prime Minister Yitzhak Shamir agreed to extradite the hijackers after he was assured by the Kremlin that they would not face the death penalty. By noon on Saturday, an Aeroflot passenger jet with a crew of technicians, police, and medical personnel was in Israel and had the hijackers in custody.[167]

With his typical bluntness, Rabin told reporters that he was stunned that the Kremlin had permitted the plane to take off. Then he posed a rhetorical question: "How can a superpower like the Soviet Union allow five simple robbers with four pistols and one hunting gun, when the children had already been freed, when not even one hostage was on the airplane, to leave?"[168]

Other Israeli officials explained it by saying that the Soviet Union, unlike Israel, had scant experience handling these kinds of hijackings.[169] Tass, the official Soviet news agency, said that the decision to acquiesce to the hijackers' demands had been made by "the country's leadership" and was carried out to save the children.[170]

Yet the political truth was obscured by these explanations. The USSR had plenty of experience with hijacking, and Gorbachev could have easily ordered an assault on the jet while it sat on the runway at Mineralnyye Vody. In March 1987, Soviet security had stormed a passenger plane during an attempted hijacking by a family of jazz musicians, and nine people had died in the shooting – including a trio of passengers and a flight attendant – which led to a loud chorus of public criticism.[171]

This solution, however, was a hallmark of the old Soviet style – unbridled force, not diplomacy. Gorbachev was in the process of building a new vision of the Soviet Union, a gentler vision he planned to describe in his speech at the United Nations. It would have been foolish to undercut himself by overreacting to this parody of a hijacking. The wiser course was to show restraint.

And Gorbachev used the occasion of Israeli assistance to signal publicly that he intended to improve the relationship between Moscow and Jerusalem – a move with obvious benefits for Soviet Jewry that would not be missed by the governments of Israel and the United States, and the organized American Jewish community.

The signal came via Gorbachev's old friend, the foreign minister,

Eduard Shevardnadze. On the Saturday that the hijackers were being flown home, Shevardnadze spoke on television, thanking Israel for dealing with this "barbaric deed" in such a "noble and humanitarian way."[172]

Then Shevardnadze invited Arye Levin, head of the Israeli consular delegation, to his office in the Foreign Ministry tower overlooking Smolensk Square. Levin had been stationed in Moscow since September, but he had been pointedly ignored by the Kremlin, finding it impossible to speak with any officials who wielded real power in the Gorbachev government.[173]

Before the meeting began, Shevardnadze and Levin had one of those highly symbolic diplomatic exchanges weighted with a meaning well beyond the spoken words. The foreign minister asked Levin if he was freezing in the harsh Moscow winter, and the Israeli replied that Moscow was cold, but there was "much warmth" in the city if one could find it.[174]

Shevardnadze was not simply being polite. Anyone who mistook his good manners for a lack of shrewdness or a weak will would have done well to remember that the charismatic silver-haired diplomat had grown up in Georgia, the same region that produced Stalin.

Perhaps the most exceptional feature of the meeting was the presence of television cameras in Shevardnadze's seventh-floor office recording the exchange.[175]

"We thank the Israeli authorities for showing such goodwill and decisive suppression of the illegal action," Shevardnadze told Levin, and everyone else in the Soviet Union who would view the broadcast. "Such norms of civilized intergovernmental relations must be firmly established in the modern world."[176]

It was left to a spokesman for the Israeli Foreign Ministry in Jerusalem to define the importance of the incident to the cause of freeing Soviet Jewry. Before the hijacking, said the spokesman, "such a meeting between Levin and Shevardnadze could not have been dreamed of."[177]

◆ ◆ ◆

On Tuesday afternoon, December 6, 1988, as Mikhail Gorbachev was touching down in New York City, members of the National Conference on Soviet Jewry were meeting with Secretary Shultz in Washington.

NCSJ had never been shy about criticizing the more heavy-handed behavior of the Soviet Union, but Shultz had apparently convinced them that Gorbachev was committed to reform, because at a news conference, Shoshana Cardin, chairwoman of the organization, said she was "optimistic that promises made by the Soviets in recent months would be implemented."[178]

Security had been stepped up for the Gorbachev visit, but during his two days in the States, no attempts were made on his life. He spent the night at the Soviet mission, and early the next day he received a telegram about an earthquake in Armenia. The extent of the damage was unclear from the communication,[179] and it wasn't until later that night that Gorbachev learned of the toll – approximately forty-five thousand people dead and five hundred thousand homeless.[180]

Shortly before 10 AM, his motorcade wended through the East Side traffic to the United Nations, passing a few thousand protesters, the majority of whom came from Jewish day schools in the Metropolitan area. It was a noticeably small turnout for a New York City Soviet Jewry protest, a result of the progress that had already been made.[181]

Rabbi Avi Weiss and members of the Student Struggle for Soviet Jewry were at the UN to let the Soviet leader know that they were still waiting for him to let the dissidents and refuseniks go. As Weiss was recounting his story about the demonstrations during the May summit in Moscow, a cameraman on the sidewalk filming the scene interrupted, saying that he remembered the demonstration at the Lenin Library, because he had been in the Canadian TV van that had ferried Weiss and others out of harm's way.[182]

Other than this coincidence, the dramatic highpoint outside the UN on this December morning was provided by fifty-eight members of SSSJ, who blocked First Avenue and were arrested for disorderly conduct.[183]

Gorbachev entered the grand assembly hall to thunderous applause, an unusual reaction in that august chamber.[184] To one of Gorbachev's advisers it seemed that his boss "was getting an honorary degree from the international community," his certification as "a world-class leader of great authority."[185]

He spoke for an hour, a remarkably brief performance given his penchant for long and winding speeches. *Pravda* entitled his address "To Put an End to the Era of Wars and Conflicts," while the *New York Times* characterized it as "The World According to Gorbachev." He introduced his plan to reduce Soviet military might by ten thousand tanks and half a million troops,[186] and renounced the persecution of dissidents and any suppression of Eastern European governments, saying that he favored "developing wide-ranging mutually beneficial and equitable cooperation among nations."[187]

Gorbachev also had an unequivocal message on Soviet Jewry, saying that "the principle of freedom of choice is mandatory. Its non-recognition is fraught with extremely grave consequences for world peace. Denying that right to peoples, under whatever pretext or rhetorical guise, means jeopardizing even the fragile balance that has been attained. Freedom of choice is a universal principle that should allow no exceptions." No Soviet citizens, he promised, would be convicted for their political or religious beliefs and those who wished to leave the USSR would be dealt with in a "humane spirit."[188]

When he was finished at the UN, Gorbachev went to lunch with President Reagan and President-elect Bush at the Coast Guard station on Governors Island in New York Harbor. While they ate, Bush tried to extract some assurances from Gorbachev that *glasnost* and *perestroika* would succeed, believing that American businessmen would require this official optimism to invest in the Soviet Union. Gorbachev couldn't provide the assurance, but he did tell the president-elect that there was "a revolution taking place in my country…. They all applauded me when I started it in 1986, and now they don't like it so much. But it's going to be a revolution nonetheless."[189]

For the most part, the organized American Jewish community had faith in Gorbachev. Shoshana Cardin, who was now the chairwoman of the National Conference on Soviet Jewry, issued a statement to the press praising the UN speech and indicating that she was convinced Gorbachev would do as he promised.[190]

Cardin had traveled through the countries of Eastern Europe and the Soviet Union and she believed that Gorbachev, even if his personal convictions wavered, would have to forge ahead regardless of roadblocks because his economy was in trouble. Cardin had watched women selling a single cabbage on the streets of Moscow, selling anything they could just to get their hands on tiny sums of money. She had seen the nationalism percolating in the Soviet republics and listened to people in Eastern Europe openly expressing their desire to step out from behind the Iron Curtain.[191]

Yet neither the most sanguine US officials nor leaders of the Soviet Jewry movement were aware of the magnitude of Gorbachev's transformation after he appeared at the United Nations, the synergy that crackled between the forward-looking general secretary and the democratic people of the West.

A poll conducted prior to his address to the General Assembly indicated that 85 percent of Americans approved of the friendlier relationship developing between the United States and the USSR,[192] and after Gorbachev left Governors Island he saw the ecstatic signs of this approval.

His motorcade was hailed by thousands of New Yorkers, who shouted their greetings and leaned out of windows high above the streets to wave at him with hands, hats, and handkerchiefs. Gorbachev had frequently claimed that he would go further in changing the Soviet Union than anyone had predicted, and in the glimmering aftermath of his visit to New York he realized that he could move more quickly and surely "in shaking off the fetters of the past."[193]

For the moment, though, geopolitics were put on hold. Gorbachev cancelled the rest of his trip abroad to return home and deal with earthquake-ravaged Armenia, and when that was behind him the Soviet leader would move faster than almost anyone dared dream.

CHAPTER 11

THE GREAT TRANSITION

On January 11, 1989, President Ronald Reagan gave his thirty-fourth speech from the Oval Office. Despite the spread of instant news during his presidency, when images of unfolding events could be beamed via satellite to TV screens around the globe, Reagan still relied on the plainspoken heart-to-heart to cajole, comfort, and inspire Americans. Friends and foes alike referred to him as the "Great Communicator," and perhaps in no other president of the television age was political strategy more wedded to the rhetoric that gave voice to it.

The rhetoric was inseparable from Reagan himself – his unshakeable, can-do optimism and moral surety, both of which appeared to spring full-blown from the long-ago tales of Horatio Alger. Consequently, Reagan had been criticized for a tendency to oversimplify modern social, economic, and geopolitical challenges – an approach some considered naïve at best, deliberately misleading at worst. However, these criticisms would now be for historians to judge. A month shy of his seventy-eighth birthday, Reagan was giving his farewell address, and the speech itself was perfectly suited to his style, crafted for one last gentle tug on the heartstrings of the nation. In simple declarative sentences, delivered through that corridor of intimacy Reagan rarely failed to establish with his audience, as if he were pouring out his deepest feelings over a cup of coffee at the local diner, the president reflected on his eight years in the White House.

He covered a range of topics, but focused on one that he clearly viewed as the greatest positive change that had occurred between 1981 and 1989: the countries that were rejecting Communism and discovering that "democracy, the profoundly good, is also the profoundly productive." He spoke of establishing a "satisfying new closeness with the Soviet Union," and the "internal democratic reforms" that had been instituted by Mikhail Gorbachev. He also highlighted his commitment to freedom for the "prisoners whose names I've given [Gorbachev] every time we've met."

Reagan left office believing that while his administration had "meant to change a nation," it had instead "changed a world."[1] And a majority of Americans agreed with him. According to the Gallup poll, Reagan's final approval rating stood at 63 percent; the *New York Times*-CBS Poll claimed it was 5 percent higher. Either way, it was the highest approval rating of any president since the era of Reagan's first political hero, Franklin Roosevelt.[2]

Despite these polling numbers, President-elect George Bush was not immediately inclined to pick up with Moscow where Reagan had left off. By nature he was cautious, and with the Soviets he was concerned that a misstep could lead to disaster – either with Gorbachev or one of the hardliners who could replace him and revive the authoritarian state.

Not long after election day, the president-elect's old friend and nominee for secretary of state, James A. Baker III, invited Anatoly Dobrynin (who had officially returned to Moscow in 1986 but still played an advisory role) to his house on Foxhall Road in Washington. During their private chat in Baker's den, Dobrynin said that there was growing concern in the Soviet Union about the potential for runaway inflation if the Kremlin imposed a market economy, since salaries would have to be increased to make up for the loss of government subsidies "on food and other staples."[3]

When Baker asked the old hand for a reading on the political climate, his reply did little to alleviate the anxieties of the incoming administration. "The danger," Dobrynin said, "is whether Gorbachev can survive."[4]

Bush was unsure of how to proceed with Gorbachev, but his newly named national security adviser, Brent Scowcroft, was not disposed to trust the Soviet leader. On a Sunday morning talk show, Scowcroft accused Gorbachev of being "interested in making trouble within the Western alliance."[5]

Secretary of State Baker agreed with the NSA adviser, believing that

"Gorbachev's strategy was premised on...undercutting the United States in Western Europe by appealing [directly]...to Western publics."[6] Baker also thought that during 1987 and 1988 his predecessor, George Shultz, should have assumed a much more forceful negotiating stance with the Soviets,[7] and now the new secretary of state wanted to "craft initiatives that [Gorbachev] would feel obliged to embrace."[8]

The initiatives would address the reduction of forces in Europe and of nuclear arms, and one especially troubling aspect of Soviet foreign policy that had escaped Gorbachev's mania for reform: his government's support for revolution in Central America. With the assistance of its client state, Cuba, the Soviet Union was still arming the Sandinistas in Nicaragua and the rebels in El Salvador. Perhaps Gorbachev could be convinced to reduce Soviet aid to Cuba itself.[9]

By February, President Bush still had not seen a satisfactory plan for dealing with the Kremlin, and so he ordered a comprehensive review of national security policy.

Secretary of State Baker would later write in his memoir, *The Politics of Diplomacy*, that the new president "was quite conscious of the need to put his own imprint on policy."[10] The review would also send a signal to "the bureaucracy, the Congress, the media, and the public at large that it was time for a reassessment of the old assumptions" in light of all the changes that had recently come to pass.[11]

Gorbachev referred to the policy review as the *pauza* (pause), and he was not happy about it. He felt that the Bush administration was dismissing his commitment to reform, refusing to recognize that he had unchained himself from the Soviet past. Why would Bush require a policy review to illuminate the obvious?[12]

As Gorbachev later recalled, "No person should be deprived of the opportunity to change his views. *Perestroika* didn't come to me as a revelation on one day. It was the sum of my entire life experience. I represent a generation of Russians who were born before the Second World War. I remember the repression [of life under Stalin]. I saw the war. I lived under the Nazis. Many people in Russia understood we needed reforms and that the old Politburo was an impediment to these changes. *Perestroika* was a conclusion I reached as an outcome of my entire previous life."[13]

Two days after Bush announced his review, as if to spotlight the monumental shift in the position of the Soviet Union, the world watched the Red Army complete their withdrawal from Afghanistan, a process that had begun the previous spring. The civil war between the Soviet-backed government and the US- and Pakistan-supported Muslim rebels would go on, but after nine years the last of the Soviet soldiers were heading back across the Amu Darya River, the long columns of tanks and armored personnel carriers rolling over the Friendship Bridge into the city of Termez in Uzbekistan.[14]

The Kremlin had taken pains to orchestrate an orderly withdrawal – so unlike the images that accompanied the frantic US departure from Vietnam in 1975 – but in the end the Soviets, like the Americans, could not escape the fallout from their war.

The Soviet Union had paid dearly for their incursion into Afghanistan.[15] In nine years of fighting, the Soviets spent over $20 billion and suffered more than twenty-two thousand dead and seventy-five thousand wounded. Although they never accomplished their goal of suppressing the rebels, the Red Army did kill approximately 1.5 million people, drove 6 million refugees into neighboring countries, destroyed half the agriculture and livestock, and one-third of the villages.[16]

But the greatest political price the Soviets paid in Afghanistan was that the illusion of their invincible power was gone. The Kremlin, it was clear now, could not control the nations in its orbit.

The disillusionment was trumpeted by an emboldened Soviet press. The *Literaturnaya Gazeta* was deeply critical of the war, and in one essay revisited an alleged atrocity carried out by the Red Army and the ensuing cover-up.[17] *Pravda* commented that while the invasion might have been justified as a means to protect Soviet borders, the war itself was undermined by tactical errors. The newspaper suggested "that in the future such vital issues as the use of troops must not be decided in secrecy, without the approval of the country's Parliament."[18]

Gorbachev did not back away from what, by past Soviet standards, would have to be categorized as a torrent of criticism. He referred to the Afghan adventure as his country's "bleeding wound."[19]

Yet the Bush administration seemed unable to assimilate the changes taking place inside the Soviet Union into a coherent new approach. In March, as the pause dragged on, Secretary of State Baker went to Vienna and had his first meeting with Soviet foreign minister Eduard Shevardnadze, a man renowned for his patience, intelligence, and impressive shock of white hair.

In his memoir, Baker recalls that he met Shevardnadze at the US ambassador's residence and adds, for no immediately apparent reason, that this was "the same place President Kennedy had met Khrushchev in June 1961."[20]

One might assume that James Baker was simply being a thorough memoirist and presenting an interesting historical nugget for his readers. However, Baker has long been regarded as a shrewd political operative with an acute eye and ear for the slightest nuance, and so it would be naïve to think that he was merely serving as a tour guide.

Understanding why the former secretary of state chose to point this out requires a glimpse backward to the Kennedy-Khrushchev summit. In 1961, Kennedy did not perform well with the Soviet leader, who knocked the young, inexperienced president back on his heels with a verbal barrage of Communist dogma.

As Kennedy later admitted to James Reston, the influential Washington Bureau chief of the *New York Times*, the worst result of his discussions was that Khrushchev came away believing that the president "had no guts."[21]

It was a disastrous impression, one that Kennedy had pledged to avoid in his Inaugural Address, stating that "we dare not tempt [our adversaries] with weakness," for it was bound to exacerbate the tensions of the Cold War.[22] Of course, Kennedy was unaware of it in 1961, but Khrushchev's conviction that he could steamroll him partially convinced the Soviet leader he could get away with a more aggressive posture toward the United States, including the placing of missiles in Cuba.

Baker was well aware of what had befallen Kennedy due to the false impression of the president that Khrushchev had taken away from Vienna. And Baker had no intention of repeating that mistake with Shevardnadze. Thus it would seem that Baker cites the Kennedy-Khrushchev summit to explain why he promised little in the way of real help to a Soviet Union that was in dire need of assistance.

Like JFK, Baker also spoke to his Soviet counterpart with just their interpreters present.[23] The secretary of state assured the foreign minister that the United States fully supported *perestroika*. Baker also said that because President Bush had such long-standing relationships with his foreign policy advisers, the administration would be free of the internal squabbling that had plagued the Reagan White House.[24]

Shevardnadze told the secretary of state that with the coming of *perestroika* his nation could be transformed into a "reliable partner" for the West."[25] He also observed that the opening up of Soviet society was so far along that it would be impossible to rescind even had the hardliners in the Kremlin tried to do so.[26]

Baker said that in the future they ought to explore the practical results of the new attitude in the Soviet Union, an exploration that could lead to "concrete actions that serve our mutual interests."[27] He then raised the issues of Soviet arms winding up in Nicaragua, and the Kremlin's refusal to criticize the radical Islamic regime of Iran and Ayatollah Khomeini's issuing of a *fatwa* that called for the killing of writer Salman Rushdie for publishing *The Satanic Verses*, a novel the ayatollah considered an insult to Islam.[28]

This part of the Baker-Shevardnadze conversation followed the predictable script from hundreds of discussions between American and Soviet officials. A pledge to work toward a better understanding between the two countries, with unspecified promises of US help, followed by a spate of criticism of Soviet behavior.

It was the carrot and stick of old, and in retrospect it is clear that it belonged to a different era, but for the moment it was the best the Soviets would get from the Bush administration.

◆ ◆ ◆

James Baker would complain that journalists were making "much of our review of US-Soviet relations," but it was not the press that was growing impatient; it was Gorbachev.[29]

Looking back at the events thirteen years later, Gorbachev recalled, "The lack of freedom was stifling our country. We had a system that could not be improved; it had to be replaced. Our choice was to remain communist and become marginal, or resume marching with history. So we took the risk. It was the right thing to do. I didn't understand why some in the United States couldn't see what was occurring."[30]

The report President Bush had requested was delivered to the Oval Office in March, but it did little to help Gorbachev. In effect, all the report did do was restate the obvious: for instance, the United States should help "make reforms [in the Soviet Union] irreversible," and that "*perestroika* is in [US] interest."[31] It did not lay out an operational plan.[32]

The president was so disappointed by the report that he did not think it necessary to convene the National Security Council for an immediate review of its findings.[33]

NSC adviser Brent Scowcroft agreed with his boss and criticized his underlings for "their lack of imagination about where to take America."[34]

Baker would eventually come to see that the administration had erred "in the way we set up the review."[35] Those in charge were holdovers from the Reagan years; they had both an emotional and intellectual investment in the current policy; and they were being asked to suggest ways in which their approach should be altered.[36] To Baker, it was "pretty much like asking an architect to review his own work."[37] Slight modifications might be made to the overall plan – a small addition here, a smaller deletion there – but the essential design would remain unchanged by a bureaucracy more interested in consensus and the status quo than in bold new strategy and tactics. Consequently, says Baker, what the administration wound up with was "mush."[38]

The reaction of the administration paled beside the disappointment of Gorbachev. The pressure on him to improve the Soviet economy was enormous. At last, after forty years, the Soviet Union had realized that playing the role of paterfamilias to an impoverished tribe of Third World nations was a pricey proposition, and one that had outdistanced their pocketbook. The retreat from Afghanistan had turned the eyes of Soviet citizens inward, and they did not like what they saw – a nation crumbling around them, a nation unable to compete economically with the West. And though Gorbachev may have been celebrated in Europe and the United States, more and more in the Soviet Union he was referred to as a "*boltun*," a chatterbox, a man whose promises far exceeded his ability to deliver.[39]

"Russians were impatient for *perestroika* to work," Gorbachev says, demonstrating his rarely used talent for understatement. "At the beginning, it brought many hardships and humiliations, and I thought the United States would be ready to ease our way. They weren't."[40]

Gorbachev recognized that his problems were rooted in the Soviet past, but he seemed to believe that the White House could, in one fell swoop, bail him out, and perhaps that explains his tendency to shift some of the blame for his situation to the United States.

In April, during a meeting with British prime minister Margaret Thatcher at Number 10 Downing Street, Gorbachev vented his frustrations with what he believed was the administration's foot-dragging on putting together some kind of aid program. Furthermore, the Pentagon had leaked information that the Soviet Union was furnishing Libya with long-range bombers, and the State Department accused the KGB of bugging the US consulate in Leningrad. It was, in Gorbachev's view, a replay of the worst of the Cold War and an approach that refused to recognize the current reality.[41]

He was particularly frustrated because Thatcher had told him that Bush could be counted on to follow the same path as Reagan. Now, Gorbachev wondered, why should there be any delay? After all, significant progress had been made with Reagan, remarkable progress. Why shouldn't it continue? What was stopping it? This current breakdown, he concluded, was "intolerable."[42]

Thatcher felt that Gorbachev was "a different kind of Soviet leader."[43] She went to great lengths to reassure him that the matter would soon be resolved, and in the wake of their discussion, the British prime minister did her best to help resolve it.

She informed Bush about their meeting, a move Gorbachev had obviously been banking on, hoping that Thatcher – no shrinking violet over the years when it came to standing up to the Soviets – would be able to convince the president that Gorbachev was sincere about ending East-West enmity. In her message to the White House, Thatcher said that Gorbachev was deeply troubled by the current state of affairs, and she had to agree with him that it seemed to be taking an unnecessarily long time for the United States to put a plan in place.[44]

The White House came under further pressure from two quarters it had not anticipated: former president Ronald Reagan and Ambassador George Kennan, the distinguished diplomat and Pulitzer Prize-winning historian who was considered the country's foremost Soviet expert and the founding father of the policy of containment.

Reagan, now living in Los Angeles, passed along to friends that he was "uneasy [with the administration's] foreign policy indecisiveness,"[45] and his opinion appeared in a *Washington Post* column written by the longtime political journalist and Reagan watcher Lou Cannon.[46]

Kennan's pronouncement had a more dramatic backdrop. He testified before the Senate Foreign Relations Committee, claiming that "whatever reasons there may once have been for regarding the Soviet Union primarily as a possible, if not probable, military opponent, the time for that sort of thing has clearly passed."[47]

When his testimony was finished, the chamber erupted in applause.[48]

Finally, in May, in a commencement address at Texas A&M University, President Bush announced the course that he wanted to pursue toward the USSR. The president offered no new initiatives, but he did declare that it was "time to move beyond containment to a new policy…that recognizes the full scope of change taking place…in the Soviet Union."[49]

The "full scope" of the changes was so rapid and vast it was difficult to assimilate into the narrative of Cold War history, which partially explains why the Bush administration found itself running in place – in a hurry to do something but not exactly sure what to do.

Political journalism, often critical of Gorbachev himself, was blossoming. For example, the magazine *Ogonyok* saw its subscriptions rise in three years from two hundred thousand to 4.6 million.[50] By spring, the USSR had held its first competitive elections since 1917. Soviet citizens elected 2,250 delegates to the Congress of People's Deputies, which then voted for members to a new Supreme Soviet that would possess true powers to legislate.[51]

Though the process was an improvement over the old Soviet system, it was not quite an exercise in Jeffersonian democracy. The Communist Party had played the most important role in nominating the candidates, and Gorbachev had worked behind the scenes to make certain that his supporters won. In due time, he would go so far as seeing to it that he was selected as president of the Soviet Union, a post with significant power that he had been instrumental in creating.

Nonetheless, the very idea of free elections reverberated through the Soviet republics and satellite countries, energizing separatist movements and nations who were anxious to replace their Communist dictatorships with democratically elected governments.[52]

◆ ◆ ◆

Regardless of how optimistic the Soviets may have been about the future, their present difficulties were hard to escape. Their feelings were summed up in a joke making the rounds and later quoted by *New York Times* columnist, Tom Friedman: Upon being asked to describe the state of his country in a single word, Gorbachev says, "Good." When he is given two words, he replies, "Not good."[53]

And the present reality was certainly "not good." The Soviet economy was splitting apart at the seams. Plumbers and electricians were being remunerated with vodka; tourists learned that cab drivers preferred being paid with foreign cigarettes; and bread, subsidized by the Kremlin, was so worthless it was being used as feed for livestock, while corn went unpicked in the fields.[54]

One evening, when the American writer Gail Sheehy was in Moscow to research her biography of Gorbachev, she went to the dining room of the Intourist Hotel, where her waiter informed her that none of the dishes listed on the dinner menu were available. When Sheehy asked him what had happened, the waiter responded with a "mordant smile," saying, "What happened, happened seventy years ago."[55]

The waiter's observation about the deleterious effects of living under the Soviet system was shared by Gorbachev, who believed that Russians "would have accomplished a great deal," had it not been for "decades of existence under conditions of totalitarianism and the personality cult [which] inevitably resulted in apathy, anemia, loss of initiative, and the extinguishing of social energy."[56]

These were the realities Gorbachev confronted, trying to bring capitalism to a collapsing superpower where citizens who tried to rise above the poverty of their neighbors were hated,[57] and where it could take fifteen or twenty years to build a single factory.[58]

Gorbachev knew that his sole hope for meaningful reform rested on a fast and sizable transfusion of capital, and this goal dictated larger questions of policy. To free up revenues, he had made deep cuts in military expenditures, and trotting the globe he encouraged democracies to invest in ventures with Soviet companies. But his best bet for grabbing an economic lifeline was to try to secure credit from the Export-Import Bank and enter into trade agreements with the United States.

These options were circumscribed by the Jackson-Vanik and Stevenson amendments, both of which resulted from the Kremlin's refusal to grant its citizens the right of free emigration.[59] Therefore, Gorbachev had no choice but to open up the doors of the Soviet Union.

Less than three weeks after the Bush speech at Texas A&M, Soviet foreign minister Shevardnadze was at the Conference on the Human Dimension in Paris, telling the audience that "the new Soviet parliament has before it a number of bills on the freedom of…entry [and] exit from the country.… We are confident that our new laws will reflect the new democratic essence of our socialist society.… The times are changing."[60]

In part, Gorbachev's overtures to Israel also grew out of his desire to win US economic support, and certainly Israel continued to encourage this movement toward rapprochement. Israel had a huge stake in the freedom of Soviet Jewry; the country desperately needed the infusion of citizens as the Arab world, particularly the Palestinians, continued their exploding birth rates.

The Israelis were especially helpful after the earthquake in Armenia. Within a week, their Hercules cargo planes were landing in the capital city of Yerevan, bringing field hospitals, dogs trained to locate bodies underneath rubble, equipment for clearing debris, and doctors and paramedics from the Israel Defense Forces, Hadassah Hospital, and *Magen David Adom*, the Israeli Red Cross.[61] Other supplies – 1,550 cartons of food, clothing, and medicine collected by Israelis – were loaded onto a ship in Ashdod. It was the first vessel flying under the Soviet flag to enter an Israeli port since 1967.[62]

Gorbachev's effort to repair the relationship between Russia and Israel and American Jewry was as rooted in the Russian past as it was in the Russian present. The Soviet leader would have agreed with the observation by historian David Biale that "the movement of Jews into the American political elite marks one of the most radical social transformations…in history."[63] Even so, like many Eastern Europeans, Gorbachev misunderstood and overrated the nature and breadth of this power.[64]

Yes, there had been an intense lobbying effort to pass Jackson-Vanik – an effort spearheaded by Jewish congressional staffers and Jewish establishment and non-establishment organizations. By American standards of grassroots-inspired lawmaking, getting the amendment written and passed was a noteworthy feat. By the standards of the Soviet Union, where the powerlessness of Jews was as common a feature of the landscape as the snow, the passage of Jackson-Vanik must have appeared to be an event as miraculous as the parting of the Red Sea.

To be sure, democracy is its own kind of miracle, but the rights of American citizenship employed by Jews to help create Jackson-Vanik was a far cry from the type of presidential and legislative power Gorbachev would need to alter American foreign policy or save the Soviet Union – if indeed it could have been saved.

This is not to say that Gorbachev was an antisemite. Personally, he despised the record of Soviet antisemitism, considering it another weapon of control wielded by a totalitarian government.[65]

And in October 1991, he would offer moving words about this tragic history during the fifty-year commemoration of the massacre at Babi Yar,[66] admitting what Soviet leaders had refused to admit for a half century – the involvement of Soviet citizens in the massacre and "that Jews were among the first Nazi victims…in our country."[67]

Still, Gorbachev, a descendent of Ukrainian Cossacks, was a child of his homeland, where the noxious fantasies of *The Protocols of the Elders of Zion* had been born, so it is not too long a reach to suggest that at some level, conscious or otherwise, he believed that by improving relations with Israel he would be influencing American Jewry, who would express their gratitude by using all of their mythical powers to convince the Bush administration to extend credits and trade to Moscow.[68]

Whatever collection of motivations set Gorbachev in motion, the result was that beginning in the final months of 1988, as the Cold War slid toward its end, Jewish emigrants began streaming out of the Soviet Union in numbers that had had not been seen in a decade.

In December, 3,652 left, and the following month, 2,796.[69] Based on these numbers, the chairperson of the National Conference of Soviet Jewry, Shoshana Cardin, predicted that perhaps thirty thousand Jews would be allowed to emigrate from the USSR in 1989.[70] Cardin was among the more experienced leaders of the organized American Jewish community with a reputation as an even-tempered realist, so her prediction was considered prudent.

"For the most part," says Cardin, "the organized American Jewish community had more faith in Gorbachev's intentions, and survival, than the incoming administration. And I believed we would see, over a period of years, a manageable increase in the numbers coming out."[71]

Anticipating this wider stream of emigrants, NCSJ appointed Martin Wenick, a career foreign service officer with a background in Eastern European affairs, as its new executive director.[72]

The Solidarity Sunday rally for Soviet Jews in New York, usually a massive demonstration, was cancelled, because, as the coalition chairman, Rabbi Haskel Lookstein, explained, "Innovative programs and a flexible approach are essential in light of Gorbachev's policies of *glasnost* and *perestroika*."[73]

Despite the growing optimism, Shoshana Cardin says, "I never thought Jews would move so fast from around the Soviet Union to apply for visas. Nor did I believe that Gorbachev would see to it that the visas would be forthcoming as quickly as they were."[74]

In 1989, the actual number of emigrants turned out to be 71,217, a staggering total that was dwarfed in 1990 when Jewish emigration from the Soviet Union swelled to 181,759. The next year, 145,005 came out.[75]

With this immense exodus in motion, it almost seemed as if the battle for freedom had been won, the drama was gone, and all that remained were the mundane details of travel arrangements and the nuts and bolts of resettlement.

That would have been a dangerous assumption. As the scholar Henry L. Feingold noted in *The Politics of Rescue*, one of the problems preventing the rescue of Jews from Hitler was that "Jewish philanthropy was not equipped to handle hordes of penniless refugees."[76]

It was a mistake that the American Jewish community vowed not to repeat.

Chapter 12

Dropouts

Twenty-two miles west of Rome, surrounded by wooded hills and the ruins of ancient stone villas, sits the Italian resort town of Ladispoli. In the off-season, through the long gray winter and rainy spring, the population numbers less than twenty thousand.

Then, as the weather turns and the sky clears, all at once it seems the overcast spring gives way to golden summer. The hotels, guesthouses, and apartments fill up with tens of thousands of vacationers. The cafés are busy; the soft, salty air swells with a jubilant glimmer as crowds gather to talk by the central fountain in Piazza Vittoria or descend on the beaches along the Tyrrhenian Sea, where they can swim and relax in the sun and gaze out toward the islands of Corsica, Sardinia, and Sicily with the sparkling blue waters of the Mediterranean beyond.

Ladispoli then is not the sort of place one associates with the hardships of refugees, their loneliness, doubt, and fear. Yet, Italy had long been a way station for refugees. First and foremost, the government was willing to provide a place for them, and Italy was a convenient location and relatively safe from terrorists, unlike some other European countries. In addition, hosting refugees was a good money-making venture, and at first, the refugees could rent inexpensively.[1] Since the 1970s, Soviet Jews had stopped there while waiting to receive their final clearance to enter the United States, Canada, and Australia. The long off-season left many of the resort apartments vacant, and in the autumn of 1988 they were being rented to emigrant families for $400 a month.[2]

At the time, there were approximately six thousand transients in Ladispoli – from Iran, Africa, Eastern Europe, and the Arab world. But two-thirds of these transients were from the USSR, so the language one most frequently heard across the main square of the town was Russian.[3]

Every day men and women would emerge from their cramped quarters to stand in the cold, blowing on their hands and stamping their feet as they gathered around the fountain. They had, at last, escaped from the Soviet Union, and now they had nothing to do but wait for a visa to the United States. So they stood around, with their breath steaming in the cold sea air, chatting about their uncertain future, worried that their journey might stop here or take them back to the harsh places they had fled. The endless waiting and uncertainty turned Ladispoli, in the words of one visiting reporter, into "an overcrowded hive of tension and despair."[4]

History is rarely short of irony, and as Ronald Reagan prepared to leave the White House and George H. W. Bush prepared to move in, the ironic was in full bloom in Ladispoli. It was this irony that spread so much anxiety among the Soviet residents of the town.

Until the fall of 1988, every Soviet Jew who filed a request to enter the United States was granted permission to enter the country as a refugee. This designation gave them financial aid to cover their travel and resettlement. Yet beginning in September, the US Justice Department's Immigration and Naturalization Service began to withhold this official status from Jews who had left the USSR and rejected their applications for admission to the United States.[5]

During the last three months of the year, 179 Soviet Jews had been denied this special status. Additionally, there were 345 more awaiting a final word from the INS,[6] and these people were soon dubbed "delayniks."[7]

Admittedly, these were not large numbers. Nonetheless, after waiting years, and in some cases, decades; after undergoing government harassment, job loss, and all manner of deprivations great and small, Soviet emigrants in Ladispoli were understandably perplexed by the change. And it wasn't just the emigrants who were flabbergasted by this turn of events.

The organized American Jewish community was also shocked. After having struggled so tirelessly to get Jews out of the Soviet Union for the last twenty years – after wending their way through the dangerous intricacies of the Cold War and working the narrow margins of cooperation between the superpowers, it seemed that a bureaucratic shuffle was about to neutralize all of their efforts.

The community was especially appalled by the fact that the sudden change negated the accomplishment of the Helsinki Final Act, which made allowances for the reunification of families and had provided a basis for substantial immigration.[8]

Pamela Cohen, president of the Union of Councils for Soviet Jews, remarked that "the recent INS policy of quizzing every Soviet Jew to prove a history of persecution and denying some Jews refugee status on that basis – repudiates everything our country has stood for since Helsinki."[9]

In keeping with the Refugee Act of 1980, the State Department was tasked with offering guidance to the INS on the current situation inside the refugee's country. Unquestionably, Mikhail Gorbachev had relaxed restrictions on Jews, and perhaps this explained why the INS, at the urging of the State Department, no longer considered Soviet Jews qualified to be classified as individuals fleeing political oppression.

During his confirmation hearing, Secretary of State Baker had pointed out that the United States had more refugees waiting in line than it could fund, and it was shortly afterwards that the consular office at the US embassy in Rome began turning down the visa applications of Soviet Jews as if they were holding back a wave of KGB agents. In January 1989, 11 percent of the applications were rejected; the next month, 19 percent; and in March the number jumped to 36 percent.

With over four thousand new rejections, the problems in Ladispoli, according to Congressman Barney Frank, became "appalling." At the beginning of the year, five thousand people had been waiting; by summer it was sixteen thousand.[10]

Making the whole situation more confusing and worrisome was the chorus of official doublespeak echoing inside the hallways of Washington. While both the State Department and the Justice Department acknowledged that visas had been denied a number of Soviet Jews who had been unable to prove their "well-founded fear of persecution," the government continued to deny that there had been any change in US policy.[11]

Of course, what had changed was the message emanating from the

Kremlin. Still, the question remained to what degree the social structure of the Soviet Union had actually been altered. After all, Gorbachev could issue any kind of decrees he wanted, but their efficacy depended on them being carried out by a bureaucracy – and accepted by a populace – whose antisemitism dated back to the dark and bloody days of the tsars.

For the Kremlin, legalizing the teaching of Hebrew and establishing a Jewish cultural center in Moscow might represent a leap forward, but many Soviet Jews and Americans who advocated on their behalf were skeptical about the power of a fast makeover to reverse the longtime historical facts on the ground. Already the increase in freedom of speech allowed by Gorbachev had resulted in presses churning out new antisemitic publications, and vandals, giving their freedom of expression full reign, had taken to desecrating the headstones in Jewish cemeteries.[12]

As David Waksberg, executive director of the Bay Area Council for Soviet Jews in San Francisco, observed, "Despite palpable improvements in immigration and the ability to travel back and forth, and some improvements that came with *glasnost*, the fundamental basis of fear on the part of the Jews in the Soviet Union has not changed."[13]

This was the view of Alexander Rabichev, a thirty-four-year-old dentist who had left the Soviet Union for the limbo of Ladispoli. Talking to a reporter in his slightly accented English, Rabichev said, "There is no difference between us and those who were accepted [into the United States]. To be a Jew in Russia is to be discriminated against. Finding a job was very difficult. To enter the institute there meant many, many problems because we are Jewish. The Americans now tell us, OK, we are restricted, but maybe not at a level that qualifies us as refugees. Where is that level? What is the criterion? Maybe it would be better if I come without an eye or an arm?"[14]

Dr. Rabichev's frustration – and the frustration of the other emigrants in Ladispoli – was understandable, but what was holding them fast in that seaside town outside Rome was not a coterie of uncooperative INS agents, but an intricate web of history, politics, funding, and philosophy. Thus, freeing the emigrants from these complexities was no small task.

Let's start with the history. The Soviet Jewry movement had finally met with startling success, and this was becoming apparent in December

1988. That month, 3,652 Jews departed from the Soviet Union, the most that had left in a single month since 1979.[15]

For 1988, though, Congress and the administration had put together a program that only allowed 24,500 refugees from Eastern Europe and the Soviet Union into the United States, with space reserved for just sixteen thousand Soviets, including Jews, Armenians, Pentecostals, and ethnic Germans.[16]

Congress was treated to a chorus of protests about these limited numbers from organized American Jewry and several grassroots groups, and on December 13, the 160 members of the Congressional Human Rights Caucus accused the Reagan administration of providing the Soviet Union with "an undeserved public relations victory by permitting them to claim that they are releasing more Soviet Jews than the United States is willing to receive."[17]

In response to the protests, the White House decided to make space for seven thousand more Armenian and Jewish refugees from the Soviet Union in the coming fiscal year. The Reagan administration found the extra room through a standard bureaucratic maneuver – robbing Peter to pay Paul. The new slots were appropriated from Southeast Asia and the Near East, which sparked a round of protests from Asian Americans. As if to demonstrate how emotionally complex this issue had become, representatives from organized American Jewry, perhaps sympathetic to the Asian plight, or feeling guilty because the Asians' loss had been their gain, also protested the appropriated slots.[18]

Had the stream of emigration continued at two thousand per month, finding a place for twenty-four thousand Soviet immigrants a year would have been challenging, but the US government and the American Jewish community would have somehow managed it.

But twenty-four thousand Soviet Jews would not have represented a stream; in reality, they were a trickle. The USSR contained the largest Jewish population outside the United States and Israel – somewhere between 2 million and 2.5 million Jews – and four hundred thousand of them had started the lengthy process of securing exit permits.[19] Even more disconcerting, as one refusenik noted, was that "when people see others leaving, they decide to try themselves."[20] Estimates put the number of

Soviet Jews who eventually hoped to emigrate at one million.[21] It was a mind-boggling number of people to move and resettle, and someone had to pay for it.

The US Committee on Refugees estimated that in total over one hundred thousand refugees would come to the United States during 1989; however, the law allowed no more than ninety-four thousand to receive the formal designation of refugee, which entitled newcomers to a host of services, such as housing subsidies and English lessons. The first year of their arrival these services cost taxpayers $2,000 per refugee, with additional funding being allocated for the ensuing years.[22]

Since the US budget was hard-pressed to come up with more money, the Jewish community saw that it would have to raise the funds. But they were already stretched to the limit by the émigrés. Back in 1987, the American Joint Distribution Committee, which functioned as "the overseas arm of the American Jewish community," helping Jews around the world who were in distress,[23] had only had to pay out $1 million to support the Jews leaving the USSR. The following year, the JDC's costs escalated to $12 million. In 1989, the estimate for moving and absorbing Soviet Jews surpassed $142 million.[24]

In December, seeking help in the waning moments of the Reagan administration, Shoshana Cardin, chairwoman of the National Conference on Soviet Jewry, took a delegation to talk to Secretary of State Shultz. During the thirty-minute meeting, Cardin explained that the crisis had developed because Jews were leaving the Soviet Union faster than they could be funded. The group also told Shultz how concerned they were that the Justice Department, through their INS representatives in Rome, was using a more exclusive application of the term "refugee," thereby denying Soviet Jews entry into the United States.[25]

Shultz assured the gathering that "those who are refugees should be able to leave and should be able to come here," and that "the doors to the US are open and will always remain open."[26]

Despite the vocal support, it was unclear exactly what Shultz, with only a month left at Foggy Bottom, could do. The group moved on to a meeting with Richard Schifter, assistant secretary of state for human rights and humanitarian affairs. Schifter also said that he would try to help, but again it didn't appear much could be done, especially by an outgoing administration when the capital was emptying out for the Christmas season.[27]

But that didn't stop the administration from trying. Two days later, at the request of Secretary Shultz, Attorney General Dick Thornburgh announced what he described as an "interim measure."[28] He pledged to extend his parole authority to two thousand Soviet émigrés a month, and all of the other émigrés in Ladispoli who had been denied refugee status.[29]

Parole status is the poor cousin of refugee status. While refugees can secure federal monies for travel, housing, and health insurance, and can apply for citizenship, parolees must have an affidavit of support from a US sponsor that promises the individual will not become a dependent of the welfare system.[30] Not only are parolees forbidden to receive public funds, they can't become citizens unless they marry a US citizen. Nor can they bring in their families from outside the United States, and they can be subject to deportation at the whim of the government. About the sole right parolees do have is to work.[31]

The humanitarian gesture was a stopgap measure, and the organized American Jewish community had a mixed reaction to the offer.

The National Conference on Soviet Jewry, focused on trying to open the doors wider for immigrants and knowing that they would need the help of another incoming Republican administration to do it, chose not to press the issue.[32]

However, Micah Naftalin, national director of the Union of Councils for Soviet Jews, deemed the AG's announcement a "positive signal that our concerns are being addressed," but characterized the response as "inadequate."[33]

Karl Zukerman, executive vice president of the Hebrew Immigrant Aid Society, took it a step further. He said that his organization had "advised Jews denied refugee status not to seek the parole authority until HIAS can appeal each case to the INS."[34]

Mark Talisman, who by now had moved on from his job with Rep. Charles Vanik to serve as the director of the Washington office of the Council of Jewish Federations, told the *Washington Post* that "the distinction on approach to citizenship [is] troubling."[35]

Talisman, as the CJF lobbyist, was in a position to discuss solutions on

Capitol Hill. Representative Charles E. Schumer, a Democrat from New York and a member of the House Judiciary subcommittee on immigration, refugees, and international law, felt that parole status was tantamount to abandoning the parolees and leaving them to linger in open-ended and hopeless "limbo."[36]

Deeply dissatisfied with Thornburgh's announcement, Schumer sent a letter to Secretary Shultz, suggesting that the "modifications that affect such sensitive issues as status should be brought to the attention of Congress and not implemented through unilateral action."[37]

Schumer had strong bipartisan support for his letter, while a Democratic senator from New Jersey and former chairman of the United Jewish Appeal, Frank R. Lautenberg, was circulating a similar letter among his colleagues in the Senate.[38]

As it was, the American Jewish community paid half the cost of resettlement for Soviet refugees, but they would have to assume the entire cost of resettling parolees.[39] And all signs pointed to the inescapable conclusion that it was going to get even more expensive. So the United Jewish Appeal began planning "Passage to Freedom," a special drive to raise $75 million for resettlement.[40]

This was a highly controversial decision by the UJA. As a rule, the organization, in concert with the local Jewish federations across the country, raises money for Israeli needs and turns the funds over to the American Joint Distribution Committee, Hebrew Immigrant Aid Society, and the Jewish Agency for Israel, a nongovernmental Israeli institution that represents the partnership between Jews in the diaspora and Israel.[41]

Historically, the UJA has geared most of its efforts toward raising money for those who wanted to come or had already arrived in Israel. Now, they were putting together a campaign that would help Jews who had recently entered or were planning to enter the United States.[42]

In January, as Bush was settling into the Oval Office, fifty-one senators signed and sent a letter to Secretary of State Baker and Attorney General Thornburgh. The senators wanted the administration to revive the past US policy of bestowing refugee status on any Soviet Jew who wanted it. Their reasoning was that the new freedoms in the Soviet Union had awakened the old beast of antisemitism.[43]

The letter did little to change the position of the White House. In April, Secretary of State Baker told Congress that he fully supported the selective designation of refugee status for Soviet Jews and the administration would not pressure the Justice Department to change its position.[44]

However, the administration would try to assist by making more room and money available for Soviet emigrants. In testimony before the House Foreign Affairs Subcommittee on International Operations, Baker said that in the next fiscal year the Bush administration would seek to raise its refugee quota to 43,500.[45] The administration would also ask Congress for an additional $85 million in funding.[46]

These arrangements became necessary not only because the Soviet Union had finally opened up her doors, but because so many of the emigrants had become what the Israelis were calling *noshrim* (dropouts).

In 1988, when 19,286 Jews left the Soviet Union, they landed in Vienna. Disembarking from their planes, they were met by representatives from Israel, who asked if they would like to board another flight, this one for Tel Aviv. It was a logical question to ask, since Israel was listed as the destination on their Soviet exit visas. Yet only 7 percent answered that they wished to go to Israel. The others, the *noshrim*, replied that they wanted to come to America.[47]

Within a week of declaring that they had decided to switch their final destination from Israel to the United States, the dropouts received their new paperwork and were taken by train to Ladispoli to join the other Soviet Jews hoping to become Americans.[48]

In mid-February 1989, the UJA's Morton Kornreich, and Sylvia Hassenfeld, president of the American Joint Distribution Committee, visited the seven thousand Soviet Jewish émigrés waiting in Ladispoli, hoping to find a way to slow the dropout rate. During a Sabbath meeting at the transit center with seven hundred emigrants who had applied for visas to the United States, Canada, and Australia, Kornreich said that his grandparents had come to America in 1860 "because there was no other choice, but today they could have gone to Israel."[49] Kornreich added that Soviet emigrants had "exaggerated notions of how life was in the US and how it was in Israel."[50]

That weekend, Kornreich and Hassenfeld flew to Israel for meetings at the Jewish Agency.[51] When the dropout problem was raised, it was suggested that the agency send people from their Immigration Department to Ladispoli to convince the *noshrim* to come to Israel.[52]

Some in the department were banking on the fact that once the funds dried up for the *noshrim* and they no longer entertained any hope of reaching the United States, they would be more open to becoming Israelis.

Yet others at the agency were concerned that if they waited that long, the dropouts would grow angry and bitter and view an agency representative in Italy as a "vulture that has come to pick over the remnants of the *noshrim*."[53]

The Jewish Agency dispatched Jonathan Davis, a member of its Immigration Department, to Italy, where he took the time to question the dropouts on an individual basis, trying to discover why they refused to come to Israel. Although Davis did convince four hundred of the *noshrim* to change their minds, his report to the Jewish Agency was dispiriting.[54]

Davis told the Agency Board of Governors that "Jews at Ladispoli had a basically negative attitude towards Israel and expressed this in terms of tremendous fears and stereotypes. They feared army service, terrorism, theocracy, and rampant unemployment."[55]

Davis tended to skip over some of the attractiveness of the United States, particularly to immigrants with skills, professionals, and academics.[56] Potential immigrants to Israel would have to be concerned about their safety because of the Intifada, which had begun in December 1987 with children throwing stones and soon included well-organized fighters attacking Israeli soldiers and civilians with hand grenades and automatic weapons.

◆ ◆ ◆

On the surface, it would appear that all of the passion tied to the exodus from the Soviet Union had come to revolve around the mundane concerns of government and philanthropic bodies – the allocation of and competition for financial resources.

Yet this would be a gross misreading of the events. In reality, the fierce debate over where the Soviet Jews should resettle was a collision of culture and philosophy between the majority of Jews in the United States and the

Israelis, and it represented the deepest ideological split, with the highest stakes, in world Jewry since the establishment of Israel in 1948.

Martin S. Kraar, who at the time was the executive vice president of the Council of Jewish Federations, illustrates the American view: "The position that the majority of us took was that the Soviet Jews were entitled to decide where they wanted to live. We may have preferred that they go to Israel, but we were not going to rescue them from an oppressive society, bring them into a free one, and then make their first personal decision for them. Nor once they entered the United States were we going to allow them to become destitute. Our mandate is to help Jews and so our services were made available to them."[57]

This view was shared by the majority of American Jewry, and it was identical to the position of the US government. George Shultz, for example, arguably the secretary of state who did the most to help Jews leave the Soviet Union, never pursued their freedom with the goal of seeing them become Israeli citizens.

Shultz recalled, "I was interested in getting [the Jews] out. I was interested in them going wherever they wanted to go. If they wanted to go to Israel, that was great, Israel needed them. If not, that was fine. It was up to them, not up to us, to decide."[58]

Opposed to this stance was the Israeli perspective. Mendel Kaplan, a South African by birth, who resided in Israel part of each year and served as the chairman of the Jewish Agency Board of Governors, says that Israelis "do not believe in Soviet Jews going to America – in moving them from one diaspora to another. To us, the freedom of choice that American Jews spoke about was a negation of Jewish leadership.... The Soviet Jews were being referred to as refugees, which means that the person is politically persecuted and has nowhere else to go. But every Jew in the world does have a place: Israel. The word 'refugee' is offensive to us because Israel is their home."[59]

In large measure, these divergent viewpoints were rooted in the differing reaction to the central event of Jewish life in the twentieth century: the Holocaust.

For Israelis, the response to this horror was the other momentous event of Jewish existence in that war-torn century: the founding of Israel and a commitment to handling their own self-defense. And in the Soviet Jews, Israel saw that their position with regard to the Arabs would be strengthened, thereby contributing to their long-term security.

The American Jewish community at large, and especially the philanthropic self-help organizations that had expanded exponentially after the Second World War, have always been haunted by their inability to rescue the six million. To these Jews, the establishment of the Jewish state was important, but rescuing Jews in danger superseded it, and so the exact nuts and bolts of the action paled beside the rescue itself.

So, for the moment, the debate went on, and dropouts piled up in Italy.

One possible fix for the problem was the instituting of direct flights between the Soviet Union and Israel. During the early winter of 1989, this looked like a possibility. In Paris, Soviet foreign minister Eduard Shevardnadze met with Moshe Arens, the Israeli foreign minister. From such a high-level meeting it seemed clear that in all likelihood the two countries would reestablish the consular relationship that had been severed after the 1967 Six-Day War. This was good news for Israelis, but some of the dropouts currently residing in Ladispoli felt that such a new beginning would work against them, since once relations between the two governments were on a secure footing, Israel would be able to arrange for Soviet Jews to be flown straight to Tel Aviv. And the dropouts who still harbored dreams of coming to America would lose their refugee status and would have to wait in line with everyone else who wanted to relocate to the United States.[60]

◆ ◆ ◆

On February 23, 1989, Arens and Shevardnadze agreed to upgrade Soviet-Israeli relations to consular status, allowing them to focus on the chief issue between the two states: emigration. Soon after this upgrade in relations, articles began to appear in the Soviet press advocating the reestablishment of full diplomatic relations with Israel. Even Soviet officials urged the resumption of ties.

The news was greeted with less than good cheer in the Arab world. Yasser Arafat had traveled to Moscow to speak with Gorbachev, who asked his advisers what point there was to meeting with the PLO leader.

Although the Palestinian Liberation Organization had its roots in intra-Arab politics, it was nurtured by the Cold War. Now that the conflict was ending, the PLO was of little use to the Kremlin. Arafat, who believed that the Soviet Jews pouring into Israel was "more ominous for the Arabs" than the founding of the Jewish state,[61] had most likely come to complain to Gorbachev, but according to Anatoly Chernyaev, Gorbachev's political adviser, the talk between his boss and Arafat "didn't really yield any results," and Gorbachev warned Arafat against escalating his uprising.[62]

Arab carping about the new immigrants reached a fever pitch once Gorbachev came to power, but the Soviet Union was casting about for new friends in the West, where the freedom to emigrate was considered a hallmark of a genuinely free society.

The leadership of the PFLP in Damascus criticized the Soviet move and asked the Kremlin to rethink its policy, since it allegedly ran counter to the interests of Palestinians.[63] Rifat Makgub, speaker of Egypt's People's Assembly, picked up the same theme in a meeting with Andrei Gromyko, who by then was occupying the largely ceremonial post of Soviet president. Makgub charged that the Russian Jews moving into the West Bank and Gaza were creating a humanitarian crisis by crowding out Palestinians.[64]

This strategy was employed because, in the words of one Israeli official, Arab leaders had finally come to understand that for people in the West, "being against immigration was like being against motherhood or apple pie. [So] they argued against [immigration into Israel], because then it would create a de facto situation in the territories and imperil the peace process."[65]

Makgub's charges popped up in the Soviet media, perhaps passed along by hardliners who wanted Gorbachev to slow his reforms.[66] Indeed, Gorbachev did threaten to curb emigration unless the Israeli government assured him that the immigrants would be required to reside within the pre-1967 borders. Israel countered that her policy was not to move immigrants around the country as though they were chess pieces, but encouraged the newcomers to make their own decisions about where they should live.[67]

On numerous occasions, Prime Minister Yitzhak Shamir, though an avid and vocal advocate of settling Jews in Judea, Samaria, and Gaza, claimed that he wasn't using the émigrés to populate the territories. His claim was borne out by statistics. In 1989, 12,887 immigrants came to Israel, and only 138 chose to go to the territories.[68]

Gorbachev must have been satisfied with the response, for emigration went on. And truthfully, it is not altogether certain that he would have acted on his threats, because emigration was intimately entwined with his vision of progress for the Soviet people.

During an interview in 2002, Gorbachev recalled his thinking in the late 1980s: "You have to look at our change in the law permitting emigration in terms of *perestroika*. I didn't believe you could have one without the other. In fact, I was convinced you couldn't have *perestroika* without free emigration. Not just for Jews but for everyone, all of the dissidents. It was one moment, and I decided. It was time to do it. It was right. It was the moral thing to do. Still, I didn't want the Jews to go. I went on television and asked them to stay. We needed their contribution. Yes, many did leave. But many stayed as well."[69]

Gorbachev was not alone in his assistance to the émigrés. The Soviet satellite countries of Eastern Europe, which for the most part adhered to the anti-emigration policies delineated by the Kremlin, were now free to alter their position. This was not a matter of altruism or a sudden uncontrollable passion for emigrants or Israel. After decades of Communist rule, the economies of the Eastern bloc were starved for foreign currency. If they allowed the Israelis to establish transit points inside their countries, then they were paid with money that could be used to purchase goods and services on the world market.[70]

During the spring of 1989, these transit points were crucial because no direct flights existed between Moscow and Tel Aviv. It seemed that Gorbachev was not quite prepared to permit them. Possibly this was his way of conceding something to his hardliners and the Arabs. He could please the West with his newly opened exit doors, yet he was still able to tell his right-wing opposition inside the Kremlin and his former patrons that he was not stocking Israel with Soviet Jews.[71] It was a minor concession, a political sleight of hand, and ultimately didn't prevent the influx of Soviet émigrés into Israel.

Still, the establishment of direct flights would have made it far easier for the American Jewish community and Israel to solve the dropout problem.

◆ ◆ ◆

In April, the conflict about the ultimate destination of Soviet Jewry erupted over "Passage to Freedom," the special $75-million fundraising campaign set up by the United Jewish Appeal.

Bernice Tannenbaum, head of the American Section of the World Zionist Organization, called the campaign "ill conceived," and speculated that "if there were a proposal to scrap the whole thing, I might have to go along with it."[72]

Her reasoning centered around her fear that Soviet Jewish "resettlement in Israel will end up getting [nothing] from the campaign. I also believe it is fundamentally out of character for the UJA to launch a campaign to resettle Russian Jews in the US. I think it was a mistaken idea."[73]

Indicative of how vehemently the sides disagreed with each other were the comments made by Simcha Dinitz, Israel's former ambassador to Washington and a very popular man both inside and outside the Beltway. Dinitz was now serving as the chairman of the Jewish Agency for Israel, which oversaw immigration, and he was so angered by "Passage to Freedom" that he publicly threatened the UJA, saying that if the organization didn't turn over half the money raised to the JAFI for settling Jews in Israel, then he would disassociate the agency from the campaign.[74]

These were harsh words from Dinitz, and they concerned the UJA chairman, Morton Kornreich, who promised that Israel would receive "a meaningful contribution."[75]

His promise was too vague for those who wanted the Soviet Jews in Israel. Furthermore, since so much additional money was needed to sustain the Jews flooding into Ladispoli to wait for US visas, it was unlikely that significant funding would remain for Israel.[76]

Zelig Chinitz, who for over forty years was intricately involved in Israel-diaspora relations, and wrote a history of the reconstituted Jewish Agency for Israel, saw the UJA-JAFI conflict as a replay of an old battle.

"American fund-raisers have raised enormous amounts of money based on the drama of Israel," says Chinitz. "For example, during the Six-Day War, a special emergency fund was established, which raised hundreds of millions of dollars in donations and bond sales. And so a fellow who normally gave a few thousand dollars a year to his local federation most likely increased his gift to $10,000. After the crisis passed, however, his gift often remained higher than his original few thousand dollars, but Israel wouldn't get any of that money. It would be kept in the United States to meet local needs – retirement homes, for instance, or a new community center. And the Israelis understandably resented it."[77]

To some degree, this ongoing battle accounted for the view on the resettlement of Soviet Jews expressed by Mendel Kaplan, who at the time was chairing the Jewish Agency Board of Governors.

"I believe that Jews should have a right to move anywhere they want," Kaplan said. "But they should not use public Jewish funds to do it."[78]

Except the lion's share of these "public" funds was raised by American Jewry, who felt that they had a right to have their opinion considered on how the money should be spent. And this desire to be heard, combined with their view that the most important goal was simply to get Jews out of the USSR regardless of where they settled, fed an already ferocious debate in which each side accused the other of short-sightedness, malfeasance, and perhaps worst of all, betraying the memory of the six million.

The human cost of this debate backed up at government offices in the Soviet Union, where those seeking exit permits formed long, hopeless lines, and at European transit stations, which served as dismal reminders of the displaced persons camps that had sprouted up across Europe after allied forces had liberated the concentration camps.

Ironically, a series of events in April and May that were unrelated to the fate of Soviet Jewry underscored just how destructive the arguments were becoming and suggested, at least for some American Jews involved in relief and rescue efforts, a possible outcome too horrible to contemplate.

In China, former Communist Party general secretary Hu Yaobang suffered a fatal heart attack. Hu had been forced out of his position in 1987 because of his alleged sympathies with student demands for democratic reform and the eradicating of official corruption. Now, two years later, students in Beijing began crowding into Tiananmen Square to honor Hu and renew their call for reform.[79]

By the day of Hu's memorial service in the Great Hall of the People, one hundred thousand students had gathered in the square, demanding that the government meet with their representatives. China's senior leader, Deng Xiaoping, and Premier Li Peng refused, and the students responded by boycotting classes and continuing their public dissent.[80]

The first step Chinese leaders took to stem the spreading protest was in keeping with the tried and true tradition of the regime: they denied it was occurring. The Communist Party newspaper, *People's Daily*, claimed in an editorial that the human sea in Tiananmen Square was due to a "handful of plotters" intent on destroying the Communist Party and the socialist system.[81]

Angered by the editorial and disregarding warnings that the government might resort to violence to break up the protests, students from over forty universities descended on Beijing. By mid-May, hundreds of students were participating in a hunger strike at the square. A dozen of China's most renowned intellectuals beseeched them to end their strike and asked the government to recognize the movement for what it was – a patriotic cry to live in freedom. By then, a number of students had grown sick from lack of food and had to receive intravenous nourishment. Yet neither the students nor China's leaders gave any ground, and hostility between the two camps escalated.[82]

It was at this incendiary moment that Mikhail Gorbachev stepped off his plane for the first meeting between Soviet and Chinese leadership since 1959.[83] A twenty-one-gun salute greeted him at the airport, and as the gunfire echoed through the spring sky, people from every segment of China's society were flooding into Tiananmen Square to support the students.[84] Within twenty-four hours the size of the crowd was estimated at 250,000. And since reporters from all over the globe had come to Beijing to record the historic Soviet-Sino meeting, the protestors took the opportunity to press their case.

One symbol they used was a hastily built, ten-meter-high statue. Students from the Central Academy of Fine Arts had constructed it from Styrofoam and papier-mâché, modeling their work on the Statue of Liberty and christening it the Goddess of Democracy. She stood gazing at the northern edge of the square, where a huge photograph of Mao brooded over the Gate of Heavenly Peace. As people massed around the Goddess, banners in Chinese, English, and Russian were raised, proclaiming,

"Democracy Is Our Common Dream.... In the Soviet Union They Have Gorbachev. In China, We Have Whom?"[85]

Gorbachev spent three days talking to Chinese leaders about a variety of issues – force reductions in Asia was high on the list, as was his desire for Communist countries to begin forging economic relationships with non-Communist nations. At bottom, his message was that he hoped the current leadership would move ahead with their own version of *glasnost* and *perestroika*.[86]

At a press conference, when Gorbachev was asked his opinion of the demonstrations, he replied, "I am convinced that we are participating in a very serious turning point in the development of world socialism.... These processes are painful, but they are necessary."[87]

After gracing China with his vision of progressivism, Gorbachev went home, and, in his wake, the world got a glimpse of what happens when a historically repressive government decides that for now reform has no place on its agenda.

On May 20, martial law was declared in Beijing, but this did not intimidate the demonstrators. They remained in the square for the next two weeks, bolstered by widespread support from the citizenry, who built makeshift roadblocks to slow down troops from the People's Liberation Army as they moved into the city with tanks and armored personnel carriers.

Finally, on June 4, the government ordered their soldiers to remove the protestors from Tiananmen Square. The troops attacked. They destroyed the Goddess of Democracy and fired on the protestors with automatic weapons, killing hundreds of them and dragging others beyond the international eyes of news cameras, where they were summarily executed. The crackdown came to be symbolized by a photograph of a single protestor blocking the path of a tank column. *Time* magazine would call him "the unknown rebel," eventually placing him on their list of the 100 Most Influential People of the 20th Century and saying that "with a single act of defiance, a lone Chinese hero revived the world's image of courage.[88]

Despite the drama of the image, for some American Jews the massacre in Beijing confirmed their private nightmares. If they had been wondering what tragedy might be in store for Soviet Jewry if Gorbachev were unseated by Kremlin hardliners, all they had to do was fix their eyes on Tiananmen Square.

One person who had been watching the news was Detroit industrialist and philanthropist Max Fisher, and he reached an inescapable conclusion: the bickering among world Jewry could easily lead to another catastrophe. The fate of the Soviet Jews had to be settled now.

◆ ◆ ◆

By the spring of 1989, as Fisher approached his eighty-first birthday, he was widely considered to be the elder statesman of American Jewry. His long history as a leader of Jewish communal organizations, combined with his philanthropic work inside Israel and his service to every Republican president since Richard Nixon, had earned him a unique spot in American political life.

As a rule, Fisher's importance to a president increased whenever there was tension in the relationship between Washington and Jerusalem, and at the moment, the Bush administration was at odds with Israeli prime minister Yitzhak Shamir. The tension had its roots in Shamir's resistance to negotiating peace with PLO representatives selected by Yasser Arafat, and Shamir's reluctance to halt settlement activity.[89] The process was further complicated by the fact that the president and Shamir appeared to have a personality conflict. By inclination, Bush was a listener, and Shamir, a talker; their phone calls often became wide-ranging monologues rather than focused, give-and-take conversations.[90]

In one respect, though, the president and prime minister had more in common than generally assumed. Both were instinctive and intellectual conservatives, slow to crawl out on a limb. So, in reality, they were at loggerheads not over their approach, but because of their differing views of what would be in their respective nations' best interest. Bush wanted to reduce the heat in the Middle East. This required that Israel talk directly to the Palestinians and halt their controversial policy of settlement expansion.

On the other hand, Shamir, seeing no genuine partner for peace among the Palestinian leadership, wanted to preserve the status quo, for as bad as things were they could always be worse. Therefore, Shamir would not stage meaningless discussions with Arafat stand-ins, nor would he relinquish what Israelis perceived as their greatest trump card in negotiations: land.

When one of the prime minister's aides suggested to him that one day Israel would have to enter into a serious dialogue with Palestinians, Shamir replied, "Yes, but what's the hurry?"[91]

Fisher had a good relationship with Shamir – so good, in fact, that Dennis Ross, the chief Middle-East negotiator for Presidents George H. W. Bush and Bill Clinton, used Fisher as a diplomatic back channel to the Israeli prime minister since, as Ross recalled in his memoir, *The Missing Peace*, Fisher was "someone [the prime minister] trusted" and because "Max was discreet and spoke nearly every Saturday to Shamir."[92]

During those phone conversations Fisher tried to explain to Shamir why the administration needed him to show some flexibility and why it was in his best interest to do so. He also assured him that Israel was not alone and would not be abandoned by the United States. Furthermore, as Fisher wrote in his notes of one discussion, he emphasized that Israel "could only make peace with the help of the U.S."[93]

Beyond the immediate conflicts between Washington and Jerusalem, Shamir was interested in where the Jews coming out of the Soviet Union would go. Shamir recognized how crucial the influx of Soviet immigrants was to long-term Israeli security, and this gave him a large incentive to be more accommodating with requests from the White House, since if Soviet Jewry was steered to Israel, the Israeli government would be faced with absorbing the equivalent of one-fifth of its population in a very compressed span of time. To do this with any moderate chance of succeeding they would need help from the United States in the form of substantial loan guarantees.[94]

Thus, although the prime minister and his government had been ardent in their support of expanding settlements in the West Bank and Gaza, Shamir put out a number of statements claiming that as a matter of official policy immigrants would not be sent to these areas.[95]

These statements, Fisher believed, might reassure the Bush administration, but they would do little to heal the rift within world Jewry, which remained hopelessly divided on the issue.[96]

The prime minister urged Fisher to see what could be done to help, but the truth was that had Fisher known what to do, he would have started doing it during the Reagan administration or soon after Bush took office.

His natural inclination was to seek some form of common ground and then go about the painstaking process of leading people there, scheduling and attending meetings around the country and in Israel, making phone calls, persuading Jewish communal leadership that his plan would be the best way to work out the situation. At heart, Fisher was a pragmatist – after all, wasn't politics the often-disappointing art of the possible? – and he had an extensive record of being able to build a consensus where none had previously existed. This didn't mean that he always got his way – far from it: the Jackson-Vanik amendment had passed, much to his displeasure.

However, where was the common ground in the argument over the ultimate destination of Soviet Jews? Most of them wanted to come to the United States, and if something wasn't done to move them along they would continue to back up at the transit centers at an enormous cost to the communal groups, using up money that would be better spent on resettlement.

Fisher's position on resettlement was well known within organized American Jewry, and to the US and Israeli governments. Beginning in the late 1960s he had repeatedly tried to convince leaders of Jewish federations to prevent the majority of Soviet emigrants from seeking American citizenship, which would force the potential dropouts to go to Israel.

This was the hope of every Israeli prime minister, whether they leaned right or left, and so over the years in meetings between Israeli government officials and American Jewish communal leaders this subject frequently led to an overwrought debate.[97]

During the course of these discussions, which began in the early 1970s and lasted until 1980, when the Kremlin cut off emigration, Fisher had been unable to impose his views, and by the late spring of 1989, with the debate reaching a fevered pitch, it would have been unthinkable.[98]

Still, he wondered, what were his options?

He discussed the possibilities with Mark Talisman, the director of the Council of Jewish Federations' Washington action office. Talisman did not have a specific approach in mind, but there was no question that the problem had to be solved, and sooner rather than later. Talisman had recently returned from Ladispoli and told Fisher in detail about the Soviet refugees he had spoken to who were stuck in the pipeline.

They were, said Talisman, people without a country and people quickly losing hope. The situation, said Talisman, was unconscionable. It was a humanitarian and financial disaster. In reality, Talisman observed, by paying for the Soviet Jews to remain in limbo, Jewish communal organizations were funding a disaster they hoped to avoid.

What could be done about all of this was unclear, but Fisher and Talisman agreed that the American Jewish community was emotionally incapable of working it out.

Talisman suggested that perhaps Congress and the State Department could help, since the crisis would ultimately become a political problem for the administration.

Perhaps, Fisher said, though government wasn't notable for its speed, and time was of the essence. Fisher had recently been to Washington to talk with the president and secretary of state about their latest Middle East peace initiative, and the situation in the Soviet Union had come up. The latest intelligence indicated that Gorbachev was meeting with strong opposition, and if he failed and the Kremlin was recaptured by hardliners, there was the chance for the Soviet rendition of Tiananmen Square and the halting of emigration. Meantime, the Jewish organizations would still be arguing over where the Soviet Jews belonged.

Fisher was disinclined to make unilateral decisions. After all, the art of compromise dictated that you get as many people as possible to accept the position and use the power of the group to push the agenda. However, another, less pleasant aspect of the pragmatic approach was the willingness to admit that occasionally it was not possible to reach a compromise on an issue – and Fisher was convinced that the issue of resettlement was one of those occasions.[99]

While Talisman contacted members of Congress, Fisher called an old friend, Deputy Secretary of State Lawrence S. Eagleburger, who was willing to help arrange a meeting in Washington. Then Fisher spoke to another old friend and fellow Detroiter, Mandell (Bill) L. Berman, who was chairman of the Council of Jewish Federations. Berman had seen the situation in Ladispoli for himself, and he said that he was anxious to start seeking a realistic solution. Finally, Fisher contacted Shoshana Cardin, head of the National Conference of Soviet Jewry.[100]

"I knew Max as a consensus builder," recalls Cardin. "But consensus wasn't what he had on his mind. I agreed with him that American Jewry would never be able to reach an agreement on where the Soviet Jews should go to live. But I was also concerned about the appearance of a small group of Jewish leaders trying to impose a decision from on high. That tactic doesn't usually work and has the potential of creating conflict among the institutions of American Jewish life — the same institutions that were going have to make a massive effort to help the Soviet Jews. Max asked me to attend a meeting at the State Department. Since the United States can't accept everyone seeking to live here, perhaps the debate over resettlement could be concluded by the US government. Once the numbers were worked out, then that decision could be presented to the American Jewish community. It was a good idea, though looking back, I wasn't sure it would work. Still, I couldn't see any other way to fix the problem, and like Max, I was worried that Gorbachev would lose his hold on the Kremlin and emigration would stop."[101]

So the stalemate over resettlement and the burgeoning humanitarian crisis in the transit camps would now be addressed by a small group whose creation was so controversial that the members were reluctant to admit its existence and chose to be known as the No Name Committee.

CHAPTER 13

THE PEOPLE WHO DO NOT FORGET

On Friday, June 9, 1989, Deputy Secretary of State Lawrence Eagleburger left his office at Foggy Bottom and headed down the hall for the first meeting of the No Name Committee. With thirty years of high-level government experience behind him, Eagleburger was legendary in the Foreign Service. After graduating the University of Wisconsin and completing a stint in the military, he had been appointed to posts by Republican and Democratic administrations, serving in embassies in Latin America and Europe, and holding a variety of positions in the State Department. He had been an executive assistant to Henry Kissinger during the Nixon administration and had helped him set up the National Security Council staff.[1]

When Secretary of State Baker was considering Eagleburger for his deputy, he consulted former president Nixon, who gave Baker a succinct, if somewhat salty, evaluation of his abilities. Eagleburger, Nixon said, "is utterly loyal, won't have his own agenda, and he's smart as a shithouse rat."[2]

What Nixon didn't know was that Eagleburger, a Protestant, had a significant emotional attachment to the issue of Soviet Jewry because of his feelings about the Holocaust.[3]

"I started thinking about the question of Jews and the world ever since I entered government," says Eagleburger. "For me, it comes down to one simple fact: there are different levels of guilt, and I cannot believe that my country is guiltless in the Holocaust. There are things we could have and should have done and we didn't. And I think we owe a debt. And to the degree I could help repay that debt, I wanted to do it. Any American who has looked at history honestly has to see that too many Americans at senior levels [of government] knew what was going on or at least suspected it and turned their backs. That doesn't mean we were directly guilty, but we were guilty to some degree. I rank my country's guilt in the Holocaust second only to slavery, and I don't think we will ever fully pay for the guilt of slavery. I grew up a Protestant, and perhaps that's part of my problem. Catholics can go to church and confess and their sins are washed away. We Protestants never escape. We suffer forever."[4]

Eagleburger's feelings about the United States not doing more to help rescue European Jewry would lead him, after retiring from government, to become the chairman of the International Commission on Holocaust Era Insurance Claims. It also fueled his sense of urgency about making certain that all the Soviet Jews who wanted to leave the USSR were able to get out.[5]

Eagleburger was also anxious about the shape of things to come. For some time, he had been telling his colleagues that they were going to regret the end of the Cold War. Despite the ever-present danger of a nuclear thrust-and-parry between the United States and Soviet Union, the two superpowers acted as a moderating influence on their allies – a geopolitical yin and yang that kept hostilities short of Armageddon. Once the Kremlin lost its grip on its erstwhile friends, it would also lose the ability to restrain them; global politics would fragment in unpredictable ways, and it was unlikely that the United States, as the lone superpower, could police the entire planet.[6]

This view ran counter to the giddiness of the current zeitgeist, which would soon be captured by Francis Fukuyama, a member of the State Department's policy planning staff, in an essay for the foreign policy journal the *National Interest*. Fukuyama postulated that the disintegration of authoritarian regimes on the left and the right signaled "the end point of mankind's ideological evolution and the universalization of Western liberal democracy as the final form of human government."[7]

Fukuyama's end-of-history argument has withered in the wake of 9/11 and the ensuing high-stakes upheaval in the Middle East – the clash of civilizations first mentioned by Bernard Lewis and later developed into a paradigm for future conflicts by Samuel Huntington.[8] Yet by the end of 1989, Fukuyama's halcyon vision seemed to be borne out by statistics. During that year, the world was plagued by less violent conflict – both by outright killing and organized warfare – than there had been since 1938."[9]

This comparative calm, regardless of how temporary, was good news for humanity, but it was not helpful to the cause of freeing Soviet citizens. Outside and inside the Jewish community, leaders began to question why everyone was making such a fuss over people who were no longer suffering under a repressive system that no longer existed.

At a Senate hearing, Senator Alan Simpson, a Republican from Wyoming, would observe that a portion of Russian Jews preferred to stay in their country and "if they would rather remain than go to Israel, that's saying something about the level of persecution."[10]

Even the venerable Jewish leader Morris Abram, an attorney and former chairman of the National Conference on Soviet Jewry, observed, in private, that Soviet Jews did not meet the legal standard of political refugees. "If you come out of a country," Abram said, "and have access and automatic citizenship to a free country, you're not a refugee. They came here because they…get the benefits of being refugees, payments of cash…medical services and other things."[11]

Yet for Eagleburger, who says that he "never had a position one way or another as to where the Soviet Jews should go," the political situation went well beyond any legal technicalities. He saw it as centered in the beating heart of the American movement to free Soviet Jewry – the memory of the Holocaust.

"I understood the frustration some people felt about Soviet Jews coming out on Israeli visas and then turning left instead of right," says Eagleburger. "But my view was that it would be [a disaster] for the American government to be seen as refusing Soviet Jews entry into the United States. I imagined that very quickly we would be charged with antisemitism, since it would appear to be precisely what the United States had done during the 1930s and 1940s."[12]

Here was one last ironic twist of fate: the major challenge was not an unsympathetic America, but a divided American Jewish community.

Max Fisher was aware that the administration was willing to do anything within reason to help, and he had tried to steer around the divisions within the Jewish community by inviting Bill Berman from the Council of Jewish Federations and Shoshana Cardin from the National Conference on Soviet Jewry to the meeting. The CJF would have to shoulder much of the financial burden of resettlement, and the NCSJ, as the foremost organization dedicated to Soviet Jews, would have to be convinced that whatever deal was finalized was fair.

The No Name Committee had three meetings in 1989: one in June, one in July, and one in August. In June, the committee – Fisher, Berman, Cardin, and Talisman – met with Eagleburger; Undersecretary of State Ivan Sellin; Dennis Ross, head of the policy planning office; and Priscilla Clapp, a Soviet expert from the policy planning staff.

"Because it was such a hot political issue," says Clapp, "it was handled at such a high level in the State Department – by Eagleburger and Ivan Sellin, who controlled all of the resources in the State Department. Larry told me to work with Ivan to formulate a policy and then handle the groundwork. So we listened to the No Name Committee present the issues, and we agreed that the problem was going to require a radical solution and we were going to have to knock some heads together to do it. We promised to keep in touch with the committee as we went along to make sure that their concerns were being met by our decisions. We knew about the horrendous fight in the Jewish community, and we knew our job was not to make the fight worse."[13]

For Clapp, the biggest challenge was to devise a realistic plan.

"There were limits to what we could do in the way of allowable slots and federal dollars," says Clapp. "We didn't want to overwhelm our ability to handle refugees worldwide. That was another part of the controversy. There were other groups in the United States who had refugee interests and were enormously resentful of the demands that were being put on us by those who represented the Soviets. There was no way we could devote the whole refugee program to them while Africa and Asia were falling apart. We still had the Vietnamese refugee interests – the boat people we were trying to take care of."[14]

At that first meeting the basic challenges were explored, with special attention paid to the Soviet Jews backed up in Italy and the ones waiting to be cleared in Moscow. Eagleburger was adamant on one point: for the State Department to go the extra mile in the short term, everyone needed to focus on devising a pragmatic long-range plan, so that the State Department would not be perceived as offering Soviet Jews a blank check forever.[15]

After the meeting, Mark Talisman returned to his office and wrote a memo about the discussion, which he faxed to the members of the No Name Committee. Talisman was so worried that what they were doing would leak to the Jewish community that his cover letter said that had he been able "to use a 'Lemon Juice ribbon' in my computer I would have been delighted. Not being able to do so, however, this will have to do. No names are used on our side. I trust that each of you will abide by the rules of non-existence of the conversations." He then instructed the committee members who wanted to fax their thoughts to him to send their faxes to his home, because he was concerned that someone in the CJF lobbying office would see them.[16]

Talisman's impression was that while the State Department was willing to go out on a limb to assist the Soviet Jews, the truth was that the No Name Committee and the American Jewish communal organizations were going to have limited input into the State Department's decisions. To avoid dragging the State Department into the community's battle, it was imperative that the committee not appear as if it were inviting Jewish leaders across the country to participate in the discussions.[17]

The aspect of the debate over freedom of choice that was most frustrating to the No Name Committee was that not all of the Soviet Jews who wanted to come to the United States could be accommodated. Philosophically, the freedom-of-choice advocates may have been on solid ground, but the administration could not allow hundreds of thousands of Soviet Jews to pour into the United States, while millions of other people around the world who wanted to come and were also facing difficult and dangerous circumstances at home were turned away. There was neither the space nor the money for every potential immigrant, and the cure for these unrealistic expectations was what the Talisman memo referred to as "a heavy dose of diplomatic reality," which hopefully would be supplied by Priscilla Clapp.[18]

◆ ◆ ◆

On July 6, the No Name Committee met again at the State Department. The meeting was recapped in a memo from Talisman stamped "confidential" and entitled "Participants of Non Meeting," a further testament to how controversial the discussion of narrowing the options for the resettlement of Soviet Jews remained.[19]

Max Fisher began by recounting a conversation that he'd had with Edgar Bronfman Sr., head of the World Jewish Congress. Bronfman had recently spoken with Aleksandr N. Yakovlev, a Soviet official close to Gorbachev. Yakovlev was a powerful voice of liberalism inside the Kremlin and had written critically of Soviet chauvinism and antisemitism; he was considered by many to be the true father of *glastnost* and *perestroika*.[20] Yakovlev, Fisher said, had told Bronfman that direct flights between Moscow and Tel Aviv were a distinct possibility, and Fisher pointed out that processing the Soviet Jews before they departed was the key to avoiding the backlog in Europe and circumventing the controversy surrounding whether they should go to Israel or the United States. Shoshana Cardin added that the Israelis had assured her that they would do whatever was necessary to help, since the government saw "Russian resettlement second only to defense as a national priority."[21]

Then undersecretary of state Ivan Sellin outlined his plan: The transit centers would be closed down; everyone leaving Moscow would have documents in hand and a known destination before they boarded a direct flight. Those with close family relationships in the United States would go there, while the others would go to Israel or elsewhere. All rules decided about who could enter the United States had to apply to every Soviet emigrant, not just Jews. The State Department and Immigration and Naturalization Service would synchronize their policies on bestowing refugee status and the flow of financial aid. Somewhere between twenty-five and fifty new staff members would be dispatched to the US embassy in Moscow to handle the applications – and all of this would be operative by the first quarter of 1990.[22]

Bill Berman interjected that the American Jewish community only wanted their "fair share" of immigration slots for Russian Jews.[23] Originally, the administration had proposed taking in twenty-five thousand Soviet refugees a year, but the members of the No Name Committee believed that forty thousand was a fairer number, and that the American Jewish community would be able to raise the money to pay for their resettlement. The number was raised to forty thousand.[24]

At this point Fisher, Cardin, and Berman said that they had arranged a meeting of Jewish communal leaders at O'Hare Airport for July 27, and that Priscilla Clapp would be in attendance to conduct a briefing. Sellin, aware that the Jewish community was still roiling over the freedom of choice issue, had one slice of reality that could be shared with the Jewish community: US immigration policy, he said, does not support freedom of choice for anyone – "why should it be different for Jews?"[25]

Two weeks before the Chicago meeting, Carmi Schwartz, the executive vice president of the Council of Jewish Federations, scheduled a five-hour planning session at the Royce Hotel across from LaGuardia Airport.[26] CJF would be out front raising money for the resettlement, but the focus of the session was to reiterate the importance of the community supporting the arrangements made between the No Name Committee and the State Department, and that while everything possible should be done to reunite immediate family members in America – spouses, children, siblings, and grandparents – the fact was that the emigrants were desperately needed in Israel.[27]

On July 19, Fisher wrote to President Bush, thanking him for helping to provide $75 million in aid to the resettlement program and informing him that the Jewish community had raised the same amount in its Passage to Freedom campaign.[28] But Fisher was still concerned about the fund-raising demands – Ivan Sellin had predicted that one hundred thousand Soviet Jews would come out in 1990,[29] and Fisher estimated that $500 million would have to be raised to help them.[30]

Even after the meeting in Chicago, where Priscilla Clapp spoke in realistic terms about the limited number of immigration spots available in the United States, some American Jews remained intransigent about freedom of choice. The actual plan to solve the dropout dilemma did not become widely known until Shoshana Cardin, as the chairwoman of the National Conference on Soviet Jewry, was invited to address the board of the Anti-Defamation League (ADL). The executive director Abe Foxman had been born a Polish Jew, and as a child he escaped the Nazis by living with his Polish nanny and being baptized into her religion, Roman Catholicism. Foxman was an ardent proponent of the two-destination option – not surprisingly, since Hitler's victims had no choice at all.[31]

"When I first walked into the room and told the board what had been arranged," recalled Cardin, "I could see that they were hostile to the approach. But I explained to them that no matter how they felt about it, our arrangement was the only realistic option if we hoped to get the Jews out of the Soviet Union in a timely fashion. By the end of the talk they had come around, and the ADL became the first national organization to go on record in support of the plan. I'm glad Abe Foxman had the courage to invite me and to support us. I know it wasn't a popular position."[32]

On August 1, Fisher, Berman, Cardin, and Talisman met alone with Ivan Sellin at the State Department. Sellin said that there was no way the denial of refugee status in Rome could be reduced below 20 percent. Talisman was infuriated by that figure and insisted that the decision, pushed by some unknown member of the "administrative apparatus," was disastrous for the Jews and Pentecostals who had been waiting to leave Italy. After the meeting, Talisman wrote to the No Name Committee that they needed to make the White House, Congress, and the State Department aware that the American Jewish community was "outraged at what continues to go on in Rome." He added that the human toll was horrendous, to say nothing of the $6 million that had already been needlessly spent "from funds we simply cannot afford to waste."[33]

There were sixteen thousand refugees warehoused in Ladispoli,[34] and the emigration lines were getting longer in Moscow. Thirty thousand Soviet citizens who had submitted applications for exit visas were waiting to be interviewed at the US embassy, and there was another line of equal length, described by a US immigration case officer as "an informal queue" of Soviets who wanted to fill out emigration applications.[35]

The State Department stepped in and cleared the backlog in Italy.

"It was Ivan Sellin who got the resources to do it," says Priscilla Clapp. "And that first year, when we unclogged the pipeline in Italy, the US government actually saved $40 million. We had budgeted $70 million to take care of those Soviet Jews, and we were able to get them out so fast that we only had to use $30 million of that and the other $40 million, from the budget allocated by the Congress, went back into the pot, and we were able to use the money in Africa, where there were some serious refugee emergencies on the ground. That made a lot of people very happy.[36]

A large hurdle to immigration was removed by Congress. Unlike the early years of Nazi persecution when the Senate and House closed off immigration, Congress threw its weight behind Senator Frank Lautenberg when he introduced the Lautenberg amendment, which attacked the reasoning behind the denial of refugee status.[37]

The denial was based in the 1980 refugee law – a law that had been strongly supported by the American Jewish community – which necessitated that potential refugees prove that they had a "well-founded fear" of persecution in their homeland. However, with *glasnost* and *perestroika* in full bloom, US immigration officials rejected the claims by Soviet refugees. Given the history of Russian antisemitism, it did not take an Oxford don to understand that the current liberal trend could easily be reversed, a point that did not change the minds of the immigration officials.[38] Instead, the Lautenberg Amendment simply exempted most Soviet emigrants from having to prove any fear at all.[39]

◆ ◆ ◆

Meanwhile, the Cold War was winding toward its end.

In August 1989, Tadeusz Mazowiecki became the prime minister of Poland, the first non-Communist leader to take power in postwar Eastern Europe.[40] Two months later, Gorbachev announced a plan that a Kremlin spokesman dubbed the "Sinatra Doctrine," meaning that the Soviet satellites were now free to "do it their way."[41] Two weeks later, on November 9, the Berlin Wall was breached by jubilant East and West Berliners, and the reunification of Germany began.[42] On Christmas Day, the peaceful revolution sweeping across Eastern Europe was marred when, after a twenty-four-year reign, Romanian dictator Nicolae Ceausescu, along with his wife, Elena, were executed by a firing squad.[43] Four days later, the writer and former political prisoner Václav Havel, after leading a Velvet Revolution during which not one shot was fired, was elected president of Czechoslovakia.[44]

The following year, as the Soviet bloc split at the seams, unrest spread through the USSR. Reform was slower than people imagined: demonstrations erupted, Gorbachev was under assault from critics on the right and the left,[45] and antisemitism was still breathing the Russian air. Shortly, Jewish writers would be beaten in public, while leaflets that could have come straight from the hatemongers of the Third Reich were being distributed on the streets.[46]

Yet Gorbachev was unwavering in his commitment to religious freedom and Jewish emigration. On a Friday evening in January 1990, following a Global Forum on the Environment in Moscow – attended by over one thousand political, scientific, and religious leaders, and concluded with a speech by Gorbachev – a group of rabbis, who had planned to go to the Choral Synagogue for the Sabbath service, were unable to travel because the sun had set. So Rabbi Arthur Schneier, the senior rabbi of Park East Synagogue in Manhattan, received permission to conduct a service in the Kremlin, the prayers echoing through the cavernous hallways.[47]

Then, in the fall of 1991, Gorbachev did something that was as remarkable as permitting a Kremlin prayer service: at a ceremony commemorating the fiftieth anniversary of the massacre at Babi Yar, Gorbachev sent his trusted adviser Aleksandr Yakovlev to the site to read Gorbachev's personal statement on the tragedy.

> The memory of irreparable losses passes from generation to generation.... Babi Yar, in the same way as...Buchenwald is not simply a geographical name now, but a frightening symbol...a place of grief... of confession. Babi Yar is now also an appeal to the politicians of our days to be vigilant, to remember everywhere and at all times that they were given the power to serve people, that a policy that is immoral should never have a place in the world. The Nazis speculated on the lowest feelings of envy, national intolerance and hatred. They used anti-Semitism as a major means to infect peoples' minds with racism.... The Stalin bureaucracy, which publicly disassociated itself from anti-Semitism, in fact used it as a means to isolate the country from the outside and strengthen their dictatorial position.... Among tens of millions of victims were almost six million Jews, representatives of the

great nation dispersed over the whole planet. Babi Yar shows that Jews were among the first Nazi victims both in our country and in the whole of Europe.[48]

After admitting the historical complicity of Soviets in the Holocaust, his remarks criticized those who still clung to their bigotry: "The right of emigration has been approved. However, to speak frankly, we [regret] that our compatriots are leaving, that the country is losing so many talented… people."[49]

At last, he concluded, "This ceremony in Babi Yar is a mournful event, but it also gives hope – the hope that we…are capable of learning lessons from history, from the tragedies, from the errors of our past."[50]

Reflecting on that day, Shoshana Cardin, who attended the ceremony, observed that Gorbachev was "brave enough to turn away publicly from the past. It is for his bravery that I will always remember him."[51]

Beyond setting the historical record straight, Gorbachev played a deciding role in establishing direct flights between Moscow and Tel Aviv. Traditionally, Aeroflot had not violated the Arab boycott, which dated to the 1940s and was designed to prevent states and companies "from directly or indirectly contributing to Israel's economic and military strength."[52] Gorbachev reversed this long-time Soviet policy with a sleight of hand that did not overtly challenge the Arab world. He put the son of the Russian minister of aviation in charge of a new company, Transaero, which was created by painting the new name on a trio of Aeroflot passenger jets.[53]

The direct flights between Moscow and New York were trickier to establish. Priscilla Clapp had contacted James Fannan, an executive at Pan American World Airways, which at the time was considered to be the flagship commercial airline of the United States.[54]

"Priscilla asked me to come to Washington," Fannan says. "I went to see her, and she told me that she wanted us to build a high-tech center in Moscow to oversee the flights. Then she asked me how long it would take. I told her six months, and she just smiled at me. Most people thought that with the dysfunction in the Soviet Union it would take three years."[55]

But Fannan was confident he could make the deadline. Pan Am had decades of experience setting up air travel in foreign countries, and he flew to Moscow and immediately set up a joint venture with Aeroflot: the Soviet-Pan Am Travel Effort (SPATE).[56]

"If you pay attention to rules and regulations you'll never get it done," Fannan says. "So we ignored them. We leased a ticket counter from Aeroflot and promised to give the company half of the money we took in."[57]

Fannan hired Soviet contractors to build the center, and he had to run the modems through the KGB telephone system, since those were the only reliable lines in the country.

"The KGB was eavesdropping on everything we did anyway," says Fannan. "I didn't care. The trick to getting things done was being as arrogant and demanding as the Soviets were and waving hard currency under their noses. We paid a premium for everything – materials, labor. Government fees were always being assessed; everyone had their hand out and wanted to be paid 'a premium.' It might have looked liked bribery, but in America we call it capitalism."[58]

The center was up and running in six months, but at two o'clock in the morning Fannan received a phone call that the first scheduled flight to New York did not take off. He hopped in his car, but en route to investigate the problem he had an accident and banged his head on the windshield.

"My forehead was still bleeding when we arrived," Fannan says. "But a border guard and a KGB colonel wouldn't let us onto the grounds – at least not until I gave them a few bottles of Scotch that I kept in the car for just such an emergency. Priscilla had to fly over the next day, and we got the Kremlin involved. The reason for the delay turned out to be that Aeroflot didn't understand that they were collecting a fee for every person who left. When that was made clear, the flights started taking off."[59]

◆ ◆ ◆

In February 1990, a special General Assembly of the Council of Jewish Federations convened in Miami Beach to begin making plans for Operation Exodus, a fund-raising campaign to resettle Soviet Jewry that had a goal of $420 million. In March, even before the official kickoff of the campaign, Max Fisher attended a United Jewish Appeal breakfast at the Regency Hotel in New York City with, among others, Charles Hoffberger, Corky Goodman, Lew Rudin, Laurence Tisch, and Leslie Wexner. Before the orange juice was served, Fisher was called to the phone. Former ambassador Walter Annenberg, a close friend from the Nixon and Ford administrations, was on the line.

"Max," said Annenberg, "I feel keenly about this. I'd like to be helpful. What are you looking for?"

Fisher replied, "How about five million a year for three years?"

"Fine," Annenberg said.

After hanging up, it occurred to Fisher that the size of Annenberg's commitment might stimulate the generosity of the big givers at the breakfast. Fisher called the ambassador back and asked if he could announce his pledge in public. Of course, Annenberg said.

"Walter's pledge," recalled Fisher, "was a real spark. I made the announcement, and by the time coffee was poured $58 million was pledged to Operation Exodus."[60]

Marvin Lender, chairman of the United Jewish Appeal, took over the campaign,[61] and by 1997 a total of $1 billion had been raised[62] – a good thing, because the resettlement would require every dollar. During 1990, Soviet Jewish immigration to Israel reached 181,759 – almost double the number Ivan Sellin had predicted. In 1991, another 145,005 arrived. In those two years, some sixty-seven thousand came to the United States.[63] The dropouts did not disappear, but their numbers drastically decreased, and by 1995 the influx of Soviet Jews into Israel had swelled the population by nearly 20 percent.[64]

◆ ◆ ◆

Gorbachev was nearly deposed by Kremlin hardliners in August 1991 while he was vacationing in the Crimea. In Moscow, tens of thousands of protestors jammed the streets,[65] and hundreds of them fought with the troops stationed outside the Russian parliament, hurling Molotov cocktails at the armored vehicles. Three protesters were killed and scores were hurt before the soldiers withdrew.[66] The coup failed, but Gorbachev was gradually losing his hold on power to Boris Yeltsin, who had gone into the streets to confront the enemies of *perestroika*. On Christmas Day, Gorbachev resigned the presidency, and that evening, as snow fell on Moscow, the red Soviet flag flying over the Kremlin was lowered and replaced by the white, red, and blue tricolor of Russia. The Soviet Union had ceased to exist.[67]

After his resignation speech, Gorbachev phoned President George Bush, who was at Camp David for the holiday. Gorbachev told Bush that the Soviet nuclear arsenal was secure, and asked him to do his best to help Russia and the new Confederation of Independent States.[68] After the phone call President Bush spoke into the small tape recorder that he had used over the years to compile his diary, predicting that Gorbachev was a man "to whom history will give enormous credit."[69]

Indeed, sixteen years later, historian John Lewis Gaddis would write that Gorbachev's decision not to use force to preserve the Soviet Union had "made little sense in traditional geopolitical terms, but it did make [Gorbachev] the most deserving recipient ever of the Nobel Peace Prize."[70]

As for Gorbachev, he was less certain of how history would remember him. In the West, the bald, stocky, energetic man with an intense gaze and a port-wine birthmark on his forehead, retained his status as a hero, and when he was spotted on the streets he rarely failed to draw an appreciative crowd. In his native land, however, he was scorned as the leader who relinquished an empire and brought about an era of terrifying uncertainty. In 1996, when the sixty-five-year-old Gorbachev ran for the presidency of Russia, he received less than 1 percent of the vote.[71]

In the late fall of 2002, when Gorbachev was asked by the author if he thought that he had carved out a spot for himself in Jewish history, he replied, "I have traveled quite a lot now – through the United States and I have been to Israel numerous times. I have spoken to many Jews. I don't know if I have a place in Jewish history, but I do know that I have a place in the hearts of the Jewish people, because they are a people who do not forget."[72]

Gorbachev was correct: Jews are a people with a long memory, perhaps because they have much to remember. They remembered the *shtetls* of eastern Europe, the fear and the poverty that had driven generations of Jews to cross the ocean to the Golden Land or to walk across Europe to reach the sand and swamps of Palestine, and the people who had stayed behind, the ancestors of the Soviet Jews who were now leaving filled with hope for a better life. Nor had Jews forgotten the six million, the principal reason that there had ever been an American movement to free Soviet Jews, and even though the Holocaust, by the size and scope of its evil, continued to occupy a central place among Jews, the American Jewish community had earned a measure of peace with the most painful chapter of its past.

More important, in terms of American history, the bands of volunteers and activists had started a movement that endured for a generation – a dazzling accomplishment in itself – and provided a potent moral weapon for the United States to wield against the Soviet Union in the latter half of the Cold War, demonstrating to the world the difference between the ways of Moscow and the ways of Washington.

That weapon was nothing more than the desire for freedom that beats in every human heart, and the promise that it was possible to escape the darkness of a cage and live in the light of the Western star.

ACKNOWLEDGMENTS

O Powerful Western Star! began during a series of conversations with Max M. Fisher in the winter of 2002, and shortly thereafter, he agreed to support the research and writing. Sadly, Max passed away in 2005, but his family – his wife, Marjorie Switow Fisher, and his children, Jane Fisher Sherman, Mary Fisher, Phillip Fisher, Julie Fisher Cummings, and Marjorie Fisher – continued to support my work. For your kindness and generosity of spirit and, above all, your patience, each of you has my deepest gratitude.

Of course, this book would not have been possible without all those who were kind enough to grant me interviews. I am grateful to each and every one of them. Their names are listed in the bibliography.

At Gefen Publishing, I'd like to thank Ilan Greenfield, Lynn Douek, Smadar Belilty, and my editors, Rebecca Maybaum, and especially Kezia Raffel Pride, who led me down the home stretch with more grace than any writer has the right to expect.

I'd also like to tip my cap to Jennifer Breasbois in Phillip Fisher's office, for her good cheer and her efficiency, and to Ben Golden and Conor Cullen for their assistance with the footnotes.

The scholars Henry L. Feingold, Jonathan Dekel-Chen, and Fred A. Lazin were generous enough to take time out from their labors to share their views and point me in the right direction, and I am particularly indebted to J. J. Goldberg and John Lewis Gaddis, whose work has informed my own.

Finally, as always, I owe much to my wife, Annis, for her love and support, and her conviction that one day this book would be done.

NOTES

PROLOGUE

1. Larry Kahaner, *AK-47: The Weapon That Changed the Face of War* (Hoboken, NJ: John Wiley and Sons, 2007), 12–13.
2. The primary assault rifle used by the North Vietnamese Army and their South Vietnamese allies, the Viet Cong, was the Type 56, a Chinese copy of the AK-47.
3. Nassim Nicholas Taleb, *The Black Swan: The Impact of the Highly Improbable* (New York: Random House, 2007), 8.
4. Ibid., 10.
5. Ibid.
6. Martin Gilbert, *Atlas of Jewish History* (New York: William Morrow, 1993), 123.

CHAPTER 1

1. The details of Nadich learning of the Lincoln assassination and his movements over the next day are outlined in his letter to Timothy C. Smith, the United States Consul in Odessa, May 2, 1865. The letter is found in the National Archives, in volume 8 of the thirteen-volume *Odessa Consulate Dispatches*, May 30, 1831– August 14, 1906. Dates in the United States and Russia differed because prior to 1918, the US operated on the Gregorian calendar, while Russia used the older Julian calendar. During the nineteenth century Russia was twelve days behind America; in the twentieth century the difference increased to thirteen days. (See Charlotte Zeepvat, *Romanov Autumn: Stories from the Last Century of Imperial Russia* [Thrupp, Stroud: Sutton, 2002], xi.) On the heels of the Revolution, Vladimir Lenin ordered the adoption of the Gregorian calendar in order to share a calendar with the West. That Abraham Nadich was a grain dealer is mentioned in the *Congressional Record*, vol. 108, no. 36, March 13, 1962.
2. Stephen B. Oates, *Abraham Lincoln: The Man behind the Myths* (New York: Harper and Row, 1984), 161.

3.   W. Bruce Lincoln, *The Romanovs* (New York: Anchor Books, 1981), 380.

4.   Shane O'Rourke, *Warriors and Peasants: The Don Cossacks in Late Imperial Russia* (New York: Palgrave Macmillan, 2000), 20.

5.   Ibid., 2.

6.   Lincoln, *The Romanovs*, 115.

7.   Abraham J. Mensch, introduction to Nathan Hanover, *Abyss of Despair: The Famous Seventeenth-Century Chronicle Depicting Jewish Life in Russia and Poland during the Chmielnicki Massacres of 1648–1649* (New Brunswick, NJ: Transaction Books, 2003), 1–2.

8.   Lincoln, *The Romanovs*, 119.

9.   Ibid., 117.

10.   Ibid., 118.

11.   Hanover, *Abyss of Despair*, 43–44.

12.   Lincoln, *The Romanovs*, 118; Cynthia Ozick, "The Good Cossacks," *New Republic* (June 2004). The precise number of Jews murdered by the Cossacks and peasantry in 1648–1649 continues to be a subject of debate. I have seen numbers as low as twenty thousand and as high as five hundred thousand. Some historians believe that half the Jews in the region were slaughtered; some say 35 percent; others 10 percent. The number most frequently cited is one hundred thousand. For instance, see Martin Gilbert, *Holocaust Journey: Traveling in Search of the Past* (New York: Columbia University Press, 1999), 219. W. Bruce Lincoln writes that two hundred thousand Jews, 35 percent of Eastern European Jewry, died in the slaughter.

13.   Boris Sandler, "History's Paradoxes," *Jewish Daily Forward*, June 2, 2006.

14.   Ibid.

15.   Irving Howe, *World of Our Fathers* (New York: Simon and Schuster, 1976), 6.

16.   Herman Rosenthal, "Catherine II," www.jewishencyclopedia.com/view_friendly. jsp?artid=275&letter=C, retrieved October 1, 2007.

17.   Howe, *World of Our Fathers*, 5; Alden Oreck, "The Pale of Settlement," www. jewishvirtuallibrary.org/jsource/History/pale.html, retrieved July 1, 2007. The territory included present-day Latvia, Lithuania, Ukraine, and Belorussia.

18.   Howe, *World of Our Fathers*, 5; Oreck, "The Pale of Settlement."

19.   "Jewish Cultural Renaissance in Imperial Russia, 1880–1922," www.idcpublishers. com/pdf/456_brochure.pdf.

20.   Benjamin Nathans, *Beyond the Pale: The Jewish Encounter with Late Imperial Russia* (Berkeley, CA: University of California Press, 2004), 83; www. jewishdatabank.org/AJYB/AJYB-1899_1900_Statistics.pdf.

21.   Ibid., 4.

22.   Oreck, "The Pale of Settlement."

23.. Howe, *World of Our Fathers*, 6.

24.. Harold Frederic, "An Indictment of Russia," *New York Times*, October 12, 1891.

25.. Howe, *World of Our Fathers*, 7.

26.. Ibid., 6.

27.   Adina Ofek, "Cantonists: Jewish Children as Soldiers in Tsar Nicholas's Army," *Modern Judaism* 13, no. 3 (October 1993): 277.

28.   Howe, *World of Our Fathers*, 6; Ofek, "Cantonists," 277–78.

29.   Michael Stanislawski, *Tsar Nicholas I and the Jews: The Transformation of Jewish*

Society in Russia, 1825–1855 (Philadelphia, PA: The Jewish Publication Society of America, 1983), 9.

30. Nathans, *Beyond the Pale*, 28.
31. Stanislawski, *Tsar Nicholas I and the Jews*, 183–84.
32. Ibid., 25.
33. Ofek, "Cantonists," 277.
34. Stanislawski, *Tsar Nicholas I and the Jews*, 29–30.
35. Nathans, *Beyond the Pale*, 28.
36. Howe, *World of Our Fathers*, 6–7.
37. Nathans, *Beyond the Pale*, 28.
38. Stanislawski, *Tsar Nicholas I and the Jews*, 185.
39. Lincoln, *The Romanovs*, 426.
40. Nathans, *Beyond the Pale*, 29.
41. Stanislawski, *Tsar Nicholas I and the Jews*, 185.
42. Howard M. Sachar, *A History of Israel: From the Rise of Zionism to Our Time* (New York: Alfred A. Knopf, 1986), 8.
43. Howe, *World of Our Fathers*, 7.
44. Lincoln, *The Romanovs*, 578–79.
45. Edvard Radzinsky, *Alexander II: The Last Great Tsar* (New York: Free Press, 2005), 152.
46. Frederic, "An Indictment of Russia."
47. Cyrus Adler and Aaron M. Margalith, *With Firmness in the Right* (New York: American Jewish Committee, 1946), 174.
48. Ibid., 175.
49. Cathy A. Frierson, *All Russia Is Burning: A Cultural History of Fire and Arson in Late Imperial Russia* (Seattle, WA: University of Washington Press, 2002), 41.
50. Ibid.
51. Zeepvat, *Romanov Autumn*, 24.
52. Lincoln, *The Romanovs*, 591.
53. Ibid., 592.
54. Gilbert, *Atlas of Jewish History*, 72.
55. Nathans, *Beyond the Pale*, 2.
56. Sachar, *A History of Israel*, 12.
57. Nathans, *Beyond the Pale*, 5.
58. Gilbert, *Atlas of Jewish History*, 73.
59. Nathans, *Beyond the Pale*, 5.
60. Sachar, *A History of Israel*, 8.
61. Nathans, *Beyond the Pale*, 5.
62. Jean-Paul Sartre, *Anti-Semite and Jew* (New York: Schocken Books, 1948), 145.
63. Sachar, *A History of Israel*, 16.
64. Ibid.
65. Ibid.
66. Edyta M. Bojanowska, *Nikolai Gogol: Between Ukrainian and Russian* (Boston: Harvard University Press, 2007), 14.
67. Sachar, *A History of Israel*, 11.
68. Ibid.

69. Ibid.

70. Ibid.; In an 1879 essay, the British novelist George Eliot anticipated the arrival of the Zionist leaders, writing, "There may arise some men of instruction and ardent public spirit, some new Ezras, some modern Maccabees, who will know how to use all favouring outward conditions, how to triumph by heroic example, over the indifference of their fellows and the scorn of their foes, and will steadfastly set their faces towards making their people once more one among the nations." See William Kristol, "The Jewish State at 60," *New York Times*, May 12, 2008.

71. Leon Pinsker, *Auto-Emancipation* (New York: Federation of American Zionists, 1916).

72. Ibid.

73. Sachar, *A History of Israel*, 15.

74. Lincoln, *The Romanovs*, 453.

75. Sachar, *A History of Israel*, 13.

76. David Vital, *A People Apart: A Political History of the Jews in Europe, 1789–1939* (New York: Oxford University Press, 1999), 400–401.

77. In Hebrew, *aliyah* means "ascent," and thus returning to the Land of Israel represents an improvement in one's condition. Leaving Israel is referred to in Hebrew as *yerida* (descent), a diminution in one's standing. The two words accurately reflect the Zionist worldview.

78. Stephen Birmingham, *Our Crowd: The Great Jewish Families of New York* (New York: Harper and Row, 1967), 7–8.

79. Henry Feingold, *"Silent No More": Saving the Jews of Russia; The American Effort, 1967–1989* (Syracuse, NY: Syracuse University Press, 2007), 2.

80. Susan Jacoby, *The Age of American Unreason* (New York: Pantheon, 2008), 83–85.

81. J. J. Goldberg, *Jewish Power: Inside the American Jewish Establishment* (New York: Addison-Wesley, 1996), 110–11.

82. Lucy S. Dawidowicz, *The War against the Jews, 1933–1945* (New York: Holt, Rinehart and Winston, 1975), 403.

83. Charles E. Bohlen, *Witness to History, 1929–1969* (New York: W. W. Norton, 1973), 12.

84. Bohlen, *Witness to History*, 39–43.

85. Arnold Beichman, "Roosevelt's Failure at Yalta," *Humanitas* 16, no. 1 (2003).

86. Arnold Beichman, "The Cold War Begins," http://www.hoover.org/publications/hoover-digest/article/8046, retrieved December 12, 2007.

87. James McAllister, *No Exit: America and the German Problem, 1943–1954* (Ithaca, NY: Cornell University Press, 2002), 34–35.

88. Ibid., 35.

89. Beichman, "The Cold War Begins."

90. Jim Smith and Malcolm McConnell, *The Last Mission: The Secret History of World War II's Final Battle* (New York: Broadway, 2003), 56.

91. World War II Conferences, box 3, "Yalta Conference Reports and Documents [memos of conversations and meetings]," RG 43, National Archives; Bernard D. Weinryb, "Stalin's Zionism," *Proceedings of the American Academy for Jewish Research*, Jubilee Volume, 46–47 (1978–1979): 555; Bohlen, *Witness to History*, 203.

92. Bohlen, *Witness to History*, 203.
93. Rudi Williams, "Holocaust Museum: A House of Learning," www.defenselink.mil/news/newsarticle.aspx?id=45778. The image was so moving that it was recreated with some of these shoes at the US Holocaust Memorial Museum in 1993 and accompanied by a wall engraving that reads: *We are the shoes, we are the last witnesses.... And because we are only made of fabric and leather, and not of blood and flesh, each one of us avoided the Hellfire.*
94. Donald Sommerville, *World War II: Day by Day* (Greenwich, CT: Dorset Press, 1989), 248.
95. Bohlen, *Witness to History*, 203.
96. Ibid.
97. Stanislawski, *Tsar Nicholas I and the Jews*, xv.
98. Bohlen, *Witness to History*, 203.
99. Ibid.
100. Ibid.
101. Ibid.
102. Rachel Bronson, *Thicker than Oil: America's Uneasy Partnership with Saudi Arabia* (New York: Oxford University Press, 2006), 36.
103. Ibid., 42.
104. Doris Kearns Goodwin, *No Ordinary Time: Franklin and Eleanor Roosevelt; The Home Front in World War II* (New York: Simon and Schuster, 1994), 547.
105. Beichman, "The Cold War Begins."
106. Photo by Hulton Archive/Getty Images.
107. Dick Camp Jr., "Leatherneck: And a Few Marines – Colonel William A. Eddy," *Aramco Expats*, May 4, 2004; www.aramcoexpats.com/Articles/Community/Annuitants-And-Former-ExPats/1430.aspx, retrieved November 3, 2007.
108. William A. Eddy, *FDR Meets Ibn Saud* (Washington, DC: America-Mideast Educational and Training Services, 1954; reprint, Vista, CA: Selwa Press, 2005), 32.
109. Eddy, *FDR Meets Ibn Saud*, 33.
110. Ibid., 32.
111. Ibid.
112. Ibid.
113. Ibid.
114. Ibid.
115. Bronson, *Thicker than Oil*, 42.
116. Eddy, *FDR Meets Ibn Saud*, 32.
117. Bohlen, *Witness to History*, 203.
118. Ibid.
119. Ibid.
120. Bronson, *Thicker than Oil*, 41.
121. Ibid., 42.
122. Harold Denny, "Captives Confirm Reich Atrocities," *New York Times*, February 17, 1945.
123. Ibid.
124. Ibid.

125. Harold Callender, "Trial of Vichyites Set for February," *New York Times*, January 28, 1944.
126. Harold Denny, "Captives Confrm Reich Atrocities."
127. Ibid.
128. "E. G. Harrison Appointed," *New York Times*, March 16, 1945.
129. Lewis M. Stevens, "The Life and Character of Earl G. Harrison," *University of Pennsylvania Law Review* 104, no. 5 (March 1956): 591–602; Larry Teitelbaum, "Harrison Report: Post-World War II Bombshell," *Penn Law Journal* 41, no. 1 (spring 2006), www.law.upenn.edu/alumnijournal/spring2006/feature3.
130. Sinai Leichter, "Kielce," *Encyclopedia of the Holocaust* 1, ed. Israel Gutman, (New York: Macmillan, 1990), 800–803.
131. David McCullough, *Truman* (New York: Simon and Schuster, 1992), 340–42.
132. Ibid., 595.
133. Michael Beschloss, *Presidential Courage: Brave Leaders and How They Changed America, 1789–1989* (New York: Simon and Schuster, 2007), 199.
134. Ibid., 200.
135. Ibid., 210.
136. Goldberg, *Jewish Power*, 157.
137. McCullough, *Truman*, 596.
138. Beschloss, *Presidential Courage*, 200.
139. "Pat Ansboury, Led Kentucky Truckers" *New York Times*, September 29, 1952.
140. Ibid.
141. Peter Grose, *Israel in the Mind of America* (New York: Alfred A. Knopf, 1984), 219.
142. "Pat Ansboury, Led Kentucky Truckers."
143. Ibid.
144. Steven L. Spiegel, *The Other Arab-Israeli Conflict: Making America's Middle East Policy, from Truman to Reagan* (Chicago: University of Chicago Press, 1985), 21.
145. Ibid.
146. "Truman's Letter Regarding the Harrison Report on the Treatment of Displaced Jews," www.jewishvirtuallibrary.org/jsource/Holocaust/truman_on_harrison.html, retrieved October 6, 2007.
147. Ibid.
148. Ibid.
149. Dan Kurzman, *Ben-Gurion: Prophet of Fire* (New York: Simon and Schuster, 1983), 74.
150. Peter Golden, *Quiet Diplomat: The Biography of Max M. Fisher* (New York: Cornwall Books, 1992), 215.
151. Kurzman, *Ben-Gurion*, 26.
152. Ibid., 33.
153. Gilbert, *Atlas of Jewish History*, 105.
154. Kurzman, *Ben-Gurion*, 248.
155. "'Never Again!' Vows IDF Commander: Chief of Staff Barak Gives Powerful Tribute to Holocaust Victims at Auschwitz," *JINSA Security Affairs*, April–May 1993.
156. Kurzman, *Ben-Gurion*, 246.

157. Ibid., 248.
158. Ibid., 262–63.
159. Larry Teitelbaum, "Harrison Report," www.law.upenn.edu/alumnijournal/spring2006/feature3/page02.html, retrieved July 10, 2011.
160. Harrison, www.jewishvirtuallibrary.org/jsource/Holocaust/truman_on_harrison.html, retrieved October 6, 2007.
161. Spiegel, *The Other Arab-Israeli Conflict*, 21.
162. "Truman's Letter," www.jewishvirtuallibrary.org/jsource/Holocaust/truman_on_harrison.html, retrieved October 6, 2007.
163. Sachar, *A History of Israel*, 221.
164. Kurzman, *Ben-Gurion*, 224.
165. Sachar, *A History of Israel*, 224.
166. Ibid., 251.
167. Ibid., 252.
168. "Great Britain: The Winners," *Time*, August 6, 1945.
169. Sachar, *A History of Israel*, 296.
170. Spiegel, *The Other Arab-Israeli Conflict*, 21–23.
171. Kurzman, *Ben-Gurion*, 264.
172. Yehuda Bauer, "Bericha", *Encyclopedia of the Holocaust* 1, ed. Israel Gutman (New York: Macmillan, 1990), 192.
173. Sachar, *A History of Israel*, 267–68.
174. Ibid., 269; Bauer, "Bericha," 192–93.
175. Sachar, *A History of Israel*, 270.
176. Bauer, "Bericha," 196.
177. Ibid., 193.
178. Birmingham, *Our Crowd*, 324.
179. Jonathan S. Woocher, *Sacred Survival: The Civil Religion of American Jews* (Bloomington, IA: Indiana University Press, 1986), 29.
180. "Post-World War I: Relief and Reconstruction," www.jdc.org/jdc-history/years/1920.aspx, retrieved September 2, 2011.
181. Barbara W. Tuchman, *Practicing History: Selected Essays* (New York: Ballantine, 1982), 215.
182. Golden, *Quiet Diplomat*, 74.
183. "Truman's Letter," www.jewishvirtuallibrary.org/jsource/Holocaust/truman_on_harrison.html;http://www.jdc.org/jdc-history/years/1940.aspx?id=296&terms=harrison, retrieved September 11, 2011.
184. David Grubin, interview with Ruth Bader Ginsburg, *The Jewish Americans*, PBS, 2008.
185. Abraham J. Karp, *Haven and Home: A History of the Jews in America* (New York: Schocken Books, 1985), 249–50.
186. Melvin I. Urofsky, *We Are One! American Jewry and Israel* (Garden City, NY: Anchor Press/Doubleday, 1978), 4.
187. Grose, *Israel in the Mind of America*, 207.
188. Irving Bernstein, *Living UJA History: As Told through the Personal Stories of Leaders of Israel and Leaders of the United Jewish Appeal* (Philadelphia, PA: Jewish Publication Society, 1997), 2.

189. Lynn Rapaport, "The Holocaust in American Jewish Life," *The Cambridge Companion to American Judaism*, ed. Dana Evan Kaplan (New York: Cambridge University Press, 2005), 888.

190. "My Homeland: Holocaust Survivors in Israel," http://www1.yadvashem.org/exhibitions/my_homeland/index.html, retrieved September 1, 2008.

191. Urofsky, *We Are One!*, 127.

192. This view is clearly articulated in Herzl's utopian novel *Altneuland*.

193. "Joseph Meyerhoff," *Maryland Online Encyclopedia*, www.mdoe.org/meyerhoffj.html, retrieved December 6, 2007.

194. "Philanthropy: The No. 1 Charity," *Time*, February 17, 1961.

195. Golda Meir, *My Life* (London: Futura, 1976), 1.

196. Albert D. Chernin, "Making Soviet Jews an Issue," in *A Second Exodus: The American Movement to Free Soviet Jews*, ed. Murray Friedman and Albert D. Chernin (Hanover, NH: Brandeis University Press, 1999), 48.

197. "History and Highlights: A Timeline," www.ajc.org/site/c.ijITI2PHKoG/b.844677/k.D891/Timeline.htm, retrieved December 3, 2007.

198. "Sister Rose Thering, Holocaust Educator and Activist," www.shu.edu/news/sister-rose-thering.cfm, retrieved December 1, 2007.

199. Stuart Altshuler, *From Exodus to Freedom: A History of the Soviet Jewry Movement* (Lanham, MD: Rowman and Littlefield, 2005), 188.

200. Fred A. Lazin, *The Struggle for Soviet Jewry in American Politics: Israel versus the American Jewish Establishment* (Lanham, MD: Lexington Books, 2005), 19–20.

201. Author's interview with William Korey.

202. Author's interview with Shimon Peres.

203. John Lewis Gaddis, *The Cold War: A New History* (New York: Penguin, 2005), 66–68.

204. Walt Whitman, "When Lilacs Last in the Door-yard Bloom'd," *Leaves of Grass*, 1855.

205. Hasia R. Diner, *A Time for Gathering: The Second Migration, 1820–1880* (Baltimore, MD: Johns Hopkins University Press, 1992), 156.

206. John T. Cunningham, *Newark* (Newark, NJ: New Jersey Historical Society, 1988), 152.

207. William B. Helmreich, *The Enduring Community: The Jews of Newark and Metrowest* (New Brunswick, NJ: Transaction, 1999), 19.

208. Cunningham, *Newark*, 164; Bertram W. Korn, *American Jewry and the Civil War* (Marietta, GA: Bellum Editions, 1995), 214.

209. Korn, *American Jewry and the Civil War*, 189.

210. Ibid., 294–95.

211. Phillip Roth, *Portnoy's Complaint* (New York: Random House, 1969), 247.

212. Korn, *American Jewry and the Civil War*, 207–9.

213. FJC News, "Jewish Community of Rostov-on-Don," September 20, 2005.

214. "The Emancipation Proclamation," www.archives.gov/exhibits/featured_documents/emancipation_proclamation, retrieved February 1, 2007.

215. "Annual Message to Congress," http://showcase.netins.net/web/creative/lincoln/speeches/congress.htm, retrieved October 4, 2006.

216. James M. McPherson, *Drawn with the Sword: Reflections on the American Civil War* (New York: Oxford University Press, 1996), 209.
217. Ibid., 214.
218. Ibid., 216.
219. Ibid.
220. Ibid., 214.
221. Alexis de Tocqueville, *Recollections: The French Revolution of 1848* (Garden City, NY: Doubleday, 1970), 98.
222. McPherson, *Drawn with the Sword*, 210–11.
223. Olga Peters Hasty and Susanne Fusso, eds., *America through Russian Eyes, 1874–1926* (New Haven, CT: Yale University Press, 1988), 6.
224. Yegor Gaidar, *Collapse of an Empire: Lessons for Modern Russia* (Washington, DC: Brookings Institution Press, 2007), 73.
225. John Noble Wilford, "Russian Princess Stands with Franklin as Comrade of the Enlightenment," *New York Times*, March 14, 2006.
226. Hasty and Fusso, *America through Russian Eyes*, 7.
227. Ibid.
228. Lincoln, *The Romanovs*, 409.
229. Hasty and Fusso, *America through Russian Eyes*, 7.
230. Lincoln, *The Romanovs*, 410.
231. Hasty and Fusso, *America through Russian Eyes*, 7–8.
232. "United States Relations with Russia: Establishment of Relations to World War Two," www.state.gov/r/pa/ho/pubs/fs/85739.htm, retrieved January 9, 2008.
233. Norman E. Saul, *Distant Friends: The United States and Russia, 1763–1867* (Lawrence, KS: University Press of Kansas, 1991), 383.
234. Ibid.
235. Saul, *Distant Friends*, 382.
236. Ibid., 382–83.
237. Korn, *American Jewry and the Civil War*, 189.
238. Ibid., 194–97, 205.
239. Ibid., 202.
240. Ibid., 122.
241. Ibid., 122.
242. Ibid., 124–25.
243. Adler and Margalith, *With Firmness in the Right*, 172.
244. Ibid.
245. Ibid.
246. Buzzy Gordon, "Revolutionary Jews," *Jerusalem Post*, July 5, 2007.
247. Eli Faber, *A Time for Planting: The First Migration, 1654–1820* (Baltimore, MD: Johns Hopkins University Press, 1992), 129.
248. Ibid., 131.
249. Natan Sharansky, *Fear No Evil* (New York: Vintage Books, 1988), 192–93.

CHAPTER 2

1. "Mayflower Compact: 1620," http://avalon.law.yale.edu/17th_century/mayflower. asp, retrieved July 9, 2007.

2. Francis J. Bremer, *John Winthrop: America's Forgotten Founding Father* (New York: Oxford University Press, 2003), xv, 39.

3. Henry L. Feingold, *Zion in America* (New York: Hippocrene Books, 1974), 26.

4. Paul Johnson, *George Washington: The Founding Father* (New York: HarperCollins, 2005), 115.

5. Ron Chernow, *Alexander Hamilton* (New York: Penguin, 2004), 432.

6. Ibid.

7. Ibid., 433.

8. Ibid., 502.

9. Ibid., 436.

10. Johnson, *George Washington*, 112–14.

11. Chernow, *Alexander Hamilton*, 489–91.

12. Ibid., 505.

13. Ibid., 505–7.

14. "Washington's Farewell Address to the People of the United States," 106th Congress 2nd Session Senate Document, no. 106–21, Washington, 2000.

15. Ibid.

16. Johnson, *George Washington*, 115.

17. Bette Roth Young, *Emma Lazarus in Her World* (Philadelphia, PA: Jewish Publication Society, 1995), 3.

18. Chernow, *Alexander Hamilton*, 17.

19. Ibid., 7.

20. Ibid., 464.

21. Chernow, *Alexander Hamilton*, 39–40.

22. Ibid., 40.

23. Author's interview with George P. Shultz, in Golden, *Quiet Diplomat*, 438.

24. Howard M. Sachar, *A History of the Jews in America* (New York: Alfred A. Knopf, 1992), 601.

25. Goldberg, *Jewish Power*, 92.

26. Feingold, *Zion in America*, 237.

27. Goldberg, *Jewish Power*, 96.

28. Feingold, *Zion in America*, 237.

29. Goldberg, *Jewish Power*, 96.

30. Danny Loss, "Catholics and Jews in the Antebellum American Mind: A Study of Reactions to the Mortara Case," http://www.dannyscl.net/academic/mortara.pdf, retrieved February 20, 2008.

31. David I. Kertzer, *The Kidnapping of Edgardo Mortara* (New York: Vintage, 1997), 149.

32. Feingold, *Zion in America*, 238.

33. Goldberg, *Jewish Power*, 97.

34. Feingold, *Zion in America*, 239.

35. Ibid.

36. Goldberg, *Jewish Power*, 98.
37. Sachar, *A History of the Jews in America*, 83–84.
38. Jacoby, *Age of American Unreason*, 64.
39. Feingold, *Zion in America*, 240.
40. Gerald Sorin, *A Time for Building: The Third Migration, 1880–1920* (Baltimore, MD: Johns Hopkins University Press, 1992), 202.
41. Feingold, *Zion in America*, 241.
42. Ibid., 242.
43. Ibid., 240.
44. "Report on Reading Deal," *New York Times*, June 11, 1892.
45. Ibid.
46. Sorin, *A Time for Building*, 202.
47. H. Lauterpacht, ed., *International Law Reports* (Cambridge, UK: Cambridge University Press, January 1, 1996), 555.
48. Paula E. Hyman, *The Jews of Modern France* (Berkeley, CA: University of California Press, 1998), 30.
49. Emile Zola, "*I Accuse!*," http://www.marxists.org/archive/zola/1898/jaccuse.htm, retrieved February 9, 2008.
50. Sachar, *A History of Israel*, 37–40.
51. Goldberg, *Jewish Power*, 101.
52. Sorin, *A Time for Building*, 84.
53. Feingold, *Zion in America*, 241–42.
54. J. J. Goldberg, "Kishinev 1903: The Birth of a Century; Reconsidering the 49 Deaths That Galvanized a Generation and Changed Jewish History," *Jewish Daily Forward*, April 4, 2003.
55. Cyrus Adler, ed., *The Voice of America on Kishineff* (Philadelphia: Jewish Publication Society of America, 1903), ix.
56. Herman Rosenthal and Max Rosenthal, "Kishinef," www.jewishencyclopedia.com/view_friendly.jsp?artid=247&letter=K, retrieved March 15, 2008.
57. Adler, *Voice of America on Kishineff*, ix.
58. Lincoln, *The Romanovs*, 641.
59. Goldberg, "Kishinev 1903."
60. Edmund Morris, *Theodore Rex* (New York: Random House, 2001), 243.
61. Irving E. Doob, "The Czar's Dove of Peace," *New York Times*, May 17, 1903.
62. Goldberg, "Kishinev 1903"; "Korolenko Describes the Kishinev Pogrom of 1903," www.shsu.edu/~his_ncp/Kishinev.html, retrieved March 9, 2008.
63. Adler, *Voice of America on Kishineff*, 124.
64. Ibid., xviii-xxiv.
65. Ibid., xvii–xxii.
66. "A Kishineff Book," *New York Times*, July 11, 1903.
67. Warren Zimmermann, *The First Great Triumph: How Five Americans Made Their Country a World Power* (New York: Farrar, Straus and Giroux, 2002), 446.
68. Morris, *Theodore Rex*, 229.
69. Feingold, *Zion in America*, 244.
70. Morris, *Theodore Rex*, 243.
71. However, to demonstrate his support, Hay would later contribute five hundred

dollars to the Jewish Relief Committee. See Feingold, *Zion in America*, 245.

72. Walter Isaacson and Evan Thomas, *The Wise Men: Architects of the American Century* (New York: Touchstone, 1986), 180.

73. Morris, *Theodore Rex*, 243.

74. Mark Gado, "Lynching in America: Carnival of Death," www.crimelibrary.com/notorious_murders/mass/lynching/lynching_2.html, retrieved March 14, 2008. The documented numbers are smaller. From 1882 to 1930, Stewart E. Tolnay and E. M. Beck, in *A Festival of Violence: An Analysis of Southern Lynchings, 1882–1930* (Champaign, IL: University of Illinois Press, 1995), were able to document, in ten Southern states, 2,805 lynchings. However, the authors admit that lynchings may well have been unknown or gone unreported in the press. See pages 260–61.

75. Jacob Rader Marcus, *United States Jewry, 1776–1985*, vol. 3, *The Germanic Period* (Detroit, MI: Wayne State University Press, 1993), 152–53.

76. Mary White Ovington, "How NAACP Began," http://leadership500.naacp.org/about/history/howbegan/index.htm, retrieved September 2, 2011.

77. Adler, *Voice of America on Kishineff*, 479.

78. Irving Filzig, "Longfellow and the Jewish Cemetery at Newport," *American Heritage Magazine*, February 1962.

79. Morris, *Theodore Rex*, 244–45.

80. Ibid., 253.

81. "Kishineff Petition Will Be Forwarded," *New York Times*, July 1, 1903.

82. Morris, *Theodore Rex*, 253.

83. Ibid.

84. Ibid.

85. Ibid.

86. "Kishineff Petition Will Be Forwarded."

87. Morris, *Theodore Rex*, 256.

88. Ibid.

89. Ibid.

90. Lincoln, *The Romanovs*, 647.

91. Ibid., 649–50.

92. "Pine and William Sts.," *Time*, February 14, 1927.

93. David G. Goodman and Masanori Miyazawa, *Jews in the Japanese Mind: The History and Uses of a Cultural Stereotype* (New York: Free Press, 1995), 9.

94. Goldberg, "Kishinev 1903."

95. Zimmermann, *The First Great Triumph*, 461.

96. Goldberg, "Kishinev 1903."

97. Zimmermann, *The First Great Triumph*, 463; "William Randolph Hearst," http://history.sandiego.edu/GEN/media/hearst.html, retrieved March 22, 2008.

98. Karp, *Haven and Home*, 376. In the opening decade of the twentieth century an estimated nine million legal immigrants arrived in the United States. By 1910, over 14 percent of Americans had been born outside the United States. See Zimmermann, *The First Great Triumph*, 455.

99. "The October Manifesto," http://euphrates.wpunj.edu/courses/hist330-60/Supplementary%20Material/HTML/October%20Manifesto.html, retrieved March 24, 2008.

100. Feingold, *Zion in America*, 246.

101. Ibid., 247.

102. Birmingham, *Our Crowd*, 182.

103. Sorin, *A Time for Building*, 205.

104. *Hearing before the Committee on Foreign Affairs, December 11, 1911* (Washington, DC: Government Printing Office, 1911), iii.

105. Sorin, *A Time for Building*, 205.

106. Albert S. Lindemann, *The Jew Accused: Three Anti-Semitic Affairs (Dreyfus, Belis, Frank), 1894–1915* (New York: Cambridge University Press, 1992), 177.

107. "United States Relations with Russia," www.state.gov/r/pa/ho/pubs/fs/85739. htm#abrogation_commercial, retrieved March 22, 2008.

108. "Break with Russia Criticized Abroad," *New York Times*, January 12, 1912.

109. Stuart Allen, "Tsarist Prejudice on Trial," www.whatson-kiev.com/index. php?go=News&in=view&id=598, retrieved March 24, 2008.

110. Ibid.

111. Goldberg, *Jewish Power*, 107.

112. Steve Oney, *And the Dead Shall Rise: The Murder of Mary Phagan and the Lynching of Leo Frank* (New York: Pantheon Books, 2003), 3.

113. Ibid, 5.

114. Steven H. Pollack, "Of Hate and Heritage: Georgia's Statue of Politician and Publisher Tom Watson Sparks a Debate over Prejudice and the Past," *Jewish News of Greater Phoenix*, October 27, 2000.

115. Leonard Dinnerstein, "Leo M. Frank and the American Jewish Community," *American Jewish Archives*, November 1968, 107.

116. Mrs. Leo M. Frank, "Mrs. Frank Pleads for Simple Justice," *New York Times*, March 1, 1914.

117. Steve Oney, "And the Dead Shall Rise," http://www.uga.edu/gm/304/Feat2.html, retrieved August 8, 2007.

118. "Texans Make Plea for Leo M. Frank," *New York Times*, January 1, 1915.

119. Oney, *And the Dead Shall Rise*, 453.

120. Ibid., 445–46.

121. "Frank Gratified, But Awaits His Complete Vindication," *New York Times*, June 22, 1915.

122. "Leo Frank's Throat Cut by Convict," *New York Times*, July 18, 1915.

123. "Lynchers Unkown, Frank Jury Finds," *New York Times*, August 25, 1915.

124. Oney, *And the Dead Shall Rise*, 566–69. Oney describes Leo Frank's nightshirt on 562.

125. Galatians 3:13, English Revised Version, http://erv.scripturetext.com/galatians/3. htm, retrieved April 1, 2008.

126. Oney, *And the Dead Shall Rise*, 589.

127. "Leo Frank Case," www.georgiaencyclopedia.org/nge/Article.jsp?id=h-906, retrieved April 4, 2008.

128. Pollack, "Of Hate and Heritage."

129. "Leo Frank Lynching Site Recognized with State Historical Marker," http://regions. adl.org/southeast/news/leo-frank-lynching-site.html, retrieved March 28, 2008.

130. Oney, *And the Dead Shall Rise*, 574.

131. Ibid.
132. Ibid., 577.
133. Ibid., 592.
134. Ibid.
135. Ibid., 578.
136. Spencer Blakeslee, *The Death of American Antisemitism* (Westport, CT: Praeger, 2000), 81.
137. Oney, *And the Dead Shall Rise*, 578–79.
138. Sorin, *A Time for Building*, 167.
139. Sander L. Gilman, *Jewish Self-Hatred: Anti-Semitism and the Hidden Language of the Jews* (Baltimore, MD: Johns Hopkins University Press, 1986), 1.
140. Ibid., 4.
141. "Jewish Massacre Denounced," *New York Times*, April 28, 1903.
142. Dan Miron, introduction to Hayyim Nahman Bialik, *Songs from Bialik* (Syracuse, NY: Syracuse University Press, 2000), xvii.
143. Alexandra Wright, "'On the Slaughter': Bialik Confronts God after Kishinev, 1903," *European Judaism*, vol. 34, 2001.
144. Bialik, *Songs from Bialik*, 11.
145. Ibid., 2–3. I have translated "killing" as "slaughter," which is the more common translation.
146. Ibid., 3.
147. Goldberg, "Kishinev 1903."
148. Ibid.
149. Shiri Lev-Ari, "The National Poet and the New Generation," *Haaretz*, May 1, 2005, www.haaretz.com/hasen/spages/527933.html, retrieved January 28, 2005.
150. Goldberg, "Kishinev 1903."
151. Herbert Spiegel and David Spiegel, *Trance and Treatment: Clinical Uses of Hypnosis* (New York: Basic Books, 1978), 15.

CHAPTER 3

1. Glen Jeannsone, *Gerald L. K. Smith: Minister of Hate* (Baton Rouge, LA: Louisiana State University Press, 1997), 2.
2. John K. Roth and Abraham Edelheit, ed., *The Holocaust Chronicle* (Lincolnwood, Illinois: Publishers International, Ltd., 2003), 145.
3. David Behrens, "Hitler's LI Legion," *Newsday*, October 7, 2005.
4. "1,300 Will Police Big Bund Meeting," *New York Times*, February 20, 1939.
5. "Congress: Hitler's Shadow," *Time*, October 10, 1938. Other estimates claimed that the Bund had twenty-five thousand dues-paying members and one hundred thousand members and sympathizers. See Clancy, "This was Yaphank," 2007; and Charles Higham, *American Swastika: The Shocking Story of Nazi Collaborators in Our Midst from 1933 to the Present Day* (Garden City, NY: Doubleday, 1985), 8. This retrospective math is problematic at best, but the ideas expressed by the Bund were hardly uncommon at the time and could be heard in the chatter at any number

of American barrooms; author's interview with Lance Golden.

6.	Higham, *American Swastika*, 7.

7.	Beschloss, *Presidential Courage*, 166.

8.	"American War and Military Operations Casualties: Lists and Statistics," www.history.navy.mil/library/online/american%20war%20casualty.htm,	retrieved August 24, 2008.

9.	C. L. Sulzberger, *The American Heritage Picture History of World War II* (New York: American Heritage, 1966), 130.

10.	Ibid., 51.

11.	Richard Bessel, *Nazism and War* (New York: Modern Library, 2004), 80–82.

12.	Ibid.; author's interview with Wolfgang Herzfeld.

13.	Roth and Edelheit, *The Holocaust Chronicle*, 144.

14.	Deborah E. Lipstadt, *Beyond Belief: The American Press and the Coming of the Holocaust, 1933–1945* (New York: Free Press, 1986), 105.

15.	Arthur D. Morse, *While Six Million Died: A Chronicle of American Apathy* (New York: Random House, 1968), 230.

16.	United States Holocaust Memorial Museum, "German American Bund," www.ushmm.org/wlc/article.php?lang=en&ModuleId=10005684.

17.	Ibid.

18.	Higham, *American Swastika*, 9.

19.	Jim Bredemus, "American Bund," www.traces.org/americanbund.html.

20.	"Kuhn Admits Lies about His Romance," *New York Times*, February 20, 1939.

21.	Ibid.

22.	Ibid.

23.	Higham, *American Swastika*, 9.

24.	David Behrens, "Hitler's LI Legion."

25.	Henry L. Feingold, *The Politics of Rescue: The Roosevelt Administration and the Holocaust, 1938–1945* (New York: Holocaust Library, 1970), 8; *Statistical Abstract of the United States*, US Census Bureau, 1941.

26.	David S. Wyman, *The Abandonment of the Jews: America and the Holocaust* (New York: New Press, 1984), 9.

27.	Robert N. Rosen, *Saving the Jews: Franklin D. Roosevelt and the Holocaust* (New York: Thunder's Mouth Press, 2006), 9.

28.	Ibid., 9–10.

29.	Stephen Schwartz, *Is It Good for the Jews?: The Crisis of America's Israel Lobby* (New York: Doubleday, 2006), 44.

30.	Peter I. Rose, *Strangers in Their Midst: Small-Town Jews and Their Neighbors* (Merrick, NY: Richwood, 1977), 139.

31.	Feingold, *The Politics of Rescue*, 42.

32.	Laurel Leff and Rafael Medoff, "New Documents Shed More Light on FDR's Holocaust Failure," April 2004, www.wymaninstitute.org/articles/2004-04-fdrdocs.php, retrieved May 9, 2008.

33.	Ibid.

34.	Ibid.

35.	Stephen H. Norwood, *The Third Reich in the Ivory Tower: Complicity and Conflict on American Campuses* (New York: Cambridge University Press, 2009), 13.

36. Leff and Medoff, "FDR's Holocaust Failure."
37. Feingold, *The Politics of Rescue*, 16.
38. Lipstadt, *Beyond Belief*, 2.
39. Sulzberger, *Picture History of World War II*, 134.
40. Goodwin, *No Ordinary Time*, 139; Sulzberger, *Picture History of World War II*, 129.
41. Sulzberger, *Picture History of World War II*, 129.
42. Feingold, *The Politics of Rescue*, 45.
43. Rafael Medoff and Cyndy Bittinger, "How Grace Coolidge Almost Saved Anne Frank," www.wymaninstitute.org/articles/2007-3-coolidge.php, retrieved June 24, 2008.
44. Ibid.
45. Feingold, *The Politics of Rescue*, 151.
46. Rosen, *Saving the Jews*, 84.
47. Ibid., 91.
48. Ibid., 94.
49. Lipstadt, *Beyond Belief*, 116.
50. Ibid., 117.
51. Goodwin, *No Ordinary Time*, 102.
52. Lipstadt, *Beyond Belief*, 119.
53. Rosen, *Saving the Jews*, 99.
54. Goodwin, *No Ordinary Time*, 101.
55. Rosen, *Saving the Jews*, 103.
56. Carl Sferrazza Anthony, *Florence Harding: The First Lady, the Jazz Age, and the Death of America's Most Scandalous President* (New York: William Morrow,1998), 310–11.
57. Wyman, *The Abandonment of the Jews*, 9.
58. Feingold, *The Politics of Rescue*, 131–32.
59. Ronald Kessler, *The Sins of the Father: Joseph P. Kennedy and the Dynasty He Founded* (New York: Warner Books, 1996), 91.
60. Richard J. Whalen, *The Founding Father: The Story of Joseph P. Kennedy; A Study in Power, Wealth and Family Ambition* (New York: New American Library, 1964), 389.
61. Kessler, *The Sins of the Father*, 91.
62. Barbara Marshall, "Inside the Everglades Club," *Palm Beach Post*, April 13, 2008.
63. Whalen, *The Founding Father*, 389.
64. Consistent with the psychological acrobatics of "exemption," Long managed to have a "warm relationship" with the Jewish financier and presidential adviser Bernard Baruch, and admired a number of Jews as individuals. See Rosen, *Saving the Jews*, 197–98.
65. Feingold, *The Politics of Rescue*, 135.
66. Memo from Assistant Secretary of State Breckinridge Long to State Department Officials, June 26, 1940, www.pbs.org/wgbh/amex/holocaust/filmmore/reference/primary/barmemo.html, retrieved June 12, 2008.
67. Goodwin, *No Ordinary Time*, 98.
68. Ibid., 175–76.

69. Beschloss, *Presidential Courage*, 162–63.

70. Sachar, *A History of the Jews in America*, 623.

71. C. D. Jackson, "Threat to Unity Deplored; Fomenting Group Discord in America Regarded as Aid to the Enemy," *New York Times*, June 7, 1941.

72. "Edelstein, Morris Michael," http://bioguide.congress.gov/scripts/biodisplay.pl?index=E000041, retrieved September 5, 2008.

73. "Edelstein Dies after House Talk," *New York Times*, June 5, 1941.

74. Ibid.

75. Ibid.

76. Lenny Ben-David, "LBJ, a 'Righteous Gentile?,'"*Jerusalem Post*, September 9, 2008.

77. Ibid.

78. Robert Dallek, *Lone Star Rising: Lyndon Johnson and His Times, 1908–1960* (New York: Oxford University Press, 1991), 169–70.

79. Michael Karpin, *The Bomb in the Basement: How Israel Went Nuclear and What That Means for the World* (New York: Simon and Schuster, 2007), 246.

80. Lenny Ben-David, "LBJ, a 'Righteous Gentile?.'"

81. Dallek, *Lone Star Rising*, 170.

82. Michael Beschloss, *The Conquerors: Roosevelt, Truman and the Destruction of Hitler's Germany, 1941–1945* (New York: Simon and Schuster, 2002), 41.

83. *Guide to the Microfilm Edition of the FBI File on the America First Committee* (Wilmington, DE: Scholarly Resources, 1999), 2.

84. Lipstadt, *Beyond Belief*, 36–37.

85. "Arthur Schlesinger on: The America First Committee," www.pbs.org/wgbh/amex/lindbergh/filmmore/reference/interview/schlesinger06.html, retrieved June 20, 2008.

86. Justus D. Doenecke, ed., *In Danger Undaunted: The Anti-Interventionist Movement of 1940–1941 as Revealed in the Papers of the America First Committee* (Stanford, CA: Hoover Institution Press, 1990), 37.

87. Ibid.

88. "Address Delivered by President Roosevelt at Charlottesville, Virginia, June 10, 1940," www.mtholyoke.edu/acad/intrel/WorldWar2/fdr19.htm, retrieved June 20, 2008.

89. "How Members from This Area Voted in Congress Last Week," *New York Times*, September 16, 1940.

90. "Children and Starvation," *Time*, August 26, 1940, www.time.com/time/magazine/article/0,9171,764456,00.html, retrieved September 2, 2011.

91. Feingold, *The Politics of Rescue*, 152.

92. Ibid., 152.

93. Ibid., 148.

94. Goodwin, *No Ordinary Time*, 100.

95. Feingold, *The Politics of Rescue*, 152.

96. Michael R. Beschloss, "Foreign Policy's Big Moment," *New York Times*, April 11, 1999.

97. Frank Freidel, *Franklin D. Roosevelt: A Rendezvous with Destiny* (Boston: Little, Brown and Company, 1990), 361.

98. "Destroyers for Bases Agreement," www.answers.com/topic/destroyers-for-bases-agreement, retrieved July 20, 2008.

99. Kenneth S. Davis, *FDR: Into the Storm, 1937–1940* (NY: Random House, 1993), 621.

100. Goodwin, *No Ordinary Time*, 189.

101. Beschloss, "Foreign Policy's Big Moment."

102. Frank Overton Brown Jr., "Jacob L. Morewitz, Eleanor Roosevelt, and the Steamship Quanza," *Senior Lawyers Conference*, April 2008, 30.

103. Goodwin, *No Ordinary Time*, 174.

104. Sulzberger, *Picture History of World War II*, 192.

105. Feingold, *The Politics of Rescue*, 154–55.

106. Goodwin, *No Ordinary Time*, 176.

107. Ibid., 102.

108. Feingold, *The Politics of Rescue*, 314–15.

109. Lewis White Beck, ed., *Eighteenth-Century Philosophy* (New York: Free Press, 1966), 3.

110. Lipstadt, *Beyond Belief*, 159–88.

111. Feingold, *The Politics of Rescue*, 326.

112. Rafael Medoff, "The Bergson Group vs. the Holocaust – and Jewish Leaders vs. Bergson," www.wymaninstitute.org/articles/2007-6-bergson1.php, retrieved March 3, 2008.

113. Ibid.

114. Sachar, *A History of the Jews in America*, 553.

115. Lipstadt, *Beyond Belief*, 225.

116. Feingold, *The Politics of Rescue*, 326.

117. Beschloss, *The Conquerors*, 41.

118. "Declaration Concerning Atrocities," www.ess.uwe.ac.uk/documents/moscwdecl.htm, retrieved August 9, 2008.

119. Beschloss, *The Conquerors*, 43.

120. Wyman, *The Abandonment of the Jews*, 242.

121. Ibid., 285.

122. Jennifer Hyde, "Polish Jew Gave His Life Defining, Fighting Genocide," CNN World, November 13, 2008, http://articles.cnn.com/2008-11-13/world/sbm.lemkin.profile_1_armenian-revolt-genocide-raphael-lemkin?_s=PM:WORLD, retrieved September 2, 2011.

123. Goldberg, *Jewish Power*, 113.

124. Ibid.

125. Morse, *While Six Million Died*, 421.

126. Ibid., 383.

127. Wyman, *The Abandonment of the Jews*, 458.

128. Ibid., 342. Since the publication of Wyman's book, the "chain of blame" has continued. For example, in *Buried by the Times*, Laurel Leff condemned the *New York Times* for refusing to treat "the news of the Holocaust as important." See Laurel Leff, *Buried by the Times: The Holocaust and America's Most Important Newspaper* (New York: Cambridge University Press, 2005), 16. In *Were We Our Brother's Keepers?*, Haskell Lookstein excoriated American Jewry for surrendering

to FDR's "policy of secrecy." See Haskell Lookstein, *Were We Our Brothers' Keepers? The Public Response of American Jews to the Holocaust, 1938–1944* (New York: Hartmore House, 1985), 33.

129. Feingold, *The Politics of Rescue*, 321.
130. Ibid., 14.
131. Ibid., 195.
132. Morse, *While Six Million Died*, 174.
133. Wyman, *The Abandonment of the Jews*, 329.
134. Sachar, *A History of the Jews in America*, 519.
135. "The Dawes Plan, the Young Plan, German Reparations, and Inter-allied War Debts," http://history.state.gov/milestones/1921-1936/Dawes, retrieved August 28, 2008.
136. "World War I War Debts," www.answers.com/topic/world-war-i-war-debts, retrieved August 28, 2008.
137. "Foreign News: Lausanne Peace on Earth," *Time*, July 18, 1932.
138. "American War and Military Operations Casualties: Lists and Statistics," www.history.navy.mil/library/online/american%20war%20casualty.htm, retrieved August 24, 2008.
139. "Resident Population: Estimates by Age, Sex, and Race: July 1, 1918," www.census.gov/popest/archives/pre-1980/PE-11-1918.pdf, retrieved August 10, 2008.
140. Robert S. McElvaine, *The Great Depression: America 1929–1941* (New York: Times Books, 1984), 93.
141. John D. Weaver, "Bonus March," *American Heritage Magazine*, June 1963.
142. Ibid.
143. Ibid.
144. Wyatt Kingseed, "The 'Bonus Army' War in Washington," www.historynet.com/the-bonus-army-war-in-washington.htm, retrieved August 28, 2008. The article originally appeared in the June 2004 issue of *American History* magazine.
145. Ibid.
146. Hans Wagener, *Understanding Erich Maria Remarque* (Columbia, SC: University of South Carolina Press, 1991), 7.
147. Michael Reynolds, *Hemingway: The Final Years* (New York: W. W. Norton, 1999), 24–25.
148. Nathan G. Hale Jr., *The Rise and Crisis of Psychoanalysis in the United States: Freud and the Americans, 1917–1985* (New York: Oxford University Press, 1995), 14–15.
149. Doris Kearns Goodwin, *The Fitzgeralds and the Kennedys: An American Saga* (New York: St. Martin's Press, 1987), 526.
150. Wyman, *The Abandonment of the Jews*, 15.
151. Ibid., 311.
152. Morse, *While Six Million Died*, 255.
153. Ibid.
154. Eleanor Roosevelt, *This I Remember* (New York: Harper and Brothers, 1949), 161–62.
155. Henry Raymont, "A Book Asserts U.S. Thwarted Rescue of Jews from the Nazis," *New York Times*, October 25, 1967.

156. Author's interview with David S. Wyman.
157. Robert Rosen, "FDR Was a Hero, Not a Villain," www.savingthejews.com/html/whywrotesavingthejews.htm, retrieved September 5, 2011. According to the website, the essay originally appeared in the *Jewish Press*, October 25, 2006.
158. Robert Shogan, *Prelude to Catastrophe: FDR's Jews and the Menace of Nazism* (Chicago, IL: Ivan R. Dee, 2010), xi.
159. Feingold, *The Politics of Rescue*, 329.
160. Bernard Susser and Charles S. Liebman, *Choosing Survival: Strategies for a Jewish Future* (New York: Oxford University Press, 1999), 47.
161. Robert Kennedy, "Jews Have Fine Fighting Force: Make Up for Lack of Arms with Undying Spirit, Unparalleled Courage – Impress World," *Boston Post*, June 4, 1948.
162. Sachar, *A History of the Jews in America*, 558–59.
163. Grose, *Israel in the Mind of America*, 207.
164. Mortimer Ostow, "The Psychologic Determinants of Jewish Identity," *Judaism and Psychoanalysis*, Mortimer Ostow, ed., (London: Karnac Books, 1997), 181–82.
165. Goldberg, *Jewish Power*, 117.
166. "Annotated Bibliography of Holocaust Writing in American-Jewish Magazines, 1945–1952," www-english.tamu.edu/pers/fac/myers/annotated_bib.html, retrieved September 1, 2008.
167. Jonathan Woocher, "'Sacred Survival' Revisited: American Jewish Civil Religion in the New Millennium," *The Cambridge Companion to American Judaism*, Dana Evan Kaplan, ed. (New York: Cambridge University Press, 2005), 283.

Chapter 4

1. Associated Press, "Stalin Sets a Huge Output Near Ours in Five-Year Plan; Expects to Lead in Science," *New York Times*, February 10, 1946.
2. Alan Bullock, *Hitler and Stalin: Parallel Lives* (New York: Alfred A. Knopf, 1993), 13, 859.
3. Robert Conquest, *Stalin: Breaker of Nations* (New York: Penguin, 1991) 282.
4. Simon Sebag Montefiore, *Stalin: The Court of the Red Tsar* (New York: Alfred A. Knopf, 2003), 515–31.
5. Bullock, *Hitler and Stalin*, 382.
6. Robert Conquest, *The Harvest of Sorrow: Soviet Collectivization and the Terror-Famine* (New York: Oxford University Press, 1986), 209–307.
7. AP, "Stalin Sets a Huge Output."
8. Ibid.
9. Conquest, *Stalin*, 281.
10. AP, "Stalin Sets a Huge Output."
11. Gaddis, *The Cold War*, 29.
12. Tim Weiner and Barbara Crossette, "George F. Kennan Dies at 101; Leading Strategist of Cold War," *New York Times*, March 18, 2005.
13. Ibid.

14. Gaddis, *The Cold War*, 29.
15. Isaacson and Thomas, *The Wise Men*, 353.
16. "Telegram," www.gwu.edu/~nsarchiv/coldwar/documents/episode-1/kennan.htm, retrieved November 30, 2010.
17. McCullough, *Truman*, 488–89.
18. "The Sources of Soviet Conduct," www.foreignaffairs.org/19470701faessay25403/x/the-sources-of-soviet-conduct.html?mode=print, retrieved September 2, 2008.
19. McCullough, *Truman*, 547.
20. Ibid., 549.
21. Ibid.
22. "Bernard Mannes Baruch," www.bartleby.com/73/233.html, retrieved November 28, 2008.
23. Feingold, *"Silent No More"*, 30–31.
24. Bullock, *Hitler and Stalin*, 619.
25. Lazin, *The Struggle for Soviet Jewry*, 21.
26. Richard Rhodes, *Masters of Death: The SS-Einsatzgruppen and the Invention of the Holocaust* (New York: Alfred A. Knopf, 2002), 172–74.
27. Ibid., 175.
28. Shmuel Spector, "Babi Yar," *Encyclopedia of the Holocaust*, vol. 1, Israel Gutman, ed. (New York: Macmillan, 1990), 133.
29. Roth and Edelheit, *The Holocaust Chronicle*, 270.
30. Rhodes, *Masters of Death*, 178.
31. "The World: Silence at Babi Yar," *Time*, July 26, 1976; Rhodes, *Masters of Death*, 178.
32. Oz Almog, exhibition notes, "Towards the Light of Dawn – Heroes of the Soviet Union," Jewish Museum Vienna, http://www.jmw.at/exhibitions-2002, retrieved September 18, 2008.
33. Daniel Weiss, "The Case of Masha Bruskina," www.youtube.com/watch?v=TkI7h VcOhOY&feature=related, retrieved September 20, 2008.
34. "Hanging Belarusian Partisans in Minsk," http://www.charonboat.com/item/36, retrieved September 20, 2008.
35. Nechama Tec and Daniel Weiss, "A Historical Injustice: The Case of Masha Bruskina," *Holocaust and Genocide Studies 11:3*, 1997, 366–67.
36. Feingold, *"Silent No More"*, 31.
37. David Bezmozgis, "Refusenik," *New York Times*, December 26, 2004.
38. Isaacson and Thomas, *The Wise Men*, 452.
39. Ibid., 451.
40. Ibid., 452.
41. Beschloss, *Presidential Courage*, 197.
42. McCullough, *Truman*, 562.
43. "Remarks of Secretary of State George C. Marshall at the Harvard University Commencement Exercises, June 5, 1947," http://usinfo.org/enus/government/forpolicy/pam-sp.html, retrieved September 19, 2008.
44. McCullough, *Truman*, 562–63.
45. "Remarks of Secretary of State George C. Marshall."
46. Tim Weiner, *Legacy of Ashes: The History of the CIA* (New York: Doubleday,

2007), 21.

47. Bullock, *Hitler and Stalin*, 13, 926.
48. Weiner, *Legacy of Ashes*, 21.
49. "Remarks of Secretary of State George C. Marshall."
50. Weiner, *Legacy of Ashes*, 28.
51. Ibid.
52. Conquest, *Stalin*, 271.
53. Ibid.
54. Beschloss, *Presidential Courage*, 224.
55. McCullough, *Truman*, 610.
56. Sachar, *A History of the Jews in America*, 615.
57. Shlomo Slonim, *Jerusalem in America's Foreign Policy, 1947–1997* (Boston, MA: Martinus Nijhoff, 1998), 18.
58. Ibid., 19.
59. Eric Lichtblau, "Jailed for Aiding Israel, but Pardoned by Bush," *New York Times*, December 24, 2008; The total number of volunteers remains a matter of conjecture: "The best estimate is that about 1,000 came from the United States with another 250 from Canada. Another 700 volunteered from South Africa, 600 from Great Britain, 250 from North Africa, 250 from Latin America, and still others from France and Belgium. There were also small contingents from Australia, the Belgium Congo, Rhodesia, Finland, and Russia. All told, volunteers, both Jews and non-Jews and men and women, came from some 37 different countries." See "About Machal," www.sabranet.com/machal/english.html, retrieved December 24, 2008.
60. Lichtblau, "Jailed for Aiding Israel, but Pardoned by Bush."
61. Ibid.
62. Sachar, *A History of the Jews in America*, 612–13.
63. Reuven Hammer, "The Dream: Thoughts for *Yom HaAtzma'ut*," *The Orchard*, Spring 2003.
64. McCullough, *Truman*, 613.
65. Arthur Schlesinger Jr., "Who Was Henry A. Wallace?," *LA Times*, March 12, 2000.
66. McCullough, *Truman*, 645.
67. Ibid., 612.
68. Beschloss, *Presidential Courage*, 231.
69. Kurzman, *Ben-Gurion*, 416.
70. Sachar, *A History of Israel*, 312.
71. Dan Kurzman, *Genesis 1948: The First Arab-Israeli War* (New York: New American Library, 1970), 251.
72. McCullough, *Truman*, 619.
73. Grose, *Israel in the Mind of America*, 242.
74. Ibid.
75. General Assembly, Seventy-Seventh Plenary Meeting, May 14, 1947.
76. Meir, *My Life*, 188.
77. Ibid., 188–89.
78. Isaacson and Thomas, *The Wise Men*, 454.
79. Bullock, *Hitler and Stalin*, 936.
80. "Blockade Lifted," www.trumanlibrary.org/whistlestop/BERLIN_A/BLOCKADE.

HTM, retrieved October 4, 2008.

81. Isaacson and Thomas, *The Wise Men*, 480.

82. Thomas L. Friedman, *From Beirut to Jerusalem* (New York: Farrar Straus Giroux, 1989), 458.

83. Meir, *My Life*, 201.

84. Ibid., 204.

85. Ibid.

86. Ibid., 205.

87. Bullock, *Hitler and Stalin*, 956–57.

88. Roman Brackman, *The Secret File of Joseph Stalin* (New York: Routledge, 2000), 377.

89. Joshua Rubenstein, "The Night of the Murdered Poets," *New Republic*, August 25, 1997.

90. Bullock, *Hitler and Stalin*, 117.

91. Meir, *My Life*, 205.

92. Conquest, *Stalin*, 293.

93. Meir, *My Life*, 206.

94. Ibid., 207.

95. Ibid., 209.

96. Bullock, *Hitler and Stalin*, 963.

97. Yaacov Ro'i, *The Struggle for Soviet Jewish Emigration, 1948–1967* (New York: Cambridge University Press, 1991), 52.

98. Bullock, *Hitler and Stalin*, 965–66.

99. William H. Orbach, *The American Movement to Aid Soviet Jews* (Amherst, MA: University of Massachusetts Press, 1979), 14.

100. Bullock, *Hitler and Stalin*, 966.

101. Ro'i, *The Struggle for Soviet Jewish Emigration*, 93–94.

102. Ehud Sprinzak, *Brother against Brother: Violence and Extremism in Israeli Politics from Altalena to the Rabin Assassination* (New York: Free Press, 1999), 67.

103. "Aliya and Absorption," www.mfa.gov.il/MFA/History/Modern History/Centenary of Zionism/Aliya and Absorption, retrieved January 4, 2009.

104. Lazin, *The Struggle for Soviet Jewry*, 23.

105. Sachar, *A History of Israel*, 461.

106. Ro'i, *The Struggle for Soviet Jewish Emigration*, 91.

107. John Lewis Gaddis, *We Now Know: Rethinking Cold War History* (New York: Oxford University Press, 1997), 75.

108. McCullough, *Truman*, 777.

109. Sachar, *A History of Israel*, 462.

110. Ro'i, *The Struggle for Soviet Jewish Emigration*, 91.

111. Meir, *My Life*, 139.

112. Nehemiah Levanon, "Israel's Role in the Campaign," in Friedman and Chernin, *A Second Exodus*, 71.

113. Lazin, *The Struggle for Soviet Jewry*, 24–25.

114. Levanon, "Israel's Role in the Campaign," 73.

115. Author's interview with Richard N. Perle.

116. Levanon, "Israel's Role in the Campaign," 72–73.

117. Lazin, *The Struggle for Soviet Jewry*, 25.
118. William Taubman, *Khrushchev: The Man and His Era* (New York: W. W. Norton, 2003), 271.
119. "Speech to 20th Congress of the C.P.S.U.," www.marxists.org/archive/khrushchev/1956/02/24.htm, retrieved December 15, 2008.
120. Taubman, *Khrushchev*, 271.
121. Orbach, *The American Movement to Aid Soviet Jews*, 15.
122. Taubman, *Khrushchev*, 306.
123. "The First Steps towards a New Era," www.guardian.co.uk/theguardian/2007/apr/26/greatspeeches4, retrieved December 5, 2008.
124. Yossi Melman, "Trade Secrets," *Haaretz Magazine*, March 10, 2006.
125. Ro'i, *The Struggle for Soviet Jewish Emigration*, 95.
126. Lazin, *The Struggle for Soviet Jewry*, 25.
127. Orbach, *The American Movement to Aid Soviet Jews*, 16–17.
128. Ibid., 17.
129. "Judaism: Russian Anti-Semitism," *Time*, April 17, 1964.
130. Orbach, *The American Movement to Aid Soviet Jews*, 16.
131. Ibid., 17.
132. Ibid., 16.
133. Edwin McDowell, "'Exodus in Samizdat: Still Popular and Still Subversive," *New York Times*, April 26, 1987.
134. Ibid.
135. Ibid.
136. Ibid.
137. Sachar, *A History of Israel*, 481.
138. Chester J. Pach Jr., and Elmo Richardson, *The Presidency of Dwight D. Eisenhower: Revised Edition* (Lawrence, KS: University Press of Kansas, 1991), 126.
139. Sachar, *A History of Israel*, 473–74, 481.
140. Spiegel, *The Other Arab-Israeli Conflict*, 67.
141. Said K. Aburish, *Nasser: The Last Arab* (New York: Thomas Dunne Books, 2004), 75.
142. Weiner, *Legacy of Ashes*, 127.
143. Pach and Richardson, *The Presidency of Dwight D. Eisenhower*, 127.
144. Aburish, *Nasser*, 104–06.
145. Spiegel, *The Other Arab-Israeli Conflict*, 70.
146. Aburish, *Nasser*, 106.
147. Ibid., 108.
148. Pach and Richardson, *The Presidency of Dwight D. Eisenhower*, 128.
149. Ibid., 129.
150. Spiegel, *The Other Arab-Israeli Conflict*, 71–74.
151. Golden, *Quiet Diplomat*, 15.
152. Spiegel, *The Other Arab-Israeli Conflict*, 74–75.
153. Sachar, *A History of Israel*, 503.
154. Burton Hersh, *The Old Boys: The American Elite and the Origins of the CIA* (New York: Charles Scribner's Sons, 1992), 391.
155. Ibid.

156. Weiner, *Legacy of Ashes*, 128.
157. A photo of the fallen head can be seen on Wikipedia's page on the Stalin monument.
158. Hersh, *The Old Boys*, 393.
159. Weiner, *Legacy of Ashes*, 130.
160. Aleksandr Fursenko and Timothy Naftali, *Khrushchev's Cold War* (New York: W. W. Norton, 2007), 129.
161. Gaddis, *The Cold War*, 109–10.
162. Taubman, *Khrushchev*, 297.
163. Pach and Richardson, *The Presidency of Dwight D. Eisenhower*, 131; Hersh, *The Old Boys*, 392.
164. Weiner, *Legacy of Ashes*, 130.
165. Pach and Richardson, *The Presidency of Dwight D. Eisenhower*, 131.
166. Weiner, *Legacy of Ashes*, 131.
167. Pach and Richardson, *The Presidency of Dwight D. Eisenhower*, 132.
168. Gaddis, *We Now Know*, 211.
169. Henry Kamm, "Hungarian Who Led '56 Revolt Is Buried as a Hero," *New York Times*, June 17, 1989.
170. Pach and Richardson, *The Presidency of Dwight D. Eisenhower*, 134.
171. Wolf Blitzer, *Between Washington and Jerusalem: A Reporter's Notebook* (New York: Oxford University Press, 1985), 12; Golden, *Quiet Diplomat*, xvi.
172. Author's interview with Richard M. Nixon, in Golden, *Quiet Diplomat*, xvi–xvii.
173. Ambrose's claims about interviewing Eisenhower have come under fire. According to Richard Rayner, "The footnotes to Ambrose's first big Eisenhower book, *The Supreme Commander*, published in 1970, cite nine interview dates; seven of these conflict with the record." See Richard Rayner, "Channelling Ike," *New Yorker*, April 26, 2010.
174. Stephen E. Ambrose, *Nixon: The Education of a Politician 1913–1962* (New York: Simon and Schuster, 1987), 420.
175. Pach and Richardson, *The Presidency of Dwight D. Eisenhower*, 237.
176. Con Coughlin, *Saddam: King of Terror* (New York: Ecco, 2002), 38.
177. Ibid., 65.
178. Ihsan A. Hijazi, "Assad Will Travel to Soviet Union," *New York Times*, December 21, 1989.
179. Author's interview with Max. M. Fisher, in Golden, *Quiet Diplomat*, xi.
180. Ibid., xviii–xix.
181. Author's interview with Richard M. Nixon, in Golden, *Quiet Diplomat*, xviii.
182. Ibid., xvii–xviii.
183. Ibid., xviii.
184. Ambrose Bierce, "The Devil's Dictionary," www.online-literature.com/view.php/devilsdictionary/16?term=strife of interests, retrieved January 5, 2009.
185. Elinor Burkett, *Golda* (New York: HarperCollins, 2008), 293.
186. William Korey, *The Soviet Cage: Anti-Semitism in Russia* (New York: Viking, 1973), 199.
187. Gaddis, *The Cold War*, 114.
188. Richard Reeves, *President Kennedy: Profile of Power* (New York: Simon and Schuster, 1993), 536–37.

189. "Israel Answers Soviet; Mrs. Meir Says 9,236 Jews Want to Leave Russia," *New York Times*, August 9, 1960.

190. Boris Morozov, *Documents on Soviet Jewish Emigration* (Portland, OR: Frank Cass, 1999), 135.

191. "Russians Say Jews Are Not a Nation," *New York Times*, February 7, 1953; Harris, "Arab Opposition to Jewish Immigration to Israel," 2.

192. Elizabeth Neuffer, "In Brooklyn Apartment, Russian Finds a Haven," *New York Times*, October 24, 1987.

193. Lazin, *The Struggle for Soviet Jewry*, 24–26.

194. Orbach, *The American Movement to Aid Soviet Jews*, 18.

195. Ro'i, *The Struggle for Soviet Jewish Emigration*, 92–96.

196. Ro'i, *The Struggle for Soviet Jewish Emigration*, 100.

197. Orbach, *The American Movement to Aid Soviet Jews*, 18.

198. Ro'i, *The Struggle for Soviet Jewish Emigration*, 113–14.

199. Ibid., 133.

200. Jacob Victor, "Moshe Decter, 85, Activist for Soviet Jewry," *Jewish Daily Forward*, July 11, 2007.

201. Charles McGrath, "A Liberal Beacon Burns Out," *New York Times*, January 23, 2006.

202. "Who We Are and Where We Came From," http://www.thenewleader.com/pdf/who-we-are.pdf, retrieved January 20, 2009.

203. John B. Judis, *William F. Buckley Jr.: Patron Saint of the Conservatives* (New York: Simon and Schuster, 1988), 175–76.

204. Pach and Richardson, *The Presidency of Dwight D. Eisenhower*, 207–8.

205. Ro'i, *The Struggle for Soviet Jewish Emigration*, 133.

206. Ibid., 186.

207. Ibid.

208. Ibid., 186–87.

209. "Address Before the 18th General Assembly of the United Nations, September 20, 1963," http://www.jfklibrary.org/Research/Ready-Reference/JFK-Speeches/Address-Before-the-18th-General-Assembly-of-the-United-Nations-September-20-1963.aspx, retrieved January 22, 2009.

210. Ro'i, *The Struggle for Soviet Jewish Emigration*, 187.

211. Ibid., 343.

212. Ibid.

213. Author's interview with Richard M. Nixon.

214. Author's interview with Shoshana S. Cardin.

215. Lazin, *The Struggle for Soviet Jewry*, 27–28.

216. Dupuy and Dupuy, *The Harper Encyclopedia of Military History*, 1309.

217. McElvaine, *The Great Depression*, 331.

218. Dean Acheson, *The Korean War* (New York: W. W. Norton, 1971), 6.

219. James Howard Kunstler, *The Geography of Nowhere: The Rise and Decline of America's Man-Made Landscape* (New York: Simon and Schuster, 1993), 104.

220. "The Battle to Enlist: Anti-Semitism in the Armed Forces," www.fathom.com/course/21701756/session2.html, retrieved January 9, 2009.

221. Rapaport, "The Holocaust," 190.

222. Jonathan Sarna, *American Judaism: A History* (New Haven, CT: Yale University Press, 2004), 282.

223. Ibid., 279.

224. Dana Evan Kaplan, "Trends in American Judaism from 1945 to the Present," *The Cambridge Companion to American Judaism*, Dana Evan Kaplan, ed. (New York: Cambridge University Press, 2005), 190.

225. Rapaport, "The Holocaust," 190.

226. Kaplan, "Trends in American Judaism," 64.

227. "The Hollywood Ten," www.mcpld.org/trumbo/WebPages/hollywoodten.htm, retrieved January 9, 2009.

228. Sachar, *A History of the Jews in America*, 647.

229. "Senate Resolution 301: Censure of Senator Joseph McCarthy (1954)," www.ourdocuments.gov/doc.php?flash=true&doc=86, retrieved January 2, 2009.

230. Arthur Herman, *Joseph McCarthy: Reexamining the Life and Legacy of America's Most Hated Senator* (New York: Free Press, 1999), 303, 330.

231. Harvey Klehr, *Communist Cadre: The Social Background of the American Communist Party Elite* (Stanford, CA; Hoover Institution Press, 1978), 4.

232. Peter Novick, *The Holocaust in American Life* (Boston, MA: Houghton Mifflin, 1999), 93.

233. "Red Regrets," *New York Post*, February 8, 2009.

234. Novick, *The Holocaust in American Life*, 92.

235. Sachar, *A History of the Jews in America*, 633.

236. AP, "Fifty Years Later, Rosenberg Execution Is Still Fresh," *USA Today*, June 17, 2003.

237. Enid Nemy, "Frederick Vanderbilt Field, Wealthy Leftist, Dies at 94," *New York Times*, February 7, 2000.

238. Novick, *The Holocaust in American Life*, 94.

239. Sachar, *A History of the Jews in America*, 635.

240. Ibid., 635–36.

241. Patricia Cohen, "But Is Madoff Not So Good for the Jews? Discuss Among Yourselves," *New York Times*, January 17, 2009.

242. Sachar, *A History of the Jews in America*, 640–41.

243. Thomas Hines, *Populuxe* (New York: Alfred A. Knopf, 1987), 60.

244. Ibid., 125.

245. McElvaine, *The Great Depression*, 332.

246. "U.S. Enrollment Exceeds Baby-Boomer Days," http://usgovinfo.about.com/od/censusandstatistics/a/schoolboom.htm, retrieved February 1, 2009.

247. Ari L. Goldman, "Long Island Interview: Egon Mayer; Intermarriage: Public Issue, Private Fear," *New York Times*, May 21, 1989.

248. Sarna, *American Judaism*, 279.

249. Novick, *The Holocaust in American Life*, 105.

250. Hasia R. Diner, *We Remember with Reverence and Love: American Jews and the Myth of Silence after the Holocaust, 1945–1962* (New York: New York University Press, 2009), ix.

251. Sarna, *American Judaism*, 296.

252. Diner, *We Remember with Reverence and Love*, 88.

253. "A Thousand Darknesses," www.powells.com/review/2006_03_23.html, retrieved March 23, 2006.
254. AP, "Holocaust Scholar Raul Hilberg Dies at 81," *LA Times*, August 7, 2007.
255. "JPS at 120 Years," http://www.jewishpub.org/about/, retrieved February 1, 2009.
256. Sarna, *American Judaism*, 296.
257. Novick, *The Holocaust in American Life*, 103–4.
258. Sarna, *American Judaism*, 296.
259. Novick, *The Holocaust in American Life*, 83.
260. Ibid., 2–3.
261. Deborah E. Lipstadt, "The Holocaust in the Western Mind: How Americans Think the Unthinkable," *The Boston Globe*, June 13, 1999.
262. Diner, *We Remember with Reverence and Love*, 8.
263. Novick, *The Holocaust in American Life*, 3.
264. Ibid., 195.
265. Ibid., 207.
266. Ibid., 104.
267. Sarna, *American Judaism*, 299.
268. Novick, *The Holocaust in American Life*, 108.
269. Diner, *We Remember with Reverence and Love*, 18, 341.
270. Richard L. Rubenstein, *After Auschwitz: Radical Theology and Contemporary Judaism* (New York: Bobbs-Merrill, 1966), x.
271. Dan Raviv and Yossi Melman, *Every Spy a Prince: The Complete History of Israel's Intelligence Community* (Boston, MA: Houghton Mifflin, 1990), 115.
272. Irving Crespi, "Public Reaction to the Eichmann Trial," *Public Opinion Quarterly* 28:1 (Spring 1964), 92.
273. Tom Segev, *The Seventh Million: The Israelis and the Holocaust* (New York: Hill and Wang, 1993), 344.
274. Walter Goodman, "Crime and Punishment: The Trial of Eichmann," *New York Times*, April 30, 1997.
275. Segev, *The Seventh Million*, 351.
276. Jeffrey Shandler, *While America Watches: Televising the Holocaust* (New York: Oxford University Press, 1999), 90–91.
277. Novick, *The Holocaust in American Life*, 128.
278. Françoise S. Ouzan, "The Eichmann Trial and American Jewry: A Reassessment," *Jewish Political Studies Review 19:1–2* (Spring 2007); Rapaport, "The Holocaust," 194.
279. Novick, *The Holocaust in American Life*, 133.
280. Paul Jacobs, "Eichmann and Jewish Identity," *Midstream* (Summer 1961), 36–37.
281. Segev, *The Seventh Million*, 330.
282. Novick, *The Holocaust in American Life*, 131.
283. Douglas Martin, "William F. Buckley Jr., Champion of Conservatism, Dies at 82," *New York Times*, February 27, 2008.
284. Novick, *The Holocaust in American Life*, 130.
285. Ibid., 129.
286. Ibid., 129, 313.
287. Ibid., 129.

288. "André Schwarz-Bart," www.timesonline.co.uk/tol/comment/obituaries/article645874.ece, retrieved February 7, 2009.

289. Howe, *World of Our Fathers*, 626.

290. "George Lincoln Rockwell," http://encyclopedia.stateuniversity.com/pages/8502/George-Lincoln-Rockwell.html, retrieved February 7, 2009.

291. Homer Bigart, "Just Took Orders, Eichmann Insists; Declares He Would Have Killed His Own Father if Told to Do So," *New York Times*, April 22, 1961.

292. Goodman, "Crime and Punishment: The Trial of Eichmann."

293. Segev, *The Seventh Million*, 365.

294. Ibid., 347.

295. Mary White Ovington, "How NAACP Began."

296. "Business Development," http://depts.washington.edu/cartah/text_archive/clark/bc_3.shtml, Retrieved February 14, 2009.

297. Mary White Ovington, "How NAACP Began."

298. George Hutchinson, *The Harlem Renaissance in Black and White* (Cambridge: MA, Harvard University Press, 1996), 373.

299. Sachar, *A History of the Jews in America*, 803.

300. Lunabelle Wedlock, "The Reaction of Negro Publications and Organizations to German Anti-Semitism," *Howard University Studies in the Social Sciences* 3, no. 2 (1942): 96.

301. Sarna, *American Judaism*, 308–9.

302. Gabrielle Simon Edgcomb, *From Swastika to Jim Crow: Refugee Scholars at Black Colleges* (Malabar, FL: Krieger, 1993), xiii.

303. Michael Lee Lanning, *The African-American Soldier: From Crispus Attucks to Colin Powell* (Secaucus, NJ: Citadel/Carol, 1999), 173–74.

304. Thomas Borstelmann, *The Cold War and the Color Line: American Race Relations in the Global Arena* (Cambridge: MA, Harvard University Press, 2001), 43.

305. McCullough, *Truman*, 588–89.

306. "Morgan v. Virginia (No. 704)," www.law.cornell.edu/supct/html/historics/USSC_CR_0328_0373_ZO.html, retrieved February 12, 2009.

307. "Desegregation of the Armed Forces," www.trumanlibrary.org/whistlestop/study_collections/desegregation/large/index.php?action=chronology, retrieved February 18, 2009.

308. Mary Price, "Baton Rouge Bus Boycott Background," www.lib.lsu.edu/special/exhibits/boycott/background.html, retrieved February 18, 2009.

309. David A. Nichols, *A Matter of Justice: Eisenhower and the Beginning of the Civil Rights Revolution* (New York: Simon and Schuster, 2007), 69.

310. Wolfgang Saxon, "E. Frederic Morrow, 88, Aide in Eisenhower Administration," *New York Times*, July 21, 1994.

311. Nichols, *A Matter of Justice*, 80.

312. Stephen E. Ambrose, *Eisenhower: Soldier and President* (New York: Simon and Schuster, 1990), 446–48.

313. Sachar, *A History of the Jews in America*, 803.

314. Marc Schneier, *Shared Dreams: Martin Luther King, Jr. and the Jewish Community* (Woodstock, VT: Jewish Lights, 1999), 26.

315. Louis Harap, "Anti-Negroism among Jews," *Strangers and Neighbors*, eds.,

Maurianne Adams and John Bracey (Amherst, MA: University of Massachusetts Press, 1999), 448.

316. Melissa Fay Greene, *The Temple Bombing* (New York: Perseus Books, 1996), 1.

317. Sarna, *American Judaism*, 309.

318. "Jacob Rothschild (1911–1973)," www.georgiaencyclopedia.org/nge/Article. jsp?id=h-1616, retrieved February 11, 2009.

319. Greene, *The Temple Bombing*, 1.

320. Harold H. Martin, *Atlanta and Environs: A Chronicle of Its People and Events; Years of Change and Challenge, 1940–1976* (Athens, GA: University of Georgia Press, 1987), 286.

321. Greene, *The Temple Bombing*, 1.

322. Ibid., 246.

323. Oney, *And the Dead Shall Rise*, 11–12.

324. Greene, *The Temple Bombing*, 260.

325. Greg Bluestain, "Atlanta Jews Remember 'Bomb That Healed,'" *USA Today*, October 13, 2008.

326. "Jacob Rothschild (1911-1973)," www.georgiaencyclopedia.org/nge/Article. jsp?id=h-1616, retrieved February 11, 2009.

327. Paul Berman, *A Tale of Two Utopias* (New York: W. W. Norton, 1996), 44.

328. Sachar, *A History of the Jews in America*, 803.

329. William Bradford Huie, *Three Lives for Mississippi* (Jackson, MS: University Press of Mississippi, 2000), 35–36.

330. Sachar, *A History of the Jews in America*, 803.

331. Lawrence van Gelder, "Rabbi Arthur J. Lelyveld, 83, Rights Crusader," *New York Times*, April 16, 1996.

332. Margalit Fox, "Betty Friedan, Who Ignited Cause in 'Feminine Mystique,' Dies at 85," *New York Times*, February 5, 2006.

333. Jerry Klinger, "American Jewish History, 1967–2005, Part 2," www.jewishmag. com/89mag/usa12/usa12.htm, retrieved October 10, 2008.

334. James Baldwin, *Notes of a Native Son* (Boston, MA: Beacon, 1955), 67.

335. Julius Lester, *Lovesong: Becoming a Jew* (New York: Henry Holt, 1988), 43.

336. Ibid., 195.

337. Natalie Weinstein, "Julius Lester: There's 'No Magic Formula' for Blacks and Jews," *The Jewish Newsweekly of Northern California*, February 16, 1996.

338. Peter Golden, "Twisting the Years Away," *New Jersey Monthly*, January 2005.

339. Norman Wain, "Mintz and Moondog 'Made' Rock 'n Roll," *Cleveland Jewish News*, April 4, 1986.

340. "Alan Freed," www.history-of-rock.com/freed.htm, retrieved February 21, 2009.

341. Wain, "Mintz and Moondog 'Made' Rock 'n Roll."

342. Nick Tosches, *Unsung Heroes of Rock 'n' Roll: The Birth of Rock in the Wild Years before Elvis* (Cambridge, MA: Da Capo Press, 1999), 135.

343. Philip H. Ennis, *The Seventh Stream: The Emergence of Rocknroll in American Popular Music* (Middletown, CT: Wesleyan University Press, 1992), 18.

344. "Moondog Coronation Ball," http://cleveland.about.com/od/springevents/p/ moondog.htm, retrieved February 21, 2009.

345. Tosches, *Unsung Heroes of Rock 'n' Roll*, 137.

346. Golden, "Twisting the Years Away"; author's interview with Carl Foushee.
347. Gerri Hirshey, *Nowhere to Run: The Story of Soul Music* (New York: Times Books, 1984), 9.
348. Ibid.
349. David Halberstam, *The Fifties* (New York: Ballantine Books, 1993), 472.
350. Linda Martin and Kerry Segrave, *Anti-Rock: The Opposition to Rock 'n' Roll* (Cambridge, MA; Da Capo Press, 1993), 63–66.
351. Halberstam, *The Fifties*, 473.
352. Ibid., 478.
353. Gayle Wald, *Crossing the Line: Racial Passing in Twentieth-Century U.S. Literature and Culture* (Durham, NC: Duke University Press, 2000), 53–55.
354. Halberstam, *The Fifties*, 477.
355. Norman Mailer, *Advertisements For Myself* (New York: G. P. Putnam's Sons, 1959), 303.
356. James Baldwin, *Nobody Knows My Name* (New York: Dell, 1961), 229–30.
357. Tom Wolfe, *Radical Chic and Mau-Mauing the Flak Catchers* (New York: Farrar, Straus and Giroux, 1970), 32–33.
358. "The Civil Rights Movement and Television," www.museum.tv/archives/etv/C/htmlC/civilrights/civilrights.htm, retrieved February 21, 2009.
359. "American Bandstand," www.museum.tv/archives/etv/A/htmlA/americanband/americanband.htm, retrieved February 21, 2009.
360. Halberstam, *The Fifties*, 474.
361. Wilborn Hampton, *Up Close: Elvis Presley* (New York: Viking Juvenile, 2007), 115.
362. Halberstam, *The Fifties*, 479.
363. Philip Norman, *John Lennon: The Life* (New York: Ecco, 2008), 82.
364. Bob Spitz, *The Beatles: The Biography* (New York: Little, Brown, 2005), 102.
365. Benjamin Jowett, trans., *The Republic* (New York: Oxford at the Clarendon Press, 1908), 424.
366. Suze Rotolo, *A Freewheelin' Time: A Memoir of Greenwich Village in the Sixties* (New York: Broadway Books, 2008), 50.
367. Taylor Branch, *Parting the Waters: America in the King Years 1954–63* (New York: Simon and Schuster, 1988), 878.
368. Ibid., 877.
369. Mike Marqusee, *Wicked Messenger: Bob Dylan and the 1960s* (New York: Seven Stories Press, 2005), 9–10.
370. Reeves, *President Kennedy*, 522.
371. Branch, *Parting the Waters*, 876.
372. "Civil Rights," www.joachimprinz.com/civilrights.htm, retrieved February 21, 2009.
373. Ibid.
374. Schneier, *Shared Dreams*, 96.
375. "The Liberty Bell," www.ushistory.org/libertybell/, retrieved February 21, 2009. The quote is from Leviticus 25:10.
376. Edward K. Kaplan, *Spiritual Radical: Abraham Joshua Heschel in America, 1940–1972* (New Haven, CT: Yale University Press, 2007), 47.

377. Ibid., 215, 217.
378. Schneier, *Shared Dreams*, 140.
379. Kaplan, *Spiritual Radical*, 176.
380. Ibid., 225.
381. Ro'i, *The Struggle for Soviet Jewish Emigration*, 193.
382. Kaplan, *Spiritual Radical*, 226–27.
383. Feingold, *"Silent No More"*, 60.
384. Louis Rosenblum, "On the National Scene," www.clevelandjewishhistory.net/sj/lr-nationalscene.htm, retrieved March 1, 2009.
385. Feingold, *"Silent No More"*, 60.
386. Taylor Branch, *Pillar of Fire: America in the King Years 1963–65* (New York: Simon and Schuster, 1998), 167–68.
387. Irving Spiegel, "Inaction Charged to Western Jews on Soviet Issue; Dr. Heschel of the Theological Seminary Scores Americans; Rabbis at Meeting in Toronto Urged to Show Concern," *New York Times*, May 17, 1966.
388. Feingold, *"Silent No More"*, 61.
389. Chernin, "Making Soviet Jews an Issue," 34–35.
390. Ro'i, *The Struggle for Soviet Jewish Emigration*, 196.
391. Ibid., 192.
392. Chernin, "Making Soviet Jews an Issue," 35.
393. Ro'i, *The Struggle for Soviet Jewish Emigration*, 198.
394. Ibid., 199.
395. Ibid., 198–99.
396. Morris B. Abram, *The Day Is Short: An Autobiography* (New York: Harcourt Brace Jovanovich, 1982), 76.
397. Elaine Woo, "Morris B. Abram; Jewish Leader Was Longtime Human Rights Advocate," *LA Times*, March 17, 2000.
398. Ro'i, *The Struggle for Soviet Jewish Emigration*, 198.
399. Chernin, "Making Soviet Jews an Issue," 43.
400. Ro'i, *The Struggle for Soviet Jewish Emigration*, 199.
401. Chernin, "Making Soviet Jews an Issue," 43.
402. Ro'i, *The Struggle for Soviet Jewish Emigration*, 199.
403. Chernin, "Making Soviet Jews an Issue," 44.
404. Ro'i, *The Struggle for Soviet Jewish Emigration*, 200.
405. Ibid.
406. "World: A Day in the Life of Yuli Daniel," *Time*, June 6, 1969, www.time.com/time/magazine/article/0,9171,941670,00.html, retrieved September 2, 2011.
407. Jeanne Vronskaya, "Obituary: Andrei Sinyavsky," *Independent* (London), February 27, 1997.
408. Ibid.
409. Lisa W. Foderaro, "Yuli M. Daniel, a Russian Writer Tried as a Dissident, Is Dead at 63," *New York Times*, January 1, 1989.
410. Spiegel, "Inaction Charged to Western Jews on Soviet Issue.
411. Ibid.
412. Ibid.
413. Ibid.

414. Elie Wiesel, *The Jews of Silence: A Personal Report on Soviet Jewry* (New York: Signet Books, 1967), See copyright page facing the table of contents.

415. Fred A. Lazin, e-mail to author, November 3, 2007.

416. Lazin, e-mail to author, November 3, 2007.

417. Spiegel, "Inaction Charged to Western Jews on Soviet Issue."

418. Ibid.

419. Kaplan, *Spiritual Radical*, 228–29.

420. Chernin, "Making Soviet Jews an Issue," 68.

421. Ibid., 50.

422. Ibid., 51.

423. Ro'i, *The Struggle for Soviet Jewish Emigration*, 133.

424. Ibid., 188.

425. Feingold, *"Silent No More"*, 61.

426. Borstelmann, *The Cold War and the Color Line*, 75.

427. Ibid., 51.

428. Ibid., 48.

429. Ibid., 57.

430. Penny Marie von Eschen, *Satchmo Blows Up the World: Jazz Ambassadors Play the Cold War* (Cambridge, MA: Harvard University Press, 2004), 16.

431. Borstelmann, *The Cold War and the Color Line*, 122.

432. Louis Armstrong, *Satchmo at Symphony Hall*, 1951, GRP Records.

433. "Louis Armstrong, Barring Soviet Tour, Denounces Eisenhower and Gov. Faubus," *New York Times*, September 9, 1957.

434. Ambrose, *Eisenhower*, 446.

435. Borstelmann, *The Cold War and the Color Line*, 204.

436. Ibid., 198–99.

437. Thurston Clarke, *Ask Not: The Inauguration of John F. Kennedy and the Speech That Changed America* (New York: Henry Holt, 2004), 127.

438. Reeves, *President Kennedy*, 40.

439. Borstelmann, *The Cold War and the Color Line*, 169.

440. Ibid., 159.

441. "Mississippi and Meredith Remember," http://edition.cnn.com/2002/US/South/09/30/meredith/index.html, retrieved Ferbruary, 26, 2009.

442. Reeves, *President Kennedy*, 529–31.

443. James M. Washington, ed., *A Testament of Hope: The Essential Writings and Speeches of Martin Luther King, Jr.* (New York: HarperCollins, 1991), 217–18.

444. David Biale, *Power and Powerlessness in Jewish History* (New York: Schocken Books, 1986), 54.

445. Author's interview with Zelig S. Chinitz.

446. Ro'i, *The Struggle for Soviet Jewish Emigration*, 136, 379.

447. Ibid., 196.

448. Author's interview with William Korey.

449. Ibid.

450. Korey, *The Soviet Cage*, 185–87.

451. Hedrick Smith, "Moscow Ratifies Two U.N. Covenants on Human Rights; Action, Viewed as Linked to Trade Issues, Is Expected to Have Little Effect," *New York*

Times, September 28, 1973.

452. Author's interview with William Korey.

453. Korey, *The Soviet Cage*, 185.

454. Wolfgang Saxon, "Rabbi Pinchas M. Teitz, 87, Founder of Schools," *New York Times*, December 29, 1995.

455. Author's interview with David H. Hill.

456. Sarna, *American Judaism*, 234.

457. Lazin, *The Struggle for Soviet Jewry*, 27.

458. Author's interview with David H. Hill.

459. Ari L. Goldman, "Rabbi Schneerson Led a Small Hasidic Sect to World Prominence," *New York Times*, June 13, 1994.

460. Ezra Mendelsohn, *The Jews of East Central Europe between the World Wars* (Bloomington, IN: Indiana University Press, 1987) 248.

461. Author's interview with David H. Hill.

462. Walter Ruby, "The Role of Nonestablishment Groups," in Friedman and Chernin, *A Second Exodus*, 220.

463. Sarna, *American Judaism*, 293.

464. Author's interview with David H. Hill.

465. Author's interview with Louis Rosenblum.

466. Louis Rosenblum, "From These Beginnings," www.clevelandjewishhistory.net/sj/lr-beginnings.htm, retrieved March 9, 2009.

467. Author's interview with Louis Rosenblum.

468. Louis Rosenblum, "Launching the Cleveland Committee on Soviet Anti-Semitism (CCSA)," www.clevelandjewishhistory.net/sj/lr-firstcontact.htm, retrieved March 9, 2009.

469. Ibid.

470. Author's interview with Louis Rosenblum.

471. Louis Rosenblum, "An American Jewish Conference on Soviet Jewry," www.clevelandjewishhistory.net/sj/lr-conference.htm, retrieved March 9, 2009.

472. Author's interview with Louis Rosenblum.

473. Author's interview with David H. Hill.

474. Rosenblum, "An American Jewish Conference on Soviet Jewry."

475. Ibid.

476. Author's interview with Louis Rosenblum.

477. Louis Rosenblum, "Transforming the Cleveland Committee on Soviet Anti-Semitism," www.clevelandjewishhistory.net/sj/lr-transforming.htm, Retrieved March 9, 2009.

478. Ibid.

479. Author's interview with Louis Rosenblum.

480. Louis Rosenblum, "Face-to-Face with Visiting Soviet Cultural Groups," www.clevelandjewishhistory.net/sj/lr-facetoface.htm, retrieved March 9, 2009.

481. Author's interview with Louis Rosenblum.

482. Ibid.

483. Yossi Klein Halevi, "Jacob Birnbaum and the Struggle for Soviet Jewry," *Azureonline* no. 17 (spring 5764/2004): www.azure.org.il/article.php?id=221, retrieved March 9, 2009; author's interview with Jacob Birnbaum.

484. Shmuel Hiley, "Solomon A. Birnbaum," Dov Ber-Kerler, ed., *History of Yiddish Studies* (Philadelphia, PA: Harwood Academic Publishers, 1991), 3–4.

485. "Yakov Birnbaum's Freedom Ride," www.jewishworldreview.com/0504/yakov_birnbaum.php3?, retrieved March 8, 2009.

486. Author's interview with Glenn Richter.

487. Halevi, "Jacob Birnbaum and the Struggle for Soviet Jewry."

488. Author's interview with Jacob Birnbaum.

489. Halevi, "Jacob Birnbaum and the Struggle for Soviet Jewry."

490. College Students' Struggle For Soviet Jewry, handout, from Jacob Birnbaum; author's interview with Glenn Richter.

491. College Students' Struggle For Soviet Jewry, handout, from Jacob Birnbaum.

492. Orbach, *The American Movement to Aid Soviet Jews*, 4.

493. Yossi Klein Halevi, *Memoirs of a Jewish Extremist: An American Story* (New York: Little, Brown, 1995), 47–48.

494. Author's interview with Glenn Richter.

495. Ibid.

496. Halevi, "Jacob Birnbaum and the Struggle for Soviet Jewry."

497. Philip Spiegel, *Triumph over Tyranny: The Heroic Campaign That Saved 2,000,000 Soviet Jews* (New York: Devora, 2008), 79.

498. Author's interview with Glenn Richter.

499. Ibid.

500. "Soviet U.N. Mission Is Picketed by 700 over Anti-Semitism," *New York Times*, May 2, 1964.

501. Author's interview with Glenn Richter.

502. "Soviet U.N. Mission Is Picketed by 700 over Anti-Semitism."

503. Ibid.

504. Spiegel, *Triumph over Tyranny*, 80.

505. Ibid.

506. Ibid, 81–82.

507. Ibid, 81.

508. Ibid., 81–82.

509. Author's interview with Glenn Richter.

510. Author's interview with Jacob Birnbaum.

511. Prayer Service For Soviet Jewry, Remarks, Jacob Birnbaum, August 25, 1964.

512. Joshua Zeitz, "Democratic Debacle," *American Heritage Magazine* 55, no. 3 (June/July 2004).

513. Ibid.

514. Author's interview with Jacob Birnbaum.

515. Ibid.

516. Irving Spiegel, "Jews' Treatment by Soviet Scored; Easing Urged by Kennedy, Keating, and Javits," *New York Times*, October 19, 1964.

517. Author's interview with Jacob Birnbaum.

518. Spiegel, *Triumph over Tyranny*, 84.

519. Irving Spiegel, "3,000 Here Protest Soviet Curb on Jews; 'Jericho March' Held on East Side Near Russian Mission," *New York Times*, April 5, 1965.

520. Author's interview with Jacob Birnbaum.

521. Spiegel, *Triumph over Tyranny*, 85.
522. Author's interview with Glenn Richter.
523. Halevi, *Memoirs of a Jewish Extremist*, 50.
524. Author's interview with Glenn Richter.
525. Halevi, *Memoirs of a Jewish Extremist*, 13.
526. Ibid., 48–50.
527. Halevi, "Jacob Birnbaum and the Struggle for Soviet Jewry."
528. Ibid.
529. *Saturday Evening Post*, November 19, 1966.
530. *Library Journal* 91, no. 21 (December 1966).
531. Hawes Publications, "Adult *New York Times* Best Seller Lists for 1966," www.hawes.com/1966/1966.htm, retrieved September 15, 2011; Hawes Publications, "Adult *New York Times* Best Seller Lists for 1967," www.hawes.com/1967/1967.htm, retrieved September 15, 2011.
532. "1967 Pulitzer Prize," http://en.wikipedia.org/wiki/1967_Pulitzer_Prize; "National Book Awards 1967"; www.nationalbook.org/nba1967.html, retrieved September 15, 2011.
533. Bernard Malamud, *The Fixer* (New York: Farrar, Straus and Giroux, 2004); Eliot Fremont-Smith, "Yakov's Choice," *New York Times*, August 29, 1966.
534. Abram, *The Day Is Short*, 150.

CHAPTER 5

1. "40 Years Ago," www.sovietjewry.org/calendar.php, retrieved March 18, 2009.
2. Author's interview with Jonathan Dekel-Chen.
3. Rachel Schnold, curator, "Jews of Struggle: The Jewish National Movement in the USSR" exhibition notes, Beit Hatfutsot, The Museum of the Jewish People, www.bh.org.il/on-line-exhibition-intro.aspx?49752, retrieved March 18, 2009.
4. Leonard Schroeter, *The Last Exodus* (New York: Universe Books, 1974), 340.
5. Spiegel, *Triumph over Tyranny*, 99.
6. Ibid.
7. Schroeter, *The Last Exodus*, 89.
8. Spiegel, *Triumph over Tyranny*, 100–102.
9. Berman, *A Tale of Two Utopias*, 9.
10. Ibid., 21.
11. Ibid., 29.
12. Gaddis, *The Cold War*, 147.
13. Associated Press, *The World in 1968: History as We Lived It* (New York: Associated Press, 1969), 103.
14. Ibid., 101.
15. Ibid., 102–3.
16. Marshall McLuhan, *The Gutenberg Galaxy: The Making of Typographic Man* (Toronto, Canada: University of Toronto Press, 1962), 21.
17. Arch Puddington, *Broadcasting Freedom: The Cold War Triumph of Radio Free*

Europe and Radio Liberty (Louisville, KY: University Press of Kentucky, 2003), 141.

18. Weiner, *Legacy of Ashes*, 36.
19. Gale Stokes, *The Walls Came Tumbling Down: The Collapse of Communism in Eastern Europe* (New York: Oxford University Press, 1993), 24.
20. Associated Press, *The World in 1968*, 103; Gaddis, *The Cold War*, 143.
21. Gaddis, *The Cold War*, 143.
22. Associated Press, *The World in 1968*, 103.
23. Edward R. Kantowicz, *Coming Apart, Coming Together: The World in the Twentieth Century, Volume 2* (Grand Rapids, MI: William B. Eerdmans, 2000), 349.
24. Associated Press, *The World in 1968*, 174–75.
25. Gaddis, *The Cold War*, 150.
26. David Talbot, *Brothers: The Hidden History of the Kennedy Years* (New York: Free Press, 2007), 255.
27. "Soviets Invade Czechoslovakia," http://www.history.com/this-day-in-history/soviets-invade-czechoslovakia, retrieved March 2, 2009.
28. Gaddis, *The Cold War*, 150.
29. Schroeter, *The Last Exodus*, 89.
30. Steven F. Windmueller, "The '*Noshrim*' War: Dropping Out," in Friedman and Chernin, *A Second Exodus*, 163.
31. Michael B. Oren, *Six Days of War: June 1967 and the Making of the Modern Middle East* (New York: Oxford University Press, 2002), 76.
32. "Yossi Peled, MK," www.mfa.gov.il/MFA/Government/Personalities/From+A-Z/Yossi_Peled.htm, Retrieved April 2, 2009.
33. Oren, *Six Days of War*, 97.
34. Ibid., 112.
35. Associated Press, *The World in 1967: History as We Lived It* (New York: Associated Press, 1968), 268.
36. Oren, *Six Days of War*, 77.
37. Ibid., 79.
38. Urofsky, *We Are One!*, 351.
39. Ibid.
40. Goldberg, *Jewish Power*, 135.
41. Urofsky, *We Are One!*, 352–53.
42. Feingold, *"Silent No More"*, 65.
43. Urofsky, *We Are One!*, 358.
44. Golden, *Quiet Diplomat*, 128–29.
45. Goldberg, *Jewish Power*, 135.
46. Urofsky, *We Are One!*, 356.
47. Eli N. Evans, *The Provincials: A Personal History of Jews in the South* (Chapel Hill, NC: The University of North Carolina Press, 2005), 107.
48. Judith A. Klinghoffer, *Vietnam, Jews and the Middle East: Unintended Consequences* (New York: St. Martin's Press, 1999), 1.
49. Urofsky, *We Are One!*, 358.
50. Ibid.
51. David H. Jones, *Moral Responsibility in the Holocaust: A Study in the Ethics of*

Character (Lanham, MD: Rowman and Littlefield, 1999), 191.

52. "Jewish Uprisings in Ghettos and Camps, 1941–1944," www.ushmm.org/wlc/article.php?lang=en&ModuleId=10005407, retrieved April 8, 2009.

53. Robert O. Freedman, "Soviet Jewry and Soviet-American Relations: A Historical Analysis," *Soviet Jewry in the Decisive Decade, 1971–80*, Robert O. Freedman, ed., (Durham, NC: Duke University Press, 1984), 41.

54. Ibid.

55. Feingold, *"Silent No More"*, 65.

56. Korey, *The Soviet Cage*, 143–44.

57. "United Nations: Jamil the Irrepressible," *Time*, December 13, 1971.

58. Goldberg, *Jewish Power*, 139.

59. Feingold, *"Silent No More"*, 66.

60. Berman, *A Tale of Two Utopias*, 44–45.

61. Goldberg, *Jewish Power*, 140.

62. Associated Press, *The World in 1967*, 193; Goldberg, *Jewish Power*, 140.

63. "A Letter from the Publisher, Apr. 19, 1954," *Time*, April 19, 1954.

64. Grose, *Israel in the Mind of America*, 310.

65. Joseph Berger, "Rabbi Arthur Hertzberg, Scholar and Blunt Advocate for Civil Rights, Dies at 84," *New York Times*, April 18, 2006.

66. Urofsky, *We Are One!*, 364–65.

67. Kaplan, *Spiritual Radical*, 226.

68. Branch, *Parting the Waters*, 873–74.

69. Associated Press, *The World in 1967*, 269.

70. Schneier, *Shared Dreams*, 180.

71. Ibid., 173.

72. Ibid., 176.

73. Baldwin, *Notes of a Native Son*, 68.

74. Alice Walker, *The Same River Twice* (New York: Washington Square Press, 1992), 168.

75. Schneier, *Shared Dreams*, 177.

76. Benjamin Ginsberg, *The Fatal Embrace: Jews and the State* (Chicago, IL: University of Chicago Press, 1993), 168.

77. Robert I. Friedman, *The False Prophet: Rabbi Meir Kahane From FBI Informant to Knesset Member* (Brooklyn, NY: Lawrence Hill Books, 1990), 85.

78. Bobby Seale, *Seize the Time: The Story of the Black Panther Party and Huey P. Newman* (New York: Random House, 1968), 64.

79. Mark Dollinger, "Black Nationalism," Richard Levy, ed., *Antisemitism: A Historical Encyclopedia of Prejudice and Persecution* (Santa Barbara, CA: ABC-CLIO, 2005), 72.

80. John Lewis, "'I Have a Dream' for Peace in the Middle East: Martin Luther King Jr.'s Special Bond with Israel," *San Francisco Chronicle*, January 21, 2002.

81. Goldberg, *Jewish Power*, 140.

82. Dollinger, "Black Nationalism," 72.

83. Associated Press, *The World in 1967*, 137.

84. Goldberg, *Jewish Power*, 140.

85. Lester, *Lovesong*, 48.

86. Martin Mayer, *The Teachers Strike: New York, 1968* (New York: Harper and Row, 1969), 12.

87. Friedman, *The False Prophet*, 92; Lester, *Lovesong*, 48.

88. Friedman, *The False Prophet*, 91–92.

89. Goldberg, *Jewish Power*, 141; "Behavior: The Black and the Jew: A Falling Out of Allies," *Time*, January 31, 1969, www.time.com/time/magazine/article/0,9171,841586,00.html, retrieved September 15, 2011.

90. Lester, *Lovesong*, 48.

91. Richard D. Kahlenberg, "Ocean Hill-Brownsville, 40 Years Later," *The Chronicle of Higher Education* 54, no. 33, (April 2008): B7.

92. Goldberg, *Jewish Power*, 141.

93. Kahlenberg, "Ocean Hill-Brownsville, 40 Years Later," B7.

94. Goldberg, *Jewish Power*, 141.

95. Joseph Berger, "Albert Shanker, 68, Combative Leader Who Transformed Teachers' Union, Dies," *New York Times*, February 24, 1997.

96. Goldberg, *Jewish Power*, 141.

97. Lester, *Lovesong*, 50–51.

98. "Behavior: The Black and the Jew: A Falling Out of Allies."

99. Christopher Hitchens, foreword to Friedman, *The False Prophet* (London: Faber and Faber, 1990), xii.

100. Urofsky, *We Are One!*, 360.

101. Friedman, *The False Prophet*, 86–88.

102. Meir, *My Life*, 319–20.

103. Author's interview with Henry A. Kissinger.

104. Halevi, *Memoirs of a Jewish Extremist*, 78.

105. Rodney Stark and Stephen Steinberg, "Jews and Christians in Suburbia," *Harper's Magazine*, August 1967.

106. Ibid.

107. Martin Weil, "Abraham Ribicoff, 87, Dies; Senator, HEW Chief," *Washington Post*, February 23, 1998.

108. "A Timeline of Unconventional Moments in U.S. History," www.blacktable.com/zoellner040831.htm, retrieved April 20, 2009.

109. Rosen, *Saving the Jews*, 444.

110. Arthur D. Morse, "…and America slept," *Washington Post Book World*, February 4, 1968.

111. Friedman, *The False Prophet*, 118.

112. "15 Jews Protest Action by N.Y.U.; Pickets Ask Retraction of Hatchett's Appointment," *New York Times*, August 6, 1968.

113. "Education: Response to Destruction," *Time*, October 18, 1968.

114. Friedman, *The False Prophet*, 91–92.

115. Ibid., 101.

116. Mark A. Stuart, *Gangster #2: Longy Zwillman, The Man Who Invented Organized Crime* (Secaucus, NJ: Lyle Stuart, 1985), 20–21.

117. Warren Grover, *Nazis in Newark* (New Brunswick, NJ: Transaction, 2003), 39.

118. Friedman, *The False Prophet*, 97.

119. Author's interview with Glenn Richter.

120. Friedman, *The False Prophet*, 93.

121. Ibid., 98.

122. Ibid., 105–6.

123. Ibid., 108.

124. Irving Spiegel, "14 Jews Arrested in Soviet Protest; League Paints Airliner, Invades Offices Here," *New York Times*, December 30, 1969.

125. Friedman, *The False Prophet*, 108.

126. Ibid., 111.

127. Irving Spiegel, "J.D.L. is Criticized by Jewish Leader; But Hoffman Also Assails Soviet and Arab 'Calumny,'" *New York Times*, October 31, 1971.

128. Friedman, *The False Prophet*, 112.

129. Author's interview with Louis Rosenblum.

130. Author's interview with Hillel Levine.

131. Ibid.

132. Ibid.

133. Associated Press, *The World in 1967*, 143.

134. "Jewish Emigration from the Former Soviet Union to Israel and the United States," www.ncsj.org/stats.shtml, retrieved April, 2, 2005.

135. Associated Press, *The World in 1969: History as We Lived It* (New York: Associated Press, 1970), 267; Freedman, "Soviet Jewry and Soviet-American Relations," 42.

136. Freedman, "Soviet Jewry and Soviet-American Relations," 42.

137. Spiegel, *Triumph over Tyranny*, 93–94.

138. Schroeter, *The Last Exodus*, 45.

139. Spiegel, *Triumph over Tyranny*, 94.

140. Schroeter, *The Last Exodus*, 45.

141. Spiegel, *Triumph over Tyranny*, 95.

142. Schroeter, *The Last Exodus*, 47.

143. Lindemann, *The Jew Accused*, 177.

144. Schroeter, *The Last Exodus*, 48.

145. "'Sowing,'" www.ajhs.org/publications/TimelineASJM/section4.cfm, retrieved May 8, 2009.

146. Spiegel, *Triumph over Tyranny*, 95–96.

147. Gitelman, *A Century of Ambivalence*, 180.

148. Korey, *The Soviet Cage*, 201.

149. Ibid., 202.

150. "Israel Knesset Asks Clemency for Soviet Jews; At Special Session, It Calls Upon Moscow to Release 11 in Hijacking Case," *New York Times*, December 26, 1970.

151. Anatoly Dobrynin, *In Confidence: Moscow's Ambassador to America's Six Cold War Presidents* (Seattle, WA: University of Washington Press, 1995), 158.

152. Ibid.

153. Ibid.

154. Edward Drachman, *Challenging the Kremlin: The Soviet Jewish Movement for Freedom, 1967–1990* (New York: Paragon, 1991), 447.

155. Ibid.

156. Urofsky, *We Are One!*, 420.

157. Harris, "Arab Opposition to Jewish Immigration to Israel," 3.

158. "Lebanon Fears Influx of Soviet Jews into Israel," *New York Times*, December 18, 1971; Harris, "Arab Opposition to Jewish Immigration to Israel," 3.

159. "Plight of Soviet Jews," *New York Times*, April 1, 1972; Harris, "Arab Opposition to Jewish Immigration to Israel," 3–4.

160. Harris, "Arab Opposition to Jewish Immigration to Israel," 4.

161. Bernard Gwertzman, "Why Did Leningrad 9 Take Such a Drastic Risk?," *New York Times*, May 16, 1971.

162. Associated Press, *The World in 1970: History as We Lived It* (New York: Associated Press, 1971), 153–57.

163. Feingold, *"Silent No More"*, 80.

164. Dobrynin, *In Confidence*, 55.

165. Irving Spiegel, "A Hannukkah Rite Attracts 20,000," *New York Times*, December 14, 1971.

166. Feingold, *"Silent No More"*, 81.

167. Golden, *Quiet Diplomat*, 257.

168. Feingold, *"Silent No More"*, 81.

169. Feingold, *"Silent No More"*, 81; Spiegel, *Triumph over Tyranny*, 115.

170. Spiegel, *Triumph over Tyranny*, 115.

171. Feingold, *"Silent No More"*, 81.

172. Spiegel, *Triumph over Tyranny*, 273.

173. "'Sowing,'" www.ajhs.org/publications/TimelineASJM/section4.cfm, retrieved May 8, 2009.

174. Spiegel, *Triumph over Tyranny*, 115.

175. Golden, *Quiet Diplomat*, 256–58.

176. Spiegel, *Triumph over Tyranny*, 115.

177. Golden, *Quiet Diplomat*, 258.

178. Freedman, "Soviet Jewry and Soviet-American Relations," 43.

179. Gwertzman, "Why Did Leningrad 9 Take Such a Drastic Risk?".

180. Stephen E. Ambrose, *Nixon: The Triumph of a Politician 1962–1972* (New York: Simon and Schuster, 1989), 439.

181. Associated Press, *The World in 1970*, 187.

182. Berman, *A Tale of Two Utopias*, 91.

183. Stanley Karnow, *Vietnam: A History* (New York: Viking Press, 1983), 610.

184. Kathy Warnes, "The Ageless Anguish of Kent State," in *Crimes and Trials of the Century*, vol. 1, *From the Black Sox Scandal to the Attica Prison Riots*, ed. Frankie Y. Bailey and Steven Chermak (Westport, CT: Greenwood Press, 2007), 318.

185. Richard Reeves, *President Nixon: Alone in the White House* (New York; Simon and Schuster, 2001), 234.

186. Ambrose, *Nixon: The Triumph of a Politician*, 367.

187. Author's interview with Richard M. Nixon.

188. Morozov, *Documents on Soviet Jewish Emigration*, 148.

189. Korey, *The Soviet Cage*, 201.

190. Friedman, *The False Prophet*, 114–15.

191. Tad Szulc, "Shots at Soviet Mission Stir Bitter Debate in the U.N.," *New York Times*, October 22, 1971.

192. Friedman, *The False Prophet*, 115–17.

193. Morozov, *Documents on Soviet Jewish Emigration*, 70.
194. Friedman, *The False Prophet*, 104.
195. Eric Pace, "Joseph Gruss, 91, Philanthropist Who Supported Jewish Schools," *New York Times*, July 5, 1993.
196. Friedman, *The False Prophet*, 115–16.
197. "*Soviet Union: The Leningrad Nine.*" *Time*, May 31, 1971.
198. Friedman, *The False Prophet*, 115.
199. Author's interview with Shoshana S. Cardin.
200. Feingold, *"Silent No More"*, 82.
201. Author's interview with Morey Shapira.
202. M. H. Naftalin, "The Activist Movement," in Friedman and Chernin, *A Second Exodus*, 231.
203. Spiegel, *Triumph over Tyranny*, 228.
204. Nadine Brozan, "Richard Maass, 79, Founder of Conference on Soviet Jewry," *New York Times*, September 12, 1998.
205. Author's interview with Jerry Goodman.
206. Ibid.
207. Ibid.
208. Ibid.
209. "Crime: Bombs for Balalaikas," *Time*, February 7, 1972.
210. Friedman, *The False Prophet*, 109.
211. Ibid.
212. "Crime: Bombs for Balalaikas."
213. Friedman, *The False Prophet*, 145.
214. "Crime: Bombs for Balalaikas."
215. Friedman, *The False Prophet*, 145.
216. Ibid., 110.
217. Jim Dwyer and Kevin Flynn, *102 Minutes: The Untold Story of the Fight to Survive inside the Twin Towers* (New York: Times Books, 2004), 8.
218. Greg B. Smith, "Bin Laden Bankrolled Kahane Killer Defense," *Daily News*, October 9, 2002.
219. "Jewish Emigration from the Former Soviet Union to Israel and the United States," www.ncsj.org/stats.shtml, retrieved April, 2, 2005.

CHAPTER 6

1. Meir, *My Life*, 325–26.
2. Leonard Garment, *Crazy Rhythm: From Brooklyn and Jazz to Nixon's White House, Watergate, and Beyond* (New York: Times Books, 1997), 191; author's interview with Leonard Garment.
3. Author's interview with Richard M. Nixon.
4. Klinghoffer, *Vietnam, Jews and the Middle East*, 30.
5. Golden, *Quiet Diplomat*, 193.
6. Meir, *My Life*, 324.

7. Burkett, *Golda*, 265.
8. David Stout, "Israel's Nuclear Arsenal Vexed Nixon," *New York Times*, November 29, 2007.
9. Richard Nixon, *RN: The Memoirs of Richard Nixon* (New York: Simon and Schuster, 1978), 478.
10. Meir, *My Life*, 327.
11. Richard M. Nixon, letter to author, June 22, 1989.
12. Nixon, *RN*, 346.
13. Golden, *Quiet Diplomat*, 193–94.
14. Robert Dallek, *Nixon and Kissinger: Partners in Power* (New York: HarperCollins, 2007), 169–70.
15. Nixon, *RN*, 339.
16. Golden, *Quiet Diplomat*, 204.
17. Burkett, *Golda*, 263.
18. Yitzhak Rabin, *The Rabin Memoirs* (Berkeley, CA: University of California Press, 1979), 171.
19. John N. Mitchell, Oral History, Max M. Fisher Archives.
20. Kenneth M. Pollack, *Arabs at War: Military Effectiveness, 1948–1991* (Lincoln, NE: University of Nebraska Press, 2002), 94.
21. Raymond H. Anderson, "Nasser, with Libya and Sudan, Seeks to Halt Jordan Fighting," *New York Times*, September 19, 1970.
22. Dallek, *Nixon and Kissinger*, 171.
23. Reeves, *President Nixon*, 254.
24. Nixon, *RN*, 483.
25. Henry Kissinger, *White House Years* (Boston: Little, Brown, 1979), 618.
26. Dallek, *Nixon and Kissinger*, 183.
27. Nixon, *RN*, 483.
28. Ibid., 485.
29. Janet and John Wallach, *Arafat: In the Eyes of the Beholder* (New York: Lyle Stuart, 1990), 292.
30. Spiegel, *The Other Arab-Israeli Conflict*, 202.
31. Goldberg, *Jewish Power*, 34.
32. Nixon, *RN*, 481–82.
33. Associated Press, *The World in 1967*, 252.
34. Klinghoffer, *Vietnam, Jews and the Middle East*, 34.
35. Oren, *Six Days of War*, 112.
36. Author's interview with Richard M. Nixon.
37. David H. Hackworth, *About Face: The Odyssey of an American Warrior* (New York: Simon and Schuster, 1989), 551.
38. Rabin, *The Rabin Memoirs*, 126–27.
39. Karnow, *Vietnam*, 632.
40. Ibid., 626.
41. Author's interview with Richard M. Nixon.
42. Author's interview with J. J. Goldberg. All quotes from this meeting, except where noted, are drawn from this interview.
43. Author's interview with David Twersky.

44. Ethan Bronner, "Israel, after 43 Years, Is Ready for Beatlemania," *New York Times*, August 28, 2008. The Israeli government, many years later, apologized for its decision in a letter to Paul McCartney and Ringo Starr and invited the two surviving members of the Beatles to perform. On September 25, 2008, McCartney gave a concert for an estimated forty thousand fans at Tel Aviv's Yarkon Park. To make the story a bit muddier: music aficionado and historian Yoav Kutner told *Haaretz* that the cancellation was really because of a fight between the music promoters Giora Godik and Yaakov Uri. See "Paul McCartney Gig Revives Israeli Beatles Tale," http://new.music.yahoo.com/paul-mccartney/news/paul-mccartney-gig-revives-israeli-beatles-tale--61660019, retrieved August 11, 2011. However, the unflattering name for the Beatles still existed, as did the government report and the later government apology. I think we are on safe historical ground to say that older Israeli leaders were not charter members of any Beatles fan clubs.

45. Bronner, "Israel, after 43 Years, Is Ready for Beatlemania".

46. Author's interview with Zev Yaroslavsky.

47. Ibid.

48. Spiegel, *Triumph over Tyranny*, 247.

49. Author's interview with Zev Yaroslavsky.

50. Ibid.

51. Ibid.

52. Author's interview with Si Frumkin.

53. Ibid.

54. Ibid.

55. Ibid.

56. Dennis McLellan, "George Putnam, Longtime L.A. Newsman, Dies at 94," *LA Times*, September 13, 2008.

57. Spiegel, *Triumph over Tyranny*, 242–43.

58. Ibid., 248.

59. Author's interview with Zev Yaroslavsky.

60. Ibid.

61. Kathleen Hendrix, "The Obsession: For Years, Si Frumkin Irked the Jewish Establishment with His Crusade to Aid Soviet Jews. Now His Cause Is in the Mainstream," *LA Times*, August 30, 1990.

62. Author's interview with Zev Yaroslavsky.

63. Ibid.

64. Spiegel, *Triumph over Tyranny*, 309–10.

65. Orbach, *The American Movement to Aid Soviet Jews*, 38.

66. Schroeter, *The Last Exodus*, 89.

67. Spiegel, *Triumph over Tyranny*, 101.

68. Raviv and Melman, *Every Spy a Prince*, 103–4.

69. Spiegel, *Triumph over Tyranny*, 101.

70. Ibid.

71. Orbach, *The American Movement to Aid Soviet Jews*, 88.

72. Ibid., 39.

73. Author's interview with Hillel Levine.

74. Friedman, *The False Prophet*, 113.

75. Author's interview with Louis Rosenblum.
76. Orbach, *The American Movement to Aid Soviet Jews*, 48.
77. Ruby, "The Role of Nonestablishment Groups," 207.
78. "Jewish Emigration from the Former Soviet Union to Israel and the United States," www.ncsj.org/stats.shtml, retrieved April, 2, 2005.
79. Windmueller, "The *'Noshrim'* War," 163.
80. Feingold, *"Silent No More"*, 45.
81. Author's interview with Mark E. Talisman.
82. Windmueller, "The *'Noshrim'* War," 166.
83. James Rosen, *The Strong Man: John Mitchell and the Secrets of Watergate* (New York: Doubleday, 2008), 127.
84. Windmueller, "The *'Noshrim'* War," 164–65.
85. Golden, *Quiet Diplomat*, 207.
86. Author's interview with Max M. Fisher.

CHAPTER 7

1. Reeves, *President Nixon*, 434.
2. Alistair Horne, *Kissinger: 1973, the Crucial Year* (New York: Simon and Schuster, 2009), 81.
3. Karnow, *Vietnam*, 636.
4. Gaddis, *The Cold War*, 150.
5. Ambrose, *Nixon: The Triumph of a Politician*, 514.
6. Karnow, *Vietnam*, 637.
7. Gaddis, *The Cold War*, 150.
8. Robert D. Kaplan, "Kissinger, Metternich, and Realism," *The Atlantic Monthly*, June 1999.
9. Ambrose, *Nixon: The Triumph of a Politician*, 526.
10. Associated Press, *The World in 1972: History as We Lived It* (New York: Associated Press, 1973), 75–77.
11. Associated Press, "Congress Gets Bills to Help Israelis Settle Soviet Jews," *New York Times*, February 9, 1972.
12. "Record Goal Set For Israel Bonds," *New York Times*, February 26, 1972.
13. Margaret MacMillan, *Nixon and Mao: The Week That Changed the World* (New York: Random House, 2007), 69–71.
14. Reeves, *President Nixon*, 438–39.
15. Gaddis, *The Cold War*, 151.
16. Ibid., 147–48.
17. Reeves, *President Nixon*, 440.
18. Ibid., 442–43.
19. Ibid., 441.
20. Arthur M. Schlesinger Jr., *The Imperial Presidency* (Boston: Houghton Mifflin, 1973), viii.
21. Ibid., x.

22. Author's interview with Richard M. Nixon, in Golden, *Quiet Diplomat*, 183.
23. Karnow, *Vietnam*, 640.
24. Ibid., 642.
25. Dallek, *Nixon and Kissinger*, 385.
26. Reeves, *President Nixon*, 474.
27. Ibid., 486.
28. Gaidar, *Collapse of an Empire*, 87.
29. Ibid., 80.
30. Ibid., 91.
31. Robert G. Kaufman, *Henry M. Jackson: A Life in Politics* (Seattle, WA: University of Washington Press, 2000), 250; Freedman, "Soviet Jewry and Soviet-American Relations," 43.
32. Gaddis, *The Cold War*, 213.
33. Ibid., 218.
34. Ibid., 213.
35. Dobrynin, *In Confidence*, 217–18.
36. Spiegel, *Triumph over Tyranny*, 236–37.
37. George Dugan, "A Huge Crowd Here Protests Soviet Imprisonment and Treatment of Jews," *New York Times*, May 1, 1972.
38. Ibid.
39. Halevi, *Memoirs of a Jewish Extremist*, 73.
40. "Rates of Intermarriage," www.ujc.org/page.aspx?id=46253, retrieved June 1, 2009.
41. Author's interview with Carmi Schwartz.
42. Author's interview with Max M. Fisher; author's interview with Richard M. Nixon.
43. Author's interview with Richard M. Nixon.
44. Eric Caldwell, "Angela Davis Acquitted on All Charges; Angela Davis Found Not Guilty by White Jury on All Charges," *New York Times*, June 5, 1972. Davis was found not guilty by a predominantly white jury.
45. Author's interview with Richard M. Nixon.
46. Author's interview with Henry A. Kissinger.
47. Henry Kissinger, *Years of Upheaval* (Boston, MA: Little, Brown, 1982), 249; Paula Stern, *Water's Edge: Domestic Politics and the Making of American Foreign Policy* (Westport, CT: Greenwood Press, 1979), 15.
48. Kissinger, *Years of Upheaval*, 249.
49. Stern, *Water's Edge*, 19.
50. Kissinger, *Years of Upheaval*, 989.
51. Dallek, *Nixon and Kissinger*, 393.
52. Alvin Z. Rubinstein, *Red Star on the Nile: The Soviet-Egyptian Influence Relationship since the June War* (Princeton: Princeton University Press, 1977), 278–79.
53. Daniel C. Thomas, *The Helsinki Effect: International Norms, Human Rights, and the Demise of Communism* (Princeton: Princeton University Press, 2001), 48.
54. "Radio and Television Address to the People of the Soviet Union: May 28, 1972," www.presidency.ucsb.edu/ws/index.php?pid=3437, retrieved June 1, 2009.
55. Author's interview with Richard M. Nixon, in Golden, *Quiet Diplomat*, 277–78.

56. Walter Isaacson, *Kissinger: A Biography* (New York: Simon and Schuster, 1992), 611.

57. Henry Kissinger, *Diplomacy* (New York: Simon and Schuster, 1994), 752.

58. David C. Geyer, et al., eds., *Foreign Relations of the United States, 1969–1976*, vol. 14, *Soviet Union: October 1971–May 1972* (Washington, DC: Government Printing Office, 2006), document 39.

59. William Korey, *The Promises We Keep: Human Rights, the Helsinki Process, and American Foreign Policy* (New York: St. Martin's Press, 1993), xviii.

60. The Academy of Sciences of the USSR, *Leonid Brezhnev: Pages from His Life* (New York: Simon and Schuster, 1978), 204.

61. Dallek, *Nixon and Kissinger*, 389.

62. Thomas, *The Helsinki Effect*, 36–37.

63. Korey, *The Promises We Keep*, 16.

64. Dobrynin, *In Confidence*, 268.

65. John F. Burns, "Of Ideology, Succession and Suslov's Big Shadow," *New York Times*, January 31, 1982.

66. Orbach, *The American Movement to Aid Soviet Jews*, 132.

67. Feingold, *"Silent No More"*, 85.

68. Petrus Buwalda, *They Did Not Dwell Alone: Jewish Emigration from the Soviet Union, 1967–1990* (Washington, DC: The Woodrow Wilson Center Press, 1997), 91.

69. Dobrynin, *In Confidence*, 268.

70. Andrei Gromyko, *Memoirs*, trans. Harold Shukman (New York: Doubleday, 1989), 293.

71. Dobrynin, *In Confidence*, 269.

72. Morozov, *Documents on Soviet Jewish Emigration*, 172.

73. Ibid., 175.

74. Feingold, *"Silent No More"*, 86.

75. Buwalda, *They Did Not Dwell Alone*, 90.

76. Ibid., 92.

77. Zavier Cornut, "The Moroccan Connection," *Jerusalem Post*, June 22, 2009.

78. Orbach, *The American Movement to Aid Soviet Jews*, 132.

79. Author's interview with Jerry Goodman.

80. Feingold, *"Silent No More"*, 86.

81. Kissinger, *Years of Upheaval*, 250.

82. Ibid.

83. Morozov, *Documents on Soviet Jewish Emigration*, 175.

84. Gaddis, *The Cold War*, 204.

85. Feingold, *"Silent No More"*, 126.

86. "Terrorism: Blackmail in Vienna," *Time*, October 8, 1973.

87. Arab Report and Record, September 16–30, 1973; Harris, "Arab Opposition to Jewish Immigration to Israel," 4.

88. Harris, "Arab Opposition to Jewish Immigration to Israel," 4.

89. Ibid.

90. Ibid.

91. Ibid., 5.

92. Ibid.
93. "Fahmi Seems to Soften Line on Immigration into Israel," *Washington Post*, May 11, 1975; Harris, "Arab Opposition to Jewish Immigration to Israel," 6.
94. Harris, "Arab Opposition to Jewish Immigration to Israel," 6.
95. Rubinstein, *Red Star on the Nile*, 172–73.
96. Kaufman, *Henry M. Jackson*, 250.
97. Stern, *Water's Edge*, 19.
98. Jerry W. Markham, *A Financial History of the United States, Volume III: From the Age of Derivatives into the New Millennium* (Armonk, NY: M. E. Sharpe, 2001), 40.
99. Kaufman, *Henry M. Jackson*, 250.
100. Ibid., 250.
101. "Business: Another Soviet Grain Sting," *Time*, November 28, 1977.
102. Kaufman, *Henry M. Jackson*, 250–51.
103. Stern, *Water's Edge*, 20; Kissinger, *Years of Upheaval*, 250.
104. Robert McG.Thomas Jr., "Dorothy Fosdick, 83, Adviser on International Policy, Dies," *New York Times*, February 10, 1997.
105. Robert G. Kaiser, "Behind-Scenes Power over Arms Policy," *Washington Post*, June 26, 1977.
106. Thomas Jr., "Dorothy Fosdick."
107. Kaiser, "Behind-Scenes Power over Arms Policy"; Stern, *Water's Edge*, 23.
108. Isaacson, *Kissinger*, 611.
109. Kaufman, *Henry M. Jackson*, 38–39.
110. Peter J. Ognibene, *Scoop: The Life and Politics of Henry M. Jackson* (Briarcliff Manor, NY: Stein and Day, 1975), 183–84.
111. "No Protest, Says Russia," *New York Times*, December 18, 1911.
112. Stern, *Water's Edge*, 10–11.
113. Louis Rosenblum, "Political Action," www.clevelandjewishhistory.net/sj/lr-action. htm, retrieved June 8, 2009.
114. Stern, *Water's Edge*, 12.
115. Rosenblum, "Political Action."
116. Feingold, *"Silent No More"*, 115.
117. Author's interview with Mark E. Talisman.
118. Stern, *Water's Edge*, 25–26.
119. Feingold, *"Silent No More"*, 116.
120. Orbach, *The American Movement to Aid Soviet Jews*, 133.
121. Buwalda, *They Did Not Dwell Alone*, 93.
122. Stern, *Water's Edge*, 26–27.
123. Author's interview with Richard N. Perle.
124. Ibid.
125. Ibid.
126. Buwalda, *They Did Not Dwell Alone*, 95–96.
127. Orbach, *The American Movement to Aid Soviet Jews*, 133.
128. Golden, *Quiet Diplomat*, 270–72.
129. Ambrose, *Nixon: The Triumph of a Politician*, 616.
130. "Sept. 6, 1972: Day 12," *LA Times*, September 6, 1972.
131. William Safire, *Before the Fall: An Inside View of the Pre-Watergate White House*

(New York: Doubleday, 1975), 571.

132. Golden, *Quiet Diplomat*, 271–72.

133. JTA *Daily News Bulletin*, September 29, 1972.

134. Ibid.

135. Bernard Gwertman, "Gromyko Invited to Nixon Retreat; President Moves Talks to Camp David for Night," *New York Times*, October 3, 1972.

136. Feingold, *"Silent No More"*, 120.

137. Buwalda, *They Did Not Dwell Alone*, 96.

138. Stern, *Water's Edge*, 44.

139. Ambrose, *Nixon: The Triumph of a Politician*, 615.

140. Ibid., 616.

141. Stern, *Water's Edge*, 54.

142. Ibid., 44–45.

143. Ambrose, *Nixon: The Triumph of a Politician*, 617.

144. Stern, *Water's Edge*, 46.

145. Elizabeth Becker, "Kissinger Tapes Describe Crises, War and Stark Photos of Abuse," *New York Times*, May 27, 2004.

146. Karnow, *Vietnam*, 623.

147. Ibid.

148. Ibid., 636.

149. Ambrose, *Nixon: The Triumph of a Politician*, 615–16.

150. Isaacson, *Kissinger*, 455.

151. Karnow, *Vietnam*, 651.

152. Alexander M. Haig Jr., *Inner Circles: How America Changed the World* (New York: Warner Books, 1992), 294.

153. Isaacson, *Kissinger*, 462.

154. Ibid.

155. Karnow, *Vietnam*, 652–53.

156. Christopher Goffard, "New Batch of Nixon Tapes Released," *Chicago Tribune*, June 24, 2009.

157. Karnow, *Vietnam*, 654.

158. Ibid.

159. Stern, *Water's Edge*, 49.

160. C. L. Sulzberger, *An Age of Mediocrity: Memoirs and Diaries, 1963–1972* (New York: Macmillan, 1973), 608.

161. Dobrynin, *In Confidence*, 337.

162. Richard, C. Thornton, *The Nixon-Kissinger Years: Reshaping of America's Foreign Policy* (New York: Paragon House, 1989), 293.

163. Stern, *Water's Edge*, 48.

164. Ibid., 46.

165. Kissinger, *Years of Upheaval*, 996.

166. Ibid., 983.

167. Kiron K. Skinner, Annelise Anderson, and Martin Anderson, eds., *Reagan: In His Own Hand; The Writings of Ronald Reagan That Reveal His Revolutionary Vision for America*, (New York: Free Press, 2001), 15.

168. Michael Lind, "A Tragedy of Errors," *The Nation*, February 23, 2004.

169. Isaacson, *Kissinger*, 609.
170. Sidney Blumenthal, "Mugged by Reality," *Salon* magazine, www.salon.com/ opinion/blumenthal/2006/12/14/jeane_kirkpatrick/, retrieved June 18, 2009.
171. Author's interview with Richard M. Nixon.
172. Kissinger, *Years of Upheaval*, 983.
173. Feingold, *"Silent No More"*, 116.
174. Author's interview with Max M. Fisher.
175. Terence Smith, "Nixon Aides, Seeing Big Gains, Plan a Drive for Jewish Votes," *New York Times*, July 7, 1972.
176. Hedrick Smith, "McGovern Urges Israeli Pullout; Links Move to Guarantees of the Nation's Borders," *New York Times*, March 3, 1971.
177. Golden, *Quiet Diplomat*, 267.
178. Author's interview with Max M. Fisher.
179. Ambrose, *Nixon: The Triumph of a Politician*, 651.
180. Feingold, *"Silent No More"*, 121.
181. Nixon, *RN*, 875.
182. Author's interview with Mark E. Talisman.
183. For instance, see Ambrose, *Nixon: The Triumph of a Politician*, 617; and Goldberg, *Jewish Power*, 165.
184. Feingold, *"Silent No More"*, 122–23.
185. Author's interview with Mark E. Talisman.
186. Nixon, *RN*, 346.
187. Stephen E. Ambrose and Douglas G. Brinkley, *Rise to Globalism: American Foreign Policy Since 1938* (New York: Penguin, 1997), 269.
188. "Statistical Information about Casualties of the Vietnam War," http://www. archives.gov/research/military/vietnam-war/casualty-statistics.html,   retrieved June 18, 2009.
189. Ambrose and Brinkley, *Rise to Globalism*, 269.
190. Kissinger, *Years of Upheaval*, 981.
191. Kissinger, *White House Years*, 1088–89.
192. Isaacson, *Kissinger*, 74–75.
193. Kissinger, *Years of Upheaval*, 50.
194. Ibid., 981.
195. Isaacson, *Kissinger*, 76.
196. Ibid., 611.
197. Kissinger, *Years of Upheaval*, 242.
198. Kissinger, *Diplomacy*, 462.
199. Philip Caputo, *A Rumor of War* (New York: Ballantine Books, 1987).
200. Dobrynin, *In Confidence*, 334.
201. "Nixon on Abortion, Vietnam and Jews," *New York Times*, June 23, 2009.
202. Safire, *Before the Fall*, 564.
203. Ibid., 577.
204. Isaacson, *Kissinger*, 28.

CHAPTER 8

1. Richard Pearson, "Wilbur Mills Dies at 82, Ways and Means Chairman," *Washington Post*, May 3, 1992.
2. "The Congress: Return of King Caucus," *Time*, December 16, 1974.
3. Pearson, "Wilbur Mills Dies at 82."
4. Stern, *Water's Edge*, 54; author's interview with Mark E. Talisman.
5. Elizabeth Auster, "Former U.S. Rep. Charles Vanik dead at 94," (Cleveland) *Plain Dealer*, August 30, 2007.
6. Stern, *Water's Edge*, 54.
7. Auster, "Former U.S. Rep. Charles Vanik dead at 94"; author's interview with Mark E. Talisman.
8. Author's interview with Mark E. Talisman.
9. Ibid.
10. Ibid.
11. Stern, *Water's Edge*, 56.
12. Ibid.
13. Associated Press, *The World in 1973: History as We Lived It* (New York: Associated Press, 1974), 69.
14. "Timeline," www.washingtonpost.com/wp-srv/onpolitics/watergate/chronology. htm#1973, retrieved June 8, 2009.
15. "Watergate Chronology," http://watergate.info/chronology/1973.shtml, retrieved June 10, 2009.
16. Stanley I. Kutler, *The Wars of Watergate: The Last Crisis of Richard Nixon* (New York: W. W. Norton, 1992), 260.
17. James R. Dickinson, "Sen. Sam Ervin, Key Figure in Watergate Probe, Dies; Ervin Was in Senate 20 Years," *Washington Post*, April 24, 1985.
18. Author's interview with Mark E. Talisman.
19. Ibid.
20. Orbach, *The American Movement to Aid Soviet Jews*, 136.
21. Wolfgang Sazon, "Irving Stone, 90, an Innovator in the Greeting Card Industry," *New York Times*, January 19, 2000; Orbach, *The American Movement to Aid Soviet Jews*, 136.
22. Orbach, *The American Movement to Aid Soviet Jews*, 136.
23. Stern, *Water's Edge*, 66.
24. Lazin, *The Struggle for Soviet Jewry*, 51.
25. Feingold, *"Silent No More"*, 123.
26. Stern, *Water's Edge*, 63–64.
27. Feingold, *"Silent No More"*, 124.
28. Orbach, *The American Movement to Aid Soviet Jews*, 137.
29. Feingold, *"Silent No More"*, 124.
30. Stern, *Water's Edge*, 64.
31. Author's interview with Mark E. Talisman.
32. Ibid.
33. Ibid.
34. Orbach, *The American Movement to Aid Soviet Jews*, 138.

35. Stern, *Water's Edge*, 67.
36. Ibid., 68.
37. Ibid., 68–69.
38. Ibid., 69.
39. Orbach, *The American Movement to Aid Soviet Jews*, 139.
40. Stern, *Water's Edge*, 69.
41. Ambrose, *Nixon: The Triumph of a Politician*, 585.
42. Stern, *Water's Edge*, 210.
43. Author's interview with Mark E. Talisman.
44. Associated Press, *The World in 1973*, 69.
45. Author's interview with Jacob Stein.
46. Author's interview with Jacob Stein and Max M. Fisher.
47. Author's interview with Max M. Fisher, in Golden, *Quiet Diplomat*, 277.
48. Author's interview with Jacob Stein and Max M. Fisher.
49. Author's interview with Richard M. Nixon, in Golden, *Quiet Diplomat*, 278.
50. Max M. Fisher notes, April 19, 1973, Fisher Archives.
51. Author's interview with Max M. Fisher; author's interview with Richard M. Nixon, in Golden, *Quiet Diplomat*, 279.
52. Urofsky, *We Are One!*, 421–22; Golden, *Quiet Diplomat*, 279.
53. Golden, *Quiet Diplomat*, 279.
54. Goldberg, *Jewish Power*, 170.
55. "7 U.S. Students Briefly Detained in Moscow for Protest on Jews; Students Identified Here," *New York Times*, April 21, 1973.
56. Irving Spiegel, "Protest Backs Soviet Jews on Eve of Israel's Birthday; Thousands March down Fifth Avenue and Rally in Hammarskjold Plaza," *New York Times*, May 7, 1973.
57. Ibid.
58. Ibid.
59. Ibid.
60. Feingold, *"Silent No More"*, 125; author's interview with Jacob Stein.
61. Nixon, *RN*, 876–77.
62. "Timeline," www.washingtonpost.com/wp-srv/onpolitics/watergate/chronology.htm#1973, retrieved June 8, 2009.
63. Dallek, *Nixon and Kissinger*, 397.
64. Orbach, *The American Movement to Aid Soviet Jews*, 141; Linda Charlton, "Security Is Tight as Brezhnev Arrives; 'Freedom March' Held," *New York Times*, June 19, 1973; author's interview with Si Frumkin.
65. Golden, *Quiet Diplomat*, 281.
66. Stern, *Water's Edge*, 83.
67. Orbach, *The American Movement to Aid Soviet Jews*, 141.
68. Author's interview with Jacob Stein.
69. Author's interview with Richard M. Nixon.
70. Golden, *Quiet Diplomat*, 282.
71. Ibid.
72. Ibid.
73. Ibid.

74. Ibid.
75. Ibid., 282–83.
76. Author's interview with Si Frumkin.
77. Ibid.
78. Ibid. All quotes between Whittinghill and the police officer are from author's interview with Si Frumkin.
79. Stephen E. Ambrose, *Nixon: Ruin and Recovery 1973–1990* (New York: Simon and Schuster, 1991), 174.
80. Feingold, *"Silent No More"*, 127.
81. Lenny Ben-David, "Washington's Elders of Anti-Zion," *Jerusalem Post*, May 5, 2009. Not surprisingly, Fulbright later registered as a foreign agent for Saudi Arabia.
82. Feingold, *"Silent No More"*, 127.
83. Golden, *Quiet Diplomat*, 283.
84. Ibid.
85. Ibid., 284.
86. Ibid.
87. Ibid.
88. Ibid.
89. Ibid.
90. Ibid., 285.
91. Ibid.
92. Ibid.
93. Ibid.
94. Ibid., 286.
95. Ibid.
96. Feingold, *"Silent No More"*, 127.
97. Orbach, *The American Movement to Aid Soviet Jews*, 142.
98. Smith, "Moscow Ratifies 2 U.N. Covenants on Human Rights."
99. Feingold, *"Silent No More"*, 127.
100. Orbach, *The American Movement to Aid Soviet Jews*, 142.
101. Ibid., 142–43.
102. Theodore Shabad, "Sakharov Gets a Backer as Soviet Critics Increase," *New York Times*, September 5, 1973.
103. Christopher S. Wren, "Interrogated and Threatened, Mrs. Sakharov Says; Refused to Answer," *New York Times*, November 22, 1973.
104. Feingold, *"Silent No More"*, 127.
105. Gaddis, *The Cold War*, 204.
106. Golden, *Quiet Diplomat*, 287–88.
107. Sachar, *A History of Israel*, 755–68.
108. Meir, *My Life*, 362.
109. Isaacson, *Kissinger*, 516–17.
110. Golden, *Quiet Diplomat*, 289.
111. Kissinger, *Years of Upheaval*, 504.
112. Isaacson, *Kissinger*, 529.
113. William B. Quandt, *Decade of Decisions: American Foreign Policy toward the Arab-Israeli Conflict, 1967–1976* (Berkeley and Los Angeles, CA: University of

California Press, 1977), 175.

114. Kissinger, *Years of Upheaval*, 485.
115. Isaacson, *Kissinger*, 514.
116. Author's interview with Henry A. Kissinger, in Golden, *Quiet Diplomat*, 291.
117. Author's interview with Richard M. Nixon, in Golden, *Quiet Diplomat*, 291-292.
118. Author's interview with Alexander M. Haig Jr, in Golden, *Quiet Diplomat*, 292.
119. John Loftus and Mark Aarons, *The Secret War against the Jews: How Western Espionage Betrayed the Jewish People* (New York: St. Martin's Griffin, 1994), 315–17.
120. Author's interview with Henry A. Kissinger.
121. Donn A. Starry, *Armored Combat in Vietnam* (Indianapolis, IN: Bobbs-Merrill, 1981), 215.
122. Isaacson, *Kissinger*, 522.
123. Nixon, *RN*, 937–39.
124. Ibid., 941.
125. Orbach, *The American Movement to Aid Soviet Jews*, 145.
126. Author's interview with Jacob Stein and Max M. Fisher.
127. Author's interview with Jacob Stein.
128. Golden, *Quiet Diplomat*, 295.
129. Author's interview with Jacob Stein.
130. Stephen Green and Margot Hornblower, "Mills Admits Being Present during Tidal Basin Scuffle," *Washington Post*, October 11, 1974.
131. Kissinger, *Years of Upheaval*, 991.
132. Ibid., 992–95.
133. Ibid., 995.
134. Ibid., 991.
135. "'Tending to the Sprouts,'" www.ajhs.org/publications/TimelineASJM/section6. cfm, retrieved July 2, 2009.
136. Kissinger, *Years of Upheaval*, 995.
137. Ibid., 996.
138. Thomas, *The Helsinki Effect*, 78.
139. Ibid.
140. Ibid.
141. Isaacson, *Kissinger*, 616.
142. Gerald R. Ford, *A Time to Heal: The Autobiography of Gerald R. Ford* (New York: Harper and Row/Reader's Digest, 1979), 138–39.
143. Ford, *A Time to Heal*, 139.
144. Ibid.
145. Buwalda, *They Did Not Dwell Alone*, 103.
146. Isaacson, *Kissinger*, 616–17.
147. Feingold, *"Silent No More"*, 137; Isaacson, *Kissinger*, 617.
148. Isaacson, *Kissinger*, 618.
149. Buwalda, *They Did Not Dwell Alone*, 103–4.
150. During the 1972 primary season, Jackson had contacted J. Stanley Shaw, a Liberal Party leader in New York, to arrange a speaking engagement before a black audience. With the help of Representative Shirley Chisholm, the first African

American woman elected to Congress, Shaw set up a speech at a chamber of commerce dinner, where half the seats were filled with black men and women. Jackson began by saying, "Ladies and Gentlemen, the main reason for my being here tonight is to call a spade a spade." Shaw glanced over at Shirley Chisholm and recalled that, "like me, she seemed to be experiencing an overwhelming desire to crawl under her chair." J. Stanley Shaw and Peter Golden, *I Rest My Case: My Long Journey from the Castle on the Hill to Home* (Albany, NY: Chestnut Street Press, 2000), 175–76.

151. Isaacson, *Kissinger*, 618.
152. Ibid.
153. Feingold, *"Silent No More"*, 138.
154. Buwalda, *They Did Not Dwell Alone*, 105–6.
155. Stern, *Water's Edge*, 169.
156. Ibid.
157. Buwalda, *They Did Not Dwell Alone*, 106.
158. Isaacson, *Kissinger*, 619.
159. Stern, *Water's Edge*, 177.
160. Kissinger, *Years of Upheaval*, 996.
161. Goldberg, *Jewish Power*, 173.
162. Buwalda, *They Did Not Dwell Alone*, 102.
163. Author's interview with Stanley J. Marcus.
164. Goldberg, *Jewish Power*, 173.
165. Kissinger, *Years of Upheaval*, 996.
166. Author's interview with Richard N. Perle.
167. Stanley J. Marcus, "New Light on the Export-Import Bank," *U.S. Financing of East-West Trade No. 22*, Paul Marer, ed. (Bloomington, IN: International Development Research Center, 1975), 280–81.
168. Ibid., 281.
169. Author's interview with Richard N. Perle.
170. Author's interview with Henry A. Kissinger.
171. Stern, *Water's Edge*, 179.
172. Buwalda, *They Did Not Dwell Alone*, 106.
173. Ibid.
174. Dobrynin, *In Confidence*, 336.
175. Goldberg, *Jewish Power*, 172.
176. Isaacson, *Kissinger*, 619–20; Goldberg, *Jewish Power*, 172.
177. Ford, *A Time to Heal*, 225.
178. Isaacson, *Kissinger*, 620.
179. "Jewish Emigration from the Former Soviet Union to Israel and the United States," www.ncsj.org/stats.shtml, retrieved April, 2, 2005.
180. "Marshall I. Goldman," www.wellesley.edu/PublicAffairs/Profile/gl/marshallgoldman.html, retrieved July, 4, 2009.
181. Marshall I. Goldman, "Jackson-Vanik: A Dissent," in Friedman and Chernin, *A Second Exodus*, 118–19.
182. Ford, *A Time to Heal*, 345.
183. Freedman, "Soviet Jewry and Soviet-American Relations," 48.

184. "Jewish Emigration from the Former Soviet Union to Israel and the United States," www.ncsj.org/stats.shtml, retrieved April, 2, 2005.

185. Natan Sharansky and Ron Dermer, *The Case for Democracy: The Power of Freedom to Overcome Tyranny and Terror* (New York: PublicAffairs, 2004), 120.

186. Ibid., 122.

187. Ibid., 123.

188. Ibid.

189. Goldberg, *Jewish Power*, 175.

190. Author's interview with Mark E. Talisman.

191. Ibid.

192. Gaddis, *The Cold War*, 222.

CHAPTER 9

1. Geoffrey Roberts, *Stalin's Wars* (New Haven, CT: Yale University Press, 2007), 264.

2. Ibid., 5.

3. Ibid.

4. Jordan Bonfante, "Remembering a Red Flag Day," *Time*, May 23, 2008.

5. All quotes in this exchange come from author's interview with Mark E. Talisman.

6. Henry Kissinger, *Years of Renewal* (New York: Simon and Schuster, 1999), 619.

7. Korey, *The Promises We Keep*, xix.

8. William Korey, "From Helsinki: A Salute to Human Rights," in Friedman and Chernin, *A Second Exodus*, 125.

9. Korey, *The Promises We Keep*, 17.

10. Ibid., 1.

11. Dobrynin, *In Confidence*, 346.

12. AP, "Nikolai V. Podgorny Dead at 79; Was Soviet President for 12 Years," *New York Times*, January 13, 1983.

13. Dobrynin, *In Confidence*, 346.

14. John M. Burns, "The Emergence of Yuri Andropov," *New York Times*, November 6, 1983.

15. Dobrynin, *In Confidence*, 346.

16. Ibid.

17. John Robert Greene, *The Presidency of Gerald R. Ford* (Lawrence, KS: University Press of Kansas, 1995), 152–53.

18. Ford, *A Time to Heal*, 301.

19. J. Peter Scoblic, *U.S. vs. Them: How a Half Century of Conservatism Has Undermined America's Security* (New York: Viking, 2008), 77.

20. Korey, "From Helsinki: A Salute to Human Rights," 125.

21. Ford, *A Time to Heal*, 300.

22. Ibid.

23. Greene, *The Presidency of Gerald R. Ford*, 153.

24. Ford, *A Time to Heal*, 302.

25. Ibid., 305.
26. Ibid., 305–6.
27. Dobrynin, *In Confidence*, 346.
28. Korey, "From Helsinki: A Salute to Human Rights," 126.
29. Dobrynin, *In Confidence*, 346–47.
30. Spiegel, *Triumph over Tyranny*, 195.
31. Dobrynin, *In Confidence*, 346.
32. Author's interview with David Satter.
33. Smith, "Moscow Ratifies 2 U.N. Covenants on Human Rights."
34. David K. Shipler, "Sakharov in Vigil at Friend's Trial; While His Wife Accepts Nobel Prize, He Stands Outside Courtroom in Vilnius," *New York Times*, December 11, 1975.
35. Korey, "From Helsinki: A Salute to Human Rights," 126.
36. Seweryn Bailer, "The Andropov Succession," *New York Review of Books* 30, no. 1, February 3, 1983.
37. Korey, "From Helsinki: A Salute to Human Rights," 126.
38. Sharansky and Dermer, *The Case for Democracy*, 129.
39. Author's interview with Kevin Klose.
40. Gaddis, *The Cold War*, 191.
41. Amy Schapiro, *Millicent Fenwick: Her Way* (New Brunswick, NJ: Rutgers University Press, 2003), 103.
42. Bruce Lambert, "Millicent Fenwick, 82, Dies; Gave Character to Congress," *New York Times*, September 11, 1992.
43. Schapiro, *Millicent Fenwick*, 168–69.
44. Feingold, *"Silent No More"*, 212.
45. Korey, "From Helsinki: A Salute to Human Rights," 126–27.
46. Thomas, *The Helsinki Effect*, 124.
47. Schapiro, *Millicent Fenwick*, 168.
48. Bennett Kovrig, *Of Walls and Bridges: The United States and Eastern Europe* (New York: NYU Press, 1991), 174.
49. Schapiro, *Millicent Fenwick*, 171.
50. Feingold, *"Silent No More"*, 213–14.
51. Korey, "From Helsinki: A Salute to Human Rights," 127.
52. Schapiro, *Millicent Fenwick*, 168–69.
53. Thomas, *The Helsinki Effect*, 127.
54. Feingold, *"Silent No More"*, 213.
55. Freedman, "Soviet Jewry and Soviet-American Relations," 48–49.
56. Feingold, *"Silent No More"*, 224.
57. Spiegel, *Triumph over Tyranny*, 189.
58. Ibid.
59. Freedman, "Soviet Jewry and Soviet-American Relations," 50.
60. Spiegel, *Triumph over Tyranny*, 188–89.
61. Freedman, "Soviet Jewry and Soviet-American Relations," 50.
62. Shelley Fisher Fishkin, "The Cruelest Assignment," *New York Times*, March 27, 1988. Orlov would not be freed until 1986, when he was allowed to emigrate to the United States in exchange for Gennadi Zakharov, a Soviet working at the United

Nations who was arrested for espionage in New York.

63. Sharansky and Dermer, *The Case for Democracy*, 131.

64. "200,000 at Rally for Soviet Jews Hear Carter Administration Pledge," *New York Times*, May 2, 1977.

65. Freedman, "Soviet Jewry and Soviet-American Relations," 50.

66. "200,000 at Rally for Soviet Jews Hear Carter Administration Pledge."

67. Freedman, "Soviet Jewry and Soviet-American Relations," 52.

68. "Excerpts from the Address by President Carter on Relations with Soviet Union," *New York Times*, July 22, 1977.

69. Dobrynin, *In Confidence*, 411.

70. Freedman, "Soviet Jewry and Soviet-American Relations," 54.

71. Dobrynin, *In Confidence*, 414.

72. Gromyko, *Memoirs*, 289.

73. Freedman, "Soviet Jewry and Soviet-American Relations," 52.

74. "Postcard From Budapest," http://news.bbc.co.uk/2/hi/europe/2559747.stm, retrieved July 12, 2009.

75. Gromyko, *Memoirs*, 292.

76. Freedman, "Soviet Jewry and Soviet-American Relations," 51–52.

77. Dobrynin, *In Confidence*, 410.

78. Gromyko, *Memoirs*, 288.

79. Vladislav M. Zubok, *A Failed Empire: The Soviet Union in the Cold War from Stalin to Gorbachev* (Chapel Hill, NC: The University of North Carolina Press, 2007), 241–42.

80. Gaddis, *The Cold War*, 213.

81. Dobrynin, *In Confidence*, 409–10.

82. Feingold, *"Silent No More"*, 215.

83. Korey, "From Helsinki: A Salute to Human Rights," 126.

84. Feingold, *"Silent No More"*, 215.

85. Ibid.

86. Korey, "From Helsinki: A Salute to Human Rights," 130.

87. Ibid., 126.

88. Ibid., 131.

89. Author's interview with William Korey.

90. Wolfgang Saxon, "Men in the News; Egypt's Shrewd, Intuitive President Mohammed Anwar el-Sadat," *New York Times*, November 21, 1977.

91. Freedman, "Soviet Jewry and Soviet-American Relations," 55.

92. Dobrynin, *In Confidence*, 403.

93. Freedman, "Soviet Jewry and Soviet-American Relations," 55.

94. Ibid., 60.

95. Feingold, *"Silent No More"*, 195.

96. David P. Forsythe, *Human Rights and U.S. Foreign Policy: Congress Reconsidered* (Gainesville, FL: University Press of Florida, 1988), 75.

97. Feingold, *"Silent No More"*, 195–96.

98. "Jewish Emigration from the Former Soviet Union to Israel and the United States," www.ncsj.org/stats.shtml, retrieved April, 2, 2005.

99. Freedman, "Soviet Jewry and Soviet-American Relations," 63.

100. "Jewish Emigration from the Former Soviet Union to Israel and the United States," www.ncsj.org/stats.shtml, retrieved April, 2, 2005.

101. Spiegel, *Triumph over Tyranny*, 201.

102. Don Oberdorfer, "Deep Differences Mixed with Air of Tolerance," *Washington Post*, June 19, 1979.

103. Ibid.

104. Gordon Stewart, "Carter's Speech Therapy," *New York Times*, July 15, 2009.

105. "Primary Sources: Crisis of Confidence" www.pbs.org/wgbh/amex/carter/filmmore/ps_crisis.html, retrieved July 12, 2009.

106. Robert E. Emery, *Marriage, Divorce, and Children's Adjustment* (Thousand Oaks, CA: Sage, 1999), 12.

107. Adam Clymer, "Jobless Rate Is Up to 10.1% in Month, Worst in 42 Years; News Analysis," *New York Times*, October 9, 1982.

108. Anthony Lake, *Somoza Falling* (Boston, MA: Houghton Mifflin, 1989), 259.

109. Alan Greenspan, *The Age of Turbulence: Adventures in a New World* (New York: Penguin, 2007), 82.

110. Gaddis, *The Cold War*, 213.

111. Thomas J. McCormick, *America's Half-Century: United States Foreign Policy in the Cold War and After* (Baltimore, MD: The Johns Hopkins University Press, 1995), 208.

112. Ibid.

113. Gaddis, *The Cold War*, 209–10.

114. McCormick, *America's Half-Century*, 208.

115. Gaddis, *The Cold War*, 210.

116. McCormick, *America's Half-Century*, 208.

117. Dobrynin, *In Confidence*, 440.

118. McCormick, *America's Half-Century*, 208.

119. Terrence Smith, "Carter Tells Soviet to Pull Its Troops out of Afghanistan; He Warns of 'Consequences,'" *New York Times*, December 30, 1979.

120. McCormick, *America's Half-Century*, 210.

CHAPTER 10

1. Dobrynin, *In Confidence*, 478.

2. Peter Schweizer, *Victory: The Reagan Administration's Secret Strategy That Hastened the Collapse of the Soviet Union* (New York: Atlantic Monthly, 1994), 17.

3. Beschloss, *Presidential Courage*, 283.

4. Ronald Reagan, *The Reagan Diaries*, Douglas Brinkley, ed. (New York: HarperCollins, 2007), 21.

5. Ibid.

6. Beschloss, *Presidential Courage*, 287.

7. Ibid.

8. Andrew Harrison, *Passover Revisited: Philadelphia's Efforts to Aid Soviet Jews,*

1963–1998 (Madison, NJ: Fairleigh Dickinson University Press, 2001), 189–91.

9. "Jewish Emigration from the Former Soviet Union to Israel and the United States," www.ncsj.org/stats.shtml, retrieved April, 2, 2005.

10. Author's interview with Norman R. Patz.

11. Author's interview with Marc Levin.

12. Author's interview with Norman R. Patz.

13. Author's interview with Martin Kesselhaut.

14. Author's interview with Norman R. Patz.

15. Author's interview with Evan Kingsley.

16. Author's interview with Morey Schapira.

17. Author's interview with Richard Stone.

18. Author's interview with Joseph Smukler.

19. Harrison, *Passover Revisited*, 115–17.

20. James Mann, *The Rebellion of Ronald Reagan: A History of the End of the Cold War* (New York: Viking, 2009), 132–36.

21. McPherson, *Drawn with the Sword*, 214.

22. William Borders, "150,000 in London Rally against Bomb," *New York Times*, October 25, 1981.

23. Beschloss, *Presidential Courage*, 289.

24. Andrew C. Goldberg, "Moscow's INF Experience," *The Other Side of the Table: The Soviet Approach to Arms Control*, Michael Mandelbaum, ed., (New York: Council on Foreign Relations, 1990), 108.

25. Kissinger, *Diplomacy*, 752.

26. Richard Reeves, *President Reagan: The Triumph of Imagination* (New York: Simon and Schuster, 2005), 6.

27. Ibid., 109.

28. Mann, *The Rebellion of Ronald Reagan*, 80.

29. Reeves, *President Reagan*, 109.

30. Schweizer, *Victory*, xiii.

31. Gaddis, *The Cold War*, 222.

32. Gaddis, *The Cold War*, 218–19.

33. Richard Owen, "Gunman Mehmet Ali Agca May Reveal KGB Plot to Kill Pope John Paul II," *Times* (London), January 18, 2010.

34. Spiegel, *Triumph over Tyranny*, 297–300.

35. Reeves, *President Reagan*, 107–8.

36. Schweizer, *Victory*, 65.

37. Gaidar, *Collapse of an Empire*, 107.

38. Schweizer, *Victory*, xvi.

39. David Satter, *Age of Delirium: The Decline and Fall of the Soviet Union* (New York: Alfred A. Knopf, 1996), 55.

40. Author's interview with David Satter.

41. Reeves, *President Reagan*, 138.

42. Dobrynin, *In Confidence*, 517–20.

43. Author's interview with Ronald W. Reagan, in Golden, *Quiet Diplomat*, 424.

44. Reeves, *President Reagan*, 138–39.

45. George P. Shultz, *Turmoil and Triumph: My Years as Secretary of State* (New York:

Charles Scribner's Sons, 1993), 1094.

46. Kenneth L. Adelman, *The Great Universal Embrace: Arms Summitry – A Skeptic's Account* (New York: Simon and Schuster, 1989), 144.

47. Shultz, *Turmoil and Triumph*, 1094.

48. Reeves, *President Reagan*, 141.

49. Beschloss, *Presidential Courage*, 292–93.

50. Gaddis, *The Cold War*, 226.

51. Lou Cannon, *President Reagan: The Role of a Lifetime* (New York: Simon and Schuster, 1991), 323.

52. Gaddis, *The Cold War*, 226.

53. Schweizer, *Victory*, 215.

54. Gaddis, *The Cold War*, 227.

55. Ronald Reagan, *An American Life: The Autobiography* (New York: Simon and Schuster, 1990), 585.

56. Kaufman, *Henry M. Jackson*, 430.

57. "Remarks on Awarding the Presidential Medal of Freedom to the Late Senator Henry M. Jackson of Washington," www.reagan.utexas.edu/archives/speeches/1984/62684c.htm, retrieved July 8, 2009.

58. "Joe Lieberman: Patriot," townhall.com/columnists/CalThomas/2007/11/13/joe_lieberman_patriot, retrieved May 8, 2009.

59. Schweizer, *Victory*, 215.

60. Mann, *The Rebellion of Ronald Reagan*, 80.

61. Reagan, *An American Life*, 593–94.

62. "Address before a Joint Session of the Congress on the State of the Union, February 6, 1985," http://reagan2020.us/speeches/state_of_the_union_1985.asp, retrieved September 4, 2011.

63. "Reagan Doctrine," http://history.state.gov/milestones/1981-1989/ReaganDoctrine, retrieved July 2, 2009.

64. Cannon, *President Reagan*, 369.

65. Maureen Dowd, "Where's the Rest of Him?," *New York Times*, November 18, 1990.

66. Reeves, *President Reagan*, 246.

67. Beschloss, *Presidential Courage*, 302.

68. Reeves, *President Reagan*, 248–50.

69. Ibid., 250.

70. Ibid., 255.

71. Kissinger, *Years of Upheaval*, 661.

72. Author's interview with Alexander M. Haig Jr.

73. Schweizer, *Victory*, 94.

74. Ibid., 232.

75. Ibid., 243.

76. Steve Posner, *Israel Undercover: Secret Warfare and Hidden Diplomacy in the Middle East* (New York: Syracuse University Press, 1987), 225.

77. Author's interview with Ronald W. Reagan.

78. "Jewish Emigration from the Former Soviet Union to Israel and the United States," www.ncsj.org/stats.shtml, retrieved April, 2, 2005.

79. Beschloss, *Presidential Courage*, 306.
80. Cannon, *President Reagan*, 783.
81. Author's interview with Mikhail S. Gorbachev.
82. Reagan, *An American Life*, 720.
83. "Jewish Emigration from the Former Soviet Union to Israel and the United States," www.ncsj.org/stats.shtml, retrieved April 2, 2005.
84. "History," www.ajhs.org/publications/TimelineASJM/section1.cfm, retrieved July 10, 2009.
85. Spiegel, *Triumph over Tyranny*, 220–21.
86. Beschloss, *Presidential Courage*, 311.
87. "The Intermediate-Range Nuclear Forces (INF) Treaty at a Glance," www. armscontrol.org/factsheets/INFtreaty, retrieved July 8, 2009.
88. Author's interview with Shoshana S. Cardin.
89. Author's interview with David A. Harris.
90. Ibid.
91. Author's interview with Shoshana S. Cardin.
92. Author's interview with David A. Harris.
93. Author's interview with Shoshana S. Cardin.
94. Author's interview with David A. Harris.
95. Ibid.
96. Ibid.
97. Shoshana S. Cardin, *Shoshana: Memoirs of Shoshana Shoubin Cardin*, (Baltimore, MD: Jewish Museum of Maryland, 2008), 116.
98. Andrew Rosenthal, "March by 200,000 in Capital Presses Soviet on Rights," *New York Times*, December 7, 1987.
99. Cardin, *Shoshana*, 116.
100. Rosenthal, "March by 200,000 in Capital Presses Soviet on Rights."
101. Cardin, *Shoshana*, 116.
102. Author's interview with Shoshana S. Cardin.
103. Mann, *The Rebellion of Ronald Reagan*, 269.
104. Ibid., 269–70.
105. Drachman, *Challenging The Kremlin*, 522.
106. Shultz, *Turmoil and Triumph*, 1101–2.
107. Ibid., 1102.
108. Cannon, *President Reagan*, 783–84; Shultz, *Turmoil and Triumph*, 1102.
109. Felicity Barringer, "Moscow Summit: Preaching to the Unconverted; President Meets with Dissidents, and Tea and Empathy Are Served," *New York Times*, May 31, 1988.
110. Susan Birnbaum, "American-Born Refusenik Abe Stolar Will Emigrate, After 13-Year Wait," JTA *Daily News Bulletin*, January 3, 1989.
111. Ibid.
112. Ibid.
113. Barringer, "Moscow Summit."
114. Ibid.
115. Naftalin, "The Activist Movement," 235.
116. Author's interview with Glenn Richter.

117. Naftalin, "The Activist Movement," 235.
118. Glenn Richter, "Cry Freedom," *Newsday*, June 30, 1988.
119. Ibid.
120. Author's interview with Glenn Richter.
121. Ibid.
122. Ibid.
123. Cannon, *President Reagan*, 786.
124. Ibid., 783.
125. Scott Ladd, "Times Square Rally Backs Soviet Jewry," *Newsday*, June 1, 1988.
126. AP, "Gorbachev Scorns Reagan Advice on Human Rights: No Change in Policies, He Declares," *Los Angeles Times*, June 2, 1988.
127. Ibid.
128. Ibid.
129. Ibid.
130. Ibid.
131. Ibid.
132. Shultz, *Turmoil and Triumph*, 1102.
133. "Shultz Prods Soviets Again on Emigration," *Washington Post*, November 9, 1988.
134. Susan Birnbaum, "Soviets Remove 'Secrecy' Ban on Large Number of Refuseniks," JTA *Daily News Bulletin*, December 2, 1988.
135. "Kislik Questions Soviet 'Secrecy,'" *Newsbreak*, January 23, 1987, NCSJ Archives.
136. "Shultz Prods Soviets Again on Emigration."
137. James A. Baker III, *The Politics of Diplomacy* (New York: G. P. Putnam's Sons, 1995), 62.
138. Dan Oberdorfer, "Baker's Evolution at State; 'Mr. Cautious' Becomes Leading Activist," *Washington Post*, November 16, 1988; Shultz, *Turmoil and Triumph*, 1106.
139. Shultz, *Turmoil and Triumph*, 1106.
140. Dan Oberdorfer; Bil McAllister, "Reagan-Bush-Gorbachev Session Expected to Be "General Conversation,'" *Washington Post*, November 16, 1988.
141. Reagan, *An American Life*, 720.
142. Ibid.
143. Ibid.
144. Michael R. Beschloss and Strobe Talbott, *At the Highest Levels: The Inside Story of the End of the Cold War* (Boston: Little, Brown, 1993), 14.
145. Reagan, *An American Life*, 720.
146. Ze'ev Schiff and Ehud Ya'ari, *Intifada: The Palestinian Uprising; Israel's Third Front* (New York: Simon and Schuster, 1989), 311.
147. Hugh Orgel, "Hungary Says It Plans to Restore Diplomatic Relations with Israel," JTA *Daily News Bulletin*, December 5, 1988.
148. Robert O. Freedman, *Soviet Policy toward Israel under Gorbachev* (New York: Praeger, 1991), 53.
149. Buwalda, *They Did Not Dwell Alone*, 224.
150. Harris, "Arab Opposition to Jewish Immigration to Israel," 8–10.
151. Dan Kurzman, *Yitzhak Rabin: Solider of Peace* (New York: HarperCollins, 1998), 412; William B. Quandt, *Peace Process: American Diplomacy and the Arab-Israeli*

Conflict since 1967 (Washington, DC: The Brookings Institution, 2001), 279–84.

152. Susan Birnbaum, "Emigration of Soviet Jews Hit a Nine-Year High in September," JTA *Daily News Bulletin*, January 3, 1989.

153. "Reclassification Gives First Hope in Nine Years – And Then He Dies," *Newsbreak*, December 20, 1988, NCSJ Archives.

154. Hugh Orgel, "Israel Team Defeats Soviets in Historic Moscow Match," JTA *Daily News Bulletin*, January 4, 1989.

155. Glenn Frankel, "Soviet Hijackers Give Up Quietly in Israel: 4 Men, Woman Seize Bus with 30 Children to Trade for Jet, Cash," *Washington Post*, December 3, 1988; Glenn Frankel, "Israel Turns Hijackers Over to Soviets," *Washington Post*, December 4, 1988.

156. Frankel, "Soviet Hijackers Give Up Quietly in Israel."

157. Ibid.

158. Andrew Silow Carroll, "United States Now Denying Refuge to Hundreds of Jews Leaving USSR," JTA *Daily News Bulletin*, December 5, 1988.

159. Frankel, "Soviet Hijackers Give Up Quietly in Israel"; "4 Soviet Hijackers Are Shipped Home," *New York Times*, December 4, 1988.

160. "4 Soviet Hijackers Are Shipped Home."

161. Frankel, "Soviet Hijackers Give Up Quietly in Israel."

162. Joel Brinkley, "'Parody of a Skyjacking' Ends Peacefully in Israel," *New York Times*, December 3, 1988.

163. Frankel, "Soviet Hijackers Give Up Quietly in Israel."

164. Orgel, "Hungary Says It Plans to Restore Diplomatic Relations with Israel"; Frankel, "Soviet Hijackers Give Up Quietly in Israel."

165. Frankel, "Soviet Hijackers Give Up Quietly in Israel."

166. Brinkley, "'Parody of a Skyjacking' Ends Peacefully in Israel."

167. Orgel, "Hungary Says It Plans to Restore Diplomatic Relations with Israel"; Frankel, "Soviet Hijackers Give Up Quietly in Israel."

168. Orgel, "Hungary Says It Plans to Restore Diplomatic Relations with Israel."

169. Ibid.

170. Frankel, "Soviet Hijackers Give Up Quietly in Israel."

171. Ibid.

172. Orgel, "Hungary Says It Plans to Restore Diplomatic Relations with Israel."

173. Ibid.

174. Ibid.

175. Ibid.

176. Ibid.

177. Mary Curtius, "Hijackers Returned to Soviet Union; Israel's Assistance Seen Improving Ties," *Boston Globe*, December 4, 1988.

178. David Friedman, "Jewish Community Will Work with U.S. to Resolve Soviet Refugee Problem," JTA *Daily News Bulletin*, December 7, 1988.

179. Anatoly Chernyaev, *My Six Years with Gorbachev* (University Park, PA: Pennsylvania State University Press, 2000), 203.

180. "Death Toll Rises in Armenian Earthquake," http://news.bbc.co.uk/onthisday/hi/dates/stories/december/10/newsid_2544000/2544077.stm, retrieved July 2, 2009.

181. Andrew Silow Carroll, "Gorbachev Says Refusenik Problem Can Be Removed

from World Agenda," JTA *Daily News Bulletin*, December 8, 1988.

182. Author's interview with Glenn Richter.

183. Carroll, "Gorbachev Says Refusenik Problem Can Be Removed from World Agenda."

184. Shultz, *Turmoil and Triumph*, 1106.

185. Chernyaev, *My Six Years with Gorbachev*, 202.

186. Steven V. Roberts, "Gorbachev's Journey; Reagan Cautious on Arms Pledge but Sees Soviet on Path of Peace," *New York Times*, December 9, 1988.

187. Mikhail S. Gorbachev speech to United Nations General Assembly, December 7, 1988, NCSJ Archives.

188. Ibid.

189. Beschloss and Talbott, *At the Highest Levels*, 10–12.

190. NCSJ News Release, December 7, 1988, NCSJ Archives.

191. Author's interview with Shoshana S. Cardin.

192. Beschloss and Talbott, *At the Highest Levels*, 10.

193. Chernyaev, *My Six Years with Gorbachev*, 203.

Chapter 11

1. Ronald Reagan, "Farewell Address," January 11, 1989, http://millercenter.org/scripps/archive/speeches/detail/3418, retrieved July 1, 2009.

2. Cannon, *President Reagan*, 894; Reagan, *An American Life*, 66.

3. Baker, *The Politics of Diplomacy*, 63.

4. Ibid.

5. Beschloss and Talbott, *At the Highest Levels*, 17.

6. Baker, *The Politics of Diplomacy*, 70.

7. Beschloss and Talbott, *At the Highest Levels*, 27.

8. Baker, *The Politics of Diplomacy*, 70.

9. Beschloss and Talbott, *At the Highest Levels*, 58.

10. Baker, *The Politics of Diplomacy*, 68.

11. Ibid.

12. Author's interview with Mikhail S. Gorbachev.

13. Ibid.

14. Michael Dobbs, *Down with Big Brother: The Fall of the Soviet Empire* (New York: Vintage Books, 1996), 233; Bill Keller, "Last Soviet Soldiers Leave Afghanistan after 9 Years, 15,000 Dead and Great Cost," *New York Times*, February 16, 1989.

15. "Soviet Invasion of Afghanistan," www.nationmaster.com/encyclopedia/Soviet-invasion-of-Afghanistan, retrieved November 4, 2007.

16. Ibid.

17. Keller, "Last Soviet Soldiers Leave Afghanistan after 9 Years."

18. Ibid.

19. Author's interview with Mikhail S. Gorbachev.

20. Baker, *The Politics of Diplomacy*, 64.

21. Reeves, *President Kennedy*, 173.

22. "John F. Kennedy Inaugural Address," www.americanrhetoric.com/speeches/jfkinaugural.htm, retrieved July 24, 2009.
23. Reeves, *President Kennedy*, 137.
24. Baker, *The Politics of Diplomacy*, 65.
25. Ibid.
26. Ibid.
27. Ibid.
28. Ibid., 65–66.
29. Ibid., 59.
30. Author's interview with Mikhail S. Gorbachev.
31. Beschloss and Talbott, *At the Highest Levels*, 28, 43–44.
32. Gail Sheehy, *The Man Who Changed the World: The Lives of Mikhail S. Gorbachev* (New York: HarperCollins, 1990), 213.
33. Beschloss and Talbott, *At the Highest Levels*, 45.
34. Ibid.
35. Baker, *The Politics of Diplomacy*, 68.
36. Ibid.
37. Ibid.
38. Ibid.
39. Dobbs, *Down with Big Brother*, 218.
40. Author's interview with Mikhail S. Gorbachev.
41. Beschloss and Talbott, *At the Highest Levels*, 49; author's interview with Mikhail S. Gorbachev.
42. Beschloss and Talbott, *At the Highest Levels*, 49.
43. Ibid., 29.
44. Ibid., 49.
45. Ibid., 50.
46. Ibid.
47. Ibid.
48. Ibid.
49. Ibid., 69–70.
50. Sheehy, *The Man Who Changed the World*, 279.
51. Ibid., 275.
52. Freedman, *Soviet Policy toward Israel under Gorbachev*, 66–67.
53. Thomas Friedman, "Elephants Can't Fly," *New York Times*, January 1, 2004.
54. Beschloss and Talbott, *At the Highest Levels*, 64.
55. Sheehy, *The Man Who Changed the World*, 17.
56. Mikhail Gorbachev, *On My Country and the World*, trans. George Shriver (New York: Columbia University Press, 1999), 31.
57. Hedrick Smith, *The New Russians* (New York: Random House, 1990), 182.
58. Ibid., 185.
59. Freedman, *Soviet Policy toward Israel under Gorbachev*, xv–xvi.
60. Drachman, *Challenging the Kremlin*, 476–77.
61. David Friedman, "Lawmakers Urge Refugee Status Be Given to All Soviet Jews," JTA *Daily News Bulletin*, December 12, 1988; Ruth E. Gruber, "In An Italian Town by the Sea, A New Class of Refuseniks Waits," JTA *Daily News Bulletin*, December

14, 1988.

62. Carroll, "Gorbachev Says Refusenik Problem Can Be Removed from World Agenda."

63. Biale, *Power and Powerlessness*, 181.

64. Freedman, *Soviet Policy toward Israel under Gorbachev*, xv–xvi; author's interview with Martin Wenick.

65. Gorbachev, *On My Country and the World*, 32.

66. Francis X. Clines, "Gorbachev Condemns Anti-Semitism, Past and Present," *New York Times*, October 7, 1991.

67. Speech of Mikhail Gorbachev delivered by Aleksandr Yakovlev, October 5, 1991, Shoshana S. Cardin Archives.

68. Freedman, *Soviet Policy toward Israel under Gorbachev*, xv–xvi; author's interview with Martin Wenick.

69. "Jewish Emigration from the Former Soviet Union to Israel and the United States," www.ncsj.org/stats.shtml, retrieved April, 2, 2005.

70. Friedman, "Jewish Community Will Work with U.S."

71. Author's interview with Shoshana S. Cardin.

72. David Friedman, "January Emigration Figures Dip; NCSJ Hires State Dept. Official," JTA *Daily News Bulletin*, February 2, 1989.

73. "Solidarity Sunday March Canceled in Recognition of Soviet Changes," JTA *Daily News Bulletin*, March 13, 1989.

74. Author's interview with Shoshana S. Cardin.

75. "Jewish Emigration from the Former Soviet Union to Israel and the United States," www.ncsj.org/stats.shtml, retrieved April 2, 2005.

76. Feingold, *The Politics of Rescue*, 14.

Chapter 12

1. Author's interview with Mark E. Talisman.

2. Clyde Haberman, "Ladispoli Journal; A Very Crowded Vestibule of the Western World," *New York Times*, February 2, 1989.

3. Clyde Haberman, "For Stranded Jews, 'When' Is Now 'If,'" *New York Times*, December 11, 1988.

4. Haberman, "Ladispoli Journal."

5. Friedman, "Jewish Community Will Work with U.S."

6. Ibid.

7. Carroll, "United States Now Denying Refuge"; Friedman, "Lawmakers Urge Refugee Status."

8. Korey, "Helsinki: A Salute to Human Rights," 125.

9. Carroll, "United States Now Denying Refuge."

10. Fred Lazin, "Refugee Resettlement and 'Freedom of Choice,'" *Center for Immigration Studies*, June 2005, 10.

11. Carroll, "United States Now Denying Refuge."

12. Norman Kempster, "Soviets Jail Fewer Dissidents, U.S. Says," *LA Times*, August

14, 1988.

13. Carroll, "United States Now Denying Refuge."

14. Haberman, "For Stranded Jews, 'When' Is Now 'If.'"

15. Birnbaum, "Emigration of Soviet Jews Hit a Nine-Year High in December."

16. Ruth Marcus, "U.S. Moves to Ease Soviet Emigres' Way; Up to 2,000 a Month Permitted," *Washington Post*, December 9, 1988; Carroll, "United States Now Denying Refuge."

17. Lazin, "Refugee Resettlement and 'Freedom of Choice,'" 11.

18. Ibid.

19. Tyler Marshall, "Despite Reforms, More Soviet Jews Seek to Leave," *LA Times*, August 14, 1988; Roger Boyes, "Locked out of the Promised Land – Emigrant Russian Jews," *The London Times*, February 7, 1989.

20. Marshall, "Despite Reforms, More Soviet Jews Seek to Leave."

21. Author's interview with Mark E. Talisman.

22. Ibid.

23. "Shalom, Romania!," www.jdc.org/who_mission.html.

24. Boyes, "Locked Out of the Promised Land."

25. Friedman, "Jewish Community Will Work with U.S."

26. Ibid.

27. Author's interview with Shoshana S. Cardin.

28. Marcus, "U.S. Moves to Ease Soviet Emigres' Way."

29. Ibid.

30. Carroll, "United States Now Denying Refuge."

31. Friedman, "Lawmakers Urge Refugee Status."

32. Marcus, "U.S. Moves to Ease Soviet Emigres' Way."

33. Friedman, "Lawmakers Urge Refugee Status."

34. Friedman, "Jewish Community Will Work with U.S."

35. Marcus, "U.S. Moves to Ease Soviet Emigres' Way."

36. Ibid.

37. Friedman, "Lawmakers Urge Refugee Status."

38. Marcus, "U.S. Moves to Ease Soviet Emigres' Way"; Friedman, "Lawmakers Urge Refugee Status."

39. Friedman, "Lawmakers Urge Refugee Status."

40. Andrew Silow Carroll, "UJA to Launch a Special Campaign to Fund Resettlement of Soviet Jews," JTA *Daily News Bulletin*, February 3, 1989.

41. Technically, funds for JAFI first go to the United Israel Appeal and then are transferred to the Jewish Agency.

42. Andrea S. Arbel, *Riding the Wave* (Jerusalem: Gefen, 2001), 29–30.

43. Lazin, "Refugee Resettlement and 'Freedom of Choice,'" 11.

44. Ibid.

45. Howard Rosenberg, "Jewish Groups Protest Sharp Rise in Soviet Jews Rejected by U.S.," JTA *Daily News Bulletin*, March 23, 1989.

46. Howard Rosenberg, "Plan to Provide $85 Million More for Soviet Refugees Wins Support," JTA *Daily News Bulletin*, March 16, 1989.

47. Boyes, "Locked out of the Promised Land."

48. Ibid.

49. Lisa Palmieri-Billig, "U.S. Jewish Leaders Due with Plan to Cut Drop-Out Rate," *Jerusalem Post*, February 12, 1989.

50. Ibid.

51. Haim Shapiro, "More Emissaries Needed to Bring Dropouts Here," *Jerusalem Post*, February 13, 1989.

52. Ibid.

53. Charles Hoffman, "Agency Will Send Envoy to Rome to Court Soviet Jews," *Jerusalem Post*, January 2, 1989.

54. Arbel, *Riding the Wave*, 28.

55. Ibid., 28, 34.

56. Windmueller, "The '*Noshrim*' War," 165.

57. Author's interview with Martin S. Kraar, in Golden, *Quiet Diplomat*, 470.

58. Author's interview with George P. Shultz.

59. Author's interview with Mendel Kaplan, in Golden, *Quiet Diplomat*, 470–71.

60. Boyes, "Locked Out of the Promised Land."

61. Arbel, *Riding the Wave*, 44.

62. Chernyaev, *My Six Years with Gorbachev*, 147.

63. "Voice of the Oppressed in Arabic to Lebanon," November 29, 1988, translated by the Foreign Broadcast Information Service; Harris, "Arab Opposition to Jewish Immigration to Israel," 10.

64. Gary Lee, "First Israeli Delegation Arrives in Moscow after 21 Years," *Washington Post*, July 29, 1988; Harris, "Arab Opposition to Jewish Immigration to Israel," 9.

65. Arbel, *Riding the Wave*, 44–45.

66. Lee, "First Israeli Delegation Arrives in Moscow"; Harris, "Arab Opposition to Jewish Immigration to Israel," 9.

67. Arbel, *Riding the Wave*, 45.

68. Ibid.

69. Author's interview with Mikhail S. Gorbachev.

70. Arbel, *Riding the Wave*, 43.

71. Ibid., 44.

72. Walter Ruby, "American Zionist Leader Blasts USA's Soviet Jewry Campaign," *Jerusalem Post*, April 9, 1989.

73. Ibid.

74. Ibid.

75. Ibid.

76. Ibid.

77. Author's interview with Zelig Chinitz, in Golden, *Quiet Diplomat*, 82.

78. Author's interview with Mendel Kaplan, in Golden, *Quiet Diplomat*, 470–71.

79. Beschloss and Talbott, *At the Highest Levels*, 83.

80. "20th Century China: A Partial Chronology," www.tsquare.tv/chronology, retrieved July 12, 2009.

81. Ibid.

82. Ibid.

83. Bill Keller, "Gorbachev Praises the Students and Declares Reform Is Necessary," *New York Times*, May 18, 1989.

84. Ibid.

85. Beschloss and Talbott, *At the Highest Levels*, 83.
86. Keller, "Gorbachev Praises the Students and Declares Reform Is Necessary".
87. Ibid.
88. "The Unknown Rebel," http://www.time.com/time/time100/leaders/profile/rebel. html, retrieved April 9, 2002.
89. Dennis Ross, *The Missing Peace: The Inside Story of the Fight for Middle East Peace* (New York: Farrar, Straus and Giroux, 2004), 58.
90. Author's confidential interview.
91. Ibid.
92. Ross, *The Missing Peace*, 61.
93. MMF Notes, March 9, 1989, Fisher Archives.
94. Ross, *The Missing Peace*, 82.
95. Arbel, *Riding the Wave*, 45.
96. Author's interview with Max M. Fisher.
97. Windmueller, "The *Noshrim* War," 166.
98. Lazin, *The Struggle for Soviet Jewry*, 98.
99. Author's interviews with Mark E. Talisman and Max M. Fisher.
100. *A CJF Oral History Project: The Response of the North American Federations to the Emigration of Jews from the Former Soviet Union to the United States and Israel* (New York: Council of Jewish Federations, 1993), 41.
101. Author's interview with Shoshana S. Cardin.

CHAPTER 13

1. Author's interview with Lawrence S. Eagleburger.
2. Baker, *The Politics of Diplomacy*, 34.
3. Author's interview with Lawrence S. Eagleburger.
4. Ibid.
5. Ibid.
6. Ibid.
7. Jeffrey C. Isaac, *Democracy in Dark Times* (Ithaca, NY: Cornell University Press, 1998), 20.
8. Michael Hirsch, "Bernard Lewis Revisited," *Washington Monthly*, November 2004.
9. Ambrose and Brinkley, *Rise to Globalism*, 349.
10. Lazin, "Refugee Resettlement and 'Freedom of Choice,'" 11.
11. Ibid.
12. Author's interview with Lawrence S. Eagleburger.
13. Author's interview with Priscilla Clapp.
14. Ibid.
15. Mark E. Talisman, "Meeting at Department of State," June 9, 1989, Fisher Archives.
16. Ibid.
17. Ibid.
18. Author's interview with Max M. Fisher; Mark E. Talisman, "Meeting at Department

of State," June 9, 1989, Fisher Archives.

19. Mark E. Talisman memo, "Participants of Non Meeting," July 6, 1989, Fisher Archives.
20. Victor Sebestyen, "Transcripts of Defeat," *New York Times*, October 28, 2009.
21. Mark E. Talisman memo, "Participants of Non Meeting," July 6, 1989, Fisher Archives.
22. Ibid.
23. Ibid.
24. Cardin, *Shoshana*, 123.
25. Mark E. Talisman memo, "Participants of Non Meeting," July 6, 1989, Fisher Archives.
26. Carmi Schwartz memo, July 11, 1989, Fisher Archives.
27. Ibid.
28. Max M. Fisher letter to George H. W. Bush, July 19, 1989, Fisher Archives.
29. Mark E. Talisman memo, "Participants of Non Meeting," July 6, 1989, Fisher Archives.
30. Ibid.
31. Author's interview with Shoshana S. Cardin.
32. Ibid.
33. Mark E. Talisman memo, "Non-Meeting with Sellin," August 1, 1989, Fisher Archives.
34. Lazin, "Refugee Resettlement and 'Freedom of Choice,'" 10.
35. Robert Pear, "U.S. Drafts Plans to Curb Admission of Soviet Jews," *New York Times*, September 3, 1989.
36. Author's interview with Priscilla Clapp.
37. Feingold, *"Silent No More"*, 265.
38. Goldberg, *Jewish Power*, 264.
39. Feingold, *"Silent No More"*, 265.
40. Gaddis, *The Cold War*, 242.
41. Beschloss and Talbott, *At the Highest Levels*, chronology inside front cover.
42. "1989: The Night the Wall Came Down," http://news.bbc.co.uk/onthisday/hi/witness/november/9/newsid_3241000/3241641.stm, retrieved July 12, 2009.
43. Reuters, "Elena Ceausescu Tried to Flee Execution," *LA Times*, January 5, 1990.
44. Dan Bilefsky, "In New Play, Vaclav Havel Looks Back on Power," *New York Times*, July 25, 2008.
45. Beschloss and Talbott, *At the Highest Levels*, chronology inside front cover.
46. AP, "Gorbachev Decries Anti-Semitism," *The Boston Globe*, October 7, 1991.
47. Susan Heller Anderson, "Chronicle," *New York Times*, January 24, 1990.
48. Cardin, *Shoshana*, 158.
49. Ibid.
50. Francis X. Clines, "Gorbachev Condemns Anti-Semitism, Past and Present," *New York Times*, October 7, 1991.
51. Cardin, *Shoshana*, 158.
52. Nancy Turck, "The Arab Boycott," *Foreign Affairs*, April 1977.
53. Arbel, *Riding the Wave*, 106.
54. "Remember the Clippers: Pan Am Dies, and So Does Part of Aviation," *Seattle*

Times, December 4, 1991.

55. Author's interview with James Fannan.

56. Ibid.

57. Ibid.

58. Ibid.

59. Ibid.

60. Golden, *Quiet Diplomat*, 474.

61. Cardin, *Shoshana*, 124.

62. "Operation Exodus: Photo Exhibit," www.ujc.org/page.aspx?id=1033, retrieved August 18, 2009.

63. "Jewish Emigration from the Former Soviet Union to Israel and the United States," www.ncsj.org/stats.shtml, retrieved April, 2, 2005.

64. Feingold, *"Silent No More"*, 288.

65. Beschloss and Talbott, *At the Highest Levels*, 427.

66. Ibid., 433.

67. Michael Dobbs, *Down with Big Brother: The Fall of the Soviet Empire* (New York: Vintage Books, 1996), 449.

68. Ibid., 448.

69. George Bush and Brent Scowcroft, *A World Transformed* (New York: Vintage Books, 1998), 561.

70. Gaddis, *The Cold War*, 257.

71. Warren Hoge, "Once Red, 'Mr. Green' Is a Hero Anywhere but at Home," *New York Times*, October 23, 2004.

72. Author's interview with Mikhail S. Gorbachev.

Sources

Selected Bibliography

Abram, Morris B. *The Day Is Short: An Autobiography.* New York: Harcourt Brace Jovanovich, 1982.

Aburish, Said K. *Nasser: The Last Arab.* New York: Thomas Dunne Books, 2004.

Academy of Sciences of the USSR. *Leonid Brezhnev: Pages from His Life.* New York: Simon and Schuster, 1978.

Acheson, Dean. *The Korean War.* New York: W. W. Norton, 1971.

Adams, Maurianne, and John Bracey, eds. *Strangers and Neighbors: Relations Between Blacks and Jews in the United States.* Amherst, MA: University of Massachusetts Press, 1999.

Adelman, Kenneth L. *The Great Universal Embrace: Arms Summitry; A Skeptic's Account.* New York: Simon and Schuster, 1989.

Adler, Cyrus, ed. *The Voice of America on Kishineff.* Philadelphia: Jewish Publication Society of America, 1904.

Adler, Cyrus, and Aaron M. Margalith. *With Firmness in the Right: American diplomatic action affecting Jews, 1840–1945.* New York: American Jewish Committee, 1946.

Altshuler, Stuart. *From Exodus to Freedom: A History of the Soviet Jewry Movement.* Lanham, MD: Rowman and Littlefield, 2005.

Ambrose, Stephen E. *Eisenhower: Soldier and President.* New York: Simon and Schuster, 1990.

——. *Nixon: The Education of a Politician, 1913–1962.* New York: Simon and Schuster, 1987.

——. *Nixon: Ruin and Recovery, 1973–1990.* New York: Simon and Schuster, 1991.

——. *Nixon: The Triumph of a Politician, 1962–1972*. New York: Simon and Schuster, 1989.

——, and Douglas G. Brinkley. *Rise to Globalism: American Foreign Policy since 1938*. New York: Penguin Books, 1997.

Anthony, Carl Sferrazza. *Florence Harding: The First Lady, the Jazz Age, and the Death of America's Most Scandalous President*. New York: William Morrow, 1998.

Arbel, Andrea S. *Riding the Wave*. Jerusalem: Gefen Publishing House, 2001.

Associated Press. *The World in 1967: History as We Lived It*. New York: Associated Press, 1968.

——. *The World in 1968: History as We Lived It*. New York: Associated Press, 1969.

——. *The World in 1969: History as We Lived It*. New York: Associated Press, 1970.

——. *The World in 1970: History as We Lived It*. New York: Associated Press, 1971.

——. *The World in 1972: History as We Lived It*. New York: Associated Press, 1973.

——. *The World in 1973: History as We Lived It*. New York: Associated Press, 1974.

Bailer, Seweryn. "The Andropov Succession." *New York Review of Books*, February 3, 1983.

Bailey, Frankie Y., and Steven Chermak, eds. *Crimes and Trials of the Century*. Volume 1, *From the Black Sox Scandal to the Attica Prison Riots*. Westport, CT: Greenwood, 2007.

Baker, James A. III. *The Politics of Diplomacy*. New York: G. P. Putnam's Sons, 1995.

Baldwin, James. *Notes of a Native Son*. Boston, MA: Beacon, 1955.

——. *Nobody Knows My Name*. New York: Dell, 1961.

Bauer, Yehuda. "Bericha." In Gutman, *Encyclopedia of the Holocaust*.

Beck, Lewis White, ed. *Eighteenth-Century Philosophy: Readings in the History of Philosophy*. New York: Free Press, 1966.

Beichman, Arnold. "Roosevelt's Failure at Yalta." *Humanitas* 16, no. 1 (2003).

Ber-Kerler, Dov, ed. *History of Yiddish Studies*. Philadelphia: Harwood Academic Publishers, 1991.

Berman, Paul. *A Tale of Two Utopias: The Political Journey of the Generation of 1968*. New York: W. W. Norton, 1996.

Bernstein, Irving, and Howard Morley Sachar. *Living UJA History: As Told through the Personal Stories of Leaders of Israel and Leaders of the United Jewish Appeal*. Philadelphia: Jewish Publication Society, 1997.

Beschloss, Michael R. *The Conquerors: Roosevelt, Truman and the Destruction of Hitler's Germany, 1941–1945*. New York: Simon and Schuster, 2007.

——. *Presidential Courage: Brave Leaders and How They Changed America, 1789–1989*. New York: Simon and Schuster, 2007.

——, and Strobe Talbott. *At the Highest Levels: The Inside Story of the End of the Cold War*. Boston: Little, Brown, 1993.

Bessel, Richard. *Nazism and War*. New York: Modern Library, 2004.

Biale, David. *Power and Powerlessness in Jewish History*. New York: Schocken Books, 1986.

Bialik, Hayim Nahman. *Songs from Bialik*. Syracuse, NY: Syracuse University Press, 2000.

Birmingham, Stephen. *Our Crowd: The Great Jewish Families of New York*. New York: Harper and Row, 1967.

——. *"The Rest of Us": The Rise of America's Eastern European Jews*. London: Macdonald, 1985.

Blakeslee, Spencer. *The Death of American Antisemitism*. Westport, CT: Praeger, 2000.

Blitzer, Wolf. *Between Washington and Jerusalem: A Reporter's Notebook*. New York: Oxford University Press, 1985.

Blumenthal, Sidney. "Mugged by Reality." *Salon* magazine. www.salon.com/opinion/blumenthal/2006/12/14/jeane_kirkpatrick/. Retrieved June 18, 2009.

Bohlen, Charles E. *Witness to History, 1929–1969*. New York: W. W. Norton, 1973.

Bojanowska, Edyta M. *Nikolai Gogol: Between Ukrainian and Russian*. Boston: Harvard University Press, 2007.

Bonfante, Jordan. "Remembering a Red Flag Day." *Time*, May 23, 2008.

Borstelmann, Thomas. *The Cold War and the Color Line: American Race Relations in the Global Arena*. Cambridge, MA: Harvard University Press, 2001.

Brackman, Roman. *The Secret File of Joseph Stalin*. New York. Routledge, 2000.

Branch, Taylor. *At Canaan's Edge: America in the King Years, 1965–68*. New York: Simon and Schuster, 2006.

——. *Parting the Waters: America in the King Years, 1954–63*. New York: Simon and Schuster, 1988.

——. *Pillar of Fire: America in the King Years, 1963–65*. New York: Simon and Schuster, 1998.

Bremer, Francis J. *John Winthrop: America's Forgotten Founding Father*. New York: Oxford University Press, 2003.

Bronson, Rachel. *Thicker than Oil: America's Uneasy Partnership with Saudi*

Arabia. New York: Oxford University Press, 2006.

Brown, Frank Overton, Jr. "Jacob L. Morewitz, Eleanor Roosevelt, and the Steamship Quanza." *Senior Lawyers Conference*, April 2008.

Bullock, Alan. *Hitler and Stalin*. New York: Alfred A. Knopf, 1993.

Burkett, Elinor. *Golda*. New York: HarperCollins, 2008.

Bush, George, and Brent Scowcroft. *A World Transformed*. New York: Vintage Books, 1998.

Buwalda, Petrus. *They Did Not Dwell Alone: Jewish Emigration from the Soviet Union, 1967–1990*. Washington, DC: Woodrow Wilson Center, 1997.

Cannon, Lou. *President Reagan: The Role of a Lifetime*. New York: Simon and Schuster, 1991.

Caputo, Philip. *A Rumor of War*. New York: Ballantine Books, 1987.

Cardin, Shoshana S. *Shoshana: Memoirs of Shoshana Shoubin Cardin*. Baltimore: Jewish Museum of Maryland, 2008.

Chernin, Albert D. "Making Soviet Jews an Issue." In Friedman and Chernin, *A Second Exodus*.

Chernow, Ron. *Alexander Hamilton*. New York: Penguin Books, 2004.

Chernyaev, Anatoly. *My Six Years with Gorbachev*. University Park, PA: Pennsylvania State University Press, 2000.

A CJF Oral History Project: The Response of the North American Federations to the Emigration of Jews from the Former Soviet Union to the United States and Israel. New York: Council of Jewish Federations, 1993.

Clarke, Thurston. *Ask Not: The Inauguration of John F. Kennedy and the Speech That Changed America*. New York: Henry Holt, 2004.

Conquest, Robert. *The Harvest of Sorrow*. New York: Oxford University Press, 1986.

———. *Stalin*. New York: Penguin Books, 1991.

Coughlin, Con. *Saddam: King of Terror*. New York: Ecco, 2002.

Crespi, Irving. "Public Reaction to the Eichmann Trial." *Public Opinion Quarterly* 28, no. 1 (spring 1964).

Cunningham, John T. *Newark*. Newark, NJ: New Jersey Historical Society, 1988.

Dallek, Robert. *Lone Star Rising: Lyndon Johnson and His Times, 1908–1960*. New York: Oxford University Press, 1991.

———. *Nixon and Kissinger: Partners in Power*. New York: HarperCollins, 2007.

Davis, Kenneth S. *FDR: Into the Storm*. NY: Random House, 1993.

Dawidowicz, Lucy S. *The War against the Jews, 1933–1945*. New York: Holt, Rinehart and Winston, 1975.

Dershowitz, Alan M. *The Case for Israel*. New York: John Wiley and Sons, 2003.

De Tocqueville, Alexis. *Recollections: The French Revolution of 1848*. Garden City, NY: Doubleday, 1970.

Diner, Hasia R. *A Time for Gathering: The Second Migration, 1820–1880.* Baltimore: Johns Hopkins University Press, 1992.

——. *We Remember with Reverence and Love: American Jews and the Myth of Silence after the Holocaust, 1945–1962.* New York: New York University Press, 2009.

Dinnerstein, Leonard. "Leo M. Frank and the American Jewish Community." *American Jewish Archives*, November 1968.

Dobbs, Michael. *Down with Big Brother: The Fall of the Soviet Empire.* New York: Vintage Books, 1996.

Dobrynin, Anatoly. *In Confidence: Moscow's Ambassador to America's Six Cold War Presidents.* Seattle: University of Washington Press, 1995.

Doenecke, Justus D., ed. *In Danger Undaunted: The Anti-Interventionist Movement of 1940–1941 as Revealed in the Papers of the America First Committee.* Stanford, CA: Hoover Institution Press, 1990.

Dollinger, Mark. "Black Nationalism." In *Antisemitism: A Historical Encyclopedia of Prejudice and Persecution*, edited by Richard Levy. Santa Barbara, CA: ABC-CLIO, 2005.

Drachman, Edward. *Challenging the Kremlin: The Soviet Jewish Movement for Freedom, 1967–1990.* New York: Paragon, 1991.

Dupuy, Ernest R., and Trevor N. Dupuy. *The Harper Encyclopedia of Military History.* New York: HarperCollins, 1993.

Dwyer, Jim, and Kevin Flynn. *102 Minutes: The Untold Story of the Fight to Survive Inside the Twin Towers.* New York: Times Books, 2004.

Eddy, William A. *FDR Meets Ibn Saud.* Washington, DC: America-Mideast Educational and Training Services, 1954. Reprinted. Vista, CA: Selwa, 2005.

Edgcomb, Gabrielle Simon. *From Swastika to Jim Crow: Refugee Scholars at Black Colleges.* Malabar, FL: Krieger, 1993.

Emery, Robert E. *Marriage, Divorce, and Children's Adjustment.* Thousand Oaks, CA: Sage, 1999.

Ennis, Philip H. *The Seventh Stream: The Emergence of Rocknroll in American Popular Music.* Middletown, CT: Wesleyan University Press, 1992.

Evans, Eli N. *The Provincials: A Personal History of Jews in the South.* Chapel Hill, NC: University of North Carolina Press, 2005.

Faber, Eli. *A Time for Planting: The First Migration, 1654–1820.* Baltimore: Johns Hopkins University Press, 1992.

Feingold, Henry L. *The Politics of Rescue: The Roosevelt Administration and the Holocaust, 1938–1945.* New York: Holocaust Library, 1970.

——. *Silent No More: Saving the Jews of Russia; The American Effort, 1967–1989.* Syracuse, NY: Syracuse University Press, 2007.

——. *Zion in America*. New York: Hippocrene Books, 1974.

Filzig, Irving. "Longfellow and the Jewish Cemetery at Newport." *American Heritage Magazine*. February 1962.

Ford, Gerald R. *A Time to Heal: The Autobiography of Gerald R. Ford*. New York: Harper and Row / Reader's Digest, 1979.

Forsythe, David P. *Human Rights and U.S. Foreign Policy: Congress Reconsidered*. Gainesville, FL: University Press of Florida, 1988.

Françoise S. Ouzan. "The Eichmann Trial and American Jewry: A Reassessment." *Jewish Political Studies Review* 19, no. 1–2 (spring 2007).

Frederic, Harold. *The New Exodus: A Study of Israel in Russia*. Boston: Adamant Media, 2005.

Freedman, Robert O. *Soviet Policy toward Israel under Gorbachev*. New York: Praeger, 1991.

——, ed. *Soviet Jewry in the Decisive Decade, 1971–80*. Durham, NC: Duke University Press, 1984.

Freidel, Frank. *Franklin D. Roosevelt: A Rendezvous with Destiny*. Boston: Little, Brown, 1990.

Friedman, Murray, and Albert D. Chernin, eds. *A Second Exodus: The American Movement to Free Soviet Jews*. Hanover, NH: Brandeis University Press, 1999.

Friedman, Robert I. *The False Prophet: Rabbi Meir Kahane; From FBI Informant to Knesset Member*. Brooklyn, NY: Lawrence Hill Books, 1990.

Friedman, Thomas L. *From Beirut to Jerusalem*. New York: Farrar Straus Giroux, 1989.

Frierson, Cathy A. *All Russia Is Burning: A Cultural History of Fire and Arson in Late Imperial Russia*. Seattle: University of Washington Press, 2002.

Fursenko, Aleksandr, and Timothy Naftali. *Khrushchev's Cold War*. New York: W. W. Norton, 2007.

Gaddis, John Lewis. *We Now Know: Rethinking Cold War History*. New York: Oxford University Press, 1997.

——. *The Cold War: A New History*. New York: Penguin Books, 2005.

Gaidar, Yegor. *Collapse of an Empire: Lessons for Modern Russia*. Washington, DC: Brookings Institution, 2007.

Garment, Leonard. *Crazy Rhythm: From Brooklyn and Jazz to Nixon's White House, Watergate, and Beyond*. New York: Times Books, 1997.

Garrow, David J. *Bearing the Cross: Martin Luther King, Jr., and the Southern Christian Leadership Conference*. New York: Vintage Books, 1988.

Gay, Peter. *Freud: A Life for Our Time*. New York: W. W. Norton, 1988.

General Assembly, Seventy-Seventh Plenary Meeting, May 14, 1947.

Geyer, David C. et al., eds. *Foreign Relations of the United States, 1969–1976*.

Vol. 14, *Soviet Union: October 1971–May 1972*. Washington, DC: Government Printing Office, 2006.

Gilbert, Martin. *Atlas of Jewish History*. New York: William Morrow, 1993.

——. *Holocaust Journey: Traveling in Search of the Past*. New York: Columbia University Press, 1999.

Gilman, Sander L. *Jewish Self-Hatred*. Baltimore: Johns Hopkins University Press, 1986.

Ginsberg, Benjamin. *The Fatal Embrace: Jews and the State*. Chicago: University of Chicago Press, 1993.

Ginsburg, Ruth Bader. Interview with Ruth Bader Ginsburg, by David Grubin. *Jewish Americans*, PBS, 2008.

Gitelman, Zvi. *A Century of Ambivalence: The Jews of Russia and the Soviet Union, 1881 to the Present*. Bloomington, IN: Indiana University Press, 2001.

Goldberg, Andrew C. "Moscow's INF Experience: The Other Side of the Table; The Soviet Approach to Arms Control." Edited by Michael Mandelbaum. New York: Council on Foreign Relations, 1990.

Goldberg, J. J. *Jewish Power: Inside the American Jewish Establishment*. New York: Addison-Wesley, 1996.

Goldberg, Jonah. "Pragmatic Reagan?" *National Review Online*, June 9, 2004. http://old.nationalreview.com/goldberg/goldberg200406090918.asp.

Golden, Peter. *Quiet Diplomat: The Biography of Max M. Fisher*. New York: Cornwall Books, 1992.

——. "Twisting the Years Away." *New Jersey Monthly*, January 2005.

Goodman, David G., and Masanori Miyazawa. *Jews in the Japanese Mind: The History and Uses of a Cultural Stereotype*. Studies of Modern Japan. New York: Free Press, 1995.

Goodwin, Doris Kearns. *The Fitzgeralds and the Kennedys*. New York: St. Martin's, 1987.

——. *No Ordinary Time: Franklin and Eleanor Roosevelt; The Home Front in World War II*. New York: Simon and Schuster, 1994.

Gorbachev, Mikhail. *On My Country and the World*. Translated by George Shriver. New York: Columbia University Press, 1999.

Greene, John Robert. *The Presidency of Gerald R. Ford*. Lawrence, KS: University Press of Kansas, 1995.

Greene, Melissa Fay. *The Temple Bombing*. New York: Perseus Books, 1996.

Greenspan, Alan. *The Age of Turbulence: Adventures in a New World*. New York: Penguin Press, 2007.

Gromyko, Andrei. *Memoirs*. New York: Doubleday, 1989.

Grose, Peter. *Israel in the Mind of America*. New York: Alfred A. Knopf, 1984.

Grover, Warren. *Nazis in Newark*. New Brunswick, NJ: Transaction, 2003.

Gutman, Israel, ed. *Encyclopedia of the Holocaust*. Vol. 1. New York: Macmillan, 1990.

Hackworth, David H. *About Face: The Odyssey of an American Warrior*. New York: Simon and Schuster, 1989.

Haig, Alexander M., Jr. *Inner Circles: How America Changed the World*. New York: Warner Books, 1992.

Halberstam, David. *The Fifties*. New York: Ballantine Books, 1993.

Hale, Nathan G., Jr. *The Rise and Crisis of Psychoanalysis in the United States: Freud and the Americans, 1917–1985*. New York: Oxford University Press, 1995.

Halevi, Yossi Klein. *Memoirs of a Jewish Extremist*. New York: Little, Brown, 1995.

——. "Jacob Birnbaum and the Struggle for Soviet Jewry." *Azure* online, no. 17 (spring 5764/2004). www.azure.org.il/article.php?id=221.

Hammer, Reuven. "The Dream: Thoughts for Yom HaAtzma'ut." *Jewish Life: The Orchard*, spring 2003.

Hampton, Wilborn. *Up Close: Elvis Presley*. New York: Viking Juvenile, 2007.

Hanover, Nathan. *Abyss of Despair: The Famous Seventeenth-Century Chronicle Depicting Jewish Life in Russia and Poland during the Chmielnicki Massacres of 1648–1649*. New Brunswick, NJ: Transaction Books, 1983.

Harap, Louis. *Anti-Negroism among Jews, Strangers and Neighbors*. Edited by Maurianne Adams and John Bracey. Amherst, MA: University of Massachusetts Press, 1999.

Harrison, Andrew. *Passover Revisited: Philadelphia's Efforts to Aid Soviet Jews, 1963–1998*. Madison, NJ: Fairleigh Dickinson University Press, 2001.

Hasty, Olga Peters, and Susanne Fusso, eds. *America through Russian Eyes, 1874–1926*. New Haven: Yale University Press, 1988.

Hearing before the Committee on Foreign Affairs, December 11, 1911. Washington, DC: Government Printing Office, 1911.

Helmreich, William B. *The Enduring Community: The Jews of Newark and Metrowest*. New Brunswick, NJ: Transaction, 1999.

Herman, Arthur. *Joseph McCarthy: Reexamining the Life and Legacy of America's Most Hated Senator*. New York: Free Press, 1999.

Hersh, Burton. *The Old Boys: The American Elite and the Origins of the CIA*. New York: Charles Scribner's Sons, 1992.

Higham, Charles. *American Swastika: The Shocking Story of Nazi Collaborators in Our Midst from 1933 to the Present Day*. Garden City, NY: Doubleday, 1985.

Hines, Thomas. *Populuxe*. New York: Alfred A. Knopf, 1987.

Hirsch, Michael. "Bernard Lewis Revisited," *Washington Monthly*, November 2004.

Hirshey, Gerri. *Nowhere to Run: The Story of Soul Music*. New York: Times Books, 1984.

Hitchens, Christopher. Foreword to Friedman, *The False Prophet*. London: Faber and Faber, 1990.

Horne, Alistair. *Kissinger 1973: The Crucial Year*. New York: Simon and Schuster, 2009.

Howe, Irving. *World of Our Fathers*. New York: Simon and Schuster, 1976.

Huie, William Bradford. *Three Lives for Mississippi*. Jackson, MS: University Press of Mississippi, 2000.

Hutchinson, George. *The Harlem Renaissance in Black and White*. Cambridge, MA: Harvard University Press, 1996.

Hyman, Paula E. *The Jews of Modern France*. Berkeley: University of California Press, 1998.

Isaac, Jeffrey C. *Democracy in Dark Times*. Ithaca, NY: Cornell University Press, 1998.

Isaacson, Walter. *Einstein*. New York: Simon and Schuster, 2007.

——. *Kissinger: A Biography*. New York: Simon and Schuster, 1992.

——, and Evan Thomas. *The Wise Men: Architects of the American Century*. New York: Touchstone, 1986.

Jacoby, Susan. *The Age of American Unreason*. New York: Pantheon, 2008.

Jeannsone, Glen. *Gerald L. K. Smith: Minister of Hate*. Baton Rouge, LA: Louisiana State University Press, 1997.

JINSA Security Affairs. "Never Again! Vows IDF Commander: Chief of Staff Barak Gives Powerful Tribute to Holocaust Victims at Auschwitz." April/May 1993.

Johnson, Paul. *George Washington: The Founding Father*. New York: HarperCollins, 2005.

——. *A History of the Jews*. New York: Harper and Row, 1987.

Jones, David H. *Moral Responsibility in the Holocaust: A Study in the Ethics of Character*. Lanham, MD: Rowman and Littlefield, 1999.

Jowett, Benjamin, ed. *The Republic*. New York: Oxford at the Clarendon Press, 1908.

Judas, John B. *William F. Buckley, Jr.: Patron Saint of the Conservatives*. New York: Simon and Schuster, 1988.

Kahaner, Larry. *AK-47: The Weapon That Changed the Face of War*. Hoboken, NJ: John Wiley and Sons, 2007.

Kahlenberg, Richard D. "Ocean Hill-Brownsville, 40 Years Later." *Chronicle of Higher Education* 54, no. 33 (April 2008).

Kantowicz, Edward R. *Coming Apart, Coming Together: The World in the Twentieth Century*. Vol. 2. Grand Rapids, MI: William B. Eerdmans, 2000.

Kaplan, Dana Evan. "Trends in American Judaism from 1945 to the Present." In *The Cambridge Companion to American Judaism*, edited by Dana Evan Kaplan. New York: Cambridge University Press, 2005.

Kaplan, Edward K. *Spiritual Radical: Abraham Joshua Heschel in America, 1940–1972*. New Haven: Yale University Press, 2007.

Kaplan, Robert D. "Kissinger, Metternich, and Realism." *Atlantic Monthly*, June 1999.

Karnow, Stanley. *Vietnam: A History*. New York: Viking Press, 1983.

Karp, Abraham J. *Haven and Home: A History of the Jews in America*. New York: Schocken Books, 1985.

Karpin, Michael. *The Bomb in the Basement: How Israel Went Nuclear and What That Means for the World*. New York: Simon and Schuster, 2007.

Kaufman, Robert G. *Henry M. Jackson: A Life in Politics*. Seattle, WA: University of Washington Press, 2000.

Kertzer, David I. *The Kidnapping of Edgardo Mortara*. New York: Vintage, 1997.

Kessler, Ronald. *The Sins of the Father: Joseph P. Kennedy and the Dynasty He Founded*. New York: Warner Books, 1996.

Kingseed, Wyatt. "The 'Bonus Army' War in Washington." *American History*, June 2004.

Kissinger, Henry A. *Diplomacy*. New York: Simon and Schuster, 1994.

——. *White House Years*. Boston: Little, Brown, 1979.

——. *A World Restored: Metternich, Castlereagh and the Problems of Peace, 1812–1822*. Boston: Houghton Mifflin, 1957.

——. *Years of Renewal*. New York: Simon and Schuster, 1999.

——. *Years of Upheaval*. Boston: Little, Brown, 1982.

Klehr, Harvey. *Communist Cadre: The Social Background of the American Communist Party Elite*. Stanford: Hoover Institution, 1978.

Klinghoffer, Judith A. *Vietnam, Jews and the Middle East*. New York: St. Martin's, 1999.

Korey, William. *The Soviet Cage: Anti-Semitism in Russia*. New York: Viking, 1973.

——. *The Promises We Keep: Human Rights, the Helsinki Process, and American Foreign Policy*. New York: St. Martin's, 1993.

——. "From Helsinki: A Salute to Human Rights." In Friedman and Chernin, *A Second Exodus*.

Korn, Bertram W. *American Jewry and the Civil War*. Marietta, GA: Bellum Editions, 1995.

Kovrig, Bennett. *Of Walls and Bridges: The United States and Eastern Europe*.

New York: New York University Press, 1991.

Kurzman, Dan. *Ben-Gurion: Prophet of Fire*. New York: Simon and Schuster, 1983.

———. *Genesis 1948: The First Arab-Israeli War*. New York: New American Library, 1970.

———. *Yitzhak Rabin: Soldier of Peace*. New York: HarperCollins, 1998.

Kutler, Stanley I. *The Wars of Watergate: The Last Crisis of Richard Nixon*. New York: W. W. Norton, 1992.

Lake, Anthon. *Somoza Falling*. Boston: Houghton Mifflin, 1989.

Lanning, Michael Lee. *The African-American Soldier*. Secaucus, NJ: Citadel/ Carol, 1999.

Larson, Erik. *In the Garden of Beasts: Love, Terror, and an American Family in Hitler's Berlin*. New York: Crown, 2011.

Lauterpacht, H., ed. *International Law Reports*. Cambridge, UK: Cambridge University Press, January 1, 1996.

Lazin, Fred A. "Refugee Resettlement and 'Freedom of Choice.'" *Center for Immigration Studies*, June 2005.

———. *The Struggle for Soviet Jewry in American Politics: Israel versus the American Jewish Establishment*. Lanham, MD: Lexington Books, 2005.

Leff, Laurel. *Buried by the Times: The Holocaust and America's Most Important Newspaper*. New York: Cambridge University Press, 2005.

Leichter, Sinai. "Kielce." In Gutman, *Encyclopedia of the Holocaust*.

Lester, Julius. *Lovesong: Becoming a Jew*. New York: Henry Holt, 1988.

Levanon, Nehemiah. "Israel's Role in the Campaign." In Friedman and Chernin, *A Second Exodus*.

Levy, Richard, ed. *Antisemitism: A Historical Encyclopedia of Prejudice and Persecution*. Santa Barbara, CA: ABC-CLIO, 2005.

Lincoln, W. Bruce. *The Romanovs*. New York: Anchor Books, 1981.

Lindemann, Albert S. *The Jew Accused: Three Anti-Semitic Affairs (Dreyfus, Belis, Frank), 1894–1915*. New York: Cambridge University Press, 1992.

Lipstadt, Deborah E. *Beyond Belief: The American Press and the Coming of the Holocaust, 1933–1945*. New York: Free Press, 1986.

Loftus, John, and Mark Aarons. *The Secret War against the Jews: How Western Espionage Betrayed the Jewish People*. New York: St. Martin's Griffin, 1994.

Lookstein, Haskell. *Were We Our Brothers' Keepers? The Public Response of American Jews to the Holocaust, 1938–1944*. New York: Hartmore House, 1985.

MacMillan, Margaret. *Nixon and Mao: The Week That Changed the World*. New York: Random House, 2007.

Mailer, Norman. *Advertisements for Myself.* New York: G. P. Putnam's Sons, 1959.

Malamud, Bernard. *The Fixer.* New York: Farrar, Straus and Giroux, 2004.

Mandelbaum, Michael, ed. *The Other Side of the Table: The Soviet Approach to Arms Control.* New York: Council on Foreign Relations, 1990.

Mann, James. *The Rebellion of Ronald Reagan: A History of the End of the Cold War.* New York: Viking, 2009.

Marcus, Jacob Rader. *United States Jewry, 1776–1985.* Detroit, MI: Wayne State University Press, 1992.

Marer, Paul, ed. *U.S. Financing of East-West Trade.* Bloomington, IN: International Development Research Center, 1975.

Markham, Jerry W. *A Financial History of the United States.* Vol. 3, *From the Age of Derivatives into the New Millennium.* Armonk, NY: M. E. Sharpe, 2001.

Marqusee, Mike. *Wicked Messenger: Bob Dylan and the 1960s.* New York: Seven Stories, 2005.

Martin, Harold H. *Atlanta and Environs: A Chronicle of Its People and Events; Years of Change and Challenge, 1940–1976.* Athens, GA: University of Georgia Press, 1987.

Martin, Linda, and Kerry Segrave. *Anti-Rock: The Opposition to Rock 'n' Roll.* Cambridge, MA: Da Capo, 1993.

Mayer, Martin. *The Teachers Strike: New York, 1968.* New York: Harper and Row, 1969.

McAllister, James. *No Exit: America and the German Problem, 1943–1954.* Ithaca, NY: Cornell University Press, 2002.

McCormick, Thomas J. *America's Half-Century: United States Foreign Policy in the Cold War and After.* Baltimore: Johns Hopkins University Press, 1995.

McCullough, David. *Truman.* New York: Simon and Schuster, 1992.

McElvaine, Robert S. *The Great Depression: America, 1929–1941.* New York: Times Books, 1984.

McLuhan, Marshall. *The Gutenberg Galaxy: The Making of Typographic Man.* Toronto: University of Toronto Press, 1962.

McPherson, James M. *Drawn with the Sword: Reflections on the American Civil War.* New York: Oxford University Press, 1996.

Meir, Golda. *My Life.* London: Futura, 1976.

Melman, Yossi. "Trade Secrets." *Haaretz Magazine,* March 10, 2006.

Mendelsohn, Ezra. *The Jews of East Central Europe between the World Wars.* Bloomington, IN: Indiana University Press, 1987.

Miron, Dan. Introduction to *Songs from Bialik,* by Hayyim Nahman Bialik. Syracuse, NY: Syracuse University Press, 2000.

Montefiore, Simon Sebag. *Stalin: The Court of the Red Tsar.* New York: Alfred

A. Knopf, 2003.

Morozov, Boris, ed. *Documents on Soviet Jewish Emigration*. Portland, OR: Frank Cass, 1999.

Morris, Edmund. *Theodore Rex*. New York: Random House, 2001.

Morse, Arthur D. *While Six Million Died: A Chronicle of American Apathy*. New York: Random House, 1968.

Naftalin, M.H. "The Activist Movement." In Friedman and Chernin, *A Second Exodus*.

Nathans, Benjamin. *Beyond the Pale: The Jewish Encounter with Late Imperial Russia*. Berkeley: University of California Press, 2004.

Newsbreak. "Kislik Questions Soviet Secrecy." January 23, 1987, NCSJ Archives.

Nichols, David A. *A Matter of Justice: Eisenhower and the Beginning of the Civil Rights Revolution*. New York: Simon and Schuster, 2007.

Nixon, Richard M. *RN: The Memoirs of Richard Nixon*. New York: Simon and Schuster, 1978.

Norman, Philip. *John Lennon: The Life*. New York: Ecco, 2008.

Norwood, Stephen H. *The Third Reich in the Ivory Tower: Complicity and Conflict on American Campuses*. New York: Cambridge University Press, 2009.

Novick, Peter. *The Holocaust in American Life*. Boston: Houghton Mifflin, 1999.

Oates, Stephen B. *Abraham Lincoln: The Man behind the Myths*. New York: Harper and Row, 1984.

Ofek, Adina. "Cantonists: Jewish Children as Soldiers in Tsar Nicholas's Army," *Modern Judaism* 13, no. 3 (October 1993).

Ognibene, Peter J. *Scoop: The Life and Politics of Henry M. Jackson*. Briarcliff Manor, NY: Stein and Day, 1975.

Oney, Steve. *And the Dead Shall Rise: The Murder of Mary Phagan and the Lynching of Leo Frank*. New York: Pantheon Books, 2003.

Orbach, William H. *The American Movement to Aid Soviet Jews*. Amherst, MA: University of Massachusetts Press, 1979.

Oren, Michael B. *Six Days of War: June 1967 and the Making of the Modern Middle East*. New York: Oxford University Press, 2002.

O'Rourke, Shane. *Warriors and Peasants: The Don Cossacks in Late Imperial Russia*. New York: Palgrave Macmillan, 2000.

Ostow, Mortimer, ed. *Judaism and Psychoanalysis*. London: Karnac Books, 1997.

Pach, Chester J., Jr., and Elmo Richardson. *The Presidency of Dwight D. Eisenhower: Revised Edition*. Lawrence, KS: University Press of Kansas, 1991.

Peters Hasty, Olga, and Susanne Fusso, eds. *America through Russian Eyes, 1874–1926*. New Haven: Yale University Press, 1988.

Pinsker, Leon. *Auto-Emancipation*. New York: Federation of American Zionists, 1916.

Pollack, Kenneth M. *Arabs at War: Military Effectiveness, 1948–1991*. Lincoln, NE: University of Nebraska Press, 2002.

Posner, Steve. *Israel Undercover: Secret Warfare and Hidden Diplomacy in the Middle East*. New York: Syracuse University Press, 1987.

Puddington, Arch. *Broadcasting Freedom: The Cold War Triumph of Radio Free Europe and Radio Liberty*. Louisville, KY: University Press of Kentucky, 2003.

Quandt, William B. *Decade of Decisions: American Foreign Policy toward the Arab-Israeli Conflict, 1967–1976*. Berkeley and Los Angeles: University of California Press, 1977.

——. *Peace Process: American Diplomacy and the Arab-Israeli Conflict since 1967*. Washington, DC: Brookings Institution, 2001.

Rabinovich, Abraham. *The Yom Kippur War: The Epic Encounter That Transformed the Middle East*. New York: Schocken Books, 2004.

Rabin, Yitzhak. *The Rabin Memoirs*. Berkeley: University of California Press, 1979.

Radzinsky, Edvard. *Alexander II: The Last Great Tsar*. New York: Free Press, 2005.

Rapaport, Lynn. "The Holocaust in American Jewish Life." In *The Cambridge Companion to American Judaism*, ed. Dana Evan Kaplan. New York: Cambridge University Press, 2005.

Raviv, Dan, and Yossi Melman. *Every Spy a Prince: The Complete History of Israel's Intelligence Community*. Boston: Houghton Mifflin, 1990.

Rayner, Richard. "Channelling Ike." *New Yorker*, April 26, 2010.

Reagan, Ronald. *An American Life: The Autobiography*. New York: Simon and Schuster, 1990.

——. *The Reagan Diaries*, edited by Douglas Brinkley. New York: HarperCollins, 2007.

Reeves, Richard. *President Kennedy: Profile of Power*. New York: Simon and Schuster, 1993.

——. *President Reagan: The Triumph of Imagination*. New York: Simon and Schuster, 2005.

——. *President Nixon: Alone in the White House*. New York: Simon and Schuster, 2001.

Reynolds, Michael. *Hemingway: The Final Years*. New York: W. W. Norton, 1999.

Rhodes, Richard. *Masters of Death: The SS-Einsatzgruppen and the Invention of the Holocaust*. New York: Alfred A. Knopf, 2002.

Roberts, Geoffrey. *Stalin's Wars*. New Haven: Yale University Press, 2007.

Robinson, Archie. *George Meany and His Times*. New York: Simon and Schuster, 1981.

Ro'i, Yaacov. *The Struggle for Soviet Jewish Emigration, 1948–1967*. New York: Cambridge University Press, 1991.

Roosevelt, Eleanor. *This I Remember*. New York: Harper and Brothers, 1949.

Rosen, James. *The Strong Man: John Mitchell and the Secrets of Watergate*. New York: Doubleday, 2008.

Rosen, Robert N. *Saving the Jews: Franklin D. Roosevelt and the Holocaust*. New York: Thunder's Mouth, 2006.

Rose, Peter I. *Strangers in Their Midst: Small-Town Jews and Their Neighbors*. Merrick, NY: Richwood, 1977.

Ross, Dennis. *The Missing Peace: The Inside Story of the Fight for Middle East Peace*. New York: Farrar, Straus and Giroux, 2004.

Roth, John K., and Abraham Edelheit, eds. *The Holocaust Chronicle*. Lincolnwood, Illinois: Publishers International, 2003.

Roth, Phillip. *Portnoy's Complaint*. New York: Random House, 1969.

Roth Young, Bette. *Emma Lazarus in Her World*. Philadelphia: Jewish Publication Society, 1995.

Rotolo, Suze. *A Freewheelin' Time: A Memoir of Greenwich Village in the Sixties*. New York: Broadway Books, 2008.

Rubenstein, Joshua. "The Night of the Murdered Poets." *New Republic*, August 25, 1997.

Rubenstein, Richard L. *After Auschwitz: Radical Theology and Contemporary Judaism*. New York: Bobbs-Merrill, 1966.

Rubinstein, Alvin Z. *Red Star on the Nile: The Soviet-Egyptian Influence Relationship since the June War*. Princeton: Princeton University Press, 1977.

Ruby, Walter. "The Role of Nonestablishment Groups." In Friedman and Chernin, *A Second Exodus*.

Sachar, Howard M. *A History of Israel*. Vol. 1, *From the Rise of Zionism to Our Time*. New York: Alfred A. Knopf, 1986. Vol. 2, *From the Aftermath of the Yom Kippur War*. New York: Oxford University Press, 1987.

———. *A History of the Jews in America*. New York: Alfred A. Knopf, 1992.

Safire, William. *Before the Fall: An Inside View of the Pre-Watergate White House*. New York: Doubleday, 1975.

Sakharov, Andrei. *Memoirs*. New York: Alfred A. Knopf, 1990.

Sarna, Jonathan. *American Judaism: A History*. New Haven: Yale University Press, 2004.

Sartre, Jean-Paul. *Anti-Semite and Jew*. New York: Schocken Books, 1948.

Satter, David. *Age of Delirium: The Decline and Fall of the Soviet Union*. New

York: Alfred A. Knopf, 1996.

Saul, Norman E. *Distant Friends: The United States and Russia, 1763–1867*. Lawrence, KS: University Press of Kansas, 1991.

Schapiro, Amy. *Millicent Fenwick: Her Way*. New Brunswick, NJ: Rutgers University Press, 2003.

Schiff, Ze'ev, and Ehud Ya'ari. *Intifada: The Palestinian Uprising; Israel's Third Front*. New York: Simon and Schuster, 1989.

Schlesinger, Arthur, Jr. *The Imperial Presidency*. Boston: Houghton Mifflin, 1973.

Schneier, Marc. *Shared Dreams: Martin Luther King, Jr. and the Jewish Community*. Woodstock, VT: Jewish Lights, 1999.

Schroeter, Leonard. *The Last Exodus*. New York: Universe Books, 1974.

Schweizer, Peter. *Victory: The Reagan Administration's Secret Strategy That Hastened the Collapse of the Soviet Union*. New York: Atlantic Monthly, 1994.

Scoblic, J. Peter. *Us Versus Them: How a Half-Century of Conservatism Has Undermined America's Security*. New York: Viking, 2008.

Seale, Bobby. *Seize the Time: The Story of the Black Panther Party and Huey P. Newman*. New York: Random House, 1968.

Segev, Tom. *The Seventh Million: The Israelis and the Holocaust*. New York: Hill and Wang, 1993.

Shandler, Jeffrey. *While America Watches: Televising the Holocaust*. New York: Oxford University Press, 1999.

Sharanksy, Natan. *Fear No Evil*. New York: Vintage Books, 1988.

——, and Ron Dermer. *The Case for Democracy: The Power of Freedom to Overcome Tyranny and Terror*. New York: Public Affairs Books, 2004.

Shaw, J. Stanley, and Peter Golden. *I Rest My Case: My Long Journey from the Castle on the Hill to Home*. Albany: Chestnut Street, 2000.

Sheehy, Gail. *The Man Who Changed the World: The Lives of Mikhail S. Gorbachev*. New York: HarperCollins, 1990.

Shogan, Robert. *Prelude to Catastrophe: FDR's Jews and the Menace of Nazism*. Chicago: Ivan R. Dee, 2010.

Shultz, George P. *Turmoil and Triumph: My Years as Secretary of State*. New York: Charles Scribner's Sons, 1993.

Skinner, Kiron K., Annelise Anderson, and Martin Anderson, eds. *Reagan: In His Own Hand; The Writings of Ronald Reagan That Reveal His Revolutionary Vision for America*. New York: Free Press, 2001.

Slonim, Shlomo. *Jerusalem in America's Foreign Policy, 1947–1997*. Boston: Martinus Nijhoff, 1998.

Smith, Hedrick. *The New Russians*. New York: Random House, 1990.

Smith, Jim, and Malcolm McConnell. *The Last Mission: The Secret History of World War II's Final Battle*. New York: Broadway, 2003.

Sommerville, Donald. *World War II: Day by Day*. Greenwich, CT: Dorset, 1989.

Sorin, Gerald. *A Time for Building: The Third Migration, 1880–1920*. Baltimore: Johns Hopkins University Press, 1992.

Spiegel, Herbert, and David Spiegel. *Trance and Treatment: Clinical Uses of Hypnosis*. New York: Basic Books, 1978.

Spiegel, Philip. *Triumph over Tyranny: The Heroic Campaign That Saved 2,000 Soviet Jews*. New York: Devora, 2008.

Spiegel, Steven L. *The Other Arab-Israeli Conflict: Making America's Middle East Policy, from Truman to Reagan*. Chicago: University of Chicago Press, 1985.

Spitz, Bob. *The Beatles: The Biography*. New York: Little, Brown, 2005.

Sprinzak, Ehud. *Brother against Brother: Violence and Extremism in Israeli Politics from Altalena to the Rabin Assassination*. New York: Free Press, 1999.

Stanislawski, Michael. *Tsar Nicholas I and the Jews: The Transformation of Jewish Society in Russia, 1825–1855*. Philadelphia: Jewish Publication Society of America, 1983.

Stark, Rodney, and Stephen Steinberg. "Jews and Christians in Suburbia." *Harper's Magazine*, August 1967.

Starry, Donn A. *Armored Combat in Vietnam*. Indianapolis: Bobbs-Merrill, 1981.

Statistical Abstract of the United States, US Census Bureau, 1941.

Stern, Paula. *Water's Edge: Domestic Politics and the Making of American Foreign Policy*. Westport, CT: Greenwood Press, 1979.

Stevens, Lewis M. "The Life and Character of Earl G. Harrison." *University of Pennsylvania Law Review* 104, no. 5 (March 1956).

Stokes, Gale. *The Walls Came Tumbling Down: The Collapse of Communism in Eastern Europe*. New York: Oxford University Press, 1993.

Stuart, Mark A. *Gangster #2: Longy Zwillman, the Man Who Invented Organized Crime*. Secaucus, NJ: Lyle Stuart, 1985.

Sulzberger, C. L. *An Age of Mediocrity: Memoirs and Diaries, 1963–1972*. New York: Macmillan, 1973.

———. *The American Heritage Picture Encyclopedia of World War II*. New York: American Heritage, 1966.

Susser, Bernard, and Charles S. Liebman. *Choosing Survival: Strategies for a Jewish Future*. New York: Oxford University Press, 1999.

Taleb, Nassim Nicholas. *The Black Swan: The Impact of the Highly Improbable*. New York: Random House, 2007.

Talbot, David. *Brothers: The Hidden History of the Kennedy Years*. New York:

Free Press, 2007.

Talisman, Mark E. "Meeting at Department of State." June 9, 1989, Fisher Archives.

———. Memo, "Non-Meeting with Sellin." August 1, 1989, Fisher Archives.

———. Memo, "Participants of Non Meeting." July 6, 1989, Fisher Archives.

Taubman, William. *Khrushchev: The Man and His Era*. New York: W.W Norton, 2003.

Teitelbaum, Larry. "Harrison Report: Post-World War II Bombshell." *Penn Law Journal* 41, no. 1 (spring 2006).

Thomas, Daniel C. *The Helsinki Effect: International Norms, Human Rights, and the Demise of Communism*. Princeton: Princeton University Press, 2001.

Thornton, Richard C. *The Nixon-Kissinger Years: Reshaping of America's Foreign Policy*. New York: Paragon House, 1989.

Time. "A Letter from the Publisher, Apr. 19, 1954." April 19, 1954.

———. "Behavior: The Black and the Jew: A Falling Out of Allies." January 31, 1969.

———. "Business: Another Soviet Grain Sting." November 28, 1977.

———. "Congress: Hitler's Shadow." October 10, 1938.

———. "Foreign News: Lausanne Peace on Earth." July 18, 1932.

———. "Philanthropy: The No. 1 Charity." February 17, 1961.

———. "Pine and William Sts." February 14, 1927.

———. "Soviet Union: The Leningrad Nine." May 31, 1971.

———. "Terrorism: Blackmail in Vienna." October 8, 1973.

———. "The Congress: Return of King Caucus." December 16, 1974.

———. "World: A Day in the Life of Yuli Daniel." June 6, 1969.

Tolnay, Stewart E., and E.M. Beck. *A Festival of Violence: An Analysis of Southern Lynchings, 1882–1930*. Champaign, IL: University of Illinois Press, 1995.

Tosches, Nick. *Unsung Heroes of Rock 'n' Roll: The Birth of Rock in the Wild Years before Elvis*. Cambridge, MA: Da Capo, 1999.

Tuchman, Barbara W. *Practicing History: Selected Essays*. New York: Ballantine, 1982.

Turck, Nancy. "The Arab Boycott." *Foreign Affairs*, April 1977.

Urofsky, Melvin I. *We Are One! American Jewry and Israel*. Garden City, NY: Anchor Press / Doubleday, 1978.

Vital, David. *A People Apart: A Political History of the Jews in Europe, 1789–1939*. New York: Oxford University Press, 1999.

Von Eschen, Penny Marie. *Satchmo Blows Up the World: Jazz Ambassadors Play the Cold War*. Cambridge, MA: Harvard University Press, 2004.

Wagener, Hans. *Understanding Erich Maria Remarque*. Columbia, SC: University of South Carolina Press, 1991.

Wald, Gayle. *Crossing the Line: Racial Passing in Twentieth-Century U.S. Literature and Culture*. Durham, NC: Duke University Press, 2000.

Walker, Alice. *The Same River Twice*. New York: Washington Square, 1992.

Wallach, Janet, and John Wallach. *Arafat: In the Eyes of the Beholder*. New York: Lyle Stuart, 1990.

Warnes, Kathy. "The Ageless Anguish of Kent State." In *Crimes and Trials of the Century*. Vol. 1, *From the Black Sox Scandal to the Attica Prison Riots*, edited by Frankie Y. Bailey and Steven Chermak. Westport, CT: Greenwood, 2007.

Washington, James M., ed. *A Testament of Hope: The Essential Writings and Speeches of Martin Luther King, Jr.* New York: HarperCollins, 1991.

"Washington's Farewell Address to the People of the United States." 106th Congress, 2nd Session Senate Document, no. 106-21, Washington, 2000.

Weaver, John D. "Bonus March." *American Heritage*, June 1963.

Wedlock, Lunabelle. "The Reaction of Negro Publications and Organizations to German Anti-Semitism." *Howard University Studies in the Social Sciences* 3, no. 2 (1942).

Weiner, Tim. *Legacy of Ashes: The History of the CIA*. New York: Doubleday, 2007.

Weinstein, Natalie. "Julius Lester: There's 'No Magic Formula' for Blacks and Jews." *Jewish Newsweekly of Northern California*, February 16, 1996.

Whalen, Richard J. *The Founding Father: The Story of Joseph P. Kennedy; A Study in Power, Wealth, and Family Ambition*. New York: New American Library, 1964.

Wiesel, Elie. *The Jews of Silence: A Personal Report on Soviet Jewry*. New York: Signet Books, 1967.

Windmueller, Steven F. "The 'Noshrim' War: Dropping Out." In Friedman and Chernin, *A Second Exodus*.

Wolfe, Tom. *Radical Chic and Mau-Mauing the Flak Catchers*. New York: Farrar, Straus and Giroux, 1970.

Woocher, Jonathan S. *Sacred Survival: The Civil Religion of American Jews*. Bloomington, IA: Indiana University Press, 1986.

Wyman, David S. *The Abandonment of the Jews*. New York: New Press, 1984.

Zeepvat, Charlotte. *Romanov Autumn: Stories from the Last Century of Imperial Russia*. Thrupp, Stroud, Great Britain: Sutton, 2002.

Zimmermann, Warren. *The First Great Triumph: How Five Americans Made Their Country a World Power*. New York: Farrar, Straus and Giroux, 2002.

Zubok, Vladislav M. *A Failed Empire: The Soviet Union in the Cold War from Stalin to Gorbachev*. Chapel Hill, NC: University of North Carolina Press, 2007.

——, and Strobe Talbott. *At the Highest Levels: The Inside Story of the End of the Cold War*. Boston: Little, Brown, 1993.

INTERVIEWS

Berman, Mandell. April 9, 1990; September 8, 2002.

Bernstein, Irving. October 13, 1988.

Birnbaum, Jacob. August, 27, 2002; September 6, 2002; September 8, 2002.

Cardin, Shoshana S. July 6, 2000; October 25, 2000.

Chinitz, Zelig. April 10, 1989.

Clapp, Priscilla. November 5, 2002.

Dekel-Chen, Jonathan. November 1, 2007.

Dinitz, Simcha. February 12, 1989.

Eagleburger, Lawrence. April 5, 2003; April 6, 2003.

Fannan, James. November 14, 2002.

Feingold, Henry. February 1, 2007.

Fisher, Max. July 6, 2002; June 8, 2003; July 30, 2003; January 21, 2005.

Foushee, Carl. September 7, 2004.

Frumkin, Si. December 22, 2007.

Garment, Leonard. August 10, 1989.

Goldberg, J. J. March 1, 2007.

Golden, Lance. November 4, 2000.

Goodman, Jerry. January 21, 2008.

Gorbachev, Mikhail. November 12, 2002.

Haig, Alexander. November 13, 1990.

Harris, David. February 8, 2008.

Herzfeld, Wolfgang. April 7, 2007.

Hill, David. January 9, 2008.

Hoenlein, Malcolm. August 24, 1989; July 16, 2002.

Kaplan, Mendel. November 20, 1990.

Kesselhaut, Martin. January 2, 2008.

Kingsley, Evan. November 8, 2008.

Kissinger, Henry. January 25, 1989; March 18, 2004.

Klose, Kevin. December 15, 2007.

Korey, William. August, 27, 2002; September 6, 2002; September 8, 2002.

Krarr, Martin. March 28, 1989.

Lazin, Fred. November 1, 2007.

Levin, Marc. December 13, 2007.

Levine, Hillel. May 9, 2009.

Marcus, Stanley. January 20, 2004.

Nixon, Richard. June 9, 1989.

Patz, Norman. January 21, 2008.

Peres, Shimon. February 10, 1989.

Perle, Richard. July 2, 2002.

Rabin, Yitzhak. February 15, 1989.

Reagan, Ronald. November, 28, 1990.

Richter, Glenn. May 12, 2003; March 3, 2009.

Robin, Edward. January 16, 2008.

Rosenblum, Louis. July 11, 2007.

Ross, Dennis. February 9, 2005.

Satter David. January 7, 2008.

Schwartz, Carmi. March 28, 1990; January 17, 2008.

Shapira, Morey. January 4, 2008; January 21, 2008.

Shultz, George. November 22, 1989; November 19, 2003.

Sislen, Samuel. December 19, 2007.

Smukler, Joseph. January 17, 2008.

Stein, Jacob. June 5, 1989; June 1, 2003.

Steinbruck, John. December 20, 2007.

Stone, Richard. December 26, 2007.

Talisman, Mark. January 9, 1990; June 3, 2002.

Twersky, David. March 19, 2009.

Wenick, Martin. November 19, 2000.

Wyman David. November 3, 2008.

Yaroslavsky, Zev. December 13, 2007.

INDEX